HUMAN
RIGHTS
WATCH
WORLD
REPORT
1 9 9 6

■ Featured in World Report 1996

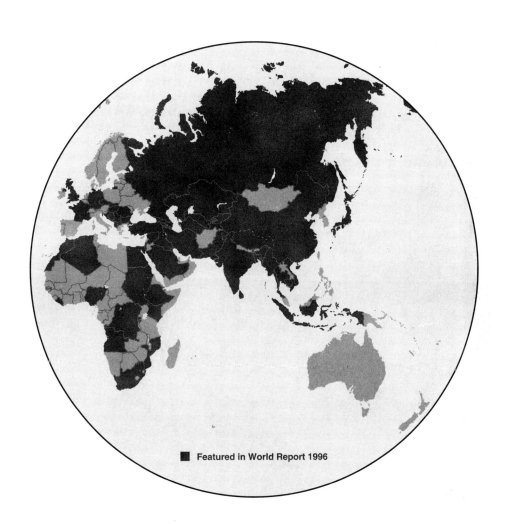

■ Featured in World Report 1996

HUMAN RIGHTS WATCH WORLD REPORT 1996

Events of 1995

New York • Washington
Los Angeles • London • Brussels

ISBN 0-300-06658-9
ISSN 1054-948X

Cover design by Margaret Marcy.

Human Rights Watch
485 Fifth Avenue
New York, NY 10017-6104
Tel: (212) 972-8400
Fax: (212) 972-0905
E-mail: hrwnyc@hrw.org

Human Rights Watch
1522 K Street, NW, #910
Washington, DC 20005-1202
Tel: (202) 371-6592
Fax: (202) 371-0124
E-mail: hrwdc@hrw.org

Human Rights Watch
10951 West Pico Blvd., #203
Los Angeles, CA 90064-2126
Tel: (310) 475-3070
Fax: (310) 475-5613
E-mail: hrwatchla@igc.apc.org

Human Rights Watch
33 Islington High Street
N1 9LH London
United Kingdom
Tel: (44171) 713-1995
Fax: (44171) 713-1800
E-mail: hrwatchuk@gn.apc.org

Human Rights Watch
15 Rue Van Campenhout
1040 Brussels, Belgium
Tel: (322) 732-2009
Fax: (322) 732-0471
E-mail: hrwatcheu@gn.apc.org

HUMAN RIGHTS WATCH

Human Rights Watch conducts regular, systematic investigations of human rights abuses in some seventy countries around the world. It addresses the human rights practices of governments of all political stripes, of all geopolitical alignments, and of all ethnic and religious persuasions. In internal wars it documents violations by both governments and rebel groups. Human Rights Watch defends freedom of thought and expression, due process and equal protection of the law; it documents and denounces murders, disappearances, torture, arbitrary imprisonment, exile, censorship and other abuses of internationally recognized human rights.

Human Rights Watch began in 1978 with the founding of its Helsinki division. Today, it includes five divisions covering Africa, the Americas, Asia, the Middle East, as well as the signatories of the Helsinki accords. It also includes five collaborative projects covering arms transfers, children's rights, free expression, prison conditions, and women's rights. It maintains offices in New York, Washington, Los Angeles, London, Brussels, Moscow, Dushanbe, Rio de Janeiro, and Hong Kong. Human Rights Watch is an independent, nongovernmental organization, supported by contributions from private individuals and foundations worldwide. It accepts no government funds, directly or indirectly.

The staff includes Kenneth Roth, executive director; Cynthia Brown, program director; Holly J. Burkhalter, advocacy director; Robert Kimzey, publications director; Jeri Laber, special advisor; Gara LaMarche, associate director; Lotte·Leicht, Brussels office director; Juan Méndez, general counsel; Susan Osnos, communications director; Jemera Rone, counsel; Joanna Weschler, United Nations representative; and Derrick Wong, finance and administration director.

The regional directors of Human Rights Watch are Peter Takirambudde, Africa; José Miguel Vivanco, Americas; Sidney Jones, Asia; Holly Cartner, Helsinki; and Christopher E. George, Middle East. The project directors are Joost R. Hiltermann, Arms Project; Lois Whitman, Children's Rights Project; Gara LaMarche, Free Expression Project; and Dorothy Q. Thomas, Women's Rights Project.

The members of the board of directors are Robert L. Bernstein, chair; Adrian W. DeWind, vice chair; Roland Algrant, Lisa Anderson, Alice L. Brown, William Carmichael, Dorothy Cullman, Irene Diamond, Edith Everett, Jonathan Fanton, James C. Goodale, Jack Greenberg, Alice H. Henkin, Harold Hongju Koh, Jeh Johnson, Stephen L. Kass, Marina Pinto Kaufman, Alexander MacGregor, Josh Mailman, Andrew Nathan, Jane Olson, Peter Osnos, Kathleen Peratis, Bruce Rabb, Orville Schell, Sid Sheinberg, Gary G. Sick, Malcolm Smith, Nahid Toubia, Maureen White, and Rosalind C. Whitehead.

ACKNOWLEDGMENTS

A compilation of this magnitude requires contributions from a large number of people, including most of the Human Rights Watch staff. The contributors were:

Fred Abrahams, Aziz Abu-Hamad, Marcia Allina, Kathleen Bleakley, Michael Bochenek, Sebastian Brett, Cynthia Brown, Samya Burney, Bruni Burres, Holly Cartner, James Cavallaro, Allyson Collins, Diana T. Cheng, Melissa Crow, Erika Dailey, Sarah DeCosse, Rachel Denber, Alison Des Forges, Richard Dicker, Jamie Fellner, Janet Fleischman, Christopher George, Eric Goldstein, Stephen Goose, Patricia Gossman, Jeannine Guthrie, Carl Haacke, Heather Harding, Steve Hernández, Elahé S. Hicks, Joost Hiltermann, Ernst Jan Hogendoorn, David Holiday, Guissou Jahangiri-Jeannot, LaShawn Jefferson, Mike Jendrzejczyk, Sidney Jones, Tanya Karanasios, Robin Kirk, Viviana Krsticevic, Sylvia Kucera, Anne Kuper, Gara LaMarche, David Aquila Lawrence, Robin Levi, Zunetta Liddell, Ivan Lupis, Bronwen Manby, Anne Manuel, Joanne Mariner, Kim Mazyck, Juan E. Méndez, Kerry McArthur, Michael McClintock, Evelyn Miah, Anna Claudia Monteiro, Ivana Nizich, Binaifer Nowrojee, Liliana Obregón, Brian Owsley, Christopher Panico, Paul Paz y Miño, Alexander Petrov, Dinah PoKempner, Regan A. Ralph, Shira Robinson, Torrance Robinson, Jemera Rone, Ken Roth, Tuhin Roy, Awali Samara, Mina Samuels, Jennifer Schense, Carol Schlitt, Kathleen Schorsch, Urmi Shah, Virginia N. Sherry, Milbert Shin, Gretta Tovar Siebentritt, Lenee Simon, Joel Solomon, Karen Sorensen, Mickey Spiegel, Dorothy Q. Thomas, Alex Vines, José Miguel Vivanco, Marti Weithman, Lois Whitman, Fatemah Ziai.

Cynthia Brown, Michael McClintock and Jeri Laber edited the report, with editing and production assistance by Nandi Rodrigo. Various sections were reviewed by Holly Burkhalter, Lotte Leicht, Juan Méndez and Joanna Weschler. Robert Kimzey, Susan Osnos, Nandi Rodrigo and Karen Sorensen proofread the report.

CONTENTS

HUMAN RIGHTS WATCH/HELSINKI

HUMAN RIGHTS WATCH/MIDDLE EAST

HUMAN RIGHTS WATCH

INTRODUCTION

For much of this decade, the major powers regularly shirked their duty to promote human rights. This year, largely due to public insistence, there were signs that human rights are slowly returning to the fore. The trend is far from uniform, particularly when commercial interests are at stake, but it suggests a renewed official commitment to these universal principles as they are increasingly embraced by the peoples of the world.

Despite the great human rights victories represented by the collapse of repressive regimes in Eastern Europe, Africa and Latin America, the first half of this decade saw a waning of will to uphold human rights among the major powers. Governments feared that the vigorous defense of these rights might offend trading partners and risk economic opportunities. While an emerging global economy demanded a new breadth of vision, political leaders grew parochial and indifferent in the human rights realm.

To soothe public disquiet over this abandonment of human rights, political leaders propounded facile theories about trade and investment inevitably leading to human rights progress. To calm outrage over their refusal to stop genocide in Rwanda and Bosnia-Hercegovina, they mustered belated humanitarian assistance. To justify inaction in the face of ethnic slaughter, they portrayed such carnage as timeless and inevitable. To allay calls to bring mass murderers to justice, they created international tribunals but denied them political and financial backing.

In the past year, there were indications that the pendulum is beginning to swing back. The utter failure of "constructive engagement" to secure human rights progress in China began to undermine the convenient proposition that trade and investment alone will automatically improve human rights. The horror of U.N. troops serving as silent witnesses to genocide in Bosnia—particularly in Srebrenica—highlighted the necessity of standing up to ethnic or sectarian slaughter. The tremendous cost of ending ethnic conflict heightened interest in preventing the human rights abuse that can transform ethnic tension into ethnic violence. The devastation wrought by abusive officials operating with impunity for their human rights crimes sparked a renewed sense of urgency behind the quest to bring official violators to justice. Increasingly, human rights were seen less as a dispensable luxury and more as an essential underpinning of global security and public well-being.

Political leaders played a disturbingly small role in this course correction. From U.N. Secretary-General Boutros Boutros-Ghali's reluctance to offend powerful governments to U.S. President Bill Clinton's persistent tendency to yield on matters of human rights principle, their support for human rights was often belated, inconsistent and grudging. However, the public repeatedly showed itself troubled by this abdication of the human rights cause. When official indifference to abuse became intolerable in Bosnia, Chechnya, China and elsewhere, public demands for action grew. A burgeoning global human rights movement played an important part in building and expressing this public reaction.

Gaining prominence most recently in Beijing at the Fourth U.N. World Conference on Women, this diverse network of activists and associations provided an increasingly powerful voice of principle and a genuinely cross-national perspective to combat the tendencies of national governments toward apathy and isolationism. It also ensured that governments pay a heavy political price for any flight from their human rights commitments.

An International System of Justice

A central issue defining the international commitment to human rights is whether to bring human rights criminals to justice. For the first time since Nuremberg, there is a chance to create an international system of justice to overcome the impunity bred by weak, corrupt or terrorized national judiciaries. The establishment of such a system would revolutionize the defense of human rights by adding a powerful threat of international prosecution and punishment to the existing tools of stigmatization and economic pressure. But the realization of this vision depends on the international community's willingness to match its supportive rhetoric with concrete action.

As the major powers debate whether to take this crucial step forward, an irrepressible longing for justice is surfacing, often in parts of the world where the proponents of amnesty and amnesia thought that the past had been forgotten and that festering wounds had healed. While abusive officials still try to exploit their positions of power to obtain impunity for their human rights crimes, many societies, particularly in Latin America but also in Africa and Asia, are demanding that the rule of law apply to all, that the book not be closed on the horrors of the past, and that the convenient compromises leading to amnesty and official forgetting be resisted in the name of rebuilding a collapsed moral order.

Illustrative was Haiti, where in September 1994 the Clinton administration through its envoy, former U.S. President Jimmy Carter, enticed military leaders to relinquish power by promising them a general amnesty for the thousands of political murders committed under their rule. Upon being returned to power by a U.N.-authorized multinational force, President Jean-Bertrand Aristide and the Haitian parliament refused to forget these crimes. Seeking to break the cycle of impunity that condemned Haiti to a succession of brutal regimes, President Aristide launched investigations of some of the more notorious murders. When Haiti's judicial system proved too feeble to secure justice on its own, he took the unusual step of inviting a team of foreign prosecutors to help. He also dismissed all senior military officials, effectively dissolved the Haitian army, and established a truth commission to create a public record of human rights crimes under military rule. (However, his frequent public support for "reconciliation and justice" was marred when, in a eulogy for a slain congressman, he contributed to a wave of vigilante killings by

urging civilian participation in police disarmament efforts.)

Breaking its own pattern of impunity, Chile convicted and imprisoned two former secret police officials, Gen. Manuel Contreras Sepúlveda and Brig. Gen. Pedro Espinoza Bravo, for ordering the 1976 car-bomb assassination of a former Chilean defense minister and a U.S. colleague. In Honduras, a special prosecutor for human rights overcame threats and violence to issue a rare criminal indictment of active-duty Latin American military officers. Among those indicted (for kidnapping, torture and attempted murder in 1992) was Lt. Col. Alexander Hernández, the chief of operations in the early 1980s of the notoriously abusive Battalion 3-16 and currently the inspector general of the military police.

In Argentina, the army chief of staff issued an historic apology for crimes committed during the "dirty war" of the 1970s. Individual prosecutors in Guatemala and Peru courageously pressed forward with investigations of particular military atrocities. The Inter-American Court on Human Rights found that the Peruvian government violated the right to life during its deadly suppression of the 1986 riots in El Frontón prison. At the urging of the Inter-American Commission on Human Rights, the Colombian government investigated and accepted responsibility for the killing and forced disappearance of thirty-four people in 1994 and fired the lieutenant colonel who was implicated.

In Africa, Ethiopia is proceeding with the trial of forty-four leaders of the government of former President Mengistu Haile Mariam for its brutally repressive rule from 1974 to 1991 (although hundreds of others remain in custody without having been formally charged). South Africa has also filed murder charges against a number of former senior officials, including a former defense minister, Gen. Magnus Malan, in connection with abuses from the 1980s. In addition, it is ready to launch a truth commission before which abusive officials must confess their crimes to be eligible for indemnity from prosecution. In Asia, South Korean President Kim Young Sam has called for legislation to permit prosecution of the country's former military leaders for the 1980 massacre of pro-democracy protestors in Kwangju.

Whether this clamor for justice sparks a trend will depend in large part on the actions of the major powers toward the former Yugoslavia. President Clinton, U.S. Ambassador to the U.N. Madeleine Albright and other U.S. officials have spoken eloquently about the need for justice to build the foundation for lasting peace, as opposed merely to a short-lived peace agreement. Behind their support lie important truths. Only justice for today's killers can deter those who might resume their bloodshed tomorrow. Only justice can offer unequivocal condemnation of warfare waged by the slaughter of civilians. Only justice can establish the rule of law to replace the cycle of summary revenge. And only justice can substitute an individualized assessment of guilt for the false assumptions of collective ethnic guilt that divide the Bosnian, Croatian and Serbian communities.

The International Criminal Tribunal for the Former Yugoslavia has made important steps toward achieving justice by indicting, through mid-November, fifty-two people for murder, torture, rape and other acts of genocide, war crimes and crimes against humanity in Bosnia and Croatia. Unlike Nuremberg, where only the losers faced justice, the tribunal for the former Yugoslavia has indicted both Serbs and Croats, and tribunal prosecutors have pledged to seek indictments against all those for whom evidence of serious crimes can be found. But securing the defendants' presence for trial will depend on how the peace agreement initialed in Dayton, Ohio at the end of November is implemented.

The agreement represents an important advance toward justice in several respects. It demonstrates that a peace accord can be reached without promising amnesty to war criminals. It obliges the parties to "cooperate fully" with the tribunal. And it bars indicted war criminals from holding public office. However, ambiguities in the agreement may be exploited, such as the lack of an explicit requirement that indicted war criminals be arrested.

Whether trials take place is thus likely to depend on the international community's willingness to impose sanctions and withhold reconstruction aid for any government that refuses to surrender indicted defendants for trial. Pressure for justice may also come from the natural reluctance to deploy international troops and field workers where indicted war criminals, with a history of broken agreements and barbaric tactics, still maintain formal or de facto authority over troops. Equivocation on the demand that indicted war criminals be made to stand trial—the unwillingness to match rhetoric with action—risks making a mockery of the quest for justice by raising the specter of international representatives in Bosnia conducting business as usual with persons accused of the most heinous crimes. It would also set a damaging precedent of indifference for future efforts to establish an international system of justice.

The International Criminal Tribunal for Rwanda has made far less progress than its counterpart for the former Yugoslavia. While evidence of the Rwandan genocide is ample and its orchestrators, in exile, are vulnerable to arrest, the Rwanda tribunal has proceeded at a snail's pace because of funding shortages, uninspired personnel, and international indifference. By tolerating this languid pace, the international community is squandering an opportunity to reduce severe ethnic tensions in Rwanda, where ascendant hardliners within the new government seek to promote the myth that all Hutus, rather than particular individuals, are guilty of genocide. The hostility of the new government toward Hutus was shown by its detention in inhumane and life-threatening conditions of some 57,000 persons accused of genocide and by the Rwandan army's massacre of thousands of displaced persons. Meanwhile, some two million refugees outside Rwanda are afraid to return home and the leaders of the former government, not yet threatened by arrest or prosecution, re-arm and mount increasingly serious incursions into Rwanda.

Progress has been particularly difficult in the effort to establish a permanent International Criminal Court (ICC). Unlike the *ad hoc* tribunals for Rwanda and the former Yugoslavia, the ICC would be available to try human rights criminals wherever national judicial systems fail in their duty to bring offenders to justice. Among its many forceful governmental proponents has been President Nelson Mandela's South Africa, which fully appreciates the difference that such a court could have made in deterring the repression of apartheid. But precisely because this court could be applied to Americans, the Clinton administration—a vocal supporter of justice elsewhere—has led efforts to undermine the independence of a future ICC. The U.S. found itself allied with such predictable opponents of international human rights enforcement as China, India, Mexico, North Korea and Pakistan.

In a speech honoring a Nuremburg prosecutor, President Clinton endorsed the ICC in principle. But his negotiators continue to insist on Security Council approval before any episode gives rise to prosecution—a transparent effort to allow the United States to veto prosecution of its own citizens or those of its allies. The other permanent Security Council members could only be expected to follow suit. The partial justice offered by such a politicized entity would sell far short the tremendous potential of the ICC.

As U.S. officials readily admit, there is little prospect that the United States in the current political climate in Washington would ratify even the watered-down version of the court they propose, meaning that U.S. citizens would not immediately be subject to it. Yet, rather than permit a strong court to go forward and simply wait until U.S. political leaders have the vision and courage to take part in an international system of justice, the Clinton administration threatens to miss this historic moment by sabotaging an institution that the U.S. government does not even plan to join.

The need for an international system of justice was made painfully apparent by the war in Chechnya. Russian troops attacked Grozny and surrounding areas with a ferocity not seen on Russian soil since World War II. Civilians faced massive indiscriminate shelling. Thousands died and hundreds of thousands were displaced.

At first, the international community responded firmly to these Russian abuses: the European Union froze an interim trade agreement and suspended ratification of a partnership and cooperation agreement; the Council of Europe suspended Russia's membership application; the Organization for Security and Cooperation in Europe established a field mission in Grozny; and the U.N. Commission on Human Rights issued a critical statement. This tough reaction generated significant pressure to curb the killing. However, this pressure soon eased—particularly when the International Monetary Fund decided to extend a major loan to Russia—without any guarantee that those behind the slaughter would be brought to justice. Russian courts did convict seven servicemen for crimes against civilians, but the generals who ordered this butchery have escaped punishment.

The creation of an ad hoc international tribunal to end this impunity is unlikely because of Russia's veto on the Security Council. Only a pre-existing ICC would have offered the possibility of justice. Moreover, an ICC offers the best chance of ensuring that this carnage is not repeated, in Chechnya or elsewhere.

Similarly in Burundi, a paralyzed judicial system cries out for international assistance. Leaders involved in assassination and mass murder continue to exercise power because judicial officials, out of fear or political interest, refuse to initiate prosecutions. In this and a score of countries around the world, only an international forum would offer any prospect of justice for the victims of violent abuse. It is thus time for the major powers, and particularly the United States, to overcome parochial fears and become active partners in building a strong international system of justice.

The United Nations

Fifty years after the United Nations was founded to, among other things, "promot[e] and encourag[e] respect for human rights and...fundamental freedoms for all" (U.N. Charter, Art. 1), Secretary-General Boutros-Ghali has grievously failed to uphold these principles. Unwilling to offend powerful governments, the secretary-general could not bring himself to criticize the Chinese government for brazenly flouting the rights of free speech and association of those attending the U.N.-sponsored Conference on Women in Beijing. Similarly, at the height of the butchery in Chechnya, the secretary-general told journalists that he had "no comment" on the brutal war. His refrain that he is merely a humble servant of 185 masters cannot mask his abdication of leadership in the human rights realm.

This leadership void turned to active obstruction in Bosnia. As Bosnian Serb forces overran the Security Council-declared "safe area" of Srebrenica, the secretary-general allowed his military commander, French Lt. Gen. Bernard Janvier, to block the protective "close air support" that Dutch peacekeepers in the enclave sought and NATO planes were ready to provide. The result was the disappearance and probable slaughter of as many as 8,000 Muslim men and boys. Rather than learning from this tragedy about the importance of stopping genocide, the secretary-general continues to embrace only the classic view of peacekeeping: he favors only the consensual deployment of lightly armed troops in the context of an established cease-fire, while relegating to others the duty to prevent mass murder. Public esteem for the U.N. diminished significantly as a result of this shirking of the U.N.'s duty to secure fundamental human rights.

The Security Council fared only slightly better in fulfilling this responsibility. Human rights issues have come to dominate the Security Council's agenda, lying at the heart of virtually every situation it addresses—in Angola, Bosnia, Burundi, Croatia, El Salvador, Georgia, Guatemala, Haiti, the Israeli-occupied territories, Iraq, Liberia, Mozambique, Rwanda, Sudan, Tajikistan and Western Sahara. This de facto recognition of the centrality of human rights to international peace and security is an important advance from the days when human rights issues were relegated to the obscurity of Geneva. Today, Security Council resolutions routinely call for respect for human rights and the establishment of field operations to protect those rights.

However, the effectiveness of these field operations varied considerably and was frequently poor. On the positive side, 6,000 peacekeepers in Haiti helped to maintain a stable environment during President Aristide's first full year in office after a U.N.-authorized military force compelled the Haitian army to relinquish power. The U.N. mission in Guatemala produced three excellent reports while providing some protection for independent human rights monitors. U.N. representatives in Cambodia also helped to check repressive governmental tendencies by issuing critical human rights reports.

By contrast, the U.N. operation in Liberia has made no public mention of human rights concerns. The U.N. operation in Western Sahara stood by quietly as Morocco worked to undermine the fairness of a planned referendum on the territory's status. U.N. peacekeepers in Rwanda sometimes contributed to the security of people at risk, but they failed to fulfill their mandate to protect civilians when Rwandan troops opened fire on displaced persons in Kibeho and mobs attacked those forced to return home. The U.N. presence in Mozambique underwrote total impunity for horrendous abuses during the recently concluded war, and the U.N. operation in Angola seemed headed in a similar direction. U.N. troops in Croatia began serious efforts to document human rights abuses only after Croatian forces retook Serb-held regions; until then, U.N. forces effectively accepted "ethnic cleansing" and spent more time evacuating non-Serbs than protecting, let alone repatriating, them.

Bosnia was the site of the U.N.'s most disturbing performance. Despite numerous resolutions calling for respect for human rights, the Security Council's repeated failure to act on these principles led to a devaluation of its condemnatory currency. Once a powerful tool, critical Security Council resolutions were cheapened. Commands issued by the score were flouted because they were so rarely backed by the will to enforce them. Instead, for most of the year, the Security Council's only concrete answer to the victims of ethnic slaughter was belated humanitarian assistance—a palliative which, while exposing vulnerable humanitarian workers to the threat of retaliation, provided a convenient pretext for avoiding more effective action. It was only after the fall of Srebrenica and Zepa and the shelling of a Sarajevo market that the need for U.N. headquarters to consent to NATO air strikes was eliminated and NATO deployed decisive force to stop the shelling of Sarajevo (although "ethnic cleansing" continued in other parts of Bosnia). This new resolve must be maintained to avoid returning to the view that, so long as officially organized mass murder takes place within internationally recognized borders, it is of no consequence to the "international peace and security" that the Security Council is charged with upholding.

Moreover, the U.N. has a particular duty to ensure that its representatives never again act as silent witnesses to atrocities. While the Dutch peacekeepers in Srebrenica justifiably cast blame for the fall of the enclave on the obstruction of General Janvier, they cannot escape responsibility for their embarrassed silence at a time when immediate and public protest might have saved thousands of lives.

One significant human rights victory at the U.N. was the reaffirmation of the universality of human rights by the U.N.-sponsored World Conference on Women. Because many repressive governments saw the conference as an opportunity to weaken or qualify the strong human rights guarantees contained in international treaties, there was a risk of retrenchment. These governments tried to use the conference to suggest that the abuse of women is a "private" matter, that it should be tolerated in the name of "custom," or that it is irrelevant to overcoming the poverty, lack of education and unequal job opportunities faced by women everywhere. Yet, women's rights activists from around the world came to Beijing to reject this cynical attack. While affirming their varying cultural and religious backgrounds, they stood together around the belief that all women deserve full respect for their human rights, that rigid concepts of privacy and tradition cannot stand in the way of these basic rights, and that violence and discrimination against women lie behind many of the economic and social problems addressed by the conference. However, because impunity for the violation of women's human rights remains the global norm, further pressure will be needed to ensure that the official commitments made at the conference to secure women's rights will be translated into effective protection.

U.N. High Commissioner for Human Rights José Ayala Lasso continued to display a disappointing tendency to avoid confrontation in his dealings with abusive governments. He was at his best during a visit to Kashmir, where his guarded comments were reported widely in the Indian press. But in Beijing, as Chinese authorities detained journalists virtually before his eyes, he ducked the opportunity to criticize this clear human rights violation by saying he would have to investigate the circumstances. In Rwanda, the human rights monitoring operation that he oversees went through much of the year without issuing a single public report, although the September appointment of an experienced human rights investigator to head the mission may signal a more vigorous reporting role.

Moreover, the high commissioner continued to treat his job as if it should be limited to the monitoring and advice traditionally offered by the U.N. Centre for Human Rights. Although he is supposed to coordinate all U.N. human rights activities, his voice was not heard at the Security Council as it deployed and managed a variety of U.N. field operations with immediate human rights consequences. The lack of human rights expertise serving the Security Council—indeed, the lack of any formal link between the council and the Human Rights Centre in Geneva—has contributed to the council's difficulty in effectively implementing its resolutions on human rights.

The high commissioner did take steps to prevent governments from substituting his relatively quiet diplomacy for the tough, public reporting of U.N. special rapporteurs, as occurred in 1994 when Cuba invited him to visit while refusing entrance to the special rapporteur for the country. Invitations for him to visit Iran, Iraq and Sudan—all countries that bar visits by special rapporteurs—were deferred.

Global Trade and Investment

The rise of a global economy has not seen a parallel global commitment to ensure respect for human rights on the part of the major economic powers. While multinational corporations look abroad for economic opportunity, Western political leaders continue to avert their gaze from parallel human rights concerns. To justify this neglect, these leaders proffer a theory that trade and investment are the best defense of human rights. Yet, as the events of 1995 exposed the hypocrisy behind this prescription, it became increasingly clear that the market is not an automatic guarantor of human rights.

The bankruptcy of this policy of "constructive engagement" was most apparent in China, where the Chinese Communist Party used the enhanced revenue generated by international trade to tighten its grip on power while ruthlessly crushing any attempt to initiate political reform. Since May 1994, when President Clinton delinked China's Most Favored Nation (MFN) trade status from its human rights record, human rights conditions in China and Tibet have deteriorated markedly. Chinese authorities have arrested additional dissidents and rearrested previously released dissidents, filed new criminal charges against democracy activist Wei Jingsheng, renewed a crackdown on Tibetans, suspended negotiations for prison

visits by the International Committee of the Red Cross (ICRC), and tightened controls on the media and on religious practices outside officially controlled churches—all in addition to their continuing practice of torture, use of forced labor, and tight restrictions on civil society.

Even the formal U.S.-China human rights dialogue, begun in 1990, has largely ended. In 1991, when MFN for China was hotly contested, nearly 800 cases of political prisoners were discussed, and a few prisoners were released. In 1994, before MFN linkage with human rights was abandoned, another 400 cases were discussed and a few additional prisoners were released. By contrast, during the October 1995 summit between Presidents Clinton and Jiang Zemin, U.S. officials quietly handed over a list of four political prisoners, and none was released. Still, the Clinton administration proclaimed the summit "highly positive."

Contrary to predictions by proponents of this trade-based human rights policy, those provinces with the most dramatic economic development and the highest level of foreign investment have shown no greater respect for civil and political rights than have other parts of China. Indeed, certain human rights violations—such as the repression of labor activists and the mistreatment of migrant laborers—appear to have increased with economic development.

A serious effort was made by the European Union, the United States, Japan and others to condemn China's abysmal record before the U.N. Human Rights Commission. While the effort failed by one vote, it represented the first time that a commission resolution to condemn a permanent member of the Security Council had survived procedural challenges to come to a substantive vote. U.S. First Lady Hillary Rodham Clinton also delivered a strong rebuke to Chinese repression in a speech at the U.N. Women's Conference.

Yet the important message sent by these efforts was undermined by the flood of Western leaders to China in search of business opportunities despite the Chinese government's deteriorating human rights record. U.S. Commerce Secretary Ron Brown continued to epitomize this approach as he traveled to Beijing to pay obeisance to Chinese rulers with nary a public word about the brutal underpinnings of China's economy. U.S. Energy Secretary Hazel O'Leary and a delegation of corporate executives joined the caravan without any public criticism of China's human rights practices. The White House did try to highlight the corporate community's potential as a force for human rights, but the Model Business Principles it issued were far too vague and broadly worded to have any impact on the specific problem they were meant to address: human rights violations in China.

Chancellor Helmut Kohl embodied similar priorities as he led a parade of German commercial supplicants to Beijing. While his delegation sought release of a list of political detainees, Chancellor Kohl stressed the need to take into account varying cultural traditions in applying universal human rights standards—the same code words used by China to justify its repression. He also became the first European head of government to visit a Chinese army base, despite a European Union arms embargo in effect since China's crackdown on the Tiananmen Square democracy movement. Canadian Prime Minister Jean Chrétien, another proponent of "constructive engagement," welcomed Chinese Premier Li Peng as a featured speaker at a conference of the Canada China Business Council, with only discreet mention of human rights. In the end, no government seemed willing to risk the economic consequences of applying consistent political and economic pressure to Beijing. Nor did any government take the lead in developing multilateral forms of pressure that would prevent less principled competitors from undercutting those who stand up for human rights.

The continued subordination of human rights to commercial concerns could be found outside of China as well. Despite the enormous leverage provided by a $20 billion economic support package, the U.S. government made only one cautious public statement about Mexican human rights abuses. (As with every country, the State Department also commented on Mexico in its *Country Reports on Human Rights Practices*, but the widespread failure to modify U.S. policy to reflect these generally accurate accounts continued to undermine their significance.) Brazil, another "big emerging market" in the U.S. Commerce Department's world view, did not warrant a single public mention about, for example, its alarming rate of police killings, even when President Clinton met with Brazilian President Fernando Henrique Cardoso. The same silence reigned over U.S. relations with Saudi Arabia, where the quest for billions of dollars in new contracts helped to foster a quiet tolerance of systematic discrimination against women, the repression of independent public expression, a crackdown on largely nonviolent Islamists, and the lack of any prospect for elections. France and Britain were equally silent about Saudi human rights practices as they vied for military sales to the kingdom.

Japan, while committed in principle to linking its Official Development Assistance (ODA) to democratization and the promotion of human rights, rarely invoked this policy in Asia. Burma was the principal exception, but even there Japan was quick to begin talks for the resumption of ODA following the release from house arrest of Nobel laureate Daw Aung San Suu Kyi, despite her own recommendation that Japan move slowly in restoring aid. Apart from Burma, Japan has cut off ODA mainly to African countries, although it has raised human rights concerns in its "policy dialogues" with some Asian governments. The United Kingdom, for its part, held its second "British Week" to encourage British business in Burma. The Association of Southeast Asian Nations (ASEAN) also prepared to admit Burma despite its highly abusive military government.

German Chancellor Helmut Kohl overlooked Indonesia's poor human rights record, including a new crackdown on free expression and association, to preside at the signing of major business deals during a visit to Germany by Indonesia's President Soeharto. Queen Beatrix of the Netherlands visited Indonesia to express regret over Holland's colonial role, but this gesture was undermined by the downplaying of Indonesian abuses as a delegation of Dutch business people pursued Indonesian contracts.

While powerful business interests lie behind these misplaced priorities, hope lies in the public discomfort periodically shown at this coddling of dictators and the accompanying vacuous pledges that unhampered trade would inevitably improve human rights. U.S. Commerce Secretary Brown typified the cynicism behind this trade with tyrants during a trip to India to clinch business deals worth billions of dollars. He announced that while "commercial diplomacy" was one way to effect human rights improvements, "one doesn't have to wait for the other." Despite a self-imposed obligation to promote human rights through trade and diplomatic channels, the European Union also approved two major development projects in India with little evidence of a serious effort to raise human rights concerns.

The power of public outrage to reassert principle over profit was seen in the reaction to China's Three Gorges dam project. The Chinese government has already tried to silence local protests over the dam's anticipated environmental damage and plans to displace forcibly over one million people. Public criticism in the West of U.S. investment banks Merrill Lynch and Morgan Stanley for vying for the right to finance the project led China to announce that it would suspend its search for foreign financing of the dam in 1995. In addition, the White House recommended, on human rights and environmental grounds, that the U.S. Export-Import Bank not fund dam-related projects.

Similarly, public outrage over Indonesia's abuse of human rights met President Soeharto's deal-signing visit to Germany. Public protests in Australia over the naming and acceptance as Indonesian ambassador of a general who had defended the military's action in the 1991 killing of demonstrators in Dili, East Timor, led to his withdrawal.

A more appropriate balance was struck between trade and human rights in dealings with Vietnam. When President Clinton opened diplomatic relations with Vietnam, he announced that normal economic relations, involving such matters as MFN trade status and coverage by the Overseas Private Investment Corporation (OPIC), would require certification of Vietnam's human and labor rights practices. The European Union, for its part, signed a trade and cooperation agreement with Vietnam conditioned on "[r]espect for human rights and democratic principles." Such linkage was needed because, despite Vietnam's increasing integration into the world economy and such other diplomatic breakthroughs as becoming the seventh member of ASEAN, it ordered new arrests and prosecution of political and religious dissidents.

Whether the major economic powers will maintain a better balance between trade and human rights will be seen in several pending decisions:

• The European Parliament is poised to decide whether to ratify a "customs union agreement" with Turkey which has been negotiated by the European Union. Ratification has been conditioned on specific improvements in Turkey's human rights practices. Turkey has taken some steps to comply, but its serious abuses against the Kurdish population continue.

• The Organization on Economic Cooperation and Development (OECD), the club of industrial democracies, is considering membership for South Korea. Its stated commitment to uphold labor rights will be measured by whether it insists that South Korea lift its extensive restrictions on independent labor activity as a condition of membership. (The South Korean government boycotted an OECD seminar on worker rights in order to avoid awkward questions about Korea's repressive laws and practices.)

- The U.S. government has announced that it will remove tariff benefits under the Generalized System of Preferences (GSP) from one of three designated imports unless Pakistan complies with unspecified commitments regarding the use of child and bonded labor. Washington is also considering a challenge to Indonesia's eligibility for GSP trade benefits because of labor rights abuses that include military intervention in peaceful labor disputes and the harassment of independent labor organizers.

- The European Union is considering a similar petition based on Pakistan's use of bonded child labor as well as Burma's use of forced labor.

These and other pending decisions provide an opportunity for the economic powers to act on the fact that unrestrained trade and investment, without a firm parallel commitment to promote human rights, offer no guarantee of human rights progress.

The World Bank is often at the center of the debate over the relationship of trade and human rights. For many years, it hid behind its charter's prohibition of involvement in "political" affairs to justify ignoring human rights. However, prompted largely by the lack of economic progress in countries governed by abusive and corrupt governments in sub-Saharan Africa, the bank now accepts that "good governance" is relevant to its development goals. But it generally still tends to define this concept narrowly to include only transparent and sound fiscal management, not the broad accountability that would be ensured by a vigorous civil society, full political participation including free elections, and the rule of law.

Human Rights Watch and other nongovernmental organizations (NGOs) are working to convince the World Bank to accept the economic significance of these human rights concerns. There is evidence that such ideas are now received more sympathetically at the bank: for example, the bank's private-sector branch, the International Finance Corporation, cited "macroeconomic" considerations to reject a loan for a gas liquification project in Nigeria just hours after the Nigerian military's execution without elementary due process of Ken Saro-Wiwa and eight ethnic Ogoni activists who were outspoken critics of the oil industry's role in that country. However, much work must still be done to integrate this perspective into the mainstream of the bank's thinking.

Because so many multinational corporations claim that their trade and investment inherently promote human rights, it is only proper that their conduct be more closely scrutinized—particularly as global trade dwarfs governmental aid programs. But while government-to-government aid is regularly conditioned on respect for human rights, multinational corporations face few if any such restrictions, even though their power often exceeds that of governments. The heightened scrutiny of corporate practices has led a growing number of businesses to adopt codes of conduct that include human rights standards for their factories and those of their suppliers. A smaller but growing number of companies are taking serious steps to implement these codes through regular monitoring. Perhaps most important, consumers increasingly want to make sure that the goods they buy are not the product of human rights abuse.

Human Rights Watch believes that all businesses have a duty to avoid direct complicity in violations of international human rights and labor rights standards such as discrimination, the use of forced and bonded labor, and restrictions on the right to free expression and association, including on the right to organize a labor union and bargain collectively. At a minimum, this duty extends to the adoption of country-specific standards for avoiding such complicity and the implementation of a concrete program to apply those standards through credible on-site inspections of factories and suppliers. When these standards are not met, immediate corrective steps should be taken or the commercial relationship should be ended.

The duty to avoid complicity in human rights abuse can also extend outside the walls of a factory or supplier, since the refusal to address broader human rights issues can come back to haunt multinational businesses unexpectedly. Illustrative is the experience of Royal Dutch Shell, whose call to Nigerian security forces to protect its oil installations from Ogoni protesters set in motion a series of military abuses that included brutal attacks on Ogoni villages and the appalling execution of nine Ogoni activists. Despite Shell's tremendous influence as the company responsible for nearly half of Nigeria's oil production, it refused to engage in anything but "quiet diplomacy" to end the atrocities and consequently is now left with a dark stain on its reputation. Unocal and Total face similar issues as they proceed with plans to build a gas pipeline across Burma, where a highly abusive military junta and the pervasive use of forced labor to build the country's infrastructure virtually guarantee their complicity in human rights abuses. Troubling issues must also be faced by businesses that manufacture in South Asia, with its widespread use of bonded child labor.

Moreover, while businesses legitimately point out that they are not human rights organizations, the more far-sighted companies increasingly recognize that the same strong judiciary and rule of law needed to protect dissidents also safeguard their own commercial interests. Similarly, a healthy civil society and democratic rule are the best guarantor of the long-term stability that business needs to thrive. Recognition of the intersecting interests of business and the human rights community should lead to the striking of a better balance between trade and human rights.

The Arms Trade

The quest for foreign markets takes on a particularly insidious form when the commodity is weapons. The flood of weapons to abusive governments can intensify repression and compound human suffering. Human Rights Watch believes that all governments have a duty to prevent the transfer of arms to abusive governments and to prohibit the production and stockpiling of weapons, such as landmines, that are inherently prone to abuse.

This duty continued to be regularly breached. Despite a European Union pronouncement in 1993 that arms sales to Nigeria would be presumptively barred, Britain continued to sell arms to the Nigerian military right up until the execution of the nine Ogoni activists. Although the European Union imposed an arms embargo following the execution, it exempted the delivery of military equipment under contracts that had already been signed.

France was revealed in 1995 to have flouted the previous year a Security Council ban on arms sales to the genocidal army of Rwanda. Britain muted criticism of severe human rights abuses to endorse India's policy on Kashmir while promoting the sale of military aircraft to Delhi. Russia and Ukraine sent weapons to the Angolan government despite a peace accord. China continued to send helicopters, armored vehicles, naval vessels and rifles to Burma. The U.S. government tried to authorize the private sale of cluster bombs to Turkey until public exposure scuttled the plan, although the U.S. continues to sell other arms to Turkey despite its use of them to wage an abusive counterinsurgency war. The United States did refuse to license the sale of weapons to Algeria's violently abusive government—unlike France, which sold Algeria nine helicopters which could easily be refitted for military purposes.

On the positive side, a South African commission of inquiry established by the Mandela government to look into arms sales by the previous government reported a "dismal picture of irresponsibility." The current government established a cabinet-level committee to authorize all future arms sales based on a review that includes human rights criteria. The government has already rejected

Nigeria as an arms recipient.

A growing coalition of 350 NGOs from some three dozen countries, led in part by Human Rights Watch, placed landmines on the international agenda by highlighting the tremendous human suffering caused by these indiscriminate weapons and by calling for a total ban on the production, stockpiling, trade and use of antipersonnel mines. To date, eighteen nations have announced support for a comprehensive ban, and thirty-one nations have unilaterally banned mine exports. However, at an international conference convened to consider restrictions on the use of landmines, the United States, Britain and other governments promoted their technologically superior "self-destruct" mines as the solution to the global landmines crisis, while China, India and others sought to avoid rendering their technologically simpler mines obsolete. As a result, negotiations on new restrictions were suspended until 1996.

A recent NGO effort to. ban blinding laser weapons was more fruitful. Revelations by Human Rights Watch and the ICRC that these inherently cruel weapons were being developed sparked a campaign which led to an international agreement that intentional blinding is an unacceptable way to wage war. Although the U.S. government insisted on a loophole to permit the use of certain blinding lasers that it has developed, the Pentagon simultaneously announced the cancellation of its program to begin full-scale production of these lasers.

Closing the Door to Refugees

From Burma to Rwanda, from Algeria to Bosnia, the spread of warfare waged through the targeting of civilians contributed to a large and continuing flow of refugees. Yet as xenophobia rises in many receiving countries, the international response to refugees has become increasingly stingy. Even the bedrock principle of international refugee law—the prohibition against forcibly repatriating refugees to face a well-founded fear of persecution—is violated routinely.

The U.S. government epitomized this disregard for refugee protection when, in January 1995, it forcibly repatriated without a hearing more than 3,700 Haitians who had been held at the U.S. naval base at Guantánamo, Cuba. Although the return of President Aristide the previous October had markedly improved respect for human rights in Haiti, some Haitians legitimately feared repatriation because many of the military and paramilitary forces that had ruled Haiti for the prior three years remained armed and at large. For a brief period before screening procedures were improved, the U.S. government violated the same principle by summarily repatriating Cuban asylum-seekers. Cuba had vowed not to prosecute the asylum-seekers for "illegal exit," but the crime remained on the books, and Cuba continued to imprison a wide range of peaceful dissidents. U.S. Border Patrol agents also continued to commit acts of violence with impunity against undocumented migrants crossing from Mexico into the United States, although the U.S. Immigration and Naturalization Service (INS) began to take corrective steps.

The reaction of Western Europe to an influx of refugees was no more generous. While Germany has taken commendable steps to prosecute those behind right-wing and xenophobic violence, police abuse of foreigners is on the rise. Both Germany and France, like a growing number of European governments, now apply summary procedures to assess the claims of asylum-seekers from countries that are deemed to be "safe" for repatriation, often despite substantial contrary evidence. France also denies asylum, with rare exception, for people facing persecution by rebel groups, even though international law does not limit refugee status to those facing persecution by governments. The cost of such narrow application of refugee law is compounded by the Schengen Agreement among several European countries, which reinforces the practice of summarily rejecting asylum applications if another country that generally observes refugee standards has already ruled against the asylum-seeker, however unjustly.

Nor is the West alone in shutting the door on refugees. Those fleeing repression and warfare in Burma were rarely granted formal refugee protection by Thailand. The result was a legal limbo which left many Burmese subject to harassment, detention, forced prostitution and deportation. The Thai military also failed for part of the year to prevent cross-border raids upon Burmese refugee camps.

Similarly, the Iranian government announced that its 1.6 million Afghan refugees must leave the country by March 1997 despite ongoing civil war in Afghanistan. Libya began expelling Palestinian refugees and immigrants to embarrass the Palestinian Authority for signing a second peace agreement with Israel. Hundreds of Palestinians were dumped on the Egyptian border, where they were forced to live in wretched makeshift camps because they lacked papers that would entitle them to enter the West Bank, the Gaza Strip, or anywhere else. Libya also started expelling a large portion of its 1.5 million African immigrants, citing alleged economic difficulties resulting from the international embargo imposed by the U.N. Following deteriorating relations with its neighbors to the east, Sudan in turn threatened to expel Ethiopian and Eritrean refugees to make room for the thousands of Sudanese deported from Libya.

The Role of Civil Society

Often the best measure of governmental respect for human rights is the visible presence of people exercising those rights by forming organizations, assembling, speaking out publicly, and publishing independently. However, because this pluralism is antithetical to the monopoly on political space that dictators seek to maintain, civil society is a frequent target of their repression. The past year was no exception.

The military government in Nigeria, seeking to silence criticism of its protracted "transition to democracy," banned independent publications, dissolved independent trade unions, and imprisoned journalists, pro-democracy activists and human rights

monitors. The Sudanese government arrested hundreds of demonstrators, shut down newspapers and, with the help of government-organized surveillance committees, detained supposed agitators for months without charge or trial. In Kenya, independent organizations, journalists, and political opponents faced shutdowns, violent attacks, and politically motivated charges.

In Peru, under the guise of combatting a guerrilla force, the government used "faceless courts" and secret military tribunals to imprison political opponents without the most basic due process. Colombia similarly misused "public order" courts in the name of combatting guerrillas and drug traffickers. Cuba continued to charge human rights activists and political dissidents with the thought and speech crimes of "enemy propaganda," "clandestine printing," "contempt of authority," "anti-social behavior," and violating "socialist morality."

The Cambodian government used a criminal defamation law to silence journalists and editors. The Indonesian government prosecuted journalists, harassed independent labor organizations and banned public appearances by popular opposition figures. Having failed to take strong action against the explosion of violence in Karachi, the Pakistani government lashed out at the press by banning newspapers and bringing lawsuits against critical journalists. The Chinese government responded to open petitions calling for greater tolerance and democracy by jailing signatories.

Azerbaijan prosecuted journalists for insulting the honor and dignity of the president. Armenia closed twelve news agencies allegedly associated with a suspended opposition party. Uzbekistan prosecuted political opponents on trumped-up charges of drug and arms possession. Turkey harassed, imprisoned and tortured journalists. Kyrgyzstan imprisoned independent journalists. Bulgaria continued to deny legal registration to forty-five "non-traditional" religions. Turkmenistan beat and arrested protesters.

Saudi Arabia arrested hundreds of members of the largely nonviolent Islamist opposition and, having prohibited an independent press within the kingdom, banned the possession of satellite dishes to curtail the spread of critical reporting from abroad. Egypt used its fight against violent Islamists as a pretext to suppress public criticism, jail political opponents, restrict political participation, and arrest and torture lawyers. Iran allowed a mob of militants to attack a prominent intellectual who was advocating a liberal interpretation of Islamic principles.

Syria's state security courts sentenced nonviolent dissidents to long prison terms. Algeria barred meetings about human rights organized by opposition political parties. Bahrain security forces used live ammunition to disperse demonstrators seeking the restoration of parliament and constitutional rule and detained hundreds of protesters. Palestinian authorities in the self-rule areas closed newspapers and, in part due to U.S. and Israeli urging that terrorism be rooted out, subjected political opponents to closed, summary trials.

Abuse of Elections

As recognition grows of the right freely to elect one's governmental representatives, more governments felt compelled to hold elections in order to gain legitimacy. However, some governments attempted to substitute an electoral charade for a free and competitive polling, without permitting the vigorous debate and broad participation that make elections meaningful.

The most outrageous attempt was in Iraq where, despite harsh repression against any independent political activity, President Saddam Hussein claimed to have received 99.9 percent approval in a referendum on his rule. In Turkmenistan, all candidates were nominated by the president and ran uncontested. Kazakstan dissolved parliament and, after a popular referendum riddled with irregularities, canceled the 1996 presidential elections and allowed the president to remain uncontested in office until the year 2000. Tajikistan held parliamentary elections flawed by intimidation and fraud.

Egypt used military courts to jail opposition candidates in advance of its elections. Algeria, determined to obtain high voter turnout for a presidential election despite a limited choice of candidates, censored the media, barred rallies and arrested activists favoring a boycott. Iran restricted candidate eligibility and closed newspapers in advance of its election in 1996. President Mobutu Sese Seko of Zaire put off scheduled elections for another two years, extending his announced "transition to democracy" to seven years. The Burmese military continued to imprison sixteen members of parliament who had been elected in the annulled 1990 elections together with some one thousand other political prisoners.

The Armenian government suspended the oldest and most popular opposition party in the months before Armenia's first post-Soviet parliamentary elections. Azerbaijan prosecuted political opponents and excluded some from parliamentary elections. Albania banned several prominent opposition politicians from elections scheduled for early 1996 under a law meant to bar officials from the pre-1991 government but worded so vaguely and so lacking in due process guarantees as to make selective application easy.

The Right to Monitor

The human rights movement continued to grow and gain a foothold in new and often hostile parts of the world. Typical of its resilience is the explosion of strong and capable groups in sub-Saharan Africa, despite chaos and repression in Zaire, a systematic crackdown on human rights activists in Nigeria, and threats and harassment in Kenya. In Latin America, the movement continues to display its sophistication and vibrancy. Parts of Asia host a diverse and growing assembly of human rights groups. Human rights groups are also slowly emerging in many of the countries of the former Soviet Union.

Because the public exposure of human rights violations is so powerful, abusive governments go to great lengths to prevent revelation of their crimes. In extreme cases, human rights monitors risk their lives to reveal abuses. The exceptional dedication and courage of many human rights monitors was illustrated by Sergei Kovalyev, the Russian human rights commissioner, who braved the massive shelling of Grozny to report on the savagery of Russian troops in Chechnya.

At least nine human rights monitors disappeared or were murdered over the last year in apparent retaliation for their work, including three in Colombia and two in Algeria:

• In Colombia, Ernesto Fernández Fester was killed by armed men who had been linked to several earlier killings of peasant and civic leaders. Javier Barriga Vergel and Humberto Peña Prieto were killed by unidentified assailants.

• In Algeria, human rights activist Abdel-Hafid Megdoud was murdered by unidentified assailants, while an armed Islamist group reportedly claimed responsibility for the killing of women's rights activist Nabila Djahnine.

• In Guatemala, one human rights monitor, Manuel Saquic Vásquez, was kidnapped and brutally murdered. A death squad associated with the military later took credit for the killing. Another monitor, Martin Quip Mocu, was seriously wounded when soldiers opened fire on an unarmed crowd.

• Jaswant Singh Khalra of Punjab, India, was arrested and disappeared after his office filed a legal petition claiming that the Punjab police had killed and secretly cremated hundreds.

• In Honduras, Pedro Espinosa Osorio, a security guard for National Commissioner for Human Rights Leo Valladares Lanza, was killed on a public bus by unknown assailants amid regular death threats to Valladares.

• Disaster relief expert Frederick Cuny was reportedly detained and summarily executed while on a mission for the Open Society Institute to assess food and medicine needs in southern Chechnya. A U.S. citizen and a member of the Human Rights Watch Arms Project Advisory Committee, he was reportedly captured by Chechen forces who may have been reacting to allegedly leaked Russian intelligence information. It is widely believed that he incurred the wrath of the Russian government because of his outspoken views on the abusive conduct of the war.

In some countries, human rights activists faced detention and trumped-up criminal charges for their bravery. Wei Jingsheng, China's most outspoken advocate of democracy and human rights, was charged with attempting to overthrow the government. Having served most of a fifteen-year sentence for seeking democratic change, he had been rearrested in April 1994 after only six months of freedom.

Those detained in Nigeria included the leaders of the major human rights and pro-democracy organizations, such as the Civil Liberties Organization and the Campaign for Democracy. Monitors in Cuba faced lengthy prison sentences for such crimes as "enemy propaganda" and, though less frequently than in the past, attacks by government-organized mobs in self-styled "acts of repudiation." Activists were also detained or remained in custody for reporting human rights information in Burma, China and Tibet, Egypt, India, Indonesia and East Timor, the Israeli-occupied West Bank, the Palestinian-administered Gaza Strip, Syria, Tunisia and Turkey.

Human rights monitors faced threats and other forms of harassment in Brazil, Burundi, Cambodia, Colombia, Egypt, Guatemala, Honduras, India, Indonesia, Kenya, Mexico, Pakistan, Peru, Rwanda, Turkmenistan, Uzbekistan and Zaire.

No overt domestic human rights monitoring was possible in Burma, China and Tibet, Iran, Iraq, North Korea, Saudi Arabia, Singapore, Sudan, Syria and Vietnam.

Human Rights Watch

Over the last year, Human Rights Watch has continued to adjust to the shifting global climate for the protection of human rights—from the spread of ethnic strife to the growing importance of trade in comparison to governmental aid as a tool for curbing abuse. Perhaps most important, as an expanding human rights movement takes root in many countries, we have endeavored to ensure closer and more effective alliances with our local colleagues. We worked jointly to set research priorities, undertake investigations, and pursue advocacy strategies. Our special contribution to this work derives from our broad mandate, our capacity to undertake lengthy and difficult field investigations, our established reputation among the international press corps, and our ability to insert human rights issues into the foreign policy deliberations of influential governments.

As the nature of human rights abuse changes in many parts of the world—with classic political imprisonment often giving way to labor rights violations, abuse related to competition over resources, or warfare among ethnic groups—we have adjusted our investigative priorities. For example, with our capacity to mount complex wartime investigations and our long history of reporting on violations of not only human rights but also humanitarian law or the laws of war, we launched repeated investigations over the past year and issued numerous reports concerning atrocities in Bosnia and Chechnya. In the aftermath of the genocide in Rwanda, we opened a field office to collect detailed evidence against those responsible and to help to deter a new outbreak of killing.

With this war-related work in particular, we sought to highlight the need to bring the authors of atrocities to justice. We worked closely with prosecutors from the International Criminal Tribunals for Rwanda and the Former Yugoslavia and devoted substantial attention and resources to securing the establishment of an International Criminal Court.

We also published a global report on communal conflict which drew on ten case studies to reveal the human rights abuse that is frequently the proximate cause of this bloodshed. Our goal was to promote preventive action by identifying the violations of human rights that can serve as an early warning sign of communal violence.

In the economic realm, we heightened our scrutiny of development efforts to ensure that they proceed with due attention to human rights. We highlighted adverse human rights consequences of such development projects as China's Three Gorges dam and of logging, mining and other extraction operations in Asia and Latin America. Our goal is not to halt this economic activity but to ensure that it is carried out with full respect for human rights and only after free public debate inside the relevant country about its desirability.

As international trade and investment dwarfs government-to-government assistance, we are paying closer attention to the human rights role of the business community. Many companies now seek advice from us on how to set and implement human rights standards for their own operations and those of their suppliers. When voluntary efforts are lacking, we have investigated and publicized business complicity in human rights violations. One special investigation that we have launched is into the use of bonded child labor by South Asian suppliers of multinational corporations.

To curtail the devastation caused by the flourishing arms trade, we continued to investigate not only abuses attributable to government and rebel forces but also the ways in which those forces obtain their arms. We conducted lengthy investigations and issued reports on the U.S. role in supplying the abusive Turkish military and the role in 1994 of France, Zaire and others in supplying the genocidal Rwandan army. We also helped to launch and lead large coalitions of NGOs to stop the use of inherently indiscriminate landmines and cruel blinding laser weapons.

The global communications revolution, with its flood of human rights information, presents both opportunity and hazard for our work. While the stigmatization of abusive governments is easier, the avalanche of news accounts about repression and abuse risks fueling isolationism and encouraging a sense of helplessness among the general public. To avoid reinforcing this despair, we have tried to move beyond simply investigating and reporting abuse to also link the information we publish to the steps that could be taken to curtail abuse.

We have worked closely with certain governments to craft pro-human rights policies. Illustrative was our positive response to a request from the Brazilian government that we help it formulate a national plan of action on human rights. We also assisted in drafting a new press law for Cambodia and provided guidance to a newly created U.S. advisory board that is reviewing the human rights practices of the INS. In addition, we are using our growing legal expertise to support and employ such international mechanisms as the Human Rights Committee and the Inter-American Court on Human Rights.

Recognizing the importance of enlisting support for human rights from all quarters, we have continued to internationalize our advocacy. We took steps to bolster our new Brussels office in order to expand our contacts with European NGOs and journalists and to extend our reach to European governments. With our new U.N. representative in place, we substantially intensified our research and advocacy directed toward the United Nations, with a special focus on U.N. field operations that affect human rights. We also continued periodic visits to Tokyo to work with local allies in encouraging the Japanese government to promote human rights more vigorously. At the World Bank, we expanded our informal contacts and our provision of information about human rights practices in countries where the bank is considering loans.

In advance of the U.N. Women's Conference in Beijing, we issued a global report on women's human rights which highlighted the broad range of rights violations confronted by women worldwide and the diverse efforts to overcome these abuses. The lengthy and detailed report helped the thousands of activists in Beijing to demonstrate that women's rights must be addressed if women are to overcome the many social and economic problems they face. It also helped to lay the groundwork for an emerging and powerful alliance between women's and human rights organizations to secure accountability for violations of women's human rights.

Our insistence that human rights standards be applied universally led us to undertake a series of investigations and reports on human rights abuses in established democracies. We investigated or reported on prison conditions in Japan and the treatment of foreigners and immigrants in France, Germany and Britain. In the United States, our investigations and reports addressed police abuse, sexual abuse of women inmates, cruel practices in supermaximum security prisons, abusive custodial facilities for juveniles, the judicial execution of juvenile offenders, Border Patrol abuse along the U.S.-Mexican border, U.S. violations of international refugee law in the summary repatriation of Cuban and Haitian asylum-seekers, and U.S. compliance with and reporting under the International Covenant on Civil and Political Rights and the International Convention on the Elimination of All Forms of Racial Discrimination. We also continued to press for U.S. ratification of, among other treaties, the International Covenant on Economic, Social and Cultural Rights; the Convention on the Elimination of All Forms of Discrimination Against Women; the Convention on the Rights of the Child; and the 1977 Additional Protocols to the 1949 Geneva Conventions.

What follows is a review of human rights practices in sixty-five countries. This report, released in advance of Human Rights Day, December 10, covers events from December 1994 through November 1995. Each chapter examines major human rights developments during the year and the response of the international community. While we continue to devote particular attention to the human rights policies of the U.S. government, this report reflects our increasing focus as well on the human rights policies of the European Union, the United Nations, Japan, the World Bank, and other international actors. Each country chapter also details restrictions on human rights monitoring and the efforts of Human Rights Watch to end abuse.

This is our sixth report on human rights developments worldwide and our thirteenth on U.S. human rights policy. The volume does not include a chapter on every country where we worked, nor does it discuss every issue of importance. The countries and issues treated reflect the focus of our work in 1995, which in turn was determined by the severity of abuses, our access to information about them, our ability to influence abusive practices, and our desire to balance our work across various political and regional divides.

HUMAN RIGHTS WATCH WORLD REPORT 1996

HUMAN
RIGHTS
WATCH

AFRICA

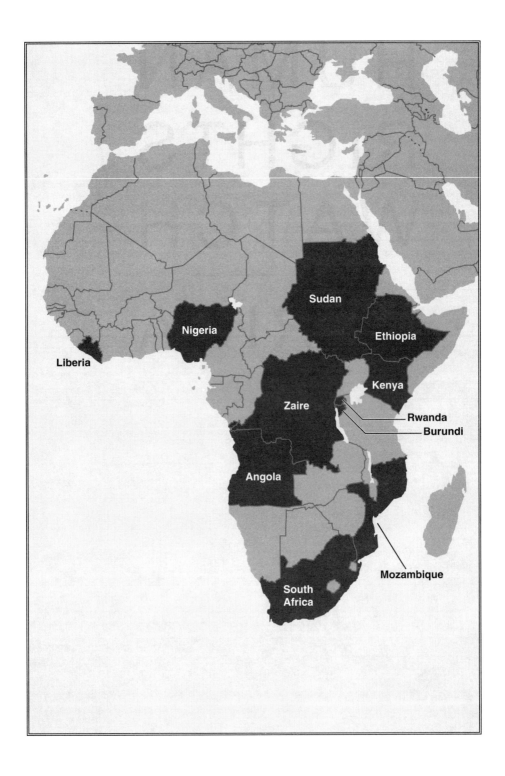

HUMAN RIGHTS WATCH/AFRICA
OVERVIEW

Human Rights Developments

Human rights in sub-Saharan Africa continued to be assaulted during 1995, despite improvements in some human rights conditions and new prospects for ending bloody civil wars. In the aftermath of genocide in Rwanda, a new government that put an end to the genocide was itself responsible for abuses this year, while Rwanda's former government threatened to return to "finish" the genocide with its Zaire-based exile army. With the dismantling of apartheid and the extraordinary changes in South Africa, in contrast, tangible progress was made toward the development of a human rights culture.

Although respect for human rights varied from country to country, the issue of impunity cut across much of Africa in 1995, as many countries grappled with the legacy of past abuses, while others suffered from direct interference with the independence of the judiciary. The support given to governments and armed opposition groups known for their abuse of human rights, by governments and state-sanctioned arms traders, also contributed to regional insecurity and widespread human rights abuses.

Throughout the continent, internal armed conflicts and autocratic governments combined to erode respect for human rights. In situations of internal conflicts—whether collapsed states like Somalia and Liberia, or the civil wars of Sudan and Angola—human rights protections were virtually nonexistent, and abuses were carried out with impunity. In situations where entrenched governments were undermining transitions to democracy—like Nigeria, Kenya, and Zaire—the weakness of state institutions and civil society were used by leaders to consolidate their personal rule and to attack their real or perceived opponents.

Proceedings to establish accountability for past abuses were underway in 1995 in Ethiopia, Rwanda, South Africa, and Malawi. In other countries, like Angola and Mozambique, governments and armed opposition alike avoided any effort to confront the issue. In Rwanda and Ethiopia, prosecutions for gross abuses of human rights under previous governments were stymied by lengthy delays.

In Rwanda, some 57,000 people remained in overcrowded and life-threatening prisons awaiting trial for genocide, yet the judiciary remained paralyzed. Although shortages of human and material resources slowed the functioning of the judicial system, this did not explain the failure to try any of those accused of genocide. Hundreds of prisoners died in Rwandan jails this year as the government failed to show the political will to move forward with trials. Nor was there much progress at the international level; a year after its creation in November 1994, the International Criminal Tribunal for Rwanda had yet to hand down an indictment.

Ethiopia presented a different situation, with a Special Prosecutors' Office created to try the 1,500 officials of the Derg government who were detained since 1991. It was only in December 1994 that the top forty-four Derg leaders were charged. South Africa took yet another course, and agreed to establish a National Commission on Truth and Reconciliation to hear applications for indemnity from prosecution for persons who committed gross human rights violations on political grounds, and to prepare a record of human rights abuses committed from March 1960 to December 1993.

Not all governments were interested in confronting these issues. One of the first things agreed upon in peace talks by Angola's warring factions was a general amnesty for illegal acts associated with the war, including human rights abuses. Similarly, the political leaders of RENAMO and the ruling party FRELIMO in Mozambique refused to acknowledge any involvement in human rights abuses, or to make either "truth-telling" or accountability a part of the peace process.

In countries that professed to be democratizing, respect for human rights was undercut by governments seeking to retain power. In Kenya, the government of President Daniel arap Moi attacked independent organizations, journalists, and opposition politicians, and effectively banned a new political party, Safina. In Nigeria, President Sani Abacha announced on October 1 that he was extending his rule and the "transition to democracy" for another two years, while keeping numerous human rights activists, pro-democracy figures, and journalists in prison. In Zaire, the promised transition to democracy was also extended for another two years in July, with no restrictions placed on the military and security forces, which continued to prey on the civilian population.

Nigeria was a clear illustration of the severely circumscribed powers of the judiciary being used to shield the government. The closed trial of alleged coup plotters, who were sentenced to terms of imprisonment and death (the death sentences were commuted to life imprisonment), was characterized by a lack of due process, without the right to choose counsel freely or the right to appeal to an independent court. The same mockery of justice prevailed in the trial by a special tribunal of Ken Saro-Wiwa and other Ogoni activists, which resulted in the death sentence for nine of the defendants. The nine men were hanged just forty-eight hours after the verdict was confirmed by the Provisional Ruling Council: no appeal was allowed as the Abacha government was determined to flaunt its power of life and death in defiance of international appeals for clemency. Chief Moshood Abiola, the presumed winner of the 1993 presidential election, remained in detention, with his trial postponed indefinitely. Human rights and pro-democracy activists were subjected to near-constant harassment or arrest, and several remained in incommunicado detention without charge or trial. The government of Sudan carried out similar practices, with security forces arresting hundreds of demonstrators, often detaining supposed agitators for months without charge or trial. Former Prime Minister Sadiq Al Mahdi, leader of the banned Umma Party whose democratically elected government was deposed by the military coup of 1989, was held in incommunicado detention for three-and-a-half months.

Africa's internal armed conflicts were characterized by widespread violations of human rights and humanitarian law. For much of the year, ongoing civil strife ravaged Sudan, Somalia, Liberia, Burundi, Angola, and Sierra Leone. However, by year's end, hopes were raised by peace agreements and cease-fires that appeared to be holding in Angola and Liberia. All these conflicts involved forces that primarily targeted civilians for killing, often on ethnic lines, causing millions to become refugees or internally displaced. Indeed, Africa is the largest producer of refugees and displaced persons in the world. Several of these conflicts have also been characterized by the extensive use of child soldiers, especially Angola, Mozambique, and Liberia.

Arms flows to abusive governments and rebel groups increased the possibility of renewed war in many areas, especially in the Great Lakes region of Central Africa. The flow of arms to the Rwandan refugee camps in eastern Zaire and military training by Hutu forces of the former Rwandan government, sometimes together with the Burundian Hutu militias, presented serious risks for the entire region. The increased number of weapons in the area fueled conflicts in eastern Zaire that predated the Rwandan crisis. Evidence of new arms deliveries and foreign military support of rival factions continued in Liberia, despite a U.N. arms embargo, and in Angola, in violation of the Lusaka Protocol. With fragile peace processes underway in both these countries, any influx of arms could undermine the prospects for peace.

More than anywhere else, the situation in Central Africa demonstrated the regional nature of conflict. Zaire and Tanzania suffered from the crises in Rwanda and Burundi, each of which exacerbated the other. Huge refugee flows had ramifications for the environmental, economic, and security conditions in neighboring countries. The regionalization of conflict was not limited to central Africa; the conflicts in Liberia and Sudan also caused massive refugee flows into neighboring countries, leading to tensions with the host population and security problems throughout the region.

The Right to Monitor

One of the most striking developments in Africa in recent years has been the growth of the human rights movement. From South Africa to Zaire, from Kenya to Nigeria, human rights activists have become an important force on the continent, often at considerable risk to themselves. Human rights activists continued to face arrest, imprisonment, and harassment in many countries; some have been tortured and even killed. Nevertheless, human rights activism continued to grow during 1995, sparked by the courageous efforts of individuals and groups all over the continent. Despite a lack of resources and the dangers involved in their work, human rights activists in Africa found new opportunities to expose abuses and to seek remedies.

The crackdown on the human rights movement in Nigeria illustrated both the challenges and the aspirations of many African activists. Several of Nigeria's leading human rights activists have been detained for prolonged periods, often without charge or trial, including Abdul Oroh, the executive director of the Civil Liberties Organisation, Chima Ubani, former general secretary of the Campaign for Democracy (CD) and the campaign officer of the Civil Liberties Organisation, and Dr. Beko Ransome-Kuti, chairman of the CD. However, human rights organizations continued to document and publicize the abuses of the Abacha government, using strategies such as filing cases in national courts against their government, publishing reports, and conducting campaigns to educate people about their rights. The reporting from Nigeria's human rights community helped keep the world informed about the deteriorating conditions in Nigeria, which increased the domestic and international pressure on the government.

The Role of the International Community

The year saw the increasing marginalization of Africa on the world stage. From the cuts in U.S. assistance to Africa to a more generalized sense of donor fatigue, a tangible sense of disengagement from Africa by the international community made attention to human rights abuses in Africa increasingly rare.

At the same time, however, a realization began to take hold that Africa's "failed states" and human rights disasters were all predictable before they exploded, and that preventive action is far less costly than massive humanitarian aid afterwards. In some isolated cases, such as Burundi, the international community seemed engaged in trying to prevent an explosion that it realized might rival the genocide in Rwanda. A series of high-level visits to Burundi from the U.N., the E.U., the OAU, France, Germany, and the U.S. indicated a more active role. The establishment of a U.N. commission of inquiry in August was evidence of an interest in combating impunity, although it remains unclear how the commission will implement its findings.

But the impact of international pressure is obviously limited. Violence in Burundi continued to spiral out of control, despite international attention. The military government of Nigeria resisted international pressures to commence a meaningful transition and to release political prisoners, despite high-level interventions. The execution of Ken Saro-Wiwa and the eight other Ogoni activists, after world appeals for clemency, demonstrated the Nigerian government's clear contempt for international pressure on human rights grounds.

The United Nations

Most areas of U.N. involvement in Africa saw repeats of the same mistakes of the past, especially concerning the role of human rights protection in U.N. peacekeeping operations. This failure to effectively incorporate human rights into the mandate of peacekeeping forces was especially evident in

Angola and Liberia, where the U.N. paid only lip service to human rights reporting. Even in Rwanda, where human rights was accorded a mission of its own, the peacekeeping force failed to protect internally displaced persons, and the human rights monitoring mission was ineffective.

The Somalia intervention showed the cost of failing promptly to address emergencies that threaten international peace and security. The peacekeeping operation excluded human rights considerations from its program, concentrating instead on bringing warleaders to the bargaining table and failing to hold them accountable for their actions. The U.N. itself violated international standards and lost sight of its humanitarian mission, resulting in an enormous toll in Somali civilian casualties. The Somalia experience makes it clear that the U.N. must make monitoring, reporting on and protecting human rights integral to its response to such emergencies.

The establishment of the International Criminal Tribunal for Rwanda in late 1994 was welcomed as an important response by the U.N. to seeking accountability in Africa. Yet as the Tribunal ended its first year in November 1994, no indictments had been handed down, and it was still hampered by a lack of resources, staff, and funding.

U.S. Policy

Africa was clearly not a priority for the Clinton administration, since no compelling issues of trade, investment, or perceived national interest galvanized attention. Given the decreased levels of U.S. assistance to Africa mandated by the U.S. Congress, the administration will have fewer tools with which to conduct its Africa policy. Nevertheless, the U.S. remained engaged in a few places, including the Great Lakes, Angola, and Nigeria. In each of these areas, the administration named a special envoy to illustrate heightened concern, and took opportunities to raise human rights concerns.

While the U.S. is credited with pressuring both sides in Angola to accept the peace process, developments in the Great Lakes

and Nigeria presented more intractable situations. To its credit, the U.S. sent a series of high-level delegations to Rwanda and Burundi to demonstrate attention to the region, but the administration did not maximize its leverage with the new Rwandan government to press for human rights improvements. In Nigeria, the administration officials held a series of secret meetings with the Abacha government in an unsuccessful effort to persuade it to proceed with the transition to democracy and to refrain from executing its alleged opponents.

In the Horn of Africa, the administration's main focus was the Greater Horn of Africa Initiative. Launched in 1994, the initiative included ten countries and sought to involve African leaders in tackling the continent's problems, notably the issues of food security, development, and political conflict. Human rights per se was not a part of the initiative, although human rights violations are among the causes of famine. In its policies on individual countries in the region, the Clinton administration denounced widespread human rights abuses by the government of Sudan, but refrained from publicly criticizing the human rights abuses of the Ethiopian government.

The use of visa denials to those obstructing the democratization process proved to be an effective way to distance the U.S. from human rights abusers. This policy was put to good effect in Liberia, Nigeria, and Zaire; during the 50th anniversary of the U.N. in October, for example, President Mobutu and General Abacha were denied U.S. visas and only permitted restricted travel to the United Nations. Although President Mobutu ultimately accepted this limited visa, General Abacha refused to come to the U.S. on such terms.

The administration's support for the International Tribunal on Rwanda and the Commission of Inquiry for Burundi were significant contributions to the establishment of accountability for human rights abuses during 1995. U.S. support for the war crimes trials in Ethiopia was also important. By taking a public stand in favor of these efforts, the administration allied itself with the struggle to end impunity in Africa.

Unfortunately, the Clinton administration made few public statements about human rights in Africa during 1995, and thus lost an important means of raising awareness in the U.S. and internationally about human rights concerns. When combined with the diminishing U.S. aid, the U.S. conveyed an image of increasing disengagement in Africa.

The Work of
Human Rights Watch/Africa

Throughout 1995, Human Rights Watch/Africa was a key source of information and documentation about human rights in Africa for journalists, government officials, the United Nations, and humanitarian organizations, among others. Human Rights Watch/Africa provided timely information about areas where human rights abuses were rampant—such as Angola, Nigeria, Liberia, Rwanda, and Sudan—as well as tracking the attacks on civil society and independent activists in places like Kenya. Human Rights Watch/Africa translated the information on human rights challenges into advocacy strategies in the U.S. and Europe, pressuring governments to adopt policies to combat human rights abuses.

In early 1995, Human Rights Watch/Africa opened an office in Rwanda to enable extended investigations of the genocide and to monitor current abuses, while assisting the local human rights groups. Its long record of reliable research in Rwanda has made Human Rights Watch/Africa a leading authority about human rights developments in Rwanda. Staff members were consulted regularly by governments and nongovernmental organizations and were interviewed extensively by U.S. and international media. Human Rights Watch/Africa worked in particular to influence the policies of the U.N., African, and European governments, as well as Canada and the U.S., to address the Rwandan government directly, and to assist in genocide-related prosecutions in Europe, Canada, and the U.S.

Human Rights Watch/Africa was active on Nigeria in 1995, reporting on the political trials, the ongoing crackdown on human rights and pro-democracy activists, and the military repression in the southeast. After a mission to Nigeria in February, Human Rights Watch/Africa published the first-ever testimony by Nigerian soldiers on the military's punitive campaign in the oil-rich Ogoni area.

The work in 1995 with the Human Rights Watch/Arms Project focused new attention on the issue of arms flows into the volatile region of the Great Lakes, and sparked international attention to the role of other governments in facilitating the arms trade. Again with the Arms Project, Human Rights Watch/Africa continued its work on landmines in Africa, and participated in the campaign to ban the sale and production of landmines. Human Rights Watch/Africa worked with the Children's Rights Project to document the use of child soldiers, notably in Sudan and Liberia, and with the Women's Rights Project on violations of women's human rights in South Africa.

ANGOLA

Human Rights Developments

Following the signing in Lusaka on November 20, 1994 of a cease-fire protocol between the ruling Movement for the Popular Liberation of Angola (MPLA) and the rebel National Union for the Total Independence of Angola (UNITA), Angola entered an uneasy period of peace. But despite continued skirmishing between the rival forces, the U.N. Security Council agreed to mount a new peacekeeping operation in Angola (UNAVEM III), authorizing a military contingent of up to 7000. Respect for human rights marginally improved in 1995, but both sides were responsible for abuses, including restrictions on freedom of movement, extrajudicial executions, conscription of child soldiers, and the intimidation, detention and killing of journalists.

By November 1994, government offensives had reduced UNITA's territorial control from 60 percent to 40 percent of the country. In October, government units had begun their final push toward Huambo, the UNITA-occupied second city in Angola, forcing UNITA into "strategic retreat." Within a month UNITA had lost most of its significant urban and commercial footholds: Soyo, Huambo, Mbanza Congo, and Uige. Retreating from these towns, UNITA's troops looted extensively and killed a number of civilians. UNITA also forcibly conscripted hundreds of civilians from these urban areas; many are still unaccounted for.

The military gains by the government forced UNITA to concede further in the Lusaka peace talks and accept the proposals on national reconciliation put forward at the talks. In return the U.N. agreed that a new set of international trade sanctions and travel restrictions on UNITA would not be implemented. As its territorial losses quickened, UNITA tried to bargain its promise to sign the Protocol against a government promise not to press further militarily. Although both sides initialed the Lusaka Protocol on October 31, with President dos Santos promising the U.S. and U.N. that government forces would not capture Huambo, government forces continued to push forward. Because UNITA forces had pulled out, the government captured the city quickly.

Despite continuing fighting, both sides finally signed the Lusaka cease-fire protocol on November 20. But significantly, neither leader signed it himself, leaving it to Foreign Minister Venacio de Moura for the government and Secretary General Eugenio Manuvakola for UNITA, thereby suggesting a continuing lack of confidence in the stability of the peace process. Human rights did not feature prominently in the Lusaka Protocol, which advocated impunity under Annex 6, No.1. A general amnesty for "illegal acts" committed prior to a cease-fire was the first issue agreed upon by both sides in the 1993-1994 Lusaka peace talks.

The Lusaka Protocol provides for the re-establishment of the cease-fire; the integration of UNITA generals into the government's own forces (which are to become nonpartisan and civilian controlled); demobilization, under the United Nations Angola Verification Mission (UNAVEM); the repatriation of all mercenaries; the incorporation of UNITA troops into the Angolan National Police (which will come under the Ministry of Home Affairs, but will retain its own organizational structure from the national to local level), and the prohibition of any other police or surveillance organization.

The major political issues covered in the Lusaka Protocol were the U.N.'s mandate, the role of observers, the completion of the electoral process, and national reconciliation. Under the provisions for reconciliation between the parties, UNITA leadership would receive up to eighty-eight private residences, political offices in each province and one central headquarters. UNITA would also hold the government posts of Geology and Mines, Trade, Health, and Hotel and Tourism; the Deputy Minister posts of Defense, Home Affairs, Finance, Agriculture, Public Works, Social Reintegration, and Mass Communication; six ambassadorships; three provincial governorships; seven deputy governorships; thirty municipal and thirty-five deputy municipal administrators; and seventy-five administrators of communes. The government retains all other positions of power and patronage.

The presidential run-off, which was to have been concluded after the September 1992 elections, was set to be held in 1996. In July, however, the National Assembly postponed the elections until the year 2000. A Joint Committee, comprised of the U.N., government, and UNITA representatives, with the U.S., Portugal, and Russia as observers (the Troika), oversees the implementation of the Lusaka protocols.

Despite the Protocol, localized fighting, including targeting of humanitarian agencies, continued throughout 1995. A World Food Programme plane was hit by several bullets in Malanje on December 9, 1994. In March 1995, UNITA fighters shot down a

UNAVEM III helicopter in Quibaxe, fired on two ICRC aircraft near Ganda and ambushed an ICRC truck convoy just west of Ganda, on the central plateau. A meeting of military leaders from both sides on January 10, 1995 failed to bring the fighting to an end. Although a second meeting in Waku Kungo in Kwanza Sul on February 2 and 3 made more progress towards consolidating the cease-fire, the U.N. recorded 235 cease-fire violations in March, 110 in July, and 52 in September.

The cease-fire violations occurred mainly in the northern parts of the provinces of Huila, Lunda Norte, Lunda Sul, Malange, Moxico, and Zaire. By September, about 45 percent of these cease-fire violations were attacks on civilians designed either to control the movement of food aid in contested areas or to stop people from moving into areas controlled by the other side. Roads previously cleared of mines had mines laid again overnight, aimed at keeping roads closed and delaying U.N. patrols. Fifteen percent of the incidents were military maneuvers aimed at reinforcing troops or gaining territory. The remaining incidents were termed "minor" by the U.N.

The spirit of the peace process was broken by the importation of new weapons. Although shipments declined in 1995, new specialized weaponry, especially from Russia and the Ukraine, reached the government, albeit on an irregular basis. In early 1995, the majority of the weaponry arriving was the tail-end of 1994 procurement. However, as the year progressed, it was evident that the government was still purchasing new, specialized equipment.

UNITA also increased its cross-border sanction-busting operations, bringing in new weapons and supplies on secret flights from Zaire to airstrips in the diamond-rich Lunda provinces. UNITA appeared determined to maintain its grip on its remaining diamond assets. Localized, and sometimes fierce, fighting continued in the diamond areas throughout 1995. In July, government forces lost 153 soldiers in fighting against UNITA along a small stretch of the Chicapa River. In order

to focus its efforts on controlling the Lunda diamond areas, Uige, and the areas north of Huambo, UNITA signaled its intention to abandon its former bush headquarters of Jamba and invited the U.N. to assist in the evacuation of some 40,000 people.

The first meeting between President dos Santos and UNITA leader Jonas Savimbi for two years occurred in Lusaka on May 6, a symbolic step forward in the peace process. Although President dos Santos had been pressed by hard-liners in the military and party not to attend, immense U.N. and U.S. pressure secured his participation. In June, the government offered Savimbi the position of vice-president of the Angolan Republic. In August, following a second summit in Gabon, Savimbi accepted the position on behalf of UNITA, without making it clear whether he would take the post himself. A third meeting between both leaders occurred in Brussels on September 25 and 26 at a Round Table donors conference in which both leaders once again pledged their confidence in peace and reconstruction. The Round Table resulted in pledges and proposals of contributions of US$993 million. This exceeded the $700 million originally requested by Angola.

The reality on the ground remained less positive. The government's ongoing suppression of freedom of the press heightened the feeling of anxiety, fear, and confusion in the country. The killing on January 18 of Ricardo de Mello, the editor-publisher of the semi-independent Luanda-based daily *Imparcial Fax*, by an unknown assailant with one shot in the chest from an AK-47 with a silencer, had a profound impact on the fledgling press. *Imparcial Fax* closed, and its other journalists left the country. Many other journalists received warnings about filing critical reports of the government. Human Rights Watch learned that journalists it visited in June also received anonymous warnings. Conditions were the same in the provinces. In Saurimo, Lunda Sul province, several local demonstrations by local pro-separatist groups were studiously ignored by the state media. A local journalist who tried to report on the situation in Lunda Sul was detained for several months by the local authorities. Attempts by the U.N. mission to set up an independent radio station, Radio UNAVEM, were frustrated by government foot-dragging over the allocation of broadcasting frequencies. Freedom of expression was even more tightly controlled in UNITA dominated areas, with no criticism tolerated.

Free circulation of persons and goods, a specific principle of the Lusaka Protocol, continued to be abused by both sides. Dozens of Angolans interviewed by Human Rights Watch in June complained of not being able to move freely to their homes and that soldiers heavily "taxed" them when they traveled.

A disturbing characteristic of the Angolan conflict has been the use of child soldiers. International law forbids the use of children under the age of fifteen as soldiers in armed conflict, but both sides continued to use child combatants. UNITA redeployed some to work as bonded labor in its diamond areas. There are no precise figures on the numbers, but UNICEF estimates suggested thousands.

Street children also suffered abuses in Angola's urban areas. UNICEF estimated that Luanda alone had 4,000 street children. The majority of these were boys, and their daily life was characterized on the streets by illness, forced labor, sexual exploitation, and arbitrary underage military conscription.

Repatriation of prisoners of conflict was slow. In March, both sides provided lists of detainees to the ICRC. In May, the government handed over 208 UNITA prisoners to the ICRC and a further two batches by late August, totaling 230. UNITA released four batches of government prisoners, totaling 230, by September.

Arbitrary detention and assault on suspects by the police remained widespread. Prison conditions across Angola were appalling. The government several times announced that it would improve over-crowded prison conditions, but there was no evidence of this. There were unconfirmed reports of sick inmates being killed by prison warders in Sao Paulo prison inLuanda to clear space for fresh detainees.

The Right to Monitor

A feature of Angola remained the absence of effective branches of civil society that publicize or lobby on human rights issues. The Luanda-based Angolan Association of Human Rights remained the sole functioning human rights group in Angola but did not publish or conduct research in 1995. The National Assembly also maintained a cross-party human rights commission, presided by Domingos Tungu. UNITA reported its human rights concerns through its Lisbon-based Association of Surviving Angolans (ACAS).

The Role of
the International Community

The United Nations

On February 8, the U.N. Security Council authorized UNAVEM III to start deploying up to 7,000 U.N. peacekeeping forces, monitors, and civilian police to act as a buffer between the two sides and to prevent the continuation of skirmishes and cease-fire violations. This force would be finally established at a strength of some 6,771 military staff, 350 military observers, 260 civilian police, and 343 international civilian staff. The expected annual cost would be $383.1 million. About twenty-two to twenty-four self-sustained infantry companies are to be deployed at fourteen quartering areas and eight main weapons storage locations in the country. In Mid-1995, military observers were stationed at fifty-four sites in the country, including all quartering areas, airports, border areas, and other strategic locations. By April, the U.N. was finally able to press ahead with expanded deployment because of the improved security situation on the ground and in its financial and logisitics situation. However, delays in deployment continued into late 1995, with U.N. supervised quartering and demobilization efforts many months behind schedule.

Between July 14 and 16, U.N. Secretary-General Boutros Boutros-Ghali traveled to Angola, visiting both Luanda and UNITA's headquarters in Bailundo in an attempt to get both sides to co-operate more fully in the peace process. On August 7, the U.N. Security Council extended the mandate of UNAVEM III until February 8, 1996.

UNAVEM III established a small subunit to deal with human rights issues. E.U. member states temporarily funded five human rights specialists from Denmark, France, and Portugal to staff it. These monitors made little impression on the ground and were not effective in bringing attention to abuses. The U.N. hoped to increase the unit's cadre to eleven so that human rights monitors could be stationed in a majority of the provinces of Angola.

The European Union

The E.U. Presidency issued a Declaration on Angola on February 21, which pledged the Union to make a practical contribution to the consolidation of lasting peace. E.U. funds have been directed towards mine clearance and deploying human rights monitors. In 1995 the E.U. provided ECU 6 million towards mine clearance operations and up to ECU 55 million on humanitarian projects. The E.U. also hosted the September UNDP Brussels Round Table Conference on Angola. On October 2 the E.U. Commission published a declaration of its Common Position on Angola. In addition to supporting the effective implementation of the Lusaka Protocol, especially demobilization of ex-combatants, the E.U. announced its support for democracy, the rule of law, and respect for human rights in Angola. In late October the E.U. committed additional funding for expanding UNAVEM III's program of human rights monitors, providing ECU 600,000 for a human rights project managed by the Netherlands-based European Parliamentarians for (Southern) Africa (AWEPA).

U.S. Policy

Angola remained one of the U.S. administration's Africa priorities in 1995, but only after detailed debate in the House of Representatives and the Senate over funding. Angola is seen by the administration as a special case for Africa because it represents the last piece in a regional settlement in which the U.S. has had significant economic and diplomatic investment. During the Cold War, Angola was the second largest recipient of covert aid from the U.S., after Afghanistan.

The U.S. continued to be Angola's largest trading partner in 1995, purchasing 90 percent of its oil exports. The U.S. also continued to play an important role by providing 30 percent of the U.N.'s running costs in Angola (some US$100 million) and some 50 percent of the costs of relief operations. At a donor conference in Geneva on February 23, the U.S. pledged $106 million. The U.S. also played an important role at the September 25-26 UNDP-assisted Brussels Angola Round Table, pledging $190 million.

In mid-December 1994 and in mid-January 1995, joint USAID/State Department missions visited Angola to review the status of the Lusaka Protocols, and assess what future administration strategy should be.

In January, Paul Hare, President Clinton's special envoy to Angola, visited several provinces. He was mandated to deliver a strong message to both sides that respect for the cease-fire protocol was a precondition for renewed international interest and assistance. According to U.S. officials, Department of Defense and Central Intelligence Agency monitoring of Angola was expanded in 1995, with evidence of Lusaka Protocol violations, especially weapons shipments, sometimes being presented through diplomatic channels to the government or UNITA for explanation and caution.

In early May, following the announcement that President dos Santos would not travel to Lusaka to meet UNITA leader Jonas Savimbi in their scheduled summit, frenetic U.S. diplomatic efforts contributed towards reversing the Angolan government decision to postpone, which turned out to be a watershed in the peace process in 1995. The U.S. threat not to fund the U.N. operation in Angola and curtail assistance unless the meeting happened was effective.

A new U.S. ambassador, Donald Steinberg, formerly senior director of African Affairs at the White House National Security Council, arrived in late July. Steinberg replaced Edmund Dejarnette who had been ambassador since May 1994. During the hearings for his nomination, Steinberg committed himself to pushing for human rights improvements in Angola. In his early months in the post, Steinberg tried to travel widely to familiarize himself with the Angola situation and was noted to take a special, if discreet, interest in human rights issues.

USAID began development assistance to Angola in 1992 but the program was suspended because of fighting. In 1995 the administration's development request was $5 million, aimed at economic projects ($4.2 million) and its Democracy and Governance program ($800,000). One significant project was for the opening of a full-time Luanda office for the Voice of America radio. The project was funded on the grounds that it would promote more journalistic coverage of sensitive issues, such as continued human rights abuses, while providing training facilities and confidence building for Angolan journalists.

The Work of
Human Rights Watch/Africa

Human Rights Watch/Africa in conjunction with the Human Rights Watch/Arms Project continued to closely monitor human rights developments and arms flows into Angola following the November 15, 1994 publication of the *Angola: Arms Trade and Violations of Laws of War Since the 1992 Elections* report, timed to put human rights back on the agenda at the time of the signing of the Lusaka Protocol and the following expansion of UNAVEM. In March, Human Rights Watch visited Angola and participated in a television documentary on the U.N. and Angola, in addition to conducting research into continued human rights abuses by both

sides. Articles drawing attention to the human rights situation in Angola were published, and Human Rights Watch also wrote to the U.N. Security Council members in July and met with U.N. diplomats to urge the U.N. to give a high priority to human rights monitoring and to act decisively against continued weapons flows into the country before extending UNAVEM's formal mandate.

BURUNDI

Human Rights Developments

In Burundi, soldiers and their civilian allies slaughtered innocent victims virtually daily. The army, composed largely of Tutsi (who make up about 15 percent of the population), operated at the command of radical Tutsi leaders rather than under the orders of the ineffective civilian government, nominally controlled by the Front for Democracy in Burundi (FRODEBU), a political party that encompasses many of the majority Hutu. Under the guise of reprisals for attacks on the military or of campaigns to disarm the population, soldiers repeatedly attacked Hutu neighborhoods in the cities as well as Hutu communities in the countryside. The military attacks were replicated on a smaller scale by army-backed militia who terrorized city populations and by killers who assassinated Hutu political and community leaders. Through a combination of violence, intimidation, and political blockage, Tutsi-dominated factions re-appropriated the political control they had lost at the polls in June 1993.

Meanwhile the largely Hutu National Council for the Defense of Democracy (CNDD), based in Zaire, and the Party for the Liberation of the Hutu People (PALIPEHUTU), based in Tanzania, won supporters away from the weakening and more moderate FRODEBU. They stepped up attacks by their own militia who targeted soldiers primarily but who also killed unarmed Tutsi civilians.

According to a July report by the U.N. special rapporteur on human rights in Burundi, some 800 civilians and one hundred soldiers were slain per month by both sides, meaning that more than 10,000 people may have been killed by the end of the year. None of the killers was brought to trial, just as none of those responsible for the 1993 assassination of President Melchior Ndadaye or the subsequent massacres was brought to trial; indeed, many of them continued to hold important positions of leadership. Media from both sides thrived on encouraging the violence between Hutu and Tutsi, while local and foreign arms dealers profited from easy and extensive sales of guns and grenades. The Hutu and Tutsi populations, who had once lived intermingled, were increasingly driven into ethnically segregated areas. As a result of military and militia attacks, Hutu fled most neighborhoods of the capital of Bujumbura. Some 300,000 Tutsi, afraid to return to the homes they had left in 1993 violence, clustered in camps near towns and urban centers where they enjoyed military protection.

The facade of a civilian democratic government was left in place, but elected officials were repeatedly held hostage by radical Tutsi leaders and youth gangs who used "dead city" demonstrations to attain their goals. In late December 1994, for example, FRODEBU officials were forced to replace the president of the National Assembly, and in February 1995 they were obliged to accept both a change in the prime minister and the inclusion of small Tutsi splinter parties in the cabinet after Tutsi youth gangs used grenades, arson, and attacks to interrupt all normal activity in the capital of Bujumbura.

In late March, in April, in June and again in July, the military, supported by militias, attacked the Hutu neighborhoods of Bujumbura, each time killing hundreds of civilians. Outside of the capital, soldiers and their civilian allies killed at least seventy people at Butaganzwa commune, Kayanza province in January; as many as 400 in Gasorwe commune in Muyinga province;

some 200 in Mutumba commune in Karuzi province in March; and an estimated 250 others in Ngozi province in late October. In addition, military operations in the hills overlooking the capital and immediately adjacent rural regions took hundreds of lives during the month of July.

Two Tutsi militia were principally responsible for terrorizing civilian in the cities, one called the *Sans Echecs* (The Infallibles) and the other, the *Sans Defaits* (The Undefeated). They recruited among high school and university students and also among the urban unemployed, and threatened moderate young Tutsi unwilling to join their ranks. Soldiers helped train these militia, and soldiers and police generally did not intervene to halt militia attacks or to arrest those involved.

The spread of violence among students was underlined by a Tutsi militia's slaughter of some two dozen Hutu students at the University of Bujumbura on June 12. Several weeks later, a Hutu militia group attacked the Kiriri university campus and killed six Tutsi, four of them students. During the funeral procession for these victims, an armed group fired sub-machine guns and threw grenades at the mourners, killing ten and wounding fourteen persons. Some thirty secondary school students were slain and scores more injured in more than a dozen attacks on schools throughout the year.

In the countryside, armed groups of displaced Tutsi frequently attacked and killed Hutu living their camps, often with the clear complicity of the local military or police.

The providers of humanitarian aid, increasingly burdened by the need to supply food also to the mostly Hutu Rwandan refugees who fled to Burundi after the 1994 genocide, decided to reduce aid to displaced persons with a goal of stopping it completely during the course of 1995. Extremist Tutsi played on the differences in aid distributed to the Tutsi displaced and that given to Hutu refugees to whip up hatred against both refugees and humanitarian workers. In April a Greek employee of a humanitarian agency was assassinated, supposedly for favoring

Hutu refugees over Tutsi displaced people.

The *Forces pour la defense de la democratie* (Forces for the Defense of Democracy, FDD), the military wing of the exiled CNDD, and its rival, the PALIPEHUTU, attacked a number of military targets during the year. The FDD, based in Zaire, operated largely in northwestern Burundi, where it was reportedly responsible for killing fifteen Burundian army soldiers at Mabayi in Cibitoke province in March. In Zaire its troops sometimes trained with the forces of the former Rwandan government, and they may have carried out joint military operations in Burundi. The PALIPEHUTU troops, based in Tanzania, attacked in northeastern Burundi, where they apparently killed a number of Burundi army soldiers in Gasorwe and Mabayi communes. Hutu forces attacked Tutsi civilians, especially those in camps for the displaced. In late October, for example, they killed some forty persons at a camp in Kayonza province. In Bujumbura, a Hutu militia known as the *Intagoheka* (Those Who Never Close Their Eyes), was responsible for random attacks against Tutsi.

Both Hutu and Tutsi used assassinations and threats to silence opposing leaders, and even moderates of their own ethnic group. In January, the governor of Muyinga province was stabbed to death. In March the minister of energy and mines, Ernest Kabusheyeme was killed at mid-day in downtown Bujumbura. Two days later a former highly ranked military officer and government official was abducted and later found killed, apparently in retaliation for the killing of Minister Kabushemeye. Some twenty other local government officials were also assassinated in the course of the year, and attacks were made on many others. Four leaders of the FRODEBU party were captured and killed in the first week of June, and the deputy who heads the FRODEBU group in the parliament escaped an attempted assassination in mid-September. In addition, five Burundian priests and one Adventist pastor had been slain as of late October.

The killers took aim at foreigners as well. On June 14, American Ambassador Robert Krueger, the special representative of the Organization of African Unity (OAU), Leandre Bassole, and Burundian Foreign Minister Jean-Marie Ngendahayo were ambushed. The dignitaries escaped unhurt, but two soldiers accompanying their convoy were killed, and nine other persons were injured. On September 30, two Italian priests and an Italian lay sister were murdered in the southern province of Bururi.

Newspapers from both sides incited violence against their opponents. *Le Carrefour des Idees* published a scorecard of Hutu leaders "who feel threatened." Next to each name was a blank square under the heading "fate." One week before the assassination of Minister Kabushemeye, the same newspaper listed him as number seven of a group of Hutu said to "have murdered Tutsi" and "spread terror." *La Nation*, a newspaper run by former president Jean-Baptiste Bagaza, published a story attacking U.S. Ambassador Krueger and the special representative of the U.N. secretary-general, Amedou Ould Abdallah, under the headline "Two to beat up or to gun down." On April 10, the newspaper *L'Etoile* accused Ambassador Krueger of "fanning the flames" of conflict and said, "The day may come when patriotic Barundis will make him pay. This would be a legitimate act." Radio Rutomorangingo (Radio Truth), which broadcasts intermittently from Zaire, called on Hutu to kill Tutsi before the Tutsi kill them first.

In late March, Army Chief of Staff Jean Bikomagu acknowledged that national police forces under his command had been responsible for massacres that had just taken place in Bujumbura. Official commissions were established to investigate the slaughter in Gasorwe commune and the June massacres in Bujumbura. After some fifty persons were slain at Choga, outside Bujumbura, in September, Ambassador Krueger asked that an inquiry be carried out into that incident as well. The first commission submitted its report, but apparently no disciplinary measures were taken in these or other military massacres, with the exception of a change in command in the post of Chief of Staff of the National Police force.

The Burundian judicial system has been paralyzed since March 1993, when the terms of the judges of the three criminal courts of appeal expired and were not renewed. In the meantime, some 4,000 persons have been detained on serious charges, virtually all of them Hutu. Given that most judges as well as soldiers and police are Tutsi, this situation suggests grave inequities in the administration of justice.

The Right to Monitor

The Burundi League of Human Rights, Iteka, has been the organization most active in criticizing human rights abuse and calling for moderation and tolerance in political life. Its members and staff have often been threatened over the telephone and by visits of armed men to their homes. At least two have been shot at. The threats led them to limit the frequency and vigor of their criticism. The association SONERA stood closer to the official Tutsi establishment and spoke with an even more muted voice.

The Role of
the International Community

The enormity of the failure of the international community in Rwanda the previous year spurred both governments and nongovernmental organizations (NGOs) to play a more active role in trying to halt violence in Burundi. Throughout 1995 there was a series of high level missions to Burundi from the U.N., the European Union (E.U.), the OAU, and from a number of individual governments, including the U.S., France, and Germany. The secretary-generals of both the U.N. and the OAU visited, as did members of the Security Council.

The United Nations

From time to time diplomats, including the secretary general of the OAU, suggested that a peacekeeping force of some kind might intervene in Burundi, but most found such an idea unrealistic. Instead, many international actors supported some form of justice to deal with Burundi's immediate past of unpunished killing and to serve as a deterrent against further large-scale slaughter. In 1994, the mainstream political parties recognized that the inadequacies of the Burundian judicial system were permitting a pattern of impunity that encouraged further massacres. They asked the international community to provide an official commission of inquiry to investigate the 1993 assassination of President Ndadaye and the massacres that had followed. An initial mission sent by the Security Council in 1993 had recommended such an international commission, as did a special envoy sent in 1995 to look into its feasibility. The five person commission, finally established by the Security Council on August 28, began its work in October. It will identify those accused of the killings and will recommend ways of bringing them to justice as well as measures to prevent a repetition of similar killings.

To stress that massive slaughter would not go unpunished, the Security Council adopted a statement on March 29 condemning the ongoing violence in Burundi, emphasizing the importance of accountability, and warning that the council would consider prosecuting any party who committed acts of genocide, just as it had done in the case of Rwanda.

After the assassination of President Ndadaye in 1993, the U.N. secretary-general asked Mauritanian diplomat Ahmedou Ould Abdallah to go to Burundi as his special representative, a post he filled until early October 1995. Although criticized by both sides and often threatened with assassination, Ould Abdallah was able to facilitate contacts among various parties on the complex political scene.

The U.N. Human Rights Centre operated a program focused on education and training. Although it intended to begin active monitoring of the human rights situation at several posts throughout the country, the center did not receive the funds needed to implement this plan.

In March the U.N. Human Rights Commission named a special rapporteur on human rights despite initial opposition from the Burundi government. The special rapporteur, Paulo Sergio Pinheiro, undertook his first mission to Burundi in July. He immediately issued a preliminary report expressing grave concern about the heavy loss of life and other human rights violations. Special Rapporteur on extrajudicial, summary or arbitrary executions, Bacre Waly Ndiaye, in July issued a report on his mission in which he expressed concern about the widespread extrajudicial executions of civilians and the pervasive insecurity.

The European Union
The E.U. stated its objectives in Burundi on March 19 (the Carcassonne statement) and in its common position of March 24. Concerned about the violence, it supported the accords known as the Convention of Government, which had been signed by the main political parties in 1994, and it offered to help in organizing the national debate, called for in the Convention. It promised support in the amount of ECU 3 million for the U.N. human rights center program in Burundi, offered to assist in training magistrates, and called for a round table of donors to facilitate aid to Burundi. In April members of the European Parliament appealed to the E.U. to prepare for military intervention in case the violence in Burundi got worse.

At the end of June, the E.U. reaffirmed its commitment to the objectives specified in March. It expressed concern about the growth of extremism and the increase in violence. It also condemned the massacres by the military in Bujumbura and reminded the Burundi government of its responsibility for the proper conduct of military operations. At that time the E.U. was providing funds to the OAU observer mission, had offered support for the sending of human rights experts, had identified needs to be met in the judicial system, and was ready to offer humanitarian aid to refugees and displaced persons. It announced also that a donors round table had been agreed to by the U.N. Development Programme (UNDP) and the Burundi gov-

ernment. It declared that member states were applying measures banning travel to their countries by certain identified extremists.

The Organization of African Unity
On April 21, the OAU decided to extend the mandate of its military observer team, which had been operating in Burundi since 1994. It also increased the number of observers from forty-seven to sixty-seven, including soldiers to accompany the Burundi military during operations as well as doctors and engineers. Because the mission was small in size and was limited by regulations which prevented it from traveling without Burundi soldiers, it was sometimes judged ineffective. But its presence appears to have restrained Burundi troops from abuses on at least some occasions.

U.S. Policy
U.S. Ambassador Robert Krueger vigorously and courageously defended human rights in Burundi throughout the year, traveling himself to investigate massacres on the spot, giving press conferences about his findings, and demanding accountability from Burundi authorities. He was supported by the White House, which issued a statement on April 21 commending him for his commitment. Radical Tutsi resented his efforts and did their best to discourage him, even to the point of threatening his life.

The U.S. strongly supported the need for accountability for past and current violence in Burundi. To this end, they favored the establishment of the international commission of inquiry, supported the sending of human rights monitors, and co-sponsored the March 29 Security Council resolution warning of prosecutions for any who became guilty of acts of genocide. They sought to support moderates and to ostracize extremists, forty-seven of whom were excluded from receiving U.S. visas. The White House issued three statements during the year calling for calm and toleration and condemning violence. The U.S. dedicated $5 million to a conflict resolution program and gave funds to develop local radio broadcasts promoting peace. The U.S. appointed a special coordinator for Rwanda and Burundi, Ambassador Richard Bogosian, who made several trips to the region. The U.S. also chaired the Rwanda Operational Support Group, a group of eleven donor nations, the U.N., the OAU, and the E.U. which met regularly to coordinate policies and promote reconciliation in Rwanda and Burundi.

The Work of
Human Rights Watch/Africa

Human Rights Watch/Africa focused primarily on the importance of justice, both for its own sake and as an effective way of cutting short the cycle of violence. In circles where other actors often sought diplomatic compromise even at the price of ignoring past abuse, we advocated for an immediate establishment of a state of law. We urged donors to concentrate on rebuilding the justice system in Burundi and on facilitating international involvement in establishing responsibilities for past slaughter. Through meetings with officials of the U.S. and other governments and of the U.N. as in contacts with the press, we helped provide factually-based assessments in a situation where deliberate misinformation or easy generalizations often distort the reality.

ETHIOPIA

Human Rights Developments

After four years, the Transitional Government of Ethiopia (TGE), established after the toppling of the Derg in 1991, handed over power to a new government named by the parliament elected in August 1995. The Ethiopian People's Revolutionary Democratic Front (EPRDF), a coalition of three ethnically-based political groups led by the Tigray People's Liberation Front (TPLF), remained the dominant force in the new government. By unanimous vote, the parliament elected the former president of the TGE (and head of the TPLF) Meles Zenawi to be prime minister. The presidency, which is mainly a figurehead position, went to Negaso Gidada, representative of the Oromo People's Democratic Organization. Although there were significant human rights improvements registered under the Transitional Government, the government continued to commit or tolerate harassment of members of opposition parties, freedom of expression was restricted, arrests were carried out without charge or prospect of trial, and suspected extrajudicial executions of opposition activists were reported.

In its inaugural session from August 20 to 24, 1995, the parliament formally declared the Federal Democratic Republic of Ethiopia. The constitution divides the country into nine ethnically-based regions and gives each virtual autonomy in legislative, executive, and judicial matters. The constitution also provides each region the right to secede following a simple majority vote in a general referendum, subject to confirmation by a subsequent two-thirds majority vote in the regional legislature.

While some observers viewed these constitutional developments as offering a new model of ethnic accommodation, others accused the government of exposing the country to risks of fragmentation and political turmoil if the liberal constitutional provisions encouraged minorities to seek secession. The thrust of EPRDF policies has been the progressive devolution of powers to the ethnic groups or nationalities. Claiming that they have been left out of the political process during the TGE reign, the major opposition groups, including the Oromo Liberation Front (OLF), the All Amhara People's Organization (AAPO), and the Southern Coalition boycotted the May parliamentary elections. In part a result of this boycott, but also because the EPRDF was in control of all state institutions, the candidates of the EPRDF gained 483 out of the 548 seats in the Council of Representatives. Independent local observers noted that the actual voting in parliamentary elections was free and fair in a majority of cases they covered, although inconsistencies and irregularities were also registered. The final declared results indicated the virtual absence of the opposition in national and regional assemblies, a situation which raised concerns about how the opposition would be able to express its views.

Significant disagreements persisted between the government and various, mostly ethnically-based, opposition groups. A number of these continued to contest the legitimacy of the EPRDF and to claim that they were unfairly represented in the power structure. The opposition repeatedly complained about political harassment by police, local authorities, and security agents. While the government continued to deny these allegations, contending that it only clamps down on armed dissidents, reports published by independent local human rights groups and the local independent media indicated that the legal opposition suffered continuing abuses. Prime Minister Meles Zenawi told the parliament that he would form a human rights commission to investigate abuses.

The issue of accountability for human rights abuses was of particular relevance in Ethiopia during 1995. About 1,500 officials of the Derg government had been detained since 1991. It was only in mid-December 1994 that the top forty-four political officials, members of the inner circle of the Derg, were formally charged with the torture and murder of thousands of people. The others, mainly high government officials and military personnel, were in custody awaiting indictment for war crimes and murder. The new rulers of Ethiopia maintained that only public trials could end the culture of official impunity that made the crimes of the Derg possible.

It is within a context of civil strife and the emergence of a vibrant and dynamic civil society that many human rights abuses occurred during 1995. The political changes in Ethiopia since 1991 and the prospects of greater regional autonomy had the effect of generating a new dynamic of political participation at the national as well as the local levels. People came forward to express their opinions and to form political parties, civil groups, and organizations in an unprecedented exercise of democratic freedoms.

The Oromo Liberation Front (OLF) broke away from the EPRDF and took up arms against it in 1992, after failing to get a larger share in the TGE. Pockets of armed insurgency persisted in 1995 in various areas of Oromia. In an official communique dated June 18, the Oromo Liberation Front accused the Ethiopian authorities of being responsible for the killing on May 20 of Ali Youssif, one of its leading members, in front of his shop in Addis Ababa. The OLF alleged that this killing was one of a series of assassinations targeting its members and supporters. It cited the death in custody of a twenty-six-year-old farmer, Henok Jonatan, arrested in Najjo, in the western Oromia region, on March 16. He and nine other Oromo prisoners were believed to have been tortured. Similarly, Jafar Ibrahim Utto, a village elder in Kiyyo, in Oborra Province (eastern Oromia), was found dead on April 8 after being detained by pro-government militiamen. Two months earlier, two of his sons had reportedly been arrested, tortured, and murdered by members of the same militia.

The Amhara, who comprise about 25 percent of Ethiopia's estimated fifty-five million people, traditionally dominated political, cultural, and religious life in Ethiopia. Most political groupings representing them, particularly the All Amhara People's Organization (AAPO), were opposed to the new constitution, arguing that EPRDF policies risked destruction of a long heritage of cultural and political unity that was painstakingly developed over time. Dr. Asrat Woldeyes, a physician and founder and leader of AAPO, continued to serve a five-and-one-half-year prison sentence on charges of conspiracy to organize armed rebellion against the government. AAPO maintained that it is committed to nonviolent political action and that Dr. Woldeyes, and four other members of the organization tried with him, were discussing complaints of abuses by government soldiers and pro-government militia against other AAPO members in the meeting that was the basis for charging them with conspiracy against the government.

Article 29 of the new constitution, as

well as the National Charter and the 1992 Press Law, provides for the right to free speech and press. However, many journalists continued to be detained, in most cases without charge. While a number of journalists were released from detention prior to the May elections, twenty-three were still detained by August, of whom fourteen were held without charge or trial. The whereabouts of three other journalists remained unknown. Of these, two have been missing for over a year and were feared to be held secretly by the security services for publishing critical articles. The authorities continued to deny that they arrested them. In July, the jury at the central high court sentenced the editor-in-chief of *Zog* newspaper to one year's imprisonment for printing "groundless allegations" about developments in the conflict in Oromia, while a second journalist from the same publication was acquitted for lack of evidence.

Following the failed assassination attempt against Egyptian President Hosni Mubarak in Addis Ababa in June, the Ethiopian Free Press Journalists' Association reported a new wave of arrests of journalists in connection with articles about the incident. Mulugetta Lule, vice-chair of EFJA and manager of *Tobia* magazine, was reported to have been detained for sixty-four hours following an article on the questions raised by the attack about the security of the Organization of African Unity, which has its headquarters in the Ethiopian capital. Lule reportedly was released after a guarantor payed a 10,000 birr bail (around US$2,000), a prohibitive amount when compared to the average monthly salary of a journalist (about 750 birr). Taye Belachew, editor-in-chief of *Tobia*, reportedly was detained for twenty-one days. Other journalists, from *Beza* and *Roha* newspapers among others, were also detained for varying periods in relation to articles on the same incident.

Article 31 of the constitution guarantees freedom of association. Although the Ethiopian government permits the existence of independent nongovernmental organizations (NGOs), a number of NGOs from various fields regularly reported harassment in the form of delays in getting official clearances to operate, the intimidation or detention of personnel, or their arbitrary deregistration. The government requires the registration of NGOs with the Relief and Rehabilitation Commission and a special permit issued by the Ministry of Internal Affairs. Following the formation of the new government in August, new registration regulations also required NGOs to register with the Ministry of Justice. In August, the Relief and Rehabilitation Commission announced the deregistration of forty-seven NGOs, of which forty-five were national and two international. The commission sent letters to the NGOs' banks asking that their accounts be closed and to donor agencies advising them of the deregistration. Most of the affected NGOs appealed the decision to the RRC directly.

In a similar development, the Oromo Relief Association (ORA) complained in August that its offices and operations in Hararghe, Wallagga, and Borena had been closed down following a decision by the Council of Oromia. Reports indicate, moreover, that ORA workers were regularly harassed and subjected to arbitrary detentions, particularly in Borena area, and that the measures to halt the organization's relief operations were politically motivated. Administrative measures have been used to curtail the operational capacity or the existence of humanitarian and welfare NGOs as well as independent human rights monitoring groups (see below).

The Right to Monitor

Criticism of the government's human rights record in the local press was common. The Ethiopian government permits the existence of independent human rights groups, although some of these groups have been the object of harassment for their critical comments about its human rights record or political direction. Groups with a human rights monitoring and education agenda include the Ethiopian Human Rights Council (EHRCO), Action Professionals Association for the People (APAP), Ethiopian Human Rights and Peace Center, the Ethiopian Congress for Democracy, and the Inter-Africa Group. EHRCO has been subjected to intimidating measures on a number of occasions in the past and this continued in 1995 as well. Steps were also openly taken to obstruct its operations. In a press release dated August 1995, EHRCO complained that the government had blocked its bank account. The government also moved against APAP, another human rights group. It was among the forty-seven NGOs whose licenses were revoked by the RRC in August.

Human Rights Watch/Africa as well as other international human rights organizations were able to conduct monitoring visits to Ethiopia in 1995. International human rights organizations and foreign journalists were invited to observe the proceedings of the war crimes trial.

The Role of
the International Community

U.S. Policy

In 1995, Ethiopia continued to be the second largest recipient of U.S. assistance in sub-Saharan Africa, after South Africa. In FY 1995, U.S. bilateral assistance was approximately $125 million, $84 million of which was food aid and $103,000 was for Democracy and Governance programs. These aid levels indicate the substantial U.S. interests in Ethiopia, which involve enlisting Ethiopia as an ally in the Horn of Africa as well as U.S. support for its democratization process. However, even as it sought to encourage the Ethiopian government in its democratization efforts, the Clinton administration was reluctant to publicly raise human rights issues in Ethiopia.

U.S. officials maintained that discussions with the Ethiopian government focused on several areas: regional issues in the Horn of Africa, especially relating to security concerns; domestic issues such as democratization, respect for human rights, and economic reform; and trade issues involving U.S. business interests. In pursuing these agendas, the U.S. had regular exchanges with Ethiopian officials, often at a fairly high level. However, the administration made no public statements during 1995 about the human rights situation in Ethiopia apart from the State Department's annual *Country Reports on Human Rights Practices for 1994*, which gave a comprehensive and critical account citing many patterns and cases of violations.

In February, National Security Advisor Anthony Lake met with representatives of the Transitional Government of Ethiopia after a series of meetings organized by the Congressional Task Force on Ethiopia. The Task Force, which was chaired by Congressman Harry Johnston, and included State Department Director of East African Affairs David Shinn, succeeded in bringing together representatives of major opposition groups and the TGE in an attempt to find a compromise that would allow the participation of the opposition groups in the political process and the May elections as a step toward the resolution of the outstanding issues in the long term. Negotiations collapsed, however, after only three days of talks. The TGE representative insisted that opposition groups accept the existing constitutional framework as a precondition for participation in future talks, a precondition that the opposition groups rejected. On February 11, a White House statement noted that the meeting with Lake "underscored the President's commitment to democracy in Ethiopia."

The Work of
Human Rights Watch/Africa

In order to focus international attention on the trials of the former government, Human Rights Watch/Africa published a report in December 1994 entitled, *Reckoning Under the Law*. The report described the role of the Special Prosecutor's Office, the rights of the victims, and the rights of the defendants. Human Rights Watch/Africa sent a mission to Ethiopia in June to update the progress of the trials.

KENYA

Human Rights Developments

Throughout 1995, the government of President Daniel arap Moi continued to undermine Kenya's multiparty system through harassment and intimidation of perceived critics. The year was characterized by attacks on organizations and publications that were critical of the government, harassment of the political opposition, and a continuation of a policy of persecution on ethnic grounds. President Moi's barrages against his critics became more pronounced, including warnings that criticism of the government would be considered treason, that any "insults" of the president would result in arrest, and that the government would be "strict" with nongovernmental organizations.

In the early part of 1995, the human rights situation notably deteriorated as the government launched a crackdown against human rights activists, opposition politicians, and internally displaced persons. The escalation of human rights abuses came in the wake of new commitments of foreign aid, pledged without strong human rights conditions, at the December 1994 consultative group meeting of Kenya's donors.

In February, two independent organizations, the Center for Law and Research International (Clarion) and the Mwangaza Trust, were banned by the government. The Mwangaza Trust was notified on January 18 that it had engaged in activities "which require it to be registered under the Societies and NGO Act," although the letter did not specify what these activities were. Another banning involved the magazine *Inooro*, which has been published by the Catholic Church for many years. On February 23, the magazine was declared "a prohibited publication" under Section 52 of the Penal Code.

The office of the Legal Advice Center (LAC), a nongovernmental organization, was violently attacked by unknown assailants in March. On February 1, the office of *Finance*, an independent magazine, was firebombed. A well-established pattern of attacks on government critics by unidentified assailants raised concerns that both were targeted for their work to publicize and stem government abuses.

The government continued to hold a monopoly on all broadcast media and refused to grant licenses for private broadcasting. Journalists came under attack for writing articles critical of the government. In January, two *Daily Nation* reporters—Alex Cege and Julius Mokaya—were dismissed in circumstances suggesting government pressures. On January 16, two other *Daily Nation* journalists were detained after investigating allegations that the Kiambu district commissioner was involved in drug trading. On April 28, government officials stormed the premises of the printer Colourprint Ltd., which prints some of the independent publications, and dismantled its printing machines. In April, *Finance* magazine editor, Njehu Gatabaki, and the director of Colourprint Ltd, were charged with sedition for publishing and printing an article that quoted an alleged guerrilla leader. The speaker of parliament prohibited newspapers from reporting the findings of a committee report on government embezzlement, known as the Goldenberg scandal.

International journalists were not exempt from government censorship. On February 17, the government canceled a license and seized three reels of film belonging to a British Channel 4 television crew that had come to film a documentary on tourism and travel. In April, President Moi threatened to expel the Nairobi correspondents of international journals *Time*, *Newsweek*, and the *Washington Post* for writing articles that highlighted the government's human rights abuses.

The political opposition parties—the Forum for the Restoration of Democracy-Kenya (FORD-Kenya), FORD-Asili, and the Democratic Party (DP)—remained divided largely on ethnic or regional lines. Throughout the year, opposition members faced harassment from the government. Frequently, licenses to hold meetings in their constituencies were denied to opposition politicians, and a number of peaceful gatherings were forcibly broken up by police.

In February, the government announced that two guerrilla groups, the February Eighteen Resistance Army (FERA) and the Kenya Patriotic Front, from Uganda, were plotting to overthrow the government by force. The government called for the alleged leader, John Odongo, a refugee in Uganda, to be forcibly repatriated. The refusal by the U.N. High Commissioner for Refugees to assist in repatriating Mr. Odongo resulted in a threat by President Moi to expel the estimated 230,000 refugees (most from Somalia and Sudan) in camps on Kenyan territory.

In early May, top members of the Kenyan opposition announced the formation of a new political party, Safina (which means Ark in Kiswahili). President Moi and several ruling party officials immediately spoke out against its registration. As a result, Safina's application for registration under the Societies Act has been stalled since June 20. On June 23, in an effort to prevent Safina's registration, the attorney general published a bill which, if enacted into law, would severely restrict the formation and registration of new opposition parties and the functioning of those already existing.

One founding member of Safina, conservationist Richard Leakey, a Kenyan of English origin, was denounced by President Moi as a racist colonialist. Shortly after, one hundred armed Maasai stormed the Leakey home demanding the departure of "the colonialist." In August, Mr. Leakey and several Safina members were attacked with whips and clubs by ruling party youth wingers and severely beaten.

The government continued to use the judiciary to silence critics and to punish political opponents. No progress was made during 1995 by the legal reform task force formed by the attorney general in 1993 to amend or repeal repressive legislation. In January, President Moi stated that none of the government's policies could be "interfered" with by the courts.

The trial of prominent opposition figure Koigi wa Wamwere, a former MP and founder of a human rights organization, on charges of armed robbery, concluded in October. He was sentenced to four years imprisonment and a flogging for attempted robbery, in a trial that did not conform to international standards.

Although the large-scale violence that characterized the ethnic persecution in the early 1990s diminished, the government continued its potentially disastrous policy of targeting certain ethnic groups. Since 1991, the government has been responsible for unleashing terror to provoke the massive displacement of people of Kikuyu, Luo, and Luhya origin. The campaign against certain ethnic groups from the Rift Valley Province caused at least 1,500 deaths and some 300,000 to be displaced. These attacks have pitted Kalenjin and Maasai, the ethnic groups of the president and his ruling elite, against those ethnic groups identified with the political opposition—Kikuyu, Luo, and Luhya. Large-scale attacks have decreased since the 1992 election, but persecution against the displaced continued in 1995. There were regular reports of acts of violence and intimidation against those who attempted to return to their land.

In March, the government repealed emergency regulations established in September 1993, under the Preservation of Public Security Act, which had given the government extraordinary powers to enforce law and order and to limit access to outsiders in some of the areas where the worst violence had occurred. The regulations had restricted the ability of journalists and human rights workers to document events in the area.

A joint Kenyan government and United Nations Development Programme (UNDP) project to resettle the estimated 300,000 driven from their land by the "ethnic" violence was failing. Since the program began almost two years ago, there has been little reintegration. The government has consistently manipulated and undermined the UNDP program, obstructing genuine resettlement efforts. In December 1994, government officials forcibly dispersed a camp at Maela, where approximately 30,000 displaced people, predominantly of the Kikuyu ethnic group, had sought refuge since October 1993. Without notice, government officials razed the camp and forcibly transported some 2,000 of the residents to Central Province; there they proceeded to question them about their ethnicity and ancestral background. It forcibly moved some of the victims for the second time in January 1995.

The forced removal of certain ethnic groups from the Rift Valley Province appeared to play a part in the growing calls by Kalenjin and Maasai politicians for the introduction of *majimboism*, a federal system based on ethnicity that would give political and economic power in the Rift Valley Province only to members of those pastoral groups originally on the land before colonialism, such as the Kalenjin and Maasai.

The Right to Monitor

Although several Kenyan nongovernmental organizations engaged in monitoring human rights in Kenya during 1995, some of their members as well as individual lawyers defending those accused of political offenses were subject to official harassment. A wide range of local human rights organizations continued to function, including the International Commission of Jurists (Kenya), the International Federation of Women Lawyers (FIDA-Kenya), the Kenya Anti-Rape Organization, the Kenya Human Rights Commission, the Legal Advice Center (LAC), the Legal Education and Aid Program (LEAP), and the Public Law Institute. The National Council of Churches of Kenya (NCCK) and the Catholic Church continued to provide relief to the displaced population and to monitor ethnic persecution.

The attacks against the LAC and *Finance* magazine in early 1995 served as an informal warning to organizations and publications critical of government policies. In March, the Law Society of Kenya, the Legal Advice Center, and the Kenya Human Rights Commission issued a joint statement in which they noted that they too were targets of intimidation meant to silence critics and feared that their lives were in danger. In

April, President Moi attacked international human rights organizations for reporting on Kenya, accusing them of adopting double standards. In July, two days before donors met to discuss Kenya's human rights record, the government announced the creation of a government Human Rights Committee.

The Role of
the International Community

Since 1991, when aid to Kenya was suspended on economic and human rights grounds, donors have failed to sustain pressure for the respect of human rights, in large part due to the justification that the government had taken significant steps towards economic reform. Donors seemed willing to countenance harassment and intimidation of government critics as long as the government continued to liberalize the economy and retain a multiparty system in name.

In December 1994, at the consultative group meeting, Kenya's bilateral and multilateral donors expressed satisfaction with Kenya's economic and human rights record. The December 1994 donor statement announcing renewed aid noted "the positive developments over the past year with respect to the democratization process, ethnic tensions and human rights issues," despite strong evidence to the contrary. As a result, US$800 million in new commitments were pledged, reversing the 1991 decision to withhold aid on human rights and economic grounds. However, the deterioration in the situation in early 1995 indicated that this rosy assessment was premature.

Donor concern at the escalation of human rights abuses resulted in an unscheduled donor meeting that was held in Paris on July 24. The closing statement of the July consultative meeting stated that: "Most bilateral donors expressed concern about the overall direction of political events since the end of 1994," and highlighted issues such as freedom of the press, freedom of association, and independence of the judiciary. However, the donors stopped short of a suspension of aid.

The European Union

While the European Union did not take a unified position of strong condemnation of human rights violations in Kenya, some European donors unilaterally expressed their dissatisfaction. Germany cut its aid levels due to "disappointment over Kenya's serious political backsliding," and offered only DM49 million (US$34.6 million) for 1995-6 purely for technical cooperation—compared to the DM138 ($97.5 million)it had pledged in 1993-4. Denmark also declined to release DKr 180 million ($32.8 million) for health projects because of doubts about human rights and government accountability. Both Denmark and Japan noted that continuing assistance would depend on improvements in Kenya's political and economic record.

However, other European countries were less willing to link aid to human rights improvements. The United Kingdom, in particular, was responsible for blocking European Union efforts to condition aid to Kenya. Britain, with aid payments of £31 million (about $49.6 million) for 1995 ranks among Kenya's leading bilateral donors. Up to £2 billion ($3.2 billion) is invested in Kenya. Following the July donor meeting, Britain's overseas minister, Baroness Lynda Chalker, publicly criticized Kenya's human rights record and warned that normal bilateral aid flows would not resume until Kenya's political climate improved. While the statement appeared to be a reversal of British policy, the British Embassy in Kenya rebutted that presumption and insisted that Baroness Chalker had been misquoted and misinterpreted.

U.S. Policy

While the United States did raise human rights issues, both with the Kenyan government and at the donor meeting in July, U.S. officials were less outspoken on human rights than in the past and appeared unwilling to take the lead to press for multilateral donor action. In 1995, U.S. aid to Kenya totaled approximately $18 million, 94 percent of which was directed to NGO sources.

Throughout 1995, the embassy in Nairobi issued several press releases and statements on a variety of human rights issues in Kenya, including backsliding on constitutional reform, attacks on judicial independence, "ethnic" violence, good governance, and restrictions on freedom of expression and association. In January, the embassy expressed its dismay at a recent outbreak of ethnic violence at Mai Mahiu, and two further statements protested the forced dispersals of the internally displaced by the government. A statement by Ambassador Aurelia Brazil publicly lamenting the government's decision to prohibit private broadcast media was criticized as a violation of sovereignty by ruling party officials. In February, the ambassador was held up by police for one hour at a police station when she tried to enter Naivasha for a lunch meeting, on the grounds that she was trying to visit a camp for the internally displaced. In August, Congressman Harry Johnston met with President Moi and raised concern over harassment of the political opposition. The embassy simultaneously released a press release criticizing the harassment of the opposition.

The Work of Human Rights Watch/Africa

Alarmed by the deterioration in the human rights situation in the early part of the year, Human Rights Watch/Africa intensified its efforts to publicize the situation. Throughout the year, Human Rights Watch/Africa was involved in advocacy for human rights in Kenya at conferences, U.S. congressional briefings, and in the Kenyan and international press. In March, Human Rights Watch/Africa wrote to President Moi to call for an end to the violations and followed up with a meeting with the Kenyan ambassador to the United States.

In anticipation of the donor meeting in July, Human Rights Watch/Africa wrote letters to Kenya's major donors, detailing the recent human rights violations, and participated in a briefing for the U.S. delegation to the donor meeting. Human Rights Watch/

Africa also issued a report entitled *Kenya: Old Habits Die Hard*. The report highlighted the abuses which had taken place since the last donor meeting in December 1994.

LIBERIA

Human Rights Developments

By the end of 1995, hopes for peace and respect for human rights in Liberia were once again rekindled. After a dozen prior peace agreements, a new accord signed in Abuja in August again seemed to be Liberia's last, best hope.

One of the hallmarks of the Liberian war has been the proliferation of armed factions, all of which targeted civilians and were responsible for systematic human rights abuses, and none of which was fighting for any recognizable cause or ideology. The war has also been characterized by the extensive use of child soldiers, boys younger than fifteen years old who were easy prey for all the factions. The massive displacement of the civilian population has been another tragic aspect of the war, leading to some 750,000 refugees and one million internally displaced, out of a pre-war population of some 2.5 million. Finally, the Liberian war has been carried out in a climate of utter impunity, with no one held accountable for the crimes committed against the Liberian people. The challenge now is to bring an end to the bloody civil war, which has cost an estimated 150,000 lives and devastated the country.

In accordance with the peace accord, a new transitional government was sworn in on September 1. The new government took over from the Liberian National Transitional Government (LNTG), which had governed the capital, Monrovia, since March 1994, backed by the West African peacekeeping force, ECOMOG. The main warring factions are: Charles Taylor's National Patriotic Front of Liberia (NPFL), which began the civil war with the incursion of its exile army in December 1989; the Armed Forces of Liberia (AFL), the army of former President Samuel Doe, made up largely of the Krahn ethnic group; the United Liberation Movement for Democracy in Liberia (ULIMO), made up primarily of former AFL soldiers, which split in March 1994 along ethnic lines, pitting the Krahn faction of Roosevelt Johnson (ULIMO-J) against the Mandingo faction, led by Alhadji Kromah (ULIMO-K); the Liberian Peace Council (LPC), another offshoot of the AFL, which has been fighting the NPFL in the southeast; and the Lofa Defense Force (LDF), from Lofa County. ECOMOG, which is mostly Nigerian, has been in Liberia for more than five years, and while its presence has helped protect many civilians living in Monrovia, ECOMOG's reputation has been tarnished by its support for various anti-NPFL, Krahn-based factions.

In August 1995, a new peace agreement was signed in Abuja, amending and supplementing the Cotonou and Akosombo accords, which includes all the warring factions and provides for a new cease-fire. The new six-person Council of State is composed of Wilton Sankawolo, as chairman; George Boley, representing the LPC, the Central Revolutionary Council of the National Patriotic Front of Liberia, and the Lofa Defense Force; Alhadji Kromah, representing ULIMO; Oscar Quiah, representing the Liberian National Council; Chief Tamba Tailor; and Charles Taylor of the NPFL. The agreement provided for presidential elections to be held in one year, in August 1996.

Liberian civilians continued to be terrorized throughout 1995. No meaningful investigation was made into the Cow Field massacre outside Monrovia in December 1994, during which forty-eight people were killed, most of them children. The perpetrators have never been identified, but many reports indicated that Krahn-speaking fighters were involved. The LNTG announced that nine AFL soldiers had been arrested, but the results of its inquiry were not publicized.

Massacres of civilians were reported in several other parts of Liberia during 1995. In Grand Cape Mount County in March, a massacre was reported in Meenkor town, apparently related to fighting between the two ULIMO factions.

In Bong County, which had been under the control of the NPFL, fighters abused civilians, burned their villages, and prevented them from receiving humanitarian assistance. International relief groups found that as many as 43 percent of children under age eleven suffered from malnutrition in parts of Bong and Margibi counties.

In the area around Buchanan in Bassa county, civilians have been caught in the fighting between the NPFL and the LPC, with both sides attacking civilians and accusing them of supporting the other faction. Many atrocities have been reported in these attacks, including beatings, rapes, cutting off of body parts, and executions. On April 10, more than seventy civilians in the village of Yosi in Bassa County were massacred; it remains unclear which warring faction—the NPFL or the LPC—was responsible. The fighters ordered the villagers to gather in an open field and then attacked them with machetes and clubs. Although the massacre was publicized by UNICEF, no investigation was opened and the killers remained unidentified. In June, UNICEF reported that 652 women had been raped in Buchanan within the prior six months.

As expected, the signing of the peace agreement did not have immediate effect throughout the country. Within two days of the start of the cease-fire, the rival wings of ULIMO fought each other near Tubmanberg, west of Monrovia. Reports of skirmishes between the LPC and the NPFL in the southeast also continued. In the northeastern town of Ganta in late September, relief workers from the World Health Organization (WHO) and the U.N. Children's Fund (UNICEF) had to abort their mission after being harassed by twelve NPFL fighters; the fighters held the relief workers at gunpoint, commandeered a WHO vehicle, and stole money and personal effects. The vehicle was later returned, although it was in poor condition. In October, new fighting broke out in Gbarnga between the NPFL and ULIMO-K.

The continued fighting among the warring factions raised serious questions about the prospects for repatriating the 727,000 Liberian refugees who fled to neighboring countries. Some 370,000 were in the Ivory Coast, 395,000 in Guinea, 14,000 in Ghana, 4,600 in Sierra Leone, and 4,000 in Nigeria. In addition, approximately one million are internally displaced.

There are no precise figures on the number of child soldiers in Liberia; even the total number of combatants in all the factions is unknown, but estimates range between 40,000 and 60,000 combatants. UNICEF estimates that approximately 10 percent of the fighters are under the age of fifteen. The NPFL and ULIMO have consistently used children under the age of eighteen, including thousands of children under fifteen. International law—the Protocols of the Geneva Conventions and the United Nations Convention on the Rights of the Child—forbids the use of children under the age of fifteen as soldiers in armed conflict. The African Charter on the Rights of the Child has a higher threshold, stating that no one under the age of eighteen can serve in armed hostilities. In spite of these clear provisions, thousands of children are being used as soldiers in Liberia.

The Right to Monitor

A number of human rights organizations were able to function in Monrovia without interference. The principal human rights organizations include: the Catholic Peace and Justice Commission, the Center for Law and Human Rights Education, the Liberian Human Rights Chapter, the Association of Human Rights Promoters, and Liberia Watch for Human Rights. However, it was often difficult for these groups to travel outside Monrovia to document human rights abuses. There were no known human rights organizations operating in NPFL, ULIMO, or LPC territory.

The Role of
the International Community

The United Nations

In September 1993, the United Nations Security Council created a U.N. Observer Mission in Liberia (UNOMIL) to help supervise and monitor the Cotonou peace agreement, in conjunctionwith ECOMOG. On September 15, 1995, UNOMIL's mandate in Liberia was extended until January 31, 1996; on November 10, the Security Council voted to strengthen the mission to 160 military observers. UNOMIL has a mandate to report on violations of the cease-fire and violations of humanitarian law, but since its creation in September 1993, it has not reported publicly about the situations it has monitored.

Human rights concerns have been notably absent from the U.N.'s reporting on Liberia. Accordingly, many opportunities were missed to insert provisions for human rights protection into the peace process. The U.N. observers must fulfill their mandate to monitor and report on human rights violations if their presence is to contribute effectively to the peace process.

A U.N.-sponsored donors meeting in New York on October 27 raised US$145.7 million to support the peace process in Liberia, with only a small portion going to ECOMOG. The main donors were the U.S., which pledged $74 million, and the E.U., which pledged $53 million for reintegration activities; the U.K. pledged $7.7 million, and France pledged $3 million.

U.S. Policy

Throughout the war, the U.S. policy has been to support the conflict resolution efforts of the Economic Community of West African States (ECOWAS) and the U.N., to withhold recognition of any of the governments until elections could be held, and to promote ECOWAS and its peace plan. However, by deferring to ECOWAS, the U.S. lost important opportunities to influence the negotiations and to insert human rights guarantees into the process.

The U.S. has been the largest donor to the Liberian relief effort. (Other U.S. aid is prohibited by the Brooke Amendment, which suspends aid to countries that have failed to repay their loans to the U.S.) The U.S. has spent some $380 million in humanitarian and peacekeeping assistance to Liberia, including assistance to the refugee communities outside Liberia. In addition, some $60 million has been provided for conflict resolution efforts such as financing the Senegalese and later the Ugandan and Tanzanian contingents to ECOMOG.

During 1994, the Clinton Administration sent several delegations to the West African region to deal with the Liberian crisis. In early 1995, President Clinton appointed Ambassador Dane Smith to be his special envoy to Liberia, and he made five trips to the region. His primary functions involved moving the peace process forward and obtaining a regional consensus on stopping the flow of arms into Liberia.

In an important move, in July 1995, the U.S. detained Momolu Sirleaf, a high official of the NPFL, at Dulles Airport for violating Article 212F of the Immigration and Nationality Act which, by presidential proclamation, prohibits entry into the U.S. of those individuals hindering the peace process. The presidential proclamation was issued on September 1, 1994, but this was the first time it was applied. Sirleaf was held for approximately forty-eight hours before being released pending a hearing, which was scheduled for early November. The U.S. action was intended to send a signal to the warring factions that they would not be allowed to continue using the U.S. as a base for financing their war effort.

By year's end, there was considerable discussion about enhanced U.S. support for ECOMOG. ECOWAS was seeking some $90 million for its peacekeeping operation in Liberia, and an additional $42 million for demobilization. The U.S. was considering how it could respond to these requests, which also include ECOMOG's need for communications support and equipment. At the donors meeting on October 27, the U.S. pledged $75 million for Liberia: $50 million in food aid, $10 million for trucks for ECOMOG, and the remaining $15 million for demobilization.

Given the history of ECOMOG's involvement in Liberia, Human Rights Watch/Africa called for close attention to be paid to ensure that their mission is conducted in an even-handed fashion without assisting or prejudicing any of the warring factions. Any future U.S. assistance to ECOMOG must be contingent upon transparency of ECOMOG operations and strict scrutiny of ECOMOG conduct. While new national contingents or military support personnel were to be introduced into ECOMOG from Burkina Faso, the Ivory Coast, Benin, Niger, Mali, and Togo, the bulk of the ECOMOG forces would remain Nigerian military, a highly problematic recipient of U.S. assistance. This situation made human rights conditions for the receipt of U.S. assistance doubly urgent.

In a statement released on October 23, the U.S. embassy warned that new violence in Liberia could threaten the peace process. The embassy advised all parties in Liberia "to demonstrate their commitment and responsibility to peace by exercising control over their supporters and intervening personally and swiftly to halt cease-fire violations and other threatening acts, including the sale or purchase of arms and their distribution."

The Work of
Human Rights Watch/Africa

With the seeming inability of the peace process to move forward, Human Rights Watch/Africa continued to monitor human rights developments in Liberia and to publicize the situation. Human Rights Watch/Africa frequently briefed journalists, government officials, and U.S. congressional staff about Liberia, and participated in discussions aimed at pressuring the warring factions to respect human rights.

After the peace accord was signed, Human Rights Watch/Africa testified in September before the U.S. Senate Subcommittee on Africa of the International Relations Committee. The testimony recommended ways that human rights protections could be incorporated into the peace process.

MOZAMBIQUE

Human Rights Developments

After Mozambique's first ever multi-party elections in October 1994, human rights practices improved throughout the country. For many observers Mozambique is seen as a success story in Africa with a bloody civil war ended and elections generally considered free and fair. However, significant human rights concerns remain, including restrictions on freedom of movement and expression in some areas controlled by the former rebel Mozambique National Resistance (RENAMO), heavy-handed and intimidatory government policing, and appalling prison conditions.

A final breakdown of the 1994 election results showed that the ruling Front for the Liberation of Mozambique (FRELIMO) took 57 percent of the vote, to just 28 percent for RENAMO in urban areas, but that in rural districts RENAMO scored a narrow victory of 41 percent to FRELIMO's 40 percent. Unlike in neighboring countries, such as Angola and South Africa, there has been no power-sharing between the government, headed by President Joaquim Chissano, and the main opposition party. This was part of a government strategy to slowly strangle RENAMO of resources by denying it access to positions of patronage and power. With few exceptions, the new administration is made up of FRELIMO supporters, although RENAMO does receive a state subsidy of about US$1.1 million yearly. Throughout 1995 RENAMO warned that it was in financial crisis and could not guarantee control of its supporters without additional resources.

Impunity for human rights abuses during the 1977-1992 civil war continued to be advocated by both FRELIMO and RENAMO officials. Officials from both sides have told Human Rights Watch that any trials or exposure of the past would undermine national reconciliation. There has been no acknowledgment at senior levels in RENAMO or FRELIMO of involvement in human rights abuses; in some cases, known human rights abusers in authority continued to generate fear and mistrust among those who knew about their past abuses.

A de facto situation of "dual administration" persisted, in which RENAMO continued to exercise administrative control over a patchwork of territory. Expanding public administration into areas dominated for many years by RENAMO remained slow. In Sofala province, RENAMO still effectively ran three districts (Maringue, Cheringoma and Muanza), and large parts of three others (Gorongosa, Chibabava and Machanga). In these areas RENAMO boycotted schools, health posts and even shops that it believed were funded by the Chissano government. This resulted in some violence and confrontation.

In Manica province, in June, a dozen police attempted to open a police station in Dombe, but the RENAMO-supported *regulos* (former colonial chiefs) expelled them and a dispute has continued ever since. Forty-four of these Dombe regulos demanded that the government buy them uniforms and pay them a wage before they permitted the police to return. In northern Nampula, western Tete province and in Sofala province, RENAMO also blocked freedom of movement and information and, as in Dombe, claimed that it had won the 1994 multi-party elections. In contrast, in some areas of Zambezia and Nampula provinces, there was better cooperation between RENAMO and the government, with increasing freedom of movement and expression.

There were several reports of extrajudicial executions. The government-appointed administrator of Mongincual district in Nampula province, Isidro Loforte, was suspended by the provincial governor in June following reports that he had ordered the execution by firing squad of a disabled former soldier and was involved in a series of other crimes.

Police behavior remained a serious concern and was the source of the majority of complaints Human Rights Watch received from Mozambique in 1995. Police units and especially the paramilitary police force, the Rapid Intervention Police, maintained a reputation for intimidation and heavy-handed tactics. Arbitrary detention, torture and bribery were common allegations. There was tangible evidence that the Rapid Intervention Police were used to intimidate RENAMO supporters. Several policemen interviewed by Human Rights Watch admitted that malpractice was common, but justified it by saying they felt it was internationally acceptable police practice: they said many U.N. Civilian Police monitors (CIVPOL) engaged in corrupt practices and did not comment on their policing style although they frequently visited their stations. Until the U.N. withdrew from Mozambique in December 1994, CIVPOL was mandated to monitor police practice.

Prison conditions and detention without trial remained a source of grave concern. According to official statistics, there were 2,572 prisoners in prisons across the country and over half, 1,451, were still waiting to be tried. The full number may have been considerably higher as the official statistics are unreliable. The recognized capacity of the central prison in Maputo was 800 but, at this writing, it had 1,576 prisoners, of which only 566 had been sentenced; 686 had been detained, pending trial. The civil prison (for lesser crimes) in Maputo also had a serious overcrowding problem. Its official capacity was 250, but it held over 550 prisoners.

The situation in the provinces was worse. In the first eight months of 1995, thirty-one prisoners died of hunger or untreated illness in Manica's provincial prison in Chimoio. Built to house 300, it held over 900. Similar reports of overcrowding and deaths of inmates in Tete, Nampula and Gaza provincial prisons were obtained by Human Rights Watch. In July, prisoners rioted in the Xai Xai jail, Gaza's provincial prison, reducing the building to a shell. The riot was in protest against the long delays in cases coming to court. Of the 164 prisoners in the jail, only twenty-one were serving sentences.

Riots and press reports on poor prison conditions prompted Justice Minister Jose Abudo to tour provincial prisons in July, resulting in a public acknowledgment that, with the exception of Niassa provincial jail, all prisons were substandard, and in a pledge that there will be a full review of the prison system.

The Information Service for State Security (SISE), the state security service, became more active after the withdrawal of the U.N. It appeared to have engaged in a recruitment drive, especially among FRELIMO supporters, offering scholarships and other incentives for joining. Human Rights Watch was concerned that this was a return to the previous practice of maintaining SISE as a branch of the ruling party.

Throughout 1995 there were incidents of banditry, occasional riots, and violent demonstrations by ex-combatants who are found reintegration into civilian society hard and had few employment prospects. Most violent incidents were believed to have been acts of economic and socially induced banditry. The thousands of guns readily available for as little as a second-hand shirt were a potential temptation to more focused violence and protest. There have also been incidents where landmines have been used by highwaymen to ambush vehicles.

The Right to Monitor

The League of Human Rights (LDH) was active in lobbying the National Assembly about the poor policing standards of the police and the performance of the interior minister, Manuel Antonio. A new Mozambican nongovernmental organization, the Center for the Promotion and Defense of Human Rights (CPDH), was launched in April. It is comprised of past members of the LDH, who found its operational style too confrontational. The CPDH pledged to defend civil, political, economic and cultural rights.

The Role of the International Community

The United Nations

Following the October 1994 elections, U.N. policy was focused on the withdrawal of its forces from Mozambique. On November 19, 1994, the then U.N. special representative, Aldo Ajello, formally declared that the elections had been free and fair. On November 21 the U.N. Security Council endorsed the results and called on all parties to accept and fully abide by them.

The United Nations Operation in Mozambique's (UNOMOZ) mandate was extended until the swearing in of the new government in December, and U.N. withdrawal continued until the end of January 1995. After this date, only the Accelerated Demining Program (ACP), the U.N. supervised mine-clearance operation, continued. This program was an attempt to compensate for the little mine-clearance that occurred during UNOMOZ's mandate. The ACP had 450 mine clearers, organized in ten platoons, plus a headquarters in Maputo. It depends on outstanding funds from the UNOMOZ budget and on personnel provided by the governments of Australia, Bangladesh, Germany, the Netherlands, and New Zealand, committed until November 1995. At a meeting in Copenhagen during the March 1995 World Summit for Social Development and at the U.N. in New York in October, U.N. Secretary-General Boutros Boutros-Ghali assured President Chissano that the U.N. remained committed to providing assistance to Mozambique for reconstruction and for its mine-clearance in particular.

The U.N. proclaims Mozambique as a success. However, the U.N. clearly had not performed well in human rights monitoring and mine-clearance. Poor CIVPOL monitoring directly influenced subsequent local policing standards and contributed to the lack of seriousness with which respect for human rights was maintained by local police. Hundreds of thousands of antipersonnel mines, manufactured by at least fifteen countries, were found in Mozambique and frequently claim victims. Until mid-1994 U.N. mine-clearance efforts were limited due to internal U.N. disputes and a lack of political will by U.N. special representative Aldo Ajello to confront the issue and quicken clearance efforts. Such failures have lessons that future U.N. operations of this kind should take into account.

U.S. Policy

Bilateral U.S.-Mozambican relations deteriorated in 1995 despite the fact that the peace process was regarded as a success. A prime reason for this was the United State's pressure, through its embassy in Maputo, to demand a power-sharing arrangement with RENAMO following the multiparty elections and the government's refusal to bow to this demand. A dispute over the style of tendering for a lucrative gas pipe-line contract in which U.S. companies had significant interest also contributed in late 1995 to keeping these already poor relations cool. The U.S. government presented a "non-paper" (*aide memoire*) to the Mozambican government on March 10. The paper was timed to coincide with the March 14-15 annual Consultative Group (donors') meeting in Paris. The paper was hard-hitting, and called for economic reform, a transparent budget, cuts in military expenditure, and efforts to curb corruption. It also called for greater efforts by the government to further reconciliation, particularly through funding for opposition parties and a halt to police harassment of RENAMO members. The Mozambican government did not respond to this non-paper; its ambassador in Washington even refused to accept a copy. U.S. policy was softer towards RENAMO, with little comment on its continued blocking of freedom of expression and movement in some of its zones.

U.S. policy after March was been aimed at keeping the Mozambican government to its commitments undertaken at the March Paris donors meeting. USAID shifted its strategy and resources from emergency relief toward longer-term development programs. Initiatives for mine-clearance, repatriation of refugees, and the re-integration of ex-combatants have featured prominently. Institutional support, especially for the new legislature, has also benefited from funds. U.S. assistance to Mozambique in 1995 stood at about $42.25 million, down from the previous year total of $70 million.

The Work of Human Rights Watch/Africa

Human Rights Watch's Mozambique program was aimed at following up recommendations made in *Landmines in Mozambique*, a report jointly produced by its Africa Division and Arms Project in 1994. The key objectives were lobbying the Mozambique government to sign and ratify the 1980 Landmines Protocol and to participate constructively in the 1995 Vienna Review Conference of the Convention on Conventional Weapons (CCW). In late October, President Chissano indicated that Mozambique supported an international ban on the production of antipersonnel landmines.

On June 14, the thirtieth anniversary of the first recorded landmine incident in Mozambique, Human Rights Watch and the Faculty of Arts at Eduardo Mondlane University, Maputo, jointly hosted a one-day conference on landmines. The conference delegates called on the Mozambican government to ban the use and transfer of antipersonnel mines. A book based upon the conference proceedings was also launched in October as a joint Human Rights Watch and Mozambique National Archives initiative.

Human Rights Watch also met government and Renamo officials both in Mozambique and in Europe and the U.S. to discuss human rights issues. It also engaged in other forms of advocacy aimed at informing interested individuals and groups on the current human rights situation and conducted numerous press interviews.

NIGERIA

Human Rights Developments

Human rights, pro-democracy, and labor activists were imprisoned; press freedom was restricted; and the powers of the judiciary were severely circumscribed in Nigeria as military rule extended into the twenty-seventh year out of the country's thirty-five years of independence. General Sani Abacha, who seized power in November 1993, announced on October 1, Nigeria's independence day, that he would remain in power until 1998, fueling skepticism in Nigeria and internationally about the military's promise of a transition to democracy. With the execution of Ken Saro-Wiwa and eight other Ogoni activists on November 10, the Abacha government demonstrated its utter contempt for the rule of law.

The closed trials of some fifty alleged coup plotters, including former Head of State General Olusegun Obasanjo and former Deputy Head of State Major-General Shehu Musa Yar'Adua, by a seven-man military tribunal, exemplified the progressive disintegration of the rule of law throughout the country. Most of the defendants were detained incommunicado and without charge between March 1995 and the start of the trials in early June 1995. They were denied access to independent and freely chosen legal counsel, although they had the option to be represented by armed forces personnel with legal training. In late July, forty of the defendants, who included active and retired military personnel as well as civilians, were convicted and sentenced, some to varying terms of imprisonment and others to the death penalty. The tribunal's decision was not subject to review by a higher court, but only to confirmation by the Provisional Ruling Council. On October 1, General Abacha announced that the Provisional Ruling Council would commute the sentences of those defendants who had been sentenced to death. Critics of the Abacha government claimed that the government "fabricated" the coup crisis to perpetuate its tenure; the government produced no compelling evidence that a coup attempt actually occurred.

Chief Moshood Abiola, the presumed winner of the annulled June 12, 1993 presidential election, also remained in detention under harsh conditions in late 1995, notwithstanding his deteriorating health. In April 1995, Abiola agreed to a conditional release on terms proposed by General Abacha. These terms included confinement to his house, a ban on future political activities, and a prohibition against leaving the country. However, Abacha later reneged on his promise on the ground that the courts were adjudicating Abiola's case. Although Abiola was charged with treason after he proclaimed himself president in late June 1994, his trial has been adjourned indefinitely.

Most of the draconian decrees promulgated by the Abacha government in the fall of 1994 remained in force throughout 1995. These decrees banned independent publications that criticized the government, dissolved the governing bodies of the trade unions, and limited the scope of judicial authority by, for example, permitting the administrative detention of persons deemed to present a "security risk" for renewable periods of three months and suspending the right of habeas corpus. The government also promulgated the Money Laundering Decree of 1995, which gave government officials the authority to tap telephone lines, monitor bank accounts, intercept mail, and access computer systems to prevent drug trafficking and money laundering.

Although the Nigerian government renewed Decrees 6 and 7, which imposed additional six-month bans on *The Punch* and *The Concord*, in early June, these decrees were lifted on October 1. The government attempted to silence outspoken journalists in 1995, including George Mbah, the assistant editor of *Tell* magazine, who was arrested and detained on May 5, 1995, reportedly after he published an article about the alleged coup attempt in March 1995. Kunle Ajibade was detained on May 23, 1995, reportedly after he refused to reveal his sources for an article in *The News* magazine, which claimed that military panels of inquiry had found no evidence of a coup attempt. Chris Anyanwu, editor-in-chief of *The Sunday Magazine*, was arrested and detained in March 1995, released without charge, and subsequently rearrested in late May or early June. Ben Charles Obi, editor of *Classique* magazine, was arrested and detained on May 9, 1995. These individuals, who were subsequently convicted of involvement in the alleged coup, were originally sentenced to life imprisonment, but their sentences were commuted to fifteen years.

Throughout 1995, the trade unions were run by government-appointed administrators. Several trade union leaders, including Frank Kokori, Wariebi Kojo Agamene, Francis Addo, and Fidelis Aidelomon, were detained in August 1994 because of their involvement in the oil workers' strike for democracy and were still imprisoned at the end of the year.

Arrests and harassment of human rights and pro-democracy activists were commonplace throughout 1995. Both Dr. Beko Ransome-Kuti, chairman of the Campaign for Democracy (CD), and Femi Falana, chairman of the National Association of Democratic Lawyers, were arrested on January 12, 1995. Both were released on January 20. Sylvester Odion-Akhaine, secretary-general of the CD, was arrested on January 17. At the time of this writing, he was still in incommunicado detention—notwithstanding a ruling by the Lagos High Court on May 25 that he should be unconditionally released. Shehu Sani, CD coordinator for Kaduna, was arrested on March 9; he also remained in detention.

As the second anniversary of the annulled June 12, 1993 presidential election approached, the Abacha government stepped up arrests of human rights and pro-democracy activists at an alarming rate, presumably in an effort to stifle criticism. On June 3, 1995, State Security Service (SSS) members broke up a meeting of the Democratic Alternative (DA), and arrested and detained without charge DA President Alao Aka-Bashorun and Dr. Onje Gye-Wado, a member of its National Coordinating Committee. Those activists who were arrested and detained without charge in the week preceding the anniversary included Olisa Agbakoba, president of the Civil Liberties Organization (CLO), CLO campaign officer Tunde Akanni, Femi Falana, and Dr. Beko Ransome-Kuti. Most of these individuals were released shortly after June 12.

General Abacha's announcement on June 27, 1995 that he was lifting a ban on political activity generated hope that arrests of government opponents would diminish. On July 3, however, the SSS arrested and detained Chief Gani Fawehinmi, National Coordinator of the National Conscience Party and one of Nigeria's most prominent human rights lawyers, shortly after he had criticized the Abacha government at a press conference. Fawehinmi was released on July 18, the same day that the SSS arrested Chima Ubani, secretary-general of the DA. As of this writing, Ubani remained in detention.

In late July, the SSS arrested Abdul Oroh, the executive director of the CLO, Dr. Beko Ransome-Kuti, and Dr. Tunji Abayomi, the chairman of Human Rights Africa and legal counsel to General Olusegun Obasanjo. These arrests appeared to be in response to a protest letter these individuals wrote to General Abacha which was published in Nigeria's *This Day* magazine on July 21, 1995. Abayomi was arrested following a press conference in his chambers, at which he alleged that the government had no concrete evidence of a coup plot.

Arrests of members of the National Democratic Coalition (NADECO), which includes politicians, retired military officials, and pro-democracy figures who support Abiola's installation as president, as well as other government opponents were commonplace in 1995. Those held as of this writing included NADECO General Secretary Ayo Opadokun and Acting General Secretary Wale Osun. Abiola's personal physician, Dr. Ore Falomo, was detained on April 20, apparently because he publicized his concerns about Abiola's deteriorating health and harsh conditions of imprisonment; Falomo was later released.

Human rights violations in Ogoniland, an oil-rich area in southeastern Nigeria, were particularly severe in 1995. The Movement for the Survival of Ogoni People (MOSOP), led by Ken Saro-Wiwa, has been at the forefront of the confrontation between the indigenous communities of the Niger Delta, the oil companies, and the government. Like other communities in oil-producing areas, the Ogoni contend that multinational oil companies, particularly the Shell Petroleum Development Company, with the active cooperation of the Nigerian government, have ravaged their land and contaminated their rivers, while providing little, if any, tangible benefit in return. In the wake of the May 21, 1994 murders by a mob of four Ogoni leaders who had been branded as pro-government, the Rivers State Internal Security Task Force embarked on a series of punitive raids on Ogoni villages. These raids were characterized by flagrant human rights abuses, including extrajudicial executions, indiscriminate shooting, arbitrary arrests and detention, floggings, rapes, looting, and extortion. The security forces continued to arbitrarily arrest, detain, and beat Ogoni civilians in 1995. In late July, security agents raided and sealed the MOSOP office in Port Harcourt.

Shortly after the May 1994 murders, Ken Saro-Wiwa and Ogoni activists Ledum Mitee, Barinem Kiobel, John Kpuinen, and Baribor Bera were detained. On February 6, 1995, the prosecution charged them with four counts of murder at the first session of the special tribunal established expressly to hear their case. The eight-month delay in filing charges in the case, in conjunction with the procedural irregularities that characterized the trials—including the presence on the tribunal of an active member of the armed forces, the highly militarized tribunal premises, and the lack of any provision for independent review—strongly suggested that the charges were politically motivated. On March 28, the special tribunal assumed jurisdiction over the cases of ten additional defendants, all of whom were formally charged on April 7 with the murders of the Ogoni leaders.

In the face of increasing evidence of the tribunal's bias against the defendants, the original defense team withdrew from all the cases by mid-July 1995 in order to avoid legitimizing the proceedings before the tribunal. The immediate impetus behind their withdrawal was the tribunal's refusal to admit into evidence a videotape or transcript of a government press conference on May 22, 1994, the day after the murders, where Lieutenant-Colonel Komo, the military administrator of Rivers State, accused MOSOP of carrying out the murders. The videotape also includes a statement by A. M. Kobani, a prosecution witness, which contradicts his testimony in the case against Saro-Wiwa, Mitee, Kiobel, Kpuinen, and Bera, in several material respects. The defense team intended to use Kobani's earlier statement to undermine his credibility.

At least one of the defense lawyers subsequently employed by the government Legal Aid Council also resigned, reportedly after being denied access to Ken Saro-Wiwa. Security agents made the representation process even more difficult when they confiscated important files and videotapes from the MOSOP office in Port Harcourt and then sealed the premises.

In late October, Ken Saro-Wiwa, Barinem Kiobel, John Kpunien, Baribor Bera, Saturday Dobee, Felix Nwate, Nordu Eawo, Paul Levura, and Daniel Gbokoo were convicted and sentenced to death; the remaining defendants were acquitted. On November 8, the Provisional Ruling Council confirmed the sentences of those convicted. Despite world appeals for clemency, all nine defendants were executed by hanging in Port Harcourt on November 10. The executions underscored General Abacha's complete disregard for human rights and international law.

The Right to Monitor

Despite severe constraints on their activities and a persistent government campaign of arrest and harassment of their staff, Nigerian human rights groups continued to document and publicize abuses due to the courage and commitment of their local activists. The Constitutional Rights Project (CRP) and the Civil Liberties Organization (CLO) engaged in fact-finding and documentation of human rights abuses throughout the country, filed cases in national courts, and in some cases filed petitions with international treaty bodies. Both the Committee for the Defense of Human Rights (CDHR) and the Nigerian Association of Democratic Lawyers (NADL) also filed cases in national courts. CDHR supplemented its litigation efforts by publishing and distributing leaflets to generate increased awareness of human rights developments and by organizing symposia and rallies to promote human rights and democracy. The Legal Research and Resources Development Center acted as a clearinghouse for human rights reports and documentation from local and international NGOs, published human rights education materials in easy-to-understand English and local languages, and trained paralegals to use these materials in reaching out to deal with the concerns of local communities. The Port Harcourt Institute for Human Rights and Humanitarian Law continued to develop its network of paralegals, who educated local communities in southeastern Nigeria about their rights, provided legal advice and assistance, monitored governmental accountability, and documented abuses. The Nigerian branch of the International Federation of Women Lawyers (FIDA) filed cases in national courts, organized educational programs, and undertook community organizing. The Campaign for Democracy and the Democratic Alternative were involved in community organizing and political consciousness-raising throughout the country, with a view to sustained mass political action.

The Role of
the International Community

The defeat of a resolution on Nigeria at the February 1995 session of the United Nations Commission on Human Rights was an indication of the divided sentiments of the international community with respect to human rights abuses in Nigeria. The draft resolution advocated a return to democratic rule and called upon the Nigerian government to reinstitute the right of habeas corpus, release political detainees, restore press freedom, lift arbitrarily imposed travel restrictions, and respect the rights of trade unionists. The resolution was rejected by twenty-one votes to seventeen, with fifteen abstentions; while most Western countries supported the resolution, most African and Southeast Asian nations opposed it. In meetings with Nigerian officials, the U.N. High Commissioner for Human Rights expressed concern about the human rights situation in Nigeria.

The execution of Ken Saro-Wiwa and the other Ogoni activists on November 10 provoked a strong reaction from the international community. The U.S., Britain, and other countries withdrew their ambassadors. The Commonwealth countries, which were meeting in Auckland, New Zealand, suspended Nigeria's membership—the first time such an action had been taken. The Commonwealth set a two-year deadline for the Nigerian government to restore democracy and constitutional rule or face expulsion. Nelson Mandela, speaking at the Commonwealth summit, called the executions a "heinous act." The European Commission suspended development cooperation with Nigeria and recalled its head of delegation. Britain announced a total ban on arms sales. The Organization of African Unity (OAU) condemned Nigeria for the executions as did U.N. Secretary General Boutros Boutros-Ghali.

The International Finance Corporation (IFC), the private sector lending arm of the World Bank, was considering a loan of US$100 million plus $50 million in equity to an entity called "Nigerian LNG, Ltd." for the construction of a liquefied natural gas plant in southeastern Nigeria and a gas pipeline through the Niger delta to the northern part of the country. The direct recipient of the funds would have been the Shell Petroleum Development Company (the Nigerian subsidiary of Royal Dutch/Shell), which is involved in a joint venture with the Nigerian government, Elf, and Agip. After the execution of Ken Saro-Wiwa and the other Ogoni activists on November 10, the IFC decided against the project. On November 15, however, Shell announced that the project would go forward.

During the summer, a delegation of the Commonwealth visited Nigeria and met with representatives of the government, the business sector, and nongovernmental organizations. Upon their return, the leader of the delegation, former Canadian Foreign Minister Flora MacDonald, confirmed that the team had found evidence of repression, including a lack of judicial independence and deteriorating prison conditions.

The European Union

On July 14, 1993, the European Political Cooperation (the foreign ministers of the European Community) issued a statement on Nigeria in which the European Community and its member states agreed to suspend military cooperation, suspend visits by members of the Nigerian military and intelligence services, and impose visa restrictions for members of the Nigerian military, security forces, and their families. In early December 1993, the E.U. reiterated these measures and further recommended travel restrictions for all military staff of Nigerian diplomatic missions; case-by-case review, with a presumption of denial, for all new export license applications for defense equipment; cancellation of training courses for all Nigerian military personnel; case-by-case review of new E.U. aid projects; and suspension of all non-essential high-level visits to and from Nigeria. In late 1995 numerous E.U. member states called for clemency for the alleged coup plotters who had been sentenced to death.

The measures adopted by the E.U. have been selectively enforced. The European Development Fund has promised substantial assistance to Nigeria, including funds for export promotion, hard currency facilities for the government, as well as aid to the telecommunications industry, news agencies, and universities.

Although the United Kingdom has endorsed virtually all the measures adopted by both the European Political Cooperation and the E.U., the British government has evaded many of the above-mentioned restrictions in practice. In September 1995, British Prime Minister John Major met in London with Chief Ernest Shonekan, General Abacha's predecessor as president, in apparent defiance of visa restrictions. Moreover, notwithstanding the U.K.'s endorsement of the provision for case-by-case review of export license applications for defense equipment, the British government has issued at least thirty export licenses for military equipment since January 1, 1994. The president of the British Board of Trade has described all of this equipment as "non-lethal," although he refused to disclose the precise nature of the equipment. The U.K. is also reportedly completing delivery of eighty Vickers tanks pursuant to a contract executed in 1991. The British Foreign and Commonwealth Office does not deny that weapons shipments have taken place since December 1993 pursuant to export licenses granted prior to the imposition of restrictions.

On October 12, the European Parliament called on the European Commission and the European Council to suspend the application of the Lomé Convention to Nigeria without delay, based on human rights concerns; this step would restrict aid and privileged access to E.U. export markets. The European Parliament also called on Commonwealth nations not to invite representatives of the present Nigerian government to the November 1994 Commonwealth meeting as an act of protest.

To protest the execution of Ken Saro-Wiwa and the other Ogoni activists on November 10, the European Commission announced it was suspending development cooperation with Nigeria and recalling its head of delegation. Fifteen individual member states had already withdrawn their envoys.

United States Policy

Nigeria assumes considerable importance in U.S. policy, due to the country's size and importance on the African continent, its vast natural resources, and its economic potential. The U.S. has $3.9 billion invested in Nigeria, primarily in the petroleum sector. Since the annulment of the 1993 election, the Clinton administration has made strong public declarations condemning the Abacha government and has undertaken policy initiatives intended to facilitate a transition to democracy in Nigeria and to promote human rights. However, the Nigerian government appears to have been impervious to this pressure. Throughout most of 1995, U.S. diplomatic efforts focused primarily on the fate of the alleged coup plotters, with the exception of intermittent references in some public statements to broader human rights concerns. The U.S. embassy occasionally sent representatives to observe the trials of Ken Saro-Wiwa and other Ogoni activists.

In response to the annulment, the U.S. canceled all foreign assistance to Nigeria, with the exception of humanitarian aid. In fiscal year 1995, U.S. aid to Nigeria amounted to $13.5 million, for projects concerning health, population, child survival, and democratization. The U.S. also ended all government-to-government military assistance and training, except counternarcotics training, requested the withdrawal of the Nigerian military attaché from the U.S., withdrew the U.S. security assistance officer, and suspended travel to Nigeria by the U.S. defense attaché. Since July 1993, when the U.S. announced that military sales would be reviewed on a case-by-case basis, with the presumption of denial, the U.S. has granted less than twenty applications for export licenses for non-lethal defense equipment.

In response to Abacha's coup in November 1993, the Clinton Administration suspended the entry into the U.S. of "immigrants and nonimmigrants who formulate or implement policies impeding a transition to democracy in Nigeria or who benefit from such policies, and the immediate families of such persons." The practical impact of these provisions has been reduced because they are waived for Nigerian government officials who seek to enter the U.S. for the purpose of attending meetings of international organizations, although the movements of such officials are restricted during their visits. In April 1994, President Clinton decertified Nigeria for its failure to control illegal drug trafficking, which meant that the U.S. was precluded from granting any foreign aid to Nigeria and from supporting Nigerian applications for loans from international lending institutions. All of the above policies remained in effect in 1995.

In 1995 President Clinton appointed a special emissary, Donald F. McHenry, who reportedly undertook at least five secret missions to Nigeria in an effort to expedite the transition to democracy and improve U.S.-Nigerian relations. General Abacha's prolonged transition timetable suggests that McHenry's efforts were at best marginally successful. Senior State Department and White House officials severely criticized the trials of the alleged coup plotters. In August, President Clinton reportedly warned General Abacha that a decision to execute the alleged coup plotters would have serious consequences for U.S.-Nigerian relations.

In response to General Abacha's October 1 statement, the White House issued a press statement criticizing the length of the proposed transition program as well as the government's failure to provide for significant civilian participation in national decision-making in any transitional government. The statement went on to welcome the decision to commute the death sentences of the alleged coup plotters, but called upon the Nigerian government to provide prompt clarification of their status. The statement also reiterated earlier calls for the prompt and unconditional release of political detainees and for an open appeal process for those convicted in secret trials.

After the execution of the Ogoni activists on November 10, the White House issued a statement strongly condemning the executions, stating that they "demonstrate to the world the Abacha regime's flouting of even the most basic international norms and universal standards of human rights." In addition to protesting the executions, President Clinton decided to recall Ambassador Carrington from Lagos for consultations; to ban the sale and repair of military goods and provisions of related services to Nigeria; to extend the ban on visas to include all military officers and civilians who actively formulate, implement, or benefit from the policies that impede Nigeria's transition to democracy; and to require Nigerian government officials visiting the U.N. or the international financial institutions to remain within twenty-five miles of those organizations.

The Work of
Human Rights Watch/Africa

Human Rights Watch/Africa issued numerous press releases denouncing arrests of human rights and pro-democracy activists, and wrote General Abacha in June to call for clemency for the coup suspects who had been sentenced to death. Also in June, Human Rights Watch/Africa sent letters to the U.N. High Commissioner for Human Rights; the U.N. Special Rapporteur on Extrajudicial, Summary, and Arbitrary Executions; and the U.N. Special Rapporteur on the Independence of the Judiciary urging them to appeal promptly to the Nigerian government to prevent the arbitrary execution of the alleged coup plotters.

Based on a fact-finding mission to southeastern Nigeria in February, Human Rights Watch/Africa issued a report entitled *The Ogoni Crisis: A Case-Study of Military Repression in Southeastern Nigeria*. This report focused on the most recent phase of the crackdown in the Ogoni area, which began in late May 1994. Human Rights Watch/Africa used the report to encourage Royal Dutch/Shell and other multinational oil companies operating in Nigeria to adhere to a set of basic human rights principles in the course of their business operations. The report also comprised the basis of submissions to the U.N. Committee on the Elimination of Racial Discrimination and the U.N. Subcommission on Prevention of Discrimination and Protection of Minorities. Letters to General Abacha in April and October protested the unfair trials of Ogoni activists charged with the May 1994 murders of four Ogoni leaders and called for them to be retried before and independent and impartial tribunal. After the execution of the last Ogoni activists on November 10, letters were sent to the European Union, the Security Council, and the multinational oil companies recommending various actions to be taken to isolate the military government of Nigeria.

Human Rights Watch/Africa provided information about human rights developments in Nigeria to the U.S. and international press, governments, and intergovernmental organizations. In July, Human Rights Watch/Africa testified on Nigeria before the Africa Subcommittee of the U.S. Senate Foreign Relations Committee. Human Rights Watch/Africa also participated in coalitions of nongovernmental organizations working on Nigeria in Washington, London, Dusseldorf, and Amsterdam.

RWANDA

Human Rights Developments

The government of Rwanda, in power only six months at the start of 1995, faced enormous problems in rebuilding a country shattered by war and a genocide that had taken the lives of between one half and one million of its citizens. In repeated declarations, authorities affirmed that bringing the perpetrators of genocide to justice was one of their most important tasks, but as the year neared its end, they had tried no one. They had, however, arrested some 57,000 people who were being detained in inhumane and life-threatening conditions, virtually all of them in violation of due process guarantees of Rwandan law.

Authorities also saw dispersing the hundreds of thousands of displaced persons clustered in camps as a central concern. During 1995, they eliminated the camps, but at the cost of thousands of lives. In the worst massacre of the displaced, at Kibeho camp in April, as in some other cases of soldiers killing civilians, military authorities justified the slaughter on the grounds of self-defense. They announced investigations into several such incidents or, in the case of Kibeho, they called for an investigation by an international commission, but they have not published the results of their own investigations. Authorities removed commanding officers and even detained several junior officers accused in these cases, but, as of late 1995, they had apparently not brought to trial anyone involved in these killings.

Outside Rwanda some two million refugees who had fled the new government in mid-1994 remained unwilling to return home, but those in Zaire, where the largest number lived, were facing the possibility that they might be forcibly expelled before the end of the year. Meanwhile leaders of the former government, which was responsible for the genocide, were training and arming soldiers for incursions to Rwanda.

At the beginning of 1995, some 15,000 persons had been jailed in official prisons, communal lockups, or regular places of detention. As the year neared its end, the number had increased to some 57,000, and arrests were continuing at the rate of more than 2,000 per month. Virtually all the detained were accused of having participated in the genocide, most on the basis of denunciations alone. Relatively few detainees had been formally charged after some form of investigation.

On April 6, 1995, the anniversary of the start of the genocide, the prosecutor in Kigali brought seven persons to trial on charges of having participated in the mass slaughter. The proceedings lasted only a few hours before the prosecutor asked for a postponement to permit further investigation. By November 1995, this trial had not resumed, nor had any other trial begun on charges of genocide.

Rwandan authorities attributed the judicial paralysis to lack of resources, both material and human. International assistance to the judicial system, promised by a number of donors in late 1994 and early 1995, trickled in. In July 1995, about a third of a promised $13 million had actually been delivered. The situation in terms of personnel was equally difficult. With only thirty-six judges, fourteen prosecutors, and twenty-six police inspectors, the government hardly had the staff necessary to prosecute tens of thousands of persons. The government initially favored bringing in foreign judges to aid in the trials, but by mid-year the Transitional National Assembly had rejected the proposed legislation needed to authorize foreign judges to sit in Rwandan courts.

Although real shortages of human and material resources slowed the operation of the judicial system, this did not account for the failure to try even one of the more than two hundred cases that were ready as early as April 1995. The authorities who ended the genocide appeared unwilling to prosecute its perpetrators, either because they lacked confidence in judges named by the previous government or because they saw some political interest in detaining large numbers of persons indefinitely.

Since the establishment of the current government, soldiers have been responsible for maintaining law and order because there has been no functioning police force: backed by some civilian recruits known as the local defense force, soldiers carried out thousands of arrests without warrants, often without the knowledge or approval of appropriate judicial or local authorities. Efforts by the minister of justice and various prosecutors to end this practice had little effect. Similarly, the military has interfered with the release of detainees by judges or prosecutors. In February, for example, soldiers refused to release the priest Joseph Ndagijimana, who was ordered freed by the prosecutor at Gitarama. In other cases, soldiers or local authorities have immediately re-arrested persons freed by magistrates.

In late 1994, Minister of Justice Alphonse-Marie Nkubito created a "Selection Commission" (Commission de triage) to review cases of detainees who might be eligible for release, and in 1995 similar commissions were established in about half the major jurisdictions in Rwanda. The commissions, however, were ineffective; they met irregularly and freed at most several dozen persons in each of the jurisdictions where they operated. Those few people released by the commissions were only provisionally at liberty and had not been cleared of the charges against them. They, as well as those freed directly by magistrates, remained at least suspect, if not already convicted in the eyes of some in their communities. Some of those released were attacked or killed, such as Deputy Prefect Placide Koloni, while others lived in hiding (see below).

The arrests of persons accused of genocide so long after the end of the slaughter raised the question of why it took so long for complaints to be registered, particularly against persons who had been living in their home communities in the interim. In February, March and April, a number of officials from the former government, including some re-appointed to their posts by the current government, were arrested, arousing concern that the arrests were politically motivated.

The capacity of Rwandan prisons is officially given as 12,250 but the number actually in jails was more than 57,000 in October. In the worst of the prisons, four inmates shared every square yard of space, unable to sit, far less to lie down. Many suffered from illness or infection. Several hundred cases of gangrene were reported at the Gitarama prison, where ill prisoners had limbs amputated in an effort to save their lives. In this worst of the Rwandan prisons, nearly 1,000 of 7,000 inmates died in the period from September 1994 to June 1995. These inhumane and life-threatening conditions drew extensive criticism from the international community, which offered aid in building new prisons. In early October, the first of these new prisons was opened and one thousand prisoners were transferred there. Immediately after the opening ceremonies, however, the prisoners were returned to their original place of detention.

Conditions at the brigades, communal lockups, and other irregular places of detention were even worse. Complaints of beating and torture were rare at the regular prisons, but detainees arriving from other facilities reported brutal and humiliating treatment.

Rwandan authorities improved the treatment of imprisoned minors, of whom there were more than a thousand. Several hundred, most of them aged seven to thirteen years old, were moved to a special facility established by UNICEF. At Butare prison, children aged fourteen to seventeen were separated from adult prisoners and given educational facilities.

At the end of 1994, the Rwandan authorities announced that they would soon close the displaced persons' camps in southwestern Rwanda that housed some 220,000 people. The vast majority of the camp residents were unarmed civilians who had fled before the Rwandan Patriotic Army (RPA) troops in June and July 1994. Hidden among the displaced were a small number of armed extremists, members of the militia and others that had participated in the genocide, who continued to kill, rob, and threaten others in the camps and in neighboring communities.

Representatives of various U.N. agencies and international nongovernmental organizations (NGOs) were discussing a plan for closing the remaining camps with Rwandan authorities when several thousand RPA soldiers surrounded four camps in mid-April. The largest of these was Kibeho, with a population of some 120,000.

On April 18, the soldiers fired in the air to herd the residents into the center of the Kibeho camp. Thousands of persons panicked and stampeded, causing the deaths of nine persons. In a series of incidents between April 20 and 22, the troops fired directly into the crowd, using machine guns as well as rock-propelled grenades, killing thousands of people. On April 23, they chased and shot at unarmed civilians, including children, who were attempting to flee the carnage. During the nights of April 20 and 21, unidentified assailants killed and wounded dozens of camp residents in attacks with machetes.

Rwandan authorities cited these attacks and the wounding and death of several RPA soldiers on April 22 as evidence that troops faced a serious threat and were justified in firing. Several hundred troops of the United Nations Assistance Mission for Rwanda (UNAMIR), the U.N. peacekeeping force, were present at Kibeho during the massacre but failed to execute their mandate to protect the displaced.

On April 23, UNAMIR soldiers assisted RPA soldiers in burying some of the dead, who were estimated by U.N. officers to number 8,000. Other victims were not buried but rather were thrown in latrines or were removed from the camp in trucks for disposal elsewhere. The Rwandan government sharply contested the U.N. figures and announced that fewer than 400 had been killed. Later, U.N. officials lowered the estimate of those killed to about 2,000.

At the request of the Rwandan government, an international commission carried out an investigation into the Kibeho killings. In a generally inconclusive and superficial report, the commission concluded that the slaughter had not been planned. It added, however, that there was evidence of serious human rights abuse by both RPA soldiers and unidentified elements among the displaced population. It gave no estimate of casualties, but indicated that the death toll was higher than the number advanced by the Rwandan government.

Following the closing of the camps, thousands of the displaced were sent home by truck, but thousands of others left Kibeho and the other camps in convoys escorted by RPA soldiers. En route, many were attacked by gangs of civilians who beat them and pillaged their belongings. Hundreds of the displaced were arrested as they arrived in their home communes and were crammed into lockups that were already full to bursting. In the commune of Rusatira, twenty-eight persons died of suffocation on April 26 after having been forced with hundreds of others into a small jail.

In early September, RPA troops killed at least 110 unarmed civilians in the north-western commune of Kanama. According to Rwandan and UNAMIR authorities, a number of militia and soldiers of the former government had made incursions into the region in the weeks just before. On the evening of September 11, an RPA lieutenant was killed by unidentified assailants on the highway that passes Kanama. At dawn the next morning, RPA soldiers assaulted local residents in three separate attacks. Many of the victims were older women and children, and some were killed while sleeping in their beds. When General Paul Kagame, vice-president and minister of defense, went to the scene, he admitted that the soldiers had committed excesses and announced that any found guilty of violations would be punished. At the same time, he warned that local residents must prevent any infiltration of their area by forces from Zaire or suffer the consequences.

In addition to the massacres described above, unidentified assailants, often in uniform, killed or caused to disappear a substantial number of Rwandans during the year. Some of the best-known cases involved government officials or local leaders, who had criticized government policy. In January, Edouard Mutsinzi, a leading journalist who had criticized the government, was attacked by a gang of five armed men and barely survived. The prefect of Butare Prefecture, Dr. Jean-Pierre Rwangabo, was shot at an improvised roadblock on March 4 along with his son and the driver of his vehicle. He had called for the release of prisoners against whom there was little evidence of guilt. On July 27, Placide Koloni, Deputy Prefect of Gitarama Prefecture, was assassinated along with his wife, two children, and the family cook. Oreste Habinshuti, Deputy Prefect of Gikongoro Prefecture until the end of July, was killed on the night of August 1. A judge, Bernard Nikuze was shot outside his home in Butare in late August, and a local government official, Jean-Baptiste Sinamenaye, was assassinated in Gisenyi at the end of September. Authorities have opened investigations in several of these cases, but no one has been brought to trial for these crimes.

Concerned with continuing insecurity and abuses by the military, Interior Minister Seth Sendashonga insisted upon some resolution to the problem of military indiscipline at a cabinet meeting at the end of August. The meeting turned hostile and ended without settling the issue. On August 28 Prime Minister Faustin Twagiramungu resigned over this issue of insecurity, as did Sendashonga. Minister of Justice Nkubito and two other ministers were ousted at the same time, eliminating the most effective voices against military influence in the government.

The two million Rwandans in refugee camps in Zaire, Tanzania, Burundi, and Uganda have suffered from intimidation and violation of their rights, by officials of the former Rwandan government and officials of host countries. Robbery, rape, and murder were frequent occurrences, although the presence of a special unit of Zairian soldiers under the supervision of the U.N. High Commissioner for Refugees improved the security of the camps in Zaire somewhat. In March, Tanzania closed its border to any new refugees, and in August, Zaire expelled some 16,000 refugees, 14,000 of them to Rwanda, the others to Burundi. Zaire has threatened to drive out the 1.2 million refugees in its territory by the end of 1995.

Reports by the Human Rights Watch/ Arms Project and others documented the flow of arms to the camps as well as military training by forces of the former government, sometimes together with militia of Burundian exiles. Although the international community repeatedly expressed alarm about the risks of renewed war in this region, the U.N. was unable to muster the forces needed to separate the soldiers from civilian refugees and to interrupt these military preparations. As the year ended, incursions from Zaire into Rwanda were increasing in number and scale. In early November the RPA killed a reported 300 soldiers of the former government in an attack on an island in Lake Kivu, nominally in Zairian territory.

The Right to Monitor

In keeping with its declared commitment to openness and improving human rights, the government permitted Human Rights Watch/ Africa and other international human rights organizations to conduct investigations in Rwanda throughout the year. Occasionally Human Rights Watch/Africa was prevented from entering an area by soldiers who cited security considerations, but such prohibitions were unusual. Since the establishment of the current government, Rwandans have been hesitant in making contacts with Human Rights Watch/Africa. Several said that they had been warned not to give information to foreigners or even to talk at length with them. Although we knew of no cases of persons having suffered from being in touch with us, field officers of the U.N. human rights operation have reported such cases among their contacts.

The once dynamic Rwandan human rights movement split this year into two groups, only one of which criticized violations effectively. Activists have been occasionally threatened and harassed by the military. Some have chosen to live abroad, saying that it is impossible to carry on human rights work in Rwanda today.

Abbe Andre Sibomana, editor of the largest newspaper in Rwanda and vice-president of the Association pour la defense des droits de la personne et des libertés publiques (ADL), has criticized human rights abuse under both the former and the current governments. Threatened by RPA soldiers and others, he was also subjected to unsubstantiated charges of involvement in the genocide.

The Role of
the International Community

Having beaten a hasty retreat in the face of the 1994 genocide, the international community tried to act more responsibly in Rwanda during 1995. But torn between the hope of redressing past wrongs and a fear of supporting a new government whose record was unproved, the international community pursued a hesitant and indecisive course. It wasted the opportunity to exercise influence through firm, coordinated action and elicited increasing distrust and hostility from Rwandan authorities. At a conference organized by the United Nations Development Programme (UNDP) in January, various foreign donors pledged US$587 million to help rebuild Rwanda, but much of that money was already committed to Rwanda before the genocide and another substantial part was designated to repay arrears to the World Bank. Of the funds pledged in January, less than $100 million had actually arrived in Rwanda six months later. In July the donors pledged another $200 million in development aid.

The United Nations

When the first UNAMIR peacekeeping force failed to protect the targets of genocide and political slaughter in 1994, U.N. officials justified its inaction on the grounds that its mandate did not extend to such protection and that the force was too small and ill-equipped to undertake the task. The second UNAMIR, created on May 17, 1994, had a broader mandate, including specifically the protection of civilians at risk, and a far larger complement of troops (5,500), but it too failed to protect unarmed civilians, both those slaughtered at Kibeho camp in April 1995 and those who were attacked on the trek back to their home communities in the days immediately after. NGO personnel working in the Kibeho area had observed the buildup of troops in the weeks before the attack and expected a potentially violent closing of the camps. Presumably UNAMIR soldiers and military observers were also well informed about these preparations. Even had they been taken by surprise when the camps were encircled, they still would have had time to reinforce their contingents before the massacre four days later.

While the failure of UNAMIR at Kibeho is clear, it is more difficult to estimate the impact of the U.N. peacekeepers on general security in the country. Many Rwandans took comfort from the presence of the international troops, and those at risk often preferred to live near U.N. posts. Proximity to U.N. locations was no guarantee of protection, however. Deputy Prefect Koloni was assassinated although he lived just next to a U.N. post and after he had specifically asked for protection (see above). UNAMIR soldiers and military observers, like human rights field officers and personnel from NGOs have played an important role in informing the world about human rights violations.

In June, the mandate for UNAMIR was extended until December 1995, but the force was to be gradually reduced to 1,800 and its duties were also to be shifted from providing security to "assisting in the normalization of the country." As financial problems worsened for the U.N., the secretary-general proposed further reductions in the number of troops in early October.

The U.N. human rights effort was a tangle of overlapping authorities destined for permanent conflicts over mandate and materials, limiting the impact of one and all on the real problems of human rights and accountability for abuses. The effort included the work of a special rapporteur named by the U.N. Human Rights Commission, a field operation run by the Geneva-based Human Rights Centre under the authority of the High Commissioner for Human Rights and an International Tribunal created by the Security Council. None of these human rights agencies had the resources required for their work. The special rapporteur operated with virtually no staff. The field operation was so short of funds that it was never able to field the full complement of one officer for each of the 147 communes of Rwanda. The International Tribunal was so restricted by lack of staff and resources that Justice Richard Goldstone, its chief prosecutor, was obliged to call a special conference in May to raise money for its operation.

The High Commissioner's field operation was supposed to gather data on the genocide, to monitor the current situation of human rights, and to assist in re-establishing the judicial system and a rule of law. When the International Tribunal was established, the field operation was directed to deliver to it all materials on the genocide. Apparently the Tribunal staff found little of the material usable for its prosecutions and, since the field operation failed to publish any of the data, its investigation has thus far served little purpose.

In monitoring the current situation, the field operation worked with such complete discretion that it was difficult to see what impact it had. Its officers had no regular reporting procedure to inform all relevant Rwandan officials of abuses. The head of the field office rarely made a clear and forceful public condemnation of even major human rights violations. Such impact as the operation had came from the local activities of some persistent and dedicated field officers. Logistical and administrative problems, enormous at the start, diminished in the course of the year.

The U.N. field operations's technical assistance unit sought to improve the judicial system and to coordinate foreign assistance to it. The unit spent many months hammering out an agreement between international donors and the Rwandan government for aid to the judicial system only to have it all delayed by conflicts between U.N. agencies over which would control the funds. An accord to bring in foreign experts at first provided for teams of four persons for each prefecture, a judge, a prosecutor, a police inspector, and a defense lawyer. But when Rwandan interlocutors indicated that the program would be approved more easily if the provision for defense lawyers were dropped, the U.N. human rights experts made that change.

As the International Tribunal ended its first year of operation, it was still dependent upon a handful of permanent staff members and a slightly larger number of others seconded by supportive governments. The Tribunal promised to announce at least one indictment before the end of 1995.

The European Union

At first reluctant to aid the new Rwandan government, reportedly because of opposition from France, the European Union (E.U.) in December 1994 decided on an aid pack-age of ECU 67 million. On April 26, following the Kibeho massacre, the E.U. suspended ECU 50 million of that aid. It restored full assistance in July. The Netherlands and Belgium also suspended portions of their bilateral assistance following the Kibeho massacre, but they resumed full assistance several months later.

U.S. Policy

The U.S. consistently insisted on the importance of bringing to justice the perpetrators of the genocide. It donated $3 million to the International Tribunal as well as supplying it with some seconded staff, and it pledged some $4 million to the Rwandan judicial system. Total U.S. government assistance to Rwanda was $274 million in humanitarian assistance, $4 million to rebuild government ministries, $2.5 million to pay Rwanda's World Bank arrears, and $860,000 for the Human Rights Field Office. In addition, a Defense Department team assisted Rwandan forces in demining several parts of the country.

In January, the Clinton administration named a special Rwanda coordinator, initially Ambassador Townsend Friedman, and after his death in June, Ambassador Richard Bogosian. The U.S. also chaired the Rwanda Operational Support Group, a group of eleven donor nations, the U.N., the OAU and the E.U. which met regularly to coordinate policies and promote reconciliation in Rwanda and Burundi.

In dealing with current human rights violations, the U.S. issued statements condemning the assassination of Pierre-Claver Rwangabo in March, expressing concern about the violence in Kibeho in April, and calling for an inquiry into the massacre at Kanama in September. It failed to press vigorously enough for progress in the judicial domain.

The Work of
Human Rights Watch/Africa

Human Rights Watch/Africa worked first to ensure that those accused of genocide be brought to justice. In order to establish a firm, detailed body of information about the slaughter, Human Rights Watch/Africa carried out a major study of the genocide in several communes in southern Rwanda, based on extensive documentary material as well as eye-witness testimony. It provided substantial expert witness testimony in the proceedings against former Rwandan officials being prosecuted outside of Rwanda, including Jean-Bosco Barayagwiza and Leon Mugesera as well as in the cases pending in Belgium. It supplied both evidence and general information to Justice Goldstone and his staff on the International Tribunal. Through contacts with U.S., European and African officials as well as with U.N. staff, Human Rights Watch/Africa sought to secure continued commitment to prosecutions for genocide. In frequent conversations with Rwandan officials, it stressed the importance of prompt trials and improvements in the conditions of detention in Rwandan jails. It sought to persuade foreign donors to provide adequate funding for the Rwandan judicial system and to use their influence with the Rwandan government to speed the beginning of trials.

Even while seeking to keep alive a sense of the horror of the genocide and the need to punish it, Human Rights Watch/Africa sought to ensure that these crimes against humanity not serve to excuse current human rights violations. Present at Kibeho during the killings, Human Rights Watch/Africa reported fully on the massacre. As a result of frequent visits to the prisons, it was able to present detailed information about the sufferings of detainees and the consequences of the paralysis of the judicial system. Human Rights Watch/Africa testified at a rare joint hearing of the U.S. House and Senate Africa Subcommittees on April 5, and published fifteen press releases and reports on human rights conditions in Rwanda.

Human Rights Watch/Africa supported Rwandan human rights activists with training and advice on methodology as the local organizations carried out their own work in documenting the genocide.

Field work was carried out during the year by a research team based in Rwanda sponsored jointly with the International Federation of Human Rights.

SOUTH AFRICA

Human Rights Developments

After the euphoria of 1994, 1995 saw the onset of realism in South Africa as the leaders of the African National Congress (ANC), the former liberation movement and now senior partner in a government of national unity, came to grips with the challenges facing them in remaking their country. While the year generally saw positive developments in the creation of a human rights culture, progress was disappointingly slow in some areas, while threats to the new democracy were also apparent. Most seriously, continuing political violence in KwaZulu-Natal province and secessionist demands by the Inkatha Freedom Party (IFP) undermined the inspirational progress of reconstruction and reconciliation.

During the course of the year, a range of legislation with important implications for human rights was passed by the National Assembly. These acts included a new Police Act, a Labor Relations Act, an Emergency Act (repealing former emergency legislation and introducing strict controls over emergency powers, in line with the interim constitution), land reform legislation, and an Education Act. At the same time, first steps were taken to developing a truly accountable parliamentary system, as committees of members of parliament (MPs), formed to monitor specific subject areas, accepted public submissions, and held hearings relating to new legislation.

Important reforms were proposed or implemented during the year in the police, prison, and court systems. Police reform included the replacement of the former commissioner of police, who was tainted with involvement in political police operations under the previous government, and the gradual amalgamation of the former homeland police forces even more abusive than the centralized police into a single new national police service. In May, however, three local organizations monitoring human rights published a report alleging that police torture of criminal suspects was continuing on a regular basis. Until the end of August, the Human Rights Committee, a nongovernmental organization monitoring human rights and political violence, recorded twenty-three deaths in police custody. However, in October, when asking for confirmation from the police, they were told that 507 had died in police custody by the end of September, far higher than anything recently recorded in South Africa. The police later stated that the correct figure was 168 deaths, including deaths resulting from injury during arrest, for the first nine months of the year. The new Police Act mandated the establishment of an "independent complaints directorate" to investigate complaints by the public of police misconduct, but human rights groups feared that it would have insufficient powers to be effective.

Prison conditions were characterized by violence both between prisoners and by guards assaulting prisoners. In May, legislation passed in 1994 was implemented by the minister of correctional services to release from prison 700 children awaiting trial. However, lack of consultation with NGOs and other government agencies meant that many of them were not housed in suitable alternative accommodation and either escaped or were released to the streets. In July, a "transformation forum," including representatives of the prison administration, parliament, unions, and NGOs, was established to examine South Africa's correctional system and began to consider proposals for prison reform.

Positive developments for the criminal justice system were threatened by a public outcry at increasing levels of violent crime, and a rise in vigilante justice by individuals frustrated at lack of action against known criminals. Government responses included aggressive police house-to-house searches, and an act to make access to bail more difficult in cases of violent crime, returning the burden of proof to an accused person to show why he or she should be released.

In 1995, the government pledged to ratify a number of international human rights instruments, including the Convention on the Elimination of All Forms of Discrimination Against Women. In September, a high-level delegation led by the minister of health attended the U.N. women's conference in Beijing and played a prominent role. Important initiatives to address the problem of violence against women were announced during the year, but real progress was hampered by lack of resources to devote to education and training of police and justice officials. Women continued to be discriminated against under customary law.

The new constitutional court, established to adjudicate disputes under the interim constitution, heard its first cases in 1995 and delivered a number of significant judgments based on the bill of rights. Most important of these was the judgment declaring the death penalty unconstitutional, delivered in June.

Political violence in the province of KwaZulu-Natal threatened to undermine the process of reform and reconciliation. Although the number of deaths in political violence in the province was well below the horrific figures preceding the 1994 election, the Human Rights Committee recorded a total of 694 deaths in the province by the end of October, of a total of 1,016 political killings countrywide. The new provincial government remained virtually paralyzed throughout the year due to conflict between the IFP and other parties, particularly the ANC; and, on a national level, the IFP withdrew from the constitutional assembly and, for a period in February, also withdrew from the National Assembly. The basis of the IFP's grievances was its continuing demand for almost total autonomy for the province of KwaZulu-Natal within a federal South Africa.

During the year, there were further revelations of illegal covert activities by the security forces of the previous regimes in Pretoria and the homelands, right up to the date of the 1994 elections. Two trials, of a former South African security branch policeman, and of three police reservists from the KwaZulu homeland, provided the main evidence, including allegations of the involvement of senior IFP and KwaZulu government officials in political assassinations and the promotion of violence. A number of former security police also spoke to the press during the year about their efforts to undermine the ANC and other black opposition groups under the previous regime. An "Investigation Task Unit" (ITU), appointed by the new government in 1994 to follow up allegations made by the Goldstone Commission of hit squad activity in KwaZulu-Natal, made a number of arrests during 1995 in connection with assassinations carried out in the province during the late 1980s. Those arrested included the former minister of defense, Magnus Malan; a personal adviser to IFP leader Chief Mangosuthu Buthelezi, M.Z. Khumalo; and a number of former high-ranking security force officials. However, human rights groups expressed concern at the apparent reluctance of provincial Attorney-General Tim McNally to prosecute less high- profile cases put before him by the ITU.

Ominously, reports from KwaZulu-Natal suggested that political assassinations and the deliberate promotion of violence were continuing. While both ANC and IFP supporters were involved in violence, the evidence suggested that systematic efforts to destabilize the province emanated, as in previous years, largely from the IFP. In January, the graduation of 600 recruits from the KwaZulu Police training college in Ulundi, the capital of the former KwaZulu, was blocked by the new national police commissioner and the minister for safety and security, after it was discovered that only fifty-four of them were qualified to graduate and forty-three had criminal records. In September, it was revealed that Inkatha "self protection units" (SPUs), many of whom had passed through paramilitary training camps before the 1994 election, had been paid from provincial government funds during 1995. Both

IFP and ANC leaders were the targets of assassination attempts, some of them successful, throughout the year.

In July, legislation to establish a National Commission on Truth and Reconciliation was finally signed into law by President Nelson Mandela, after long negotiations between the various parties to the government of national unity. The commission will hear applications for indemnity from prosecution for persons who committed gross violations of human rights on political grounds, prepare a record of human rights violations committed during the period March 1, 1960 to December 6, 1993, and make recommendations for reparations to the victims. In September, a panel of respected individuals was appointed to oversee the process of selection of the commissioners and make recommendations to the president. It was expected that the Commission itself would not start operations until early in 1996, when it would have a maximum of two years to complete its work.

The transition in South Africa resulted in an increasing number of economic migrants and refugees seeking to enter the country from southern and central Africa. Estimates of the number of illegal aliens in South Africa ranged as high as eight million, or almost 20 percent of the population. A number of attacks on "foreigners" were reported throughout the year, although both the ANC and the Congress of South African Trade Unions (COSATU) urged tolerance and stated that illegal immigration to South Africa should be seen in the light of the previous government's policies of regional destabilization. New legislation tightened regulation of visas and work permits, and made citizenship more difficult to acquire. In June, the army requested finances for the extension of the electric fence currently bordering Mozambique to cut off the borders of Zimbabwe and Botswana. However, ratification of the refugee conventions of both the U.N. and Organization of African Unity was approved by parliament in October.

Addressing its history of illegal weapons dealing to abusive states, South Africa's arms industry underwent a major restructuring during 1995. A commission of inquiry headed by Mr. Justice Edwin Cameron published an interim report in July, finding "a conclusive and dismal picture of irresponsibility" under the previous government, and urging greater openness in and control over South Africa's arms trade. In August, the cabinet announced the introduction of a new process to authorize weapons exports that would forbid the export of South African arms to governments that violate human rights. South Africa attended the September conference in Vienna on the Convention on Prohibitions and Restrictions on Certain Conventional Weapons, acceding to the convention on September 13. The government disappointed human rights and humanitarian organizations, however, by arguing that, while "long-life" landmines should be banned, "short-life" landmines should be permitted under international law. During October, ratification of the two protocols to the Geneva Conventions was approved by parliament.

The Right to Monitor

No restrictions on human rights monitoring were maintained by the government of national unity. South Africa's human rights community continued the process of adjusting to life under a democratic government. While many individuals active in the human rights and anti-apartheid fields left to join government in one form or another, those remaining in the NGO movement stated their commitment to independent criticism of their former colleagues.

The Role of
the International Community

The European Union

Negotiations for South Africa's accession to the Lome Convention, by which the relations of the African, Caribbean, and Pacific (ACP) states with the European Union are regulated, continued throughout the year. The European Commission stated its preference for South Africa to have limited access to Lome Convention benefits, due to its relative wealth compared to other ACP states, but for a bilateral trade agreement to be agreed. The commission also announced that it would support the government's Reconstruction and Development Program through the "European Program for Reconstruction and Development" (EPRD). The EPRD budget for 1995 was ECU 125 million, while that for 1996 to 1999 would be ECU 500 million, making the European Union South Africa's largest donor of development assistance. This money would be spent in the fields of education, health, job creation, rural infrastructure, and the promotion of representative and efficient government and balanced regional development.

U.S. Policy

The U.S. embassy in South Africa made no statements relating to human rights issues during the year. The State Department human rights report for 1994 reflected a generally thorough and accurate picture of the human rights situation in the country, but, as in previous years, chose to play down allegations of deliberate promotion of political violence, especially by senior members of the IFP and officers in the police force of the former KwaZulu homeland.

The budget of USAID for South Africa totaled U.S.$186 million for FY 1995. $25 million of the total assistance was devoted to the Democracy and Governance Program, which included support for human rights. The priorities of the program in South Africa were strengthening the rule of law and respect for human rights, promoting free and fair elections (for the next national elections in 1999), strengthening civil society, and promoting more accountable governance.

The new South African government's friendly relations with Cuba and a proposed deal for storage of Iranian oil in South Africa caused conflict with the U.S. A longstanding U.S. prosecution being brought against various companies, including Armscor and a U.S. company, International Signal and Control, for sanctions-busting arms deals during the 1980s, also soured U.S./South Africa relations for much of the year, as the U.S. blocked further arms trade between American companies and South Africa as a result. Negotiations for a plea-bargain settlement of the case, after which remaining U.S. arms sanctions against South Africa could be lifted, centered around the payment of heavy fines by Armscor and the other accused.

The Work of
Human Rights Watch/Africa

A representative of Human Rights Watch/Africa was based in South Africa throughout the year, at the local human rights group Lawyers for Human Rights. Several letters were sent to the South African government urging the government to take a strong stand on human rights issues. In May, a report following up on previous reports on political violence was published, titled *Threats to a New Democracy: Continuing Violence in KwaZulu-Natal.* In November, a book length report, *Violence Against Women in South Africa: The Response of the State to Domestic Violence and Rape,* was published to coincide with the international day of no violence against women and a national conference on domestic violence.

SUDAN

Human Rights Developments

The self-proclaimed government of National Salvation is in its seventh year of power in Sudan. The government sought to consolidate its military gains of the last two years by pursuing an outright military victory over the southern rebels, the Sudan People's Liberation Movement/Army (SPLM/A) and Southern Sudan Independent Movement/Army (SSIM/A). The military government of President Lt. Gen. Omar Hassan Al Bashir continues to be dominated by the National Islamic Front (NIF). The politicization of religion and ethnicity under the NIF agenda of Islamization, together with the protracted civil war, remained a main source of human rights abuses in the country, north and south.

In the north, prospects for the Sudanese people to exercise their right to change their government peacefully remained curtailed as the government continued to hold opposition activists in administrative detention. Draconian emergency laws, instituted after the toppling of the previous democratically-elected government in 1989, ban political parties and independent unions and deny freedom of expression and assembly.

Thirteen years of civil war have shattered the civilian population of southern Sudan. Sudanese continued to flee the war-torn south and to seek relative safety in neighboring countries; by mid-1995, some 553,000 were refugees, and 650,000 internally displaced lived a marginal existence in the north.

As in previous years, both the government of Sudan and the rebel factions continued to commit abuses against civilians in the war zone. War resumed in the south in August after four months of a cease-fire negotiated by former U.S. President Jimmy Carter. The government forces captured Kaya, a key town on the Ugandan border. In September, government planes bombed Mundri, Badiet, Ombasi, and Chukudum among other localities, causing dozens of civilian casualties. An SPLA force attacked thirty-five villages in the Nuer area of Ganyliel of Upper Nile on July 30, killing over 210 persons, more than half of whom were children. These clashes, between the SPLA's main force and splinter-factions drawn on largely ethnic lines served as reminders of the deeper divides that underlie the political and strategic divisions among the rebel groups.

All parties to the conflict took actions that hampered Operation Lifeline Sudan (OLS), the U.N.-led relief operation that seeks to extend much needed assistance to the war-affected population. The Sudan government continued to issue permits for relief flights to land only selectively. Flights are the only means of emergency food deliveries to a number of southern locations. The barge operation on the White Nile, one of the vital routes of OLS food and relief supplies deliveries, was repeatedly delayed and interrupted after incidents of attacks, hostage-taking, and looting, all of which involved human rights abuses, violations of the rules of war, and violations of the ground rules between the OLS and the rebels. On May 7, a Nuer militia, probably aligned with the government, held two World Food Programme (WFP) workers as hostages as it diverted a barge to off lift supplies. Before the end of this attack, soldiers from the rebel faction led by Lam Akol intervened and took the barge under their own control. Remaining WFP workers were taken hostage, as the soldiers looted the barge and stole the hostages' personal belongings. In May, the government captured two doctors, one Italian, one Sudanese, working for the Italian NGO Comitato Collaborazione Medica (CCM) in Pariang, an SPLA area in Upper Nile. To pressure for their release, the SPLA took hostage three U.N. relief workers, two government officials, and a WFP pilot who came to Pariang in late May to pick up the doctors. The government released the doctors in June 18, and the SPLA set its hostages free the next day.

Civilians had no respite from human rights abuses in the Nuba Mountains. The government continued to forbid any U.N. or nongovernmental assistance or visits to thousands of needy civilians living in rebel areas of the Nuba Mountains, pursuant to its abusive counterinsurgency policy of "draining the sea."

New evidence brought to public attention during 1995 demonstrated that the government was methodically and cruelly starving the Nuba people into government straight-jacket. The government bombed the village of Regifi on June 21 and July 9, killing six villagers and wounding thirteen, mostly children. Hundreds of mostly non-Muslim children were sent to traditional Koranic schools in northern Kordofan. Further north, Nuba children, as well as children displaced from the south, remained prime targets for "collection campaigns" in which unaccompanied children are swept from streets of northern cities and towns into government camps,

where children are held without notifying their families and are given Islamic education regardless of their religion.

The government adopted a military strategy of integrating pre-existing tribal militia into its forces to stem the rebel gains in the south and the north. Arabized nomadic tribes were integrated into the Popular Defense Force (PDF), a government paramilitary force created in 1989. These militia were responsible for indiscriminate killings of civilians, abduction, and sometimes enslavement of women and children and looting of cattle and other property.

Increasing economic difficulties in Sudan resulting in severe power failures and interruptions in water supplies led to demonstrations in various neighborhoods in the capital and other cities in April. Government security forces arrested demonstrators by the hundreds and then released some of them in small groups. Pro-government mass organizations, such as the Popular Committees for Surveillance and Services operating at the neighborhood level, pro-government unions in workplaces, and NIF-dominated student unions helped security agents identify supposed agitators, who were detained for longer periods, up to five months in some cases, without charge or trial and without access to family or lawyers.

In March, the government closed down the so-called Citibank ghost house (also known as "the Oasis"), one of the best known unacknowledged detention centers called ghost houses, where ill-treatment and torture of administrative detainees was widely practiced. About sixty security detainees were moved from Citibank ghost house to a specially-constructed security wing in Kober Prison. However, the fact that these detainees remained under the authority of the Sudan Security Service and not of the Prisons Department of the Ministry of Interior meant that they did not benefit from legal guarantees and protections that prison regulations provide for political prisoners.

Ex-Prime Minister Sadiq Al Mahdi, leader of the banned Umma Party, whose democratically elected government was deposed in the military coup of 1989, was arrested in May following a public sermon he gave in which he listed government weaknesses and called on his followers to undertake peaceful political opposition to the government. At least 200 members of his party were detained, some for a few weeks, others for several months. The government failed to charge him with any crime in the three-and-a-half-months during which he was held in incommunicado detention.

In August, officials announced the release of "all political detainees and prisoners" in a general amnesty, and invited exiled opposition leaders to return to the country and engage in legal opposition, although the controls over political life were not lifted. A committee of appeal was established to review petitions from thousands of people dismissed from their jobs in the public sector since 1989.

A total of thirty-two detainees and eighteen convicted political prisoners were released in late August. Authorities also released some 200 old, sick and disabled prisoners from Kober Prison in Khartoum in August. This followed the reported release of all women imprisoned for minor offenses and mothers of young children. The releases may also have been motivated by deteriorating conditions in prisons: Sudan's director-general of prisons said prisons suffered from diminishing budgets, leading to situations of hunger among inmates or even cases of death from lack of medical care. In July, he said there were 1,000 sick women in jail and 300 children imprisoned with their mothers.

Students of the University of Khartoum protesting the September 2 detention of three colleagues took to the streets starting September 9. This triggered three days of violent demonstrations as others joined the protest, with clashes between demonstrators and riot police, security forces, and others. At least five demonstrators were reportedly killed, although unofficial sources reported up to forty casualties. Riot police and security forces fired live ammunition and tear gas to disperse crowds. Dozens were wounded and hundreds detained. Security agents detained alleged "trouble makers" for longer periods, typically people with a history of detentions under this government. They were sent to "ghost houses" which re-opened and were kept busy during September, October, and November. Among those detained were leaders of the banned political parties, trade union and labor movement, lawyers, student activists, and professionals.

The most alarming development during the demonstrations was the appearance of plain-clothed young men at road blocks, checking identities and intimidating crowds into dispersing by threatening them with their automatic hand weapons. The young men were apparently private—but government sanctioned—NIF party militia.

Freedom of the press and freedom of expression remained severely restricted since the 1989 coup. In March 1995, the government-appointed Press and Publications Council withdrew the licenses of two independent newspapers, *Zilal* (Shadows) and *Dar Fur al Jadidah* (New Darfur), following the publication of critical articles. *Zilal* was authorized to resume publication in September.

In a bid to prevent the free flow of information in and out of the country and to prevent free expression, security agents in July searched, without warrant, the offices and homes of private businessmen, looking for fax and telex machines, which they confiscated. New strict licensing measures that require Security's prior approval for the installation of faxes and the purchase of photocopiers were put into effect. A security censorship office remained in charge of inspecting incoming regional and international newspapers, magazines, and books. Any independent publications carrying reporting deemed critical of the government were confiscated. The same censorship office also inspected incoming and outgoing mail.

The Right to Monitor

Following the 1989 coup, the government banned the Sudan Bar Association and the Sudan Human Rights Organization (SHRO). Both had a record of independent human rights monitoring and involvement in public education, legal representation and advocacy. In their place, government supporters established the General Union of Sudanese Lawyers and an official organization also called SHRO. These two organizations continued to demonstrate unconditional support of the government human rights record. The original SHRO still functioned out of Cairo and London as an organization in exile, informing the public and the international community about developments in the Sudan.

The government issued entry visas to Human Rights Watch/Africa, the Lawyers Committee for Human Rights, the International Commission of Jurists, and a delegation of the European Parliament to conduct human rights missions to Sudan during 1995. The government, however, continued to deny the U.N. Human Rights Commission's special rapporteur on Sudan, Dr. Gaspar Biro, entry to the country, accusing him of being an "enemy of Islam" because of critical reports. It addressed the same accusation to Amnesty International following the start of its 1995 campaign about Sudan's human rights record.

The Role of
the International Community

Sudan continued to be marginalized internationally, and its human rights record was often criticized in 1995. On March 8, 1995, for example, the United Nations Human Rights Commission condemned human rights violations in Sudan in a resolution expressing "deep concern at continued serious human rights violations." Nevertheless, bilateral and multilateral partners in the relief operations in Sudan, including the U.N. agencies, failed to challenge the government's virtual blockade of the people of the Nuba Mountains and its exclusion of U.N. relief agencies and international nongovernmental organizations from delivering relief supplies to war-affected populations.

The European Union

The European Parliament condemned the human rights record of the government of Sudan on July 13, and called on member states of the European Union to exert pressure on the U.N. for sanctions, particularly the imposition of an arms embargo. The aim of such sanctions would be to "bring pressure to bear on the Sudanese government to stop the massacre of its southern population and respect human rights throughout the entire country." In mid-September, the European Union presidency welcomed the releases of political prisoners and detainees in Sudan as an important step towards respect for human rights and democracy in Sudan.

U.S. Policy

The U.S. government condemned the human rights records of both the Sudan government and the southern rebel factions in the State Department's *Country Reports on Human Rights Practices for 1994*. Because of a 1993 U.S. State Department decision that placed Sudan on the list of countries it said supported "international terrorism," the Sudan continued to be ineligible for all U.S. assistance, except humanitarian aid.

In a welcome move, the U.S. rejected the nomination of al-Fatih Erwa as ambassador of Sudan to Washington. It was widely assumed that a principal reason for this rejection was his presence as a senior official in Juba in 1992 after an aborted SPLA attack on the town, when the government summarily executed or made "disappear" hundreds of alleged rebel supporters, including four employees of U.S. Agency for International Development. Although the government promised an investigation of these events, three years have passed with no report.

In March, the U.S. Embassy in Khartoum ruled out any recognition of the local elections of state councils on the grounds that they were not free. In mid-August, the Embassy condemned the SPLA for the massacre of some 200 civilians and the displacement of thousands of other people in Ganyliel, Upper Nile. It called upon the rebel group to investigate the massacre and take appropriate measures. Following the government releases of political detainees and prisoners in September, the U.S. Embassy in Khartoum described the gesture as "encouraging."

The Work of
Human Rights Watch/Africa

Human Rights Watch/Africa continued to closely monitor the situation on all sides of the conflict and maintain regular advocacy activities. A Human Rights Watch/Africa fact-finding mission visited Sudan for six weeks in May and June at the invitation of the government. This was the first-ever Human Rights Watch mission to Khartoum. Before the mission commenced Human Rights Watch asked for assurances that it would be permitted to set up and attend meetings with private individuals without notice to the government. The delegates interviewed many individuals in private, with no visible interference in Khartoum. In Juba, however, the insistence of security agents to be present at all times, in a clearly intimidating manner, made private meetings impossible.

One of the outcomes of this visit was the publication of a report with the organization's Children's Rights Project in September 1995, *Children of Sudan: Slaves, Street Children, and Child Soldiers,* detailing the human rights violations to which children and their families were subjected by all parties.

Human Rights Watch also responded to the main human rights developments in the country. When Khartoum authorities released political detainees in September, Human Rights Watch/Africa inquired about the fate of those detained or imprisoned on political grounds whose names failed to appear among those released. Human Rights Watch/Africa called on President Al Bashir to halt the use of the NIF security apparatus to suppress student demonstrations that occurred in September 1995 and to stop mobilizing NIF popular organizations to confront the demonstrators. Human Rights Watch urged the government to either charge the hundreds of student and other detainees with a crime in a regular criminal court, or free them immediately and to prosecute, with full due process, all those government and other agents responsible for injuries or deaths. In October, Human Rights Watch/Africa addressed letters to the SPLA concerning the attack on Ganyliel in Upper Nile in July 1995, and about the disappearance of Dr. Karlo Madut in Uganda in 1994, both being crimes in which the SPLA was implicated.

ZAIRE

Human Rights Developments

November 1995 marked thirty years of President Mobutu Sese Seko's reign in Zaire, and more than five years since he announced the country's so-called transition to democracy. Yet no meaningful transition is on the horizon, and Mobutu continues to control the military and therefore dominates the economy and the justice system. Zaire was plagued by massive corruption and widespread human rights abuses, all of which took place in an atmosphere of utter impunity. Mobutu's government also sought benefits from the Rwandan crisis which, while burdening Zaire with 1.2 million refugees, also gave Mobutu opportunities to bring about his international rehabilitation and to protect the former Rwandan government and military.

The elections scheduled for July 9, 1995 were put off for another two years, thus extending the announced transition to democracy to seven years. In June, the High Council of the Republic-Transitional Parliament (HCR-PT) voted to extend the transition, during which presidential and parliamentary elections are supposed to be held.

The main organized political actors in Zaire are the Political Forces of the Conclave (FPC), comprising the Popular Revolutionary Movement (MPR) and other Mobutu supporters, and the Union for Democracy and Social Progress (UDPS), headed by Etienne Tshisekedi, who also heads the coalition of parties known as the Radical Opposition. Although these two forces have been struggling for power since 1990, in 1995 allies of Mobutu opposed to Prime Minister Leon Kengo wa Dondo combined with elements of the opposition to block Kengo and attempted to oust the president of the HCR-

PT, Archbishop Laurent Monsengwo.

The opposition also sought the ouster of Prime Minister Kengo, whose election was deemed by many to be illegal. Tshisekedi was never lawfully removed as prime minister in 1993, and the subsequent election of Kengo took place under disputed circumstances. In 1994, a compromise was negotiated by Mgr. Monsengwo ensuring that the prime minister would be drawn from the opposition, although the deal created an unwieldy parliament dominated by Mobutu supporters.

The ongoing political crisis also accelerated the economic disaster. With four digit inflation, a fast disappearing transportation and communications infrastructure, and virtually no state provision of educational or health care facilities, Zairians faced a life of terror and misery. In a pastoral letter dated February 21, 1995, Zaire's Roman Catholic bishops denounced "the harmful character of the power that is progressively driving the country to its ruin and the state to its disintegration." The bishops also denounced the armed forces and security services, which terrorized the population.

The massive influx of Rwandan refugees in July 1994 caused rising tensions in Eastern Zaire. According to the United Nations High Commissioner for Refugees (UNHCR), an estimated 1.2 million Rwandans were in Zaire, more than half of whom were in the Goma area. The U.N. effort in Eastern Zaire did not benefit the local populations; rather, they suffered from the devastation of the environment and the increased insecurity in the region.

Throughout the Rwandan crisis, the government of Zaire has supported the former Rwandan authorities and facilitated the training and arming of its troops and militia in the refugee camps (see Rwanda section and the Arms Project section). Former Rwandan government officials, the former Rwandan Armed Forces (ex-FAR) and Hutu militias led by them continue to enjoy impunity from arrest and prosecution for their involvement in last year's genocide. The government of Zaire has permitted its territory and facilities to be used as a conduit for weapons supplies to the ex-FAR, and cargo companies based in Zaire have acted under contracts with Zairian officials to transport these weapons.

In February, the UNHCR deployed Zairian troops to keep order in the refugee camps, known as the Zairian Camp Security Contingent (ZCSC). The UNHCR will spend some US$13 million to pay, clothe, and equip the Zairian troops. The decision to deploy the Zairian troops, despite their well-established reputation for brutalizing their own population, came after other U.N. member states refused to send their troops to Zaire. The ZCSC has a mandate to provide security in the camps, to restrain anyone intimidating the refugees from going home, and to escort repatriation convoys to the Rwandan border.

One cause of the growing problems in North Kivu involves ethnic tensions in that region that have exploded into violence before; in 1993, some 6,000 people were killed and some 250,000 displaced in clashes that pitted the Nande and Hunde (considered to be indigenous to the region) against the Banyarwanda (Rwandan and Burundian immigrants, some of whom have been in North Kivu for generations). While the 1993 conflict focused on issues of nationality and land, the influx of Rwandan refugees has made the situation much more volatile, as has the influx of arms into the region. In 1995, these tensions were close to the surface, forcing many of the Tutsis who had lived in Zaire for many years to leave for Rwanda. In late May and June, the area of Walikale and Masisi in North Kivu witnessed new violence. According to some estimates, some forty people were killed in fighting involving youth bands of Hunde and Hutu. The Zairian military exacerbated the tensions, and pillaged on both sides.

The situation of the refugees in eastern Zaire exploded in August, when the government of Zaire began forcibly repatriating the refugees, apparently in response to the lifting of the U.N. arms embargo against Rwanda. Zairian troops engaged in a range of human rights abuses against the refugees, including beatings, burning of tents, looting, and the expulsion of refugees being treated at hospitals and health centers to Rwanda.

After four days, the government finally suspended the repatriations, but only after expelling more than 15,000 refugees and forcing some 173,000 other into the hills. The government of Zaire warned that all the refugees must leave Zaire by the end of 1995. At this writing, the fate of the refugees in Zaire is very uncertain.

In Shaba province, there have been an increasing number of incidents between the military and the civilian population since 1994. Many of these incidents involve soldiers, including troops of the Special Presidential Division (DSP), who have not been paid for many months and are consequently abusing the civilians. In 1995, the Shaba branch of the Zairian security service, the National Intelligence and Protection Service (SNIP), was responsible for a range of human rights abuses, including detention and torture of political activists, threats against human rights activists, and the expulsion of a foreign human rights researcher (a U.S. citizen).

On July 29, a demonstration was organized by PALU, the Lumumbist Unified Party, in Kinshasa to protest the Mobutu government. Security forces broke up the demonstration, killing at least nine protesters. Antoine Gizenga, the PALU leader, was arrested and charged with organizing an unauthorized demonstration and with possessing an M-16 rifle, which authorities claimed they found when they searched his home. He was released on bail on August 3. Mobutu promised to arrest and prosecute those responsible, although at this writing there is no sign of any progress.

A considerable array of human rights, pro-democracy, development, and church groups have emerged in Zaire in recent years. These groups are responsible for much of the education, health care, training and human rights sensitization that is taking place in Zaire. The Kengo government threatened the operations of NGOs in January 1995, when the Council of Ministers resuscitated a decree from 1965 requiring NGOs to be authorized by the government. Since many of these groups have tried in vain to gain legal status, this attempt to undermine their work was seen as a new effort to harass and threaten them.

The Right to Monitor

The human rights community in Zaire continued to be a vibrant force during 1995. The principal human rights groups in Kinshasa include the Zairian Association for the Defense of Human Rights (AZADHO), the Zairian Human Rights League (LIZADHO), and the Voice of the Voiceless for Human Rights (VSV). Human rights groups have also emerged in various regions, including: in South Kivu—Heirs of Justice and the Justice and Peace Commission of South Kivu; in North Kivu—Grace, the Justice and Peace Commission of North Kivu, and Muungano; in Upper Zaire—Justice and Liberation, Friends of Nelson Mandela, Lotus, and Haki Za Binadamu; in Shaba—the Center for Human Rights and Humanitarian Law and the Justice and Peace Commission.

As in the past, human rights activists have suffered threats, arrest, and harassment from the security services.

The Role of
the International Community

Since early 1992 the U.S., France, and Belgium have periodically collaborated to support the transition process begun by the National Conference. These three countries—known as the troika—have repeatedly called on the opposition and the Mobutu government to proceed with the transition. The E.U. suspended all but humanitarian aid to Zaire in 1992; the U.S. suspended aid in 1991. However, the troika never froze Mobutu's assets or pursued his financial sources abroad, despite promises to do so.

In April, the troika pressured Zaire to end its political impasse and move forward with democratization. According to a statement by State Department spokesman Nicholas Burns, the three governments were "deeply disturbed" by the political situation in Zaire and had approached the Zairian leaders to "advance the transition, to cease tactics of obstruction, and to work together in good faith to bring democracy to Zaire." The troika was attempting to pressure the Zairian government to announce when elections would take place.

Due to visa restrictions imposed by the troika, Mobutu's travel has been limited in recent years. The visa restrictions were applied almost universally until 1995, when Mobutu made a number of visits to Portugal and France (he attended last year's francophone summit in Biarritz, France, and has been able to use his transit visa to visit his luxury villa in the south of France). Official policy on visa restrictions has not changed, however.

The United Nations

In March, the U.N. Commission on Human Rights passed a resolution on the human rights situation in Zaire. While "recognizing that some progress has been achieved" by the Zairian government with respect to human rights, the resolution went on to express serious concern about arbitrary arrests and detention, summary executions, torture and inhuman treatment in detention centers, serious shortcomings in the justice system, and the impunity of human rights violators. The resolution also extended the mandate of the special rapporteur on human rights in Zaire for one year, and "invited" the high commissioner for human rights to consider establishing an office of the Human Rights Center in Kinshasa, a recommendation made in the special rapporteur's report.

In July, U.N. Secretary-General Boutros Boutros-Ghali met with Mobutu at his palace in Gbadolite, and invited Mobutu to New York for the 50th anniversary of the U.N. in October. There is no indication that Boutros-Ghali raised human rights concerns in his meeting with Mobutu.

U.S. Policy

While the Clinton administration has generally distanced itself from Mobutu, some U.S. officials, in keeping with the United States'

decades of close covert and overt association with him, still see Mobutu as an indispensable actor in Central Africa. This attitude was fueled by the U.S.'s general disdain for the Radical Opposition, and its support for Kengo's initiatives. Accordingly, U.S. policy revolved around support for Kengo's government and a growing willingness to re-engage Mobutu diplomatically.

In June, the State Department announced that the U.S. would be sending a new ambassador to Zaire, as a sign of support for Prime Minister Kengo's efforts. The ambassador designate is Daniel Simpson, a career diplomat with experience in Africa. The last ambassador was Melissa Wells, who was not replaced in May 1993 to protest President Mobutu's continued rule. State Department spokesman Nicholas Burns added that "We continue to view President Mobutu as the chief obstacle to democracy in Zaire." The Clinton Administration hopes that the presence of a new U.S. ambassador will help promote reform.

Mobutu and his family have been banned from receiving U.S. visas since 1993, an indication of U.S. disapproval of Mobutu's rule. U.S. officials have maintained that they will not deal directly with Mobutu or grant him a U.S. visa unless he demonstrates progress toward democratization, including announcing an election timetable and allowing international observers to monitor the process. In July, Mobutu supporters in the U.S. launched an effort to obtain a visa for him for his trip to the U.N. General Assembly in October. Responding to congressional concern about the possibility that Mobutu would get a visa, Assistant Secretary of State Wendy Sherman wrote in June: "The visa sanction has been, and remains, one of most effective measures to influence Mobutu and his entourage, and we have seen no change on the part of the Zairian president which would warrant a reversal of this policy."

The Work of
Human Rights Watch/Africa

Human Rights Watch/Africa continued to

focus attention on the widespread human rights abuses by the Zairian government. To this end, Human Rights Watch/Africa briefed government officials and journalists about human rights in Zaire, and met with visiting Zairian human rights activists. After the publication in May of *Rearming with Impunity: International Support for the Perpetrators of the Rwandan Genocide* by the Human Rights Watch Arms Project, Human Rights Watch/Africa was engaged in advocacy in the U.S. and Europe to press for an end to assistance to the former Rwandan government and military in Zaire as well as the investigation and prosecution of all those in Zaire who directed the genocide in Rwanda. In August, when the Zairian military forcibly expelled thousands of Rwandan refugees, Human Rights Watch/Africa issued a press release denouncing the expulsions as a violation of international law.

HUMAN RIGHTS WATCH

AMERICAS

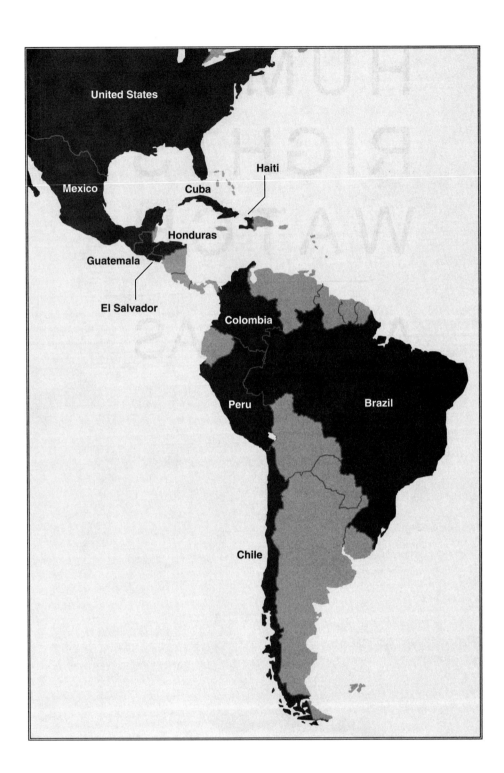

HUMAN RIGHTS WATCH/AMERICAS OVERVIEW

Human Rights Developments

Over the last fifteen years, many Latin American and Caribbean countries have undergone the important transformation from military dictatorship to civilian government. Unfortunately, respect for human rights has not kept pace with progress in democratization. More than a decade of civilian rule has allowed for a blossoming of civil society, yet the limits of political space were still defined by torture, disappearances, and extrajudicial executions in 1995. In societies with wide income disparities, economically vulnerable sectors—children, indigenous people, women, peasants, workers, and the homeless—were disproportionally affected by violent human rights abuse.

The states of the hemisphere must adopt effective measures to prevent future human rights violations and to punish abuses by agents of the state and those operating with official acquiescence. Just as it is unacceptable for a state to adopt torture or disappearance as official policy, a government may not condone such violations or decline to protect those subject to its jurisdiction. Nearly every state in the region has assumed the affirmative obligation under international law to secure the unconditional exercise of the rights enshrined in that law. They have thus assumed the responsibility to bring domestic legislation into accord with international human rights standards and develop independent and impartial judiciaries capable of prosecuting and punishing the perpetrators of human rights violations.

The spread of institutional democracy in the region has given national legislatures unparalleled opportunities to enact human rights reforms and to provide oversight of state security agencies, a challenge that has yet to be met. In 1995, most civilian governments in the region had yet to reform penal codes to criminalize explicitly human rights violations such as torture, disappearances, and extrajudicial executions; guarantee due process; restrict the jurisdiction of military courts; and repeal *desacato* (contempt) laws and other legislative artifacts of authoritarian regimes that penalize the free expression of ideas. Further, national legislatures did not exercise sufficient diligence in bringing human rights considerations to bear on the foreign policy of their governments.

Frequently, judiciaries in the hemisphere abdicated their central role in the defense of rights. Judicial authorities took an excessively formalistic view of their role, forgetting that procedural requirements are a means of reaching justice and not justice in themselves. Their failure to take even minimal steps to protect people whose rights were violated guaranteed impunity for the perpetrators of abuses. Peru's "faceless courts" and secret military tribunals, for example, robbed civilians accused of terrorism or treason of their most basic due process guarantees. Colombia's secret "public order" courts, used to prosecute individuals charged with rebellion and drug trafficking, raised similar due process concerns. In Chile, the judiciary, especially the Supreme Court, remained ineffectual, with the notable exception of the prosecution of the security police officers responsible for the 1976 slaying of Orlando Letelier and Ronni Moffitt in Washington, D.C. Fear of the army permeated the Guatemalan judicial system, rendering it incapable of resolving disappearances and extrajudicial executions. Disorganization and a lack of resources plagued the Haitian judiciary, which had not prosecuted any member of the armed forces by November 1995.

Military justice systems, which failed in most cases to meet international standards of impartiality and independence, continued to foster a climate of impunity for perpetrators of human rights violations. In Peru, military courts achieved a near-perfect conviction rate against civilians (97 percent in 1994), while compiling an equally impressive acquittal rate when judging soldiers accused of human rights violations.

A Human Rights Watch/Americas review of internal Mexican army documents on the 1994 Ocosingo clinic massacre in Chiapas found military prosecutors more interested in accusing human rights groups of dishonesty than in investigating and prosecuting those responsible. In Brazil, military courts made little more than perfunctory inquiries into gross abuses by the military and police, despite the existence of ample evidence. National legislatures, meanwhile, neglected to take the necessary steps to ensure that human rights violations committed by members of the armed forces were judged in civilian courts.

Not all the news emanating from judges' chambers during the year was bad. Courageous prosecutors and judges did pursue human rights cases in some countries, despite considerable pressure to abandon their investigations. Peruvian prosecutor Ana Cecilia Magallanes reopened the investigation into the 1991 massacre in the Barrios Altos district of Lima, and Judge Antonia Saquicuray Sánchez found Peru's sweeping amnesty law inapplicable to the case. Sonia Marlina Dubón de Flores, the Honduran special prosecutor for human rights, initiated the hemisphere's first investigation of active-duty military officers for human rights violations, and Judge Roy Medina issued arrest warrants in October for three of the ten Honduran military officers under investigation. Special prosecutor Abraham Méndez García vigorously investigated the 1993 killing of Jorge Carpio Nicolle in Guatemala. Until he resigned from the case of Efraín Bámaca Velásquez under threat in July, Guatemalan special prosecutor Julio Arango Escobar showed integrity and initiative in pursuing the case. Stella Kuhlman, a Brazilian prosecutor in charge of the case of 111 detainees who were killed in Carandiru prison in 1992, diligently investigated the prison case and other instances of police abuse and corruption despite threats to her life; in 1995, she and seven other prosecutors in São Paulo's military justice system challenged military jurisdiction in cases of crimes against civilians. Colombia's Constitutional Court issued a number of decisions in 1995 demonstrating both a commitment to the defense of human rights and a resistance to political control; in one of these, it found unconstitutional President Ernesto Samper's August 1995 declaration of a "state of internal commotion."

In most instances where jurists worked to promote justice in human rights cases, however, they did so against the prevailing sentiment of elected civilian officials. This was clearest in Peru, where President Alberto Fujimori signed the most sweeping amnesty law in the region. He granted amnesty to all military, police, and civilians who had committed serious crimes in the course of the counterinsurgency effort between 1980 and 1995. In Colombia, where President Ernesto Samper began the year by admitting state responsibility for a spree of extrajudicial killings and disappearances in Trujillo in 1990, the president went on to support continued military jurisdiction over human rights cases, despite the impunity that military courts have fostered.

President Cardoso of Brazil introduced legislation to compensate the victims of disappearances during the military regime. This otherwise positive step proved cosmetic but the new law failed to provide any mechanism for determining the circumstances of the disappearances, identifying those responsible, or rendering justice.

In Argentina, the army chief of staff, Gen. Martín Balza, issued an historic apology to the nation for the crimes of the "dirty war" of the 1970s; yet the administration of President Carlos Menem failed to compel officers to disclose what they knew about the fate of thousands of disappearances to the families and to Argentine society.

In addition to the failure of elected civilian leaders to consolidate human rights protections in the new era of democracy, these leaders also often failed to prevent ongoing human rights violations. Extrajudicial executions, disappearances, and torture persisted in the region. In Guatemala, soldiers killed eleven repatriated refugees, a bitter reminder that the advancing peace process had not fundamentally changed the human rights situation there. In Brazil, state police officials in Rio de Janeiro, São Paulo, and Rio Grande do Norte and Mato Grosso do Sul participated in extermination squads to dispose of *marginais* ("lowlives")—street youth, the homeless, and others suspected of general lawlessness but often no particular crime. The prevalence of these grave violations in Colombia led the U.N. special rapporteurs for extrajudicial executions and torture to issue a joint report characterizing the situation as "alarming."

Disappearances were documented in such formally democratic countries as Brazil, Colombia, Guatemala, and Peru. Even in Argentina, provincial police were tied to several cases of disappearance, revealing that this tactic of repression had not been eradicated despite earlier, temporarily successful attempts to end it.

Torture during 1995 was also documented by local and international human rights groups and multilateral organizations in countries such as Brazil, Colombia, Guatemala, and Peru. The methods used differed little from those employed by military dictatorships during the 1970s and 1980s. Although Cuba ratified the U.N. Convention Against Torture and Other Cruel, Inhuman, or Degrading Treatment or Punishment in 1995, both political and common-crime prisoners reported suffering denial of medical attention, beatings, violent and arbitrary searches, and other degrading treatment for minor infractions or nonviolent protests such as hunger strikes. In Mexico, police employed severe physical and psychological torture to obtain confessions, which judges—to their shame—accepted as evidence.

The positive model for the region, as a response to torture, was the Argentine Supreme Court ruling in 1981 that confessions obtained by torture were inadmissible, even with corroborating evidence. The Alfonsín government codified this judicially adopted ruling at the federal level in 1984, and the prohibition was retained in the 1992 revision of the criminal procedure code. Even Argentina did not achieve this standard, however, in 1995. Unfortunately, some appellate courts continued to admit as presumptive evidence confessions as the result of torture. Regionwide, the failure of judges to reject confessions obtained through torture and of legislatures to prohibit their use provided an incentive for state agents to continue to torture.

In Mexico, Brazil, and to a lesser extent in Argentina, which have federal systems of government, federal authorities sought to avoid responsibility for abuses committed by security forces of state governments. This was the case, for example, in Mexico's state of Guerrero, where state police gunned down seventeen peasants in June but federal officials maintained they could not intervene to ensure justice was done. The American Convention on Human Rights holds national governments responsible for abuses committed by state government officials.

Freedom of expression, too, remained restricted in several countries. Cuba continued systematically to violate this right, frequently charging human rights activists and political dissidents with "enemy propaganda," "clandestine printing," "contempt of authority," "anti-social behavior," or the violation of "socialist morality." In Chile, several individuals were arrested and punished for remarks deemed offensive to the honor of military and civilian authorities or government institutions.

A study of desacato laws by the Inter-American Commission on Human Rights published in February noted that thirteen states in the region had some form of legislation criminalizing expression that offends, insults, or threatens a public official, in violation of the American Convention on Human Rights.

Guerrilla groups in several countries of the region violated international humanitarian law, killing civilians or destroying their homes or other property. All sides in an internal armed conflict, whether government or guerrilla, are bound by the provisions of common article 3 of the Geneva Conventions, the principal international treaty delineating the laws of war.

The Shining Path (Sendero Luminoso) of Peru continued consistently to violate international humanitarian law, targeting local authorities, members of peasant patrols, and its political opponents for assassination, threats, or humiliating and degrading treatment. Some killings followed "popular trials" in which the guerrillas mimicked a judicial process but provided no semblance of independence or impartiality. In May, the group slaughtered an entire community for its failure to pay a "war tax."

In Colombia, the Revolutionary Armed Forces of Colombia (Fuerzas Armadas Revolucionarias de Colombia, FARC) were implicated in numerous cases of hostage-taking and assassination, including a massacre in September in which twenty-three people were killed near Urabá. In June, members of the FARC apparently executed two abducted American missionaries. Other Colombian guerrilla groups, notably the Camilist Union-National Army of Liberation (Unión Camilista-Ejército de Liberación Nacional, UC-ELN), carried out executions and took hostages during the year. In Guatemala, guerrillas failed to exercise care to minimize danger to civilians during attacks on military targets and imposed "war taxes" on civilians with the implicit threat that those who did not pay would suffer bodily harm or damage to their property. In addition, several civilians were killed by land mines laid by the Guatemalan guerrillas.

The Right to Monitor

Throughout the region, a network of human rights nongovernmental organizations continued to develop. With the exception of Cuba, where human rights monitoring continued to be illegal and monitors were subjected to criminal prosecutions, the majority of states imposed few, if any, formal obstacles to human rights monitoring. A growing number of governments established or acted to strengthen human rights ombudsmen, although it was less clear whether these governments were willing to use ombudsmen's information to prosecute hu-

man rights violations. In Honduras, the National Commission on Human Rights was granted constitutional status, formalizing its permanent mandate to investigate and report on abuses in the country. In Peru, the congress created a *defensor del pueblo* (ombudsman) but severely limited his power to enter military installations or compel officials to cooperate with investigations. The position had not been filled as of this writing.

As in previous years, independent monitors ran the serious risk of injury or death, especially in Colombia and Guatemala. At least three human rights activists—Ernesto Fernández Fester, Javier Barriga Vergel, and Humberto Peña Prieto—were killed in Colombia in 1995. In June, Guatemalan rights monitor Manuel Saquic Vásquez disappeared. His decapitated corpse was found the following month with thirty-three stab wounds. Human rights monitors in other countries, such Brazil, Honduras, Mexico, and Peru faced threats and other forms of harassment for doing their work.

The Role of
the International Community

The United Nations

The United Nations played a fundamental role in human rights monitoring and promotion in Haiti and Guatemala. Six thousand peacekeepers of the U.N. Mission in Haiti (UNMIH) and over 800 U.N. Civilian Police (CivPol) monitors contributed to the marked improvement in human rights conditions during the first year since President Aristide's reinstatement. The U.N. Human Rights Verification Mission in Guatemala (MINUGUA), established in November 1994, produced three reports documenting cases of torture, extrajudicial execution, and disappearance by security forces as well as government links to organized crime and "social cleansing" operations. The U.N. presence throughout the year provided some protection for the human rights community in Guatemala and may have had some effect in reducing human rights abuses. Nevertheless, the security forces and their agents continued to commit gross abuses with impunity.

The U.N. High Commissioner for Human Rights announced plans to study the possibility of opening a permanent office in Colombia. The initiative stood a chance of helping improve the human rights situation if conducted in coordination with, not instead of, other U.N. human rights projects in Colombia, including the special rapporteurs on extrajudicial executions and torture and the Working Group on Enforced or Involuntary Disappearances. Human Rights Watch/Americas echoed the concern of Colombian human rights groups that a U.N. High Commissioner office should not preclude other U.N. initiatives, such as the appointment of a country rapporteur for Colombia.

The Inter-American System

Latin America and the Caribbean have one of the world's most progressive systems for the international protection of human rights. The two autonomous human rights institutions of the Organization of American States (OAS)—the Inter-American Court of Human Rights, a tribunal that applies and interprets the American Convention on Human Rights, and the Inter-American Commission on Human Rights, a quasi-judicial investigatory and advisory body—have played a vital role in guaranteeing fundamental human rights to those living in the hemisphere.

The court fills the valuable role of the tribunal of last resort for the region in cases of human rights violations. As it observed in the now-famous case of *Velásquez Rodriguez*, the sentences pronounced by the court serve as a form of reparation by establishing the facts, identifying with precision the nature of the violations committed, and establishing the state's responsibility to take concrete steps to prevent, investigate, punish, and disclose violations, and restore an individual's rights or provide reparations to victims or their relatives. In 1995, the court found Peru responsible for violations of the right to life in the deadly suppression of the 1986 prison riot in El Frontón. However, when Venezuela accepted full responsibility for the massacre in El Amparo, the court merely noted this admission without issuing a declaratory judgment of Venezuela's violation of the convention or determining the resulting legal consequences. As representatives of the victims, Human Rights Watch/Americas urged the court to cure this deficiency in the context of determining the nature and scope of reparations.

The work of the commission was marred in 1995 by the deficient performance of its secretariat. Over the course of the year, management anomalies made it nearly impossible to discern what, if any, criteria were used to guide the secretariat's proceedings. The secretariat's disinclination to grant requests for precautionary measures—instrumental in saving the lives of countless victims of disappearances and threats throughout the hemisphere—reversed its decades-long tradition of responsiveness in such cases and, exemplified a growing inconsistency in its work. Other procedural irregularities included unwarranted delays in the release of reports; arbitrary and illegal refusal to admit new complaints; impeding the resolution of cases before the commission; and affording certain government representatives access to documents and petitions even before they came under the consideration of the commissioners. Under these circumstances, some government representatives were able to use personal or political influence with the secretariat, thus undermining the independence of the commission and the credibility of the OAS as a protecter of human rights.

Human Rights Watch/Americas was extremely concerned about these developments at the commission; the weight and influence of the commission's resolutions and recommendations depend not only on their content but also on the moral authority of the institution itself.

As a consequence of the irregularities at the secretariat, the commissioners informed the secretary-general of the OAS in September that they lacked confidence in the commission's executive secretary. Nevertheless, some governments, particularly Venezuela and Chile, sought to maintain the executive secretary in her position. As of this writing, the secretary-general had not acted to solve a situation that threatened the autonomy and integrity of the commission.

U.S. Policy

The Clinton administration remained sensitive to human rights concerns in the hemisphere but failed to make human rights a centerpiece of its policy towards the region. In relations with Mexico, the administration muted human rights concerns so as not to jeopardize economic policy. Even while providing a $20-billion economic support package to Mexico, the administration failed to raise publicly human rights concerns. Although the U.S. ambassador in Mexico assured us he privately raised human rights concerns at the highest levels of government in Mexico, the issuance of only one cautious public statement focusing on human rights, lent legitimacy to abuses in Mexico.

In a similar vein, the administration failed to seize the opportunity presented by the Summit of the Americas in December 1994 to advance human rights protection in the hemisphere. Human rights concerns were included in the final plan of action approved at the summit, but no specific follow-up meetings or reporting provisions were included to ensure that human rights would be actually addressed over the coming years. Other subjects in the plan of action, such as trade, included detailed follow-up mechanisms.

In Bolivia, human rights principles were sacrificed to the pursuit of counternarcotics programs. Bolivia's rural counternarcotics forces—created, funded, and trained by the U.S.—rode roughshod over residents in coca-growing areas, beating them, stealing their money and goods, and arbitrarily searching their homes at all hours. The U.S. Drug Enforcement Administration (DEA) was intimately involved in counternarcotics operations in Bolivia; yet the results of the agency's internal investigations into alleged complicity or acquiescence in abusive interrogations were not made public.

In the wake of its successful restoration of the democratically elected government of Haiti, the Clinton administration rushed to return Haitians who had found "safe haven" at the U.S. naval base in Guantánamo Bay, Cuba, without first determining if they qualified as refugees under international law. The January 1995 forced repatriation of more than 3,700 Haitians from Guantánamo violated the U.S.'s obligation under the 1967 Protocol Relating to the Status of Refugees not to return (*refouler*) a refugee to a territory where his or her life or freedom would be threatened on account of persecution. The Department of Defense also restricted independent monitoring of the Guantánamo facilities, making it difficult to investigate reports of mistreatment and to independently verify the claims of those detained there. In the first months of 1995, unaccompanied Haitian minors reported some abuses by U.S. military personnel, including shackling and isolation. The U.S. military did not release the results of its investigation into these complaints or its regulations governing discipline.

On May 2, the Clinton administration announced a new policy to interdict and repatriate Cuban asylum seekers based on an agreement struck with the government of President Fidel Castro. Under the agreement, most of the 20,000 Cubans remaining in Guantánamo camps would receive humanitarian parole into the U.S.; those found excludable because of past criminal activity or other statutory reasons would be repatriated. After returning several groups of Cubans without adequate refugee screening, the U.S. improved its procedures to adhere to international requirements.

U.S. covert links to human rights violators in the hemisphere became front page news in 1995 with the revelation that a Guatemalan military officer paid by the Central Intelligence Agency (CIA) had been involved in two extrajudicial executions, including the 1990 murder of American citizen Michael DeVine. The CIA's links to human rights violations in Guatemala followed a similar pattern previously disclosed in El Salvador, Haiti, Honduras, and Peru. The Clinton administration announced several executive branch inquiries to deal with the crisis, disciplined several CIA officials, expanded a review of its foreign agents, and began writing new rules governing their recruitment. No review appeared to be underway, however, of the so-called liaison programs that the CIA routinely establishes with foreign intelligence services without informing Congress or the public. As the details of the CIA relationship with Guatemala became public in March and April, it was revealed that the agency had spent millions of dollars in such a program with Guatemala's notoriously abusive military intelligence service after overt military aid had been suspended in the wake of Michael DeVine's murder.

The initial steps taken to curb the CIA were positive but insufficient. Human Rights Watch called for the enactment of legislation—rather than classified internal regulations—that would prevent the agency from keeping murderers and torturers on its payroll and would prohibit liaison relationships with units that consistently violate human rights.

The Work of
Human Rights Watch/Americas

Our work in 1995 focused on seven countries—Brazil, Colombia, Cuba, Guatemala, Haiti, Mexico, and Peru—in which the nature and extent of the violations and the response of the state raised urgent human rights concerns. We conducted missions, wrote and released publications, and advocated for change in these countries' human rights practices as well as highlighting discrete issues in other countries, such as the human rights violations associated with the drug war in Bolivia and the need for accountability for past CIA activities in Honduras. We called attention to the need of the Chilean government to enforce the judgment of its highest court against the head of the intelligence agency during the dictatorship, and we emphasized the obligation of the Chilean state to investigate, prosecute, and punish those responsible for human rights abuses. In an *amicus* brief prepared jointly

with the Center for Justice and International Law (CEJIL), we urged the Argentine Supreme Court to guarantee the right of the victims of human rights violations and their families to know the truth about the role of the state in the abuses—an indispensable step to prevent future abuses and provide compensation for the victims of past cruelty.

Among our efforts to press for accountability for past human rights violations, we cosponsored an international conference on amnesties in Guatemala with the Myrna Mack Foundation, which concluded that grave human rights violations and breaches of the laws of war should never be amnestied, and we worked with the national commissioner for human rights of Honduras, to press the Clinton administration to declassify documents relating to disappearances carried out by a U.S.-funded death squad in the 1980s. In Mexico, we released new information on a 1994 massacre of civilians in Chiapas which helped advance domestic efforts to investigate the crime. Our work on Peru and Bolivia drew attention to the lack of due process guarantees for out-of-favor groups or individuals such as those accused of drug offenses or support for terrorists. We also continued our traditional monitoring of laws of war violations by all sides to the region's armed conflicts, including violations of international humanitarian law by guerrillas in Colombia and Peru.

In partnership with CEJIL and several national human rights organizations, we are involved in nearly one hundred cases at the Inter-American Commission on Human Rights, which has referred ten of these to the Inter-American Court of Human Rights.

BRAZIL

Human Rights Developments
The assumption of power in 1995 by the largest contingent of newly elected federal and state officials in Brazilian history, and in particular, of President Fernando Henrique Cardoso, widely viewed as a long-term de-

fender of the rights of the excluded, brought high hopes for the improvement of human rights in Brazil. Indeed, in his first year as president, Cardoso took several important steps toward ameliorating many of Brazil's chronic problems. Nonetheless, government agents and private parties continued to violate fundamental rights in Brazil in 1995.

The magnitude of human rights violations that face Brazil were exemplified by two high-profile incidents. On March 4, before dozens of onlookers outside the Rio Sul shopping center in Rio de Janeiro's prosperous southern zone, Military Police Corp. Flávio Ferreira Carneiro dragged robbery suspect Cristiano Moura Mesquita de Melo behind a parked van and summarily executed him with·three shots at point-blank range. The entire incident was filmed by a camera crew from the TV Globo network and broadcast throughout Brazil and the world. The banality of this event for Brazilians was underscored by flash polls taken in subsequent weeks showing that a majority of Rio residents supported the actions of Corporal Ferreira Carneira.

Second, in the pre-dawn hours of August 9, 187 military police conducted a search of the Santa Elina *fazenda* (ranch) in the northern state of Rondônia to remove 200 families of *sem terra* (landless squatters) who were occupying the land. With violence on both sides, two police and several squatters were killed in the conflict. After the police had subdued the squatters, however, they killed several more, tortured dozens, and beat more than one hundred men. The military police humiliated the squatters, forcing one man to eat the brains of a dead companion so that he would overcome "his fear of the dead." In all, the police killed nine people, including a seven-year-old girl shot in the back, and injured more than one hundred, thirty of whom were hospitalized in serious condition. Nine people remained unaccounted for.

These two incidents were not isolated events: in Rio alone police killed 191 civilians in the first seven months of 1995. Figures from the Pastoral Land Commission (Comissão Patoral da Terra, CPT) for the first eight months of 1995 showed that at least twenty-six people had been killed in land conflicts. Of these, the CPT attributed six cases to hired gunmen, four to civil police, and two to military police.

These two incidents also demonstrated the serious problems in the military justice system, the entity charged with the prosecution of violations committed by military police. Corporal Ferreira Carneiro, though eventually convicted in the aftermath of the televised shooting, had been involved in the killings of several other civilians, but none of these cases had been prosecuted by the military justice system. In the weeks after the Santa Elena ranch incident, although the ordinary courts took statements from 121 squatters and indicted seventy-four for the crime of resisting the judicial order to abandon the fazenda, only nine military police had given statements to the military court investigating police violence in the event.

Finally, the two incidents demonstrated that reforms instituted solely at the federal level are insufficient. Significant steps must be taken at the state level if human rights abuses are to be brought under control. In both instances, the prosecution of the police officers involved rested in the exclusive jurisdiction of state authorities, as do the overwhelming majority of cases of human rights abuse.

Urban police violence continued to be a severe human rights problem throughout Brazil in 1995, as exemplified by the televised execution. In several major cities, reports of extrajudicial killings and torture were commonplace. In Rio de Janeiro, an October 1994 massacre of thirteen residents of the Nova Brasília *favela* (slum) by the state civil police resulted in federal intervention in Rio de Janeiro. Dubbed "Operation Rio" by the press, the joint military and state police initiative provoked great expectations but little relief from the city's surging criminality and violence. Perhaps this was because the operations failed to target police criminality, widely viewed as inextricably linked to drug-related violence. In late November 1994, in the Borel and Chácara do Céu favelas of Rio de Janeiro, troops tortured detainees with electric current, near drowning, and severe beatings. Despite ample evidence of these and other abuses, the prosecutors failed to charge any of the troops involved.

State police forces were also responsible for serious violations during 1995. In May, Rio civil police raided the Nova Brasília favela, killing thirteen young men. After the killings, police loaded the corpses of their victims into a sanitation department pickup truck and drove them to the hospital for "first aid." This technique—a flagrant violation of Brazilian law—is a common technique among abusive police to undermine crime scene investigations. In the aftermath of the operation, favela residents reported that they had seen a number of the victims being executed after having surrendered to police. Human Rights Watch/Americas obtained copies of the coroner's reports, which established conclusively that several victims had been shot numerous times in the head and chest, consistent with a massacre but not a shootout. Nonetheless, Rio de Janeiro Gov. Marcello Alencar declared that he would not accept any criticism of the police action, and at this writing—six months after the events—the public ministry had still not indicted any of the police involved.

In São Paulo, police killings of civilians rose to shocking levels in 1995, significantly higher than those registered in 1994. During the first half of 1995, military police in the state of São Paulo killed 338 civilians, reversing what had been a downward trend over the previous three years. The discovery in April of a clandestine deposit for corpses on the outskirts of São Paulo and evidence that police used the site to dump the corpses of their victims raised the possibility that, as alarming as the official figures for civilian killings were in São Paulo in 1995, they might not accurately reflect the actual total number of homicides by the police.

Unfortunately, urban police violence in 1995 and impunity for abuses, particularly when directed against criminal suspects, were not limited to Rio de Janeiro and São Paulo. For example, on January 23, 1995, a group of police in Maceió (capital of the northeastern state of Alagoas), under the direction of Secretary of Public Security José de Azevedo Amaral, raided a housing complex purportedly to capture bank robbery suspects, killing nine and arresting only one. The lone prisoner taken, Wellington Santos, was photographed handcuffed outside the residential unit, but his body was later found at the morgue. According to newspaper reports, three other detainees disappeared from this police station without having been registered. Summarizing the operation to the press, the secretary of public security stated, "We identified the lowlives (*marginais*) and we sent them bullets."

In May, in the northeastern state of Rio Grande do Norte, the state attorney general formed a special commission to investigate allegations that Under Secretary of Public Security Maurílio Pinto had been involved directly in the oversight and operations of a death squad that included off-duty police known as the *Meninos de Ouro* (Golden Boys). Witness and victim testimony presented to the special commission established that the Meninos de Ouro had killed eight people and "disappeared" two others since 1988. In addition, among the allegations that surfaced were Pinto's direct supervision of torture sessions. In a televised interview, Pinto admitted that he instructed—and would continue to instruct—his officers to beat "lowlives." Nonetheless, he was retained in his position overseeing all police in the state of Rio Grande do Norte.

The national news program "SBT Reporter" aired a program on September 12 denouncing the suspected involvement of a special police force, the Border Operations Group (Grupo de Operações da Fronteira, GOF), in Mato Grosso do Sul, in dozens of extrajudicial killings. Speaking on the program, the GOF's commander admitted that the group had killed "marginals."

Street children and other youths continued to be killed at a frightening pace in Brazil's major cities. According to the Center for the Mobilization of Marginalized Populations (Centro de Articulação dos Povos Marginalizados, CEAP), a Rio de Janeiro human rights group focusing on issues of racial discrimination and violence against persons of color, 574 minors were killed by guns in the state of Rio in 1994; some 1,274 were victims of violent death. In the first three months of 1995, 189 minors in Rio were killed by gunfire as compared with 151 in the same period in 1994. Despite these alarming figures, police and other authorities failed to protect urban youths; in some cases, off-duty police officers and participants in death squads were responsible for the killings.

A critical factor in the persistence of these abuses was the impunity virtually guaranteed to military police who violated human rights. Impunity continued to be particularly extreme in the case of the São Paulo justice system. In 1995, high-profile cases remained stalled in the São Paulo courts, including the 1992 massacre of 111 prisoners in the Carandiru prison and the 1989 killing of eighteen detainees by beating and asphyxiation in Parque São Lucas, despite federal government pressure to address these matters. In a meeting also attended by representatives of the Center for the Study of Violence at the University of São Paulo (Núcleo de Estudos da Violência), Minister of Justice Nelson Jobim raised both cases with the president of the São Paulo military appellate court. In his September 7 speech on human rights, President Cardoso noted the message of impunity sent by the lack of progress in the Carandiru case.

In an Independence Day speech on September 7, President Cardoso recognized the pervasiveness of impunity, noting in particular the slaughter of 111 prisoners by São Paulo military police in October 1992 and the massacre of eight street children by off-duty police in then-named Candelária plaza in Rio in July 1993, among other grave violations. In the second half of 1995, the president and his cabinet created a division within the federal police to investigate human rights abuses, prepared draft legislation

to provide federal jurisdiction for certain human rights violations, and announced the creation of a national human rights plan.

In 1995, the Cardoso administration also took an important step forward by introducing legislation to compensate relatives of those forcibly "disappeared" by state agents during the military dictatorship (1964-1985). Unfortunately, the legislation, stalled in the Senate, would not provide any means of investigating these disappearances or of including those executed for political reasons (though not "disappeared") among those whose deaths were to be compensated. This continued failure to investigate disappearances and extrajudicial executions constituted ongoing violations of Brazil's duty under the American Convention on Human Rights and the International Covenant on Civil and Political Rights to ensure justice and an effective remedy to the victims of human rights abuses.

Another important development in 1995 was the creation of a human rights commission within the federal Chamber of Deputies. Presided by the chamber's president, Nilmário Miranda, the commission followed its establishment in March with outstanding work in drawing public attention to severe human rights problems in Brazil, including those whose denunciation was politically unpopular, such as police abuse committed against criminal suspects. Despite limited resources, the commission managed to become an effective voice in denouncing human rights abuses and in pressing the federal and state governments to address human rights concerns.

Of particular concern in 1995 were renewed reports of disappearance in rural Brazil. On June 30, 1995, police arrested José Carlos B. Matos and another unidentified individual, in Conceição do Araguaia, in southern Pará state in the heart of Amazônia, for their alleged involvement in the theft of a motorcycle. The arresting officers took the two men to the local precinct and later that evening turned the two detainees over to a group of four men, one of whom was also a police officer. Three days later, two corpses were found by the side of a local highway, burnt almost beyond recognition. Matos's mother identified the remains of her son from police photographs.

On July 12, five prisoners accused of bank robbery and other assaults were called to testify before a judge in the interior of Alagoas. While returning from their court appearance, the prisoners disappeared from police custody. Authorities stated that the prisoners had been kidnaped by a group of heavily armed men, although not a single shot was fired.

Sergio Gomes, one of those missing following the August 9 Rondônia massacre, was later seen by a local city councilman entering a police vehicle. Days later, his corpse was found floating in the nearby Tanarú river.

CPT investigations revealed the continued increase in reported cases of forced labor and near-forced labor in 1994, the practice by which rural laborers are enticed with promises of high wages to toil at distant work sites. These laborers are often bonded to their employers by heavy, ever-increasing debt and are confined to the site by armed guards. While the CPT documented twenty-seven such cases involving 4,883 people in 1991, and eighteen cases involving 16,442 victims in 1992, these numbers increased to twenty-nine cases involving 19,940 laborers in 1993 and twenty-eight cases involving 25,193 workers in 1994.

The Cardoso government's response to allegations of forced labor was open and constructive. In an April radio address, President Cardoso recognized the seriousness of the problem and established an interministerial commission to address it. Although much needed to be done to eradicate forced labor—for instance, the federal police investigated only two of more than a dozen cases denounced during 1995—the president's recognition of the issue and his preliminary efforts to address it constituted a positive first step.

Although Brazilians generally enjoyed the right to free speech, in several instances in 1995 the judiciary was employed to impose limits on the full enjoyment of this right, in direct violation of article 13 of the American Convention on Human Rights and article 19 of the International Covenant on Civil and Political Rights. In March, an appellate court affirmed the conviction of human rights activist Father Júlio Lancellotti for the crime of disrespect of authority. In a television interview in 1992, Father Lancellotti had accused the military police of acting as a death squad. In that year, the military police in São Paulo killed 1,470 civilians, including 111 disarmed prison inmates in a single episode.

In May, after more than a year, *O Calvário de Sonia Angel*, a text in which former military officer João Luiz de Moraes' describes his twenty-year ordeal in discovering how his daughter had been tortured and murdered by security forces during the dictatorship, was finally permitted to circulate. In 1994, a Rio de Janeiro court had granted Air Force Gen. João Paulo Burnier, one of those implicated by Moraes's book, a restraining order prohibiting the book's circulation.

In June, on petition from Bonifácio de Andrada, counsel for the Chamber of Deputies of the Federal Congress, a court in the capital Brasília prohibited the rock band Paralamas do Sucesso from playing a song of their own composition based on a speech given by former presidential candidate Luiz Inácio da Silva ("Lula"). The song, "Luiz Inácio (300 Picaretas)," accuses the majority of Congress of being scoundrels (*picaretas*).

The Right to Monitor

The Brazilian government imposed no formal obstacles to human rights monitoring, and Brazil continued to maintain a well developed network of human rights nongovernmental organizations (NGOs). These groups promoted the rights of women, children, indigenous groups, rural laborers and activists, prisoners and others victimized by human rights violations. These groups, however, did face threats, intimidation, and physical violence from police and *fazendeiros* (ranchers).

Wagner dos Santos, who survived gunshot wounds from the July 1993 Candelária massacre of eight street children and had come forward as a witness, once again survived an attack by off-duty police. In September, dos Santos fled Rio de Janeiro and abandoned the case, underscoring the need for an effective national witness protection program.

Human rights activists in southern Pará continued to operate under death threats from a vigilante group directed by Jerônimo Alves de Amorim, owner of the Nazaré fazenda. The Rev. Ricardo Rezende and the Rev. Henri des Roziers of the CPT were among those on a list of forty targeted persons that continued to circulate in the region. In 1994, five of those on the list were killed. During 1995, authorities failed to detain Alves de Amorim, despite of outstanding warrants for his involvement in several homicides.

In June, all eight prosecutors in the São Paulo military justice system signed a document calling for the transfer of crimes committed against civilians to the ordinary courts. This important reform proposal, an attempt to bring some measure of due process to an important set of cases, flew in the face of the military high command. A week afterwards, two of the eight prosecutors began to receive anonymous death threats. A third, responsible for the prosecution of 120 military police responsible for the October 1992 massacre of 111 prisoners in the Carandiru prison, had already received threats for more than two years. Despite the frequency and similarity of the threats, in more than two years the authorities charged with investigating them had been unable to identify those responsible.

U.S. Policy

In April, President Fernando Henrique Cardoso visited the United States and met with senior officials, including President Clinton. Despite pressure from the NGO community, including Human Rights Watch/Americas, Clinton failed to raise the issue of Brazil's human rights record with his Brazil-ian counterpart. With the exception of the Brazil section of the retrospective *Country Reports on Human Rights Practices for 1994*, the Brazil desk officer for the State Department could point to no public human rights statement on Brazil made by the State Department or the U.S. Embassy in Brasília during 1995.

The State Department's 1994 country report for Brazil generally presented a fair portrayal of the human rights situation. Nevertheless, the report's summary and treatment of Operation Rio failed to note the abuses committed by military troops and police forces, noting instead that the joint operations were "essentially nonviolent and popular with the city's residents" and repeating the military authorities' contention that they "worked closely with judges to obtain the necessary warrants." Human Rights Watch/Americas investigations established that troops engaged in Operation Rio committed numerous abuses, including torture, massive arbitrary searches and arrest, and extended detention without adequate legal basis.

In December 1994, the U.S. Embassy's human rights officer traveled to Belém, in the state of Pará, to attend the trial of those charged in the 1991 assassination of rural activist Expedito Ribeiro de Souza. The two defendants present at the trial were convicted; the third, fazendeiro Jerónimo Alves de Amorim, remained a fugitive.

In 1995, the U.S. gave relatively little direct assistance to Brazil. For fiscal year 1996, the administration requested $200,000 for training through the International Military Education and Training Program (IMET) and $1 million in anti-narcotics assistance. The U.S. government should use both aid grants to press police and military to take steps to eliminate human rights abuses by their forces and to respond to reports of violations when they occur.

The Work of
Human Rights Watch/Americas

Given the seriousness and range of human rights violations in Brazil, Human Rights

Watch/Americas decided to establish permanent representation in the country, opening a joint office with the Center for Justice and International Law (CEJIL) in Rio de Janeiro. Having a permanent office in Brazil allowed us to participate more closely in the public debate concerning human rights violations and to press government officials concerning measures to be taken to address these violations.

In March, together with several Brazilian human rights groups, we submitted an agenda for human rights to newly-elected President Fernando Henrique Cardoso. That document, an open letter released to the press, summarized our reports and main concerns in Brazil since our first report in 1987. Several of the recommendations contained in that letter, such as the need to create federal jurisdiction for human rights abuses and modify the jurisdiction of the military justice system, led to public debate and government action in 1995.

In April, along with several organizations in Washington, we met with President Cardoso, Minister of Justice Jobim, and other members of a visiting Brazilian official delegation. We later followed up by meeting other senior officials of the Cardoso administration to discuss human rights concerns.

In September, we released in Brazil a Portuguese version of the Human Rights Watch Global Report on Women's Human Rights (see the Women's Rights Project section) emphasizing the chapter that addressed human rights abuses of women in Brazil. The release received vast press coverage in the television, radio and print media.

Throughout 1995, we continued to use international mechanisms to pressure the Brazilian government to comply with its international obligations. In conjunction with CEJIL, we brought several cases to the attention of the Inter-American Commission on Human Rights, including the August massacre in Ronônia. In February, on the application of Human Rights Watch/Americas and CEJIL, the Inter-American Commission requested that the Brazilian government take measures to protect the life of Father

Rezende, who was honored by Human Rights Watch in its December 1994 for the CPT's sustained work on human rights in the southern Pará state in the Amazon region. In 1995, after years of pressure by Human Rights Watch/Americas and CEJIL, the Brazilian government decided, in an April meeting with Human Rights Watch/Americas and other NGOs, to permit the Inter-American Commission on Human Rights to visit Brazil to investigate human rights conditions.

CHILE

Human Rights Developments

The issue of accountability for past human rights violations continued to divide the nation; and constitutional restraints on full democracy, out-of-date penal standards, and ingrained police abuses remained major obstacles to the full enjoyment of basic human rights in Chile.

On May 30, the Supreme Court unanimously confirmed a prison sentence of seven years for Manuel Contreras Sepúlveda, a retired army general and former head of Chile's secret police, the National Intelligence Directorate (Dirección de Inteligencia Nacional, DINA), and a sentence of six years for Brig. Gen. Pedro Espinoza, Contreras's former deputy. These two had been convicted in 1993 by a special judge appointed by the Supreme Court to resolve the 1976 Washington, D.C., car-bombing murders of Orlando Letelier, a former Chilean defense minister, and U.S. citizen Ronni Moffitt. Contreras was finally incarcerated in Punta Peuco prison in the early hours of October 21. The Letelier-Moffitt case is the only one in which senior DINA officials—responsible for a widespread campaign of disappearances and political murders between 1973 and 1978—have been fully prosecuted or imprisoned.

On June 19, after three weeks of uncertainty in which police officials tried in vain to carry out an arrest order, the army discharged Espinoza, and an army escort took him to a prison constructed especially for military officers in Punta Peuco, on the outskirts of Santiago. It took almost five months for the court sentence on Contreras to be executed. On learning of his conviction, Contreras promised that he would "never spend a day in jail" and took refuge in his ranch in southern Chile. On June 13, after police received authorization to arrest him there, army commandos working under cover of night spirited him away to the naval base in Talcahuano, where he was admitted to hospital allegedly suffering from diabetes and high blood pressure, disorders from which he had not been known previously to suffer. Citing ill health, Contreras's attorneys launched a series of appeals against his imprisonment, prompting a sequence of medical examinations. Finally, Contreras underwent a hernia operation at the hospital, having received permission by the court to begin serving his sentence there. When his doctors had pronounced him fit and all further avenues of appeal had been exhausted, Contreras finally joined Espinoza in prison on October 21.

In response to the civil-military crisis, right-wing opposition parties, which have historically rejected concerns about human rights issues stemming from Pinochet's military rule (1973-90), pressed for a new law to interpret the 1978 amnesty that provided immunity from punishment for human rights violations committed between 1973 and 1978. Opposition senators introduced a bill in July proposing what amounted to a "full stop law," a deadline for judicial investigations into human rights cases. The bill would make it easier for courts to close unresolved human rights cases by requiring that they need only establish the type and date of the human rights violation that took place to mandate the permanent closure of the case. In recent years, trial-level courts have made significant advances in the opposite direction, including reopening human rights cases and prosecuting suspected human rights violators.

At issue was the ability of Chilean courts to investigate human rights violations and prosecute perpetrators, which the Supreme Court itself threw into further question. The amnesty clearly made punishing human rights violators impossible but did not definitively address investigations and prosecutions. Trial-level courts had previously considered disappearance cases open pending confirmation of the fate of the victim. In August, however, the Supreme Court ordered the final closure of the case of the 1976 disappearance of Joel Huaquiñir Benavides, a Socialist Party leader. The court ruled that Huanquiñir be legally considered deceased from the time of his disappearance, even though his fate remained unknown. By November, the Supreme Court had confirmed the application of the amnesty law to seven other cases, and its president, Roberto Dávila, indicated publicly that the court would shortly close the remaining cases before it.

In response to the proposed bill to "reinterpret" the amnesty, the government countered with a proposal of its own. In an unusually frank television address to the nation on August 21, President Eduardo Frei stressed that the Letelier-Moffitt case had brought Chile face to face with the limitations of its democracy and that the truth about past human rights violations, especially disappearances, had to be confronted for national reconciliation to be possible.

After his speech, Frei presented three bills to parliament, the first dealing with human rights investigations and the second and third with constitutional reforms aimed at phasing out military restrictions on the full exercise of democracy. The human rights bill promised to streamline court investigations, but its general effect would be to reinforce and extend the negative effects of the amnesty law by offering to keep secret the identity of human rights violators in exchange for information about the fate of the "disappeared". The bill would mandate the appointment of superior court judges devoted for two years exclusively to disappearance cases. The judges would receive special investigative powers, including access to classified documents, military installations, and police stations, which are normally off-limits for members of the civilian judiciary. Judges would also take over all cases currently filed in military courts. Cases could be closed finally only if the judges were able to establish either the physical whereabouts of the victims' remains, or the fact of their death. However, to accomplish this, the identities of military suspects would be protected permanently in exchange for their testimony.

Other bills introduced by Frei would reduce some, but not all, of the military privileges left in place by the army when Pinochet left the presidency in 1990. With respect to human rights, they would restore the president's power to retire military officials, which could be used to remove human rights violators from service even if they could not be tried in the courts. Human Rights Watch/Americas encouraged a review under these provisions of cases such as those of Brig. Miguel Krasnoff Marchenko and Lt. Col. Fernando Laureani Maturana, former DINA agents directly implicated in several cases of disappearance in 1974. At this writing, Krasnoff was on active service in Santiago and Laureani was serving in a regiment in the northern city of Iquique.

In early November, President Frei announced on television that the government had made significant concessions to the right-wing opposition. Cases would only be opened at the express wish of relatives, those in military courts would not be transferred to civilian judges, and the grounds on which judges could close cases were relaxed. In an open letter to the Chilean Congress, Human Rights Watch/Americas criticized the government's failure to establish clear norms ensuring that cases were kept open until the fate of the victims had been determined. The congressional debate on the proposals was continuing as of this writing.

While past military abuses received considerable national attention, ongoing abuses by Chile's police forces did not, even though they continued to constitute a human rights problem in the country. Police, particularly the uniformed *carabineros*, operated without effective judicial control, often arbitrarily arresting, mistreating, or torturing detainees. Though Chilean police forces instituted internal mechanisms for investigating complaints of torture, their internal investigations rarely, if ever, led to successful court prosecutions. In a meeting with Human Rights Watch/Americas in July, officials of the Ministry of the Presidency and the Ministry of Justice failed to provide evidence that any police officers had been convicted of torture since the return to democracy, although the Ministry of Interior reported that courts received some sixty complaints of torture between March 1990 and October 1994. In July, U.N. Special Rapporteur on Torture Nigel S. Rodley visited Chile.

Although the government officially recognized the importance of freedom of expression, it continued to apply laws that limited this right, including the Law of State Security, which the former military government used to stifle political dissent. Police continued to arrest people for expression-related "crimes" under this law, and prosecutors based indictments on it. In January, both branches of the legislature voted to file a lawsuit, based on the law, against Francisco Javier Cuadra, a former Pinochet minister, because of remarks he made in the news magazine *¿Qué Pasa?* In the interview, Cuadra said that he had information that "some parliamentarians and other persons holding public office take drugs." Members of parliament deemed the comment an affront to their honor. On June 19, police arrested Cuadra and took him to Capuchinos prison in Santiago. He was released on bond on July 7. In August, police jailed Chilean Socialist Youth leader Arturo Barrios, accused of violating the law, on charges of "insulting" General Pinochet. Two weeks later, Pinochet sued Christian Democrat Congressman Rodolfo Seguel under the same law for observing that "after well-irrigated lunches he [Pinochet] is wont to say stupid things."

The state also restricted freedom of

expression in other ways. In August, the Supreme Court refused permission for Channel 7 television to interview Miguel Estay Reyno, a jailed former police undercover agent, who was believed to have information about the fate of the people who had disappeared during the military period. That same month, in an apparent case of self-censorship, a music video by the hit Argentine rock group Los Fabulosos Cadillacs was edited to delete an image of Pinochet. The video, titled "Mal Bicho" (Bad Bug), showed the general along with Argentine dictator Rafael Videla, Hitler, Mussolini, and Saddam Hussein. According to the Chilean newspaper *La Epoca*, Sony Music (Chile), which distributed the video, said that it received the version already cut from the company's Miami office and that the cut had been made to avoid problems with Chilean law.

The Right to Monitor

Human Rights Watch/Americas did not receive any reports that the government prevented or restricted human rights organizations from conducting their investigations and reporting their findings during 1995.

U.S. Policy

Human rights remained a low priority in United States relations with Chile, as both the Chilean and U.S. governments focused their attention on Chile's proposed entry into the North American Free Trade Agreement (NAFTA). In mid-1995, representatives of Chile, Mexico, the United States, and Canada met to begin official negotiations on Chile's accession to the treaty. Neither the U.S. nor the Chilean government opposed the labor rights components of the existing accord.

The Supreme Court ruling on the major issue of historic contention between the two governments, the Letelier-Moffitt case, motivated a brief official note of congratulations to the Chilean government. Although the Clinton administration was outspoken about the human rights implications of the Letelier-Moffitt case, the United States failed to voice concern about other human rights problems, including Chilean proposals to expand the amnesty law, justice for past human rights violations, current police abuses (including torture), and freedom of expression.

During 1995, the Chilean and United States militaries continued to expand their links. The U.S. continued to provide aid to the Chilean military for training in the United States and began to program military training for civilian members of Chile's defense management. The U.S. also transferred to the country excess military equipment, including a Landing Ship Tank (LST), trucks, and other vehicles. In 1995, for the first time since the 1976 Kennedy Amendment blocked U.S. military aid to Chile, the Chilean army participated in joint military exercises with the U.S. Southern Command. Congress had lifted the aid restriction in 1990.

The U.S. Agency for International Development (AID) provided an estimated $3,598,000 in assistance to Chile, focused basically on administration of justice. The Agency for International Development's justice-related programs will end by 1996, when the AID Chile mission is expected to close down.

The Work of
Human Rights Watch/Americas

In Chile, where a Human Rights Watch/Americas representative was based, the organization focused its energies on advocacy work, particularly related to proposed legislative changes in Chile likely to affect human rights. In June, we wrote to U.S. Assistant Secretary of State for Democracy, Human Rights and Labor John Shattuck, urging that he commend Frei's stand on implementing the court verdict in the Letelier case and encourage the Chilean government to support the principle of accountability in the negotiations over the amnesty law.

In July, the division's executive director visited Santiago to urge government officials to include greater human rights protections in its penal code and eliminate military jurisdiction over civilians. He and our Chile representative met with several high-level government officials. In August, on a second visit to study the Frei proposals on investigations into the disappearances covered by the amnesty law, they were received by the minister of the interior and other authorities, as well as members of human rights organizations.

In November, Human Rights Watch/ Americas sent an open letter to members of the Chilean Congress urging them not to approve measures that would prevent a full clarification of the truth in each case and criticizing Frei's proposals on secrecy as an extension of the effects of the amnesty law of 1978.

We also continued to cooperate with intergovernmental human rights bodies to promote human rights in Chile in other ways: by providing information to the United Nations special rapporteur on torture during his visit to Santiago and by continuing to litigate several cases on behalf of relatives of the disappeared before the Inter-American Commission on Human Rights. In hearings before the commission, we argued that Chile had a duty to investigate these human rights violations and prosecute those responsible. We also argued the case of Francisco Martorell, a Chilean journalist whose book, *Impunidad diplomática* (Diplomatic Impunity), was published in Argentina in 1994 and banned in Chile.

COLOMBIA

Human Rights Developments

Dogged by mounting evidence linking his campaign to drug money, and spurned by some guerrillas and members of the army who opposed his peace initiative, in 1995 President Ernesto Samper implemented authoritarian measures to govern Colombia. Although the president repeatedly promised to respect human rights and significantly expanded the country's human rights bureaucracy, the contrast sharpened between the government's sophisticated rhetoric in support of human rights and its meager accomplishments. Extrajudicial executions,

forced disappearances, reports of torture, evidence of paramilitary groups operating with the assistance and tolerance of the security forces, and impunity for security force members implicated in human rights crimes continued. Guerrillas also shared blame for Colombia's dire record, murdering, kidnaping, and attacking civilians as a method of combat, in violation of international humanitarian law.

In August, Samper exercised his constitutional authority to declare a state of "internal commotion." Like the states of siege used to rule Colombia for most of its history in this century, the declaration gave him the power to suspend fundamental rights and created a climate of fear. Human Rights Watch/Americas was particularly troubled by the government's intention to lower the age at which children could be tried as adults from eighteen to fourteen, in violation of Colombia's obligations under the Convention on the Rights of the Child. Although the decree was struck down in October by the Constitutional Court, Samper declared a new state of internal commotion after the November 2 assassination of political leader Alvaro Gómez Hurtado. The executive also supported legislators who planned to codify into law emergency measures that would violate certain human rights, like the right to due process and freedom from unwarranted search and seizure.

According to the Andean Commission of Jurists-Colombian Section (Comisión Andina de Juristas-Seccional Colombiana, CAJ-SC), ten civilians a day fell victim to political violence. Of those killings where a perpetrator was known, 65 percent corresponded to government security forces while 35 percent corresponded to guerrillas. The Intercongregational Commission on Justice and Peace (Comisión Intercongregacional de Justicia y Paz), a human rights group, indicated that ninety-six people were forcibly "disappeared" between January and September. Another 121 fell victim to so-called "social cleansing" killings, mostly indigents, homeless persons, and street children.

A March report to Congress by the

public ombudsman termed the marked rise in complaints of human rights violations to his office "chilling" and described the government's response as "apathetic." Most complaints that the ombudsman had received in 1994 involved the military, followed by police. "It is undeniable," the report noted, "that a profound impunity favors the perpetrators of these crimes through silence, indulgence, group solidarity, and cover-ups." The ombudsman said guerrillas continued to violate international humanitarian law, "completely ignoring the distinction between combatants and noncombatants."

Violence by all sides continued to spur forced displacement. A report by the Colombian Episcopal Conference published in late 1994 concluded that over 586,000 people had been forcibly displaced since 1985, 2 percent of the country's population. In 1995, forced displacement was especially acute in the city of Necoclí, in the banana-growing region known as Urabá, where local authorities registered a population increase of approximately 7,800 people between February and April, almost all rural families fleeing political violence.

Paramilitary groups expanded their area of operation in 1995, following a purported November 1994 "paramilitary summit," and appeared to be mounting a nationally coordinated offensive against Colombians deemed subversive or sympathetic to guerrillas. The paramilitary advance was particularly marked in the departments of Cesar, Norte de Santander, Bolívar, Meta, and region known as the Magdalena Medio, where they operated with the tolerance and often open support of the security forces. In the town of San Alberto, Cesar, nineteen people were killed in the month of April, most by men identifying themselves as members of Peasant Self-Defense Groups of Colombia (Autodefensas de los Campesinos de Colombia, ACC). In areas like San Vicente de Chucurí, department of Santander, paramilitaries unhindered by local police or military openly charged local merchants a war tax.

The Colombian government accepted the binding nature of Protocol II Additional to the Geneva Conventions, which means that the parties involved in an internal conflict, including the government forces, would be bound by its precepts. Nevertheless, the government continued to violate international humanitarian law. The public ombudsman's office documented one particularly flagrant incident, in which soldiers belonging to the army's Bomboná Battalion simulated a guerrilla attack in the town of Segovia, department of Antioquia, after guerrillas successfully stole a dynamite shipment on March 3. Soldiers executed a guerrilla captured hours later, killed a civilian with a grenade, wounded four children, and fired on civilian dwellings, including an elementary school, to fabricate guerrilla-army cross fire.

Although guerrillas repeatedly called on the government to respect human rights, their own record was seriously compromised by a series of massacres and kidnapings. According to press investigations, in March, in Ituango, department of Antioquia, the Revolutionary Armed Forces of Colombia (Fuerzas Armadas Revolucionarias de Colombia, FARC) killed several residents, including a four-year-old girl and three prisoners in the local jail. In September, the FARC apparently massacred twenty-six people, including two children, less than a quarter-mile from a military base in Urabá. The Camilist Union-National Liberation Army (Unión Camilista-Ejército de Liberación Nacional, UC-ELN) also carried out executions. In Saravena, department of Arauca, for example, community leaders accused the UC-ELN of killing seven girls, all minors, who had befriended local soldiers, a clear violation on the prohibition against the murder of noncombatants. The UC-ELN continued to use mines in civilian areas, although it expressed its willingness to negotiate with the government on limiting their use.

Kidnaping remained a prime source of income for guerrillas, who, according to police, captured 304 people in the first seven months of 1995, 52 percent of the total number of kidnapings reported. Victims included businesspeople, educators, government officials, journalists, landowners, a Venezuelan mayor, and five American missionaries. Two of those missionaries, Steve Welsh and Timothy Van Dyke, were kidnaped in early 1994 and apparently executed by their FARC captors near Medina, department of Cundinamarca, on June 19, 1995.

Among the areas most devastated by political violence was Urabá, on Colombia's Caribbean shore. During 1995, hundreds fell victim to political violence or fled the region out of fear for their lives, including civic leaders, trade unionists, farmers, banana workers, and indigenous leaders. Five massacres took place there in August alone, two of which local leaders blamed on paramilitaries believed to be working with the security forces, local landowners, and businesspeople. The Popular Alternative Commands (Comandos de Alternativa Popular), a self-proclaimed group of former guerrillas and others pledged to wiping out subversion, claimed responsibility for the August 12 massacre of eighteen unarmed people at the Aracatazo bar in Chigorodó.

Other massacres occurred in the context of clashes between guerrillas of the FARC, guerrillas of the Popular Liberation Army (Ejército Popular de Liberación, EPL), and former guerrillas who had laid down their arms and become part of the political party Hope, Peace, and Liberty (Esperanza, Paz y Libertad). In March, the party released a report saying that 274 of its 3,000 members had been murdered since it was formed four years ago. Most were victims of EPL guerrillas who had refused the government amnesty. On August 29, guerrillas believed to belong to the FARC stopped a truck near Carepa, department of Antioquia, selected sixteen members of the party, and bound and executed them.

In this generally bleak panorama, there were some advances for human rights. On January 31, President Samper accepted a report that concluded that government forces were responsible for the killings and forced disappearance of at least thirty-four people in and around the town of Trujillo, department of Valle, in 1990. Subsequently, Fernando Bolero, then the defense minister, discharged Lt. Col. Alirio Urueña, implicated in the killings, over the unanimous objections of the Joint Chiefs of Staff. A joint government-NGO commission was created to monitor the government's compliance with its promises to prosecute and punish alleged perpetrators of the Trujillo killings, continue the investigation, and negotiate compensation to surviving family members. In September, a committee composed of government and non-government representatives was set up to study three additional cases before the IACHR. In October, the government formed a special unit to advance criminal investigations of members of paramilitary groups implicated in serious human rights violations.

Nonetheless, government action to end impunity remained scarce. In a February report to the United Nations Human Rights Commission, the U.N. special rapporteurs for extrajudicial executions and torture concluded that, even though Colombia's human rights situation was "alarming," the government had failed to implement most of their previous recommendations. On August 18, the U.N. Subcommission for the Prevention of Discrimination and Protection of Minorities approved a declaration of concern about human rights violations in Colombia.

Colombia's civilian and military court systems contributed to the violation of human rights during 1995. The public order courts, used to prosecute individuals charged with rebellion and drug trafficking, violated the right to due process. Tried before secret judges and prosecutors, suspects were prevented from knowing the identities of the witnesses used against them and were subjected to prolonged pre-trial detention. Colombia's Congress voted to maintain the system until 1999 however.

Military tribunals continued systematically to cover up human rights crimes and absolve the military and police officers involved, using the broad categories of "acts of service" and "due obedience" to place crimes like murder, rape, and torture within their jurisdiction. In a case in which former navy intelligence officers in Barrancabermeja, department of Santander, accused Col. Rodrigo Quiñonez of ordering the murders of dozens of trade unionists, human rights activists, and local leaders, military courts absolved him of any wrongdoing, while a public order court issued warrants for the arrests of the officers who accused him.

In 1995, the government began to study reforms to the military justice system. One set of proposed reforms suggested major changes to protect human rights, while another set would maintain most current military court characteristics, including the power to handle cases involving extrajudicial execution, forced disappearance, and torture. Human Rights Watch/Americas was troubled by President Samper's support for the latter initiative, which continued the tradition of Colombian governments winking at impunity. As if to underscore its defiance of governmental human rights investigators, the Defense Ministry decorated Army Brig. Gen. Alvaro Hernán Velandia Hurtado, commander of the Cali-based Third Brigade, for "distinguished service," just one month after the attorney general's office ordered the officer discharged for his role in the forced disappearance of captured guerrilla Nydia Erika Bautista in 1990. After widespread protest by human rights groups, General Velandia was formally dismissed. In an October speech, Samper termed allegations that the security forces committed human rights violations as "without foundation, presented by their enemies," and vowed to defend military jurisdiction. A proposal to reform the constitution, supported by the executive and before Congress at this writing, would reassign active-duty officers to military tribunals, a practice struck down by the Constitutional Court.

The Right to Monitor

Local human rights monitors, including members of civic associations, unions, and religious groups, continued to play an important role in gathering and disseminating information on human rights and pressuring the authorities for change. As in previous years, however, this work put monitors at serious risk, especially those who lived and worked in Colombia's smaller cities and towns.

At least three human rights monitors were murdered during 1995. Ernesto Fernández Fester, a teacher, trade unionist, human rights activist, and founding member of the Pailitas Movement for Civic-Community Integration, was killed on February 20 by armed men who had been linked to several earlier killings of peasant and civic leaders around Pailitas, department of Cesar. Javier Barriga Vergel, a lawyer who defended Colombians accused of rebellion, was shot and killed in Cúcuta, department of Norte de Santander, on June 16. Barriga was a member of the Bogotá-based Committee in Solidarity with Political Prisoners (Comité de Solidaridad con los Presos Políticos, CSPP). Humberto Peña Taylor, a law student at Bogotá's National University who took part in a free legal clinic for poor Colombians, was hunted down and killed by two armed men who entered the university campus on June 15, apparently with the collusion of university security personnel. When fellow law student Gabriel Riaño Prieto, a member of a university human rights group, later led a campaign to press for an investigation of Peña's killing, he received telephone death threats.

Several human rights monitoring groups disbanded, or members fled, after being attacked or threatened. The Ocaña-based Human Rights Team closed its doors in early 1995, and the Civic Committee for Human Rights abandoned its offices in Villavicencio in April. Bogotá-based lawyer Luis Pérez, a member of the "José Restrepo Alvear" Collective Lawyers Association (Corporación Colectivo de Abogados "José Restrepo Alvear,") was forced to leave the country with his family after harassment and repeated threats. In May, Miguel Olaya Pabón, a member of the Pailitas Movement, was threatened by three soldiers and a civilian army informer.

The Regional Association for the Defense of Human Rights (Corporación Regional para la Defensa de los Derechos Humanos, CREDHOS) was the target of repeated telephone death threats and harassment by men traveling in unmarked vehicles, believed to be connected to the security forces. In April, two CREDHOS members were part of an international delegation including Human Rights Watch that was reportedly the target of a failed assassination attempt near Sabana de Torres, department of Santander.

On August 4, three members of MINGA, a Bogotá-based human rights organization, were arrested in Aguachica, department of Cesar, by members of the Anti-kidnaping and Extortion Unit (Unidad Anti-Secuestro y Extorsión, UNASE), who kept them for several hours in an effort to harass them and instill fear. Two weeks after their return to Bogotá, MINGA received a telephone death threat."

Aida Abella Esquivel, the president of the Patriotic Union (Unión Patriótica, UP) also reported that she was a target of harassment by unidentified men believed to work for the security forces since they operated with the unmarked cars and communications equipment used by police.

U.S. Policy

The drug war dominated relations between the U.S. and Colombia, with traded accusations and mistrust prevailing. Human rights issues received low priority in diplomatic and public exchanges between the two countries. In a brief March visit, Assistant Secretary of State for Democracy, Human Rights and Labor John Shattuck met with government officials and human rights groups and praised Colombia for recent advances. He did not balance his statements with a more detailed review of how the government failed to address serious human rights problems.

Joined by Senate Foreign Relations Committee Chairman Jesse Helms Secretary of State Warren Christopher and other administration officials threatened not to certify Colombia for continued aid and loans based on what they characterized as a poor drug-fighting performance. A bitter diplo-

matic exchange peaked in March, when the State Department issued a "conditional" certification with a national security waiver.

In 1995, U.S. embassy personnel conducted reviews of the human rights records of Colombian security force personnel scheduled to receive U.S. training. The U.S. military held two human rights training sessions for Colombian officers and a session for field commanders. However, the United States did not screen Colombian diplomats for their human rights records. For example, only widespread protest convinced Colombia in August to withdraw retired army colonel Luis Plazas Vegas as its San Francisco consul general. Government inquiries had uncovered links between Plazas Vega and paramilitary groups in the departments of Meta and Cundinamarca. Plazas Vega was also suspected of having ordered the forcible disappearance of an M-19 guerrilla after that group's assault on the Palace of Justice in 1985.

Units within the security forces continue to receive U.S. aid, yet the officers in charge were not screened, a necessary complement to any serious end-use monitoring. In 1994, most aid went to police. However, a significant amount of aid from previous years remained in the hands of the military, including M16 rifles, M60 grenade launchers, radios, ammunition, and vehicles. Among those that received U.S. aid were army units engaged in systematic human rights violations, including the Cali-based Third Brigade and Mobile Brigade I, headquartered in La Uribe, department of Meta. In his annual report to Congress, Colombia's public ombudsman singled out Mobile Brigade I commander Brig. Gen. Néstor Ramírez Mejía as an officer who tolerated human rights violations and had refused to cooperate with official investigations of the troops under his command.

In contrast to earlier years, aid to Colombia in the proposed budget for fiscal year 1996 sought to consolidate all funding into a single counternarcotics account, with $35 million requested, continuing an upward trend. About half of those funds, $15 million, were destined for the military, while most of the balance went to police, despite what Human Rights Watch/Americas believed were serious human rights concerns that merited the suspension of aid.

The United States also continued to offer "qualified support" for Colombia's six public order courts through a $36 million, six-year program funded by the Agency for International Development. Although Human Rights Watch/Americas research shows that these courts commit systematic violations of due process, U.S. government officials have termed them "acceptable."

In an improvement over previous years' reports, the State Department's annual *Country Reports on Human Rights Practices for 1994* avoided characterizing violations by state security agencies and guerrillas as equal, and accurately described the human rights situation as "critical." However, the report continues to downplay violations inherent in the public order courts.

The Work of
Human Rights Watch/Americas

Human Rights Watch/Americas sought to focus attention on institutionalized human rights problems in Colombia, such as those created by the civilian and military justice systems, impunity, and the government's failure to protect vulnerable sectors of the population from violence by state and private actors. We worked in Colombia and international fora, like the United Nations and the Organization of American States, to press the Colombian government to live up to its international human rights obligations. At the same time, we called on guerrillas to cease violating international humanitarian law.

During the year, we sent two missions and our representatives met with senior U.S. and Colombian officials as well as human rights groups, humanitarian organizations, and victims of abuses, raising our concerns along with concrete recommendations for change, including reforms to the military justice system, public order courts, and government support for investigations into hu-

man rights crimes.

We registered frequent protests with the Colombian government regarding human rights abuses. With the CAJ-SC and the Center for Justice and International Law (CEJIL), we represented victims of abuses before the Inter-American Commission on Human Rights in an effort to compel the government to accept responsibility for the actions of its agents.

We also continued to press the U.S. government, including the Congress, to publicly express its concern over human rights violations in Colombia. Given the importance to Colombia of the United States as a diplomatic and trade partner, Human Rights Watch/Americas considered this a crucial step to convincing the Colombian government to address the serious situation. Working closely with the Congressional Friends of Human Rights Monitors as well as individual congressional offices, we helped generate a series of letters to Colombian officials in defense of human rights monitors and trade unionists. Another facet of our work involved continuing efforts to foster greater accountability regarding the use of U.S. aid by the Colombian security forces.

At the U.N. we highlighted our concerns about human rights in Colombia in a written statement submitted to the Commission on Human Rights. Along with Colombian groups, we urged the Commission on Human Rights to appoint a special rapporteur for Colombia. This campaign continued at this writing, such that Colombia had become a leading issue at the commission.

After the U.N. High Commissioner for Human Rights sent a delegation to investigate the possibility of opening a permanent human rights office in Colombia, we joined with other human rights groups in recognizing the importance of the high commissioner's initiative and urging that any office opened in Colombia work in strict coordination with other U.N. human rights initiatives and not in their stead.

In June, we filed a petition with the U.S. trade representative requesting that Colombia's status be reviewed pursuant to section 502(b)(8) of the Trade Act of 1974, as amended. Our petition argued that attacks on trade unionists and the overwhelming impunity enjoyed by perpetrators, in many cases agents of the state, merited a suspension of Colombia's trade benefits under the Generalized System of Preferences. A Spanish translation of the petition was also released in Colombia. At the time of this writing, the petition was still pending.

In September, Human Rights Watch/Americas released a Spanish translation of *Generation Under Fire: Children and Violence in Colombia*, with a foreword by noted human rights leader Gustavo Gallón. The presentation was accompanied by a detailed letter to President Samper on human rights violations against children.

CUBA

Human Rights Developments

During 1995 the Cuban government quickened the pace of its economic reform program without making commensurate progress toward compliance with international human rights standards. Still, it did take several positive steps in the area of human rights. These included, most notably, the release of at least twenty-four political prisoners prior to the expiration of their sentences, a decline in the number of political prosecutions and "acts of repudiation," a commitment not to prosecute for "illegal exit" persons who were repatriated to Cuba by the United States, consent to a limited degree of human rights monitoring, and the ratification of the Convention Against Torture and Other Cruel, Inhuman or Degrading Treatment or Punishment.

None of these steps, however, indicated any fundamental change in the Cuban human rights situation. In the absence of necessary structural reforms, the Cuban government continued to violate systematically the rights to freedom of expression, association, assembly, privacy, and due process of law. Although the government promised not

to prosecute citizens who were repatriated by the United States after exercising their internationally protected right to leave the country, the law against "illegal exit" was not repealed.

Numerous Cubans remained imprisoned for peacefully expressing their disagreement with government policy, including one man jailed for writing a letter to the secretary-general of the United Nations that criticized Cuban government policies. Although the government prosecuted fewer people, state security police continued to arrest, detain, harass, and intimidate human rights monitors, labor organizers, and pro-democracy activists, to refuse them travel visas, and otherwise to restrict their movements. These individuals, whom the authorities assailed as "counterrevolutionaries," were kept under strict surveillance and discriminated against in employment. The civic and political organizations to which they belonged were denied official recognition. Political prosecutions were held in courts—including military tribunals—that flouted basic due process norms.

The Cuban penal code provided a firm legal foundation for the repression of political dissidence. Laws defining such crimes as "enemy propaganda," "clandestine printing," and "contempt of authority" curbed speech. Laws prohibiting "rebellion" and "illicit association," among other crimes—which, if properly defined and carefully applied, might be consistent with international standards—continued to pose a threat to Cubans expressing dissident views. State security forces continued to employ the "dangerousness" provision against perceived opponents of the state. Vaguely worded and broad, with an almost limitless potential for discriminatory application, the dangerousness provision authorized up to four years of preventive detention of those who conducted themselves in a manner that contradicted "socialist morality," even without having committed a crime. Under this provision, dozens of human rights monitors and dissidents received an "official warning," the first step toward detention.

Subordinate to the executive, courts in Cuba lacked the necessary procedural guarantees to protect defendants from unfair prosecutions. Public and press access to trials was often narrowly limited or denied, defense witnesses were often barred, and defendants were almost always convicted. Before trial, or often simply as a form of harassment, government officials commonly detained human rights activists and perceived opponents of the state—sometimes for short periods, sometimes for extremely long periods. Though authorities did not physically torture detainees, they commonly held them in incommunicado detention in extremely severe conditions.

Prison inmates reported that minimal infractions or nonviolent protests such as hunger strikes spawned retaliation in the form of beatings, confinement in harsh isolation cells, violent and arbitrary searches, confiscation of belongings, denial of medical attention, suspension of visits, and transfer to prisons far from their relatives. Besides serious shortages of food and other supplies, Cuban prisons were plagued with overcrowding, poor hygiene and vermin. Prisoners typically lost weight while in confinement due to the insufficient diet provided them.

The evangelical Christian movement was the target of government harassment, including prosecutions. In December 1994, Miguel Angel León García, a lay pastor of the Baptist Church in San Fernando de Camarones, Camagüey Province, and Jorge Luis Brito Rodríguez, a member of that church, were sentenced to six years' imprisonment for the crime of enemy propaganda. Pastor Orson Vila Santoyo, a Pentacostal minister in Camagüey who refused to refrain from holding religious services in his home, was arrested in May 1995. In blatant disregard for due process, he was tried for "illicit association" on the day of his arrest, receiving a sentence that was reduced on appeal to eighteen months. During the same month, the Cuban authorities closed scores of other *casas culto*, evangelical meeting places operating out of homes.

During the summer, independent journalists suffered harassment as they became increasingly active and organized. In July, the authorities detained and threatened several journalists and confiscated the equipment of another, in an official effort to prevent them from reporting on "sensitive subjects." One such subject was the anniversary of the tragedy of the hijacked tugboat *Trece de Marzo*, which was rammed by a Cuban government boat on July 13, 1994, causing the deaths of about forty civilians fleeing Cuba. As the anniversary of the incident drew near, Cubans in Miami organized a flotilla to go into or near Cuban territorial waters to honor the victims, hoping that Cubans on the island would commemorate the occasion with them. Human rights monitors reported that a notable police and military presence began building up all over the country after July 1. In the week prior to July 13, and particularly on the 13th itself, the Cuban authorities detained and harassed journalists, dissidents and human rights activists: in all, about three dozen people were detained, while others were placed under house arrest.

Independent journalists also reported serious government harassment in September, with the establishment of the Bureau of Independent Journalists of Cuba (Buró de Periodistas Independientes de Cuba, BPIC), and continuing through November. During this period, the authorities detained or threatened several journalists, including Olance Nogueras Roce. Nogueras, who had just written an article on the Juragua nuclear power plant under construction in Cuba, was arrested on October 20, held for a few days in a maximum security prison, released on October 25, and then detained again and threatened with prosecution. In addition, the authorities barred Roxana Valdivia, the Ciego de Avila representative of the BPIC, from traveling outside her province; and gave Hector Perraza, the Pinar del Rio correspondent of the Havana Press, an official warning that he would be jailed for dangerousness unless he gave up independent journalism.

In a positive step, Cuba ratified the

U.N. Convention Against Torture and Other Cruel, Inhuman or Degrading Treatment or Punishment. In addition, over the course of the year, authorities released at least two dozen political prisoners prior to the expiration of their sentences. Many of these prisoners were, however, freed on the condition that they abandon the country. Although such releases gave prisoners an alternative to continued illegal detention, they clearly did not evidence the government's greater openness to political dissent. From the government's perspective, freeing dissidents into exile was beneficial for at least two reasons: internationally, it eliminated the embarrassment to the country's image caused by having known political prisoners; internally, it helped nip nascent human rights and opposition movements in the bud by expelling potential leaders. Because the technique of releasing political prisoners into exile increasingly became the norm, the unconditional release in May of Yndamiro Restano and Sebastián Arcos was particularly significant. Up to that moment, they were the two most prominent political prisoners in Cuba; international pressure for their release enabled them to refuse exile. Nonetheless, many other pro-democracy activists and rights monitors continued to languish in prison, including Dr. Omar del Pozo of the National Civic Union, Ileana Curra Luzón of the Nationalist Agenda Movement, and Domiciano Torres Roca of the Democratic Civic Party.

The Right to Monitor

Human rights monitoring continued to be illegal in Cuba, and monitors continued to be punished for their activities. Common forms of harassment included long- or short-term detention; the practice of calling monitors into the headquarters of state security forces for questioning, cajoling, and threatening; attacks by anonymous thugs or collisions with vehicles in suspicious circumstances; arbitrary house searches; anonymous threatening phone calls, often late at night; constant surveillance, including telephone taps; discriminatory visa denials; and discriminatory firings.

"Acts of repudiation"—a once-common tactic by which a government-assembled mob gathers outside the home of a "counter-revolutionary" to shout slogans and insults, sometimes defacing or otherwise damaging property—were infrequent. One such incident occurred on August 10, however, at the Havana home of Victoria Ruíz Labrit, president of the Cuban Committee of Peaceful and Independent Opposition (Comité Cubano de Oposición Pacífica e Independiente). A crowd of sixty to eighty people armed with pipes and chains reportedly surrounded her home to prevent a planned meeting of dissidents.

Human rights monitors also faced criminal prosecution. In April, Francisco Chaviano González, president of the National Council for Civil Rights in Cuba (Consejo Nacional para los Derechos Civiles en Cuba), was sentenced to fifteen years' imprisonment by a military tribunal on charges of "revealing state secrets" and "falsifying documents." Not only did his trial violate basic due process guarantees, but the suspicious circumstances of his arrest in May 1994 cast serious doubt on the evidentiary basis of his conviction. Pedro Arguellez Morán of the Cuban Committee for Human Rights (Comité Cubano Pro Derechos Humanos, CCPDH) suffered political persecution in September, when he was convicted of "enemy propaganda" and received a seven-month sentence. In May, prosecutors charged thirteen members of the Cuban Human Rights Party (Partido Pro Derechos Humanos Cubano) with spreading enemy propaganda, and another member with "illicit association." Although the defendants were released after short stints in detention, and were never tried for these offenses, the sudden crackdown was clearly meant to intimidate both them and other human rights monitors.

In July, Genaro Cortés, the Cienfuegos representative of the CCPDH, was detained for two months and charged with "falsifying documents." Since Cortés had provided material support to Sebastián Arcos of the CCPDH while Arcos was held at Ariza prison, the charges were believed to be a form of retaliation.

There was relatively more openness toward international monitoring in 1995. For the first time since 1988, the Cuban government invited an international delegation to investigate its treatment of political prisoners. The delegation—which included the executive director of Human Rights Watch/Americas—arrived in Cuba in April. Although in a surprise move the authorities hampered the delegation's ability to assess the prisoners' treatment by limiting its access to the administrative areas of prisons, the delegation still enjoyed long, private, and informative conversations with prisoners.

In contrast, the Cuban government firmly rejected the possibility of independent monitoring—either by international or domestic groups—of its treatment of Cubans repatriated under a new migration agreement with the United States. While promising that it would not take reprisals against repatriated Cubans, the Cuban government permitted monitoring only by U.S. Interests Section personnel.

The Role of
the International Community

Under the pressure of a continuing economic crisis, Cuba worked to improve its image internationally. Seeking strengthened political and, more critically for the Cubans, economic relations, the government adopted a series of economic reform measures. Though reform in the areas of democracy and human rights lagged far behind, Cuba was notably successful in obtaining improved diplomatic relations and increased foreign investment.

Other countries' resentment of the extraterritorial aspects of the U.S. economic embargo on Cuba—and of U.S. legislative efforts to tighten the embargo—continued to divert their attention from Cuba's human rights record. In November, the U.N. General Assembly voted 117-3 (with thirty-eight abstentions) to condemn the U.S. embargo; among the countries supporting the U.N.

resolution were all of the other permanent members of the Security Council save Britain.

The United Nations
and the European Union

In its November/December 1994 session, the U.N. Human Rights Commission's Working Group on Arbitrary Detention issued a decision that termed as arbitrary the detention of Patricio de la Guardia, a former general who was sentenced to thirty years' imprisonment for drug trafficking in 1989. The working group concluded that de la Guardia's summary trial before a special military tribunal violated his right to due process.

In addition, U.N. High Commissioner for Human Rights José Ayala Lasso visited Cuba in November 1994. During his stay, he met with high-level Cuban officials, including President Castro, as well as numerous representatives of unofficial human rights, labor rights and political opposition groups. At the close of his trip, however, he made no public comment on the human rights situation in Cuba, missing an important opportunity to bring public pressure on the Cuban government to institute reforms.

The monitoring efforts of U.N. Special Rapporteur Carl-Johan Groth contrasted markedly both with Ayala Lasso's access to Cuba and with his failure to condemn abuses. Though barred from entering the country, the special rapporteur released a detailed report on the Cuban government's human rights practices. Once again, the U.N. Human Rights Commission, which voted 22-8 (with twenty-three abstentions) in favor of a resolution condemning Cuba's human rights abuses, extended the special rapporteur's mandate for another year. The commission's persistent monitoring of abuses kept needed pressure on Cuba to improve its human rights record.

With Spain's accession to the presidency of the European Union, relations between the European community and Cuba progressed rapidly. Although Cuba remained the only Latin American country with which the E.U. had not signed a cooperation agreement, the E.U. took preliminary steps toward negotiating such an agreement, while individual European countries continued to expand their economic relations with Cuba. Unlike the U.S. government, which continued to insist upon a market economy and political pluralism in Cuba as preconditions to the initiation of economic relations, E.U. officials argued that strengthening relations would facilitate the process of political and economic reform. To their credit, many Europeans appeared serious about using their growing influence in Cuba constructively, urging the government to free political prisoners and move toward compliance with international human rights standards.

U.S. Policy

In 1995, U.S. policy toward Cuba took two seemingly divergent paths—one drawn by the executive branch, the other by the Republican-dominated Congress. In May, in what seemed to herald improved relations between the two countries, the administration announced a sweeping change in its reception of Cuban asylum seekers. Ending the blanket welcome that Cubans fleeing Cuba had enjoyed for over three decades, it declared that it would repatriate rapidly all Cubans intercepted at sea. (Simultaneously, the administration stated that it would accept into the United States almost all the 21,000 Cubans then held in indefinite detention in U.S. camps in Guantánamo Bay, Cuba.) Other signs of normalizing relations included the July visit of Deputy Assistant Secretary for American Affairs Anne Patterson, who became the highest-ranking U.S.official to visit Cuba in more than a decade, the lifting in October of the U.S. ban on permanent news bureaus in Cuba, and the partial lifting of travel restrictions that bar most Americans from visiting Cuba.

Although the decision to end the prolonged arbitrary detention of the Cubans held in Guantánamo camps brought U.S. treatment of them into compliance with its international obligations, the accompanying interdiction policy was flawed. Most notably, the standard originally employed for assessing the claims of asylum seekers—by which Cubans had to show that they were in imminent danger of serious human rights violations—was more restrictive than that prescribed under international law, as U.S. authorities relied on the availability of in-country refugee processing to justify a generalized policy of repatriation.

The screening procedures were, however, revised some weeks after being initially instituted. With these revisions, screening officers were reportedly instructed to employ the appropriate international standard, and the government insisted that it would respect the obligation of non-*refoulement*: its duty not to repatriate any Cuban with a well-founded fear of persecution. Although the new policy appeared generally to comply with international requirements, certain aspects of it remained problematic. Notable among them were procedural problems associated with shipboard screening, such as the difficulty in ensuring that asylum seekers were guaranteed adequate time to rest and recover from the trauma of their voyage before being interviewed.

At the same time, in Congress, a bill intended to strengthen sanctions against Cuba moved toward passage, reflecting the Republicans' desire for a more confrontational Cuba policy. Known as the Helms-Burton bill for its original sponsors, Sen. Jesse Helms and Rep. Dan Burton, the bill represented a congressional attempt to internationalize the American economic embargo on Cuba by, among other things, punishing foreign companies doing business there. Viewed as a U.S. effort to impose its Cuba policy on the rest of the world, it was widely and vociferously condemned by the international community. Largely because of the international outcry against the legislation, the later version of the bill omitted its strongest and most controversial provisions.

Even the weakened version of the Helms-Burton bill raised human rights concerns, however. A provision designed to strengthen the enforcement of restrictions on travel to Cuba would, like the restrictions themselves, violate article 19 of the International Covenant on Civil and Political Rights (ICCPR). Article 19 protects the "freedom to seek, receive and impart information and ideas of all kinds, regardless of frontiers": as it suggests, one of the key methods by which information is shared is through travel and human contact.

In contrast to Congress's efforts to tighten enforcement of the ban on travel, a more constructive element of U.S. policy toward Cuba was revealed in the administration's October decision to lift the ban on permanent news bureaus in Cuba and partially lift the ban on travel. Although these measures were only a first step toward bringing U.S. policy toward Cuba into compliance with its international obligation to protect the free flow of information, they were an important first step.

To its credit, the U.S. government extended sympathetic treatment to the embattled human rights community in Cuba. For example, a member of U.S. Interests Section staff attempted to attend the trial of human rights activist Francisco Chaviano, and over the course of the year the State Department issued several statements condemning abuses. Using information collected by the U.S. Interests Section, the State Department produced a reliable annual human rights report on Cuba, as it had since 1989.

The Work of
Human Rights Watch/Americas

In 1995, the ability of Human Rights Watch/Americas to monitor human rights conditions in Cuba was significantly improved when the division's executive director was invited to visit Cuban political prisoners as part of an international delegation. The April mission marked the first time since 1988 that a representative of Human Rights Watch/Americas had been officially granted access to examine the human rights situation in Cuba. During the week he spent in the country, he and the other delegates met with a number of top Cuban officials, including President Castro, and discussed the government's continuing human rights violations. In October, Human Rights Watch/Americas released a lengthy report on Cuban human rights developments, titled *Improvements Without Reform*.

Human Rights Watch/Americas continued to press the U.S. government to comply with international standards in its policy toward Cuba. In May, when the administration announced that it would begin repatriating Cubans picked up at sea, we wrote a letter to Attorney General Janet Reno and Immigration and Naturalization Service Commissioner Doris Meisner expressing concern over objectionable aspects of the new policy, most of which were later revised. We also wrote a letter urging the administration to lift its ban on permanent news bureaus in Cuba, an action finally taken in October.

EL SALVADOR

Human Rights Developments

Human rights violations in 1995 did not take place on the massive scale to which human rights monitors had become accustomed prior to the signing of the 1992 peace accord. Nonetheless, several troubling developments did take place during the year, including vigilante killings and police-related abuses. As yet, it is too early to know if promising reforms in the police will resolve these problems or if the diminishing presence of the United Nations will adversely affect the human rights situation.

Since presidential elections in 1994, which brought the Nationalist Republican Alliance (Alianza Republicana Nacionalista, ARENA) to a second five-year term, the United Nations has increasingly withdrawn from El Salvador after playing a key role in bringing the peace process to fruition, monitoring human rights abuses, and restructuring the country's abusive security forces. Scheduled to withdraw in April 1996, the U.N. mission, known as MINUSAL since May, reduced its staff to only a dozen by mid-1995. MINUSAL was responsible for monitoring unfinished commitments in the peace accords, especially land transfers and public security issues. As the mission wound down, so too did its influence and ability to monitor closely issues related to human rights. Regional offices were closed in early 1995, and the human rights division as such ceased to exist at the end of March.

The formation of a professional, apolitical police force was generally seen as the most transcendent potential contribution of the historic 1992 peace accords, which ended the twelve-year civil war. The most disturbing indication of setbacks in the establishment of this new force, the National Civilian Police (PNC), came with the news in March of the involvement of a PNC agent in the 1993 assassination of FMLN leader Francisco Velis, leader of the Farabundo Martí National Liberation Front (Frente Farabundo Martí para la Liberación Nacional, FMLN). The suspect, Carlos Romero Alfaro, had been a former National Police (PN) investigator working within the Criminal Investigations Division of the PNC at the time of the October 1993 assassination. The attorney general's office showed reluctance in pursuing Alfaro, who fled El Salvador. The whereabouts of Alfaro remained unknown until mid-September, when he was arrested on an immigration violation in Houston, Texas, where he awaits extradition to El Salvador.

The new force, which struggled in 1995 to establish itself as the autonomous and professional police service it was intended to be, found itself at a crossroads: either it would begin to terminate the impunity that long characterized El Salvador's administration of justice or it would come to resemble the abusive security forces it sought to replace. Given the important role played by the United Nations on human rights issues, Human Rights Watch/Americas ended the year concerned about the extent to which positive development in the PNC would continue with a diminishing U.N. presence. The United Nations Observer Mission in El Salvador (ONUSAL, as the U.N. mission was called between July 1991 and May 1995)

played an important role in the Alfaro case by pressuring authorities to move forward. The case showed the continuing importance in El Salvador of the U.N. mission, but it also highlighted ongoing concern about the extent to which former members of the pre-1992 security forces exercised authority in the PNC. The U.N. also played an important role in dismantling the Anti-Delinquency Battalion, which was made up of former National Police agents.

At mid-year, the ARENA government signed a political pact, known as the Pact of San Andrés, with the Democratic Party. The government committed itself to increase the size of the PNC from its current 8,000 to 20,000 by the end of 1996. But there was growing concern that the ARENA government has yet to address a number of serious problems with the PNC. In late September, at the request of President Armando Calderón Sol, MINUSAL presented the government with a detailed critique of the PNC. According to press reports, the report urged that the government remove greater numbers of former PN members from new force.

Problems remaining in the PNC included excessive use of force and the preponderance, since July, of former PN officers in key positions. Anti-riot units of the PNC used excessive force in a number of cases involving labor protesters or demobilized soldiers, while in other cases they exercised admirable restraint. In one particularly grievous example in March, the PNC dispersed a demonstration of wounded war veterans with tear gas and rubber bullets, wounding sixteen protesters and briefly arresting 200. Although the PNC was to be composed primarily of civilians, by year's end, most of the key leadership posts at the PNC were held by former PN officers. Internal systems to account for abuses by PNC officers were lacking; for much of 1995, the post of inspector general remained empty. In addition, MINUSAL found that the internal disciplinary unit, while sanctioning police misconduct such as drunkenness and violation of internal police regulations, rarely penalized PNC abuses committed against civilians.

The continuing crime wave, which the PNC was unable to stem, drew significant public attention to the PNC's problems in 1995. The response of the Calderón Sol government to rampant crime raised human rights concerns; the government involved the military in rural patrols in an operation called "Plan Guardián." While these patrols were ostensibly mixed army-PNC efforts under PNC direction, in practice they tended to be run primarily by the armed forces. Public security officials cited a decrease in criminal activity as a result of these patrols, while critics charged that crime simply moved from one area to another. Given the army's lack of training for internal policing, Human Rights Watch/Americas was concerned that Plan Guardián could lead to increased human rights violations. In the second half of the year, there was also discussion of extending the joint military-PNC patrols under Plan Guardián to urban areas.

Another alarming response to the crime wave was the emergence of clandestine vigilante groups, whose stated aim was to "cleanse" society of criminals. The Black Shadow (Sombra Negra), a vigilante group operating in San Miguel, issued public death threats against several judges, saying they should resign to help weed corruption out of the judicial system. The Black Shadow, which is thought to be made up of some forty members, has claimed responsibility for several dozen murders, mostly in the eastern part of the country.

In July, the Organized Crime Unit of the PNC rounded up sixteen alleged members of Black Shadow, including four members of the PNC. Uncovering PNC collusion with vigilante operations ratified, in a startling way, the findings of the report issued in 1994 by the Grupo Conjunto, the working group established to investigate death squad killings. That report found that illegal armed groups continued to exist and were "directed, supported, covered-up or tolerated by members of the military and police institutions, and the judicial and municipal organs." Furthermore, while the fact that the PNC was willing to capture some of its own members (including the head of the San Miguel PNC delegation) was positive, the Black Shadow prosecution made little progress in the ensuing months. Meanwhile, the PNC agent who testified to her fellow officers' involvement was demoted, and high-level PNC officials tried to discredit her testimony.

Several municipalities, particularly those in San Salvador and its environs, moved to strengthen their municipal police structures. While theoretically limited to administrative detentions, the municipal police were identified as responsible for serious human rights abuses; furthermore, the existence of these municipal police undercut the constitutional provision that the PNC be the only body to carry out public-security functions.

Perhaps the most encouraging development in the overall human rights situation in 1995 was the March election for a three-year term of an active, articulate human rights ombudsman, Victoria Marina de Avilés. Avilés took public positions on many important human rights issues. She criticized police excesses in handling demonstrations, unequivocally opposed the death penalty, and challenged the nomination of an unsuitable candidate for PNC inspector general. The ombudsman's office still required a number of internal reforms to improve its effectiveness.

In addition, the Legislative Assembly discussed constitutional and secondary law reforms that had been recommended by the United Nations Truth Commission for El Salvador and ONUSAL's human rights division. If approved, these reforms would, among other things, invalidate extrajudicial confessions, strengthen the right to defense and the presumption of innocence, reduce the maximum period for administrative detentions from fifteen to five days, and classify torture and enforced disappearances as crimes. The legislature also recognized the jurisdiction of the Inter-American Court of Human Rights and ratified the Optional Protocol to the International Covenant on Civil and Political Rights, the Iner-American Convention on the Prevention, Punishment, and Eradication of Violence Against Women (known as the Convention of Belém do Pará), and the Additional Protocol to the American Covenant on Human Rights in the Area of Economic, Social, and Cultural Rights (known as the Protocol of San Salvador).

The Right to Monitor

The consolidation of regional offices of the human rights ombudsman in each of El Salvador's fourteen departments by early 1995 was an important benchmark in promoting the right to monitor in El Salvador. The ombudsman's office initiated better coordination with nongovernmental human rights organizations, and began to employ directly many former members of these organizations. However, the ARENA government sought to discredit the new human rights ombudsman, both in officials' public remarks and in the government's news bulletins. This campaign began shortly after Avilés refused to endorse the nomination of the public security minister's legal adviser for the post of inspector general.

To our knowledge, the only incident involving a direct threat to human rights workers occurred on October 4, when two armed men forced themselves into the offices of the Human Rights Institute of the Central American University (Universidad Centroamericana, UCA), tying up the institute's director and another worker. The apparent motive was robbery, but one intruder remarked on the institute's attitudes toward the ruling ARENA party. One suspect was caught, and the case was under investigation.

U.S. Policy

U.S. assistance continued to decline in 1995, although $27 million provided in 1992 to bolster the peace process was still being spent during the year. The U.S. continued to provide support to the National Civilian Police (PNC) and the judicial system. But U.S. officials maintained a very low profile in public, rarely making any statements on human rights or any other issues. While supportive of the U.N.'s leadership on issues of compliance with the peace accords, the U.S. did not take the initiative to head off problems with the PNC such as excessive dependence on former National Police (PN) personnel. The United States was one of two international donors to the country's new Public Security Academy, which trains PNC officers, and to the anti-drug and criminal investigations units of the police. In addition, the United States maintained throughout 1995 a trainer's office in the PNC building.

The Work of
Human Rights Watch/Americas

Human Rights Watch/Americas continued to monitor developments in El Salvador, watching in particular the development of a new civilian police force to replace the former National Police, which committed systematic human rights violations in the past. Also of continuing concern was the persistence of death squads. In July, we wrote to President Calderón Sol expressing concern about a raid on the office of FUNDASIDA, the only nongovernmental AIDS-awareness organization in El Salvador.

GUATEMALA

Human Rights Developments

The human rights situation remained deeply troubling in Guatemala in 1995, despite the deployment since November 1994 of a United Nations verification mission dedicated exclusively to human rights. The team of nearly 200 observers in thirteen offices across the country conducted a more comprehensive study of the human rights situation than had been possible in the past and helped pinpoint the sources of violations. Moreover, the U.N.'s presence most likely had a dissuasive impact on human rights violations and provided some protection for the beleaguered domestic human rights community. Nonetheless, Guatemalan security forces and their agents continued to commit egregious human rights violations with impunity. On October 5, soldiers massacred a group of refugees who had returned from Mexico in a village in the department of Alta Verapaz, killing eleven (including two children) and seriously wounding more than thirty.

The reports produced by MINUGUA, as the U.N. mission was known, highlighted numerous cases of torture, extrajudicial execution, and disappearances by the security forces, as well as official links to organized crime and "social cleansing" operations. The victims included students and teachers, trade unionists, human rights workers, peasant activists, individuals resisting participation in army-organized civil patrols, and common criminals.

The government adopted a two-pronged approach to MINUGUA's presence: maintaining a considerable openness in public at the same time that members of the military or its agents sought to undermine MINUGUA's work behind the scenes, without suffering any sanction for this obstruction.

Two positive steps in 1995 were the naming of a respected attorney as interior minister and the removal of a high-ranking military official who served as vice-minister. In addition, the announcement by President Ramiro de León Carpio that the function of military commissioners—civilians employed by the army, responsible for many human rights violations—would be abolished, was a welcome step, although its impact was not immediately clear.

As had been the case in prior years, the government of Guatemala failed to investigate or punish those responsible for human rights violations. Under such conditions, human rights violators felt no compunction about their behavior. Indeed, while the de León Carpio government consistently failed to bring to justice those responsible for human rights violations, a sort of underground system regularly meted out retaliation against those who pursued justice through the courts. Not only were witnesses, plaintiffs, and relatives of victims of human rights violations

targeted for violence and intimidation, but prosecutors, judges, and police who attempted to bring violators to justice also suffered reprisals.

With rare exceptions, the team of prosecutors headed by Attorney General (*fiscal general*) Ramsés Cuestas Gómez was notorious for its negligence, ineffectiveness, and infiltration by the security forces. However, blame for the failure to prosecute human rights violations lay not entirely at the attorney general's feet. Cuestas's weakness and lack of leadership simply opened the door for the military to infiltrate and intimidate the institution charged with perhaps the country's most sensitive task: investigating crimes.

Failures of omission included lack of investigation and prosecution of the steady stream of well documented cases MINUGUA provided the government. More direct obstruction was evident as well. In the months preceding MINUGUA's full deployment in late 1994, and to some extent in 1995, the army and its civilian auxiliaries—the civil patrols and military commissioners—in several rural departments spread disinformation about the mission's presence.

Perhaps the most serious attack on MINUGUA occurred on June 28, when a local civil patrol chief in the Ixcán village of San Antonio Tzejá took hostage five international humanitarian workers, including two MINUGUA observers, for twenty-six hours. Although a warrant had been outstanding for the arrest of the patroller, Raúl Martínez Pérez, since May, as of this writing the authorities had made no effort to detain him.

A MINUGUA military officer came under direct attack by the guerrillas of the Guatemalan National Revolutionary Union (Unión Revolucionaria Nacional Guatemalteca, URNG) on March 27 in the Ixcán. Guerrillas fired on the MINUGUA military liaison officer as he inspected a URNG poster after talking to a group of peasants. The officer was wearing a uniform displaying the United Nations emblem and driving a marked U.N. vehicle. Although the officer was not hit, one of the vehicle's tires was.

In addition to firing on the MINUGUA observer, the guerrillas continued to commit violations of international standards applicable to internal armed conflicts, with "war taxes" and attacks in which care was not taken to minimize danger to civilians. The demand for payment of war taxes usually was accompanied by the direct or implicit threat of violence against civilian property owners, prohibited by the laws of war. On March 28, according to MINUGUA, a guerrilla projectile aimed at a military base at Raxrujá, Alta Verapaz, killed fifteen-year-old Ofelia de la Cruz García as she walked on an adjacent road. In addition, several civilians died after stepping on mines apparently laid by the URNG during 1995.

MINUGUA argued that the sabotage of internal infrastructure such as electric pylons by the guerrillas violated the rules of proportionality derived from principles of international humanitarian law. On January 23, MINUGUA won agreement from URNG leaders in Mexico to desist from this type of attacks. The URNG had lived up to this pledge as of late 1995.

MINUGUA also found cases of participation of minors under age fifteen in the army and in guerrilla units, as well as in the army-organized civil patrols, in violation of the Convention on the Rights of the Child, ratified by Guatemala in 1990.

After the October 5 army massacre of eleven returning refugees, President de León Carpio obtained the resignation of Defense Minister Mario Enríquez Morales, and the Cobán military commander responsible for the patrol. He also named a special investigative commission, and stated that those responsible for the killings would be punished. The soldiers involved in the incident were remanded to a military tribunal in Jalapa, where they have been charged with homicide and inflicting injuries. Guatemalan refugees in Mexico suspended indefinitely the repatriations of roughly 2,000 people which were planned for the following months. The office of the United Nations High Commissioner for Refugees (UNHCR) denounced the massacre as a violation of the "principles that inspire the return process and the fundamental instruments that govern it." This marked the largest army massacre of civilians since the December 1990 slaying of thirteen villagers of Santiago Atitlán who had gathered outside a stockade to protest army violence.

Several trade unionists suffered threats and attacks, including incidents of kidnapings related to their organizing activities. Debora Guzmán Chupén, an organizer in a maquiladora (garment assembly plant) in Amatitlán and the wife of union activist Felix González, was kidnaped on February 28 by heavily armed men who drugged her, beat her, and threatened to kill her. Her captors forced her to telephone the office of the Guatemalan Workers' Federation (UNSITRAGUA), and warn that she would be killed unless her husband left the union affiliated to the Lunafil thread plant. Guzmán and her colleagues at the maquiladora MJ Modas had also received death threats before her kidnaping.

Alexander Yovani Gómez Virula, the treasurer of the RCA maquiladora, was kidnaped on March 13. His body was found in a ravine on March 19, evidently beaten to death.

Violence and the threat of violence continued to stalk members of the news media, especially those covering human rights issues. On February 13, men driving a pickup truck that was later determined to belong to a military officer followed and threatened José Rubén Zamora Marroquín, director of the daily *Siglo Veintiuno.*

Other journalists—including North American film producer Sky Callahan and Guatemalan reporter Gerson López—were briefly abducted, threatened, and beaten by armed men apparently linked to the security forces.

Street children continued to suffer abuse at the hands of police and private security forces. On June 23, 1995, a group of street children were gathered on a Guatemala City street when two of the youths attempted to rob a pedestrian. A plainclothesman who identified himself as a member of the police Criminal Investigations Directorate (Dirección de Investigaciones Criminológicas, DIC) fired shots into the air and then shot Edwin Americo Orantes, seventeen, in the face and eighteen-year-old Nicolás Cruz in the ankle. The gunman reportedly shot and killed Americo as he lay on the ground, saying, "All the thieves on 18th Street will end up like this."

MINUGUA's reports described several cases in which the security forces tortured detainees. In one case in November 1994 in which the victim's name was withheld by MINUGUA, soldiers picked up a man whom they accused of being a guerrilla. They denied having detained the individual for several days, until MINUGUA contacted the armed forces general staff. During his interrogation, soldiers placed a plastic bag over the victim's head to suffocate him, inserted a spike into his palate, beat him on the soles of his feet, and removed a gold crown from one of his teeth with a knife.

Cases in which there was considerable publicity provoked some movement. Unfortunately, as the case of "disappeared" guerrilla combatant Efraín Bámaca Velásquez showed, each positive step taken in these high publicity cases was accompanied by obstruction. Bámaca disappeared after a firefight with the army in the department of Retalhuleu on March 12, 1992. The government for years maintained that Bámaca had shot himself to avoid capture and was buried in the general cemetery in the departmental capital, but an exhumation failed to locate him. After the third hunger strike by Jennifer Harbury, Bámaca's North American wife, a U.S. lawmaker revealed that her husband had indeed been secretly detained, tortured, and extrajudicially executed by the army, with the direct participation of an informant in the pay of the Central Intelligence Agency, Col. Julio Roberto Alpírez.

This news breathed new life into the investigation. In May, Julio Arango Escobar launched a vigorous investigation after being named special prosecutor for the case. A military specialist, Nery Urízar García, testi-fied that he saw Bámica, chained to a bed, being interrogated at an army base. Shortly after Urízar testified, the U.S. Embassy received a tip that Bámaca might be buried in a military base in San Marcos called Las Cabañas, information which the State Department passed on to Harbury. The army blocked a court-ordered exhumation, however.

Army officers or government officials sought repeatedly to challenge MINUGUA's right to follow the case, despite language in the human rights accord establishing the mission which gives it authority to verify due process violations and accompany government officials investigating human rights cases.

Shortly after being named special prosecutor in the Bámaca case, Arango, who pursued the case with integrity and courage, began to receive threatening phone calls and to be followed. On June 22, while Arango worked at his desk on the sixth floor of the Public Ministry, a shot fired through a window lodged in the fifth floor ceiling below his desk. In early July, Arango resigned from the case, which was paralyzed thereafter.

The judicial process for the 1993 slaying of Jorge Carpio Nicolle, the president's first cousin, and three of his traveling companions was also punctuated by repeated threats and harassment of the victims' relatives and the special prosecutor, Abraham Méndez. In addition to threats and surveillance, Méndez suffered an assassination attempt on a highway in November 1994. Like Arango in the Bámaca case, Méndez had worked hard to bring the perpetrators of the crime to justice.

Torpor and fear marked the judicial investigation into the possible participation of senior military officers in the September 1991 extrajudicial execution of anthropologist Myrna Mack, in the hands of a military court. While tremendous pressure brought the conviction in 1993 of army Sgt. Noel de Jesús Beteta for murder, the Public Ministry and the courts failed to proceed against the intellectual authors of the crime, in what

MINUGUA called "a denial of the right to justice."

Armed civil patrollers violently obstructed the return of Guatemalan refugees from Mexico to villages in the Zona Reina del Ixcán, Quiché province, endangering the safety of repatriating refugees. A regional association called ARAP-KSI, composed mainly of civil patrollers headed by local strongman Raúl Martínez Pérez, physically obstructed access to Zona Reina villages, using death threats, assaults, and hostage-taking to intimidate Guatemalans and international officials involved in the repatriations.

Following an accord signed with the Guatemalan government, roughly 300 refugees crossed the border in April to return to the Zona Reina. On May 7, Martínez and ARAP-KSI detained, in Kaibil Balam, an International Organization for Migration employee, a government official, and an army major. They freed the detainees unharmed on May 9 when the defense minister personally intervened and, contradicting previous accords, publicly acceded to their demands for permanent land titles and a halt to refugee returns to the area. Nonetheless, on June 27, the returnees who had been sheltered by the church in Cantabal walked for two days to their village, San Antonio Tzejá. Just outside the village, ARAP-KSI members forced them to halt. The following day, ARAP-KSI members led by Martínez seized as hostages two MINUGUA observers, a UNHCR official, a representative of the World Council of Churches, and a nurse with Doctors of the World. An army colonel present in San Antonio Tzejá throughout the incident refused to report the detentions by radio, in violation of the government's commitments to cooperate in guaranteeing the security of U.N. mission members. Following the incident, government-led negotiations with the perpetrators and returnees led to the latter group's resettlement on lands south of San Antonio.

Although a judge issued an arrest warrant against Martínez on May 25 after the first hostage incident, the authorities failed to apprehend him. And while the police and local military commander told Human Rights Watch/Americas they could not locate Martínez, our researcher had no difficulty finding and interviewing Martínez at his home in early August. On August 29, the judge issued seven additional warrants for patrollers and others involved in the hostage incident; these warrants were also ignored.

Ongoing insecurity from the simmering armed conflict in Chiapas, Mexico, made it an increasingly inhospitable place for Guatemalan refugees. Organized repatriations to other areas in Guatemala proceeded slowly, mostly due to the laborious and often contentious process of securing lands and credits. Guatemala's National Commission for Attention to Repatriates, Refugees and Displaced (CEAR) reported that 6,256 refugees had repatriated from Mexico during the first half of 1995.

The Right to Monitor

On June 23, 1995, Manuel Saquic Vásquez, Presbyterian pastor and coordinator of the Human Rights Office of the Kakchiquel Presbytery, disappeared. His corpse, exhumed and identified on July 7, was partially decapitated and had thirty-three stab wounds. After the murder, repeated threats against Saquic's widow forced her to flee her home.

Three days after the exhumation, a death threat signed by the "Avenging Jaguar" (Jaguar Justiciero, a name believed to be used by members of the security forces to sow terror) was delivered to the Human Rights Committee of Panabajal, a village in Chimaltenango. The threat referred to Saquic's murder as the first of twenty-four on a "black list" that included Vitalino Similox, general secretary of the Conference of Evangelical Churches of Guatemala (CIEDEG); Blanca Margarita Valiente de Similox, his wife and president of the Kakchiquel Presbytery in Chimaltenango; Sotero Similox, his father; and Lucio Martínez of the Human Rights Office of the Kakchiquel Presbytery. A second, similar threat was delivered to the Kakchiquel Presbytery a month later. On August 7, a Chimaltenango judge issued a warrant for the arrest of military commissioner Víctor Román Cutzal for the Saquic murder, but as of this writing, the Guatemalan police had not arrested him. Saquic's murder and the subsequent death threats appeared to have been a reprisal for efforts to bring Román to justice for the August 1, 1994 murder of Pascal Serech of the Panabajal Human Rights Committee.

Other human rights monitors faced threats and harassment, and the government failed to investigate these threats. In January, a member of the security forces warned Amílcar Méndez Urízar, until recently the leader of the Council of Ethnic Communities Runujel Junam (CERJ), that a plot to kill him was being organized by the head of military intelligence for the department of Quiché, where Méndez lives, and the Quiché head of the Treasury Police. In April, Méndez's teenage son, José Emanuel Méndez, was twice threatened with death by armed men in Guatemala City. CERJ is a rural, grassroots human rights movement formed in 1988; more than twenty members of CERJ had been the victims of disappearance or extrajudicial execution as of late 1995. In October, after Méndez joined the electoral campaign of the New Guatemalan Democratic Front, his home was ransacked by armed men.

On April 9, María de León Santiago, a member of the National Coordinating Committee of Guatemalan Widows (CONAVIGUA), was attacked at her home in the hamlet of Vitzal, in the municipality of Nebaj, Quiché, by unidentified individuals, who hit her with a rock and punched and kicked her. Santiago, who had been threatened and harassed previously for her membership in CONAVIGUA, was hospitalized for her injuries. Military commissioners threatened to burn down the house of CONAVIGUA member María M. Miranda in April, according to MINUGUA.

U.S. Policy

The Clinton administration's human rights policy toward Guatemala was driven by unprecedented public attention to the plight of U.S. citizen Jennifer Harbury, wife of disappeared guerrilla leader Efraín Bámaca. Harbury's struggle against the lies, intimidation, and extravagant coverup mounted by Guatemalan authorities brought to U.S. public attention a reality all too familiar to Guatemalans. In addition, her pressure for answers from the U.S. government prompted the unraveling of a series of revelations about the Central Intelligence Agency's secret assistance to abusive military institutions and officers in Guatemala. Indeed, the scandal revealed a secret policy that for many years had made all but irrelevant Washington's public postures on human rights in Guatemala.

Harbury pressed both the U.S. and Guatemalan governments to account for her husband's whereabouts as of late 1993. On March 10, 1995, days before Harbury was to begin her third hunger strike, this time in front of the White House, the Clinton administration announced a suspension of military training for Guatemalan officials. To explain the suspension, the State Department cited the lack of progress in five notorious human rights cases: the disappearance of Bámaca, the extrajudicial executions of Myrna Mack, Michael DeVine, Nicholas Blake and Griffin Davis, and the secret detention and torture of Dianna Ortiz—all U.S. citizens excepting Mack and Bámaca.

While U.S. officials had met with Harbury and discussed her case with Guatemalan officials, it later became clear they had not told her about information the U.S. government had about her husband's fate. Washington was shaken when, on March 22, Cong. Robert Torricelli wrote to President Clinton revealing that Bámaca had indeed been tortured and murdered by the Guatemalan army—with the apparent participation of an officer paid by the CIA. Torricelli's letter also alleged that the CIA informant, Col. Julio Roberto Alpírez, was involved in the June 1990 slaying of Michael DeVine, an American innkeeper in the department of the Petén, whose unresolved murder provoked the Bush administration to cut off military aid and arms sales to Guatemala in December 1990.

A Defense Department document declassified in response to a Freedom of Information Act request by Harbury revealed that as early as September 1993, U.S. sources knew Bámaca had been killed in secret army detention. But Harbury was told nothing of the sort until Torricelli's revelations in March 1995, nineteen months and two hunger strikes later.

In the ensuing cascade of revelations, it became clear the agency had secretly provided millions of dollars in assistance to Guatemala's notoriously violent military intelligence unit even after the Bush administration cut off overt military aid and sales. Clinton ordered most of the spy agency's assistance to the Guatemalan military—with the exception of anti-narcotics funding—suspended in the wake of the scandal.

The career of Alpírez, the Guatemalan colonel implicated in both the Bámaca and DeVine cases, showed how closely the United States had embraced the most abusive elements of the Guatemalan army. Alpírez twice attended the School of the Americas at Fort Benning, Georgia, with a curriculum including human rights training. In the late 1980s, the CIA reportedly recruited him while he was working at the notorious intelligence unit "Archivos," a presidential agency which for decades has exerted central control over political repression. The CIA did not cease payments to Alpírez even when he became implicated in the 1990 murder of U.S. citizen DeVine and the subsequent coverup. Indeed, sometime in 1992, when Alpírez was again implicated in an extrajudicial execution—this time of Efraín Bámaca—the CIA rushed to pay him $44,000 upon severing the relationship.

The scandal prompted President Clinton to order an executive branch probe by the never-before convened Intelligence Oversight Board, whose study was due by the end of 1995. The CIA inspector general produced a report of more than 700 pages on the issue, of which a four-page summary was made public on July 26. The summary suggested the report was a whitewash, concluding: "No evidence has been found that any employee of the Central Intelligence Agency in any way directed, participated in, or condoned the murder of Michael DeVine." Perhaps Alpírez, an agency informant in the field, was not considered "an employee."

Nonetheless, the new CIA director, John Deutch, announced on September 29 unprecedented sanctions against eleven CIA officials, including firing the chief of the Latin American Division of the Directorate of Operations, for their role in the affair. Deutch stressed that the Guatemala scandal required greater "management control" of assets in the field and keeping congressional oversight committees informed. Deutch's actions were important, but insufficient to ensure that the agency would not again become complicit in human rights violations. Human Rights Watch presented specific reform proposals to President Clinton and the congressional intelligence committees.

A group of U.S. lawmakers requested that the Clinton administration declassify government documents regarding dozens of the most notorious human rights violations over the past twenty years. The administration had not yet announced a decision as of this writing. A thorough and timely declassification would be extremely helpful to many victims' relatives, who—against incredible odds—have persisted in seeking to prosecute those responsible for human rights violations. Moreover, it would greatly facilitate the work of the planned Historical Clarification Commission, which was foreseen in the peace negotiations as a means to establish the truth about human rights abuses during the thirty-four-year armed conflict, once a final peace agreement is signed.

U.S. military aid to Guatemala remained suspended in 1995 and was not requested for fiscal 1996. Several million dollars in military aid which had been appropriated for Guatemala before the 1990 cut-off was channeled into a peace fund to support the work of MINUGUA and the peace process.

In October, Congress approved an amendment to the Foreign Aid Appropriations bill for fiscal 1996 which would cut off all security assistance—including police training and anti-narcotics support—pending progress in the prosecution of several dozen notorious cases. At this writing, the bill had not yet become law.

The chapter of the Department of State *Country Reports on Human Rights Practices for 1994* on human rights conditions in Guatemala was overall an accurate portrayal of the discouraging situation. In addition, the U.S. Embassy remained extremely receptive and open to both domestic and international human rights monitors.

The Work of
Human Rights Watch/Americas

Our work in 1995 focused on establishing accountability for human rights violations in Guatemala, an agenda we addressed at the U.N., through U.S. policy, and through legal activism. In late 1994 and early 1995, we successfully campaigned for the renewal of the mandate of the U.N. Independent Expert for Guatemala, whose public reports on the human rights situation provided an important source of pressure for reform. In March, we published a report on the denial of justice in the Bámaca case.

We worked both in Washington and in Guatemala to preempt an amnesty for gross violations of human rights in Guatemala. In Washington we pressed the Clinton administration to take a clear position against such a sweeping amnesty and in August, we co-sponsored an international conference on amnesties in Guatemala City with the Myrna Mack Foundation.

At this writing, we had undertaken litigation in nearly a dozen cases of human rights violations in Guatemala through the inter-American system of human rights protection. One of these cases, regarding the disappearance, torture, and extrajudicial execution of several students in 1988 by treasury police agents, became in 1995 the first case against Guatemala referred to the Inter-American Court of Human Rights for trial. Two other cases we presented—the extrajudicial executions of Jorge Carpio Nicolle and companions and of a human

rights monitor in Colotenango—prompted the court to issue injunctions calling on the Guatemalan government to protect the lives of witnesses who have been threatened. The Carpio injunction, in which we sought protective measures for the government's own prosecutor, Abraham Méndez, marked the first time the Inter-American Court had ordered a government to protect one of its own officials.

HAITI

Human Rights Developments

Human rights conditions in Haiti improved markedly in 1995, due in large part to the presence of over 6,000 international peacekeepers. The significant progress was not fully consolidated at year's end however, and the imminent departure of international forces in early 1996 loomed as a critical juncture.

After three years of repression, 1995 marked the reemergence of Haitian civil society. Popular and political organizations reorganized and rediscovered their rights to freedom of expression and association. Street demonstrations against the prime minister and even the president proceeded without incident. Freed from the threat of violence, the media ended self-censorship. From October 1994 to October 1995, only some 1,000 Haitians sought refuge outside their country.

The restored Haitian government and international forces in Haiti, particularly those provided by the U.S. government, undertook the dramatic reshaping of Haiti's security forces. The Haitian government largely dismantled the military and dismissed the despised section chiefs (*chefs de sections*) who had exercised near-total control in rural areas and small towns during the period of military rule. Parasitic paramilitary structures that were responsible for severe human rights abuses—including the Front for the Advancement and Progress of Haiti (Front pour l'Avancement et le Progrès Haïtien,

FRAPH), a particularly violent organization—were not formally dismantled or disarmed but were weakened by the military's demise.

In December 1994, the Haitian government passed a law mandating the creation of a new police force, the Haitian National Police, that would gradually displace the recycled soldiers serving as interim police. Approximately 5,000 new police were scheduled to be deployed by February 1996, in time for the planned withdrawal of U.N. peacekeeping forces.

The U.S. Justice Department's International Criminal Investigations and Training Assistance Program (ICITAP) ran every stage of the selection, classroom training, and on-the-job training of the Haitian National Police. The ICITAP-led recruitment relied on a rigorous examination but did not fully explore human rights concerns. New police officers were involved in a handful of shooting incidents that involved the use of excessive force. In September, the Haitian government suspended two new officers implicated in the use of excessive force but did not initiate prosecutions against them.

Over 3,000 former Haitian soldiers remained on the streets in 1995 as members of the interim police force after a superficial human rights screening. Public recognition of their military past made the force unpopular in many areas. The force also included approximately 900 former Haitian refugees recruited at the U.S. naval base in Guantánamo. In several towns, the cowed interim police refused to patrol. Where they did play an active role, some interim police were implicated in incidents of unnecessarily using deadly force in apprehending suspects. Although several members of the force were disciplined and removed for these incidents, the results of internal investigations were rarely made public. As of this writing none of those disciplined were being prosecuted for criminal violations. The interim police were demobilized in stages as each group of new police was deployed.

The structural shift from an autonomous, abusive military to a police force

answerable to civilian authority was a positive development. The initial efforts of the police inspector general's office and the adoption of a police code of conduct were also encouraging steps. Nonetheless, greater attention to human rights concerns in the selection of recruits and leaders, and in the training and deployment of the new police, would have improved the performance of the new force and diminished the risk of its committing abuses in the future.

While state-sponsored human rights violations declined following the demise of the military government, there was an increase in common crime. Some of this was linked to former Haitian soldiers. A disturbing pattern of vigilante killings also emerged in which large crowds often violently attacked suspected collaboraters with the military or suspected criminals. Beating and stoning deaths, which local leaders attributed to a perception that the justice system was not working, reached a high of forty-five in March. The government publicly condemned such killings, but it rarely took legal action against those responsible for vigilante violence. President Aristide made no major public intervention to denounce vigilante actions. In a eulogy for a slain congressman on November 11, the president encouraged civilians to take the law into their own hands by "ordering" them to accompany the Haitian police in disarmament efforts. Despite the president's admonishment to act within the law, this invitation for active civilian participation in police functions contributed to eruptions of violence in several cities and a number of deaths. As of mid-November, Prime Minister Claudette Werleigh had clarified that the only appropriate civilian assistance to police disarmament efforts was in providing information, but President Aristide had not retracted his earlier statement.

From February to November 1995, over twenty people were killed "execution-style" in murders committed with heavy weaponry where robbery did not appear to be the primary motive. The victims included a recently elected congressman, former soldiers, officers, members of paramilitary groups, businessmen, an attorney, and gas station owners and employees. Specific allegations of the involvement of agents of the Aristide government emerged in regard to one case, the slaying of anti-Aristide activist Mireille Durocher Bertin and pilot Eugene "Junior" Baillergeau, who were killed in March. As of mid-November 1995, neither the Haitian government nor the F.B.I. team assigned to the case had produced further evidence to confirm any state involvement. The Ministry of Justice formed a special investigation unit in October to probe all of these cases.

In December 1994, the Haitian government announced the formation of a National Commission for Truth and Justice (Commission Nationale de Vérité et Justice), presided by Haitian sociologist Françoise Boucard. The government later named three Haitian and three foreign commissioners to serve with Boucard. The commission's mandate directed it to document the most serious human rights violations committed under military rule, paying special attention to "crimes against humanity" and "aggressions of a sexual nature" against women, and to prepare a public report of its findings together with recommendations to the Haitian government. While not empowered to initiate prosecutions, Boucard announced in September that the commission's report would identify perpetrators by name where there was sufficient evidence to do so. The commission initially was plagued by insufficient means and disorganization, and investigators did not begin field investigations on rights abuses until July. Boucard maintained, however, that the commission would finalize its report in December.

The Haitian Ministry of Justice, with the assistance of a team of foreign lawyers, investigated some of the most notorious extrajudicial executions of the military period. Seven men closely linked to the military government and a member of a paramilitary group were found guilty in absentia in one such case—the murder of Aristide supporter Antoine Izméry—and a soldier received a sentence of life at hard labor for another infamous killing.

The Haitian government also successfully carried out prosecutions in several less well known cases of abuses committed under military rule. However, some judges refused to investigate and prosecute reputed members of the paramilitary—the infamous *attachés*—and former members of the Haitian military, fearing retribution after the departure of international forces in February 1996. As of early October 1995, no member of Haiti's armed forces had been successfully prosecuted and sent to prison for human rights abuses, thereby continuing a legacy of impunity.

The Haitian government, with international support, initiated justice, prison, and electoral reforms in 1995, but these efforts lagged behind police reform. Prison reform began with several concrete steps, such as creating a new civilian prison authority and raising the salaries of prison guards. International efforts played a dramatic role, particularly in the registration of detainees, providing materials for physical repairs, and feeding prisoners. While the participation of some minimally screened former soldiers in the new prison authority was troubling, prison conditions improved significantly. The Haitian government closed unofficial detention centers, and the new prison authority instituted some critical reforms, including the separation of women and children from adult males at the National Penitentiary in Port-au-Prince.

The rampant abuse of prisoners that existed under the military government and for the first months after the September 1994 multinational intervention diminished dramatically in 1995. Cruel and inhuman treatment of detainees became the exception rather than the rule. Nevertheless, prisoners rioted in the National Penitentiary in February and April 1995, partly because many did not know why they had been arrested. Judges compounded prison overcrowding by continuing to sentence debtors to prison despite the clear prohibition on imprisonment for debt in international law that is binding on

Haiti. Several minors were reportedly beaten while in detention in June, and the failure to segregate adults from minors and convicts from pre-trial detainees persisted in provincial prisons. During a transfer of prisoners in early May, some interim police officers reportedly kicked and beat detainees with rifle butts while they were handcuffed. The same officer the detainees accused of ordering their mistreatment was later named to head the Fort National prison for women and minors.

One of the government's initial steps in addressing problems with the judicial system was to replace some judges and prosecutors that were named by the illegal military government with Aristide's 1991 appointees. In addition, the minister of justice increased court officials' wages, and copies of the basic Haitian legal texts and office materials were distributed to some courthouses. While the Haitian government took some concrete steps to improve the judicial system, in many districts the courts denied detainees full legal protection. Judicial officials ordered some arrests of questionable legality, including several based on warrants lacking details of specific acts, dates, or places. The Haitian legal system's reliance on public denunciations (*la clameur publique*) substituted for criminal investigations or rigorous proof. The extremely limited calendar for criminal trials virtually ensured lengthy pre-trial incarceration of anyone charged with a violent crime.

Following Aristide's return, the Haitian government created a new electoral law and named a Provisional Electoral Council (CEP). The June 1995 electoral period was marred by several cases of violence directed against CEP staff members or political party supporters. On voting day, national and international security forces cooperated to maintain a relatively peaceful climate. Nonetheless, in some areas ballots were destroyed and voting places and electoral offices were attacked, causing the CEP to cancel and then reschedule the vote. Haitian poll watchers representing political parties turned out in impressive numbers as did international observers.

Although press freedoms were extensive, Information Minister Henry Claude Ménard seized 1,500 copies of the government newspaper *L'Union* in July following the publication of a story criticizing the government's "abandonment" of the newspaper.

The Right to Monitor

Human Rights Watch/Americas was not aware of any Haitian government interference in the work of human rights monitors.

The Role of
the International Community

The international community's support for Haiti was largely responsible for the decrease in human rights violations in 1995. That support came in part through the deployment of the U.S.-led multinational force that arrived in September 1994, and in part through the presence of over 6,000 United Nations Mission in Haiti (UNMIH) peacekeepers and over 800 U.N. Civilian Police monitors (CivPol). Significant international assistance was critical to judicial and prison reform and the running of elections.

The United Nations and the
Organisation of American States

UNMIH's presence in Haiti contributed to an environment of relative security, where individual freedoms began to flourish. While UNMIH's mandate prohibited its troops or CivPol from taking an active part in law enforcement, they repeatedly filled that role, either by accompanying Haitian security forces or patrolling individually. The CivPol served a particularly important function by acting as role models and on-the-job trainers for Haiti's new police. The United Nations forces were scheduled to remain in Haiti until late February 1996, with a small U.N. police operation possibly taking their place.

The U.N. and OAS continued to support the International Civilian Mission in Haiti (Mission Civile Internationale en Haïti OEA/ONU, MICIVIH), an international human rights monitoring team that had 190 observers as of October. MICIVIH was present in Haiti for two periods under military rule and returned in late 1994. The MICIVIH's leadership and respected work in Haiti contributed to a continued focus on human rights issues. At the same time, the MICIVIH did not fully take advantage of its potential to publicly voice human rights concerns, preferring in most cases to work behind the scenes. The MICIVIH monitors conducted field research, provided expert assistance to the truth commission, and participated in some human rights education efforts. Although the MICIVIH's mandate was due to expire in February 1996, Human Rights Watch/Americas encouraged the extension of its mission further into 1996.

The OAS Election Monitoring unit posted a significant number of impartial observers throughout the country for all of the elections held in 1995 and provided thorough reporting on those elections.

The European Union

The European Union began to play a more significant role in Haiti, particularly with development assistance. It undertook special programs to address human rights and elections concerns, but was most active in the elections area, particularly with a grant to the CEP's Unit for Surveillance and Control and support for the OAS electoral observation team.

Dominican Republic

In 1995, the government of the Dominican Republic invoked a 1991 decree, calling for the expulsion of foreigners, to justify the detention and expulsion of approximately 1,000 Haitians, many of whom had obtained legal residency. The Dominican authorities reportedly exacted several days of forced labor from some Haitian detainees held at the Dajabon prison before expelling them to Haiti, and mistreated scores of others.

U.S. Policy

The Haiti entry of the Department of State *Country Reports on Human Rights Practices for 1994* presented a largely accurate portrayal of the violent political repression of Haitians by the Haitian military and its paramilitary counterparts in the period prior to the U.S.-led multinational intervention on September 19, 1994. As it had throughout the period of military rule, however, the State Department downplayed the magnitude of refugee flight from Haiti. Its report also failed to mention the military government's order to deter departures, drownings caused when the army fired on a departing vessel, and army beatings and extortion of refugees forcibly repatriated by the U.S. government. The report understated the relationship of FRAPH to the Haitian army and its organized mechanisms of repression, particularly the cooperation between FRAPH and the military in a pattern of highly destructive neighborhood searches in Port-au-Prince and other areas.

In late 1994 and 1995, the prominent U.S. involvement in Haiti overshadowed that of other countries or institutions. The U.S. presence included leadership of the multinational forces, significant involvement in UNMIH with almost 3,000 U.S. troops, and a prominent role in virtually every aspect of institutional reform, including the evolution of Haiti's new national police force and reforms of the Haitian judiciary and prison system.

U.S. leadership of these efforts contributed to the diminution of human rights abuses in Haiti. In some respects, however, the U.S. involvement in Haiti in 1995 paid insufficient attention to human rights concerns. The U.S. role in forming the interim police force, for example, utilized inadequate human rights screening of former Haitian soldiers for previous human rights abuses. After reneging on an earlier pledge, in September 1995, well after the truth commission was underway, the U.S. said it would contribute $50,000 to the commission's work, but as of late October had not delivered the funds.

Furthermore, the U.S. did not offer full cooperation with Haitian government efforts to prosecute those who committed abuses under the military government—former Haitian soldiers or members of

FRAPH—even where the U.S. reportedly possessed critical evidence. For example, the U.S. failed to provide Haitian prosecutors with evidence seized from U.S.-led raids of FRAPH headquarters in Port-au-Prince and Cap Haïtien in September and October 1994.

FRAPH leader Emmanuel "Toto" Constant fled Haiti in December 1994, entered the United States on a tourist visa, which U.S. immigration authorities later said was a mistake, and was arrested in New York in May. The Haitian courts had previously issued a warrant for his arrest for crimes committed under military rule, and the Haitian government filed for his extradition. In September, a U.S. immigration judge ordered Constant, a CIA informant who had potentially embarrassing information to disclose about U.S. involvement in Haiti, deported to Haiti. Constant's case was the most egregious of hundreds of potential cases against FRAPH members that would have benefited from the immediate release of documents held by the U.S. government to Haitian prosecutors.

Additional reports of prior U.S. links to human rights violators under military rule appeared in the magazine *The Nation* (New York), which cited U.S. officials in Haiti as stating that Marcel Morissaint, the alleged gunman in the 1993 assassination of Minister of Justice Guy Malary, had been an informant paid by the U.S. Drug Enforcement Agency from 1991 to 1995. Jean-Joseph Exumé, the justice minister, told *The Nation* that Morissaint had been "under U.S. protection" and was removed from custody with U.S. assistance. National Security Advisor Anthony Lake and State Department officials denied the *Nation* report.

A U.S. Army captain, Lawrence Rockwood, was detained by U.S. military police, forced to return to the U.S., and subsequently court-martialed for his September 1994 effort to investigate human rights conditions at the notorious National Penitentiary in Port-au-Prince.

The U.S. Agency for International Development took a leading role in judicial reform by awarding a comprehensive administration of justice project to a U.S. firm. However, the minimal consultation with Haitian experts in designing the program raised questions about its appropriateness.

The U.S. government continued practices that violated international refugee protections. In January 1995, the U.S. forcibly repatriated nearly 4,000 Haitians who had been interdicted and brought to the U.S. naval base at Guantánamo, Cuba, under a safe haven policy established during military rule. The U.S. government forced the Haitians to return without first allowing them, as is required in international law, to explain the reasons for their departure. International refugee protections adopted by the U.S. require that persons with a well-founded fear of political persecution should not be forced to return to their country. From October 1994 to September 1995, the U.S. Coast Guard repatriated 200 interdicted Haitians without a refugee hearing. Attorney General Janet Reno refused relief to 300 Haitian minors at Guantánamo while Cubans held there were granted humanitarian parole because of harsh conditions. In early 1995, there were credible reports that some American military personnel at Guantánamo were involved in incidents of physical and psychological abuse of the minors, including the use of solitary confinement and shackling. Of the over 20,000 Haitians taken to Guantánamo, not a single one left the camps as a recognized refugee in spite of having fled a brutal military government.

The Work of
Human Rights Watch/Americas

Our 1995 work on human rights in Haiti stressed accountability and building respect for the rule of law as critical parts of all institutional reform efforts and as the fundamental foundations for the lasting improvement of human rights protections in Haiti.

In March, with the National Coalition for Haitian Refugees, we published *Security Compromised: Recycled Haitian Soldiers on the Police Front Line*, which examined and expressed concerns about the Haitian and U.S. government's selection and retraining of former Haitian soldiers for the interim police force. We highlighted security concerns and organizational irregularities in a pre-electoral report, *Human Rights Conditions Prior to the June 1995 Elections*, urging heightened security for electoral officials and candidates and full clarification of problems in the voter registration and candidate review process conducted by the Provisional Electoral Council. In October, we released a comprehensive joint report with the National Coalition for Haitian Refugees, *Human Rights in Haiti After President Aristide's Return*, that pointed to dramatic improvement in human rights in Haiti tempered by a need to consolidate gains with heightened efforts to establish accountability for past wrongs and improve institutional reforms.

We undertook several additional initiatives to address impunity concerns, particularly in areas where we had conducted previous intensive research and advocacy. We provided the truth commission with all of our reports detailing the repression under military rule, and in May we co-authored a joint letter signed by nine international human rights organizations urging international support for the commission. We applauded the truth commission's special focus on sexual violence and internal displacement as tools of political repression. In September, we announced in Haiti the release of *The Human Rights Watch Global Report on Women's Human Rights*, highlighted the report's coverage of politically motivated rape, and urged the Haitian government to intensify prosecution efforts against those responsible for government-sponsored sexual violence committed under military rule. Our French translation of the June election report was released in September with a letter to President Aristide urging prosecutions for all crimes committed during the pre and post-electoral period.

Human Rights Watch/Americas actively engaged the U.S. government with regard to human rights protections in Haiti and for Haitian refugees. In January, we vigorously protested the illegal repatriation of Haitians from Guantánamo communicating our concerns to the State Department, the National Security Council, and the Immigration and Naturalization Service. We filed two Freedom of Information Act requests with the Departments of Justice and Defense regarding reported U.S. military personnel involvement in abuses of Haitian minors at Guantánamo. Both requests were denied and were under appeal at year's end. We visited the ICITAP-directed police academy in Haiti and held meetings with their Haiti and U.S.-based staff. We also engaged the State Department, the National Security Council, members of congress, the Department of Justice, U.S. AID, and other U.S. government agencies in direct dialogue concerning police selection and training, elections, and other concerns.

HONDURAS

Human Rights Developments

During 1995, the Honduran government took significant initial steps toward establishing accountability for gross human rights violations that occurred in the 1980s. An investigation begun in July of ten former and current members of the armed forces led to the issuing of arrest warrants for three army officers on October 17. These courageous initiatives by the administration of President Carlos Roberto Reina have been hampered by the refusal of the accused to appear in court, thinly-veiled threats, and outright violence from the military.

The special prosecutor for human rights brought charges in July against eight retired and two active-duty members of the armed forces for their role in the kidnaping, torture, and attempted murder in 1982 of six student activists: Guillermo López, Edwin López, Milton Jiménez, Marlen Jiménez, Gilda Rivera, and Suyapa Rivera. The six were taken from a Tegucigalpa apartment early on the morning of April 27, 1982, by fifteen armed men dressed in civilian clothes. They survived their captivity in a clandestine prison because two of those abducted were the daughters of a government official.

On October 17, Judge Roy Medina, assigned to oversee the investigation, concluded that there was sufficient evidence to order the arrest of three of the ten officers. (The arrest warrants were suspended on October 18 pending a review by the Court of Appeals.) Of the three, the most prominent is Lt. Col. Alexander Hernández, who was the operational commander of the infamous Battalion 3-16 in the early 1980s and is now inspector general of the military police. The other two wanted officers, both retired, are Police Maj. Manuel de Jesús Trejo Rosa and Capt. Billy Fernando Joya Améndola.

With the exception of one suspect, those under investigation were connected with Battalion 3-16, a secret Honduran military unit whose members were instructed by and worked with CIA officials. The battalion detained scores of leftist activists, including students, teachers, unionists, and suspected guerrillas who then disappeared. Members of the unit employed torture techniques including electric shock and suffocation to interrogate their victims, later killing and burying them in unmarked graves.

In what was widely viewed as a "saber rattling" reaction to the charges brought by the special prosecutor, the military deployed armored personnel carriers and artillery in the capital for one day in early August. This move came immediately after Leo Valladares Lanza, the National Commissioner for Human Rights, announced that he had submitted a second request to the U.S. government for documents relating to the military's role in the abuses of the 1980s. General Luis Alonso Discua, commander of the armed forces and a former commander of Battalion 3-16, stated that "the armed forces will adopt actions if there is any problem of partiality in the courts." Afterward, Discua explained that the tanks had been deployed as an "exercise" in preparation for a military celebration the next day. In fact, the celebration was never held.

In early October, threats of violence escalated against those involved in the trial of the ten officers. Two men in a vehicle reportedly opened fire on the courthouse where the trial was being held. As they did so, according to the Baltimore *Sun*, they shouted, "Where is that [expletive] Medina? Tell him to come out so we can kill him!"

Violent tactics were accompanied by an unwillingness of the officers to rely on standard legal means of defense. On October 10, Carlos López Osorio, the lawyer for the ten officers, announced that his clients would not present themselves in court despite a summons to appear. Calling the proceedings a farce, he declared that the disappearances and other abuses were covered by the amnesty laws passed in 1987 and 1991.

As a matter of law, the amnesty does not cover the egregious violations committed by members of Battalion 3-16. Unlike the sweeping amnesties passed in Peru, in Guatemala under military rule, and in El Salvador after the Truth Commission report, the Honduran amnesty is extremely restrictive. The grant of amnesty applies only to "persons sentenced, prosecuted, or subjected to judicial investigation" at the time the law went into force in 1991. Because none of the officials involved in Battalion 3-16's human rights violations was subject to any form of judicial proceeding in 1991, the amnesty does not preclude judicial investigation or prosecution of their cases. Further, the amnesty law covers political acts executed *in opposition* to the state. In contrast, the military undertook its campaign of human rights abuse *in support of* the state and as a matter of state policy. The military's argument that the amnesty applies to the actions of Battalion 3-16 is fundamentally in contradiction with the letter and intent of the legislation.

The government took several other encouraging steps during the year. In December 1994, a team of forensic anthropologists identified the remains of Nelson Mackay Chavarría. Mackay, a lawyer who, despite his connections to the military, was detained and "disappeared" on February 21, 1982, at the age of thirty-one. Mackay's alleged co-

conspirator, Miguel Carias, testified that the two were held together in a house in Tegucigalpa used by Battalion 3-16 as a secret jail. Carias was locked in a closet, where he could hear Mackay repeating the Hail Mary, his voice growing louder with each recitation. The investigation into Mackay's disappearance, conducted at the request of the attorney general's office, was still in its initial stages as of this writing.

In April, the National Assembly ratified an amendment to the Honduran Constitution providing for a system of voluntary military service. The amendment represented a rejection of the arbitrary and abusive enlistment methods employed by the military during the 1980s, when army press gangs regularly dragged young men from buses, theaters and other public places, and off the streets, selecting the best for forced recruitment and returning the rest to their families for a price.

Local rights groups noted that reported cases of torture and other abuses by police diminished in 1995. At the same time, public confidence in the authorities appeared to increase, making it more likely that such cases would be reported. These improvements followed the reassignment in June 1994 of the main police investigatory branch to civilian control. Most reports of torture charged the abuses to FUSEP, the military police, rather than the civilian Department of Criminal Investigations.

The government failed to make headway in improving prison conditions, such as the practice of illegally detaining minors with adult prisoners in penitentiaries. An August 1 report prepared by the National Commission for Human Rights documented over 200 cases of minors jailed together with adults in seventeen of the twenty-four adult prisons in Honduras. The detention of minors under these conditions is in violation of the Convention on the Rights of the Child and the American Convention on Human Rights, as well as the Honduran Constitution. The children jailed in these conditions are frequently the target of abuse or sexual assault at the hands of their adult cellmates,

as a commission composed of members of the judiciary, the Public Ministry, and the public defenders organization acknowledged in April. To date, only three or four prisons have announced plans to provide separate facilities for minors.

The Right to Monitor
In May 1995, Commissioner Valladares reported that he and his family had been the subject of continual death threats from the time he took office. As a result of these threats, he sent two of his children abroad for their protection. One of Valladares' security guards, Pedro Espinosa Osorto, had been shot to death on a public bus one week earlier.

Judge Roy Medina, who was hearing the inquiry against the ten army officers, reported that he has received numerous death threats. After two men fired upon the criminal courthouse in Tegucigalpa while shouting threats against his life, the judge accepted a bodyguard. Increasing tensions throughout Tegucigalpa and elsewhere in Honduras led the Honduran Supreme Court to post security agents at courthouses and at the homes of Supreme Court judges and other judges who were hearing cases sensitive to the military.

Local human rights monitors reported that the military has conducted a campaign in the media to denounce those who have leveled charges of human rights violations against the military. In particular, the military targeted the six former student leaders who were temporarily "disappeared" in 1982.

U.S. Policy
The Honduran government has taken important and courageous steps to account for the horrific history of Battalion 3-16; the United States has still to do the same. The U.S. role in providing training, equipment, and funding to Battalion 3-16 is well documented. Many of the Honduran participants and several of the commanders of Battalion 3-16 have publicly described CIA officials' close supervision of the battalion's operations, including the interrogation of clandestine

prisoners. Although Human Rights Watch/ Americas has pressed for several years for an accounting of U.S. involvement, the Clinton administration did not take steps to begin to examine the complicity of the United States in Honduran abuses until 1995. In mid-June, CIA Director John Deutch began an internal review of the agency's relationship with the Honduran military during the 1980s. Deutch stated that the investigation, which he characterized as an "independent review," would yield "new information" and "lessons about how not to do things while I'm director and in the future."

Deutch's announcement came after the Baltimore *Sun* published a four-part series in June on U.S. support given to Battalion 3-16. *Sun* staff correspondents Gary Cohn and Ginger Thompson obtained formerly classified documents and interviewed three former Battalion 3-16 torturers to document the breadth and depth of the battalion's close relationship to the CIA. The *Sun* series followed revelations in March that linked the CIA to serious human rights violations in Guatemala (see Guatemala section).

In addition, various U.S. government agencies agreed jointly in October to proceed with declassification of U.S. government records pertaining to disappearances and other human rights abuses in Honduras. The decision to declassify came just as the *New York Times* was preparing an editorial criticizing the administration's lack of response to requests from Honduran officials. Prior to the *New York Time*'s decision to publicize the administration's failure to act, all U.S. agencies had balked at Commissioner Valladares' two requests for documents and a third from the office of the Honduran attorney general's office. The State Department insisted that Valladares provide a more narrow list of materials for declassification. The National Security Council, the CIA, and the Department of Defense simply ignored the requests.

The administration's decision also followed the Senate's passage of an amendment to the Foreign Aid Appropriations Bill on September 20. The amendment, spon-sored by Senators Leahy (D-VT), Dodd (D-CT), and Sarbanes (D-MD), called upon the Clinton administration to declassify documents relating to disappearances in Honduras.

A meeting in September between Commissioner Valladares and State Department officials in Washington resulted in the release of some documents. These included State Department cables on the disappearance and murder of Father James Carney in 1983, excerpts from an interrogation manual, and reports from an investigation and closed hearings on Battalion 3-16 by the Senate Select Committee on Intelligence in 1988. However, these documents had already been declassified as the result of prior FOIA requests, and most had already been made public through other sources.

Human Rights Watch/Americas called upon the Clinton administration to muster the political will to let the truth be known about the disappearances, torture, and extrajudicial executions that took place in Honduras and the U.S. role in those violations. We welcome the executive branch's decision to proceed with declassification of documents. The administration's announcement is an important first step. In particular, the administration should resist the temptation to delete materials on the grounds that they would cause embarrassment to U.S. officials or harm relations with the Honduran military and intelligence services.

In 1995, the Honduran police received training in criminal investigations techniques as well as aid to the judiciary. The armed forces received an estimated US$400,000 in military training and $1.5 million in arms sales. Human Rights Watch/Americas urged the U.S. government to use its training programs as a means of conveying to the Honduran military the need for subordination to the civilian authorities and the importance of allowing trials of military officers to go forward. We urged the U.S. to cut off all assistance as a response to any further efforts by the Honduran armed forces to obstruct justice or intimidate witnesses, prosecutors, or judges in these cases.

The Work of
Human Rights Watch/Americas

In 1995, Human Rights Watch/Americas continued its efforts to press the U.S. to examine its role in the disappearances and extrajudicial executions in Honduras, a matter we have been pursuing for several years. During Commissioner Valladares' two visits to the U.S. in September, Human Rights Watch/Americas arranged for him to meet with U.S. officials. Earlier, in June, Human Rights Watch/Americas led a coalition of human rights groups in writing to President Clinton in an effort to widen the focus of the executive branch examinations of the CIA's involvement in Guatemala to include Honduras as well. We published letters to the editor and opinion articles pressing for accountability and reform at the CIA. In a meeting with National Security Advisor Anthony Lake on October 31, the executive director of Human Rights Watch/Americas urged an open examination of the CIA's involvement with Battalion 3-16.

Human Rights Watch/Americas has prodded the Clinton administration and congressional oversight committees to enact reforms of CIA rules and procedures so that the abuses of the 1980s cannot recur. In August, a letter summarizing our reform proposals was published in *The New York Times* (see Human Rights Watch/Americas Overview).

In November, Human Rights Watch/Americas sent letters to Honduran government officials regarding the cases of over twenty minors detained in three prisons in Yoro and La Ceiba.

MEXICO

Human Rights Developments

Ernesto Zedillo Ponce de León ended his first full year as president unable or unwilling to halt Mexico's triple evils of political killings, military and police abuses, and impunity. In February, Zedillo himself kicked off a crackdown on guerrillas in the southeastern state of Chiapas, but despite his assurances that security forces would respect human rights, government officials arbitrarily detained, tortured, and forced confessions from suspects. Investigators appeared to make headway in the official probe into the 1994 murder of presidential candidate Luis Donaldo Colosio, though new high-profile killings added to a growing list of such deaths, including Abraham Polo Uscanga, the judge in a politically charged union case, and seventeen peasants gunned down by police in Guerrero state. Throughout the country, labor and human rights activists also suffered attacks.

The crackdown on the Zapatista Army of National Liberation (Ejército Zapatista de Liberación Nacional, EZLN) exposed a breach between presidential words and governmental actions. On the one hand, President Zedillo recognized the problems of human rights violations and impunity, stating in his first state-of-the-union address, "The frequency of crimes and the impunity of those who break the law are an affront to society; and people have every reason to feel exasperated when they see that the very people who are entrusted with safeguarding order and imparting justice are in many cases those who disregard it." However, Zedillo's government continued to commit the very abuses that he himself condemned.

In Chiapas, an uneasy stand-off between the EZLN and the government ended suddenly on February 9, when Zedillo ordered the army to recover by force territory in which the EZLN had operated since January 1994. In a televised address from the presidential palace, Zedillo informed the nation that he had ordered the army offensive to assist the attorney general's office in carrying out arrest warrants against five alleged EZLN commanders, whose names he read on the air, including that of the EZLN leader, "Subcommander Marcos."

During the crackdown, combined police and army operations netted more than twenty people, whom prosecutors later charged with crimes such as "terrorism" and "rebellion." All except two of eighteen February detainees interviewed in prison by

Human Rights Watch/Americas reported that they gave coerced statements to government officials after being blindfolded, subjected to incessant and loud music, and deprived of liquid or food for up to forty-eight hours. Initially, none had adequate legal assistance. At least four of seven people detained in Yanga, Veracruz, suffered severe torture and, under threat, signed confessions incriminating themselves. One of them, Alvaro Castillo Granados, told Human Rights Watch/Americas that police forced him into the back of a car, stuffed a rag into his mouth, and forced mineral water up his nose. The police who interrogated Castillo shocked him with an electric baton and almost suffocated him with a plastic bag. In committing the seven for trial, a judge dismissed the torture allegations, claiming that even if proved, they would not detract from the value of the detainees' confessions. In October, a judge reviewing the earlier decision threw out several of the charges after finding that the attorney general's office failed to substantiate the government's allegations; but as of this writing the prisoners remained in detention. The judge did not refer to the treatment received by the detainees.

The Fray Bartolomé Human Rights Center (Centro para los Derechos Humanos "Fray Bartolomé de las Casas"), in San Cristóbal de las Casas, Chiapas, reported dozens of cases of torture, beatings, and intimidation committed by government officials in the context of the crackdown. Most of the abuses occurred as army troops rounded up and questioned villagers about the Zapatistas. An agreement reached between the government and EZLN in September paved the way for future negotiations between the warring parties. In October, discussions began on the topic of indigenous rights and culture.

The detentions during the crackdown and previous military abuses in Chiapas made clear that existing Mexican safeguards designed to eliminate torture and forced confessions would only be effective if political leaders, including President Zedillo, issued clear directives to their subordinates that such laws must be followed and that any breach would be fully and immediately prosecuted.

The war in Chiapas exacerbated the longstanding conflict between ranchers and the state's largely landless indigenous population. Indigenous groups, drawing inspiration from the EZLN, continued to occupy farming land across the state, while landowners and ranchers reacted by arming and training their own private police, known as *guardias blancas*, or white guards. In some cases, police sided openly with the guardias, which human rights groups have identified as responsible for serious human rights violations. On January 10, for example, guardias blancas in Chicomuselo, along with municipal police and ranchers, participated in a clash against members of the opposition Party of the Democratic Revolution (Partido de la Revolución Democrática, PRD), leaving seven people dead and several others wounded. Despite a report by the National Commission for Human Rights (Comisión Nacional de Derechos Humanos, CNDH) on the incident that identified collusion between the white guards and uniformed police, the federal Ministry of Government reported that it could find no evidence of guardia blanca activity in Chicomuselo. During the run-up to October local elections in Chiapas, guardias blancas killed some nineteen PRD activists, according to the Fray Bartolomé Human Rights Center. Three members of the ruling Institutional Revolutionary Party (Partido Revolucionario Institucional, PRI) were kidnaped or murdered, according to the *New York Times*, which cited the PRI.

Another indication of tensions in Chiapas came with the expulsion in June of three priests working in the state: Argentine Jorge Barón Gutlein; U.S. citizen Loren Riebe; and Spanish national Rodolfo Izal Elorz. Without warrants for their arrest, state judicial police detained the priests in different parts of the state on June 22. While at the airport, the priests learned that they had been accused of encouraging land occupations and preaching about national politics, which they firmly denied in later interviews. Human Rights Watch/Americas recognized the government's right to decide which foreigners to admit and which to exclude, but also found that the government failed to fulfill its obligation to provide due process. Following the expulsions, the Mexican government refused to allow two other foreign Chiapas-based priests to re-enter the country after they had voluntarily departed.

Four months after the crackdown on suspected EZLN members, the national government found itself faced with another human rights crisis of national and international dimensions, this time in the southern state of Guerrero. On June 28, members of several communities in the state made their way toward Atoyac de Alvarez to attend a protest called by the Southern Sierra Peasant Organization (Organización Campesina de la Sierra del Sur, OCSS). Outside the town of Aguas Blancas, state judicial police and public security officers, also known as *policía motorizada*, erected a roadblock and stopped two trucks heading in the direction of the protest. Police opened fire on one of the vehicles, killing seventeen people and wounding fourteen others. Two police officers were wounded by a machete. After the killings, the police planted weapons on the victims and claimed they had returned fire in self-defense. In the months prior to the massacre, authorities and members of indigenous communities had clashed frequently, and attacks by unidentified assailants left more than three dozen people dead, including political activists, police, and peasants.

In a detailed report on the incident, the CNDH determined that even if the peasants had opened fire (which the CNDH doubted), the police had reacted in a "disproportionate, irresponsible, and illegal" manner. The CNDH found overwhelming proof that police and other state officials tried to cover up the incident, and documented evidence of at least one extrajudicial execution at the scene of the massacre.

On July 1, the state attorney general accused ten police officers of manslaughter and abuse of authority, but after the CNDH released its report in August, several of the state's top political leaders—including the attorney general—lost their jobs pending investigation, in fulfillment of a recommendation made in the report. Only the governor remained in his post. Three special prosecutors have been named to head the case, but none made progress on resolving the killings. By the time this report went to press, several important questions remained unanswered, including the identity of the occupants of a helicopter that flew above the massacre and the degree to which government officials planned the killings.

Federal officials maintained that they would not and could not intervene after the massacre because the federal system of government in Mexico prohibited them from doing so. Nonetheless, Human Rights Watch/Americas believes that based on the American Convention on Human Rights, to which Mexico is a state party, the national government cannot hide behind federalism to justify state or local violations of its international obligations. The convention's federal clause, article 28, holds that national governments shall "immediately" take steps to "the end that the competent authorities of the constituent units may adopt appropriate provisions" for the fulfillment of the convention.

Although the governor made a commitment to fulfill a CNDH recommendation to restructure the police, Human Rights Watch/Americas' field investigations revealed that the state government had taken no effective steps to address impunity or restructure the police to prevent future abuses.

The government of Mexico committed human rights violations in the context of labor issues, including limiting freedom of association and failing to live up to its international obligations to prevent discrimination. A labor tribunal refused to re-register the independent union of the former Fishing Ministry, which the government transformed in December 1994 into the Ministry of Environment, Natural Resources, and Fishing. Following several questionable legal rulings, a pro-government union federation called new elections and eliminated the independent union members from the new union's Leadership. Human Rights Watch/Americas began to study other cases in 1995, including the government's confrontation with the Union of Route 100 Urban Transportation Workers, commonly referred to as Ruta-100. The government declared a publicly-financed bus company bankrupt, declared the union dissolved, and jailed several of its leaders. Three people have lost their lives so far in the struggle, including Judge Abraham Polo Uscanga. Polo denounced threats from court officials after he refused on legal grounds to issue arrest warrants for Ruta-100 leaders, and subsequently sought leave from the court. On June 19, assailants shot him dead in Mexico City. Two days earlier, unidentified gunmen shot to death the government's special prosecutor in the Ruta-100 case. In April, Mexico City's transportation secretary, the official in charge of breaking the union's control over city transportation, died after receiving two gunshots in his chest. Government investigators ruled the death a suicide.

Throughout northern Mexico's *maquiladora* sector, the government also failed to enforce statutes contained in domestic and international laws that prohibit discrimination on the basis of gender. The Human Rights Watch Women's Rights Project documented routine discrimination against women in the maquiladora industry, which required prospective women employees to reveal their pregnancy status and denied jobs to pregnant women. In addition, the Women's Rights Project documented cases in which private maquiladora companies mistreated or fired women who became pregnant (see the Women's Rights Project section).

As has been the case in past years, journalists in Mexico faced danger or harassment for reporting on sensitive issues. On July 24, gunmen shot and wounded Tijuana-based journalist Dante Cortez as he traveled to a press conference to denounce alleged drug traffickers in Baja California. Cortez had been investigating his son's murder in June, which he believed took place at the hands of drug traffickers. In March, Veracruz state officials closed Radio Huayacocotla, arguing that technical deficiencies at the station posed life-threatening danger to its employees. According to station employees, government officials had accused Radio Huayacocotla of instigating violence among Veracruz's indigenous population, a serious allegation within the context of the guerrilla war in nearby Chiapas. For decades, Radio Huayacocotla had broadcast educational and community-oriented information.

The Right to Monitor

Attacks on human rights monitors took place throughout the country during 1995. On February 13 and 14, news media citing official sources reported that police had discovered an arsenal being shipped to Arturo Lona, the bishop of Tehuantepec, Oaxaca, who is also president of the Tepeyac Human Rights Center (Centro de Derechos Humanos "Tepeyac"). On June 29, two men shot at Bishop Lona, hitting the truck he was driving with eleven bullets. Oaxaca officials ruled the attack an attempted robbery, but the harassment suffered by Bishop Lona earlier in the year led Human Rights Watch/America to suspect a political motive.

In March, the Binational Human Rights Center (Centro Binacional de Derechos Humanos) discovered that someone had wiretapped its offices, after private investigators contracted by the center conducted a thorough sweep of the group's Tijuana installations. The investigators found tapped phone lines and an expensive microphone in a telephone handset.

In August, the Rev. David Fernández, a priest who heads the Mexico City-based Miguel Agustín Pro Juárez Human Rights Center (Centro de Derechos Humanos "Miguel Agustín Pro Juárez", known as Prodh), received a series of threats against him and his family. Prior to the threats, *Proceso* magazine published a hard-hitting interview with Father Fernández, who severely criticized the government's handling of human rights issues. In September, Prodh personnel received several additional threats. José Lavanderos, a human rights lawyer working on the cases of the alleged Zapatistas detained during the crackdown, received threats in October.

An October report by the human rights coordinating group National Network of Human Rights Groups (La Red Nacional de Organismos de Derechos Humanos "Todos los Derechos para Todos," known as La Red) documented a series of threats or attacks against human rights monitors throughout Mexico, including the Mahatma Gandhi Regional Human Rights Commission (Comisión Regional de Derechos Humanos "Mahatma Gandhi") in Tuxtepec, Oaxaca; the Miguel Hidalgo Human Rights Committee (Comité de Derechos Humanos y Orientación "Miguel Hidalgo") in Dolores Hidalgo, Guanajuato; Citizens in Support of Human Rights (Ciudadanos en Apoyo a los Derechos Humanos) in Guadalupe, Nuevo León; the Tabasco Human Rights Committee (Comité de Derechos Humanos de Tabasco); and the Northern Sierra Human Rights Committee (Comité de Derechos Humanos de la Sierra Norte de Veracruz) in Huayacocotla, Veracruz. Human rights activists in Guerrero working on the June massacre also received threats. In most of the cases documented by La Red, the identity of the people making the threats could not be confirmed.

U.S. Policy

As it has in the past, the Clinton administration went out of its way to avoid criticizing the Mexican government on human rights issues. In its public statements on Mexico, the United States showed great support for the Zedillo government, rallying to provide billions of dollars in a financial package for Mexico after the peso collapsed in December 1994. Repeated praise for the Mexican government in the context of the financial package and the North American Free Trade Agreement (NAFTA), with virtually no public mention of human rights problems, made it clear that the economic relationship between the two countries mattered to the United States far more than human rights problems.

Throughout 1995, the State Department made only one public statement focusing on human rights in Mexico. The U.S. Embassy in Mexico City made none. On February 10, as the crackdown on alleged Zapatistas continued, acting State Department spokeswoman Christine Shelly justified, "Governments have the right and responsibility to protect their citizens against violence, while, at the same time, respecting their human rights." When it became clear that the Mexican government had flagrantly violated the rights of suspected guerrillas, the United States issued no follow-up comment. To his credit, U.S. Amb. James Jones did meet with Mexican human rights activists on at least one occasion.

The U.S. Agency for International Development continued to plan a rule-of-law program in Mexico, with a pilot initiative to focus on judicial reform in the state of Hidalgo. The State Department requested $2 million to assist with judicial reform issues in Mexico in 1996, including training for Mexican jurists and police, and sought another $1 million for the International Military Education and Training Program (IMET), up from $200,000 in 1994 and an estimated $400,000 in 1995. U.S. Defense Secretary William Perry visited Mexico in October and publicly announced the IMET program.

In an interview in Mexico City, Ambassador Jones assured Human Rights Watch/Americas that the United States raised human rights concerns "at the highest levels of government" in Mexico, though he emphasized that it never did so publicly. "Our message is that respect for human rights is a factor in whether people will invest in Mexico," he said. "The most effective tool is the investment community." The ambassador cautioned that nationalism in Mexico would cause the government to reject any public criticism made by the United States. Human Rights Watch/Americas found the caution to be misplaced because U.S. statements on Mexico that ignored serious human rights issues yet praised other developments effectively helped the Mexican government avoid responsibility for the violations committed by its agents. Reporting on Mexico in the Department of State's *Country Reports on Human Rights Practices for 1994* noted serious problems in Mexico, including "extrajudicial killings by the police, torture, and illegal arrests," but the existence of such violations appeared not to be factored into U.S. policy on Mexico. Further, since the State Department requested $3 million in aid to train Mexican soldiers, police, and jurists in 1996, the U.S. government should have been particularly careful to issue public criticism of human rights abuses in Mexico. By doing otherwise, the United States sent the message to Mexican officials that not only did committing or tolerating human rights abuses carry no cost, but the United States would continue to provide financial support to state agencies responsible for violating human rights.

The United States encouraged the Mexican government to accept donated helicopters and airplanes to strengthen the ability of the attorney general's office to interdict illegal drugs. In October, the United States transferred twelve Huey helicopters to the attorney general's office on a no-cost-lease basis and slated another twelve to be sent for spare parts.

During 1995, the U.S. Labor Department reviewed one complaint about labor rights violations in Mexico. The department's National Administrative Office (NAO), created in 1994 by the NAFTA accord, released a report on a complaint filed the previous year by three U.S. groups and one Mexican organization. The complaint alleged that Sony Corporation had violated freedom of association, the right to organize, and minimum employment standards. The NAO deemed "plausible" a complaint of wrongful dismissal and recommended further study of the problems. The labor ministries of Mexico and the United States agreed to study the problem of union registration in Mexico and educate Mexicans about their labor rights. While the process highlighted the lack of

enforcement mechanisms in NAFTA's labor side agreement, it also showed positive signs of facilitating much-needed discussions of important labor rights issues in Mexico. At this writing, the U.S. Congress had yet to debate a Republican-sponsored bill that would effectively curtail presidential authority to include labor rights side agreements in future trade accords in cases where the president wanted fast-track negotiating capabilities.

The Work of Human Rights Watch/Americas

Human Rights Watch/Americas continued to focus attention on human rights abuses committed in the context of the Zapatista uprising, but also sought during the year to highlight broader human rights problems in Mexico, such as impunity for violations committed by the police and military and torture. In addition, with the goal of submitting cases to the National Administrative Office of the Department of Labor, we began to investigate freedom of association cases related to Mexico's labor unions.

In April, Human Rights Watch/Americas sent a fact-finding mission to Mexico to investigate abuses committed during the February crackdown on alleged Zapatistas and, as part of its ongoing focus on impunity in Mexico, to gather new information about the 1994 Ocosingo clinic massacre in Chiapas. In June, Human Rights Watch/ Americas published *Army Officer Held "Responsible" for Chiapas Massacre: Accused Found Dead at Defense Ministry.* Based on internal military documents, the report analyzed the army's handling of the massacre, finding serious methodological flaws in the military's investigation. In publishing the report, Human Rights Watch/Americas sought to bring attention to continuing military impunity and urged that an exhaustive investigation by civilian authorities lead to the punishment of those found responsible for the killings. In addition, we urged the adoption of legislation to ensure that the investigation and prosecution of crimes involving military personnel that may constitute human rights violations are conducted under strict civilian jurisdiction.

Human Rights Watch/Americas called for a cut-off of U.S. Foreign Military Sales (FMS), estimated at $3,500,000 in 1995 and $3,600,000 in 1996, until the Mexican army completes adequate investigations into human rights violations committed by the army during the Chiapas uprising and until prosecutions of those found responsible are underway. IMET funding should be used as a lever to reach these same goals; if progress is not made, the administration should seriously consider cutting off IMET.

In August and September, Human Rights Watch/Americas conducted another fact-finding trip in Mexico to gather further information on the February crackdown, research labor rights cases, and investigate the June massacre of seventeen peasants in Guerrero state. The resulting analysis of the torture and other ill treatment during the February crackdown was being prepared for publication at this writing.

PERU

Human Rights Developments

After a comfortable victory in presidential elections held on April 9 and with a majority in the legislature, President Alberto Fujimori began his second term of office on July 28 with an agenda to modernize Peru. On June 14 the Democratic Constituent Congress (CCD) passed a sweeping amnesty benefiting scores of military and police personnel implicated in serious human rights crimes during the fifteen-year war against Shining Path (Sendero Luminoso) and other violent groups. This scandalous gift of impunity to the army and police, which was repudiated by public opinion and by many of Fujimori's own supporters, was not balanced by any relaxation of the draconian anti-terrorist measures in force. In October, Congress passed a law extending for a further year the system of so-called faceless courts, set up in April 1992 to facilitate summary trials of

terrorist suspects. These courts had resulted in hundreds of arbitrary convictions after unfair trials, but no measures were taken to review them. In August, the government promulgated a law defining the functions and powers of a *defensor del pueblo* (ombudsman), a new institution contemplated in the 1993 constitution to monitor and protect human rights.

In spite of frequent government statements claiming that the violence of Shining Path had been brought under control, 45 percent of Peru's population continued to live under states of emergency, effectively military rule. Pockets of the country were still significantly affected by political violence, especially the jungle region of Huánuco, San Martín, Ucayali, and Loreto, parts of which are also centers of narcotics trafficking. Lima was not immune either: in May its inhabitants suffered a dramatic reminder of the violence of earlier years when a car bomb planted by a Shining Path squad exploded in the center of the Miraflores business district, killing five people.

Tactics used by violent groups, particularly Shining Path, continued to violate basic standards of international humanitarian law, and killings of civilians by this group this year outnumbered those committed by government forces. They included selective assassinations of local authorities and reprisals against civilians accused of betrayal or collaboration with the army and peasant self-defense groups (rondas campesinas), as well as indiscriminate violence against civilians, such as the María Angola attack. On May 12, about twenty Shining Path guerrillas entered the community of San José de Belén, Huancavélica, whose inhabitants had recently returned after leaving the zone for the relative safety of Huancayo. The guerrillas demanded payment of a war tax of 1,000 soles (approximately US$450), which the villagers were unable to pay. A survivor told how the guerrillas then murdered six of the villagers and burned their homes.

The number of extrajudicial executions and disappearances attributed to government forces continued to decline. Human rights groups documented three extrajudicial executions and nine disappearances in the first nine months of the year. All but two of the disappearances occurred in the department of Ucayali, which is under emergency rule by a political-military command garrisoned by the Navy (Marina de Guerra). The navy base at Aguaytía has been the site of several documented cases of torture, extrajudicial executions, and disappearances. Marines from Aguaytía were allegedly responsible for the death in April of seventeen-year-old Indalecio Pomatanta Albarrán. While searching his home for terrorists, marines doused him with gasoline and set him on fire, according to his parents' testimony to a court investigator. Pomatante died in the hospital of second degree burns over 65 percent of his body. In a televised death-bed interview he told reporters that his Navy attackers made two unsuccessful attempts before setting him alight. Torture was endemic and systematic in this zone: Justiniano Hurtado Rorres, detained on November 21, 1994, and Tomás Flores Huanío, detained on April 19, 1995, died subsequently of their injuries. The whereabouts of six people detained by the marines between January and July in the area is still unknown.

The practice of torture is not limited to counterinsurgency but is a routine adjunct to police investigation in Peru, although its severity seems to depend on the social class and resources of the victim. The public prosecutor's office, which is nominally required to safeguard the rights of detainees is ineffective, in part because it is also responsible for leading criminal prosecutions. A case in which the prosecutor notably failed to protect a victim was that of student Jhoel Huamán García, who was beaten to death by police in Cerro de Pasco. Huamán's captors, acting without a warrant, pulled him out of a football game on May 26, following an apparently mistaken accusation by a robbery victim, and took him for interrogation. His father testified in court that drunken police celebrating a birthday in the precinct tortured and beat Huamán mercilessly. They then ordered him to be taken to a hospital,

where he was dead on arrival from a cerebral hemorrhage and severe internal injuries, according to an autopsy report. The police claimed that Huamán "fell on his back after suffering convulsions provoked by the interrogation." Asked to clarify Huamán's legal situation, the prosecutor told Huamán's father, "We'll sort it out tomorrow." By the next day the youth was dead.

The special faceless courts set up under the anti-terrorist law of May 6, 1992, which allow suspects to be tried through one-way mirrors by prosecutors and judges whose identity is concealed, continued to violate the most basic due process guarantees. Secret military tribunals which hear cases under the Treason Law provide even fewer guarantees: only one of the panel of five judges is an attorney, and the remainder are career officers on active service. In *Peru: The Two Faces of Justice*, released in July, Human Rights Watch/Americas highlighted nine terrorism and treason cases in which innocent people had been handed down sentences ranging from ten years to life imprisonment by these courts. The probable number of unjust convictions was close to seven hundred, according to Peruvian nongovernmental human rights organizations. Confessed guerillas who gave themselves up under the 1992 Repentance Law implicated many innocent people in order to get their own sentences suspended or reduced. On April 19, with the support of both the public prosecutor's office and the Supreme Court, the CCD passed a reform abolishing the faceless courts with effect from October 15, on the grounds that the menace of political violence had abated. However, on September 27 President Fujimori sent an urgent bill to Congress for the deadline to be extended, and Congress voted that the courts should continue to function until October 1996. In striking contrast with the celerity of this decision, a proposal suggested by Fujimori in July for Congress to appoint a special commission to review cases of unfair imprisonment came to nothing.

In an ominous new development, the Supreme Court began to overrule acquittals by faceless courts on purely procedural grounds and ordered cases to be reopened, placing former prisoners in danger of rearrest. Thus the procedural vices of the faceless courts are now prejudicing those the courts find innocent as well as those they have convicted.

In the early hours of June 14, Congress passed a law granting amnesty to military or police personnel and civilians convicted or implicated in human rights crimes during the fifteen year counterinsurgency war. The law required the immediate release of all those convicted or indicted, as well as that all mention of them in police or court records be struck out. It also expressly prohibited new investigations or prosecution of perpetrators who had not yet been identified. The law, one of the most sweeping ever passed in the hemisphere, was presented to Congress without warning, scarcely debated, and promulgated on the following day by Fujimori before the populace and international public opinion had time to react. During the next week, eight members of the Colina Group, an army death squad, who had been convicted and imprisoned for the abduction and murder of nine students and a teacher from the La Cantuta University, walked free. So did those responsible for a 1986 prison massacre and an army lieutenant sentenced to ten years for the slaying of fifteen peasants in Santa Bárbara, Huancavelica, in 1991. The law also granted amnesty to some twenty-six military officers who participated in discussions about ousting Fujimori in November 1993, and to a group of officers who had been charged and imprisoned for criticizing government policy during the border conflict with Ecuador (see below).

The law was sprung on Congress by a pro-Fujimori deputy soon after the surprise reopening of a case involving the slaying in November 1991 of fifteen people at a party in the Lima neighborhood of Barrios Altos, in which members of the Colina group were also implicated. Prosecutor Ana Cecilia Magallanes reopened the case in April and named five army officers, including General Julio Salazar Monroe, head of the National Intelligence Service (Servicio de Inteligencia Nacional, SIN) as responsible. Four of them had been convicted already for involvement in the Cantuta case. Judge Antonia Saquicuray Sánchez opened a formal investigation and ordered the commander-in-chief of the army, Nicolás de Bari Hermosa Ríos, and Vladimiro Montesinos, a close Fujimori advisor and intelligence figure, to appear as witnesses. Following the promulgation of the amnesty law, Judge Saquicuray ruled that the it was inapplicable to the Barrios Altos case on the grounds that it violated Peru's constitution and international obligations under the American Convention on Human Rights. Despite a warning by the public prosecutor that she might be charged with *prevaricato* (breach of public duty), Saquicuray insisted to the Supreme Court on her duty to continue the investigation, and the court's senior prosecutor ruled in her favor. The government reacted by railroading a new law through Congress on June 28 which effectively obligated judges to grant the amnesty. On July 13 the court ruled two to one to apply the amnesty, closing the case. Other cases were closed in the weeks that followed.

Freedom of speech remained a precarious right. In April two retired army generals, Walter Ledesma Rebaza and Carlos Mauricio Agurto, were detained and prosecuted before a military tribunal for "insulting the armed forces and the nation" solely because they had commented critically on the army's conduct of the border conflict with Ecuador in February 1995. Both former officers were supporters of opposition candidate Javier Pérez de Cuellar. Ledesma, who was retired prematurely in 1994, was sentenced in May to forty days in detention because of an interview he gave to the weekly magazine *Caretas*. Ledesma and Mauricio were absolved under the amnesty law.

The Right To Monitor

The position of *defensor del pueblo* (ombudsman), created in August, had not been filled as of this writing. The appointment requires a two-thirds majority in Congress.

Although an initial version of the legislation establishing the position would have given the defensor the authority to enter military premises, have access to classified information, and order the prosecution of officials who refused to cooperate with his or her investigations, these powers were cut from what became law.

In June and early July several human rights lawyers working on the Barrios Altos case, as well as relatives of the victims, received anonymous death threats. The circumstances suggested a concerted operation by military intelligence agents to scare them off the case. Gloria Cano Lengua, of the nongovernmental Association for Human Rights (Asociación Pro-Derechos Humanos, APRODEH) received death threats by telephone in her office. Dr. Guido Gallegos of the Vicaría de Derechos Humanos de Juli, a church-based group in Puno, received an anonymous death note and threatening phone calls from a group calling itself the Patriotic Military Front. On July 8, the Lima offices of the Ecumenical Human Rights Commission (Comisión Ecuménica de Derechos Humanos, COMISEDH) were broken into in the early morning; files were searched and diskettes and other materials handled. General Rodolfo Robles Espinoza, who was cashiered from the army for revealing the participation of the Colina Group in disappearances, received death threats following his return in June from exile in Argentina.

U.S. Policy

The Clinton administration continued to push behind the scenes for piecemeal improvements in Peru's human rights performance, while trying to avoid giving Fujimori an opportunity to dismiss human rights concerns by claiming to be "standing up to the U.S.," as he has done on several occasions in the past. While this "quiet diplomacy" has been useful in some cases, we have consistently urged the administration to use public pressure when private communication fails.

The State Department issued an unusually forthright statement condemning the amnesty law promulgated in June. The June 15 statement by spokesman Nicholas Burns read in part: "We are deeply concerned at both the substance of the law and the peremptory manner in which it was passed. We regret that President Fujimori has signed the bill into law. Doing so demonstrates to the world a lack of serious commitment to the protection of human rights, a principle on which there is broad hemispheric consensus." This statement was an unprecedented declaration of principle on the issue of accountability, giving valuable moral support to relatives of victims of human rights violations and human rights groups. Regrettably, the State Department was silent when Fujimori renewed the faceless courts in October. The administration may have been seeking to avoid a repetition of the Peruvian government's hostile reaction to the findings of the Goldman Commission, a panel of international jurists established in 1993 by the Clinton administration, with the acquiescence of the Fujimori government, to review anti-terrorist legislation. Since the commission reported, the State Department has implicitly distanced itself from the commission's recommendations rather than press publicly for their immediate implementation. While the Goldman Commission called for the government to end trials of civilians by military courts, the Clinton administration apparently believes that this system is reformable.

Plans are underway for a program of U.S. human rights training for military prosecutors and judges to begin in early 1996, according to officials of the U.S. Embassy, a move we consider ill-advised. Military courts, which have a deplorable record of due process violations and a lack of independence and impartiality, should not receive U.S. assistance or training. Any assistance provided to the judiciary should be channeled instead to support an independent review of unfair convictions by military tribunals and faceless courts. In addition, State Department should deny visas to military and former military personnel released under the amnesty law.

The need to secure Peruvian government cooperation with the U.S. anti-narcotics program has been another factor limiting a more public administration profile on human rights. The administration will spend approximately $18 million assisting Peru's anti-narcotics police force in fiscal year 1996, roughly the same level of assistance provided in past years. An effort by the administration to provide approximately $1 million in military assistance as part of its counternarcotics package for fiscal year 1996 was dropped in the wake of strong congressional opposition. Aid to the military has been limited to training since fiscal 1991. Human Rights Watch/Americas strongly opposes police aid on the grounds that the Peruvian police continue to engage with impunity in systematic human rights abuse, particularly torture. Furthermore, drug traffickers, like violent oppositionists, continued to be tried by military tribunals for "treason," with attendant due process violations.

The Work of
Human Rights Watch/Americas

Of Peru's many human rights problems, the deplorable state of the justice system stands out insharp relief, and the main focus of our work was to bring this concern to international attention. In July we published a fifty-page report, *Peru: the Two Faces of Justice*, which analyzed the workings of the anti-terrorist law, the faceless courts, and military tribunals, describing in detail the Kafkaesque situation faced by innocent people accused of terrorism and the mechanisms which have ensured impunity for those guilty of horrific human rights crimes. The report also described and condemned the so-called popular trials carried out by Shining Path, which were often a prelude to cold-blooded murder. In a speech to the U.N. Human Rights Commission in Geneva in February, we highlighted the use of torture and arbitrary detention in Peru through the faceless courts system. In addition, we litigated several cases through the Inter-American Commission on Human Rights and the Inter-American Court of Human Rights. In one of these, the *Case of Neira Alegría* (commonly known as "El Frontón," after the prison where the petitioners were detained), the court found in January that Peru had violated the right to life and the right of habeas corpus of three detainees, ordering Peru to pay their families compensation in an amount to be agreed upon by Peru and the commission.

In February a Human Rights Watch/Americas representative visited Peru during Fujimori's campaign for re-election. Irregularities such as the distribution of pro-Fujimori propaganda by military officers and public officials, the illegal issuing of voting credentials to members of the military, and harassment of opposition candidates, marred the campaign at numerous junctures, at times throwing into question the credibility of the electoral process. In March we wrote to President Fujimori describing abuses we had confirmed during our visit, and calling on him to prevent their repetition. We also sent our findings to César Gaviria, the Secretary General of the Organization of American States (OAS), which had a mission in Peru monitoring the elections, urging him to make the commission's findings public. During the last week of March, the OAS official in charge of the monitoring effort announced that his report would be made available to Peruvian political parties, as well as the government.

HUMAN
RIGHTS
WATCH

ASIA

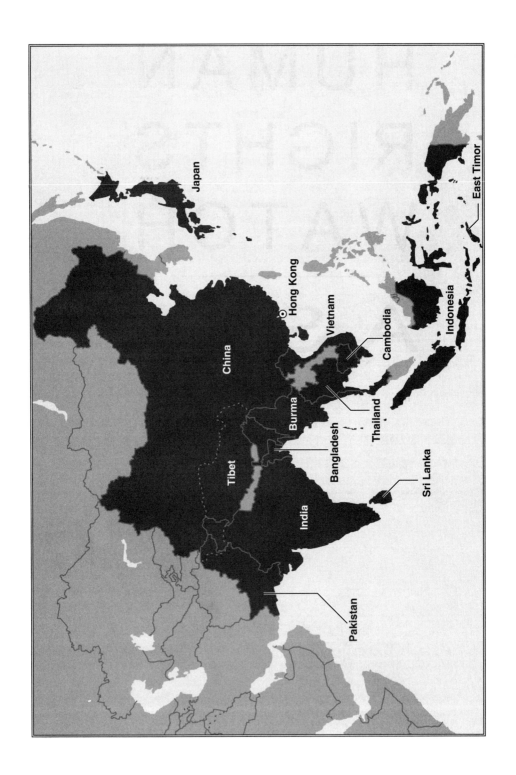

HUMAN RIGHTS WATCH/ASIA OVERVIEW

Human Rights Developments

Human rights was the issue that would not go away for Asia in 1995. It entered security discussions, as fighting resumed or continued in Sri Lanka, Kashmir, Afghanistan, northwestern Cambodia and along the Thai-Burmese border. It became an economic issue, a determinant of aid and an irritant to trade from Burma to Indonesia. Worker rights practices in the region intensified debate over the desirability of a "social clause" in multilateral trade arrangements such as the Asian-Pacific Economic Cooperation (APEC), and human rights abuses led to demands at home and abroad for increased corporate responsibility on the part of foreign businesses as investment in the region continued to grow. The capacity of human rights issues to disrupt bilateral relations was underscored with the row between the Philippines and Singapore over the latter's hanging of Filipina domestic worker Flor Contemplacion and between China and the U.S. concerning China's arrest of American human rights campaigner Harry Wu. Peaceful domestic challenges to authoritarian governments in the region were more often than not couched in terms of a demand for human rights.

At the same time that human rights became so central to political and economic developments in the region, however, the formulation of policies to promote and protect those rights became increasingly complicated. On China, no government succeeded in integrating human rights concerns with other policy interests, and the formula for doing so eluded nongovernmental organizations (NGOs) as well. The release of Burmese opposition leader and Nobel Peace Prize laureate Aung San Suu Kyi on July 10 provided one of the few bright spots in the human rights picture during the year, but it raised new questions about appropriate policy responses from governments, NGOs, and international aid agencies.

In the midst of the policy confusion, however, several trends became apparent. Domestic demands for increased freedom of expression intensified across the region. Local NGOs, foreign businesses, and the international human rights community found common ground in recognizing the importance of an impartial legal system and strengthening the rule of law; Vietnam was increasingly becoming a test case of how law, human rights protection and foreign investment interacted.' The vulnerability to abuse of specific groups, such as women, indigenous peoples, minorities and migrant workers was very much at issue, with growing concern that their vulnerability in many cases increased with economic growth. The exclusion of an Asian NGO voice in regional trade and security fora began to be an issue, and for the first time, a parallel NGO conference took place in Japan in November at the time of the APEC summit. While the U.N. and donor governments continued to be major targets of advocacy efforts, both local and international NGOs increasingly turned their attention to the private sector and to multilateral lending institutions, such as the World Bank and Asian Development Bank.

Human Rights Developments

The gravest human rights abuses in Asia continued to take place in areas of armed internal conflict, where both sides were often responsible for summary executions. The resumption of fighting in Sri Lanka in April led to massacres of villagers by the Liberation Tigers of Tamil Eelam (LTTE) and to the "disappearance" and execution of young Tamil males by the Sri Lankan Special Task Force. International outrage over the beheading of a Norwegian tourist by militants in Kashmir tended to obscure the ongoing human rights violations by the Indian armed forces in the Kashmir Valley, and Burmese military operations along the Thai-Burma border led to refugee outflows, an increase in the internally displaced, and a wide range of army abuses against villagers.

For all the criticism by some Asian governments of the tendency of the West to focus too much on individual civil rights at the expense of communal obligations, it was one of those civil rights—freedom of expression—that became perhaps the paramount political demand of Asians in 1995. In China, Hong Kong, Singapore, Cambodia, Vietnam, Malaysia, Pakistan, India and Indonesia, the freedom to express opinions critical of government leaders and policies became a major issue. On the one hand, the prevalence of the issue supported those who argued that economic growth in Asia would lead to demands for greater civil liberties, as middle-class professionals, for the most part, were the most vocal in seeking greater freedom. On the other hand, the governments in question showed no disposition to make concessions.

In Cambodia, the government's ·systematic campaign against former finance minister, independent parliamentarian and corruption fighter Sam Rainsy, together with the passage of a new press law, symbolized the steady narrowing of the political space opened up by the United Nations Transitional Authority in Cambodia during its eighteen-month peace-keeping operation. Journalists and editors were charged with criminal defamation for articles, and in one case a cartoon, critical of the government.

In China, delegates to the Fourth World Conference on Women got some inkling of the restrictions faced by ordinary Chinese when they found themselves under surveillance, their meetings restricted or canceled, their papers confiscated and their press coverage censored. Wei Jingsheng, the country's most outspoken advocate of political change and respect for human rights who was re-arrested in April 1994 after only six months of freedom, was formally charged on November 21, 1995, with "conducting activities in [an] attempt to overthrow the Chinese government." As of this writing, Wei continued to be held at an undisclosed location. Other critics remained in prison or faced other forms of persecution. Chinese media were ordered to put a favorable spin on sensitive issues and to rely exclusively on Xinhua, the government news agency, when breaking a story.

In Indonesia, members of the urban middle class protested a range of violations of free expression, from the arrest and conviction of three members of an independent journalists' association, to the police investigation and harassment of a parliamentarian who criticized President Soeharto while on a speaking tour of Germany. These actions, and the government's ban on public appearances of popular opposition figures such as Muslim leader Abdurrachman Wahid, seemed designed more to punish and humiliate outspoken individuals than to restrict the flow of information.

In South Asia, the governments appeared more determined to prevent anti-government views from reaching the public. As civil strife between government forces and the Mohajir Qaumi Movement or MQM intensified in the Pakistani city of Karachi, Prime Minister Benazir Bhutto banned six newspapers and canceled the publishing licenses of 122 other publications under a law that had not been used since the 1960s; public pressure forced her to lift the ban after six days. The Indian government likewise curbed independent access to information about developments in the troubled states of Jammu and Kashmir in an effort to portray all outbreaks of violence there as caused directly by Pakistani machinations.

In Hong Kong, the Hong Kong Journalists' Association noted with alarm the increasing tendency of editors to apply self-censorship on issues related to China as 1997, the year of the colony's return to Chinese rule, approached. The firing of a popular political cartoonist seemed a disturbing harbinger of things to come in a place known as having one of the freest presses in all of Asia.

Controls on freedom of expression throughout the region ran counter to calls from the international community for increased "transparency" as a sign of good governance. Another hallmark of good governance on which Asian governments had a very mixed record was respect for the rule of law. Impartial legal systems, free of corruption and with full independence of the judiciary are as important to businesses as they are to the human rights community, but they have been hard to find in Asia. Developments on this front in 1995 were mixed. In Malaysia, the effect of Prime Minister Mahathir's destruction of judicial independence became clear when a national scandal erupted over a company's purchase of a judge to rule in its favor in a takeover bid. In Hong Kong, pro-democracy activists were outraged at Britain's capitulation to Chinese pressure over the creation of a Court of Final Appeal that is to take the place of the Privy Council after 1997; they believed that implementing legislation approved by the two countries would compromise judicial independence and subject the court to political pressure from China. On the other side of the balance sheet, however, Indonesian courts, generally regarded as among the most corrupt and politicized in the region, made three courageous decisions during the year that went counter to government wishes. One was a ruling that a press law used to ban a popular magazine was unconstitutional; one declared the sacking of a dissident professor to be illegal; and one overturned the conviction of eight people convicted through the use of coerced confessions in a celebrated murder trial.

Several countries in the region repealed or drastically reduced the use of broadly-worded internal security laws that had been the target of international and domestic criticism. In most cases, however, other laws, equally broadly worded, were substituted for the offending legislation and used to arrest government critics. Thus, the Chinese government appeared to use the 1993 state security laws to arrest dissidents in place of the heavily criticized laws on "counterrevolution." Those in Indonesia who five years ago would have been charged under the 1963 Anti-Subversion law were charged instead with "spreading hatred of the government" under Article 154 of the Criminal Code. In one much more positive develop-

ment, India allowed the notorious Terrorist and Disruptive Activities (TADA) act to lapse, largely in response to domestic pressure. However more than 6,000 people detained under TADA remained in custody during the year. Vietnam undertook a major overhaul of its criminal code; the results were not yet apparent by the end of the year.

Worker rights issues were a major concern throughout the region, with bonded labor a particular concern in South Asia, abuses of migrant labor a growing concern of NGOs in East and Southeast Asia, and freedom of association and the right to strike an ongoing issue in South Korea, Indonesia and China, among other countries. The South Korean government, seeking entry into the Organization for Economic Cooperation and Development (OECD), the club of industrial democracies, boycotted an OECD seminar on worker rights in Seoul in order to avoid awkward questions about Korea's repressive labor laws and practices. A crackdown on labor activists in May and June led to arrests of key Korean organizers. Throughout the region, concern about violations of worker rights was such that a major NGO meeting to address this issue was planned to take place in Japan just prior to the APEC summit in November.

Ratification of international instruments on human rights proceeded at a snail's pace during the year, and Asia continued to have a poor record on acceptance of international standards. On July 5, 1995, Malaysia ratified the convention on Elimination of all Forms of Discrimination Against Women, just in time for the Beijing Women's conference. At the same time, the generally useful role played by national commissions of human rights in India and Indonesia suggested that the formation of these bodies elsewhere in the region where a strong NGO community was present might aid in the promotion of human rights and acceptance of international standards.

The Right to Monitor

The pattern of restrictions on human rights monitoring was much the same as in previous years. No overt human rights monitoring was possible in North Korea, China/Tibet, Burma, Vietnam, or Singapore. Human rights monitors faced severe difficulties, including denial of access, legal restrictions, or intimidation, in areas marked by civil strife or conflict in the region, such as East Timor, Irian Jaya, Kashmir, Assam (India) and the Jaffna peninsula in Sri Lanka. In the latter case, the main obstacle to monitoring was as much if not more the activities of the LTTE as it was the Sri Lankan government.

In India, Burma, China, Tibet, Indonesia and East Timor, people were arrested or continued to languish in prison for passing information on human rights abuses to outsiders, publishing reports on human rights violations or organizing demonstrations in support of human rights. At least one Indian human rights monitor "disappeared" after being arrested during the year, apparently in connection with such reporting.

Human rights NGOs in many Asian countries faced harassment for their monitoring activities. In Malaysia, Irene Fernandez, director of the women's rights organization, Tenaganita, was called to police headquarters in Kuala Lumpur in late September for interrogation in connection with possible criminal defamation charges after her organization published a report on abuses in Malaysian immigration detention centers. The U.S. company Freeport McMoran urged the U.S. embassy to cut off funds to the Indonesian human rights and environmental organization, Walhi, after Walhi reported on links between Freeport security guards and the local military in the commission of human rights abuses. In China, where independent human rights organizations do not exist, individuals who tried to circulate petitions demanding more respect for human rights were harassed or imprisoned, with twenty-two people still detained as of November. In Pakistan, human rights lawyers representing Christian defendants were attacked by extremist religious groups. The government has done little to prevent such attacks or to punish those responsible.

The Role of the International Community

Multilateralism on Asian human rights issues seemed moribund in 1995. There were almost no examples of international cooperation to set concrete human rights goals and develop strategies for achieving them. The amount of time and resources required to coordinate strategy on human rights was clearly more than most individual governments were willing to spend. The one exception may have been the U.S. effort, ultimately unsuccessful, to push through a resolution on China at the U.N. Commission on Human Rights in Geneva in March.

Even individual governments that professed concern about human rights in Asia found it extremely difficult to come up with coherent, consistent or effective policies to reflect that concern, especially when strategic and economic interests were also strong. The desire to strengthen trade and investment ties to Asian countries often pushed human rights to the sidelines, although there were some efforts in the U.S., Australia and elsewhere to define principles for businesses operating in repressive countries. In some cases, conflicting signals on human rights were the result of contradictory domestic pressures on governments: U.S. policy on China was probably the best example of a grab bag of competing concerns, which ended up addressing none effectively. Within Asia, donor governments were strong on some countries and weak on others, again as the result of different pressures: the business lobby in Germany was stronger on China and Indonesia than on Burma, for example, while the Australian government clearly had to take public opinion more into account in addressing East Timor than in formulating policy on India.

In some cases, what appeared to be lack of coherence may have been a conscious policy choice. Japan, for example, the region's largest aid donor, was willing to exert human rights pressure through the United Nations but emphasized economic incentives rather than economic pressure in its bilateral relations.

The dilemmas that governments face in formulating human rights policy were brought into stark relief with the release of Aung San Suu Kyi. As welcome as it was unexpected, her release raised several questions. To what extent did world attention on Suu Kyi's detention make it more difficult to keep other human rights concerns on the international agenda after her release? Did her release prove the value of economic and diplomatic pressure from the West, or the success of economic incentives (resumed aid) from Japan, or neither? What was the appropriate mix of punitive measures and incentives in approaching a country like Burma? What were the relative strengths and shortcomings of "constructive engagement" as practiced by the Association of Southeast Asian Nations (ASEAN) or distinct from political isolation, as practiced by the U.S. and most of Europe? How effective was the latter when the same governments placed no curbs on investment? Did governmental and commercial undertakings have to be coordinated for a human rights policy to be successful? How should human rights pressure and humanitarian needs be balanced? These questions remained unanswered, as governments and NGOs sought effective ways of continuing pressure for fundamental reforms and compliance with successive U.N. General Assembly resolutions on Burma.

U.N. staff and agencies had a mixed record in the region. U.N. High Commissioner for Human Rights José Ayala Lasso's critical, if guarded comments during his visit to Kashmir were widely reported in the Indian press, and that in itself was useful. The U.N.'s sponsorship of talks on East Timor in July 1995 were an important first step in bringing key East Timorese factions together, but by the end of the year, it was too early to tell whether they would have any impact on a worsening human rights situation there. The U.N. Special Representative in Cambodia and the office in Phnom Penh of the U.N. Center for Human Rights continued to perform admirably, despite the unhappiness of the Cambodian government with their criti-

cal reports. At year's end, it seemed as though Yozo Yokota, U.N. Special Rapporteur on Burma, might recommend an ongoing human rights monitoring presence in Burma.

In Thailand, the office of the U.N. High Commissioner for Refugees (UNHCR) failed to protect refugees from Burma. Indeed, the office in Bangkok did not even complain publicly when refugees were attacked in the camps or when Thai authorities refused to allow refugees asylum from fighting in the Shan State. Meanwhile, Burmese dissidents seeking asylum in Bangkok were subject to a new UNHCR ruling in June that allowed very few of them to be considered refugees. They were left with the option of returning to Burma, with no guarantees for their safety, or seeking illegal employment in Thailand.

The Work of
Human Rights Watch/Asia

The year was marked by a heightened emphasis on cooperation and consultation with local NGOs, by an effort to reach out to new constituencies and to establish connections between the business and human rights communities, and by an effort to shift our research agenda to reflect concerns in the region.

We created a new position of NGO liaison to better maintain communication with local NGOs across Asia, understand their priorities and facilitate exchanges of information. The position, filled by a long-time researcher, is still evolving, but in addition to improving overall ties to the NGO community in Asia, it is expected to help researchers formulate more effective strategies for working with local partners on human rights concerns. Individual researchers gave high priority to consultation with local and international NGOs: we responded to a plea from Pakistani NGOs to send an observer to a blasphemy trial in February, we organized roundtable discussions in Europe and the U.S. for organizations active on Burma issues, and we helped arrange visits abroad for Cambodian and Indonesian NGOs. Where possible, advocacy work in Japan, the U.S. and Europe was preceded by consultation with domestic NGOs. That consultation was particularly important on labor rights issues. The Fourth World Conference on Women in Beijing provided an important forum for communication and cooperation on women's human rights. A brochure written for delegates to that conference, introducing them to Chinese law and practices that might affect their ability to hold meetings, circulate material or take part in demonstrations, was eagerly received and translated into several languages.

Throughout the year, we sought to examine the role of trade and investment in Asia as it affects human rights issues. At one level, this meant continuing our efforts to identify common interests linking the business and human rights communities, such as increasing the transparency of government procedures, strengthening the rule of law and improving industrial relations and the treatment of workers. Recognition of these interests facilitated dialogue with businesses working on Indonesia, Vietnam and China, in particular. At another level, we did not hesitate to criticize companies whose practices we believed contributed to human rights abuses, and we became a major voice within the human rights community seeking enhanced corporate responsibility for businesses operating in Asia. We urged a freeze on all investment in Burma until the Burmese government was willing to provide verifiable guarantees that the use of forced labor had ceased. We met with representatives of the Swiss pharmaceutical corporation, Sandoz Limited, Basel, Switzerland, the producer of the main drug used in Chinese transplant operations, and stressed their responsibility to press for an end to the use of executed prisoners as organ donors.

Human Rights Watch/Asia called on foreign investors to avoid any involvement with the Three Gorges Dam project until the Chinese government provided verifiable guarantees that the rights of the more than one million people scheduled to be relocated would be protected. In the spring, we met with representatives of a major U.S. company involved in the construction of the Three Gorges Dam. We raised concerns about the use of forced or prison labor in the project.

We strengthened direct communication with Asian governments during the year and were in regular and ongoing dialogue with Pakistani, Sri Lankan, Vietnamese, Cambodian, and Indonesian officials, as well as with the Hong Kong government. In meetings with representatives of the Indian and Indonesian national human rights commissions, we raised the possibility of discussing our policy recommendations prior to the publication of our reports. The exact nature of our relationship to those commissions was still being discussed at year's end.

During the year, we made a concerted effort to reach out to the broader human rights community, especially those organizations working on development, environment, and migrant worker issues. A report on human rights and forest management in the Philippines, for example, and another on the Three Gorges dam in China, as well as ongoing concerns about logging in Cambodia and mining in Indonesia, helped strengthen ties to environmental activists. One result was a much wider advocacy network.

Widening of advocacy possibilities was also furthered by much more frequent discussions with staff of the World Bank and other multilateral lending institutions such as the Asian Development Bank (ADB.) After the ADB opened an office in Washington, D.C., and adopted a policy on "governance" late in the year, we laid the groundwork for a series of meetings with senior staff there to discuss the possible human rights impact of specific ADB projects.

Reflecting priorities in the region, our long-term research and advocacy agenda included a strong focus on worker rights, including migrant workers. A mission to the Republic of Korea in June focused exclusively on labor rights, a report on Pakistan examined bonded labor, and a petition to the U.S. Trade Representative urging a review of Indonesian labor rights practices was based on new research on abuses against workers in export-oriented manufacturing. For the first time, Human Rights Watch mounted a campaign to raise labor rights concerns in conjunction with deliberations by the Organization of Economic Cooperation and Development (OECD) as it considered the Republic of Korea's bid to become a member. We also worked through our Brussels office to forge a coalition with international labor groups that filed the first ever petition under the terms of a new European Union Generalized System of Preferences (GSP) scheme linking tariff benefits to human rights; the petition was on bonded child labor in Pakistan.

At year's end, research was underway on abuses against migrant workers across the region: Burmese in Thailand, Thais in Japan, Indonesians in Malaysia and Filipinas in Hong Kong and Taiwan.

BURMA

Human Rights Developments ·

The most significant human rights event in Burma in 1995 was the release on July 10 of Nobel laureate and opposition leader Daw Aung San Suu Kyi after six years of house arrest. Paradoxically, the governing military State Law and Order Restoration Council (SLORC) took an increasingly hard-line stance during the year, and there was no overall improvement in the human rights situation. In some areas abuses increased, notably in the Karen, Karenni and Shan States where there was fighting, while throughout the country thousands of civilians were forced to work as unpaid laborers for the army. The SLORC continued to deny basic rights such as freedom of speech, association and religion and the right of citizens to participate in the political process.

Daw Suu and more than 200 other political prisoners were released in 1995, but at least 1,000 people, including sixteen members of parliament elected in 1990—all representing Daw Suu's party, the National League for Democracy (NLD)—remained in jail, and there were new political arrests.

In February, nine students were arrested at the funeral of former prime minister U Nu when they began singing a pro-democracy anthem and were later sentenced to seven years in prison. A month later, six more students were arrested for allegedly obstructing soldiers preparing for Armed Forces Day. In June, four veteran politicians in their late sixties were arrested and sentenced to seven years in prison. On September 27, a student, Ye Htut, was arrested for having sent information to Burmese abroad; as of November, his trial was still pending. All of these people were tried under Section 5 (j) of the 1950 Emergency Provisions Act, for "spreading false news about the government."

The treatment of those detained remained an issue of concern. Two of the students were known to have been beaten immediately after their arrest, but the fate of the other is not known. In June, Dr. Thida, a twenty-nine-year-old medical doctor who was sentenced to twenty years of imprisonment in 1993 under the 1950 Act, was reported to have contracted tuberculosis while in Rangoon's Insein jail. She was also diagnosed in June as needing surgery to remove ovarian cysts. Dr. Thida reportedly received inadequate medical treatment.

The year opened with a renewed offensive against the Karen National Union (KNU) following a split within the KNU and the formation of the Democratic Karen Buddhist Army (DKBA), which was supported by the SLORC. By January 27, the KNU headquarters at Manerplaw near the confluence of the Salween and Moei rivers had fallen, and on February 23 the KNU retreated from its base at Kawmoora. Since early November 1994, the SLORC army had arrested as many as 5,000 men from towns and villages in the Karen and Mon states and even from Rangoon to work as porters in preparation for this offensive. Although the offensive was relatively short, scores, and possibly hundreds, of forced porters are believed to have died from beatings or exhaustion compounded by lack of food. Others were caught in the cross fire during the fighting or were killed by landmines laid by both the SLORC and the KNU.

In early February the offensive took a new turn as DKBA and SLORC troops launched the first of several raids into refugee camps in Thailand. There were already more than 70,000 refugees in these camps, joined by some 10,000 people after the fall of Manerplaw. Many camps were situated along the banks of the Salween and Moei rivers, which mark the border between Burma and Thailand, and were easily accessible by the DKBA/SLORC troops. The raids, which were intended to terrify the refugees into returning to Burma, continued from February to May. They left fifteen refugees and Thai civilians dead, scores injured, and at least 1,000 houses in different camps razed. In addition, the DKBA/SLORC forces kidnaped more than twenty-five individuals and took them back to Burma at gunpoint, forcing hundreds of others to return through a campaign of fear and intimidation (see Thailand section). Following its defeat in these areas, the KNU made several offers to the SLORC to engage in cease-fire talks. While there were meetings between the two sides, at the end of October there was no sign of any progress.

Talks with other ethnic groups were more successful, but the weakness of the military cease-fires as solutions to long-term ethnic insurgencies became apparent as the SLORC failed to deliver the promises of reconciliation and economic development that formed the basis of the agreements. Moreover, the SLORC continued to refuse to discuss lasting political solutions with the ethnic groups, claiming that as a temporary, military government, it had no authority to discuss political matters.

In the Karenni State, the Karenni Nationalities Progressive Party (KNPP) signed a cease-fire agreement at a ceremony in Loikaw on March 21, making it the fourth and final armed group in the Karenni State to do so. But on June 28, the KNPP issued a statement claiming that the SLORC had broken the terms of the agreement by sending an additional 2,000 troops into its territory and

continuing to take porters from the area. Two days later, fighting broke out after the SLORC launched an attack on the KNPP headquarters near the Thai border. The SLORC insisted that the offensive was launched in order to chase away illegal Thai loggers and to secure a route through the KNPP territory to that of drug warlord Khun Sa. In later addresses, the SLORC also claimed that it had positioned so many troops in the area, close to the Thai border, because of possible threats to national security during the time of the general election in Thailand.

During the fighting some porters escaped into Thailand, but these were relatively few, given the total numbers believed to have been taken in Loikaw township alone. Those who did arrive in Thailand told of witnessing the deaths of fellow porters from landmines, stories which were confirmed by medical workers who reported that in just one day seven porters arrived in a refugee camp all close to death as a result of landmine injuries. These reports led observers to believe that landmines planted by both sides may have killed many porters who fled.

The fighting died down during the rainy season in August and September, though skirmishes were still reported. By October, despite the arrival of SLORC intermediaries in Thailand, there was no sign of any new settlement, and the KNPP claimed that the SLORC was preparing for a major offensive against it and had brought in a further 6,000 troops.

In the south, the New Mon State Party (NMSP) signed a cease-fire on June 29. Discussions that had started between the NMSP and the SLORC in 1993 were helped in 1995 by three intermediaries, one of whom was an elected member of parliament for the Mon National Democratic Front who had been in jail from 1991 until November 1994. While the agreement itself, like all other previous agreements, was not made public, it was known to have included the right of NMSP troops to retain their arms within twenty small circles of territory. However, the SLORC did not agree to the right of the

Mon to receive developmental assistance from international nongovernmental organizations (NGOs) in Thailand, nor were there clear decisions made on rights to the natural resources of the area, especially logging and fishing rights. The agreement did include a program to repatriate the 11,000 Mon refugees in Thailand, with no international monitoring or guarantees of safety on return, fueling speculation that Thailand had played a major part in pressuring the Mon to accept the terms.

In the northeast, fighting continued against drug warlord Khun Sa in the Shan State. In January the SLORC had announced its resolve to crush his Muang Tai Army (MTA) by the end of the year. SLORC had also made this promise in 1994, but by October the much-heralded final offensive had not materialized. However, Khun Sa suffered a major blow in August when one of his military commanders broke off to form his own Shan nationalist group, taking between 1,000 and 2,000 troops with him. Then, in September, the United Wa State Party, a group that has had a cease-fire agreement with the SLORC since 1989, joined in the attack against Khun Sa, allegedly in order to secure its own stake in the drug trafficking market.

As in other areas, the Burmese army impressed thousands of civilians to work as porters in the offensive against Khun Sa. In January, indiscriminate aerial bombardments by the SLORC forced hundreds of people to flee from villages near Kengtung, and in March and April heavy fighting forced others to seek refuge in Thailand (see Thailand section).

At the same time, inside the Karen State, thousands of villagers living in areas where the Karen had been active were forcibly relocated to areas under DKBA/SLORC control. At first these relocations were restricted to areas in Hlaingbwe township near the DKBA headquarters, but by July relocations were also reported to have taken place as far south as Kyaukkyi, Kawkereik and Pa-an townships. Relocated families either were forced to live in encampments guarded by the army, or they fled to the forests. From the camps, they were forced to work as laborers on road-building and other infrastructural projects for the army.

Indeed, forced labor was endemic in Burma. As the SLORC sought to open up the economy to international investors, it forced tens of thousands of civilians and prisoners to rebuild the country's long-neglected infrastructure. During the year, scores of people died on such projects from beatings, lack of medical care and food, and sheer exhaustion. In the southwest, at the site of the Rangoon-Kyaukpyu road in Arakan State, at least twelve people died during December 1994 and January 1995 from untreated fevers. In the far north, some 3,000 people were taken from Putao, Kachin State, in late 1994 to work at a remote site on the Putao-Sumprabum road. After walking for six days to reach the site, they found that the rice supplies that had been promised by the army had not arrived, and they had to walk back. Many died on the journey from malaria and other diseases, exacerbated by lack of food. In the northwest, soldiers supervising the work killed a woman working on the Pakokku-Kalemyo railway line in Chin State after she had stopped working twice to feed her young baby. In the south, in Mon State, two to three families each week fled from the site of the Ye-Tavoy railway to refugee camps in Thailand.

In Arakan, Burma's most western state, refugees who had fled into neighboring Bangladesh in 1992 returned to Burma. Of the 270,000 refugees, only 40,000 remained in camps by October, though it was unclear how many of these would eventually be accepted by the Burmese authorities. Despite the presence of fifteen UNHCR staff in Arakan and two NGOs running programs to reintegrate the refugees, reports continued of abuses of Muslims, especially of those Muslims who had not left Burma in 1992. In their *Bulletin* of June, the UNHCR claimed that it had succeeded in getting an agreement to limit the amount of forced labor for returnees to one day a week. However, the government had plans to build more than 1,200 miles of road in the area, and it was unclear how the UNHCR would be able to monitor the many forced labor sites in Maungdaw and Buthidaung townships. Muslims who remained in 1992 were also subject to forced relocations and forced labor and religious persecution, and villages in Mro Haung and Myauk Oo townships were forced to move to Buthidaung, forming a Muslim enclave on the border with Bangladesh.

Following Daw Suu's release from house arrest in July, members of her party, the NLD, were able to visit her freely. Among her first visitors were former chairmen of the NLD, U Tin Oo and U Kyi Maung, who had been released from jail in March. She was also able to meet foreign journalists, ambassadors and other international representatives, including the U.S. ambassador to the U.N. Madeleine Albright, who visited in early September. Daw Su's international profile was enhanced by the showing of a videotaped speech she gave to open the NGO Forum of the U.N. Women's Conference in Beijing. Daw Suu also held regular Sunday morning gatherings outside her home, at which up to 200 people would come to hear her speak. She made her first trip outside Rangoon on October 4, visiting the famous Thanmanyat monk in the Karen State. In press interviews Daw Suu continued to take a reconciliatory line, calling on the SLORC to begin dialogue with her. On October 11, the NLD re-elected Daw Suu, U Tin Oo and U Kyi Maung as general secretary and vice-chairmen of the party respectively. This was a move intended to deprive the SLORC of their main justification for not talking to her: she was not just an ordinary individual, but re-instated as a party representative.

The National Convention, the SLORC's constitutional assembly, had begun deliberations on a new constitution in January 1993, sat for six months from September 1994 to March 1995 and was then suspended for six months until October 24. Nearly 600 of the 700 delegates were hand-picked by the SLORC. During this session, the question of representation at the local and national level for ethnic groups was discussed, including representation for those groups that were not included under previous constitutions—the most contentious issue for Burma's political future. Despite strong statements opposing the government proposals by ethnic representatives and members of the NLD, the National Convention approved the formula of 'self-administered zones' entitling groups to one representative in the House of Nationalities. In early October the convention was again postponed for a further month, leading analysts to suggest that the SLORC feared an NLD walk-out if Daw Suu was not invited to attend the convention.

The Right to Monitor

There are no indigenous human rights organizations in Burma, and no international human rights organizations were permitted to visit the country during the year.

U.N. bodies, however, were given limited access. In January the International Labor Organization conducted a preliminary mission to investigate the government's compliance with Article 87 of the ILO Convention concerning freedom of association. By the end of the year, however, the ILO had not decided to conduct a formal mission. In October, U.N. Special Rapporteur to Burma Prof. Yozo Yokota went to Burma for the fourth consecutive year and met with Daw Aung San Suu Kyi for the first time; his previous requests to see her had all been denied.

At the same time, the government refused to allow international monitoring of prisons. The International Committee of the Red Cross (ICRC) announced on June 16 that it would close its office in Rangoon the following month due to the failure of negotiations with the SLORC on allowing the ICRC regular and confidential access to prisoners.

The Role of
the International Community

On December 13, 1994, the U.N. General Assembly passed the toughest ever resolution on Burma. A key part of the resolution called on the secretary-general of the U.N. to assist in implementing the resolution, including facilitating a political dialogue between the SLORC, the democratic opposition and ethnic minorities. On that basis, Alvaro de Soto, the assistant secretary-general for political affairs, spent two days in Rangoon in February 1995 to follow up meetings held in Rangoon in November. At the U.N. Commission on Human Rights in March, the mandate of the special rapporteur to Burma was once again renewed. At the same meeting, the U.N. secretary-general presented a report in which he complained that Mr. de Soto had not been permitted to meet with Daw Suu, but made it clear that meetings with the SLORC would continue in the spring. No further meetings took place until after the release of Daw Suu. Mr. de Soto went to Burma again in August and met with Daw Suu, but was unable to see Gen. Khin Nyunt, the Secretary-1 of the SLORC. Press reports suggested that the SLORC was not prepared to enter into meaningful discussions with the U.N.'s representatives.

The efforts of the secretary-general's office failed to receive adequate support from the international community. No governments took concerted action to exert pressure on the SLORC to ensure that the resolution's recommendations were implemented. Indeed, when the SLORC launched its attack against the KNU, just days after the resolution was passed, only the U.S. government reacted with a strong statement, condemning the use of civilian porters in the January offensive. In mid-February, the European Union issued a similar statement, but days later the German Deputy Foreign Minister, Helmut Schaefer visited Rangoon to continue the policy of "critical dialogue" adopted by the European Union in 1994.

Worse yet, governments did not back up their rhetoric on Burma by denying the SLORC the benefit of bilateral aid and investment. Instead, at the end of February, the British embassy in Rangoon launched the second "British Week" aimed at encouraging British business in Burma. On March 18—as the SLORC-backed DKBO attacks

on refugees in Thailand were at their height—Japan announced an agreement to give Burma an $11 million grant for "agricultural development." In April, Tokyo also granted Burma debt relief worth $4 million.

Following the release of Daw Suu in July, the attitude of some governments toward the SLORC further softened—notably Japan, which had previously maintained support for the international consensus on Burma. Differences in approach emerged even on the the day of her release, with Western countries reacting in a spirit of "cautious optimism" and Asian governments, such as Japan and Thailand, welcoming the move as "substantive progress." Later, Tokyo indicated it planned to resume some Official Development Assistance (ODA) projects suspended in principle since 1998 (see Japan section). South Korea also rewarded the SLORC with a government loan of $16.8 million in October.

China continued to be a key supporter of the SLORC. The relationship was enhanced by the visit to Rangoon of Chinese Premier Li Peng in December 1994, followed by a flurry of diplomatic trips between the two countries during the year, including a delegation of 150 Burmese officials and businessmen who took part in the Yunnan trade fair in August. Arms supplies remained a crucial element of the Sino-Burmese relationship. Throughout the year, arms shipments arrived in Rangoon from a November 1994 deal reportedly including $400 million worth of helicopters, armored vehicles, rifles and parachutes. Several Chinese naval vessels, purchased with a $40 million interest-free loan, also arrived in June.

The ever increasing closeness between China and Burma was disquieting for Burma's other neighbors, notably India, and prompted India to reopen official border trade in April for the first time since the 1962 military coup. The Association of South East Asian Nations (ASEAN) also sought to increase its economic influence in Burma, and by March Singapore had become the second largest investor, with projects totaling $294 million.

However, relations with Thailand, which had been the originator of ASEAN's "constructive engagement" policy, soured during the year. When DKBA/SLORC troops attacked refugees, Thai police and villagers in Thailand, the Thai government maintained a policy of appeasement, barely even criticizing the SLORC for the attacks. The SLORC, on the other hand, showed no such restraint in condemning what it saw as Thailand's un-neighborly acts. It accused Thailand of supporting Khun Sa by allowing his forces to seek medical care and obtain food supplies in Thailand, and in August the SLORC condemned the murder of a Burmese fisherman by his Thai bosses, who were also illegally fishing in Thai waters. The construction of the Mae Sot-Myawaddy "Friendship Bridge" was suspended in June, and by September all border crossings between the two countries were closed.

Nevertheless, Thailand still supported the SLORC in its bid to become a member of ASEAN. Bangkok's position was made public at the ASEAN Ministerial Conference in July when Foreign Minister U Ohn Gyaw acceded to the Treaty of Amity and Cooperation, the first step towards membership. During the ASEAN meeting, Australia and the European Union urged the ASEAN countries not to grant Burma membership too rapidly, insisting that the SLORC needed to do much more than release Daw Suu. But the ASEAN governments ignored this warning and arranged for a special conference to take place in December to assess ways in which they could facilitate Burma's and Cambodia's entry into the forum in the shortest possible time. In the U.S., the Clinton administration faced congressional pressure to respond to the "further deterioration of human rights in Burma," as described by sixty-one members of the House of Representatives in a letter to President Clinton on June 1, 1995. On June 21, the administration announced that it would reward SLORC's cooperation in allowing the Drug Enforcement Administration (DEA) to undertake a joint opium yield survey by stepping up some forms of anti-narcotics assistance to Burma. This included an agreement to provide limited in-country training for SLORC's anti-narcotics enforcement agencies as well as an exchange of information on anti-drug operations. This decision contradicted earlier administration statements that without progress on each of the three fronts of human rights, democratization, and narcotics control, an upgrading of U.S. cooperation could not take place. In June, the House of Representatives adopted by a decisive 359-38 vote an amendment to the fiscal year 1996 foreign appropriations bill prohibiting anti-narcotics assistance to Burma, including training. As of the end of October, the bill was still awaiting final approval by Congress.

Following the release of Daw Suu, President Clinton issued a statement welcoming the news but expressing "concern about a number of serious and unresolved human rights problems in Burma." The White House then dispatched Ambassador Albright to visit Daw Suu and senior members of the SLORC in early September. She delivered a tough message, calling for "fundamental progress toward democracy and respect for human rights" before relations with the U.S. could be improved or the U.S. would consider lifting the ban on World Bank loans to Burma imposed since 1988.

However, while the State Department did not rule out the possibility of further economic sanctions, such as prohibitions on private U.S. investment, the administration took no moves to implement this option. By 1995, the U.S. was the fourth largest investor in Burma, with investment primarily in the oil sector, totaling some $203 million. An abortive attempt to impose comprehensive sanctions, including a ban on all U.S. investment in Burma, was led by Senator Mitch McConnell, who introduced legislation in July. But he failed in his attempt to insert the bill as a last minute amendment to the 1996 foreign aid legislation.

The Work of
Human Rights Watch/Asia

Human Rights Watch/Asia continued to press governments and the international community to exert effective political and economic pressure on the SLORC for fundamental improvements in human rights. It sponsored regular "Burma Roundtable" meetings in Washington, London and Brussels; sent missions to discuss Burma policy with government officials in Paris and Tokyo and at conferences in Europe and Seoul; and maintained close contacts with key offices of the European Union, the U.S. State Department, the World Bank, and the relevant U.N. agencies carrying a mandate on Burma. Human Rights Watch/Asia also provided information and briefings to the U.N. special rapporteur to Burma throughout the year. When Daw Aung San Suu Kyi was released, Human Rights Watch/Asia laid out specific recommendations for an international response, putting her release in perspective and laying the groundwork for a long-term strategy aimed at focusing attention on the broader situation in Burma. These recommendations were presented in congressional testimony in both the House and Senate and in a major report.

Human Rights Watch/Asia published three reports on Burma during the year. The first, *Burma/Thailand: The Mon—Persecuted in Burma, Forced out by Thailand,* was published in December 1994 and documented abuses by the Burmese army of forced laborers on the Ye-Tavoy railway and the history of the treatment that refugees from the area received in Thailand. A second report released on March 27, *Abuses since the Fall of Manerplaw,* was based on research in Thailand in January and February and included testimony from more than fifty men who had been taken to work as porters for the army. The third report, *Entrenchment or Reform?: Human Rights Developments and the Need for Continued International Pressure,* released on July 26, assessed the human rights situation in light of the release of Daw Suu.

CAMBODIA

Human Rights Developments

The human rights situation deteriorated markedly during the second year of Cambodia's new Royal Government, which continued to avoid punishing abuses committed by its own military and police forces and instead vigorously attacked opposition political figures and the press. The governing coalition also condoned the expulsion of dissident parliamentarians from the legislature despite worldwide protests, and encouraged the legislature to enact a series of laws that left the independence of the judiciary and freedom of the media on an insecure footing. In September, the worst political violence since the 1993 election broke out, raising the prospect of yet further violence should local elections proceed in 1996.

Low-level war with the Khmer Rouge continued. In late 1994 and continuing into 1995, the guerrillas shifted tactics, directly attacking civilian settlements in an effort to exacerbate internal displacement and food shortages. A stream of defections from Khmer Rouge ranks continued even after the official amnesty period expired, and some defectors reported that in response the guerrilla leadership mounted purges and stepped up extrajudicial executions of those it deemed disloyal. The kidnaping of civilians for profit and political advantage continued to be a staple Khmer Rouge tactic, and finally came to the attention of the international community when a series of young Europeans were abducted, and in some cases, killed. The Khmer Rouge continued to engage in and endorse the planting of landmines and hidden booby traps even while the government declared a ban on the use of landmines, a ban that has not been scrupulously enforced. Both sides to the conflict engaged in instances of rape and widespread pillage, in contravention of the international laws of war.

The government outlawed the Khmer Rouge in July 1994, and the first prosecutions under the law took place at the conclusion of a statutory amnesty period in February 1995 (amnesties for voluntary military defectors, however, continued). These cases, involving two men accused of laying mines in Battambang, realized fears that the law could be misused for abusive prosecutions. The accused, both returnees from a Khmer Rouge border camp in Thailand, were convicted and sentenced to twenty-five years of imprisonment each, although the government's case rested on confessions obtained by torture; the cases are now on appeal on the basis of numerous substantive and procedural flaws. The political pressures and lack of due process evident in these trials cast in an ominous light the tendency of government authorities to accuse all critics of being "Khmer Rouge," an accusation voiced by Second Prime Minister Hun Sen as recently as September 23.

Sam Rainsy, a former finance minister and member of the royalist FUNCINPEC party and the most prominent political critic of the government, came in for repeated attack throughout the year, including threats to his life and safety that appeared to emanate from the highest levels of the government. In March 1995, the government withdrew his bodyguards, some of whom later left the Ministry of Interior and continued in Sam Rainsy's private employ. In May, the FUNCINPEC party expelled Rainsy in an irregular proceeding, and on June 22, the National Assembly expelled him as a parliamentarian, despite concerns raised as to the legality of such a move by the Interparliamentary Union, the U.N. Special Representative, former U.N. officials closely involved with the drafting of Cambodia's constitution and election law, and legislators around the world. On the night of July 13-14, three of Rainsy's bodyguards and another man were abducted and taken to a Ministry of Defense installation where several dozen soldiers beat one and pointed guns at their heads, demanding that they identify Rainsy as a "Khmer Rouge."

The government confirms that the four men were interrogated, but denies there was any wrongdoing and claims that they spontaneously and inexplicably drove to the military base on their own accord.

Sam Rainsy's expulsion opened the prospect that other independent legislators would be stripped of their position and their parliamentary immunity. In July, a rift opened in the small Buddhist Liberal Democratic Party (BLDP) between Ieng Mouly, currently minister of information, and Son Sann, the party's founder. Ieng Mouly called an ad hoc party congress (boycotted by Son Sann's supporters) at which his faction voted to expel Son Sann's from the executive committee and announced a vote of "no confidence" in Son San and five other BLDP members; the Ieng Mouly faction subsequently voted to expel the six in August, among them four sitting legislators. The prime ministers recognized Ieng Mouly as the new party leader and warned Son Sann not to proceed with his own party congress unless he first reconciled with Ieng Mouly. Son Sann's group went ahead with plans, asking the Interior Ministry for protection, which was denied. On the evening before the congress, September 30, grenades were thrown at a pagoda and at the party headquarters where Son Sann's supporters had gathered, injuring between thirty and fifty bystanders. The meeting proceeded anyway on October 1, with more than a thousand participants crowding the party headquarters and the street outside. Government military police, however, waited until the U.S. ambassador had left the meeting and then dispersed most of the participants on the excuse that they were blocking street traffic; the police then cordoned off the street.

Although government officials strongly condemned the attacks by unknown perpetrators, these statements rang hollow in view of the government's condemnation of Son Sann's plans to go ahead with the meeting against its wishes. Both Second Prime Minister Hun Sen and Minister of Information Ieng Mouly prior to the incident had predicted that were the meeting to go ahead, agitators might disrupt it by throwing "grenades." Once the attacks occurred, broadcast stations reported they were told to limit their coverage of the meeting to a government-provided script that implied Son Sann was to blame for rejecting government protection at party headquarters. In fact, BLDP members had asked the government for protection and permission to hold the meeting at the Olympic Stadium, and they moved it to party headquarters only after these requests were denied.

Government efforts to control the press included criminal prosecution as well as intimidation. In February, the Phnom Penh municipal court sentenced Chan Rotana, the editor of *Samleng Yu Vachon Khmer* (Voice of Khmer Youth) to a year of prison and a U.S. $2,000 fine for publishing a cartoon of First Prime Minister Ranariddh carting a bag of money on his head and an essay that criticized him as both autocratic and subservient to Hun Sen; his appeal was rejected in October but he will appeal to the Supreme Court. Thun Bun Ly, the editor of *Odom K'tek Khmer* (Khmer Ideal) was charged with "disinformation" for five articles and editorial cartoons that satirized government leaders; mid-trial, the prosecution added the charge of defamation over the objection of defense counsel. He was convicted of all charges, fined approximately $4,000 and ordered to spend two years in jail should he fail to pay; the court also ordered his newspaper closed pending appeal. The government confirmed it was pressing charges against at least five other newspapers that had yet to receive official notice; one was the English-language *Phnom Penh Post*. The government also acted during the year to confiscate print runs and suspend publication of several critical newspapers, all under dubious legal authority, and banned from the country two foreign correspondents from the French newspaper *Libération* who had reported on atrocities by government military personnel in the northwest. According to the *Phnom Penh Post*, the government has also tried to limit the influence of critical reporting by forbidding teachers to discuss politics or use newspaper articles critical of the government in teaching foreign languages.

After intensive pressure from the international community and King Sihanouk, the government did free six men who had been arrested for tying petitions onto balloons at the time of U.S. Secretary of State Warren Christopher's visit to Phnom Penh in August.

The most recent journalist to be murdered was Chan Dara, who was shot to death on the night of December 8, 1994, just after he was seen leaving a restaurant in Kampong Cham with a colonel named Sath Soeun. A correspondent with the newspaper *Koh Santepheap* (Island of Peace), Chan Dara had also published exposés of corrupt timber and rubber deals by government and military figures, among them Sat Soeun, in the paper *Preap Noam Sar* (The Carrier Pigeon). Ministry of Interior police arrested Sat Soeun, who still continued to send threats to the two papers and to Chan Dara's wife. The colonel, however, was acquitted at trial and released, although two other serious criminal charges were still pending against him. The government has not apprehended any further suspects in the case. Violence directed at journalists continued when a grenade exploded in front of the office of *Damneung Pelpreuk* (Morning News) on September 7, exactly a year from the date that Noun Chan, former editor of *Samleng Yu Vachun Khmer,* was gunned down in public by still-unknown perpetrators. Although a neighbor was hit by shrapnel, *Damneung Pelpreuk* editor Nguon Nonn was upstairs at the time.

The threat to the press was not lightened by a new press law adopted in July that left open the possibility of criminal prosecution for material that negatively "affects national security or political stability." The government has usually prosecuted journalists under criminal "misinformation" or "defamation" charges, with judges typically refusing to make distinctions between articles purporting to report fact and opinion pieces or editorials. The new law also gives government ministries broad powers to suspend or confiscate publications. Positive features of the new law include a prohibition on pre-publication censorship and guidelines for access to official information.

Other legal developments included the passage of a law establishing the Supreme Council of Magistracy, a body charged with ensuring the independence and integrity of the judiciary and supervising the appointment, promotion and discipline of judges and prosecutors. The law, however, gives the minister of justice or his representative a place on the council, which some observers feared might perpetuate the ministry's close direction of the judiciary. A council stipulated by the Cambodian constitution to rule on the constitutionality of laws and government decisions had yet to be created, although King Sihanouk had put forward his nominations two years before. The government supported programs designed to help professionalize the legal system and to improve military accountability, although the actual impact of these programs has yet to be measured.

The justice system remained plagued by corruption, however, and government officials, particularly police and military, continued with rare exceptions to enjoy virtual impunity for criminal behavior. Symptomatic of this was the way an official inquiry into the behavior of military intelligence officers accused of abducting, extorting and murdering civilians in the northwest stalled this year. Following several trips by a special commission of inquiry to Battambang province that interviewed witnesses in this sensitive case in the presence of the military and a press corps, the commission concluded that the temple of Che K'mau was not being used as a "secret prison" for victims. This conclusion hardly closed the matter, as human rights monitors had alleged that imprisonment and murders had taken place in a variety of locations in Battambang over a period of at least eighteen months.

Cold-blooded murder of ethnic Vietnamese civilians in Cambodia continued, with the Khmer Rouge the likely perpetrators in most instances. On May 20, approximately thirty men identified as Khmer Rouge killed four ethnic Vietnamese, one Khmer policeman, and wounded at least five others in Phat Sandai village in Kompong Thom province. In September, another band of men identified as Khmer Rouge attacked the floating village of Tonle Chhmar in Siem Reap province, killing an as yet unconfirmed number of ethnic Khmer and Vietnamese civilians. Ethnic Vietnamese in Cambodia also faced harassment from the government, as local officials confiscated identity documents and drew up plans for large-scale confinement of ethnic Vietnamese as "illegal aliens" pending repatriation. Although local officials sometimes hindered international delegations from gaining access to ethnic Vietnamese who were stranded at the Vietnamese border at Chrey Thom since 1993, by mid-year the government had agreed to allow a small number of these families to return to their homes in Cambodia.

In September, First Prime Minister Ranariddh called for reinstatement of the death penalty in Cambodia for drug trafficking and murder during robberies and abductions. The Cambodian constitution currently forbids the use of the death penalty, and King Sihanouk went on record as opposing its reintroduction.

The Right to Monitor

Human rights groups continued to raise concern over abuses despite the worsening political atmosphere and persistent government attempts to register and monitor their members and activities. Important work continued in prison monitoring, education, and investigations, with groups often able to interact constructively with government authorities as advocates or intermediaries. The independence and vigor of the Cambodian nongovernmental movement was reflected in a series of international conferences hosted in Phnom Penh during the year, among them an international conference on the banning of landmines, a regional conference on child prostitution, and several other conferences that raised human rights in the context of environment and development problems.

However, the government's increasing intolerance of criticism produced an intimidating atmosphere for all groups. In the days following the international donors' meeting in April, the prime ministers called for the closure of the U.N. Human Rights Centre office in Phnom Penh, a request that was withdrawn under intense local and international pressure. The government, however, continued to criticize Justice Michael Kirby, the special representative of the U.N. secretary-general. Justice Kirby's detailed reports on the human rights situation and his frank criticism of serious abuses led the government to complain it had been inadequately consulted; nevertheless, the prime ministers were unavailable to meet with Kirby on his most recent visit.

Kem Sokha, the head of the National Assembly's human rights commission, also received death threats at various points in the year and became a target of condemnation by both prime ministers, particularly Hun Sen who in July called for his removal as commission chairman. Other members of the commission who come from the two governing coalition parties were instructed by their party leadership to cease cooperating with Kem Sokha in investigations of human rights complaints and other matters. Kem Sokha is also one of the six BLDP members who have been "expelled" from the party on the initiative of Ieng Mouly.

The Role of
the International Community

The U.S. administration expressed concern about the government's abuses through private diplomatic channels but publicly tended to downplay the Cambodian government's dismal human rights performance, urging the swift passage of legislation that would grant Cambodia Most Favored Nation trading status and celebrating "progress" as gauged from the darkest years of Cambodia's recent history. Mid-year the administration certified Cambodia as an "emerging democracy" for the purpose of eligibility for agricultural credits, a designation that by law requires a country to be taking steps toward respect for internationally recognized human rights. In August, Warren Christopher was the first U.S. secretary of state to visit

Cambodia in forty years, signing aid agreements and hosting a lunch that included government officials, NGO representatives, and dissident politicians. Christopher praised Cambodia's democracy, but warned that "elections are not enough" and suggested that U.S. aid levels would depend on the government's human rights performance. As usual, Congress was less reticent in publicly voicing dismay at the deteriorating state of human rights, with Senators Thomas, Feinstein and Roth and Representatives Neal, Frank and Rohrabacher among others offering strong statements and letters of concern.

The ASEAN countries that were investors in Cambodia, particularly Malaysia, assumed more prominent influence as the government concluded major deals with them, such as logging concessions, a casino project, and an airlines contract; this support was especially important as an alternative source of government revenue apart from international aid. International donors, on the other hand, expressed concerns regarding the government's accountability and transparency at the 1995 donors' conference, and a proposal for a special working group to address these concerns was aired, but at years' end not implemented. Japan, Cambodia's largest aid donor, protested the government's request to close the Phnom Penh office of the U.N. Human Rights Centre, but otherwise kept a low profile on human rights issues.

Thailand continued to play a pivotal role in the Cambodian conflict, diplomatically supporting the Royal Government on the one hand, while continuing to allow trade in logs and gems across its borders, a critical and vast source of revenue for the Khmer Rouge. According to the London-based environmental monitor Global Witness, Thailand was still issuing import permits for logging businesses operating in Cambodia that inevitably pay the Khmer Rouge protection money for safe passage of their haul. The summary of the U.S. administration's report to Congress on Thai military support for the Khmer Rouge (the only unclassified part of the document) acknowledged "unofficial" contacts between Thai military personnel and the Khmer Rouge, "generally in the context of business transactions."

In its March 1995 report *Cambodia at War*, Human Rights Watch documented gross violations of the international laws of war committed by both sides and called on all nations to halt aid and trade in arms and military equipment to the parties. Among the nations that have supplied arms to the Khmer Rouge in the past were China and Thailand; the guerrillas still draw on these stockpiles and buy current supplies from local arms brokers who sometimes deal in weapons intended for the Royal Cambodian Armed Forces (RCAF). The RCAF, in turn, has purchased military supplies and upgrades from North Korea, South Africa, the Czech Republic, Israel, Poland, Russia, Singapore, Indonesia and Malaysia since 1994.

The U.N. Commission on Human Rights passed a resolution expressing concern about the continuing serious violations of human rights and requested Special Representative Michael Kirby to present a report to the General Assembly and to the 1996 session of the commission.

The Work of
Human Rights Watch/Asia

In March, on the eve of the Paris donors' meeting, Human Rights Watch/Asia issued a major report titled *Cambodia at War*. The book-length report detailed grave military abuses on both sides and the increasing constraints placed upon the press. It called upon participants in the donors' meeting to insist on accountability and transparency in Cambodia's justice system, and called on all nations to cease supplying the warring sides with weapons. Human Rights Watch/Asia also sent numerous letters and press releases concerning the press law and legal actions against journalists to the Cambodian authorities throughout the year. In September, the organization followed up with a short report on the government's actions against the press and published an English translation of Cambodia's new press law. Human Rights Watch/Asia staff met with visiting

Cambodian officials and explained its concerns on these issues. Throughout the year, Human Rights Watch/Asia urged U.S. and other government representatives to protest human rights abuses. The organization provided extensive information on Cambodia's human rights situation to the U.S. House and Senate committees considering bills that would grant Cambodia Most Favored Nation Trading status and urged that any grant be accompanied by a requirement that the president report at least once a year on human rights developments, in addition to the annual report on human rights prepared by the State Department.

CHINA
AND TIBET

Human Rights Developments

Throughout 1995 the Chinese government continued to demonstrate its disdain for fundamental human rights guarantees and the rule of law. Obsessed with national "stability" as inflation, unemployment, and corruption worsened and an internal power struggle intensified, authorities continued to round up, imprison, and physically abuse activists engaged in peaceful dissent. Security officials continued to hamper independent religious practice, censored the media and publications industry, and escalated their efforts to stamp out "splittism" in Tibet. Some dissidents continued to be "disappeared"; others remained in lengthy incommunicado pre- or post-trial detention; still others had their movements constantly monitored. Members of dissidents' families were threatened and harassed.

The Chinese government continued to subvert the rule of law, violating its own criminal procedure code, using trumped-up criminal charges against political dissidents, and re-interpreting some laws and regulations to ensure specific outcomes. The November 21 formal arrest of Wei Jingsheng for "conducting activities in [an] attempt to overthrow the Chinese goverment" was the most blatant example. Wei, China's most famous dissident, has been missing since April 1, 1994, and as of his arrest date, his whereabouts were still unknown. At the time of his disappearance, in violation of China's own Criminal Procedure Code, no warrant for his arrest was issued and family members were not notified. Authorities also moved to blunt criticism of the use of counterrevolutionary charges to sentence political dissidents, by turning to the 1993 State Security Law to charge dissidents with the crime of "leaking state secrets." On September 19, former student Li Hai became the latest to be so charged. Bi Yimin, director of the Institute of Applied Science and Technology of Beijing, was sentenced to a three-year prison term in February 1995 for allegedly misappropriating public funds. The money in question was legally transferred to two well-known dissidents serving thirteen-year terms for 1989 pro-democracy activities. In December 1994, Tong Yi, Wei Jingsheng's former secretary, was sentenced to "re-education through labor" on a trumped-up charge of "disturbing the public order." An attempt to pin a morals charge on her for cohabiting with Wei had already failed, and the original charge of forging an official seal on an application for study in the U.S. was deemed too minor to prosecute.

Chinese courts levied harsh sentences, up to twenty years, on those who challenged the one-party system. Where evidence was weak, courts substituted spurious criminal charges, or "re-education committees" administratively imposed shorter "labor re-education" terms, a form of punishment that the U.N. Working Group on Arbitrary Detention had earlier labeled "inherently arbitrary in character." Severely ill political prisoners remained in detention under conditions that violated the U.N.'s Standard Minimum Rules for the Treatment of Prisoners.

Chinese officials blatantly attempted to censor delegates' participation in and press coverage of the Fourth World Conference on Women and the parallel nongovernmental

organization (NGO) Forum held in Beijing and Huairou in August and September. Even before the meetings convened, China challenged the U.N. accreditation of independent organizations with whose views it disagreed. Despite U.N. challenges and China's public promise to issue visas to all those registered by the NGO Forum, China used its position as host to deny visas to selected individuals. Security personnel monitored and disrupted NGO workshops and meetings, videotaping participants, their materials, and members of the audience. There were also attempts to confiscate NGO videotapes and to remove video equipment. Members of human rights organizations attempting to monitor Chinese violations of free expression and association were themselves under surveillance.

Members of the press were hampered in their coverage of the conference. Some hotel managers selectively refused reporters prearranged access to guests. As a condition of publishing, editors at the *Earth Times*, a daily newspaper that had been freely distributed at all major U.N. conferences and summits since 1992, were forced to comply with Chinese restrictions, including prohibitions on distribution at hotels and at the NGO Forum site and a ban on criticism of the host country.

In preparation for the conferences, Chinese officials cleared Beijing of prominent dissidents not already in custody so as to prevent meetings with outsiders. Tong Zeng, a leading campaigner for Japanese compensation to Chinese war victims, had expected to participate in a workshop about Japan's use of conquered "comfort women" during World War II. Instead, he was ordered to go on "vacation." Wang Zhihong, wife of dissident Chen Ziming who is serving a thirteen-year term for his 1989 pro-democracy activities, was "offered" a two-week prison visit with her husband. Dai Qing, who exposed fallacies and inconsistencies in the government's assessment of the Three Gorges dam project, had to leave the city. In yet another move to "ensure the security" of delegates, the government announced the executions of sixteen "criminal elements."

That same month, Shanghai activist Dai Xuezhong, a member of the unofficial Human Rights Association, received a three-year sentence for alleged tax evasion. On April 10, labor activist Xiao Biguang went on trial on "swindling" charges; as of November, a sentence had not been announced. On August 18, Ding Zilin and her husband Jiang Peikun were detained in Wuxi, Jiangsu Province, for some forty days for "economic reasons," then released without explanation. The couple, whose seventeen-year-old son was killed during the June 1989 massacre in Beijing, compiled a list of those killed and maimed in the crackdown and tried to persuade the government to reverse its finding that the 1989 demonstrations were counter-revolutionary. Gao Yu, a dissident journalist imprisoned in October 1993, was finally sentenced in November 1994 to a six-year prison term after the procuracy twice returned the case to the court. Despite a ruling that "the evidence...is partial....," no new evidence was ever offered to justify the verdict.

In December 1994, in one of the most important political trials since those that followed the 1989 protests, the Beijing Intermediate Court sentenced nine dissidents, including medical researcher Kang Yuchun, lecturer Hu Shigen, Democracy Wall activist Liu Jingsheng, and printing plant worker Wang Guoqi, to terms ranging from three to twenty years. They were among sixteen arrested in May and June 1992 and charged with "leading a counterrevolutionary group and with "counterrevolutionary propaganda and incitement." A human rights monitor, U.S. citizen Harry Wu, was arrested on June 19, sentenced on August 24 to a fifteen-year prison term for spying and immediately expelled from the country.

Despite the release in July of Shanghai activist Yang Zhou for treatment of an esophageal condition, reports of serious and untreated illness among jailed political prisoners continued in 1995. One of the most egregious cases was that of Chen Ziming, sentenced to a thirteen-year term in early 1991 and released on medical parole in May 1994. Still under treatment for urinary tract cancer, he was returned to Beijing No. 2 Prison on June 25, 1995, on the pretext that the skin condition that had led to his parole had cleared up. The medical condition of long-term prisoner Bao Tong, former principal aide to ousted Party Secretary Zhao Ziyang, did not improve; he remained in a prison hospital, and his family lacked access to his medical records and was refused permission to choose his doctor.

Released dissidents and the families of those still imprisoned continued to be harassed. Five months before he was re-arrested in May, Public Security Bureau officials threatened Wan Dang with death if he continued to speak out. Liu Gang, released in June after completing a six-year term, was prohibited from leaving his home in Liaoning Province for two years and from talking with foreign journalists. Police broke into Liu's house in June and July, tried to run over family members on the street, and threatened friends and relatives who maintained contact with him. On September 1, Liu was again detained, this time for ten days, for refusing to "share his thoughts" with security officials. Gou Qinghui, the wife of Xiao Biguang, was prohibited from returning to her job at Yanqing Theological Seminary, attending church or meeting at home with co-religionists. Tong Yi's father was warned that his job could be jeopardized if his daughter refused to comply with prison regulations. On January 16 and 17, Tong was beaten by fellow inmates in collusion with prison guards after protesting sixteen-hour work days.

Restrictions surrounding religious practice continued during 1995, and the official drive to register and subject to lay control all congregations, including the smallest family churches, escalated. Harsh crackdowns came in areas where foreigners were active proselytizers and trainers of lay leaders, where evidence of indigenous networks of unofficial churches surfaced, where evangelists were especially active, and where "underground" church members challenged the authorities through public worship. In April, during the Easter season, more than forty Catholics were detained in Jiangxi Province. Most were released, but several were sentenced to terms ranging between two and five years. At the end of October, Catholic lay persons and clergy arrested between February and June in Hebei, Inner Mongolia, and Jilin Provinces, remained in detention. But the more usual pattern during 1995 was to detain and physically abuse Catholics and Protestants until their families, the local church community or foreign evangelical organizations paid onerous fines. During a gathering of some 500-600 Protestants in Jiangsu Province in late January or early February, Protestant leaders from the province and from Wenzhou in Zhejiang Province were detained, severely beaten, heavily fined, and released. More than 300 were detained in Yingshang County, Anhui Province, at the end of May.

During 1995, Chinese officials tightened restrictions on freedom of expression. At the beginning of the year, the press was notified that it was required to put a favorable spin on sensitive issues, such as double-digit inflation, failing enterprises, and demonstrations by unemployed workers. On May 19, the party's propaganda chief ordered the twenty largest national newspapers not to cover issues that "have not been resolved" or are "impossible to resolve" and to use reports by *Xinhua*, the official news agency, for all breaking stories. In July, the Hong Kong-based *Apple Daily* was banned from covering a Beijing meeting about the colony's future. Its owner had angered the government with criticism of Premier Li Peng.

Information flows were further restricted in connection with the sixth anniversary of the June 4, 1989, crackdown. At the end of May, Nick Rufford of the London *Sunday Times*, was questioned for thirteen hours by officials who demanded the names of his Chinese contacts. From June 2-6, officials cut the CNN feed to hotels in Beijing, concerned that commemorative footage might include shots of the 1989 massacre. Also in June, the Ministry of Post and Tele-

communications moved to limit local users' access to the Internet. Invoking China's sovereign status, he declared that "by linking with Internet, we do not mean absolute freedom of information." In August, when Greenpeace members from outside China tried to stage a demonstration in Tiananmen Square protesting China's nuclear testing, they were detained for thirty hours, interrogated about the involvement of Chinese citizens, and deported.

Films did not escape censorship. When New York Film Festival officials refused to cancel a showing of *The Gate of Heavenly Peace*, about the June 1989 crackdown in Beijing, Chinese officials asked Zhang Yimou, whose *Shanghai Triad* opened the festival, to cancel plans to attend. He agreed. Zhang's work as a filmmaker in China has been entirely dependent on government approval.

Officials further curtailed freedom of association and assembly during 1995. An April law forbade Chinese citizens from attending foreign-run schools. That same month, police broke up a peaceful demonstration against corruption by some thirty entrepreneurs in Guangzhou. In April, security agents broke up a series of marches by former Nanjing residents who had been banished to the countryside during the Cultural Revolution (1966-76) and who were attempting to return. In June, authorities denied permission to two female war victims to demonstrate outside the Japanese embassy.

Human rights conditions in Tibet deteriorated throughout 1995. During the first quarter of the year, at least 123 dissidents were detained, more than in all of 1994. The government intensified its campaign challenging the legitimacy of the Dalai Lama, even as a religious leader, and the battle over who was to choose the new Panchen Lama, the second most important spiritual leader and the most important Tibetan leader residing there, resulted in the detentions of at least forty-eight people between May and July. The six year old identified by the Dalai Lama as the legitimate successor, but rejected by Chinese officials, disappeared, along with his immediate family. Authorities further curtailed religious activity by limiting the number of monks and nuns in any one nunnery or monastery, and by instituting an absolute cap on the total number in all of Tibet and a ban on the building of monasteries and nunneries.

Pro-independence activities, such as possession of the Tibetan flag, resulted in raids on the offending monasteries. In May, after independence posters surfaced at Labrang Monastery in southern Gansu Province, an area inhabited by Tibetans, five monks were arrested and two badly beaten, one so severely he suffered neurological damage. In 1994-95, two nuns, Gyaltsen Kelsang and Phunstog Yangkyi, were unexpectedly released from custody shortly before they died from injuries sustained in prison. In an attempt at restricting news flows, on three separate occasions women tourists leaving Tibet were stopped at the airport and strip-searched. Confiscated items included private letters, film, audio cassettes, and a diary.

The Right to Monitor

There is no right to monitor in China. To form a legal human rights or monitoring organization, members would have to comply with the 1989 "Regulations on the Registration and Management of Social Groups," which require approval by the "relevant professional leading organs," presumably the official China Society for Human Rights Studies. Furthermore, the "monopoly" stipulation in the regulations, which mandates that an "identical or similar social group cannot be set up within the same administrative area," further restricts independent organizational efforts. In 1995, the authorities blocked several informal attempts at monitoring, such as the dissident petition drives which began in March and culminated in May, and which initially resulted in the detention and questioning of some fifty dissidents. In November, some twenty signatories were still detained.

The Role of the International Community

In 1995, human rights concerns were further marginalized on the international agenda, as governments actively pursued trade and investment with China unhindered by any linkage to human rights. Chinese authorities aggressively offered human rights "dialogues" in exchange for business deals, sending the president and premier to visit Western capitals. At the U.N. Human Rights Commission, China defeated the most intensive, high-level campaign yet waged on behalf of a mildly worded resolution. As if to underline its growing confidence, the Chinese government made a travesty of its commitments to NGOs at the U.N. Fourth World Conference on Women with nearly total impunity.

The Clinton human rights policy of "constructive engagement" toward China lacked both substance and clout, with a few notable exceptions. The administration indicated in October that certain post-1989 sanctions would remain in place for the time being, namely a prohibition on weapons sales, denial of licenses for transfer of dual-use technology, and suspension of the Overseas Private Investment Corporation (OPIC) program in China. But for the most part, the administration downplayed human rights while concentrating on "stabilizing" relations with China at the economic and political level. The detention of the Chinese-American human rights activist Harry Wu pushed human rights to the top of the U.S.-Sino agenda, but only temporarily. The Chinese government used both Wu's detention and the controversy over the Taiwanese President Li Teng-hui's visit to the United States in June 1995 as bargaining chips to secure a summit meeting between Clinton and Jiang Zemin which took place in New York on October 24.

Clinton raised human rights concerns in his discussions with Jiang Zemin, but he declined to issue a public appeal for the release of any specific political prisoners, as he had following a previous meeting with Jiang in 1993. The two presidents agreed to meet again in Osaka in November, and the administration described the summit as "very positive" though it resulted in no concrete progress on human rights.

"Constructive engagement" got off to a shaky start in 1995 with the United States threatening a trade war over Chinese copyright and trademark violations. As the administration set a deadline for imposing sanctions, Energy Secretary Hazel O'Leary led a "presidential mission" to China in February, accompanied by more than seventy-five corporate executives. O'Leary used the opportunity to go after business deals in the energy sector, signing more than U.S. $1 billion worth of agreements. In meetings with Premier Li Peng and other senior officials, she raised human rights concerns privately but avoided any public criticism of China's human rights practices.

In March, Vice-President Al Gore held a frosty meeting with Li Peng in Copenhagen around the edges of the U.N. Social Summit. Li Peng denounced U.S. interference "in other people's affairs," while the vice-president stressed the administration's desire to maintain "constructive relations" with China while "strengthening dialogue" in areas where the two governments have differences. Gore was publicly silent about human rights.

The Copenhagen meeting occurred just days after a vote in the U.N. Human Rights Commission on a resolution criticizing China's human rights practices. Co-sponsored by the European Union, the U.S., Japan and others, the measure attracted broad support from Eastern Europe, Latin America and Africa. For months, the United States, in particular, had lobbied in capitals around the world to line up votes in favor of the resolution. China responded in kind, warning European governments, for example, that support for the resolution could endanger their prospects for doing business in China and offering to engage in bilateral "human rights dialogues" with various governments in lieu of facing action at the United Nations. Although the Chinese government failed to prevent passage of a no-action motion, resulting in the first-ever debate on a China resolution, it narrowly won the final vote, with twenty-one countries voting against, twenty for and twelve abstaining.

It was clear by May that the international community would do little to come to the defense of beleaguered activists in China waging a petition campaign. At the height of their protests in the weeks leading up to the June 1989 anniversary, President Clinton renewed Most Favored Nation (MFN) trading status for China for one more year. The president reiterated his belief that "broad engagement with China, including on human rights issues, offers the best prospect in all areas of concern to us." He denounced China's human rights record as "unacceptable," but defended the administration's "vigorous" approach to human rights, including bilateral and multilateral efforts, as well as its work with the private sector to develop "voluntary business principles."

Nearly a year after the president's initial promise to develop a voluntary code of conduct for businesses, the White House officially announced the fruit of its efforts just prior to the MFN decision. The principles did not focus exclusively on China, as originally promised, but instead were designed for universal application. Halfheartedly endorsed by eight major companies who said they would serve as a "useful reference point" in framing their own codes, the principles did contain several positive elements, but were vaguely worded and lacked any concrete details as to how they would be implemented.

In Congress, resolutions to overturn the president's MFN decision never came to a vote in the House. Instead, a consensus bill (the 1995 China Policy Act) was formulated and adopted by a huge bipartisan margin (416 to 10) in July, demanding that the administration take diplomatic initiatives to improve human rights in several specific areas. In addition to giving the administration a clear human rights mandate, the bill required a report in thirty days on what actions had been taken at the World Bank, the U.N. and elsewhere. The Chinese government expressed "strong resentment" and opposition to the bill, but clearly was relieved that MFN was not challenged. The bill was referred to the Senate; as of November, no action had been taken.

The administration reacted strongly to the reimprisonment of Chen Ziming in late June; he had been released on medical parole in May 1994 as a gesture just prior to Clinton's MFN decision. Shortly thereafter, Harry Wu was detained, and the administration launched a campaign of high-level public and private lobbying to secure consular access to Wu and, ultimately, his release. Wu's case was a top item of discussion at a key meeting between Secretary of State Warren Christopher and Chinese Foreign Minister Qian Qichen in Brunei on August 1, in conjunction with the annual conference of the Association of South East Asian Nations. The meeting coincided with a decision by the World Bank's executive directors on a $260 million non-basic human needs loan for a major highway project. Several influential members of Congress wrote to the administration and World Bank officials urging the Bank to postpone considering the loan as a way of indicating concern over Wu and the deterioration of human rights in China generally. But the Treasury Department opposed the suggestion, and the administration claimed that it did not have the authority to hold up a loan on its own, although it had previously prevented loans to Vietnam and Iran from being considered by the executive directors. Furthermore, the administration argued that seeking a delay would "undercut [its] ability to pursue our human rights objectives in our ongoing bilateral discussions with China." World Bank lending to China, despite occasional abstentions or no votes by the U.S., continued to outstrip loans to any other government. According to the Bank's annual report, in the fiscal year ending June 1995, China received $2.9 billion from the Bank.

Meanwhile, the White House continued an interagency review on possible Export-Import Bank funding for U.S. companies involved in the highly controversial Three Gorges dam project in China. In late September, the White House completed the review and recommended against Ex-Im Bank funding the project, both on environmental and human rights grounds. By November, no decision had been made by the Bank on an initial request from a U.S. company seeking funding.

As the year ended, prospects for developing a multilateral strategy to promote human rights in China through concerted political or economic pressure appeared dim. In July, the European Union's trade commissioner, Leon Brittan, outlined a long-term strategy to expand dramatically the E.U.'s ties with China while removing human rights as an impediment. His proposal acknowledged that both public pressure and private discussion would be needed to bring about human rights improvements, but stressed cooperative efforts to develop the rule of law in China over the long-term, rather than pressure. He also endorsed the E.U.'s political dialogue as a venue for raising human rights concerns. A meeting of the E.C.-China Joint Committee took place in Brussels in early October to review overall Sino-E.U. relations. Human rights concerns were discussed only briefly; Leon Brittan again affirmed the E.U.'s interest in playing a "constructive role" to improve China's judicial system. While Brittan was unveiling his proposal, President Jiang Zemin was preparing to visit Germany, Hungary and Finland. The visit was aimed at countering the effect of the Taiwanese president's trip to the U.S., but it also provided Jiang with an opportunity to generate greater recognition and acceptance, as well as new trade deals. In 1994 and 1995, Germany was China's largest European trading partner, with bilateral trade in the first five months of 1995 totaling over $4 billion. The president of Germany, Roman Herzog, and Foreign Minister Klaus Kinkel presented China's foreign minister with a list of political detainees; Chancellor Kohl stressed the universality of human rights, but undercut these moves by stating that different levels of economic development and varying cultural traditions had to be taken into account. Demonstrators were kept away from Jiang, as the German government tried to prevent a replay of Li Peng's visit in 1994 which was cut short by protests. With economic and political relations on track, Kohl planned another visit to China in mid-November.

In the weeks preceding Jiang Zemin's meeting with President Clinton in New York, Canada's prime minister, Jean Chretien, welcomed Li Peng to Montreal in mid-October as a featured speaker at a conference of the Canada China Business Council. Canada's policy towards China was similar to that of the U.S. and Europe, discreetly raising human rights in official discussions and U.N. fora, while concentrating on improving relations through "constructive engagement." In an even more subdued way, Japan followed a similar approach (see Japan section).

By the end of 1995, Beijing had successfully insulated its economic and political relations and ambitions from being seriously affected by its human rights record. For the most part, the Chinese government escaped accountability for its egregious violations of human rights, even as it sought recognition as an emerging superpower. No government was willing to exert the consistent political and economic pressure needed to compel the Chinese government to comply with its international obligations. The prospect of instability and greater repression in the wake of Deng Xiaoping's passing, however, raised doubts about the long-term prospects for economic reform and development of the rule of law in China without greater attention to human rights by the international community.

The Work of
Human Rights Watch/Asia

In 1995, Human Rights Watch/Asia worked to keep attention focused on human rights in China and to counter the trend towards downplaying rights concerns. Simultaneously, we attempted to widen the circle of those willing to work for improved human rights conditions by appealing to new constituencies, broadening our research to en-

compass abuses committed in conjunction with environmental and medical concerns.

After the February publication of *The Three Gorges Dam in China: Forced Resettlement, Suppression of Dissent and Labor Rights Concerns*, Human Rights Watch/Asia campaigned to limit involvement in the dam project by U.S. investment houses. Major institutional investors, many of whom represented public employee pension funds, were apprised of the human rights abuses and asked to eschew purchase of Three Gorges bonds. The initiative represented a continuation of our ongoing corporate social responsibility project which has included advocacy for a code of conduct for corporations active in the Chinese business community. We also provided our information to the Export-Import Bank, the White House, and to U.S. agencies involved in a review of possible U.S. funding for companies involved in the Three Gorges project.

Throughout the year, our New York, Washington, Brussels and Hong Kong offices engaged in advocacy, pressing for the release of prominent prisoners and detainees such as Wei Jingsheng, Tong Yi, Chen Ziming, and Harry Wu, and making specific policy recommendations to the European Union and the U.S. government. A major campaign was conducted on behalf of the U.N. Human Rights Commission resolution. The Brussels and Washington staff routinely briefed European Union commission staff, members of the European Parliament, and the U.S. Congress and State Department, including those traveling to China. Human Rights Watch/Asia followed up Energy Secretary O'Leary's February visit to China by contacting members of the corporate delegation who traveled with her. China was a major focus of discussions in Japan during a Human Rights Watch/Asia mission in September.

Human Rights Watch/Asia maintained an ongoing dialogue with U.S. companies involved in China regarding human rights/worker rights, the Three Gorges project, and the administration's voluntary code of conduct. Human Rights Watch/Asia urged U.S.

businesses to intervene on behalf of Harry Wu, and some companies and trade associations did make private appeals for his release.

In May, the Senate Foreign Relations Committee held a hearing on the harvesting of executed prisoners' organs for medical transplantation purposes, at which Human Rights Watch/Asia testified, updating information contained in our 1994 report. The issue of organ transplants received new prominence as part of the broader debate in Congress on China's human rights record.

At the United Nations Commission on Human Rights, a speech by Human Rights Watch condemned the practice of re-education through labor, arbitrary detentions, and overall prison conditions in China.

Reports and press releases kept the focus on Chinese attempts to find new avenues for limiting dissent. *Enforced Exile of Dissidents* revealed the Chinese policy of effectively exiling dissidents under the guise of permission to go abroad for medical treatment or scholarly pursuits. In response to the crackdown on dissident activities before the sixth anniversary of the June 1989 Beijing crackdown, we published *China: Keeping the Lid on Demands for Change*, an assessment of human rights between the June 1994 decision "delinking" MFN and human rights and May 1995. A similar analysis was given in congressional testimony in the House of Representatives.

Your Rights in Beijing: A Brief Guide for Delegates to the 1995 NGO Forum on Women was the culmination of efforts to document attempts by the Chinese government to restrict NGO participation in the Fourth World Conference on Women and the parallel forum meeting. With the help of other human rights and women's rights organizations, some 10,000 copies of the brochure were distributed. A French translation was available, and the document was posted to several sites on the Internet.

HONG KONG

Human Rights Developments

Tension over Hong Kong's future continued in 1995, even as the people of the territory voted for their first completely elected legislature. Upsetting predictions, the September elections gave a decisive victory to candidates who favored a more confrontational attitude toward China, such as those of the Democratic Party. Yet even before the polls closed, the Chinese government repeated its promise to dissolve the legislature when China resumes its rule on July 1, 1997. The new legislature, the first not to have appointed members, is likely to present a more confrontational face to the Hong Kong government as well, revisiting a number of the year's most controversial issues in the next legislative session.

Prominent among those issues is the Court of Final Appeal described in the 1984 Joint Declaration between China and the U.K. that was to replace the Privy Council in London as the court of last resort. The agreement provided that the Court "may as required invite judges from other common law jurisdictions to sit, "a provision designed both to ensure an adequate pool of high-caliber judges and to insulate the court from political pressure after the transition. A 1991 bilateral agreement that only one foreign judge would be able to sit on at most half of the Court's sessions drew protests from legislators and the bar, as did the restriction of the Court's jurisdiction to exclude "acts of state," a common law term that might be expansively interpreted by China to include a large range of cases involving government interests.

Nevertheless, in June of this year China and the U.K. agreed on implementing legislation that would preserve the limit of one foreign judge, the acts of state exception, and delay the establishment of the Court until the 1997 transition. This foreclosed the possibility that some of the jurisdictional uncertainty might be resolved in advance through the precedent of the Court's own decisions.

The Legislative Council narrowly approved the legislation in July of this year, but key political figures such as Martin Lee, the leader of the Democratic Party, remained convinced that the compromise has jeopardized Hong Kong's judicial independence, and appeared eager to try to amend the legislation. The government, for its part, argued that these features do not threaten the Court's independence and that the alternative was to risk having China dissolve the Court and fashion its own institution in 1997.

The power of this argument illustrated how profoundly Beijing's threats have begun to shape the future of the territory. The Chinese government has promised to appoint a temporary legislature in place of the one elected this year, and it is this appointed body that would be called upon to approve the most basic institutional arrangements for the post-colonial era, including confirming the judges for the Court of Final Appeal. The Chinese government has also threatened to repeal the 1991 Bill of Rights, and it has so far refused to report to the U.N. Human Rights Committee on the application of the International Covenant on Civil and Political Rights (ICCPR), a breach of its bilateral obligation to ensure the covenant's application to Hong Kong. The Chinese government has also threatened to dissolve the lower tiers of elected representation in Hong Kong, the municipal councils and district boards, and in October a Beijing-appointed committee declared that the system of executive appointments to these bodies should be reintroduced.

While strenuously lobbying for its own legislative proposals, the Hong Kong government opposed initiatives by individual legislators, such as a trio of anti-discrimination bills introduced by appointed member Anna Wu. Private discrimination, particularly in employment, remained endemic in Hong Kong, where job advertisements frequently specified age, sex and even race as qualifications. Arguing that the measures were too radical, the government proposed its own more limited version and successfully lobbied to have Wu's drafts voted down in July. Other legislators promised to reintroduce the bills. The governor also refused to allow the legislature to consider a bill for an equal opportunity commission.

The Hong Kong government made progress in reforming the archaic colonial laws of the colony to be in conformity with the Bill of Rights, although the pace and extent of reform did not satisfy many human rights advocates. One example was the government's striking out a number of restrictive subsidiary laws enacted under the authority of the Emergency Regulations Ordinance, including provisions that allowed the government to censor and suppress publications. The government, however, left untouched the ordinance itself, which permits the governor to declare an emergency and issue laws and regulations on any subject, leaving open the prospect that new regulations will be promulgated under its authority. In October, a Beijing-appointed committee called for reinstatement of the emergency regulations, of the governor's power of censorship, of the former ban on societies not registered with the police, and an end to the Bill of Rights' power to override legislation.

Other government-proposed legislative amendments scrapped or modified licensing, permit or registration procedures for demonstrations, megaphones, public performances, and news organizations. A bill introduced by legislator Martin Lee passed in December 1994, repealing a section of the Film Censorship Ordinance that had been used to censor Taiwanese films, such as a documentary on the pro-democracy movement, because they might "seriously damage relations with other territories." The government submitted to China its proposed legislative amendments to the Official Secrets Act, and it planned to submit amended laws on treason and sedition to the legislature later next year.

Self-censorship in the media continued to be a serious problem, albeit difficult to document. A poll of journalists conducted in February by the University of Hong Kong revealed that more than 80 percent believed that self-censorship took place occasionally or frequently and that press freedom would decrease during the next three years. The Hong Kong Journalists Association reported several potential incidents of self-censorship. ATV television in December 1994 dropped the popular talk show *News Tease* after its confrontational host, Wong Yukman, was accused by pro-Beijing newspapers of being "anti-China" and "hostile." In January, Hong Kong's two land-based television stations refused to air a British Broadcasting Corporation documentary on the sale of organs from executed prisoners in China. In May, the *South China Morning Post* abruptly canceled the popular and controversial "Lily Wong" cartoon strip, citing financial reasons but refusing to run the balance of cartoons that were already paid for. One of the last strips had shown a Chinese official assuring an observer that there will be no future shortage of organs for sale from executed prisoners because "by then it'll be 1997 and we got all the democrats and over a dozen cartoonists!"

Pressure on journalists took less subtle forms as well. Both Xi Yang, a reporter for *Ming Pao*, and Gao Yu, a free-lance contributor to Hong Kong publications, continued to languish in Chinese prisons for their reporting, which the Chinese government prosecuted as "espionage" (see China section). The Chinese government continued to deny entry to journalists it considered untrustworthy.

The Chinese government also tried to control access to the mainland by perceived political opponents. In July, it denied an entry permit to Cheung Man-Kwong, a member of the government's Education Commission and a Democratic Party legislator. Rosie Young, the chairwoman of the commission, canceled its planned official visit to China in response. Later in the month, China banned Martin Lee from attending a law seminar.

Serious abuses against Vietnamese asylum seekers took place again this year, as Hong Kong authorities increasingly resorted to force in connection with deportation procedures and camp inmates resisted ever more violently. The most serious incident took place on May 20, when police and correctional service officers moved some 1,500 asylum seekers from a section of the Whitehead Detention Centre to High Island in preparation for deportation. The officials fired 3,250 tear gas canisters during a period of eight hours, also using truncheons and mace against the Vietnamese. The asylum seekers responded initially by barricading themselves, but as the assault progressed, neighboring sections hurled home-made spears and projectiles at the oncoming force. Nearly 170 officers were treated for injuries, most for heat exhaustion, and seventy-eight Vietnamese reported injuries from batons, gas canisters, mace and shields, in addition to the hundreds who suffered the effects of tear gas, among them women, children and babies. Among the injured was a sixty-five-year-old woman who was sprayed with mace, kicked in the ribs and struck by a truncheon, and a baby who had fainted from the tear gas and was accidentally scalded when an inexperienced officer tried to revive her under what turned out to be a hot water tap. Few Vietnamese complained to the authorities, however, because of the experience of almost 400 other asylum seekers who pressed complaints of injury and loss of property from a similar raid that took place on April 7, 1994; few of these complainants had yet had their request for legal aid processed, and many were deported in the meantime.

Despite the massive use of tear gas and the injuries produced during the raid, the Hong Kong government refused to appoint a commission of inquiry, or indeed, to release video footage of the operation. It relied on its own account of events and a sketchy report by four independent monitors, two of whom questioned the use of tear gas. In the next operation, on June 8, authorities again deployed large amounts of tear gas in response to what they said was violent resistance, a claim disputed by Vietnamese who witnessed the events. Independent monitors arrived after the conflict was virtually over, as the authorities did not notify them that disturbances had caused police and correctional officers to move in ahead of the scheduled time. Incidents of violence by both officials and Vietnamese continued to plague camp transfers and deportations, and the authorities continued to incarcerate Vietnamese whom they deemed "troublemakers" or "protesters" without any legal hearing or review in punitive detention facilities such as Victoria Prison. In July, Vietnamese brought allegations that camp guards had beaten two Vietnamese youths during an otherwise peaceful demonstration of children protesting the decision to terminate secondary schooling for asylum seekers; officials denied the allegations but again refused to release videotapes they had made of the incident.

The Right to Monitor

Hong Kong remains one of the most hospitable environments in the region for local human rights and civil liberties advocates. In October, approximately a dozen nongovernmental organizations lobbied and observed Great Britain's report to the U.N. Human Rights Committee on its application to Hong Kong of the ICCPR. To emphasize the urgency of China assuming the reporting requirement, the Legislative Council also dispatched a delegation to the Geneva hearing.

The government continued to restrict press access to detention centers for Vietnamese asylum seekers, and in August banned reporters from observing deportation actions as well. Lawyers for asylum seekers continued to have access to their clients, but under highly restricted conditions.

The Role of
the International Community

The U.S. administration tended to frame its interest in Hong Kong in terms of achieving a "smooth transition," a term raised repeatedly by Deputy Assistant Secretary of State Kent Wiedemann before a House hearing on July 27. The administration generally supported Hong Kong government positions, from the electoral reforms to the compromise on the Court of Final Appeal, and tended to gloss over human rights issues and

the Chinese government's threats to reconstitute basic governmental arrangements in favor of expressing confidence in the territory's future. Members of Congress were more forceful in reflecting the concerns raised by Hong Kong residents and legislators, with Senator Craig Thomas and Representatives Benjamin Gilman and Howard Berman taking particular interest in transitional arrangements and the continuity of the legislature.

The administration continued to support Hong Kong's deportation policy regarding Vietnamese asylum seekers and expressed no concern at the increasingly forceful measures used and the violence they provoked. It was taken by surprise when a legislative measure to facilitate U.S. resettlement of boat people proposed by Representative Chris Smith passed the House by a wide margin. The measure, premised on concerns that the screening process to identify genuine refugees was flawed or corrupt, would have made reintegration assistance for returnees in Vietnam conditional on the re-screening of the more than 40,000 Vietnamese asylum seekers in the region for determination of their refugee status. The bill had an immediate effect in both Asia and Washington: voluntary repatriation dropped sharply as asylum seekers waited to see the fate of the legislation, and the administration then produced an alternative proposal whereby Vietnamese who volunteered to return home would be eligible for resettlement screening by U.S. officials in Vietnam.

The Sino-British agreement over the Court of Final Appeals marked one of the first significant points of cooperation between the two countries since Governor Patten's proposals for electoral reform in 1993. At an October meeting the foreign ministers of China and the U.K. agreed on further measures, including the establishment of liaison structures between Chinese officials and Hong Kong government offices and civil servants, an agreement to resolve disputes over port development, and a committee to oversee the transition ceremonies. Critical issues such as the survival of the current legislature, however, did not come up at the talks, although Britain did agree to provide China with approximately $150 million in soft infrastructure loans. In September, Governor Patten mentioned that Britain ought to give the 3.2 million holders of British Dependent Territories Citizen passports in Hong Kong the right of abode in Britain, a proposal immediately ruled out by Home Secretary Michael Howard.

At the conclusion of its hearing in October, the U.N. Human Rights Committee told a joint U.K.-Hong Kong government delegation that it considered China obligated to continue to report on the application of the ICCPR to the territory, and called on the delegation to return next year to explain exactly how this responsibility would be transferred. Members of the committee stated that China should maintain Hong Kong's Bill of Rights and the recently elected legislature, and also criticized the British administration's treatment of Vietnamese asylum seekers.

The Work of
Human Rights Watch/Asia

Human Rights Watch/Asia brought its concerns regarding human rights in Hong Kong to the attention of Congress twice this year, once in testimony submitted to the Senate in May and again in testimony given before the House in July. Among its principal recommendations were that the U.S. urge China to live up to its obligations in the Joint Declaration, and that it urge the Hong Kong government to act swiftly on law reform and allow legislators to introduce private bills on subjects such as a human rights commission and an equal opportunity commission. Also in July, Human Rights Watch/Asia wrote Governor Patten expressing concern over the pattern of escalating violence between government authorities and Vietnamese asylum seekers, recommending that the government conduct a public review on the use of tear gas against confined populations and allegations of excessive use of force, that it release all videotapes of these incidents and increase the use of independent monitors.

The government responded, denying that it had in any way mishandled the situation.

INDIA

Human Rights Developments

The Indian government took several significant steps toward addressing human rights concerns in 1995, most notably by agreeing to permit the International Committee of the Red Cross (ICRC) to visit detention facilities in the disputed territory of Kashmir and by allowing a widely-criticized security law to lapse. However, the government continued to deny human rights groups access to Kashmir, the site of the most severe abuses by security forces and armed militant groups. The government's proclaimed policy of "transparency" offered little protection for human rights activists in Kashmir and Punjab, who continued to be arrested and "disappeared." Other endemic abuses, including trafficking of women, officially-sanctioned communal violence and police abuse, received scant attention from the government or from India's allies and trading partners.

Two dramatic events focused international attention on the continuing crisis in Kashmir. A two-month-long standoff between militants and the Indian army at a Sufi shrine in the town of Charar-e Sharief ended in catastrophe on May 11 when the shrine was torched and it and most of the town burned to the ground. It was not clear who set the fire; the Indian government blamed the militants while most Kashmiris blamed the army. Because the press was barred from the site, no independent reports were available. Several Kashmiri leaders who attempted to visit the area were arrested. According to the Committee for Initiative on Kashmir, a human rights group, the government claimed that twenty-nine militants were killed in the fighting, yet only fourteen bodies were recovered, five of which were identified as civilians, including a disabled seventy-year-old woman. The disaster forced the Rao government to cancel its plans to hold elections in July; polls were tentatively scheduled for later in the year, but as of November, no date had been announced. All the militant groups in the valley vowed to boycott any election, demanding instead that a plebiscite be held under U.N. auspices.

In July, a previously unknown militant group, Al Faran, kidnaped six tourists in Kashmir: two Americans, one of whom later escaped, two Britons, one German and one Norwegian. The group, believed to be associated with Harakat-ul-Ansar, a militant organization responsible for several 1994 kidnapings and bus bombs, demanded the release of twenty-one detained militants. On August 13, police discovered the beheaded and mutilated body of the Norwegian hostage, Hans Christian Oster. The murder was widely condemned by political leaders and most other militant groups in the Kashmir valley. As this report went to press, the remaining hostages were still in Al Faran's custody. Other groups also engaged in kidnapings; at least four Kashmiris were kidnaped by militant organizations in the same month that the foreign hostages were taken.

Throughout the year, Kashmiri militant groups resorted to the indiscriminate use of explosives, including car bombs and letter bombs, not only in Jammu, but in heavily-trafficked areas of Srinagar, where such attacks had been rare. Civilians were the principal victims. As with the kidnapings, many of these attacks appeared to be the work of Islamist groups whose leadership included Afghans and other non-Kashmiris. Harakat-ul-Ansar claimed responsibility for a July 20 bomb blast in Jammu that killed sixteen and wounded forty-five. According to a statement by the group, the attack was meant to frighten Hindus on pilgrimage to the area. On September 7, a letter bomb delivered to the office of the British Broadcasting Corporation (BBC) in Srinagar killed photojournalist Mushtaq Ali, and wounded BBC correspondent Yusef Jameel. A militant group was believed responsible.

Militant violence also resumed in Punjab. Beant Singh, the chief minister of the north Indian state of Punjab, was assassinated by a car bomb explosion on August 31. His driver and twelve security officers were also killed, and some thirty others were injured. The militant organization Babbar Khalsa claimed responsibility. On September 26, bomb blasts in Delhi and Panipat in neighboring Haryana injured nine. The Khalistan Liberation Force, a Punjab militant group, claimed responsibility for blasts that injured about fifty persons in Delhi on September 25.

Victims of abuse in Punjab and their families continued to file court cases against police responsible for torture, disappearances and extrajudicial executions during the government's decade-long conflict with Sikh separatists in the state. According to the official National Human Rights Commission (NHRC), the government initiated prosecutions of fifteen Punjab police officers in five cases of disappearances and other abuses. No convictions were announced. In May, the NHRC decided to intervene in the case of Harjit Singh, who disappeared after being arrested by the Punjab police in April 1992. The commission appointed an advocate to pursue an inquiry at the High Court. At the same time, human rights groups continued to report "disappearances," including that of Jaswinder Kaur, who disappeared after she and her father were arrested on February 26, 1995. Her father was later released, but police, seeking to arrest her husband, continued to deny that Jaswinder Kaur was in custody. Human rights activist Jaswant Singh Khalra disappeared after being taken into custody on September 6. (See The Right to Monitor, below).

In Assam, police continued to murder detainees in what they claimed were "encounters." On February 16, Ripunjay Acharjya and Hem Chandra Sharma were arrested from their homes in Nayakpura, Assam, and accused of links with a militant organization, the United Liberation Front of Assam (ULFA). Their bodies, bearing bullet injuries, were later found at a local hospital. In another case, Samarendra Sharma of Tamuligaon village was arrested on February 2. After his body was discovered at a local hospital, the police superintendent claimed that Sharma had been killed in an "encounter."

On May 16, the government decided not to renew the Terrorist and Disruptive Activities Act (TADA), a widely criticized security law that permitted, among other things, the use in trial of coerced confessions. The law had prohibited any act that questioned the integrity of India, thereby criminalizing free speech. The government's decision appeared to be prompted by its interest in winning Muslim support in the 1996 general election; TADA had been widely used against Muslims and other minorities. A draft bill for a criminal law to replace TADA and incorporate many of its offensive provisions was submitted to parliament, but no action was taken. Meanwhile, some 6,000 prisoners detained under TADA remained in custody; human rights groups and the NHRC called for a review of their cases.

Official complicity in "communal" violence received scant attention from either the central or state governments. Following elections in the western state of Maharashtra, the extremist Hindu Shiv Sena party formed a coalition government with the Hindu nationalist Bharatiya Janata Party (BJP). The Shiv Sena, believed to have wide support among the Bombay police, was responsible for instigating violence against Muslims that left hundreds dead in the January 1993 "riots." Police participated in many of the attacks, and, nearly two years later, an official inquiry into the violence dragged on without result, despite criticism by human rights groups and the NHRC which urged that the authorities take action to expedite the work of the commission. With the election of the Shiv Sena-BJP government, however, it appeared increasingly unlikely that any police would be prosecuted. The election also raised fears about the security of Muslims in Bombay, particularly migrant workers from other parts of India. Almost immediately after the government was formed, Shiv Sena leader Bal Thackery vowed to deport "illegal Bangladeshi immigrants," and police raids targeted poor Muslim neighborhoods of the city.

Women and girls continued to be trafficked from Nepal into Indian brothels in Bombay and other cities for the purpose of prostitution and kept in conditions tantamount to slavery. Held in debt bondage for years at a time, they have been raped and subjected to severe beatings, exposure to AIDS, and arbitrary imprisonment. Both the Indian and Nepali governments have been complicit in the abuses suffered by trafficking victims, and neither government took significant steps to end the practice by arresting and prosecuting traffickers and punishing police who protect brothel owners.

The Right to Monitor

Although many human rights groups continued to function freely throughout India, those working in areas of conflict, such as Kashmir, the northeast, and Punjab, faced considerable risks.

In Punjab, Jaswant Singh Khalra, general secretary of the human rights wing of the Akali Dal political party, was arrested outside his home in Amritsar on September 6. In January 1995, his office had filed a petition in the High Court claiming that hundreds of individuals had been killed and secretly cremated by the Punjab police. As of November, Khalra had not been produced in court and his whereabouts were unknown.

On the night of June 15, Sheikh Mohammad Ashraf, president of the Baramulla branch of the Jammu and Kashmir bar association, which regularly documented abuses by Indian security forces, was arrested by the Rashtriya Rifles unit of the Indian army. He was released on September 9; throughout his detention, his family was denied access to him. Earlier, on May 1, Mohammad Ashraf, an advocate at the High Court in Srinagar, was reportedly arrested and charged under the Public Safety Act, a preventive detention law. On April 22, two unidentified gunmen opened fire on Mian Abdul Qayoom, president of the Jammu and Kashmir bar association, seriously injuring him. Qayoom had vigorously investigated human rights violations by Indian security forces in Kashmir.

On April 14, Parvez Imroz, secretary of the local branch of the People's Union for Civil Liberties (PUCL, a human rights group), was shot and injured, reportedly by militants who later claimed that Imroz had been shot by accident. On March 31, journalists protesting against human rights abuses by security forces were beaten by police in Srinagar.

India's official human rights commission, the NHRC, continued to perform a useful though limited role, undertaking investigations of a range of abuses, particularly deaths in custody, and recommending prosecutions of police officers responsible. According to the commission, state governments initiated prosecutions of police involved in eighteen cases of deaths in custody; the NHRC intervened to recommend prosecutions in two additional cases, and the accused police officers were arrested and tried. In other cases, however, the commission appeared to accept at face value official accounts of alleged abuse, despite contradictory reports by local human rights groups. Earlier in the year, the NHRC pushed for the repeal of TADA and for granting the ICRC access to Kashmir.

On June 22, the government of India signed an agreement to permit the ICRC to visit detainees and undertake its other humanitarian services in Kashmir. The ICRC was scheduled to begin its operations by November 1. The government decision followed years of pressure by domestic and international human rights groups. Earlier in the year, the ICRC conducted human rights training courses for Indian security personnel.

In July, the Indian government unsuccessfully attempted to prevent the accreditation of two human rights groups—Physicians for Human Rights (PHR) and Freedom House—at the U.N. committee on NGO consultative status. Both groups had been critical of India's human rights policies, particularly in Kashmir.

The Role of the International Community

In April, U.N. High Commissioner for Human Rights José Ayala Lasso made an unprecedented visit to Kashmir. As had been the pattern in his visits elsewhere, Ayala Lasso opted for caution over clout, expressing concern about reports of human rights violations while refraining from hard-hitting criticisms about Indian abuses in Kashmir. However, he criticized the lack of judicial action against police officers accused of human rights violations and urged the government to grant access to international human rights groups. The high commissioner also joined with other human rights groups to call for the repeal of TADA.

European Community Policy

Under the provisions of the cooperation agreement between India and the European Community which came into force in 1994, the European Union has an obligation to raise human rights concerns and to make an effort to improve human rights through trade and diplomatic channels. However, while the E.U. actively pursued commercial interests in India in 1995, there was little evidence of any effort to raise human rights concerns. Early in the year, Daniela Napoli, head of the human rights and democracy unit of the European Commission, traveled to India to evaluate possible human rights projects with Indian NGOs, and, to some extent, with the Indian government. The European Commission approved two major development projects in India in July.

Commercial interests dominated British Foreign Secretary Douglas Hurd's visit to India in January. Endorsing India's policy on Kashmir, he promoted the sale of British military aircraft to India.

U.S. Policy

The U.S. continued the policy adopted in 1994 not to criticize India's human rights record publicly and to raise human rights concerns only in private. The administration also continued to promote commercial relations, dispatching a stream of high-level officials to India early in the year.

In January, U.S. Commerce Secretary Ron Brown led a trade delegation to India, clinching business deals worth billions of dollars, and stating publicly that since "commercial diplomacy" was a way to effect human rights improvements, "one doesn't have to wait for the other." In the first such visit by a defense secretary since the mid-1980s, Secretary William Perry signed a historic "framework of understanding" to pave the way for more military cooperation between India and the U.S. In a welcome move, Secretary Perry called on India to permit the ICRC to operate freely in Kashmir.

Visits to India by senior administration officials reflected the administration's concern with reassuring Indian government officials anxious about a U.S. "tilt" toward Pakistan. On a visit to India in March, Assistant Secretary for South Asia Robin Raphael denied that the U.S. had downplayed human rights issues for the sake of commercial interests. However, her harshest public criticism—that human rights in practice was "not always consistent with the guarantees in the Indian constitution"—was conspicuously mild in contrast to her praise for government measures and what she called the end of India's "denial" phase about human rights abuses.

In testimony before Congress on March 7, Secretary Raphael again praised "positive developments, " particularly the work of the official NHRC, but acknowledged that "more needs to be done." Her observation that the Punjab police "often do not respect normal criminal procedures" was notably lame. In fact, the Punjab police have routinely resorted to torture and murder. Her remarks suggesting that the conflict with Pakistan over Kashmir would hinder Indian efforts to gain a seat on the U.N. Security Council angered Indian officials, and the administration was quick to respond. Visiting India several weeks later, Under Secretary for Political Affairs Peter Tarnoff reassured Indian officials that the U.S. had not ruled out a seat for India on the security council.

In its efforts to walk a fine line on the question of elections in Kashmir, the administration sent mixed messages on its view of the value of such a vote. While reiterating the administration's official policy recognizing Kashmir as a disputed territory, Secretary Raphael observed in January that "it would be premature" to say whether the government's controversial plans for elections in Kashmir would be an appropriate part of the political process. Later in the year, Ambassador Frank Wisner called for Kashmiri leaders to participate, even though most have questioned India's right of control over the territory and have raised questions about whether a fair election would be held.

First Lady Hillary Rodham Clinton visited India on her South Asia tour in March, and although she met with a wide range of women's organizations, her public remarks did not focus on human rights abuses affecting women.

The human rights officer and other staff at the U.S. Embassy met regularly with Indian human rights groups. In a welcome move, Ambassador Frank Wisner raised the case of "disappeared" human rights activist Jaswant Singh Khalra during a visit to Punjab later in the year.

The Work of
Human Rights Watch/Asia

Throughout 1995, Human Rights Watch/Asia put pressure on the Indian government, exposing its failure to live up to its publicized policy of "transparency" and pointing out where it had fallen short in holding its security personnel accountable for abuses. In April, the Indian government granted a visa to Human Rights Watch/Asia Executive Director Sidney Jones, reversing two years of government policy. She met with local human rights groups, members of the NHRC and officials of the Home Ministry, who stated that the government would not permit Human Rights Watch/Asia to undertake a mission in Kashmir.

While furthering its contacts with the official NHRC and nongovernmental human rights groups, Human Rights Watch/

Asia continued its work on areas of endemic abuse, particularly communal violence and the trafficking of women and girls.

In July, Human Rights Watch published *Rape for Profit: Trafficking of Nepali Women and Girls into India.* The report documented Indian and Nepali police complicity in the trafficking and abuse of Nepali women and girls, thousands of whom have been abducted or coerced into prostitution in Indian brothels.

In March, Human Rights Watch published *Playing the "Communal Card": Communal Violence and Human Rights,* a report that analyzed the role of the police and other government agents in many parts of the world in fostering "ethnic" and "communal" violence. The chapter on India documented the government's failure to prosecute police and security forces responsible for abuses in incidents of violence following the destruction of the Babur mosque in Ayodhya in December 1992 and in the Bombay "riots" of January 1993.

Human Rights Watch/Asia pressured U. N. High Commissioner for Human Rights José Ayala Lasso to visit detention centers in Kashmir and to be outspoken about abuses by all parties. We also urged that human rights issues be raised by India's donors at the World Bank-convened meeting in June.

Human Rights Watch/Asia also challenged the U.S. government's new "commercial diplomacy" in India and its failure to speak out critically about continuing abuses in India. In January, we wrote to Commerce Secretary Ron Brown and Defense Secretary Perry, asking them to meet with nongovernmental human rights groups and raise human rights issues publicly. Following Secretary Brown's visit, Human Rights Watch/Asia published an opinion piece in the *Boston Globe,* accusing Secretary Brown of squandering an important opportunity to demonstrate the administration's avowed commitment to human rights.

INDONESIA AND EAST TIMOR

Human Rights Developments

As Indonesia celebrated the fiftieth anniversary of its independence in 1995, widespread abuses of basic human rights continued, including arbitrary arrests and detentions, a renewed assault on freedom of expression, and restrictions on freedom of association. A long-standing pattern of abuses by members of the Indonesian military persisted with cases of arbitrary detention, the use of torture and summary killings of civilians in East Timor and Irian Jaya. Top army officials warned of communist-inspired "formless organizations" as a way of explaining criticism of the government and discrediting individual dissidents. The government-appointed National Commission on Human Rights (Komnas), operating within the limits of its mandate, continued to play a useful and active role, conducting investigations and issuing reports on sensitive, high-profile cases.

The government renewed its crackdown on freedom of expression with the arrest of two journalists and an office assistant from the Alliance of Independent Journalists (AJI) in March 1995. The journalists, Ahmad Taufik and Eko Maryadi, both officers of AJI, and staff member Danang Kukuh Wardoyo were charged with "spreading hatred against the government" and publishing the AJI newsletter, *Independen,* without a government license. *Independen* was cited by the prosecution for printing articles critical of President Soeharto and other government officials. In September 1995, Taufik and Maryadi were sentenced to two years and eight months each in prison; Danang Kukuh Wardoyo earlier received a sentence of twenty months.

Also in September, Tri Agus Susanto, a journalist who edited a newsletter for the Pijar Foundation, a Jakarta-based nongovernmental activist organization, was sent to prison for two years after being convicted of insulting the president. The newsletter, *Kabar dari Pijar*, had published an article in 1994 quoting a human rights lawyer's criticisms of Soeharto.

Freedom of expression was also curbed through the break-up of seminars and other public discussions. In June 1995, the police broke up a seminar on democracy and detained seven people, including the sole speaker, Robert Hefner, an American professor from Boston University; they were held overnight for questioning.

Gag orders were issued in an attempt to silence controversial speakers, such as Abdurrahman Wahid, leader the largest Islamic organization, Nahdatul Ulama, who was banned twice from giving speeches in East Java. Coordinating Minister for Political Affairs and Security Soesilo Soedarman stated in June 1995 that the government would pass new regulations on permits for public speaking, declaring that many of the bans imposed by security forces represented an effort to prevent actions that might jeopardize national stability.

The government tried to prosecute some of its most outspoken critics. Sri Bintang Pamungkas, a parliamentarian from the United Development Party, was charged with "defaming the president" for a lecture he delivered in Berlin in April 1995. The lecture coincided with demonstrations against Soeharto, who was visiting Germany at the time. In October, it was announced that the case would come to trial in November. In May, the president issued an executive order terminating Bintang's term as a member of parliament, and he was banned from all foreign travel. Bintang filed a lawsuit challenging the international travel ban in July; in a separate suit, he demanded reinstatement in the parliament. As of November, neither case had yet been heard.

Similar tactics were used against Permadi, a lawyer, NGO activist and mystic who was accused of blasphemy for remarks he made about the Prophet Mohammed during a 1994 seminar. He was arrested in May 1995, tried and convicted in September and released on a technicality immediately after the verdict. It was widely believed that his arrest and conviction stemmed more from critical remarks he made about government leaders than from his references to Islam. George Aditjondro, a lecturer at Satya Wacana University and frequent critic of government policy in East Timor was accused in April 1995 of insulting the government during a lecture he gave in 1994 at the Indonesian Islamic University in Yogyakarta. When the charges were announced, Aditjondro was in Australia as a guest lecturer and Canberra said it had no plans to return Aditjondro.

In a positive development of at least symbolic value, the Jakarta Administrative Court ruled in May that the ban by Minister of Information Harmoko on the popular magazine *Tempo* in June 1994 was arbitrary and illegal. Harmoko, backed by Soeharto, said he would appeal the verdict at a higher court. The Semarang (Central Java) Administrative Court made a similarly courageous ruling that dissident Arief Budiman, sacked by Satya Wacan University for his outspokeness, had been fired illegally.

In a move apparently aimed at quelling complaints about it's limits on openness, the government announced in August 1995 that it planned to abolish the practice of requiring permits for public gatherings, including political gatherings. It said that police notification would still be required, and a 1965 law on political activities still gave the government great discretion in defining and repressing "political gatherings."

In an effort to dampen criticism of its worker rights record, the government implemented various labor reforms announced in 1994, including an increase in the minimum daily wage which took effect in April 1995. But these reforms failed to address the core issues of the denial of freedom of association and the widespread intervention of the military in peaceful labor disputes.

In May, Mochtar Pakpahan, chairman of the banned Serikat Buruh Sejahtera Indonesia (SBSI, or Prosperous Workers Union), an independent labor union, was released from prison while an appeal was pending with the Supreme Court. Pakpahan was arrested in 1994 and sentenced to four years in prison in January 1995. He was charged under Article 160 of the Penal Code with inciting a riot in conjunction with a huge rally in Medan, Sumatra, in April 1994, although he was not even in the area at the time. The Supreme Court overturned Pakpahan's conviction in October 1995. Other SBSI leaders sentenced for their alleged involvement in the Medan riot were also released.

Throughout the year, SBSI and other independent labor organizations were harassed, unable to organize meetings without military interference, and detained and interrogated.

There was no perceptible change in the widespread involvement by the security forces in labor negotiations or peaceful demonstrations by workers. For example, a strike and demonstration by workers at the Great River Garment Company took place in Bogor, West Java, in July 1995. Security forces used sticks to beat demonstrators and prevent workers from reaching the nearby provincial parliamentary compound where they planned to meet with representatives after attempts at negotiation had failed. Police later charged seven students—members of a nongovernmental labor rights organization, Pusat Perjuangan Buruh Indonesia (PPBI or Center for Worker's Struggle)—with instigating and organizing the protests. As of November, their trials had not yet taken place.

In a surprise move in May 1995, the Supreme Court ordered the release of eight individuals convicted and sentenced for the torture and murder of Marsinah, a young labor organizer. The defendants were all company staff at the watch factory where Marsinah worked before her abduction and murder in 1993. Indonesian human rights groups had long suspected military involvement in the murder. The Supreme Court's decision prompted a reopening of the investigation into the case. The police finally named five new suspects, but did not reveal whether any of them were members of the military.

In October, the chief of staff of the armed forces, Lt. Gen. Soeyono, began warning of the "latent threat" of communism, saying that the communist-inspired "formless organizations" were gaining in influence, using the struggle for human rights and democracy as their cover. Others in the government and military picked up the theme, and by the year's end, it seemed as though a witch hunt of known dissidents might be underway.

Human rights conditions in East Timor deteriorated significantly following the Asia-Pacific Economic Cooperation (APEC) conference in Indonesia in November 1994. There were several riots and demonstrations early in 1995, all of which were broken up violently by the Indonesian military. The most egregious case occurred in Liquica, outside of Dili, on January 12, when six East Timorese civilians were shot and killed by Indonesian troops.

Initially the army reported that six guerrillas had been killed in cross fire during an army clash with a Fretilin rebel group. This report was contradicted by local clergy, who said that the victims were innocent civilians. International attention to the killings spurred President Soeharto to order a military investigation, and the National Commission on Human Rights (Komnas) announced it would conduct its own investigation. Both the military's report and the Komnas inquiry, announced in March 1995, concluded that the six men had been summarily executed. But the military was adamant in insisting that the six men were guerrillas, while Komnas maintained that the victims were all civilians who had been tortured prior to being killed. A lieutenant and a private under his command were tried by a military court; in June 1995, they received sentences of four years and six months and four years in prison respectively. However, the soldiers were punished not for the killings, but for violating an order from a superior and for failing to report the incident.

In September, riots broke out in Maliana and in Dili, sparked by religious and ethnic tensions. Dili's Roman Catholic bishop, Carlos Belo, said an underlying cause was the government's failure to address the underlying problems in East Timor, a view echoed by Komnas.

In the Timika area of Irian Jaya, a remote province dominated by copper and gold mining interests, a series of incidents took place between October 1994 and May 1995, involving the detention, torture, killing and "disappearance" of indigenous people by Indonesian security forces. Some of the incidents reportedly took place on property and using facilities and equipment owned by a U.S. mining company, Freeport McMoran. A highly credible report by the Catholic church of Jayapura, based on eyewitness testimony, was released in August, documenting the abuses. After two missions to Timika, Komnas issued a report in late September, confirming that sixteen people had been killed, including women and children, in conjunction with military operations against a separatist group, the Free Papua Movement (OPM). It called on the government and armed forces to investigate and punish those responsible, to identify the whereabouts of four missing people, and to "clarify" the respective roles of the military, local government and Freeport management in maintaining security and protecting the human rights of the region's residents. Freeport flatly denied any involvement in the abuses. The army said that four soldiers would be prosecuted in January 1996 for "violations of military procedures."

The Right to Monitor

Prior to the November 1994 APEC meeting, the Ministry of Interior drafted a presidential decree imposing tighter restrictions and monitoring requirements on nongovernmental organizations (NGOs), including human rights groups, provoking widespread domestic and international complaints; as of November 1995, it had not yet been issued. But a crackdown on NGOs continued nonetheless, with human rights groups, labor rights organizations and other NGOs facing routine harassment and surveillance. The Indonesian Legal Aid Institute reported that its offices and vehicles in Jakarta and Palembang were vandalized in January and February 1995. There was no attempt by the government to investigate or prosecute those responsible.

The Role of
the International Community

The Indonesian government was only partially successful in blunting criticism by extolling the work of its own human rights commission and by enhancing its economic and military ties abroad. East Timor and Irian Jaya were potent lightning rods for international criticism, as was the government's clamp down on journalists.

Soeharto's visit to Germany in April was disrupted by protest rallies focusing attention on Indonesia's poor human rights record, though a trade fair in Hanover and the signing of major business deals overseen by Chancellor Helmut Kohl were obvious successes for the government. Similarly, in September Queen Beatrix of The Netherlands visited Indonesia to mark the fiftieth anniversary of the country's independence and express regret over Holland's former colonial role. Human rights concerns in East Timor were clearly de-emphasized; Dutch business people traveling with her completed some $800 million worth of contracts.

Also in September, Australian Prime Minister Paul Keating met with Soeharto in Bali and emphasized the two governments' common interests at the upcoming APEC meeting in Japan. East Timor was also on the agenda, fueled in part by the domestic controversy over the Australian government's initial acceptance of Indonesia's newly nominated ambassador, a general who had defended the military's actions in the Dili, East Timor, killings in 1991. The nomination was withdrawn in July. The incidents in Irian Jaya also sparked official concern, particularly since the abuses were first publicized by an Australian-based development organization. Australia's ambassador in Jakarta conducted an inquiry, and Gareth Evans, foreign minister, raised "serious" concerns with his Indonesian counterpart in August.

At the World Bank-convened consultative group donor meeting in Paris in July, a number of governments, including the U.S. delegation, expressed concern, either publicly or privately, about East Timor and the Liquica killings in particular, as well as the issue of press freedom and free expression. However, the bank's public statement following the meeting did not reflect these concerns. When the World Bank's vice-president for the Asia-Pacific region met with Soeharto in March, there was no indication that "governance" issues were addressed. The bank pledged $1.2 billion to Indonesia in 1995.

The Clinton administration dispatched Assistant Secretary of State for Democracy, Human Rights and Labor John Shattuck to Indonesia and East Timor in April. Shattuck criticized the government's muzzling of the press, urged the government to give the people of East Timor "more influence over their affairs," and pressed for greater freedom of association for workers. He made no comments publicly about the administration's efforts to restore International Military Education and Training (IMET) to Indonesia, cut off by Congress in 1992 in response to the massacre that took place in Dili in 1991, or about the worker rights case pending before the U.S. Trade Representative.

Just prior to his trip, Shattuck testified before the House International Relations Committee and condemned the "deteriorating" human rights situation in East Timor at precisely the same time as a senior Pentagon official, Admiral William Owens, was in Jakarta calling for a renewal of IMET training because "appropriate action" had been taken to ease the situation in East Timor.

In fact, the administration seemed determined to deepen its ties to the Indonesian military, despite its atrocious human rights record, arguing that greater engagement and training would produce a more professional armed forces. At a meeting with Indonesia's foreign minister in August, Secretary of State Warren Christopher offered to sell to Jakarta F-16 fighter planes originally ordered by Pakistan; by October, it was clear the deal was going through. Admiral Owens, on another visit to Jakarta in September, announced that the U.S. and Indonesian military would begin regular bilateral meetings in Honolulu in November.

The administration made a deal with Congress in September, agreeing to continue its ban on the sale or licensing of small and light weapons and crowd control equipment in Indonesia in exchange for congressional approval of expanded-IMET (military education and training, which is said to include a human rights component) for the Indonesian military in the budget for fiscal year 1996. The administration requested $600,000 for IMET. The U.S. Trade Representative (USTR) planned to send a delegation to Indonesia in early November, but had not yet ruled on a petition by Human Rights Watch/Asia submitted in June 1995 urging the USTR to reinstate the formal review of Indonesia's access to Generalized System of Preferences (GSP) trade benefits in light of the government's failure to make meaningful progress on labor rights. The review had been suspended in February 1994 after Jakarta promised to make certain reforms.

The administration supported adoption of a compromise "chairman's statement" on East Timor at the U.N. Human Rights Commission in Geneva in March. U.S. Ambassador to the U.N. Madeleine Albright, meeting with Soeharto in Jakarta in early September, expressed concern about the unrest in East Timor and expressed support for a continuing dialogue under U.N. auspices. U.N. High Commissioner on Human Rights José Ayala Lasso was expected to visit East Timor late in the year.

The European Parliament, responding to reports of further killings and arrests in East Timor in September, decided to send a fact-finding delegation to East Timor. It passed a joint resolution condemning abuses and calling on governments to cease arms sales and military assistance to Indonesia.

On October 27, President Clinton welcomed President Soeharto to the White House for their first summit meeting in the United

States. Clinton privately raised concerns about human rights, particularly in East Timor.

The U.S. embassy in Jakarta was supportive of Indonesian NGOs and outspoken on human rights. The embassy publicly protested the arrests of the AJI members in March and sent observers to their trial.

The Work of
Human Rights Watch/Asia

Human Rights Watch/Asia continued to place a high priority on Indonesia and East Timor, publishing a short report, *Press Closures in Indonesia One Year Later*, plus a report on the government's attack on freedom of association, *Soeharto Retaliates against Critics*, as well as an analysis of worker rights based on our GSP petition. We used various advocacy strategies to press for specific improvements: briefing U.S. Assistant Secretary Shattuck before his trip to East Timor; testifying on East Timor before the U.N. Decolonization Committee in July and on human rights in Indonesia before Congress in March; filing a petition with the U.S. Trade Representative on worker rights in June; participating in a briefing for the newly appointed ambassador to Jakarta in August.

In advance of Soeharto's visit to the U.S., our Washington office worked with members of Congress to circulate a letter urging President Clinton to stress human rights and worker rights and making specific recommendations.

Recognizing the growing importance of the private sector, Human Rights Watch/Asia expanded an ongoing dialogue with U.S. companies involved in Indonesia. We also hosted a meeting between NGOs and a delegation of Indonesian corporate officials visiting the United States in September.

JAPAN

Human Rights Developments

Within Japan

While Japan generally had a good human rights record, social and legal discrimination continued against indigenous people, Koreans, alien workers and residents. In addition, women experienced discrimination in the workplace, despite legal protections; at least three executions took place; and trafficking of women from Southeast Asia was a major problem. But the most serious abuses of all were those that occurred in prisons and during pre-trial detention.

In March 1995 the results of a 1994 Human Rights Watch delegation's visit to Japan were published, simultaneously in English and Japanese, in a major report, *Prison Conditions in Japan*. The report analyzed the Japanese prison and police detention systems, and criticized the widespread use of solitary confinement, restrictions on legal representation, and other abuses. It called on the government to undertake a thorough reform of the system and to adopt new prison legislation in conformity with international standards. The Justice Ministry declined to make any public comments on the report.

In February, the United Nations Special Rapporteur on Torture raised concerns about the Japanese practice of extended police detention, a case of severe mistreatment of a Chinese resident by police, and another case of prolonged solitary confinement.

In Japan's Foreign Policy

Under socialist Prime Minister Tomiichi Murayama, Japan continued to emphasize its ties with its Asian neighbors while maintaining a fundamental security relationship with the U.S. The Foreign Ministry tried to strike a balance in its human rights policies toward other countries by supporting the universality and importance of human rights in general terms, while at the same time avoiding creating political tensions with its most important trading and aid partners over their abusive rights practices. In the process, Tokyo tended to downplay human rights and often failed to use its substantial political and economic leverage to promote human rights in the Asia-Pacific region.

According to the Foreign Ministry's annual "white paper" (published in September 1995), Japan's Official Development Assistance (ODA) bilateral aid program was the world's largest in 1994, totaling over $13.2 billion. In 1995 the government also indicated that it planned in the future to redirect some of its ODA away from Asian countries with booming economies and toward Africa, the Middle East and elsewhere, while within Asia the ODA program would increasingly be used to enhance the development of "democratization" and free-market economies in countries such as Cambodia, Vietnam, and Mongolia. However, the bulk of both yen loans and grant assistance was again given to Asian governments (slightly less than 60 percent of all ODA), with China the number one aid recipient.

The "white paper" reiterated the government's commitment to its ODA Charter, first adopted in 1992, which specifies promotion of human rights and democratization as well as opposition to military exports/imports and nuclear proliferation as guiding principles for ODA decisions. But application of the Charter's human rights provisions remained spotty and highly inconsistent. The Foreign Ministry's Annual Report on ODA in 1994 (published in March 1995) stated that "when there are clear problems in light of these principles...Japan reviews its aid policy to such countries" but avoids applying the guidelines "mechanically because it could hinder flexible implementation of official development assistance." The report gives several examples of situations in which ODA was actually suspended, at least in part, on human rights grounds, most of them in Africa (Sudan, Nigeria, Kenya, Malawi and Sierra Leone—see *Human Rights Watch World Report 1995* for details); no examples were cited in Asia, except for Burma (described below).

The Foreign Ministry also invoked the Charter's human rights language, but usually only in general terms, in its regular "policy dialogues" with ODA recipient governments and also at the time of high-level political visits. For example, in the case of Vietnam, Prime Minister Murayama met with Communist Party Secretary Do Muoi when he visited Tokyo in April 1995 and alluded to the ODA Charter's human rights clause. But the Japanese government did not link specific ODA decisions to Vietnam's human rights performance, nor did it intend to raise human rights concerns at the November 1995 donors' meeting convened by the World Bank. In 1995, Japan was again Vietnam's largest single aid donor. In January, notes were signed committing the Overseas Economic Cooperation Fund to $480 million infrastructure loans for 1995, initially pledged at the November 1994 international donors' meeting. During Do Muoi's visit, Japan pledged a $700 million infrastructure loan plus $36 million in grant assistance.

On the other hand, in the case of Indonesia, Japan's representatives used the occasion of an annual development aid conference in Paris in July 1995 to raise concerns about restrictions on press freedom in Indonesia, as well as human rights problems more generally. Tokyo alsopledged $1.8 billion in ODA to Jakarta. Following the killings by Indonesian troops of six civilians in Liquica, East Timor, in January 1995, the Japanese government quickly urged an investigation into the incident, but did not hint that Indonesia's response would affect foreign aid flows.

Japan did use ODA to promote a key foreign policy objective in August 1995 when the government announced it would freeze most grant assistance to China to protest Beijing's nuclear testing program, thus reducing it from $81.5 million in fiscal year 1994 to only $5.2 million for the new fiscal year beginning in April. The Chinese government reacted angrily, saying the move would affect bilateral relations. But the decision on grant aid was clearly a compromise in response to calls from some political parties and politicians for a freeze on all ODA lending to Beijing. It also appeared to be a token gesture, given that the Japanese Foreign Ministry said a new three-year package of $6.9 billion in low-interest yen loans would go forward in 1996 as planned. In its ODA report, human rights is not even mentioned in the discussion of the ODA Charter and its application to China. Meanwhile, two-way trade between Japan and China increased to a record $50 billion, making Tokyo China's largest trading partner after the United States.

Japan's willingness to risk offending China on the nuclear testing issue contrasted sharply with its reluctance to exert pressure on human rights concerns through its ODA program with China or in its bilateral relations with Beijing. But it did join other governments in multilateral human rights initiatives. At the U.N. Commission on Human Rights in March, Japan again cosponsored a resolution criticizing China's human rights record.

Following the release of Daw Aung San Suu Kyi in July, Japan signaled a fundamental shift in its policy toward Burma, where ODA had in principle been suspended since the 1988 crackdown except for some limited humanitarian grant assistance. Within days of her release, a senior Foreign Ministry official went to Rangoon to meet with Daw Suu. But at a conference of the Association of South East Asian Nations (ASEAN) in late July, Foreign Minister Yohei Kono told his counterpart from Burma that Japan was considering resuming some ODA projects following Rangoon's "great and brave decision" to free the democracy leader from house arrest. In the interim, Tokyo would give $15 million in grant aid for a nurses training school. Despite a rebuke by Daw Aung San Suu Kyi herself in a press interview in which she cautioned Japan not to move too quickly, and despite pressure from its Western allies including the United States, Tokyo said in August it was firmly committed to restoring aid, saying it was "unavoidable" that Japan would follow its own policy on Burma.

An ODA mission visited Burma in October and it appeared that a $48 million ODA loan was being prepared to upgrade Rangoon's electrical infrastructure; this was one of the projects suspended in 1988. Privately, Japanese officials also indicated that they now shared ASEAN's "constructive engagement" approach to Burma—a departure from Japan's previous posture acting as a bridge between the "isolationist" policy of the U.S. and the approach taken by Burma's closest neighbors. In late October, General Maung Aye, a top official in the Burmese government, visited Tokyo to encourage Japanese investment in Burma.

The Foreign Ministry vaguely indicated that progress towards "democratization" in Burma, including adoption of a new constitution and transfer of power to a democratically elected government, would somehow affect future ODA decisions. But Tokyo refrained from directly conditioning ODA on any specific human rights improvements. Meanwhile, at the U.N. Human Rights Commission in March, Japan supported a resolution on Burma which was adopted by consensus.

Japan endeavored to protect the gains made in Cambodia since the peace settlement as well as to demonstrate its willingness to make a constructive contribution to peacekeeping and democratization in the region. Japan continued to be the number one aid donor to Cambodia. It pledged over $89.3 million at a conference on Cambodian reconstruction held in Tokyo in 1994. In addition, Japan gave $2.5 million for landmines clearance through the U.N. voluntary fund.

Japan was more active on human rights in various multilateral fora, including at the Fourth U.N. Conference on Women in Beijing, but it also faced criticism for some of its policies and positions at the Subcommission in Geneva and at the Sixth Committee of the U.N. General Assembly.

In Geneva, the Subcommission on Prevention of Discrimination and Protection of Minorities adopted a resolution in August welcoming the Japanese government's decision to establish a private, voluntary fund for women sex slaves and forced laborers. But the subcommission also urged Tokyo to establish immediately an administrative tribunal to handle claims for state compensation from the World War II "comfort women."

In New York, at an August meeting of a working group to review a draft statute establishing an International Criminal Court to consider "crimes against peace and security," Japan was criticized by Human Rights Watch for adopting an obstructionist position when it urged further review of the draft statute, considerably slowing down the process. The Japanese delegation said it strongly supported creation of the Court, but claimed that both substantive problems with the draft and a lack of support for the Court among many developing countries warranted a delay.

One indication of the Foreign Ministry's ongoing interest in developing a distinctive human rights policy for Japan was a decision in July to co-host with the U.N. University in Tokyo a high-profile symposium on "Human Rights in the Asia-Pacific Region: Towards Partnership for the Promotion and Protection of Human Rights." The meeting had academic, governmental and NGO participants from the region; the ministry planned to hold such seminars on an annual basis.

The Right to Monitor

Human rights groups in Japan faced no legal restrictions on their activities.

U.S. Policy

There was little demonstrable progress in the U.S.-Japan dialogue on cooperation on human rights, initiated in 1994. At Japan's urging, human rights were omitted from the broad "Global Partnership" agenda of issues on which the U.S. and Japan formally cooperate, such as environmental and population problems, and therefore human rights concerns were not raised during bilateral meetings on the Partnership in 1995. There was, however, informal contact and coordination between the administration and Tokyo on some specific issues, such as resumption of ODA to Burma and the U.N. resolution on China.

The Work of
Human Rights Watch/Asia

Human Rights Watch/Asia concentrated its efforts in the area of advocacy, attempting to influence Japanese foreign policy and highlighting Japan's potential role in promoting human rights given its enormous political and economic clout, particularly in the Asia-Pacific region. In 1995, Human Rights Watch also turned its attention to the domestic human rights situation in Japan and published its first major report on Japanese prisons; it also embarked on a study of the trafficking of women in Japan, due to be completed in 1996.

The report on prison conditions in Japan was released at a press conference in Tokyo in March that received wide coverage, and a Human Rights Watch representative spoke at a conference in Japan that launched a new penal reform organization, the Center for Prisoners' Rights and at the Japan Federation of Bar Associations.

Human Rights Watch/Asia traveled to Japan in September to engage in a dialogue with policy makers, NGOs and others on Japan's ODA policies, its activities at the United Nations, and other aspects of Japanese foreign policy. In November, our representative participated in NGO activities surrounding the Asia-Pacific Economic Cooperation forum in Osaka. During the year, the Washington office of Human Rights Watch/Asia continued a regular dialogue and exchange of information on human rights matters with the Japanese embassy.

PAKISTAN

Human Rights Developments

Politically-motivated violence stemming from the ongoing conflict throughout urban Sindh remained the most pressing human rights issue in Pakistan, where guerrilla warfare and counter-offensive measures by government forces brought Karachi, the capital of Sindh, to a standstill several times during the year. For nearly a decade, the ethnic Mohajir Qaumi [National] Movement (MQM) and, later, its breakaway faction, the MQM-Haqiqi, have been fighting the government for greater economic and political power for the Mohajir community. Throughout 1995, all parties to the conflict routinely committed serious human rights violations by using random violence to create a climate of fear, by actively targeting political opponents, and by failing to control abusive forces. This created an environment of rampant lawlessness, disorder, and official corruption in Karachi, a city of twelve million, where militants and abusive security forces enjoyed virtual freedom from accountability for illegal actions.

The government demonstrated a lack of resolve to deal with Karachi's chronic security crisis and to enforce the rule of law uniformly. Rather, state intelligence agencies reportedly continued sponsorship of the Haqiqi faction, which was responsible for the most egregious acts of violence, intimidation, and extortion in the city. Human rights groups accused government forces, particularly the paramilitary Rangers and the police, of endemic civil rights violations against suspected members and supporters of the MQM, including indiscriminate house-to-house searches in targeted areas, random firing in riot-torn neighborhoods, arbitrary arrests and detentions, torture, custodial deaths, and extrajudicial executions. MQM members also engaged in killings of opponents, torture, kidnaping, robbery, and extortion.

On July 11, the government and the MQM entered into negotiations in Islamabad. With both sides bent on settling political scores, however, the talks appeared to deadlock from the start. Karachi, in the meantime, continued its slide towards anarchy, with more than 200 deaths from torture, sniper fire, and police sharp-shooters in the month of July.

Contributing to the carnage in Karachi and civil strife across the country was the rising strength of militant religious and sectarian groups, such as the extremist Sunni group, the Sipah-e-Sahaba-e-Pakistan (SSP), and its Shia counterpart, the Sipah-e-Mohammad. These groups were responsible for widespread attacks on and intimidation of secularists and minorities. The SSP and other hard-line religious groups waged a nationwide campaign to oppose proposed changes in Pakistan's blasphemy law and to protest the appeal and subsequent acquittal in February of two Christians charged with blasphemy. As part of the campaign, the SSP and its allies organized numerous strikes throughout the country and held several public rallies in which activists freely brandished weapons and threatened to silence dissenting voices. On August 24, SSP militants ransacked the office of the British Broadcasting Corporation (BBC) in Islamabad, and attacked two BBC correspondents. SSP chief Ziaur Rehman Farooqi was arrested in connection with the attack, after his group claimed responsibility for it. Some of the worst incidents of sectarian violence occurred in the Islamic holy month of Ramadan, when a number of crowded Shia mosques were attacked in Karachi, with heavy casualties among the worshipers. On February 6, gunmen killed eight people in a west Karachi mosque.

Early in the year, to combat the escalation of sectarian violence, the government announced plans to restrict foreign funding for religious groups. However, despite vows to crack down on extremist religious organizations, made prior to her official visit to Washington in April, Prime Minister Bhutto's government made no systematic effort to protect civilians from the militants or to ensure that the latter abided by the law.

Instead, the government resorted to draconian and misguided methods, implementing the harshest media crackdown since General Zia ul Haq's military dictatorship. On June 29, the government, invoking the notorious and arbitrary Maintenance of Public Order ordinance (MPO) of 1960, banned for sixty days six Karachi-based news dailies with a combined circulation of several million. In addition, the government canceled the publishing licenses of another 122 publications linked to the banned papers, in an apparent move to prevent the latter from appearing under new names. The government justified its action on grounds that the newspapers' reporting on Karachi events was "spreading sensationalism" and "inciting people to violence against the government." Press organizations condemned the ban as a violation of due process of law and the press freedom guarantees of the Pakistani constitution, and called for the repeal of the most repressive clauses of the MPO. Although a vigorous protest campaign by journalists unions and newspaper owners associations forced the government to lift the ban after six days, other aspects of the government's anti-press stance remained in evidence, including official harassment of journalists, and the failure to protect newspaper offices and employees from attacks by militants.

On September 14, Farhan Effendi, a field correspondent for the Karachi-based Urdu daily, *Parcham*, was arrested by the paramilitary Rangers, reportedly severely beaten, and kept in detention blindfolded with his hands tied behind his back. *Parcham* is considered sympathetic to the views of the MQM, and, although Effendi was charged with the illegal possession of a firearm and involvement in terrorist activities, his arrest was widely viewed as an attempt to intimidate the press. Bux Ali Jamali, a reporter for the newspaper *Kawish*, suffered a fate similar to Effendi's after he wrote stories critical of government development initiatives in Nawabshah, the hometown of Bhutto's husband, Asif Zardari.

The prime minister filed a defamation suit against Kamran Khan, a reporter for the *News* in Karachi, for writing that Bhutto, during a meeting with British Foreign Secretary Douglas Hurd, had requested that Britain expel MQM leader Altaf Husain. Another defamation suit was initiated against Razia Bhatti, editor of *Newsline*, one of Pakistan's most influential and outspoken

magazines, by Sindh Governor Kamal Azfar, who also issued a warrant for her arrest. After the prime minister intervened, all charges against Bhatti were dropped. However, journalists with less public stature than Bhatti continued to be victimized by the government. The press also suffered from violence by militants, whom the government made no serious effort to identify or punish. For example, the perpetrators of a grenade attack on June 21 that damaged the Karachi offices of the Urdu daily, *Nawa-e-Waqt*, and the English daily, *The Nation*, remained at large.

Politically-motivated abuse of the state's judicial and law enforcement mechanisms was a common feature of Pakistan's political landscape during 1995. The Bhutto government resorted to preventive detentions and spurious lawsuits to promote its own political agenda and to sideline political opponents. Politicians and members of parliament from opposition political parties, most notably the Muslim League, remained under arrest, continued to be refused bail, and, contrary to the law, were even denied permission to attend parliamentary sessions. Muslim League supporters, including businessmen, were harassed and had false cases lodged against them, and judges and public officials who supported victims of government abuse were transferred from their posts to different jurisdictions. On September 5, President Farooq Leghari suspended the Punjab Assembly and imposed direct governor's rule on the province for up to two months. Subsequently, on September 13, the assembly was reconvened and a chief minister more palatable to the federal government was duly elected. This episode perfectly echoed the 1994 incident when the president's suspension of the North West Frontier Province legislature similarly resulted in the installation of a new provincial chief minister. The legislation that allows the president to dissolve the national and provincial assemblies, a holdover from military rule, has been repeatedly invoked by the Bhutto administration; there was no indication at year's end that the government would change it.

Pakistan's religious minorities continued to have second-class status in their own country. Despite assurances given by the Bhutto administration that it would reform, if not repeal, Pakistan's discriminatory blasphemy laws, the government abandoned all reform proposals in the face of stiff opposition from extremist religious groups. In a much publicized proceeding in February, the Lahore High Court overturned the death sentences of two Christians—one of whom was a fourteen-year-old boy—accused of blasphemy. Appellate review of the convictions revealed that the blasphemy charges against the two Christians were entirely unsubstantiated, and that the trial court had acted under pressure from religious zealots in a climate of emotionalism and fear. Religious militants also made their presence felt at the appellate hearing, which was conducted under tight security. The lead defense attorney's car was smashed on the High Court grounds, and her driver was almost strangled to death by a militant mob. Nobody was arrested in connection with the attack. Because of the threat of violence by religious zealots and the lack of adequate government protection, the two acquitted Christians immediately left for a European country where they had been granted asylum. Similarly, all the Christian families residing in Ratta Dhotran, the acquitted defendants' home village, were forced to flee their homes permanently by religious zealots. Scores of blasphemy cases remained pending before the lower courts, particularly against Ahmadis and Christians.

Violent attacks on Ahmadis by sectarian militants also continued with impunity. On April 9, three Ahmadis were attacked in Shab Qadar in the North West Frontier Province, within the premises of a court. The Ahmadis were there to file a bail petition for another member of the Ahamdiyya community who had been arrested by the police under dubious circumstances. One of the victims of the attack was stoned to death, and his dead body stripped and dragged through the town on a rope. A second was seriously injured, while the third escaped unhurt. Despite the public nature of the attack, no arrests were made. The government's failure to prosecute the perpetrators of anti-Ahmadi violence sent a message of official complicity in the crimes.

Protests continued over the system of separate electorates for non-Muslim citizens, under which religious minorities have been allocated a specific number of seats in the provincial and national assemblies. Minority leaders have argued that the system marginalizes their constituencies and leaves them without genuine representation. On August 14, three Christian speakers at a rally organized by the Christian Liberation Front to protest the separate electorates system and other discriminatory legislation were charged with "inciting enmity among people." The three defendants were subsequently granted pre-arrest bail by the Islamabad Sessions Court while the case was investigated.

Despite Bhutto's election-time promises, Pakistani women continued to be subordinate in the eyes of the law. By the end of the year the Bhutto administration had made no effort to repeal or limit the scope of the Hudood Ordinances, which discriminate against women as drafted and as applied. Between 50 and 80 percent of all female detainees in Pakistan were imprisoned under this body of law, while police abuse of women, including custodial rape and other forms of torture, continued. Although the government took a few positive, if symbolic, steps such as announcing a cabinet decision to ratify the Convention on the Elimination of Discrimination Against Women, setting up a Senate inquiry commission on women, and establishing police stations staffed by women, in practice most women continued to be denied due process and equality before the law, and few abusive police officers were prosecuted.

The use of bonded industrial and agricultural labor, including bonded child labor, in Pakistan remained pervasive. At least thousands and possibly millions of adult and child workers throughout Pakistan were forcibly employed, restricted in their freedom of movement, and denied the right to negotiate the terms of their employment. Employers and landlords coerced workers into servitude through physical abuse, forced confinement, and debt bondage, whereby a member of an indebted family is obliged to work for a creditor, but unable to liquidate the debt. Bonded laborers in Pakistan were subjected to beatings, rapes, and torture by land and factory owners, and by local police when they attempted to escape. The state virtually never prosecuted or punished employers who held workers in servitude, illegally confined them, or physically and sexually abused bonded laborers. Since most of the country's political elite hails from rural areas where bondage is an entrenched and customary practice, it appeared unlikely that the government would act quickly or forcefully to eradicate the institution.

On April 16, Iqbal Masih, a twelve-year-old child labor activist and former bonded worker in a carpet-making factory, was shot dead while riding his bicycle in his village north of Lahore. Early investigations suggested that he had been killed by a villager whom he had seen involved in an illicit act. The gunman, who was arrested a week after the boy's death, confessed, but later recanted. The initial murder investigation was believed to have recommended a re-investigation of the case.

The Right to Monitor

Human rights groups in Pakistan generally functioned freely during 1995, with a few significant exceptions. Lawyers representing defendants in blasphemy cases were repeatedly threatened, with impunity, by religious groups. Asthma Jehangir, lead defense counsel in the highly publicized blasphemy trial of Salamat Masih and Rehmat Masih, received numerous death threats from religious militants and was forced to seek private armed protection. On October 19, seven armed men broke into Jehangir's home, where they were discovered by her bodyguard. Her brother was wounded in the ensuing exchange of fire. A suspect later told police that the men were members of the Sunni Tehrik sect and had intended to "punish" Jehangir and her sister, lawyer Hina Jilani, for their role in the blasphemy appeal case.

The Pakistani government's repression of the press during the year fostered a climate in which journalists became regular targets for violence and intimidation. Journalists reporting on Pakistan's bonded labor problem, for example, faced harassment from both official and unofficial sources. On June 29, Elfinn Haug, a Norwegian television cameraman, was attacked and beaten while filming a child-labor workshop in the Sialkot area north of Lahore. The unidentified assailants grabbed his camera, which the police later recovered without its film. On June 5, Zafaryab Ahmad, a journalist known for his reporting on bonded labor, was arrested by a Federal Investigation Agency (FIA) team on charges of sedition and kept in incommunicado detention. In July, Ahmad was temporarily released on bail for health reasons. On the same day as Ahmad's arrest, sedition charges were brought against the chairman of the Bonded Labour Liberation Front (BLLF), Ehsanullah Khan, who was then out of the country and has not since returned. A few days later, the FIA arrested two staff members of the BLLF and imprisoned them without charge or trial in the harshest category of cell in Lahore's Camp Jail. The arrests were part of a government clamp-down on the BLLF, in the wake of the organization's protests about the murder of its most prominent child activist, Iqbal Masih.

The Role of the International Community

The plight of fourteen-year-old Salamat Masih and forty-year-old Rehmat Masih, both sentenced to death for blasphemy, received enormous attention from governments and the media worldwide. The outrage expressed by the world community prompted Prime Minister Bhutto to ensure that the two defendants received a speedy and impartial appeal hearing. After their acquittal, the two received several offers of asylum. Shortly thereafter, during an official visit to Pakistan in April, German President Roman Herzog criticized the country's blasphemy laws and urged the government to amend them swiftly.

The European Community

In May, the European Commission responded to a question from the European Parliament noting that it was aware of the substantial use of child labor in certain industries in Pakistan and supporting the efforts of the International Labour Organization (ILO) to ensure compliance with international conventions on the use of child labor.

U.S. Policy

Human rights considerations took a back seat in U.S. efforts to improve U.S.-Pakistan relations in 1995. There were concerted efforts on both sides to resolve ongoing disputes over Pakistan's nuclear policy and rising narcotics production and the United States' refusal, pursuant to the Pressler Amendment, to deliver military equipment for which Pakistan had already paid. The Pressler Amendment cut off economic and military aid to Pakistan in 1990 in an attempt to force the country to give up its nuclear program. In January, Secretary of Defense William Perry visited Pakistan, the first such visit by a U.S. defense secretary since the mid-1980s. At the conclusion of Secretary Perry's visit, the countries agreed to revive a previously disbanded consultative group to discuss defense cooperation.

The March 8 killing of two U.S. consulate employees in Karachi by unidentified gunmen focused attention on the Bhutto government's inability to stem rising violence in the city. The State Department expressed concern about the "continued violence because two Americans paid the price as the object of that violence....We hope, for the sake of the Pakistani people as well as for the Americans who are there, the level of violence in Karachi can be reduced." In February, the State Department expressed concern about the two Christians charged with blasphemy.

Prior to an official visit to Washington in April, Prime Minister Bhutto initiated a spate of moves aimed at enhancing bilateral ties. In January, her government introduced sweeping anti-narcotics legislation, which prompted President Clinton not to apply drugs-related sanctions to Pakistan. Bhutto also extradited to the United States seven narcotics suspects, as well as Ramzi Ahmed Yusuf, who was wanted in connection with the World Trade Center bombing in New York. On the U.S. side, the United States Senate, backed by the Clinton administration, voted to release $368 million in military equipment that Pakistan had paid for but that had not been delivered since the imposition of sanctions in 1990.

During Prime Minister Bhutto's visit, the administration privately raised concerns about human rights issues, including Pakistan's blasphemy laws and treatment of minorities, and the violence in Karachi. Throughout the year, the administration continued to raise concerns about reports of official Pakistani support for Kashmiri militants who have committed abuses.

In a gesture toward warmer relations, First Lady Hillary Clinton visited Pakistan in April. Human rights discussions were again absent from the public agenda.

Following the visit of a delegation from Pakistan in June, U. S. Trade Representative (USTR) Mickey Kantor announced on July 24 that an unspecified commitment had been made on the issue of child and bonded labor. The review was extended until October 1 to confirm that these, and other reforms, were actually carried out. In October, the administration notified Pakistan that the office of the USTR would invoke GSP provisions removing tariff benefits from one of three designated imports if the government did not act on the reforms. This would be the first time that the USTR removed GSP for a specific product.

The Work of
Human Rights Watch/Asia

Human Rights Watch/Asia's principal advocacy effort on Pakistan in 1995 was to mobilize U.S. and E.U. economic pressure on the issue of bonded child labor. These efforts began in advance of the July publication of our major report, *Contemporary Forms of Slavery in Pakistan*, based on an earlier fact-finding mission to the country. In addition to documenting rights violations against bonded workers, the report made a series of detailed recommendations to end the practice of debt bondage. Human Rights Watch/Asia supplied information on bonded child labor to the U. S. Trade Representative's (USTR) office, State Department and Labor Department for use in their review of Generalized System of Preferences (GSP) benefits for Pakistan, begun in 1993 (see U.S. Policy above).

The report was also distributed to the members of the U.N. Subcommission on Prevention of Discrimination and Protection of Minorities at its July meeting, and to diplomats and other NGO delegates. We also submitted a written statement to the subcommission.

On August 30, Human Rights Watch/Asia wrote to the Commission of the European Union in support of a joint application by the International Confederation of Free Trade Unions and the European Trade Union Conference for a review of Pakistan's GSP benefits, under the terms of the new E.U. GSP scheme allowing for whole or partial withdrawal of GSP if there is "practice of any form of forced labor." This would be the first test case of the new GSP scheme. As this report went to print, a decision on accepting the petition and beginning a formal review had not yet been made.

Pakistan's blasphemy laws and abuses against minorities also continued to be a high priority. In February, Human Rights Watch sent an observer to Pakistan to attend the appeal hearing in the two blasphemy cases. Human Rights Watch/Asia appealed to the president and prime minister of Pakistan to ensure the safety of all involved in the case.

Human Rights Watch/Asia also continued to focus on bringing international attention to abuses against women. In March, prior to First Lady Hillary Rodham Clinton's visit to South Asia, Human Rights Watch/Asia communicated its key regional human rights concerns to her and called on her to push for the rights of women, minorities, and bonded laborers during her trip to Pakistan. Human Rights Watch provided briefing material on human rights concerns in Pakistan to members of Congress and the administration and urged them to raise these issues in meetings with Prime Minister Bhutto and her delegation. On April 5, Human Rights Watch raised human rights concerns directly in a meeting with Foreign Minister Sardar Aseff Ahmad Ali in Washington.

SRI LANKA

Human Rights Developments

The human rights situation in Sri Lanka remained grave in 1995 despite a series of promising human rights initiatives by the newly-elected People's Alliance (PA) government. The PA, led by President Chandrika Bandaranaike Kumaratunga, came to power in late 1994 on a human rights platform that promised a negotiated settlement of Sri Lanka's twelve-year civil war with the Tamil separatist Liberation Tigers of Tamil Eelam (LTTE), increased accountability for past human rights abuses, and an end to government corruption. The enormous popularity of these goals allowed the new party to oust the United National Party (UNP), which had ruled the country for seventeen years.

The PA inherited a legacy of severe abuse, including tens of thousands of "disappearances," extrajudicial killings and torture of political opponents and suspected insurgents. The vast majority of these abuses were never investigated, prosecuted or punished. Indiscriminate bombardment of civilian areas affected by the war was also a hallmark of the former government's campaign against Tamil insurgents. In 1995, many of the perpetrators of these abuses remained free and in positions of authority, and the abuses that occurred during the year, though only a fraction of those committed in previous years, were strikingly similar to crimes committed under earlier governments.

In January 1995, a cease-fire was declared between the government of Sri Lanka and the LTTE, and the two sides entered into negotiations, raising hopes that the parties might finally reach a political settlement. Those hopes were short-lived. The LTTE broke the cease-fire on April 19, sinking two patrol boats and then shooting down two troop transport planes, killing all ninety-seven persons on board. An LTTE massacre of forty-two Sinhalese villagers in a coastal town north of Trincomalee and the assassination of a Buddhist priest, both on May 26, along with new reports of "disappearances," extrajudicial executions and torture by Sri Lankan security personnel, were indications of how far the country was from the peace envisioned only months before. By the time the government unveiled its proposal for a political settlement in August, featuring a plan to devolve central control to regional councils determined in part along ethnic lines, the war was again in full swing. Renewed fighting led to hundreds of civilian deaths in government air raids and LTTE mortar fire on the Jaffna peninsula between July and November and to large-scale displacement. Among those killed in the fighting were families caught in a compound of church buildings sheltering displaced persons that was damaged during an air force raid in July; about seventy civilians, including about twenty-five school children, who medical workers reported were killed in government bombings in September; and nine elderly men whom the army claimed had been killed by an LTTE mortar that hit a rest home in October. By early November, the Sri Lankan military was poised to occupy the city of Jaffna, headquarters of the LTTE. Most of the city's residents, including LTTE members, had fled; total estimates of those displaced by the fighting reached 400,000.

More than one hundred villagers, most of them Sinhalese, were killed in a series of attacks by LTTE members in villages in the east and northeast beginning on October 21, the day after the LTTE blew up the island's two main oil depots near Colombo. In May, human rights organizations received more than fifteen reports of killings or "disappearances" of civilians by members of the security forces in eastern Sri Lanka. In Batticaloa, politicians, human rights activists and journalists reported that civilians had been used by soldiers as shields against LTTE attacks or for mine clearance.

The LTTE has also engaged in hostage taking and the use of civilians as shields. On August 29, members of the LTTE hijacked a government-chartered ferry it alleged was run by members of a rival Tamil group. The ferry, which was used by the LTTE to attract and sink two naval boats near the eastern port of Trincomalee, killing some twenty sailors, had sailed from Trincomalee on August 28 with more than 130 passengers, including fifteen children and several expectant mothers. It was boarded by the LTTE the next morning. The passengers and crew were held hostage until September 6, when 121 passengers, including three newborn babies, were released. As of early November, the ferry's crew members, accused by the LTTE of links to a rival Tamil group, remained in LTTE custody, and some fifteen other people reportedly aboard the hijacked ferry were unaccounted for.

The practice of using child soldiers has been a trademark of the LTTE for many years. Of the estimated 50,000 persons killed since the war began in 1983, many have been children recruited as fighters by the LTTE, some of them as young as thirteen. The recruitment of young children continued in 1995. When the LTTE led an abortive attack on four army bases in late July and several hundred LTTE fighters were killed, the army reported finding many young girls and boys among the dead. In September, the University Teachers for Human Rights-Jaffna (UTHR), a group that has monitored human rights conditions in the north and east, reported that the LTTE had stepped up recruitment drives and that families unwilling to give up their children were forced to pay large ransoms. It was also reported that the LTTE had stepped up arrests and executions of suspected informants.

Nineteen ninety-five saw the re-emergence of death-squad-style killings by members of the Sri Lankan security forces. In the vicinity of Colombo, between May 31 and August 14, twenty-one bodies were found in and around Bolgoda Lake. Some showed signs of starvation and torture, some had been strangled. Thirteen of the bodies were identified as young Tamil men abducted by armed men in civilian clothes from city lodges and security checkpoints. According to an official of the Criminal Investigation Department (CID), some of the youths had been detained for three or four days and strangled with plastic handcuffs in an unused toilet in the headquarters of the Special Task Force (STF), an elite counterinsurgency unit of the police. In August, CID announced the arrest of at least eighteen Special Task Force members and military personnel in connection with these killings. More arrests followed in September, bringing the total to around thirty. The Tamil press reported that among those arrested was a man known as Captain "Munaz" who had been implicated in the "disappearances" of more than 150 persons from a refugee camp in Batticaloa in 1990. The government announced in September that it would suspend all operations of the Intelligence Wing of the STF and disband its network of informants. Despite the arrests, bodies continued to appear in Colombo through September.

Reports of arbitrary arrests of Tamils by the police in Colombo and in other parts of the country continued throughout the year. Large-scale sweeps intensified following the resumption of hostilities in April, with reports of as many as 500-1,000 arrests on some days. In Colombo, most arrests were carried out by the police, and the majority of detainees were released within forty-eight hours. In the east, arrests were carried out by military personnel, police and members of auxiliary forces, such as former militant groups. Human rights organizations reported "disappearances" and deaths of persons detained during these search operations. Though young men were typically the target of round-up operations, in September Tamil women in Colombo also complained of ha-

rassment after rumors that a female LTTE suicide squad was on its way to the city.

Nineteen ninety-five saw several new efforts to restrict freedom of expression in Sri Lanka. In July, the Colombo office of the National Christian Council (NCC) was raided by some forty armed police, allegedly searching for subversive literature. Police confiscated a computer-drawn graphic of a bleeding lotus (the white lotus is a PA symbol of peace and support for the government's war effort). The letter-sized poster, which contained text calling for a halt to the killing of civilians in the July military offensive, was seized, and its author, an American intern named Kenneth Mulder, was detained. Mulder, who was in Vavuniya with a church delegation traveling to Jaffna at the time of his arrest, was transported back to Colombo for questioning and deported five days later. The homes of ten young Tamil women who worked in the NCC office were also searched.

Also in July, journalist Pearl Thevanayagam of the *Sunday Leader* was arrested and detained for nineteen hours on suspicion of carrying information to the LTTE, following a visit she made to LTTE-held territory. Thevanayagam had traveled to the north posing as a teacher but was arrested when she could not provide an address to a soldier who stopped her at the border on the way south. A spokesperson for the Free Media Movement, a Sri Lankan organization that monitors freedom of the press, charged that although there was no official ban on journalists traveling to the north, the army only permitted access to the state-run media. On September 22, as the army launched a major offensive on the Jaffna peninsula, the government imposed censorship curbs on war-related reporting, citing national security concerns and fear that reporting would inflame communal tensions. Those restrictions were lifted for foreign media four days later, but curbs on the domestic media remained in force. Among the first stories to be subjected to these censorship requirements were reports that on September 21 and 22, heavy shelling and aerial attacks by government forces on the northern Jaffna region had killed some seventy civilians, including many school children. A Reuter news story from September 23, which noted that the army had denied the incident, also indicated that the story had been "subjected to military censors, who deleted quotes from civilians on the reported deaths of twenty children."

Throughout 1995, the Free Media Movement and other human rights organizations continued to report incidents of harassment and threats made against journalists by security personnel assigned to guard government officials and their families, and authorities seeking to learn the sources of leaked stories. Several defamation suits were lodged against journalists reporting on government officials, including the editor of the *Sunday Times* who was summoned to the Colombo High Court on June 13 to face charges of criminal defamation of the character of President Kumaratunga. After attempts to reach an out-of-court settlement failed, hearings in the case were set for January 31, 1996. The editor and publisher of the *Sunday Leader* were also charged with criminal defamation of the president.

In 1995, The PA government made a number of administrative changes designed to curb abuses and account for the "disappeared." In addition to the creation of an advisory committee composed of local human rights experts and a proposal before parliament for the establishment of a national human rights commission, the government created three regional presidential commissions of inquiry into "involuntary removals and disappearances," mandated to investigate killings and disappearances that occurred as far back as 1988. Human rights organizations in Sri Lanka and abroad have urged the government to extend the scope of these inquiries even further back, noting that the systematic pattern of disappearances in Sri Lanka began before 1984. These commissions, which began hearing evidence in January, had received 35,500 complaints by mid-1995 and had heard evidence in several hundred cases. Two interim reports for each commission had been forwarded to the presi-

dent by September, but none have been made public. Witnesses who testified before the commission investigating disappearances in Central, North Central, North Western and Uva provinces complained in April that they were the target of death threats and intimidation by security personnel. The commission noted that some of the accused still remained on active duty in the areas from which they had operated during the period under investigation. However, based on the report of one commission, in October three senior police officers responsible for past abuses were sent on "compulsory leave," and the Minuwangoda magistrate ordered the detention of eight others: six police officers charged with raping two girls between 1988 and 1990, and two subinspectors accused of the 1989 murder of two young men.

The government also created a commission to look into detentions under the Prevention of Terrorism Act and the emergency regulations, in order to ascertain the number and identity of detainees under these laws, expedite cases, recommend releases and improve conditions of detention.

On June 7, in response to criticism over the continued abuse of detainees, the government announced the establishment of the Human Rights Task Force (HRTF) charged with monitoring arrests and detentions. A similar body was already in existence, but its powers had been limited because the emergency regulation that created it had been allowed to lapse. On June 16, the government issued a directive to the police and armed forces ordering them to cooperate with the HRTF and to respect the rights of those arrested. The directive mandated special treatment for women and children and ordered that detainees be told why they were being held, that the person making the arrest be identified, and that an arrest receipt containing the name and rank of the arresting officer be provided to the detainee. It also provided that the detainee be allowed to communicate with a relative or friend, and make statements in a language of his or her choice. Human rights groups criticized the stipulation that the detainee must request a receipt, thus putting the onus on the person arrested rather than on the arresting officer.

Sri Lanka has been under a state of emergency almost continuously since May 1983. The emergency regulations grant extraordinary powers to Sri Lankan security personnel to arrest and detain suspects, and have contributed to abuse. When the PA assumed control of the parliament in August 1994, the emergency was temporarily lifted in most parts of the country. It remained in place in the north and east where the war continued. The emergency was reimposed in Colombo after the October 24, 1994 bombing that killed UNP presidential candidate Gamini Dissanayake. In 1995, the emergency remained in effect in the north and east, in Colombo and its suburbs, and was extended to include certain portions of central and western Sri Lanka. Several of the most troubling regulations were allowed to lapse when the PA came to power. Among them was a requirement that householders in Colombo and other areas under the state of emergency must register all residents and guests with the local police, a regulation that led to harassment and arrest of Tamils in the city. But although police officials announced in August that this regulation was no longer on the books, there were complaints that the police in some areas were requiring that Tamils carry proof of registration. The regulation itself was reimposed in September.

Torture has been an almost routine part of police work in Sri Lanka throughout the conflict. In January 1994 the government acceded to the U.N. Convention on Torture. However, the government has not signed the declaration under Article 22 of the Torture Convention, which allows individuals to make complaints to a committee set up under the Convention. A parliamentary bill passed in November 1994 made torture punishable by seven to ten years of imprisonment and a fine of between Rs. 10,000 and Rs. 50,000 (up to about US $1,000). To our knowledge, no members of the security forces had been punished under this law by the end of 1995.

On June 20, the minister of justice announced that the government was considering resuming executions under the death penalty, which had not been invoked in Sri Lanka since 1976. In the face of international and domestic protest, the government announced that it would not carry out any death sentence until there had been a full debate on the issue.

On September 11, the Sri Lankan government unveiled a draft law to deter sexual abuse of children which mandated a minimum sentence of five years in prison for both pimp and client with a maximum sentence of twenty years. The draft bill targets the procurers, clients and others who benefit from or contribute to the sexual exploitation of children and is designed particularly to address sex tourism, a serious problem in Sri Lanka.

The Right to Monitor

Human rights activists have enjoyed increased freedom from harassment by government forces in recent years, although by late 1995 government pressure to curb criticism related to the war, augmented by actions by extra-governmental forces, led to an upsurge in anti-NGO rhetoric in both the state-owned and independent media, incidents of mob violence and anonymous threats against journalists and members of Sri Lanka's human rights community. Concerns also remained over possible threats to human rights activists from other political forces such as the LTTE.

Sri Lanka's vibrant human rights community played a crucial role in monitoring the implementation of the government's human rights policies in 1995, by publicizing abuses and educating the public. In early 1995, human rights organizations took advantage of the new government's apparent openness to human rights concerns to make a number of recommendations aimed at bringing Sri Lanka in line with international standards and improving human rights protections. Among their recommendations were calls for the government to ratify the Optional Protocols to the ICCPR, declarations under articles 21 and 22 of the Torture Convention, and Additional Protocol II to the

Geneva Conventions.

When fighting resumed in April, human rights organizations called for an end to attacks on civilians and urged both parties to resume the peace process. In late May, the Movement for Inter-Racial Justice and Equality (MIRJE), among others, publicly denounced both the army and Tamil separatists for the violence and called on the government to announce its long-awaited peace plan. In September, groups repeated these criticisms of combatant violence against civilians. In November a MIRJE appeal expressed concern over the increasing number of displaced persons in the Jaffna Peninsula, shortages of food and other supplies, and fears that neither party to the conflict appeared to be observing basic humanitarian norms with regard to noncombatants. The Sri Lankan government denounced the appeal in a public statement.

The Role of
the International Community

Western nations were virtually unanimous in their support of the peace process, and many issued public statements congratulating the Sri Lankan government on its human rights reforms. They were equally united in their condemnation of the LTTE's breach of the cease-fire agreement in April and the abuses that followed. Abuses by Sri Lankan forces received less attention.

In March, the E.U., the U.S., U.K., Canada and Australia began exerting heavy pressure on the LTTE to begin serious negotiations to end the conflict. The United Nations Human Rights Commission in Geneva echoed these concerns.

On April 21, the E.U. called on the LTTE to refrain from initiating an escalation of hostilities, condemned the April 20 attacks and urged the LTTE to enter into negotiations with the Sri Lankan government on the elements of a political solution.

At the end of April, the Sri Lanka Aid Group of donor nations pledged $850 million for the forthcoming year and said that additional funds could be provided for reconstruction of the north and east, if peace was achieved. The vice-chairman of the World Bank said that the donors' pledge "reflects the strong support of the international community to the Sri Lankan government."

On May 18, the European Parliament adopted a resolution on human rights in Sri Lanka condemning the LTTE's withdrawal from negotiations and "deliberate acts of violence." The resolution called on both parties to "adopt a conciliatory attitude regarding the resumption of the peace talks" and urged the Sri Lankan government to avoid indiscriminate reprisals against civilians. It invited the commission to boost its cooperation with the government of Sri Lanka, to offer it all necessary support to achieve peace and reconciliation, and called on the E.U. and its member states to introduce restrictions on arms sales to the LTTE. On May 29, the E.U. released a statement condemning the LTTE's massacre of Sinhalese villagers and the killing of the Buddhist priest and urged the LTTE to resume negotiations.

On May 31, in Canada's first ministerial visit to Sri Lanka since 1983, Raymond Chan, a junior foreign minister and secretary of state for Asia and the Pacific, met with Sri Lankan Prime Minister Sirima Bandaranaike and with Foreign Minister Lakshman Kadirgamar during "an information gathering visit" to see whether Canada could help promote the resumption of peace talks. Chan also expressed Canada's concern over the resumption of hostilities by the LTTE. Before talks broke down, a Canadian had been chairman of one of four committees that were set up to monitor the peace process.

Amid the international outcry that followed the violence in April, Sri Lanka sought and secured new sources of military aid. In June, Britain announced that it would lift its embargo on the sale of arms to Sri Lanka. But as reports of serious violations by Sri Lankan security forces escalated, some nations held back. On July 14, Australia's acting foreign minister Bob McMullan appealed to the Sri Lankan armed forces and Tamil rebels to avoid killing civilians during fighting on the Jaffna peninsula, saying that "the resumption of full-scale fighting in Sri Lanka underlines the urgent need for a negotiated political settlement to the long-standing ethnic conflict, which will require restraint and compromise on both sides." Nevertheless, he said the Australian government accepted that "it is unreasonable to expect the Sri Lankan government to acquiesce in the face of the use of force" by the Liberation Tigers of Tamil Eelam (LTTE).

On September 1 at a press briefing in Colombo, U.S. Assistant Secretary of State Robin Raphael announced that the United States would not sell lethal weapons to Sri Lanka, in part because it remained concerned about the government's human rights record, although she noted improvements. According to Raphael, the U.S. had "a limited military program with the government of Sri Lanka," which included training and the sale of some non-lethal equipment. However, she also suggested: "That cooperation could be upgraded." The International Military Education and Training (IMET) program to which Raphael referred amounted to $100,000 in 1994. It was projected at the same amount for 1995. The amount requested for fiscal year 1996 was $175,000. Human rights training was described as an important component of the IMET program and the IMET program summary noted,

> In the past, official efforts to contain the war have led to serious violations of human rights by the government and security forces. The incidence of such violations poses a grave threat to the stability of Sri Lanka's longstanding democratic tradition... IMET training for key members of the security forces will emphasize human rights training, respect for human rights and civilian control of the military.

There were $204,000 in foreign military sales to Sri Lanka in fiscal year 1994. According to the U.S. Department of State's congressional presentation of foreign operations for fiscal year 1996, no estimated sales were envisioned for 1995 or 1996. The U.S. reported delivery of only $7,000 worth of commercial military exports licensed or approved under the Arms Export Control Act (AECA) in 1994; estimated deliveries in fiscal year 1995 were $3,997,000 and for fiscal year 1996, $1,998,000.

Raphael said President Chandrika Bandaranaike Kumaratunga's government had taken important measures to check abuse. "Overall, one can say, they have clearly improved, and this government has committed itself to very high standards of observance of human rights...but...we maintain a keen eye on [Sri Lanka's human rights] and it is an issue for us."

In September, the U.S. House of Representatives Committee on International Relations adopted a resolution congratulating the Sri Lankan government for its human rights improvements, denouncing the resumption of hostilities and political violence, and urging both parties to resume negotiations toward a political settlement and to respect human rights.

On June 16, a three-member German parliamentary delegation headed by Willy Wimmer of the foreign affairs committee of the German parliament condemned the LTTE for breaking the cease-fire, but told journalists in Colombo that the country's human rights record had improved so significantly under People's Alliance government that there was no longer a need for Germany to provide asylum to Sri Lankans.

At the twelfth European Commission/Sri Lanka joint meeting in Brussels on June 27-28, the two parties stressed that the economic development of Sri Lanka required a peace process based on respect for human rights and democratic principles. The Commission also expressed its willingness to aid in rehabilitation and reconstruction in Sri Lanka's north and east, if a lasting peace were achieved. Trade relationships grew in importance, as new prospects for trade began appearing and Sri Lanka opened up to foreign investment. Between 1993 and 1994,

European exports to Sri Lanka rose 41 percent, and Sri Lankan exports to the E.U. rose 20 percent. The two parties also discussed opportunities for increased trade offered by the E.U.'s new generalized system of preferences and announced the intention to establish a permanent European Commission presence in Colombo by September 1995.

Article 1 of a cooperation agreement between the European Community and the Sri Lankan government, which came into force in April 1995 and provided for "substantial development and diversification of trade," stated that the basis for cooperation and for the agreement itself was "respect for democratic principles and human rights," which "constitute an essential element of the Agreement."

The Work of
Human Rights Watch/Asia

For several years, Human Rights Watch/Asia has focused its efforts on encouraging the Sri Lankan government to investigate and provide accountability for abuses by government forces, and on strengthening combatants' respect for humanitarian law. These efforts have included calls for better training and discipline of security force personnel, including paramilitary groups and auxiliary forces such as the Special Task Force, home guards and former militant groups now aiding the government in counterinsurgency. Human Rights Watch/Asia has called for investigations of all reported violations by these forces and for prosecution of those found responsible. To this end, Human Rights Watch/Asia has maintained contact with the heads of Sri Lanka's presidential commissions charged with investigating disappearances and has provided these bodies with recommendations and informational materials designed to aid them in their efforts. These efforts continued in 1995.

In February, Human Rights Watch/Asia staff met with Sri Lankan Foreign Minister Lakshman Kadirgamar to discuss implementation of various governmental human rights initiatives and urged that the country ratify key international instruments, including the Optional Protocols to the ICCPR, Additional Protocol II to the Geneva Conventions and that it make declarations under articles 21 and 22 of the Torture Convention.

In July, in response to reports of serious violations of humanitarian law by both military personnel and the LTTE, Human Rights Watch/Asia released a short report *Stop Killings of Civilians*, calling on both parties to uphold their obligation to protect noncombatants.

In September, Human Rights Watch/Asia staff attended a meeting with President Chandrika Kumaratunga to discuss human rights concerns and government initiatives to address abuses.

THAILAND

Human Rights Developments

The fragility of Thailand's elected government continued to hamper progress this year on many of the country's human rights problems. These included restrictions of press freedom, trafficking in women, and, most prominently, Thailand's continued mistreatment of Burmese refugees and migrant workers.

Thailand's fledgling democracy was seriously threatened in May, as the coalition government headed by Chuan Leekpai was forced to call an election. In March, after two and one-half years in office, Chuan's government became the Thai's longest serving government, only to fall to charges of corruption. The government had been at odds with the powerful military, particularly over the issue of relations with Burma and the treatment of Burmese refugees. But fears that the army might attempt a coup d'etat were not realized, and a new election took place on July 2, bringing into power a coalition led by Prime Minister Banharn Silpa-archa.

Freedom of the press was challenged in August when a newspaper delivery truck was fired on and parcel bombs were sent to the editor and proprietor of a major Thai daily newspaper, *Thai Rath* (The Thai Nation), after it published articles critical of the annual reshuffling of police posts. The police dismissed the bombs as merely a threat, not intended to harm anyone. In October, Thailand invoked the *lèse majesté* laws, which forbid any criticism of the king, to deny work visas temporarily to all Australian journalists. The action was taken in response to an unflattering cartoon of the king published in *The Age* newspaper.

Refugees from Burma increased to 90,000 after an additional 10,000 refugees fled to Thailand following the fall of the Karen National Union's headquarters at Manerplaw in January. From February onwards, the safety of some 50,000 of these refugees was threatened by groups of Burmese government troops (SLORC) and their allies, the Democratic Karen Buddhist Army (DKBA), who made frequent incursions into Thailand to force the refugees back to Burma (see Burma section). Although Thailand has not ratified the international convention on the protection of refugees, when the refugees first began to arrive, the Thai government pledged that it would offer sanctuary.

As the attacks on the refugee camps began, the head of the parliamentary Foreign Affairs Committee called for an urgent review of Thai policy toward Burma. He led a delegation of members of parliament to the border to assess for themselves the situation in the refugee camps and called for increased security for the refugees.

On March 16, approximately 8,000 refugees fled from a camp in Ban Huai Manok after thirty DKBA and SLORC troops entered the camp and tried to kidnap the camp leader. One refugee was killed and three others were seriously injured in the attack, which was repelled by Thai soldiers. The refugees moved deeper into Thailand, into an area where the roads made access very difficult for nongovernmental organizations trying to provide aid. The situation continued to deteriorate, and refugees lived in constant fear of attack. Between April 19 and 28, the DKBA entered three different camps and torched 1,172 houses, leaving two refugees dead and more than 6,000 homeless. On May 3, DKBA/SLORC troops entered a Thai village, Ban Mae Ngao in Sob Moei district, in the early hours of the morning and attacked a Thai police checkpoint, also razing the village market and the refugee shelters. Three policemen and one refugee were killed, and two other policemen were injured.

Only after this incident did the Thai army step up its presence in the border area, bringing in troops, tanks and helicopter gunships in a demonstration of strength aimed at preventing further incursions. Just days before, the commander-in-chief of the army, Wimol Wongwanich, was quoted in the Thai press: "If we were not afraid of being criticized by the world community on humanitarian grounds ...then this army chief would take only one week to push [the refugees] all out...I used to do this with over 40,000 Cambodian refugees." The discrepancy between the civilian government's reassurances and the army's actions revealed a sizeable gap in attitude between them.

Once the Thai army intervened, the incursions ceased, though armed men continued to enter camps and harass refugees. The DKBA and SLORC remained in positions on the Burmese bank of the Moei and Salween Rivers (which mark the Thai-Burma border) and the refugees' security remained a concern at the end of the year. In the two weeks between September 23 and October 10, nine refugees were abducted in separate raids. On October 6, the DKBA entered Shoklo camp looking for a KNU officer, and there were clashes which left two Karen refugees dead. By that time, camps in the Mae Sot area had been consolidated, and the Ministry of the Interior had set up an office in the largest camp, Mae La, which housed over 20,000 refugees.

Further north in Mae Sai district, Thai authorities prevented refugees from entering Thailand altogether. The Thai military had kept this part of the border closed for more than a year to prevent supplies from reaching drug warlord Khun Sa. On March 20, more than 1,000 Shan refugees fled heavy fighting in the Burmese border town of Tachilek. They were permitted to stay for only three days, when the Thai military pushed back all but 300 of them. By the end of April, the rest were also forced to return to Burma. As fighting continued in Burma's Shan State, more Shan and Lahu villagers were forced to flee and seek refuge in Thailand, but Thai authorities denied them permission to cross the border. By September, there were more than 2,000 refugees living in makeshift camps on the Burmese side of the border, but non-governmental organizations were not permitted to provide aid to them.

Thousands more Shan are believed to have entered Thailand seeking work as laborers, joining an estimated 400,000 migrant workers from Burma. During the year they faced increased harassment, arrest and deportation by the Thai authorities, in addition to abuse by their employers. On March 14, the Ministry of the Interior ordered a crackdown on illegal immigrants on grounds of national security. Two months later the crackdown began in earnest, and 1,200 people were arrested in Bangkok in the first three days of May. There were also arrests in Mae Sot and Chiang Mai, until the Chiang Mai Chamber of Commerce protested, worried that buildings for the South East Asian Games, scheduled for December, would not be completed in time without the Burmese laborers.

Following arrest, the workers were held in appalling conditions in detention centers for one month or until they paid their immigration fine of 2,000 Baht (though this was reduced in some areas). In many cases, they suffered abuse while in detention; women and girls were routinely strip-searched. From the detention centers, they were transported to the border in cattle trucks, where most then paid agents who collaborated with Thai police to get them back into Thailand.

The Right to Monitor

Thailand continued to be the regional center for international human rights organizations, a place where they could operate with a fair degree of freedom. Local human rights organizations were also able to operate without interference. But those addressing issues that touched on the commercial or political activities of the Thai military were subject to government monitoring and restrictions. In April, a Thai nongovernmental organization (NGO) worker was arrested at a seminar providing management training to Burmese dissidents in Chiang Mai, charged on immigration offenses, then tried and sentenced to three months of imprisonment. He was later released on bail, pending an appeal. Thirty-four Burmese, also arrested at the seminar, were released after paying a fine.

Groups working on child prostitution and the trafficking of women were also targeted for close surveillance, and in March Prime Minister Chuan Leekpai attacked these groups for exaggerating the problem and tarnishing Thailand's image abroad. In June, workers at a relief center for HIV/AIDS carriers were harassed by local municipal authorities and the police in order to get them to move away from the area. The center closed after workers received death threats and the center was bombed. No one was injured, and there was no official inquiry into the incident.

The Role of
the International Community

Several governments, including the United States, Australia and the European Union strongly condemned the attacks on refugee camps by DKBA and SLORC troops and called on Thailand to increase security measures in the area. When the refugees from the Shan State arrived in Thailand in March, the U.N. High Commissioner for Refugees (UNHCR) sent a protection officer to the area to investigate the situation. UNHCR officials also visited the Karen refugee camps. The UNHCR did not make any public statements critical of Thai policy in either case.

In June, more than sixty members of the U.S. House of Representatives wrote to President Clinton on U.S. Burma policy, urging him to "secure a commitment from the government of Thailand that they will continue to provide a haven for these refugees [from the attack on Mannerplaw]."

Congress also remained active on the issue of trafficking. In January 1995 the State Department submitted a report, requested by the House in 1994, on trafficking of Burmese women and girls into Thailand. The report said there was no evidence of the systematic involvement of the Thai government, but noted that the sex industry and trafficking networks "flourish through police corruption" and criticized the ineffective enforcement of existing laws against prostitution and trafficking.

In 1995, the U.S. embassy in Bangkok implemented an "action plan" on trafficking, approved in 1994, including educational efforts, support for NGOs, and diplomatic interventions with Thai officials. The embassy planned to distribute a Thai-language version of the Human Rights Watch report, *A Modern Form of Slavery*.

Congress also scrutinized the Thai military's support for the Khmer Rouge. In February the State Department released a report, required by 1994 legislation, on Thai involvement in cross-border trade and arms shipments. A declassified version noted that official Thai policy prohibits arms transfers to the Khmer Rouge and asserted there was no evidence, since a highly-publicized discovery of an arms cache in December 1993, that the Thai military was supplying the Khmer Rouge with weapons or ammunition. The report acknowledged, however, that some arms transfers still took place through "unofficial contacts, not sanctioned by the Thai government." On the issue of the lucrative cross-border logging and gem trade, as well as shipments of rice, fuel and medicine to the Khmer Rouge, the State Department said the Thai government had begun unspecified "efforts to stop such contacts and trade," but did not evaluate their effectiveness.

Some key senators were far more skeptical of Thai policy. Senator Craig Thomas released a statement in July highlighting eyewitness accounts of cross-border logging shipments published by a credible London-based NGO (Global Witness). He warned that unless the Thai government took significant steps to investigate and stop the timber shipments, he would urge the administration to invoke a law requiring the cutoff of all assistance to any country that is found to be cooperating with Khmer Rouge military operations.

Meanwhile, the U.S. continued a heavy flow of arms sales to the Thai military. Estimated foreign military sales in fiscal year 1995 totaled $120 million, and estimated shipments for fiscal year 1996 were expected to reach $145 million.

The Work of
Human Rights Watch/Asia

Human Rights Watch/Asia focused primarily on refugee concerns, both in our monitoring and advocacy efforts. We closely monitored developments in the refugee camps and issued a press release in April, calling on Thailand to step up its protection of the camps. We also met with senators and members of parliament in the United States and Europe, urging them to write to their colleagues in the Thai government and ask for a more robust response to the attacks on refugees.

Human Rights Watch/Asia continued to follow developments in the situation of Burmese migrant workers, especially of women trafficked into sex slavery in Thailand and from there to other countries. In September we sent a researcher to Thailand to investigate the treatment of Burmese asylum seekers and UNHCR-registered persons of concern. A report was scheduled for publication early in 1996.

VIETNAM

Human Rights Developments

A year of diplomatic break-throughs did nothing to improve Vietnam's human rights record; indeed, the country's increasing integration into the world community appeared to trigger a nervous reaction at home, with fresh arrests and prosecutions of dissidents and the tightest security situation in several years. In contrast to previous years when the government amnestied numerous political dissidents on the occasion of national holidays, only one political prisoner was known to have been freed in a year when Vietnam celebrated the twentieth anniversary of the reunification of the country and the fiftieth anniversary of its declaration of independence.

Vietnam was formally admitted to the ASEAN standing committee as an observer on January 26 and joined ASEAN as its seventh member on July 28. On July 11, the United States announced normal diplomatic relations with Vietnam. Then, on July 17, the European Union signed an economic cooperation accord with Vietnam that had been in negotiation for two years, much of the disagreement centering on a standard human rights clause.

At the same time as these developments unfolded, the Vietnamese government moved to imprison and prosecute internal critics. On January 4, Thich Quang Do, the second-highest leader of the Unified Buddhist Church, was arrested because of his role in organizing flood relief in the name of the church and his protest of the arrest of five other Buddhists who had participated in the charitable effort. The sixty-eight-year-old Venerable Quang Do had the previous year written a long essay alleging that the Vietnam Communist Party had persecuted, and in some cases caused the deaths of, senior figures in the church. He sent this essay to party leader Do Muoi asking why the country was officially mourning the death of Korean dictator Kim Il Sung, but not commemorating the death of Buddhist martyrs. On April 14, Venerable Quang Do and the five other Buddhists were convicted of national security offenses for their flood relief activities; the senior monk was sentenced to five years of imprisonment, and the others to terms of four to two and one half years. One laywoman who asked for clemency at trial was released. Dozens of adherents of the Unified Buddhist Church remained imprisoned, although one monk, Thich Hai Chanh, was the only political prisoner to be freed in an amnesty of prisoners to celebrate the April 30 anniversary of the reunification of the north and south parts of the country.

On December 29, 1994, in an effort to cut him off completely from all followers, security police moved the head of the church, Thich Huyen Quang, from the Hoi Phuc pagoda in Quang Ngai province where he was confined under house arrest to a one-room structure they built and guarded at the tiny Quang Phuc shrine in Nghia Hanh district. On August 16, a Voice of Vietnam broadcast called for Thich Huyen Quang and another monk under house arrest, Thich Long Tri, to be put on trial as well, but as of this writing no trial had gone forward. Thich Huyen Quang is seventy-seven years old and in poor health; since his confinement the authorities have denied him visitors, doctors and medicine for his high blood pressure.

Protestants also faced arrest in 1995, particularly in highland regions, for preaching or holding house church services. Human Rights Watch/Asia received information on arrests and confiscation of property from Protestants in Song Be, Long An, Quang Ngai and Lam Dong provinces who had distributed religious materials or held illegal prayer meetings. Relations with the Catholic church continued to show tension, with the government in April rejecting all candidates the Vatican nominated for clerical positions, including the candidate who was to assume the administrative duties for the elderly and ailing archbishop of Ho Chi Minh City; the archbishop died later in the year, leaving the administrator-designate's status uncertain.

On April 11-12, a Vietnamese court convicted Nguyen Dinh Huy and eight other members of the self-proclaimed "Movement to Unite the People and Build Democracy." This group, whose stated goals were to promote peaceful political change leading to free elections, had attempted to organize a conference on development and democracy in November 1994 that the government abruptly canceled, arresting them. Nguyen Dinh Huy was sentenced to fifteen years of imprisonment for "attempting to overthrow the government"; others received sentences of four to fourteen years, including two American citizens, Nguyen Tan Tri and Trung Quang Liem. A U.S. consular officer was allowed to observe the trial, and on November 5, the two Americans were deported from Vietnam.

On June 14, the government took into custody two prominent communist dissidents, Do Trung Hieu in Ho Chi Minh City and Tran Ngoc Nhiem, known by his alias, Hoang Minh Chinh, in Hanoi. Do Trung Hieu was formerly the Communist Party cadre in charge of religious affairs in Ho Chi Minh City; he had written and circulated an autobiographical essay describing the party's efforts to dismantle the Unified Buddhist Church after the war. Hoang Minh Chinh, a well-known and now elderly communist intellectual, had been imprisoned twice before for advocating "revisionist" lines, in 1967 and 1981 respectively. He had sent petitions to the highest levels of the Party demanding that his name be cleared from his previous jailings. The two cases are related, possibly because Do Trung Hieu had asked Hoang Minh Chinh to circulate a letter the former had written to Vietnam's leadership. Both men were put on trial in Hanoi on November 8 and sentenced to fifteen months and twelve months respectively.

A third well-known communist figure, Nguyen Ho, was visited by police on June 23, who attempted to take him into custody. Nguyen Ho had been detained twice previously, once for his role in leading an unofficial association of war veterans and another time for circulating an autobiographical essay that exposed and criticized abuses committed by the party. In one of his essays, he noted the "unprecedented speed" with which the party had moved to reconcile with its former enemies, such as the United States, France, Japan, South Korea, Japan, ASEAN and China. He asked, "Why can't the Vietnam Communist Party reconcile with its own Vietnamese brothers whom it has oppressed and victimized? Are dollars the condition for reconciliation?" Nguyen Ho

handed copies of this essay to the police and informed them he would prefer to take his life than to be imprisoned again. Although he was not arrested, he has been kept under close surveillance, which has tightened progressively since September.

The government's insistence that political and religious dissidents were being punished not for their opinions or religion but because they had broken the law rang hollow, given that Vietnam's legal system criminalized acts that are unambiguously protected by international guarantees of civil and political rights. National security offenses, for example, included peaceful expression deemed "counterrevolutionary propaganda" and activities that can be construed as "causing divisions" between the party and various social sectors; likewise, charges of "attempting to overthrow the government" were often based on no more than acts of peaceful expression or association. The justice system in these sensitive cases remained politicized, and it was not possible for dissidents to receive trials that met minimum standards of procedural fairness.

The death penalty continued to be applied in Vietnam. On March 5, the government executed Nguyen Tung Duong, a policeman convicted in October 1994 of robbing and shooting a young man he had pulled over for a traffic violation. The case became a cause celebre in Hanoi when the defendant was initially given an extremely light sentence; popular outrage caused the authorities to rehear the case and go to the other extreme by sentencing him to death. Also executed in June was a Hong Kong-born British citizen who had been convicted of trying to smuggle heroin into the country.

Press censorship also continued, with the government confiscating what it considered subversive newspapers and tapes mailed into the country, and even travel guidebooks. The Ministry of Culture shut down the weekly Ngoi Ha Noi (People of Hanoi) for publishing an article criticizing the government's decision to ban fireworks at New Year, and recalled an issue of the monthly magazine of the Casting and Metallurgy Association for containing too many sensational stories that were unrelated to metal works. Both dissident intellectuals and foreign correspondents reported heightened surveillance following the U.S. decision to normalize relations, reflecting an overall tightening of security.

In April, the Ministry of Labor, War Invalids, and Social Action banned the employment of children under the age of sixteen in conditions "injurious to health and spirit." A foreign expert at a conference held by UNICEF and the Ho Chi Minh City Communist Youth Union at the beginning of 1995 estimated that child prostitution had risen steadily during the past five years and accounted for between a quarter and a third of all urban prostitutes.

There were further labor strikes in 1995, particularly at foreign-invested enterprises. The government pushed to organize unions in all such enterprises; Vietnam's law requires all unions to belong to the state-controlled Vietnam Confederation of Labor. A new labor code passed in 1994 also recognizes the right to strike, but not for enterprises that provide "public services" or those "essential to the national economy or national defense." Nor is a strike legal if it "exceeds the scope of the enterprise," compromising the ability of workers to engage in sympathy strikes. Vietnam has not ratified the International Labor Organization convention that guarantees freedom of association and the right to organize freely.

The Right to Monitor

The government does not allow the people of Vietnam to form human rights associations or to engage in human rights monitoring, and it is highly resistant to foreign examination of its human rights record. The government denied permission for Human Rights Watch/ Asia to conduct an official visit to Vietnam in 1995.

In 1994, the government allowed the U.N. Working Group on Arbitrary Detention to visit three labor camps under controlled conditions. The Working Group reported in February 1995 that the government refused to release statistical information on the number of prisoners or the dimensions of the penal system, that it banned the delegation from visiting pre-trial detention centers, and that lower-level officials were not always cooperative. The delegation regretted these shortcomings while acknowledging the historic nature of the visit and the need to build trust and further cooperation; it also recommended that the twentieth anniversary of the reunification of the country would be an appropriate time "to grant amnesty to persons still detained in camps for offences relating to the preceding period," a recommendation that was apparently ignored. The Foreign Ministry condemned media coverage of the report, stating that the delegation did not investigate human rights but merely studied the legal system.

The Role of the International Community

On July 11, President Clinton announced normalization of diplomatic relations in a speech that noted that progress in relations, such as providing MFN Trading status or OPIC, would involve certifications regarding human rights and labor rights. He also declared that the United States would pursue its bilateral dialogue on human rights, "especially issues regarding religious freedom." On August 5 and 6, Warren Christopher visited Vietnam, the first U.S. secretary of state to do so in twenty-five years. Secretary Christopher spoke at a top foreign policy school, emphasizing the importance of accelerated economic reform, courts that provide due process, newspapers that are free to expose corruption, and business people who have free access to information. He told students, "When you hear American talk about freedom and human rights, this is what we mean. Each of you ought to have the right to help shape your country's destiny, as well as your own." Both speeches were the clearest and most high-level statements on human rights to date from the administration, and both drew criticism from the official Vietnamese press. Nevertheless, the United States also publicly criticized Vietnam for continuing political detentions, particularly the sentencing of two Vietnamese-Americans in August, as unhelpful to progress in advancing trade relations. The United States pursued talks with Vietnamese officials on human rights issues in May and October. During the May visit, a State Department official called for the release of all political prisoners, and characterized the talks as "positive" while warning that results would be a long way off. Australia also sent a delegation to Vietnam to discuss human rights issues of concern in April.

Congress was divided over the decision to normalize relations, but united in concern for human rights abuses, with numerous members writing letters and making personal communications on behalf of political and religious prisoners. In late June-early July, senators Tom Harkin and Frank Lautenberg traveled to Vietnam, revisiting the infamous "tiger cages" and also raising contemporary human rights concerns. In the immediate wake of their visits, the Vietnamese government issued passports to two dissidents whom it had obstructed in their efforts to apply for emigration through the Orderly Departure Program.

Japan became Vietnam's most generous donor, but generally remained silent on human rights concerns. In April, Communist Party leader Do Muoi visited Japan, winning pledges of a $700 million loan and a $36 million grant, in addition to a $480 million package of infrastructure loans approved earlier in January. Prime Minister Tomiichi Murayama only raised human rights privately and in very general terms (see Japan section).

In July, the European Union signed a cooperation agreement that included as Article 1 a clause stating "Respect for human rights and democratic principles is the basis for the cooperation between the Contracting Parties and the provisions of this Agreement, and it constitutes an essential element of the Agreement." The European Parliament had yet to endorse the agreement as of November. Earlier in the year, the parliament had expressed concern over Vietnam's imprisonment of religious figures. Since signing the cooperation agreement, the European Commission stated an intention to increase significantly its economic and development cooperation activities in Vietnam, both bilaterally and within the context of European Union-ASEAN cooperation.

The Work of
Human Rights Watch/Asia

Human Rights Watch/Asia continued to engage the Vietnamese government in a dialogue on issues of concern while publicizing instances of abuse to the international community. Human Rights Watch/Asia was twice forced to cancel plans to visit Vietnam to look at the formation and regulation of private associations when the government refused to issue visas because of "inconvenience." Nevertheless, the organization followed events closely, issuing press releases criticizing the detention of political and religious prisoners throughout the year, and a report on law and dissent in August. "Human Rights in a Season of Transition" recommended that the international community press the government of Vietnam to release religious and political prisoners, ratify and implement the International Labor Organization conventions guaranteeing freedom of association, and improve the neutrality and transparency of the legal system. The report was translated into Japanese and widely distributed in Tokyo to members of the Japanese government and others. Human Rights Watch/Asia testified on human rights conditions in Vietnam in March before the House of Representatives and again in August. Human Rights Watch/Asia also provided briefings throughout the year on human rights issues to members of Congress, to the U.S. State Department, foreign embassies, and to the Japanese Ministry of Foreign Affairs.

HUMAN
RIGHTS
WATCH

HELSINKI

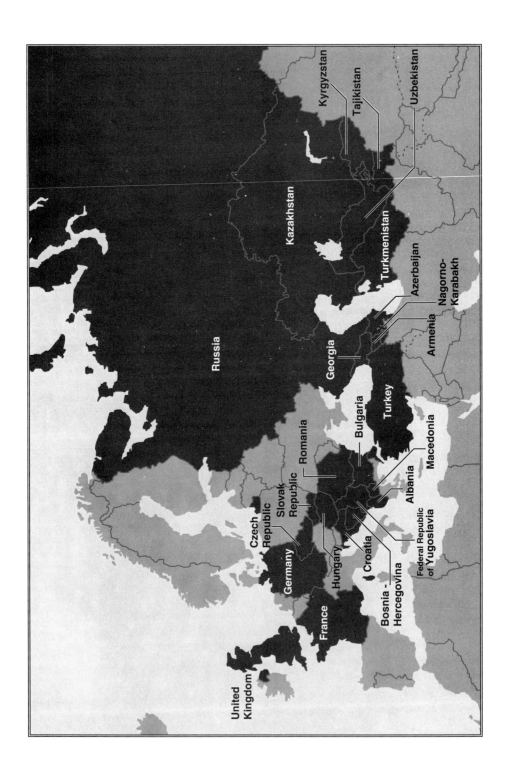

The Helsinki region encompasses fifty-three dramatically diverse countries, from developed democracies with comprehensive human rights protections, to countries making the transition from severely repressive governments to fragile new democracies, as well as a number of governments that have never faltered in the severity of repression and governmental control. Genocide, crimes against humanity, and violations of the laws of war—the worst abuses in the region—remained systematic in the former Yugoslavia, and a new conflict erupted in Chechnya, with massive violations by Russian forces, as well as by Chechen fighters. In other areas where armed conflict finally subsided, there was no corresponding effort to establish the foundations for a lasting peace. Accountability for war crimes was strikingly absent throughout the region, with the notable exception of the important work of the International Criminal Tribunal for the former Yugoslavia, which issued fifty-one indictments during the year.

One of the most devastating and long-term consequences of these conflicts was the massive dislocation of vulnerable populations. There were an estimated seven million refugees and internally displaced persons (IDPs) in the region in 1995, including over two million displaced by the war in the former Yugoslavia. Hundreds of thousands of IDPs and refugees were unable to return to their homes long after the cessation of hostilities in other areas because of the absence of a secure peace with guarantees for their safety, as well as for the prosecution of abusive government agents. In addition, hundreds of thousands of refugees from non-European countries sought refuge in the Helsinki region during the year.

This phenomenon of massive dislocation produced social and political instability in some areas, as well as an enormous economic burden on host countries and international organizations, that are likely to reverberate for years to come. One of the most pervasive repercussions was the escalation in xenophobia throughout the region, manifesting itself in state-sponsored abuses as well as both private and state-sponsored acts of violence. Refugees and IDPs, as well as immigrants and migrant workers, continued to be the most vulnerable populations and were often made scapegoats for a host of economic and social ills. Moreover, government officials often exacerbated xenophobic sentiment for their own political purposes.

Human rights featured prominently in foreign policy debates throughout the region during the year, reflecting the extent to which most governments now recognize that their human rights records are a legitimate concern in bilateral and multilateral relations. International organizations and governments were reluctant, however, to insist on concrete human rights improvement when faced with competing political and economic interests, unwilling to recognize the inextricable link between these goals. The tendency to opt for short-term political gains could be seen in numerous examples in the region, most notable of which was Bosnia. At the end of 1995, Europe faced an important challenge: to exploit immediate opportunities to resolve the region's worst conflicts without neglecting the prerequisites for long-term political stability and fundamental principles of tolerance and respect for individual liberties.

Human Rights Developments

There were two particularly disturbing human rights developments in the Helsinki region during 1995. Some of the most appalling atrocities committed to date in the four-year war in the former Yugoslavia occurred during the summer of 1995 in areas of Bosnia that had been declared "safe areas" by the United Nations. Despite early warnings of a massive Bosnian Serb offensive and substantial intelligence information of imminent danger to the civilian population, the international community apparently made a decision to let the enclaves fall to Bosnian Serb control without taking the necessary steps to safeguard the civilian population. In a misguided effort to facilitate an end to the warring parties' territorial disputes, the international community handed over the "safe area" of Srebrenica to Bosnian Serb forces, who then carried out systematic executions of hundreds, possibly thousands, of men and boys, and terrorized, raped, beat, and otherwise abused civilians being deported from the area.

There was also a decided deterioration in human rights in several countries that had only recently emerged from repressive communist systems and begun the transition to democracy. During 1995, a number of Helsinki countries backtracked in their commitments to human rights and democratic reform, ending the year with significantly poorer human rights records than in the recent past, among them Armenia, Azerbaijan, and Russia.

Russia's brutal war in Chechnya contributed to, and was the most glaring example of, the general deterioration in human rights in the Russian Federation during 1995. Throughout much of the war's first six months, government forces committed massive violations of humanitarian law, resulting in thousands of needless civilian casualties and hundreds of thousands of displaced persons. Chechen fighters also committed serious violations of humanitarian law. Despite a cease-fire agreement reached in July, little progress was made toward the withdrawal of Russian troops or the disarmament of Chechen fighters, and in early October, low-level hostilities resumed.

The Russian government too, in the area of individual rights, retreated from its human rights commitments, as it failed to continue needed legal reforms or to hold government agents accountable for a wide range of abuses. Instead, it introduced legislation, such as the Law on the Federal Security Services (FSB, formerly the KGB), which jeopardized individual rights and increased the unrestricted power of the state.

The government of Azerbaijan's Presi-

dent Heydar Aliyev, in its second year of crackdown against the political opposition, attempted to exclude parties from its parliamentary election and, when that failed due to international pressure, resorted to the arrest and criminal prosecution of political opponents. The Armenian government presided over a crackdown on religious minorities and suspended the largest and most popular opposition party. Similarly, Kazakstan's president dissolved parliament and in a popular referendum, reportedly riddled with irregularities, the 1996 presidential elections were canceled, allowing the president to remain uncontested in office until the year 2000.

Political dissent continued to be suppressed in Turkmenistan. In December 1994 elections, all candidates were nominated by the president and ran uncontested. In Uzbekistan, political opponents were arrested on fabricated charges of drug and arms possession; others were arrested and prosecuted for their nonviolent criticism.

The independent press, always a threat to abusive governments, came under systematic attack in several countries in the region. In Azerbaijan, the government arrested and prosecuted several journalists for critical speech perceived as insulting to the honor and dignity of the president. Armenian President Levon Ter-Petrossian closed twelve newspapers and news agencies allegedly associated with the suspended Armenian Revolutionary Federation (ARF). Similar restrictions were reported in numerous other countries. In Turkey, journalists reporting on sensitive topics were systematically harassed, imprisoned, tortured and, in several cases, murdered.

Torture and other inhumane treatment in detention continued. Russian forces systematically beat and tortured Chechen men suspected of being rebel fighters in detention centers known as filtration camps. Two women in Uzbekistan were forced to undergo abortions while being held in detention by the National Security Service (former KGB). Peaceful Turkmen protesters were detained and some were reportedly severely beaten in Ashgabat. Death squad-style executions and deaths in detention continued in Turkey, although not at the record levels reported in 1993 and 1994. Torture continued to be systematic and disappearances while in police custody or after being detained by persons claiming to be police were widespread. Abusive authorities were rarely held accountable.

Police brutality was a chronic problem throughout the region, not only in the countries of eastern and central Europe and the Commonwealth of Independent States, but also in western Europe, especially against ethnic and racial minorities and foreigners. Institutional and legal mechanisms to ensure accountability for such abuse and redress for the victims remained weak in many of the former communist countries.

The fighting in the former Yugoslavia came full circle during 1995. In July, Bosnian Serb forces summarily executed hundreds and possibly thousands of men and boys following the fall of the U.N.-declared "safe area" of Srebrenica. By November, 8,000 remained missing, many of them feared killed, from the fighting in northeastern Bosnia. Croatian forces also committed atrocities during and immediately following the recapture of the Krajina region. Property belonging to Serbs was looted, Serbian villages were burned, and elderly Serbs were summarily executed following the Croatian army's recapture of the area.

There was little or no effort to hold perpetrators accountable for gross violations in areas of former conflict. While cease-fires continued to hold in Abkhazia and South Ossetia (Georgia), Nagorno-Karabakh, Moldova, and Tajikistan, the absence of accountability and justice for victims to varying degrees jeopardized human rights protection and hampered the return of some refugees and IDPs.

Those perceived as "different," whether minority citizens or foreigners, were made the scapegoats for a variety of social, economic and political ills. State-sponsored or -tolerated discrimination and violence against people of color was pervasive. Spurred by the war in Chechnya, the Russian government's campaign against dark-skinned people grew more brutal during 1995.

Xenophobic violence was rampant throughout eastern Europe, especially against the Roma minority, and in western Europe, hostility toward foreigners, immigrant workers, and national minorities also continued to be widespread. In Romania and Bulgaria, in a pattern consistent with recent years, law enforcement officials not only tolerated frequent attacks on Roma but often perpetrated them. "Skinhead" violence against Roma increased in the Czech and Slovak Republics and Hungary. Throughout the region, ethnic and racial tensions were often exacerbated by government officials for their own political gains. The lack of a concerted government response to such violence was routine in all of these countries. Victims of xenophobic violence rarely had adequate legal redress.

The Right to Monitor

Domestic and international human rights monitors continued to document and expose abuses throughout most of the Helsinki region, contributing greatly to public pressure on many of the abusive governments.

Although human rights groups monitored the conflict in Chechnya, Russian authorities blocked access to several areas in the republic and Russian soldiers harassed some monitors. In Uzbekistan, in what appeared to be a bid for international support and approval, the government became more open to the presence of international governmental and nongovernmental organizations, but it remained hostile to domestic groups.

Human rights monitoring was severely restricted in Bosnian Serb-held territory throughout the year. Bosnian Croat forces and Bosnian government troops also obstructed access to territory they recaptured in western Bosnia in August and September. And Croatia denied access to both international governmental organizations and NGOs during and immediately after the Croatian Army offensive in western Slavonia in May and in the Krajina region in August. Serbia continued to impede access by international organizations to monitor abuses in Kosovo, Sandzak and Vojvodina.

The Turkish government systematically interfered with the efforts of both domestic and international human rights monitors. Many domestic human rights monitors, especially those working in or reporting on the southeast, were arrested, tortured and otherwise mistreated in custody. Others faced prosecution, primarily for their nonviolent expression.

The Role of
the International Community

The international community's passivity in the face of massive human rights violations, including genocide, was the most appalling development during 1995, and had the most devastating implications for the future of international human rights protection. It became increasingly clear during the year that, despite international treaty obligations, there was insufficient political will to stop or prevent genocide. In a chilling show of indifference, the international community allowed the U.N.-declared "safe area" of Srebrenica to fall and its inhabitants to be slaughtered. As the U.S.-led peace negotiations between the warring parties convened in Dayton, Ohio in November, Human Rights Watch was deeply concerned that peace be negotiated, not at any cost but on the basis essential for a lasting peace: protection for endangered populations, the right to repatriation, and accountability for the perpetrators of atrocities.

By contrast, in the CIS, the international community was able to make a valuable contribution, helping to mitigate abuses. European institutions, in particular, forcefully condemned human rights violations in the region and linked economic and diplomatic assistance to concrete human rights improvements.

The United Nations

The United Nations had an inconsistent record on human rights in the Helsinki region, suffering the worst failure in its history during 1995, but also achieving a few significant human rights goals. The United Nations political organs were unable to broker an end to the war in the former Yugoslavia or to bring about a cessation of human rights abuses. However, this ineptitude was contrasted with its success at maintaining a peace in Macedonia, as well as the work of the International Criminal Tribunal for the former Yugoslavia, which the U.N. established in November 1993 to adjudicate violations of humanitarian law in the former Yugoslavia.

The United Nations remained impotent in the former Yugoslavia, particularly in Bosnia. The U.N.'s insistence on neutrality translated into yet another year of inaction on preventing war crimes and crimes against humanity and protecting civilian victims of such abuses. Arguably the U.N.'s largest failure in the former Yugoslavia came in July, when the U.N. refused to protect the so-called "safe area" of Srebrenica and its residents from massacre. Action against abusive Bosnian Serb troops was taken only after NATO assumed control of the decision-making process governing the use of force in Bosnia. By mid-1995, NATO had eclipsed the U.N. mission and the first sustained bombing campaign against Bosnian Serb military targets took place. Such strong action eventually forced the Bosnian Serbs to lift their siege of Sarajevo, allow humanitarian aid to reach the besieged enclave of Gorazde, and come to the negotiating table.

After three and a half years of watching rebel Serb forces expel non-Serbs from the so-called Krajina area of Croatia, U.N. personnel finally launched a serious effort to protect human rights in the region, mostly of Serbs who remained in the western Slavonia and Krajina regions after the Croatian Army recapture of these areas. The U.N. maintained a presence in Macedonia, successfully working to prevent the outbreak of war in that country. In Abkhazia and Tajikistan, United Nations personnel played an important peacekeeping role, preventing the renewal of widespread hostilities and facilitating peace talks among the parties.

The European Institutions

Perhaps recognizing the political and economic consequences of armed conflicts and massive human rights abuses in the region, European institutions were prompt to condemn violations of human rights and humanitarian law especially in the countries of the CIS, using their leverage to seek an end to the most serious violations. However, in Bosnia, European institutions, like the United Nations, failed either to insist on the protection of vulnerable populations or to bring an end to the conflict. They registered concern about human rights abuses throughout the region. But it remained to be seen whether human rights principles would factor into negotiations on trade and cooperation with several abusive governments.

From the outset, the European Union, the Council of Europe and the Organization for Security and Cooperation in Europe (OSCE) strongly condemned humanitarian law violations in Chechnya and linked economic and diplomatic agreements with Russia to the cessation of violations and of military activities. Having played such a crucial role at the beginning of the conflict, however, the European institutions eased pressure on the Russian government before there had been any significant progress on accountability, and just as low-level hostilities again erupted in Chechnya.

The E.U. and the OSCE took a strong stand on human rights abuses in a number of other countries in the region, including: issuing *démarches* concerning a case of forced abortions in detention in Uzbekistan; adopting a resolution calling for commutation of the death sentences of two defendants who had been tortured in Georgia; adopting a resolution condemning Armenia for banning the Armenian Revolutionary Front and criticizing the government's closure of twelve newspapers.

In an important expansion of its work, the OSCE made a contribution to resolving the conflict in Chechnya by establishing the OSCE Assistance Group, headquartered in Grozny, to facilitate peace negotiations and monitor human rights. Unfortunately, its role in the peace negotiations took precedence over monitoring efforts, exhausting its resources and overwhelming its small staff. A similar mission in Tajikistan, despite expanding its mandate in July 1995 to include protection work for refugees and IDPs, as of this writing had not committed the necessary resources to allow it to successfully implement its mandate.

The European Union and its member states used their leverage to bring pressure to bear on the Turkish government's human rights record. Although the E.U. signed a "customs union agreement" with Turkey on March 6, it insisted that Turkey improve its human rights record as a condition for ratification. Similarly, while welcoming positive steps in legislative reform during the year, the E.U. insisted on additional progress on democratization and reduction in human rights abuses.

U.S. Policy

Confusion and inconsistency were prominent features of the U.S. response to serious human rights violations in the Helsinki region during 1995. The administration failed to exploit key opportunities throughout the year to further respect for human rights. There were some notable exceptions, such as Uzbekistan, and especially after mid-year, the former Yugoslavia, but in general the administration was slow to respond and erratic.

The Clinton administration's initial response to massive violations of humanitarian law by Russian forces in Chechnya was to dismiss the conflict as an "internal matter." The administration altered its position after its European partners condemned the slaughter by Russian forces. To its credit, the Clinton administration supported and actively lobbied for the establishment of the OSCE mission and addressed issues of accountability during high-level meetings with Russian officials.

Inconsistency emerged as the U.S. ambassador to Kazakstan hailed the dissolution of that nation's parliament as a "move to strengthen the rule of law", while Defense

Secretary Perry criticized the move. The Clinton administration's criticism of human rights abuses in Turkey, notably strong public criticism by Assistant Secretary of State John Shattuck, was rendered less effective by frequent and clear government statements that human rights would not interfere with relations between the two countries. The administration's human rights policy in the former Yugoslavia was similarly confused throughout the first half of the year, with numerous policy shifts.

By mid-year, however, the Clinton administration had finally assumed a leadership role in resolving the former Yugoslavia conflict, supporting NATO's use of force against Bosnian Serb forces in July and intensifying its own peace efforts. A U.S.-brokered cease-fire went into effect in Bosnia on October 12, and peace negotiations got underway in early November. Although the administration remained committed to accountability in the former Yugoslavia throughout much of the year, the U.S. opposition to an amnesty for war criminals became less clear once peace negotiations began.

The U.S. was the only country known to have placed human rights on its bilateral agenda with Turkmenistan and Uzbekistan. It played an active role in monitoring violations and was willing to raise human rights concerns publicly in neighboring Uzbekistan, but shied away from public criticism in Turkmenistan.

The Work of
Human Rights Watch/Helsinki

Recognizing that the language of human rights is now an accepted part of international discourse, but that the policies of international organizations do not always reflect the professed commitment to human rights principles, Human Rights Watch/Helsinki viewed it as critical to bridge the gap between governments' words and actions. Human Rights Watch/Helsinki devoted significant resources during 1995 not only to documenting and exposing human rights abuses, but to formulating concrete

recommendations for and entering into a dialogue with the international community to ensure that their policies were logically related to the success of their stated human rights goals.

One of Human Rights Watch/Helsinki's top priorities was to focus the attention of international and regional organizations on the human rights records of the region's most abusive governments, especially those that were seeking diplomatic and economic concessions, and to insist that all available leverage be used to obtain specific human rights commitments. We provided influential governments and international and regional organizations with regular, up-to-date documentation and analysis of human rights developments and recommended specific actions to address these concerns.

Having exposed clear and systematic violations of humanitarian law by Russia forces during three missions to Chechnya, we successfully urged the European Union to freeze its interim agreement with Russia, and the Council of Europe to suspend Russia's membership application. Our research staff, just back from documenting massive violations in the region, briefed the OSCE Permanent Council in February and called on that body to establish a semi-permanent presence in Chechnya. Again in July, we briefed the OSCE in Vienna, as well as the U.N. Human Rights Committee in Geneva, pressing for criminal accountability and urging that a special envoy be appointed to monitor and assist Russia in holding violators accountable.

In Bosnia, we concentrated on bringing pressure on the international community, and especially the U.S. government, to take action to protect the civilians in the U.N.-declared "safe areas" and insisting that international negotiators include comprehensive and specific human rights guarantees in any overall peace settlement.

We remained committed to documenting war crimes, crimes against humanity and acts of genocide. Our research staff documented the slaughter of men and boys by Bosnian Serb forces, as well as the U.N.'s mismanagement, during and immediately after the fall of Srebrenica in July, and investigated reports of large-scale disappearances in the Banja Luka area thereafter. Relying on our documentation of systematic violations in these regions, as well as on violations during and immediately after the Croatian offensives in western Slavonia and the Krajina region, we emphasized that accountability for the victims of abuses would have to be a critical component of any legitimate and stable peace agreement. We continued to supply evidence of war crimes and crimes against humanity in Bosnia to the Tribunal and issued numerous appeals to ensure the tribunal's funding.

For Turkey and Georgia we found extensive evidence of torture and disappearances, and in Turkey's case death squad-style killings. Given abuses so serious, we insisted that the U.S. government and the European Union use their influence to elicit human rights progress. With regard to Turkey, we recommended that its approval as a member of the European customs union be delayed until human rights conditions improved and the government permitted international human rights investigators, including U.N. representatives, to carry out missions unimpeded.

Our staff investigated, among other things, the government's efforts to intimidate Turkish citizens who, having suffered serious human rights violations, had applied to the European Commission on Human Rights for redress. We also reported on violations of humanitarian law by the PKK guerrillas in Turkey and called on its leaders to abide by their December 1994 assertion that they would respect the Geneva Conventions.

As part of an ongoing campaign against xenophobia, Human Rights Watch/Helsinki documented not only government-tolerated or -perpetrated violence but the ways in which governments often foster and manipulate xenophobic tensions for their own political gains. During 1995, we focused on manifestations of xenophobia in England, France, Hungary and Russia.

Our Moscow office devoted significant effort throughout the year to raising concerns about Russia's deteriorating human rights record, including critiquing numerous laws that limit individual liberties. Our office in Dushanbe monitored human rights abuses in post-war Tajikistan, focusing primarily on the treatment of those who had been displaced by the civil war and who were now trying to return to their homes. We initiated a dialogue with the OSCE regarding its missions to Tajikistan, Georgia and Chechnya.

ALBANIA

Human Rights Developments

Four years after Albania's first free elections, the country has yet to establish a democracy with full respect for human rights. The Stalinist nature of Albania's past and its legacy of one-party rule were reflected in the government's ongoing attempt to silence its critics. Political trials, media campaigns and police violence were all used against members of the political opposition, as well as against others who expressed views different from the state.

Of particular concern was the state's continued intrusions on the independence of the judiciary. Throughout the year, a number of judges were transferred or released for judicial decisions that were at odds with the policies of the president or government. The most prominent case involved Zef Brozi, chief justice of the Supreme Court, who was discharged from his duties by parliament in mid-September for allegedly having issued illegal orders to lower courts. Once a supporter of President Sali Berisha and his Democratic Party, Brozi had publicly expressed concern about the judiciary's independence. Brozi was also about to review the controversial case of Fatos Nano, leader of the Socialist Party, who was sentenced to prison in July 1993 on corruption charges despite protests from numerous human rights organizations and the Council of Europe.

Despite positive developments in recent years—such as a new Bill of Rights—some of Albania's new legislation has a decidedly undemocratic character. In September 1995, the Albanian parliament passed a law that bars from public office any person who held power in a pre-1991 government or was a collaborator with the former secret police. The law does not provide for any due process guarantees or establish criteria to determine who should be banned from public office, and it is so vaguely worded that it can be applied selectively to eliminate political rivals of the government. Upon coming into force, the law was used to ban a number of prominent opposition politicians from participating in the parliamentary elections scheduled for early 1996.

Freedom of the press remained a serious concern in 1995. The state-run broadcast media, which is heavily slanted in favor of the government, remained the main provider of news for the majority of the population. No legislation was adopted to allow for private radio or television. Two local attempts to open private radio stations were prevented by the government.

Many private newspapers exist in Albania, but their effectiveness is limited by high taxes, inefficient distribution and occasional legal action against journalists. The most publicized case of 1995 occurred in June when Ilir Hoxha, the eldest son of the former communist dictator Enver Hoxha, was sentenced to one year of imprisonment for calling the government a "pack of vandals" in an interview.

Another ongoing human rights concern was the high level of police abuse reported throughout the year. Police often used excessive violence against members of the political opposition, primarily the Socialist Party or the Democratic Alliance. But other non-violent political protestors were also victims, including former political prisoners, striking workers and homosexuals. In addition, there is overwhelming evidence of police mistreatment of detainees during the time of arrest or during pre-trial detention. The treatment of the Greek minority

improved slightly in 1995. A new law on minority education was passed in late 1994, and in February 1995, the Supreme Court decided to release from prison four Greek activists. But ethnic Greeks continued to complain about the lack of Greek-language schooling and under representation in the state administration, armed forces and police.

The Right to Monitor

Human Rights Watch/Helsinki received no reports during 1994 of human rights groups that were hindered in their monitoring efforts. However, the local Albanian Helsinki Committee for Human Rights was sometimes attacked in the state-run media after criticizing a human rights abuse by the government.

The Role of
the International Community

European Policy

In June Albania became a full member of the Council of Europe. Albanian representatives promised to adopt a new constitution, further reform the judiciary, and improve press freedom within three years. Council of Europe advisors work closely on Albania's new legislation and reform of the judiciary.

A declaration by the Presidency of the European Union in February welcomed the release of the four Greek Omonia activists. One month later, the European Commission released the first 15 million ecus of a total 35 million ecu grant designated for Albania. The rest will be released when Albania has made satisfactory progress in its macroeconomic situation and in the process of democratization and respect for human rights.

U.S. Policy

The United States continued to be a vocal supporter of the Albanian government, as illustrated by an official visit by President Berisha to the United States in September 1995. During the trip, President Berisha offered further use of Albanian ports and airfields for NATO forces. An agreement on military cooperation with the U.S. was signed one month later in Washington.

During Berisha's visit, the U.S. government commented on the importance of an independent judiciary, but did not make direct reference to the removal of Chief Justice Zef Brozi, which took place during the visit. Two State Department communiques denouncing Brozi's removal were leaked to the Albanian press later in September. A White House spokesman did relay President Clinton's concerns about the rights of the Greek minority. The State Department's *Country Report on Human Rights Practices for 1994* provided accurate information on some human rights violations, but failed to describe fully some of the more serious abuses, such as the case of Fatos Nano.

The Work of
Human Rights Watch/Helsinki

Human Rights Watch/Helsinki focused on bringing public and government attention to the violations of civil and political rights in Albania. In February, Human Rights Watch/Helsinki published a newsletter, *Albania: The Greek Minority*, which called on the Albanian government to respect minority rights. A comprehensive report documenting in detail the major abuses committed by the Albanian government since 1992 was under preparation.

In August, Human Rights Watch/Helsinki sent a letter to President Berisha protesting the arrest of Ilir Hoxha and the detention of another journalist, Filip Çakuli. In September, Human Rights Watch/Helsinki sent a letter to President Clinton asking him to raise human rights concerns with President Berisha during their meeting in Washington. Another protest letter was sent to President Berisha in October to criticize the law banning former collaborators from holding public office.

ARMENIA

Human Rights Developments

The Armenian government blatantly reneged on its commitments to democracy, making 1995 the worst year for human rights in Armenia since independence. The government that once claimed to be the most stable and legitimate democracy in the Caucasus suspended the oldest and most popular opposition party months before Armenia's first parliamentary elections in the post-Soviet era, presided over obvious due process violations, tolerated a vicious crackdown on religious minorities, and failed to reform its criminal justice system, notorious for physical abuse of detainees.

On December 28, 1994, President Levon Ter-Petrossian suspended the Armenian Revolutionary Federation (ARF), a major opposition party, and ordered the closure of twelve newspapers and news agencies allegedly associated with the ARF. The decree claimed that the party had become a mere cover for "Dro," a secret organization within it allegedly responsible for terrorism, drug trafficking and illegal arms trade. Within hours of the decree, which the president broadcast on television, Interior Ministry troops sealed off the ARF headquarters and the offices of the twelve newspapers and news agencies allegedly linked to the ARF. Police confiscated archives, computers and other office equipment.

On January 13, 1995, the Supreme Court of Armenia upheld the ARF's suspension for a six-month period citing not threats to national security, but the presence of foreigners in the party's ruling board. The government claimed that it was by mere coincidence that the six-month suspension was to lapse just after the July 5 elections. Several weeks after the elections, police arrested the ARF's leader, Vahan Hovanesian, on terrorism charges.

The government allowed individual ARF members to run for parliament, but the party's absence paved the way for a resounding victory of the Armenian National Movement, the pro- government party. To its credit, the government allowed weekly mass demonstrations by the political opposition.

Due process violations marred the trial of "Dro" defendants, which began on August 7. Investigators frequently and arbitrarily denied defense attorneys access to their clients; on March 13 the attorney general's office issued new rules reinstating the old Soviet practice of allowing a defendant access to an attorney only after an investigation's completion. The prosecution allowed defense attorneys only fifteen days to peruse eighteen tomes of prosecution materials. A well known paramilitary group attacked a "Dro" defense attorney on March 21, leaving him severely injured. Investigators failed to resolve the case and dropped it after twelve days. Unknown assailants attacked another "Dro" defense lawyer on April 28 in broad daylight in downtown Yerevan. Two "Dro" defendants were reportedly beaten during their investigation.

At least two individuals died in custody in 1995. On May 17, Artavast Manukian, a "Dro" defendant, died of pneumonia—clearly the result of inadequate medical attention—in a prison hospital. The republic prosecutor had denied three separate requests by Manukian's attorney to transfer his client to a civilian hospital.

Romik Grigorian was beaten to death on May 9 in police custody. Police in the Kamo district had arrested him without a warrant on May 8, and family members reported that Grigorian's corpse bore several bruises, including one on the nape of his neck. As of this writing, no police officer has been held responsible. Similarly, police officers from the Spandaryansky district station in Yerevan, who beat to death Rudik Vartanyan in 1993, had not been brought to justice by November 1995.

The Armenian constitution, adopted on June 7, provides for individual rights, clearly a positive development, but allows most of these rights to be limited or suspended in times of emergency, which in most cases are determined by the president. The president now appoints judges nominated by the Justice Council, whose members have, in turn, been appointed by the president, thus removing judges from any public vetting process. The constitution also reduced to six the number of parliamentary committees, thereby abolishing the human rights committee.

Newspapers expressing a variety of views continued to publish in Armenia, but the government exerted indirect pressure on the press mainly by rigidly controlling the purchase of newsprint. According to reliable sources, the government was directly involved in the temporary eviction in May of *Golos Armenii*, a Russian-language opposition daily with no ties to the ARF, from its offices in the press building. The government denied any involvement, and President Ter-Petrossian personally intervened to reinstate the newspaper.

On April 18, paramilitary gangs attacked religious groups, rounding up nine members of the Jehovah's Witness, Pentacostalist, Hare Krishna, and other churches, beating several Krishnas, stealing property, and tossing the nine men into a military police prison, where they languished for two weeks. No government agency claimed to be involved, yet the military police told detainees that they were merely following orders.

The Right to Monitor

Local human rights groups reported no government threats or harassment. In June the government denied a visa to an ethnic Armenian with some ties to the ARF who had sought to monitor the "Dro" trial. The government did not prevent local and other international observers from attending the trial.

The Role of the International Community

The European Union

An April 6 European Union (E.U.) resolution condemned the ban on the ARF as an "attack on the basic principles of democracy" and criticized the related closing of twelve newspapers. It remained to be seen whether the E.U. would factor in these concerns as it negotiated a major trade and cooperation agreement with Armenia, which was supposedly premised on conformity with human rights principles.

U.S. Policy

Armenia received $41 million in U.S. assistance in 1995 (mostly in energy credits), far more per capita than any other state of the CIS. The Clinton administration did not use this assistance as a lever for improving the Armenian government's human rights record, but did criticize the closure of the ARF. A State Department spokesperson declared in January that "the suspension of a major political party . . . runs counter to the established principles of democracy and free speech. This is all the more important given that Armenia will be holding parliamentary elections," and urged the government to open a dialogue with the ARF. Commenting on July 18 on parliamentary elections, a State Department spokesman pointed to their "inherent unfairness" but praised them as "an important step in Armenia's democratic development." In a speech delivered to Armenian-Americans prior to the elections, senior presidential advisor George Stephanopoulos sharply criticized the ARF's suspension and restrictions on the media and stated that "our relationship will rest in large part on Armenia's commitment to democratic principles and human rights."

The U.S. Embassy in Yerevan was well informed on human rights issues, but generally chose to raise such issues with Armenian officials behind closed doors. In a welcome departure from this pattern, it sent an observer to the "Dro" trial.

The Work of
Human Rights Watch/Helsinki

In 1995, Human Rights Watch/Helsinki shifted its focus from documenting Armenia's violations of humanitarian law in Nagorno-Karabakh to exposing the hollowness of the government's professed commitment to human rights. To this end we conducted a fact-finding mission in Yerevan in June which will result in a comprehensive report. A Human Rights Watch/Helsinki representative monitored the "Dro" trial in August; an *amicus curie* brief to the Armenian Supreme Court expressed our concerns over due process violations in this trial. A May letter demanded that the Armenian government fully investigate the death of Artavast Manukian and criticized the crackdown on the political opposition.

AZERBAIJAN

Human Rights Developments

Two coup attempts rocked Azerbaijan in 1995, the year a US$7 billion "deal of the century" oil contract made that country a prized international business partner in the CIS. The government of President Heydar Aliyev continued its two-year crackdown on the political opposition, allegedly to achieve the stability required for business, by pursuing a two-pronged attack: against major parties, largely by attempting to exclude them from the November 12 parliamentary elections, and against individual leaders.

The government's attempts to exclude six parties from the country's first parliamentary elections since independence failed under international pressure in September, resulting in the Ministry of Justice registering the Popular Front Party and the Social Democratic Party, among others. This action followed weeks of systematic government intimidation and harassment aimed at preventing people from signing party petitions required for registration, a practice that continued until the end of the petition period. On October 17, the government excluded Musavat, one of the oldest and largest opposition parties in Azerbaijan, claiming that 5,000 of its signatures were false.

The increasingly repressive atmosphere in Azerbaijan canceled out the gains made by the registration of some opposition political parties. Arrests and criminal investigations of party leaders in 1995 seemed aimed at eliminating President Aliyev's political opponents. Most dramatic of these was the September 19 arrest of Tofiq Qasimov, foreign minister under the Popular Front government from May 1992 through July 1993, a prominent member of the Musavat Party and an outspoken critic of President Aliyev. Qasimov was accused of providing "ideological support" to the March coup attempt. The government's shoddy evidence in this case includes a speech Qasimov made, in which he said that the Aliyev government's strategy of eliminating the opposition was likely to give rise to illegal forms of opposition. Other opposition leaders in custody included Social Democratic Party Deputy Chair Aypara Aliyev, in pre-trial detention for more that one year in connection with a 1994 coup attempt; former Interior Minister Iskander Hamidov, sentenced in September to fourteen years' imprisonment for abusing military authority and theft of state property (his lawyer was arrested one month before trial for allegedly striking a police officer in 1994); and Popular Front leaders Arif Pashaev and Fakhraddin Safarov, in connection with the loss of Shusha and Lachin to ethnic Armenian forces in Nagorno-Karabakh in 1992. Former Defense Minister Rahim Qaziyev was sentenced to death *in absentia* under the same charges, having escaped prison in September 1994.

The government began a new pattern of harassing family members of opposition politicians. Police arrested and beat relatives of those arrested in the wake of the March coup as they sought assistance from the International Committee of the Red Cross (ICRC) and the U.S. embassy. Police searched the home of Jovdan Rovshanov, deceased leader of the March coup attempt, without a warrant and stole family valuables. (In a positive move, President Aliyev ordered the arrest of the sixteen officers involved) On August 6, Baku police searched the home of Rahman Qaziyev (Rahim Qaziyev's son) and took him, his wife, and his one-year-old child into custody. While the latter were released the following day, Qaziyev remained in custody for allegedly assisting his brother's escape. The same day

police arrested the wife and five-year-old child of Rahab Qaziev (Rahim Qaziyev's brother), effectively holding them hostage for three days, until Rahab Qaziyev returned to Baku, and one week later arrested two of Qaziev's cousins in Sheki. Police also repeatedly threatened to arrest the wife of ethnic Talysh leader Aliakram Hummatov (who fiercely opposed President Aliyev's 1993 bid for power and sought to create an autonomous republic for the Talysh people) and evicted her and her three children from their home, driving her into hiding. Her two brothers received fifteen-day administrative sentences.

The government strictly controlled critical speech in the press and in public fora. Government censors had to approve each article before any newspaper went to press, a Soviet-era practice, often resulting in large blank spots in newspaper columns. In March, four journalists from the satirical newspaper *Cheshme* were arrested and charged with insulting the honor and dignity of President Aliyev (Article 188-6 of the criminal code) in connection with a political cartoon. The Baku District Court refused to release them on their own recognizance (even though two of the men needed serious medical attention), and on October 19 sentenced them to two, three, and five years respectively. On November 11, on the eve of parliamentary elections, President Aliyev amnestied them. At least one other individual faced similar charges during 1995, but as of this writing had not been tried. In June, two journalists from the Massaly district received eight-year prison sentences reportedly for bribing $400 from a government official. The charges, which did not justify such a harsh sentence, appeared specious, as the journalists had reportedly written satirical articles in the weekly *Ari* (The Bee) about the same official.

The prosecutor's office investigated Leila Yunusova, chair of the Independent Democratic Party of Azerbaijan, for telling a political joke, which it interpreted as calling for the violent overthrow of the government, at a public forum. Police raided the opposition daily *Azydlyg* in October, allegedly claiming to be searching for weapons.

Despite minor skirmishes, both parties to the Nagorno-Karabakh conflict generally respected the cease-fire signed in May 1994. Azerbaijan released thirty-five Armenian prisoners of war following the release of twenty-seven Azeris by the Armenian authorities. The Karabakh Armenian authorities also released at least twenty Azeris in June and July. Still, the fate of hundreds of persons missing and detained during the conflict remained uncertain.

The Right To Monitor

The government generally allowed monitoring related to the internally displaced from the Nagorno-Karabakh war and allowed visits with Armenian prisoners of war, but impeded monitoring of political cases. It withheld information from a well established human rights organization on the number of persons arrested in the wake of the March coup attempt, forbade local organizations access to political prisoners, and refused to register a human rights committee connected with the Musavat Party. In January, police arrested, then released, activists gathering signatures for a petition on the rights of imprisoned opposition leaders. At least one active unregistered group worked unimpeded.

U.S. Policy

The Clinton administration balanced its keen oil interests in Azerbaijan—U.S. oil firms have a 20 percent share in a $7 billion deal reached in 1995—with some criticism of Azerbaijan's poor human rights record. Congressional restrictions on all forms of U.S. assistance to the Azerbaijan government (related to Azerbaijan's blockade of Armenia), made oil investment the only economic lever available to pressure for change. President Clinton personally telephoned President Aliyev on the eve of the October decision on early pipeline routes to argue in favor of two pipelines—through both Russia and Georgia. In a letter to President Aliyev on Azerbaijani Statehood Day, President Clinton expressed hope that the country would develop democratic reforms, ignoring the deliberately anti-democratic actions so vividly described in the State Department's *Country Reports on Human Rights Practices for 1994.*

More positively, the U.S. embassy in 1995 led the international community in criticizing the government's failure to register the Popular Front Party. At an August 10 press conference, a spokesperson urged the Aliyev government to reconsider the registration, a strategy that, in combination with private *démarches* by the U.S. and European embassies, proved successful. U.S. Ambassador Richard Kauzlarich reportedly raised human rights issues at each of his private meetings with President Aliyev.

U.S. humanitarian aid to Azerbaijan, desperately needed to support the approximately 750,000 internally displaced from the Nagorno-Karabakh war, remained limited to grants to nongovernmental organizations: on June 29, Congress rejected legislation that countered the Clinton administration's request for more humanitarian aid.

The Work of
Human Rights Watch/Helsinki

After releasing a major report in March on humanitarian law violations, *Seven Years of Conflict in Nagorno-Karabakh,* and encouraged by the cease-fire in effect in Nagorno-Karabakh, Human Rights Watch/Helsinki decided to focus the rest of its work in 1995 on drawing public attention to Azerbaijan's grim record on civil and political rights. We participated in two press conferences on the topic in Moscow, the second timed to coincide with the announcement of the oil pipeline route decision. Two letters to President Aliyev protested the trial of the Cheshme journalists, and letters to European Union presidency and the OSCE chairmanship urged these bodies to press for the release of the journalists.

BOSNIA-HERCEGOVINA

Human Rights Developments

Attacks against U.N.-declared "safe areas," the expulsion of Muslims and Croats from Bosnian Serb-held areas, and the displacement of thousands of Serbs in western Bosnia following an offensive by Bosnian and Croatian forces resulted in gross human rights violations and forcible transfers of populations in 1995.

In an attempt to break the two-year siege of the Bihac "safe area," Bosnian government and Bosnian Croat forces launched a joint offensive in November 1994. However, by mid-November, Bosnian Serb forces, aided by Croatian Serb troops and rebel Muslims loyal to Fikret Abdic, had recovered most of the territory and begun an assault against the "safe area." The siege of the Bihac pocket lasted until August 1995, when an offensive by Croatian Army, Bosnian Croat and Bosnian Army units in the Krajina region of Croatia and in western Bosnia broke the siege. Thousands of Serbs fled the advancing Bosnian-Croat troops and sought refuge in the Bosnian Serb-held areas near Banja Luka.

Throughout late 1994, Bosnian Serb forces indiscriminately shelled the "safe areas" of Sarajevo, Tuzla, and Gorazde. By mid-November 1994, Bosnian Serbs were repeatedly attacking Sarajevo with heavy weapons that were supposed to have been under U.N. control, and threatened to attack the humanitarian airlift, thus leading to the closure of Sarajevo's airport and the delivery of relief supplies. Although humanitarian aid destined for Sarajevo since November 1994 finally arrived in February 1995, Bosnian Serb authorities once again refused to guarantee the safety of U.N. relief flights. Aid had to be delivered through a treacherous route along Mount Igman, which was also exposed to Bosnian Serb attacks. Only in September were deliveries of aid regularized.

At the request of rebel Bosnian Serb leader Radovan Karadzic, former President Jimmy Carter traveled to Bosnia as a private mediator on November 19, 1994. To secure Carter's mediation, Karadzic vowed immediate respect for human rights in Bosnian Serb-held territory, free movement for relief convoys, and the reopening of Sarajevo's airport; none of these promises was kept. Nevertheless, during his visit, Carter negotiated a four-month cease-fire between the Bosnian Serbs and the Bosnian government. On December 31, 1994, in a more ambitious "cessation of hostilities" accord, the Bosnian government and rebel Bosnian Serb leadership agreed to the reopening of supply routes, exchange of prisoners of war, free movement of U.N. troops and aid convoys, protection of the "safe areas," restoration of utilities to Sarajevo, removal of foreign troops, and stationing of U.N. peacekeepers at front lines between the warring parties. Neither Fikret Abdic, whose rebel Muslim troops aided Bosnian Serb forces in the assault against Bihac, nor the Croatian Serbs were party to the accord, and attacks by those parties against the Bihac "safe area" continued until mid-1995. Also, rebel Serbs in Croatia and Abdic's forces repeatedly prevented food convoys from reaching the "safe area" of Bihac in early and mid-1995.

Bosnian Serb authorities resumed several rounds of "ethnic cleansing" in northern Bosnia in late 1994 and throughout 1995. Persistent harassment of non-Serbian civilians induced 300 non-Serbs to flee Banja Luka in late February, and prompted 490 to request U.N. assistance in leaving the area. In April, Bosnian Serb authorities expelled another one hundred Muslims from Bijeljina. Bosnian Serb authorities also used non-Serbian civilians as forced labor, commanding them to dig trenches and remove dead Bosnian Serb soldiers. In May, ostensibly avenging the Croatian government's offensive in the western Slavonia region of Croatia, Bosnian Serbs in Banja Luka expelled and harassed Catholic clergy and nuns, destroyed or damaged church property and beat Croatian and Muslim civilians. During and after the

Bosnian Croat and Bosnian and Croatian Army offensives in the Krajina region of Croatia and western Bosnia in August, scores of Muslims and Croats were expelled from Bosnian Serb-held areas in northern Bosnia, where thousands of Serbs displaced from Krajina and western Bosnia had sought refuge. The displaced Serbs expelled Muslims and Croats from their homes and occupied their property. Local authorities organized the non-Serbs' deportation to Bosnian government-held areas or to Croatia. In September and October, Zeljko Raznjatovic (widely known as Arkan) and his paramilitary units arrived from Serbia proper into the Banja Luka area, where they expelled thousands of Muslim and Croatian women, children and elderly persons. Approximately 5,000 non-Serbian men were taken to detention centers or were disappeared reportedly by Arkan's troops, which also were responsible for looting, raping, beating and otherwise terrorizing non-Serbs in northwestern Bosnia.

In April, Bosnian President Alija Izetbegovic informed international mediators that the Bosnian government would not extend the Carter-brokered cease-fire. Bosnian Serb forces responded to Bosnian government offensives by intensifying their siege of Sarajevo throughout April and early May. Bosnian Serb troops responded to NATO air strikes against their positions by shelling Tuzla on the evening of May 25, killing seventy-one civilians and injuring more than 150, making it the deadliest single bombing during the three-year war. Karadzic also announced in May that his forces would capture U.N. peacekeepers if the U.N. called on NATO to launch air strikes and threatened to overrun the eastern enclaves of Srebrenica, Zepa and Gorazde. He carried out his threat, and Bosnian Serb forces took approximately 370 U.N. peacekeepers hostage in late May and June and overran the U.N.-declared "safe areas" of Srebrenica and Zepa in July. Following the fall of Srebrenica, Bosnian Serb forces summarily executed hundreds—possibly thousands—of men and boys at various mass execution sites near the Srebrenica area and during

their flight from Bosnian Serb-held territory to Bosnian-government-controlled areas. Women, children and elderly persons deported from the area were also terrorized, and thousands of persons remained disappeared.

The Right to Monitor
Human rights monitoring continued to be severely restricted in Bosnian Serb-held territory. The ICRC was given only limited access to persons detained following the fall of Srebrenica in July. Bosnian Serb officials escorted foreign journalists to view the damage caused by NATO bombing but did not allow them to conduct independent investigations. In early September, Human Rights Watch requested access to Bosnian Serb territory to investigate possible violations of the rules of war by NATO, but never received a response. Following the joint Bosnian government, Croatian government and Bosnian Croat militia offensive in western Bosnia in August and September, access was impeded by those forces.

The Role of
the International Community

The United Nations and NATO
The U.N. peacekeeping mission was increasingly eclipsed by NATO in 1995. U.N. commanders consistently argued that it was essential to maintain strict neutrality in order to avoid retaliation against U.N. troops. In practice, U.N. neutrality meant inaction. U.N. troops failed to protect the "safe areas" of Srebrenica and Zepa and did little if anything to protect Srebrenica's men and boys from execution, to ensure regular delivery of humanitarian aid, and to maintain operation of Sarajevo's airport. NATO officials grew increasingly frustrated by the U.N.'s persistent reluctance to punish the Bosnian Serb troops for repeated violations of U.N. resolutions and agreements and complained that, as a result, the credibility of the U.N. and NATO had been compromised. By mid-1995, however, NATO's call for a more robust response against Bosnian Serb forces prevailed,

and the first sustained bombing campaign against Bosnian Serb military targets took place in June 1995.

In late January 1995, the commander of U.N. forces in Bosnia, Lt. Gen. Michael Rose, was replaced by Lt. Gen. Rupert Smith, a fellow Briton. Smith's willingness to penalize Bosnian Serb forces for violations of agreements or in retaliation for attacks on "safe areas" contrasted with his predecessor's hesitation to use military force against Bosnian Serb forces. However, although the U.N. command in Bosnia was more willing to use force against abusive Bosnian Serb forces in 1995 than in previous years, U.N. military and civilian personnel—especially Yasushi Akashi, the secretary-general's special representative to the former Yugoslavia—were also reluctant to employ force to defend civilians and often vetoed requests from officers in the field. Only after the decision-making process governing the use of force was revised and Akashi's consent was no longer required to launch air strikes, did NATO begin to take punitive actions against Bosnian Serb forces in response to continuing attacks against Sarajevo.

Throughout 1995, U.N. peacekeepers and military observers found themselves increasingly harassed by all the warring parties, especially by Bosnian Serb forces. Serbian forces in Croatia and in Bosnia repeatedly blocked efforts to resupply U.N. troops in Bosnia, effectively preventing them from carrying out their mandate to protect the "safe areas" and escort relief convoys. Bosnian Serbs frequently stole vehicles, ammunition, and flak jackets from the U.N. and intensified other forms of harassment. Serbian forces repeatedly fired on U.N. peacekeepers and vehicles, killing at least two peacekeepers, and fired on planes at the Sarajevo airport in an attempt to disrupt the airport's normal operation. Bosnian Serb soldiers downed an American F-16 jet monitoring the "no-fly" zone near Banja Luka on June 2, and two French airmen were shot down and captured by Bosnian Serb forces near Pale on August 30. The U.S. pilot was discovered alive and rescued on June 7. The French airmen were detained by Bosnian Serb forces but, in mid-October, rebel Bosnian Serb leader Radovan Karadzic announced that the airmen had been "kidnaped" from the hospital where they allegedly were being held.

The Bosnian Army also detained U.N. soldiers at their compounds in Gorazde and Visoko, in May and June, respectively. In response to what was perceived as U.N. inaction to Bosnian Serb attacks against the Srebrenica "safe area" in July, a Bosnian government soldier shot and killed a Dutch soldier stationed in the enclave.

In late 1994 and mid-1995, Bosnian Serb forces took scores of U.N. soldiers hostage as a means to deter NATO air strikes. In late May and June, approximately 370 peacekeepers were taken hostage after NATO warplanes bombed several ammunition bunkers near Pale on May 25 and 26. At the end of May, the Bosnian Serb leadership announced that it would free the peacekeepers on the condition that NATO formally renounce its use of air strikes.

In order to negotiate the release of the U.N. hostages, Serbia proper dispatched Jovica Stanisic, the chief of Yugoslav state security, to Bosnian Serb territory, ostensibly to convince Karadzic to release the hostages. On June 2, 122 peacekeepers were released; on June 7, 108 were released; and on June 13 another twenty-eight were released. Then the Bosnian Serbs demanded the return of the four Serbian soldiers captured by U.N. troops on May 27 during the confrontation at Vrbanja bridge in exchange for the release of the remaining twenty-six U.N. hostages. Despite the U.N.'s demand for the unconditional release of the hostages, it capitulated to Bosnian Serb pressure, releasing the Bosnian Serb soldiers captured at the Vrbanja bridge. U.N. troops had also abandoned all the weapons collection points around Sarajevo, thus allowing Bosnian Serb forces to retrieve the weapons contained therein and to intensify the siege of Sarajevo. In return, the Bosnian Serbs had freed the remaining U.N. peacekeepers by June 18.

On June 1, as the situation in Bosnia

sharply took a turn for the worse, Secretary-General Boutros Boutros-Ghali released a report suggesting several alternatives for the peacekeeping mission in Bosnia. He declared the current mission untenable, but opposed a complete withdrawal of troops. Instead, he suggested either stationing a reinforced multinational force under the command of contributing countries, or his preferred option of completely abandoning military force and reducing the scope of the mandate. On June 25, the U.N. Security Council agreed to send another 12,500 soldiers as part of a "rapid reaction force" that was meant to respond forcefully to any attacks on U.N. peacekeepers in Bosnia. But financing of the force remained a matter of contention, because the Clinton administration had already expressed reservations about the U.S. having to pay part of the cost of the force. The force was eventually deployed but, on October 5, the U.N. announced that it would scale back its mission in Bosnia from 30,000 to 21,000 troops and that part of the rapid reaction force would also be withdrawn and placed on standby in their home countries. On August 19, U.N. forces began moving out of the Gorazde "safe area" and only a handful of U.N. monitors remained in the enclave by year's end.

After the fall of the "safe area" of Srebrenica and Zepa, on July 21 NATO threatened Bosnian Serb forces with air strikes if they attacked the Gorazde "safe area." On August 1, the threat was extended to include Bosnian Serb attacks against the other remaining "safe areas," including Sarajevo, Bihac, and Tuzla. In response to the killing of thirty-seven people by a Bosnian Serb shell in a Sarajevo market on August 29, NATO air strikes were initiated against Bosnian Serb positions around Sarajevo on August 30. The scope of the air strikes was expanded over the course of early September, when Bosnian Serb military targets in the southeast and north were also targeted or destroyed by NATO warplanes. After sustained NATO air raids were conducted for several days, Bosnian Serb forces removed their heavy weapons from around Sarajevo

and agreed to resume negotiations to discuss a peace accord to end the war.

In 1995, the International Criminal Tribunal established by the U.N. to adjudicate violations of humanitarian law in the former Yugoslavia issued a series of indictments. In February, the tribunal indicted twenty-one Bosnian Serbs for various violations of international law, including the crime of genocide. In July, Karadzic and Mladic and twenty-one other Serbs were indicted. In addition to other crimes, the tribunal charged Karadzic and Mladic with genocide. A Bosnian Croat military officer accused of commanding troops in a 1993 massacre of Muslims in the village of Stupni Do also was indicted by the tribunal in September. In October, the court began hearing evidence against Dragan Nikolic, the former commander of a Bosnian Serb-run camp who had been indicted by the tribunal in 1994. In November, six more Bosnian Croats were indicted in connection with abuses against Muslims in the Lasva valley in 1993.

U.S. Policy

Plagued by the absence of a clear goal or overall approach for resolving the war or ending human rights abuses in Bosnia, the Clinton administration's policy remained confused and erratic in the latter part of 1994 through mid-1995. By late 1995, the Clinton administration had finally assumed a leadership role in the Balkans, deeply involving itself in a war that it had earlier characterized as a "European problem," and embracing, where it had often rejected, the use of force as a necessary supplement to diplomacy. By late 1995, the U.S. encouraged NATO to counter U.N. impotence in the field, thus forcing a response to the continued siege of Sarajevo and the isolation of the Gorazde "safe area." The Clinton administration assumed control over diplomatic efforts of the so-called contact group—comprising representatives from the U.S., France, Germany, Britain, and Russia—by dispatching Assistant Secretary of State Richard Holbrooke to negotiate a cease-fire and general outlines of a peace plan between the warring parties.

Although the U.S. had urged and won adoption of a September 1994 U.N. Security Council resolution discouraging any diplomatic contact with the Bosnian Serb leadership as long as it continued to reject the contact group plan that would divide Bosnia roughly in half, with 51 percent of the land going to the Muslim-Croat federation and 49 percent to the Bosnian Serbs, U.S. and European diplomats traveled to Pale in January 1995 for direct discussions with Karadzic. Their main goal was to seek Karadzic's acceptance of the contact group plan as a "starting point" for negotiations. Karadzic, however, refused to accept the contact group proposal, even as a basis for initial discussion.

In light of Bosnian Serb intransigence, U.S. and other contact group negotiators generally ceased direct contact with the Bosnian Serb authorities in February. They then turned to Serbian President Slobodan Milosevic, asking him to influence the Bosnian Serbs to accept the contact group plan, to grant diplomatic recognition to Bosnia and offering him concessions—including the easing or lifting of sanctions—in exchange for his cooperation. This proved an extremely embarrassing policy shift when, in early March, a CIA report disclosed that Serbian forces—often with the support of Serbia proper—had committed 90 percent of "ethnic cleansing" in Bosnia.

Following repeated and unsuccessful attempts at persuading Milosevic to recognize Bosnia and to reinforce his isolation of the Bosnian Serbs in early 1995, the Clinton administration turned again in mid-May to the use of force. The U.S. pressured its allies for several weeks to make use of air strikes to revive the U.N.'s authority and applauded the use of NATO air strikes against a Bosnian Serb ammunition depot on May 25. However, the Clinton administration fell silent after approximately 370 U.N. peacekeepers were taken hostage in late May and June. The Clinton administration once again deferred to the Europeans, and approved measures against the wishes of Congress. In June, President Clinton promised $100 mil-

lion to support a "rapid reaction force" of French, British and Dutch troops to help protect U.N. troops in Bosnia and vetoed a congressional measure to lift the arms embargo against the Bosnian government in early August.

By late August, however, the U.S. released evidence indicating the probable execution of hundreds, possibly thousands, of Muslims by Bosnian Serb forces following the fall of Srebrenica and was under increasing pressure to respond to continuing attacks against Sarajevo. Following sustained NATO bombings of Bosnian Serb positions in late August, U.S. negotiators intensified peace efforts, eventually winning, on September 8, an agreement from the three warring parties to nominally maintain Bosnia as a single state that would be divided roughly in half into two entities—the Muslim-Croat federation and the self-proclaimed "Republika Srpska." Subsequent negotiations in Geneva established the outline for a new constitution, and follow-up talks were scheduled for late October in the U.S. A U.S.-brokered cease-fire went into effect throughout much of Bosnia on October 12, after gas and electricity were restored to Sarajevo and aid routes to and from the capital and the Gorazde "safe area" were opened. On November 1, U.S.-led peace talks among Bosnian, Croatian and Serbian representatives began in Dayton, Ohio.

In mid-1995, the Clinton administration issued strong support for accountability in the Balkans, expressly rejecting amnesty for war criminals as a possible bargaining chip at the negotiating table. But as peace talks opened in Dayton, Ohio, in early November, U.S. opposition to an amnesty and support for prosecution of indicted war criminals became less clear.

The Work of
Human Rights Watch/Helsinki

In addition to ongoing efforts to document and obtain accountability for violations of the rules of war in Bosnia, in 1995 Human Rights Watch/Helsinki concentrated its efforts on two areas: bringing pressure on the international community, and especially the U.S. government, to take action to protect the civilians who were under attack in the U.N.-declared "safe areas" and insisting that international negotiators include comprehensive and specific human rights guarantees in any overall peace settlement.

In an appeal to world leaders attending the summit meeting of the then-Conference on Security and Cooperation in Europe (CSCE) in December 1994, we argued that failure to protect the "safe area" of Bihac—that was then under attack by rebel Serb forces in Bosnia and Croatia—and accommodation, rather than punishment, of those besieging the enclave, would legitimize "ethnic cleansing." In a June 2 letter to members of the Security Council and the U.N. secretary-general, Human Rights Watch/Helsinki urged the U.N. not to withdraw from the "safe areas" in eastern Bosnia as part of efforts to regroup and redeploy U.N. forces in Bosnia, such abandonment, we stressed would lead to the probable slaughter or displacement of the areas' inhabitants, mostly Muslims.

On July 31, Human Rights Watch/Helsinki and twenty-six other humanitarian, human rights, religious and other groups formed a coalition to increase pressure on the international community to respond to the deepening crisis in Bosnia in particular the unabated human toll of "ethnic cleansing." A statement was issued calling for multilateral military action to stop genocide in Bosnia, as well as for protection of the remaining "safe areas," immediate access to all detainees from Srebrenica and Zepa, the delivery of humanitarian supplies to civilians in the "safe areas," stigmatization of those who direct, assist and supply abusive troops, and the maintenance of sanctions against Belgrade until such time as it cooperated with the investigation and extradition of indicted war criminals.

In late October and early November, Human Rights Watch/Helsinki representatives met with European and U.S. officials to present a proposal for a series of steps to be incorporated into any peace proposal for Bosnia, aimed at ensuring respect for human rights and accountability for past crimes. We also proposed that international observers dispatched to monitor the peace be empowered to work toward the betterment of human rights in the region. Specifically, our proposal recommended the establishment of an international civilian monitoring mission and the establishment of measures to strengthen a proposed Bosnian Human Rights Commission and a Commission for Displaced Persons. We also urged that NATO forces dispatched to Bosnia to monitor the ceasefire be empowered and required to report, or intervene to prevent or stop, human rights abuses and that all parties cooperate and assist the work of the International Criminal Tribunal for the Former Yugoslavia.

Human Rights Watch/Helsinki remained committed during 1995 to documenting violations of humanitarian law and to supporting efforts to obtain accountability for the victims of abuses. After the fall of the safe areas of Srebrenica and Zepa in July, we sent a mission to investigate, and in October issued a report, *The Fall of Srebrenica and the Failure of U.N. Peacekeeping*. The report documented violations of the rules of war and the U.N.'s mismanagement during and immediately after Srebrenica's fall. In response to the Bosnian Serbs' capture of the two enclaves in mid-July, we issued calls for the U.N. to demand access to and allow ICRC to register all those detained by the Bosnian Serbs and called on the U.N. to take steps to defend the remaining "safe areas."

Our monitoring efforts were conducted with a view to identifying perpetrators of the crimes and providing the international tribunal with additional evidence of war crimes and crimes against humanity in Bosnia. In November 1994, we issued a report about continuing human rights abuses in the Banja Luka area.

Throughout the year, Human Rights Watch/Helsinki also urged U.N. bodies and the U.N. secretary-general to ensure proper funding for the international tribunal for the former Yugoslavia. We maintained regular contact with the prosecutor's office and continued to forward our documentation to the tribunal's staff. In June, Human Rights Watch/Helsinki released a report critiquing domestic war crimes trials in Bosnia, Croatia and the FRY, pointing to their politicization and lack of due process. The report also highlighted the paucity of trials in which members of the parties' own forces are tried for violations of human rights.

BULGARIA

Human Rights Developments

Despite some improvements in Bulgaria's overall human rights record, ethnically motivated violence and the failure of the authorities to provide redress for victims of such crimes continued to be a dominant human rights problem in 1995. There were also frequent reports of police misconduct and use of excessive force, as well as of government restrictions on freedoms of expression and religion.

Widespread impunity for crimes perpetrated by police officers remained common in 1995. Human Rights Watch/Helsinki received numerous reports of police brutality, which is no longer a problem only for minority groups. For example, in a case reported by the Bulgarian daily *Twenty-Four Hours*, the sergeant who shot a man from Velingrad on June 6, 1993, escaped punishment for the killing when the Plovdiv Military Prosecutor's Office abandoned the indictment in 1995 for lack of sufficient evidence. However, the prosecutor had failed even to interrogate the victim before he died of his injuries months after the incident.

The Roma minority continued to be the target of much police violence. Anguel Anguelov, a Roma, was killed by a police officer in Nova Zagora on March 20, 1995. According to eye witnesses, Anguel was shot when he approached the police and asked why they were beating his brother. Similarly, in March, two Roma children from Vidin were severely beaten by two police officers from the regional police de-

partment. The two officers took the boys out of school and broke one boy's arm, allegedly because the two boys had harassed a colleague's son. As of November 1995, no charges had been brought against the police officers in either case.

In addition to numerous cases of police brutality, reports of xenophobic attacks and mob violence intensified during 1995. For example, on February 4, nine Roma from the village of Skobeleov were attacked by unknown people with guns and bats. Toma Yordanov Marinov was beaten to death during the incident. Similarly, four days before the anniversary of Adolf Hitler's birthday on April 20, an arsonist destroyed the homes of at least seven Roma families in Sofia. According to witnesses, approximately one hundred Roma were in the houses; one man died from injuries suffered during the fire, and several others were injured. Human Rights Watch/Helsinki received reports that, in these and other similar cases, the Bulgarian police and prosecutors failed to take prompt and forceful steps to bring the perpetrators to justice.

In addition, other groups not recognized in Bulgaria as national minorities confronted racial attacks. On June 15, a group of unidentified "skinheads" assaulted an African-American in the center of Sofia. Similarly, "skinheads" beat three Arabs in the city of Pleven on May 18.

During 1995, the Bulgarian government continued to restrict the free expression and association of certain Bulgarian citizens who identify themselves as ethnic Macedonians. As in previous years, the leaders of United Macedonian Organization Ilinden (OMO Ilinden) were banned from assembling at the Rozhen Monastery in April to celebrate the eightieth anniversary of the death of Yane Sandanski, a Macedonian leader. In July, the members of OMO Ilinden were again banned from meeting at the Samuil Castle to commemorate, among other anniversaries, the foundation of the Republic of Macedonia. It was widely reported that a Bulgarian court upheld the ban stating that, "the territory of Bulgaria cannot be used as a place to celebrate events that have no relation to Bulgarian history."

The Bulgarian government continued to restrict religious diversity in 1995. Forty-five "non-traditional" religious groups have been denied legal registration since February 1994, when a new law on non-profit organizations was adopted. Legal registration is a prerequisite to being recognized as a legitimate denomination with contractual and organizational rights to, for example, rent public halls and publish materials in the organization's name. On February 24, police in Veliko Tarnovo disbanded a meeting of members of the "Word of Life" religious sect because the assembly was "illegal." Similarly, in July, an investigation was opened concerning two pastors of the Jehovah's Witnesses, Gueorgui Boyadzhiev and Elena Karinkiova, who were accused of representing and circulating information about an unregistered denomination.

Among some positive human rights developments in Bulgaria during 1995, the Council of Ministers amended the penal code on May 18, 1995, providing for life imprisonment as an alternative to the death penalty in certain cases. However, despite the continued enforcement of a 1990 moratorium on the death penalty, capital punishment remained legal.

The 1992 law for "Additional Requirements Toward Scientific Organizations and the Higher Certifying Commission," known as the "Panev law," was abolished in 1995. The Panev law barred former secretaries and members of the Communist Party from a variety of high-level positions. This law had carried with it an inherent presumption of collective guilt that conflicted with international human rights standards. The abrogation of the Panev law entered into force on April 3, 1995.

The Right to Monitor

Human Rights Watch/Helsinki was not aware of any attempt by the government to impede human rights activists in their investigations and reporting during 1995.

U.S. Policy

The Clinton administration failed publicly to raise human rights concerns, especially the deteriorating conditions for Roma, during its review of Bulgaria's Most Favored Nation trade status in June. Bulgaria is expected to be graduated to permanent MFN status in late 1995. The State Department's *Country Reports on Human Rights Practices for 1995* was accurate and comprehensive in its portrayal of the human rights situation in Bulgaria.

The Work of
Human Rights Watch/Helsinki

Human Rights Watch/Helsinki continued to focus attention on human rights violations against minorities in Bulgaria, especially the Roma. Following the release of "Increasing Violence Against Roma in Bulgaria" in November 1994, Human Rights Watch/Helsinki raised concerns with the Bulgarian Embassy to the U.S. on the treatment of Roma and the failure of authorities to provide redress for the victims of these abuses. In late 1994, these concerns were raised with the U.N. Commission on Human Rights. On December 29, 1994, Human Rights Watch/Helsinki also sent a letter to the Bulgarian ambassador to the U.S., Snezhana Botusharova, calling on the Bulgarian government to establish an independent commission to review cases of police brutality against Roma and determine whether investigatory, prosecutorial and judicial decisions have been influenced by the ethnicity of the victims. In December 1994, Human Rights Watch/Helsinki invited Dimitrina Petrova, supervisor of the Human Rights Project in Bulgaria, to be honored for her work providing legal assistance to Roma victims of police violence at Human Rights Watch's annual tribute to human rights monitors.

CROATIA

Human Rights Developments

Two Croatian Army offensives against the western Slavonia and Krajina regions, in May and August respectively, caused the displacement of hundreds of thousands of Serbs from Croatia and a myriad of human rights violations after Croatian government control was reestablished in both areas. Violations of civil and political rights also continued in Croatia, with the Croatian military again perpetrating most of the human rights abuses in the country, both on and off the battlefield.

During and immediately after the Croatian Army's offensive in western Slavonia and Krajina, access for international observers was restricted or denied and much forensic and other evidence pointing to the possible commission of human rights abuses during or immediately after the offensives may have been destroyed. Although the Croatian government accounted for some of those reported missing after the western Slavonia offensive, officials refused to disclose the fate of others. Graves reportedly containing the remains of Serbs killed during the offensive and buried by Croatian officials in the western Slavonia region were not exhumed to determine the number and cause of death of those interred. Some Serbian men captured and detained by Croatian authorities after the offensive were beaten while in custody.

Croatian Army soldiers burned entire Serbian villages and summarily executed more than 120 mostly elderly Serbs in the two months following the Croatian government's recapture of Krajina. An August 31 decree "temporarily" revoked property rights of most Serbs who fled the Krajina region and placed such property under the control of the Croatian government, which then allotted the property to Croats who had been displaced or expelled by rebel Serbian forces in 1991 and thereafter. Croatian authorities also obstructed delivery of humanitarian aid to rebel Muslims loyal to Fikret Abdic and rebel Serbian forces following the Croatian Army's recapture of the Krajina region in August.

Forcible evictions from state-owned housing, and the violence that often accompanied such evictions, continued in 1995, but the Croatian government took virtually no action to address the human rights abuses associated with the evictions. Although the Croatian Interior Ministry had taken steps since 1992 to purge its ranks of abusive police officers, prosecution of such officers and, more particularly, of abusive members of the Croatian Army remained inadequate in 1995.

From late 1994 to mid-1995, rebel Serbian forces in Croatia aided Bosnian Serb forces and rebel Muslim troops loyal to Fikret Abdic in attacking the U.N.-declared "safe area" of Bihac. Aerial attacks against the enclave were launched from the rebel Serbian-controlled air strip at Udbina, and rebel Croatian Serbs obstructed the delivery of humanitarian aid to the besieged pocket.

Following the Croatian government's offensive in western Slavonia, rebel Serb forces in the Krajina region launched rocket attacks against the capital city of Zagreb, killing six and wounding 177. Rebel Serbian troops and Serbs displaced as a result of the Croatian Army offensive in Krajina expelled Croats and other non-Serbs from their homes in eastern Slavonia, the only area in Croatia that remained under rebel Serbian control by November 1. Bosnian Serb forces also shelled civilian targets in Dubrovnik in April and August.

The Right to Monitor

Human rights monitoring efforts in Croatia increased dramatically in mid-1995, but obstruction of such efforts by the authorities also increased. During and immediately after the Croatian Army offensives in western Slavonia and Krajina, access for international observers and local nongovernmental organizations was restricted at various times. In general, however, international and domestic human rights groups conducted wide-ranging monitoring projects and maintained contact with the Croatian government. A U.N.-established human rights monitoring effort and local nongovernmental human rights organizations monitored human rights and set up a presence in both western Slavonia and Krajina.

The Role of
the International Community

The United Nations

From its inception and deployment in 1992, the U.N. mission in Croatia had done little, if anything, to protect non-Serb civilians living in the so-called United Nations Protected Areas (UNPAs), and it similarly failed to protect the UNPAs from attack by the Croatian Army in 1995. The recapture, in 1995, of what were formerly known as Sectors West, North, and South by the Croatian military effectively ended most of the U.N.'s mission in Croatia, although U.N.human rights monitors remained in the recaptured areas.

A U.N. "Humanitarian Crisis Cell" was formed following the Krajina offensive in August, and the U.N. finally undertook a serious, concerted effort to document human rights abuses in the Krajina region—primarily against Serbs by Croatian Army soldiers—and to bring those abuses to the attention of the Croatian government and the international community. Such efforts were rarely undertaken by the U.N. when rebel Serbian forces controlled the areas from 1991 to mid-1995, partly because Serbian forces obstructed such work by U.N. monitors, but also, in part, because U.N. officials accepted "ethnic cleansing" in the UNPAs as a *fait accompli*, spending more effort evacuating non-Serbs than protecting them.

On January 2, Croatian President Franjo Tudjman announced that he would not renew the mandate of the U.N. peacekeeping mission in Croatia when it was due to expire on March 31. Tudjman justified his decision by claiming that the U.N. had not fulfilled its mandate and that the U.N. presence in Croatia consolidated rebel Serb control over 30 percent of Croatia. On February 3, the U.N.

Security Council approved a new configuration for the U.N. mission in Croatia, which was renamed the United Nations Confidence Restoration Operation (UNCRO) and was cut back from a 14,000 to 8,000 troops. U.N. troops were caught in the cross-fire and did not react to protect the UNPAs when Croatian Army forces attacked rebel Serbs in both western Slavonia and Krajina. With the recapture of three of the four UNPAs by Croatian government forces, the U.N. was thus left with a diminished role and announced that it planned to pull out most of its troops in November.

Following attacks in early and mid-November 1994 against the Bihac safe area from Serb-held areas in Croatia, the U.N. Security Council extended the "no-fly" zone to Croatian air space, thereby permitting NATO to follow and attack warplanes flying from Bosnia into Croatia. On November 21, 1994, NATO bombed the rebel Serbian-controlled Udbina air strip, but it was quickly rebuilt and rebel Serb forces in Croatia continued to attack the Bihac "safe area" until August. During this period, the U.N. did nothing to prevent such attacks, although U.N. forces were mandated to demilitarize the so-called UNPAs in Croatia.

On July 24, the International Criminal Tribunal established to adjudicate violations of international law in the former Yugoslavia indicted Milan Martic, the "president" of the self-proclaimed Republic of Serbian Krajina, for ordering attacks against civilian targets in May. Shortly before he was indicted by the tribunal, in November, the Bosnian Croat commander was promoted by Croatian President Tudjman as an inspector in the army of Croatia proper.

European Union

Croatia's efforts to negotiate a trade and cooperation agreement with the E.U. were halted after the Croatian Army offensive in western Slavonia. On June 12, the E.U.'s General Affairs Council agreed to resume negotiations with Croatia but warned Croatia to respect human rights and work toward peace in the former Yugoslavia. The E.U.

also reserved the right to take into account, at any time up to and including the conclusion of the agreement, Croatia's attitude toward the implementation of U.N. resolutions and peace efforts regarding the former Yugoslavia. In a statement issued at its Cannes Summit of June 26-27, the European Council of Ministers confirmed the authorization to open negotiations for a trade and cooperation agreement with Croatia but reiterated its warning against recapturing Krajina through military means. In response to the Croatian Army offensive in the Krajina region, the E.U., on August 4, immediately suspended negotiations with Croatia on the trade and cooperation agreement and suspended implementation of the PHARE aid program for Croatia.

U.S. Policy

In its efforts to contain the fighting in the Balkans, the Clinton administration pressured Tudjman to rescind his threat to expel U.N. peacekeepers from Croatia and worked to broker peace plans between the Croatian government and rebel Serbian forces. Human rights violations committed by Croatian Army soldiers following their August offensive met with criticism from U.S. officials, but the U.S. issued few public *démarches* against other violations of civil and political rights in Croatia.

On January 29, Peter Galbraith, the U.S. ambassador to Croatia, put forth an internationally brokered peace plan for Croatia (known as the Z-4 plan) that offered the Krajina Serbs virtually complete self-government within Croatia. Both the Croatian government and rebel Serbian authorities eventually rejected the plan but, when Croatian government troops began amassing along the front lines and war appeared imminent, the Croatian Serbs announced that they would consider the plan. The Croatian government ignored the Croatian Serbs' reported consideration of the proposed plan and launched its offensive in western Slavonia, rendering peace efforts moot. Galbraith believed the proposed plan could have been made to work, but Wash-

ington reportedly disagreed and appeared to have sanctioned the Croatian Army offensive.

Members of the U.S. administration denounced human rights abuses committed by Croatian forces in the Krajina region. John Shattuck, U.S. assistant secretary for democracy, human rights and labor, traveled to Croatia on two separate occasions to investigate, and then denounce, abuses by Croatian troops in the Krajina area. Ambassador Galbraith, incensed by Croatian civilians' stoning and harassment of retreating Serbs and police inaction to stop such harassment, rode as part of the refugee convoy to demonstrate his protest against the treatment of the Serbian civilians.

Although most of his efforts were aimed at brokering a peace accord in neighboring Bosnia, U.S. Assistant Secretary of State Richard Holbrooke also worked to address the status of eastern Slavonia, the only part of Croatia that remained under rebel Serbian control by November 1. On October 3, Thorvald Stoltenberg, the U.N. envoy to the former Yugoslavia, and Holbrooke announced that a preliminary agreement on the future of eastern Slavonia had been reached. The agreement called for the administration of the area by a transitional authority that would allow for the eventual return of Croatian government authority over eastern Slavonia, with guaranteed minority rights for Serbs. However, in mid-October, Croatian Army troops began to mass along the confrontation line in eastern Slavonia, and both parties were prepared for war by November 1.

The Work of
Human Rights Watch/Helsinki

Throughout 1995, Human Rights Watch/Helsinki continued to monitor and protest violations of humanitarian and human rights law, and to demand accountability for such abuses, in Croatia.

In May, Human Rights Watch/Helsinki conducted a mission to Croatia to investigate violations of the laws of war and subsequent violations of human rights during and after the Croatian Army offensive in western Slavonia. A subsequent report highlighted abuses that had taken place and pointed to issues that required further investigation. In a letter to Croatian President Tudjman, Human Rights Watch/Helsinki urged that all those responsible for abuses in western Slavonia be held accountable for their crimes.

Similarly, following the Croatian Army offensive in the Krajina region, Human Rights Watch/Helsinki sent a letter to President Tudjman on August 10 expressing concern about abuses against civilians and the destruction of Serbian property in areas recaptured by the Croatian Army. We also called on the Croatian government to protect the rights of Serbs wishing to remain in, or return to, the Krajina area. Human Rights Watch/Helsinki and twenty-six other humanitarian, human rights, religious and other organizations sent President Tudjman a similar letter condemning the burning and looting of Serbian homes in Krajina, the failure of the Croatian police to protect Serbs leaving Croatia from Croats who stoned their convoy, and military attacks against civilians fleeing the fighting. From August to November, Human Rights Watch/Helsinki sent missions to Serbia and Croatia to investigate abuses during and after the Krajina offensive and planned to publish the findings of those missions in early 1996.

Throughout the year, Human Rights Watch/Helsinki met with U.N. and governmental officials to press for proper funding for the international tribunal established to adjudicate war crimes and crimes against humanity in Bosnia and Croatia, as well as continued funding for the field operation of the special rapporteur for the former Yugoslavia of the U.N. Commission on Human Rights. Two reports and numerous letters sent to U.N. and governmental bodies underscored the need to properly fund the tribunal and to insist that all states cooperate with international efforts to ensure accountability in the region.

In October, in order to draw attention to human rights abuses committed off the battlefield, Human Rights Watch/Helsinki issued a book-length report on the status of civil and political rights in Croatia from 1992 to mid-1995. The report examined abuses associated with the granting of citizenship, forcible evictions from state-owned property, treatment of minorities and refugees, freedom of the press, trials of alleged war criminals and accountability for human rights abuses committed by Croatian government agents. In June, Human Rights Watch/Helsinki released a report critiquing domestic war crimes trials in Croatia, Bosnia and the Federal Republic of Yugoslavia, pointing to their politicization and lack of due process. The report also highlighted the paucity of trials in which members of the parties' own forces were tried for violations of human rights.

THE CZECH REPUBLIC

Human Rights Developments

The Czech Republic had a mixed record on human rights in 1995. The government demonstrated its commitment to human rights by, for example, ratifying the European Convention on the Prevention of Torture and Inhuman Treatment in September. Parliament also passed an amendment to the criminal code on June 29, 1995, under which perpetrators of hate crimes will face tougher sentences. At the same time, however, "skinhead" violence increased and became increasingly brutal, especially against the Roma minority. A restrictive citizenship law, which negatively affects the Roma minority, codified widespread resentment against that minority.

Provisions of the Law of the Czech National Council on Acquisition and Loss of Citizenship, which had granted citizens of the Slovak Republic more favorable conditions than non-Slovak citizens for acquiring citizenship, expired in July 1994. Yet, the government did not resolve the fate of many Roma who were effectively left without Czech citizenship by the law. The Tolerance

Foundation, a human rights organization in Prague, has documented more than 400 cases in which Slovak citizens of Roma ethnicity living in the Czech Republic have not been able to acquire Czech citizenship. The majority of those Roma who were denied Czech citizenship are long time or lifelong residents of the Czech Republic.

Although the law does not specifically refer to Roma, its requirements on residence, ancestry, and petty criminality appear to have a disproportionate impact on Roma, and as such are discriminatory. What is more, the law imposes criminal penalties that were not in existence at the time the crime was committed. Those denied citizenship are unable to vote, run for office or receive full social benefits.

There continued to be reports of violent attacks on Roma. In May, four youths armed with a baseball bat forced their way into the home of Tibor Berki, a Roma, in the town of Zdar nad Sazavou. Mr. Berki, a bakery worker, was clubbed to death in front of his wife and five children. On October 7, ten "skinheads" armed with baseball bats attacked and severely injured a Roma couple who were waiting for a bus in Breclav. Approximately thirty Roma have been killed by racist violence in the Czech Republic since the fall of communism in 1989. Human Rights Watch/Helsinki received credible reports that police failed to protect Roma from racist violence and rarely conducted a prompt and thorough investigation into such incidents.

On September 27, the Czech parliament extended the 1991 "lustration law"(screening law) that bans former high-ranking Communist Party officials and secret policemen from holding important political, economic, and judicial posts until the year 2000. The lustration law, which was to have expired at the end of 1996, has affected some 140,000 people since its adoption. Human Rights Watch/Helsinki is concerned that persons prosecuted under the lustration law are not being prosecuted for acts that were criminal at the time they were committed, but for having belonged to a now-dis-credited group. With regard to evidence provided in the former communist government's police files, the law does not take into consideration the possibility that false information might have been planted. Hundreds of people have protested that they were registered as police collaborators without their knowledge. Many have sued the Ministry of Internal Affairs and won, because there was inadequate evidence of their guilt.

The Right to Monitor

Human Right Watch/Helsinki was not aware of any attempt by the government of the Czech Republic to impede human rights activists in their monitoring activities.

U.S. Policy

Several high-level meetings between representatives of the Czech Republic and United States were held during the year to discuss privately such issues as the citizenship law and its effects on the Roma minority, as well as the extension of the lustration law. The section on the Czech Republic in the State Department's *Country Reports on Human Rights Practices for 1994* was accurate in reporting on the human rights situation, giving a particularly comprehensive evaluation of abuses against the Roma minority.

The Work of Human Rights Watch/Helsinki

Human Rights Watch/Helsinki's primary concern in the Czech Republic continued to be the treatment of the Roma minority and, in particular, the impact that the citizenship law has on Roma. Human Rights Watch/Helsinki maintained contacts with local human rights organizations throughout the year, especially with regard to the Roma situation.

ENGLAND

Human Rights Developments

Racial violence and police misconduct in responding to racist incidents continued to be a serious human rights concern in England during 1995. Racial violence has increased dramatically in recent years, according to police figures. In the five years between 1989 and 1994, the number of violent attacks rose over 200 percent, from 4,383 to 9,762. It was widely recognized, however, that these reported figures significantly underestimated the actual level of violence. The official British Crime Survey estimated that racially motivated violent attacks for 1991, for example, were as high as 32,500, ranging from intimidation to verbal threats.

The government was outspoken against racial violence and encouraged initiatives by the police, community organizations, and legal organizations to find effective solutions. Positive steps to improve police response to racial violence, however, were offset by significant failures.

In addition to numerous incidents of police brutality, victims and community groups often reported that police were unable or unwilling to respond to racial violence, and that the police sometime threatened those who reported a racist crime or even arrested the victim. Many victims of racist violence ultimately stopped reporting such incidents because the police appeared unable or unwilling to investigate the crimes effectively. As a practical matter, it was sometimes difficult to determine to what degree and in which cases poor response by the police was due to a lack of resources, a lack of professionalism of senior officers, the inexperience of junior officers, a lack of effort, and/or racial bias. However, solicitors, victims, and community groups indicated that in cases where a lack of effort and racism played a clear role, there were few effective means for making the responsible officers accountable for their behavior.

The Right to Monitor
Human Rights Watch/Helsinki received no information to indicate that human rights observers in England were prevented from conducting their investigations and reporting on their findings during 1995.

U.S. Policy
The only significant statement by the U.S. government regarding racial violence in England appears in the State Department's *Country Reports on Human Rights Practices for 1994.* The report highlighted the continuing and substantial problem of racial discrimination throughout the criminal justice system, as well as in areas of employment. However, the report made no reference to police brutality against minority groups or to the inability or unwillingness of many police officers to respond effectively to incidents of racial violence.

The Work of
Human Rights Watch/Helsinki
Human Rights Watch/Helsinki focused its efforts during 1994 on monitoring racist violence and investigating the ability of the criminal justice system to respond. In June and July, a fact-finding mission was sent to interview victims of racial violence, community organizations, solicitors, as well as with police and government officials. A report was in preparation as of this writing.

FRANCE

Human Rights Developments
Institutional xenophobia and incidents of anti-immigrant violence were the primary human rights concerns in France in 1995. Disparate treatment and harassment were particularly directed against persons of North African origin. The strong showing of the anti-immigration Front National Party (FN), which garnered 15 to 20 percent of the vote in presidential and municipal elections, encouraged the major political parties to endorse anti-immigrant positions.

France's restrictive immigration policy remained a matter of concern. The French government adopted a highly restrictive definition of refugee, limiting the notion of "agent of persecution" to state actors. The number of applications for refugee status granted in France dropped from 23.5 percent for 1994 to less than 11.5 percent for the first five months of 1995. Representatives of foreigners' rights organizations reported that France's policy on safe third countries resulted in violations of the fundamental principle of non-*refoulement*. There were reports of France's attempt to send Iraqis to Jordan, Afghans to Russia and Zairians to Cameroon to seek asylum with no assurances that they would have a fair opportunity to state their claim. In addition, the French authorities decided categorically that certain countries were incapable of producing refugees. Asylum seekers, such as Roma from Romania, were denied the opportunity to state their claims for asylum despite evidence of well-founded fears of persecution.

Sporadic incidents of violence against foreigners continued in France throughout 1995, and were of particular concern when committed by law enforcement officers. For example, on August 11, 1995, following a routine identity check, three uniformed policemen in Marseille beat a French citizen of Algerian origin. The victim was driven by police to a deserted quarry where he was beaten and allegedly robbed by police. The police were apprehended when one of them returned to the scene of the crime to recover his club. The officers were suspended and imprisoned for three weeks. During the investigation, one of the officers testified that the police hierarchy was aware of the use of intimidation tactics and did not condemn such practices.

Further, police officers convicted of violence against foreigners or immigrants appeared to receive light sentences in contrast with the gravity of the crimes. For example, on November 3, 1994, a twenty-four-year-old police officer sodomized an Algerian detained in the Paris Retention Center for Foreigners (*Le Dépôt des Etrangers de la Préfecture de Police de Paris)*, which was formerly located in the basement of the Ministry of Justice. The European Committee for the Prevention of Torture of the Council of Europe reported on the inhumane and degrading conditions of the retention center. Following protests by French NGOs, human rights lawyers and activists, the Paris center was closed on April 26, 1995. The officer convicted of sodomy was sentenced to eighteen months in prison, of which twelve months was a suspended sentence.

Government bans of books violated the right to free speech and expression. In April 1995, the Interior Ministry banned the book *The Legal and Illegal in Islam*, by the Egyptian theologian Youssef Qaradawhi, on the grounds that it was anti-Western. The ban was later rescinded. On August 17, 1995, the government banned *The White Book on the Repression in Algeria (1991-1994)* published by Hoggar publications in Switzerland. According to the Interior Ministry, the book was "FIS [*Front islamique du salut*] propaganda" whose "appeal to hate" could lead to "incidents of public disorder."

The Right to Monitor

Human Rights Watch/Helsinki has received no information to indicate that human rights monitors in France were prevented from conducting their investigations and reporting on their findings during 1995.

U.S. Policy

The only significant public statements by the U.S. on human rights in France were found in the State Department's *Country Reports on Human Rights Practices for 1994.* Its section on France, while generally accurate, omitted credible reports by human rights groups of police ill-treatment, especially of non-Europeans, and failed to note that minimal sanctions for excessive use of force by police appeared to be systematic in France.

The Work of Human Rights Watch/Helsinki

As part of an ongoing project to analyze and help reduce xenophobia throughout Europe, Human Rights Watch/Helsinki conducted a three-month mission to France in 1995 to assess the treatment of foreigners and immigrants. Human Rights Watch/Helsinki focused its efforts on an investigation of violations of international refugee law in the treatment of asylum seekers in France. A report on the findings of that mission and our recommendations were in preparation at this writing.

GEORGIA

Human Rights Developments

In 1995, the Georgian government strengthened human rights mechanisms, and the U.N. Mission in Georgia (UNOMIG) and Commonwealth of Independent States (CIS) peacekeepers in Abkhazia continued to prevent renewed hostilities in that former war zone. However, political stalemate over the proposed federative status of Georgia's breakaway regions of Abkhazia and South Ossetia jeopardized human rights there and prevented some 250,000 internally displaced persons from repatriating. Also, despite some positive new steps, such as requiring police to wear identifying badges on duty, the government was unable to reduce chronic abuses such as police brutality; politically motivated killings, violent attacks and detentions; and violations of due process rights.

On March 10, 1995, Georgia adopted a law enshrining minority rights and, on August 24, passed its first post-independence constitution. On April 17, a new independent human rights group, the All-Georgian Human Rights Council, was created. The government maintained an open dialogue about human rights problems, admitting for the first time that law enforcement bodies had practiced torture, and distanced itself from the Mkhedrioni (Horsemen), an abusive paramilitary group the government had tolerated for years as an unspoken arm of law enforcement.

Sadly, one of the greatest government achievements in Georgia—curbing organized crime—came at the expense of respect for human rights. Within hours of the explosion of a car bomb that narrowly missed Head of State Eduard Shevardnadze on August 29, law enforcement agents detained some 200 individuals as suspects and searched countless offices and homes, all reportedly without court orders. This aggressive, arbitrary sweep stood in stark contrast to the relatively passive investigations conducted in connection with the approximately six actual or attempted assassinations against other leading political figures this year, reflecting politics' influence in law enforcement in Georgia.

The eighteen-month trial of criminal case No. 7493810, which was a microcosm of abuse including torture and gross violations of due process, ended with convictions in two sets of sentences on March 6 and in May, 1995. The nineteen defendants, most of whom credibly asserted they were tortured during investigation and denied proper legal defense, had been charged with offenses ranging from murder and terrorism to petty theft. They received prison sentences of one and one-half to fourteen years; two of them—Irakli Dokvadze and Petre Gelbakhiani—were sentenced to death. The subsequent Supreme Court review had reached no decision as of this writing, six months after it began.

The May 14, 1994 cease-fire continued to hold in Abkhazia, although the U.N.-mediated peace talks failed to make notable progress toward a lasting peace. Violence broke out in Abkhazia's Gali region on March 12-13 and April 2 when, according to the U.N., Abkhazian policemen beat and tortured some thirty-five people, murdering at least ten of them and forcing the temporary displacement of some 1,500 inhabitants. The combating parties systematically failed to investigate and punish war crimes dating back as far as 1992.

The Right to Monitor

The authorities prevented access to the Gali Canal along the Inguri River and to some Georgian weapons storage sites, thus hindering somewhat the work of UNOMIG; UNOMIG also faced some security problems. In a reversal of past practices, the Georgian government allowed International Committee of the Red Cross (ICRC) personnel access to imprisoned rebel leader

Vakhtang "Loti" Kobalia, but it continued to deny them access to former Defense Minister Tengiz Kitovani, who was arrested in January 1995 for alleged illegal armed activity.

The Role of
the International Community

U.N. Policy

UNOMIG extended its presence in Abkhazia through January 12, 1996. In June 1995, the Security Council augmented the responsibilities of the collective peacekeeping forces in Abkhazia, and the secretary-general and the Human Rights Centre submitted several situation reports. However, the UNHCR repatriated only 1 percent of the internally displaced people (IDP), leaving some 40,000 to repatriate at their own risk.

European Union and OSCE Policy

These bodies played an active role in promoting human rights in Georgia this year. The OSCE monitored and reported on the human rights situation in Abkhazia, helped build human rights protections into new legislation, conducted prison investigations, and forcefully condemned prison conditions and other aspects of abuse. It failed to hold the pertinent authorities accountable for war crimes in South Ossetia and Abkhazia, however.

On March 9, at a meeting of the Permanent Council of the OSCE, France, on behalf of the European Union, expressed concern about the legal proceedings for defendants in case No. 7493810, and on March 23 issued a follow-up statement. On April 6, the European Parliament adopted a resolution calling for the commutation of the two death sentences and for proper appellate procedures in the cases, among other measures.

U.S. Policy

U.S. human rights policy in 1995 appeared confused, with stronger protests seeming to emanate from Washington than from the embassy in Georgia. The Helsinki Commission devoted a March 28 hearing to human rights in Georgia and spoke out on specific violations, but the embassy appeared to limit its response to closed-door and tardy reprimands.

Among other important contributions, the embassy frequently intervened on behalf of victims of human rights and exhibited a sound understanding of the scope of human rights abuse in the State Department's *Country Reports on Human Rights Practices for 1994*. However, the report was uneven. For example, regarding Case No. 7493810 it noted the problem of denied access to defense counsel but failed to note the even more glaring problem of torture. Moreover, the report concluded that there were no political prisoners in Georgia in 1994, but failed to indicate the fate of the approximately 100 claimed in the previous year's State Department report.

The U.S. approved a much-needed rule of law program that provided in part for training and reform in Georgia's law enforcement. However, the program that included work with Georgia's notoriously unreformed Ministry of Internal Affairs (MVD) was not accompanied by a clear public statement of goals and a strict timetable for implementation, thus leaving the unfair impression that the U.S. was unaware of or unconcerned with curbing the ministry's abuse.

The Work of
Human Rights Watch/Helsinki

This year Human Rights Watch/Helsinki worked to inject human rights concerns into the peace process in Abkhazia and to protest entrenched civil rights abuse by documenting and publicizing abuse and monitoring trials.

In March 1995, the Arms Project and Helsinki divisions of Human Rights Watch released the report *"Georgia/Abkhazia: Violations of the Laws of War and Russia's Role in the Conflict"* at a Moscow press conference (see the Human Rights Watch Arms Project section). We traveled to the capital and to Abkhazia to communicate the report's findings and recommendations to the necessary authorities and gather updated information about unfolding concerns in Abkhazia. In March we began an exchange of views with the UNHCR regarding the difficult repatriation process, and on May 16 wrote to Secretary-General Boutros-Ghali enumerating our concerns in Abkhazia. In July we wrote to the Abkhazian authorities regarding nine Georgians reportedly in their custody.

In January Human Rights Watch/ Helsinki again observed the trial of case No. 7493810 and raised concerns with pertinent government authorities. That same month we released *"Urgent Update: Trial in Georgia Draws to a Close"* at a Moscow press conference. In March we met with OSCE missions in Vienna, and in July with the OSCE's Amb. Audrey F. Glover to offer updates on developments and urge action. We also submitted an evaluation of the OSCE's human rights work in Georgia to help strengthen its ongoing programs.

On March 28, we testified before the U.S. Helsinki Commission on Georgia's human rights record, and in August wrote to key U.S. officials urging them to build clear public goals into the U.S.'s assistance program to the Georgian MVD.

GERMANY

Human Rights Developments
The primary human rights concern in Germany was the government's response to violence against foreigners and non-ethnic Germans. While government actions helped to reduce the number of attacks against foreigners in 1995, xenophobic violence continued to be a serious problem. In addition, human rights organizations reported a rise in cases of police brutality against foreigners living in the country.

Due, in part, to more forceful government measures to combat right-wing violence, there was a significant decrease in the number of violent crimes against foreigners in Germany during 1995. The government expanded the number of police and prosecu-

tors trained to investigate and prosecute cases of xenophobic violence. Some local police stations took on liaison officers to deal directly with ethnic and minority communities.

Despite these improvements, however, the number of violent attacks against foreigners was still significantly higher than before German unification. According to foreigners' rights groups, a large number of attacks also went unreported. In addition, 1995 saw an increase in police violence against foreigners. Especially in Berlin, human rights organizations reported numerous cases of police ill-treatment against foreigners, including illegal arrests and beatings during detention. Investigations into reported cases were often initiated, but very few police officers were disciplined and none of the victims were compensated.

While violence against foreigners decreased in 1995, other forms of xenophobic violence appeared to be on the rise. Anti-Semitic crimes soared during 1994 and continued to be a serious problem in 1995. A growing number of right-wing crimes against other minorities, such as the handicapped and homosexuals, was also reported, including a "skinhead" attack against seven handicapped people on a Magdeburg streetcar in August.

The government's firmer measures to combat right-wing violence, which included increased surveillance of far-right groups, sometimes went further than necessary by excessively restricting expression, association and assembly. In total, ten right-wing organizations were banned in Germany from 1993 to 1995, including the Free German Workers' Party, one of the country's largest extremist groups, and the National List. Police conducted numerous raids on the offices and homes of their members, confiscating propaganda materials and some weapons and making numerous arrests.

In April 1995, the German government signed an agreement with Vietnam that guaranteed $140 million of development aid if Vietnam would take back 40,000 Vietnamese citizens who had not yet received legal asylum in Germany. The first four deportees arrived in Vietnam on October 18, and the Vietnamese government promised they would be treated in a "humanitarian manner." But German human rights groups and Vietnamese in Germany expressed concern that some of the deportees, many of whom had been long-time residents of Germany, might face persecution if returned to Vietnam. In addition, there was concern that Vietnamese would be more hesitant to report cases of violence to police for fear of deportation.

Criticized in the past, the judiciary did improve its response to racist violence in 1995. In October, a Dusseldorf court imposed stiff prison sentences on three German youths found guilty of murdering five Turks in a firebomb attack on their home in Solingen in 1993. However, the number of prosecutions dismissed for insufficient evidence remained alarmingly high, suggesting that the prosecutors' offices, as well as the police forces, were not preparing thorough cases. In addition, many violent attacks against Turks were attributed to Kurdish terrorists. Although there is evidence to support this claim, foreigners' rights groups fear that the blame for some right-wing attacks will be shifted away from German citizens.

U.S. Policy

The State Department's *Country Report for Human Rights Practices* recognized far-right violence as a problem in Germany in both 1993 and 1994 reviews. The report on 1994, however, generally applauded the German government's responses without commenting on the work that remained to be done. Official relations between the two states remained very friendly; no high-level criticism was directed publicly at the German government's response to violence against foreigners.

The Right to Monitor

Human Rights Watch/Helsinki was not informed of any restrictions on the right to monitor human rights in Germany.

The Work of Human Rights Watch/Helsinki

Human Rights Watch/Helsinki focused all of its attention in 1995 on right-wing violence and the German government's response. In April, a comprehensive report, *"Germany for Germans:" Xenophobic and Racist Violence in Germany,* was released at a press conference in Germany. The report outlined the positive measures the German government had undertaken, as well as those areas needing improvement.

HUNGARY

Human Rights Developments

Hungary continued to make significant strides toward the protection of human rights. Adding to its international human rights commitments, on September 25 Hungary signed the Council of Europe Convention on the Rights of Minorities. Despite these legal protections, Hungary experienced a dramatic rise in xenophobia and right-wing-violence during 1995. The most serious human rights abuses involved police brutality, primarily directed at the Roma minority. In addition, "skinhead" and community violence increased during 1995, and the lack of a concerted response on the part of the authorities to such violence was troubling.

A large-scale incident of "skinhead" violence against Roma occurred on May 1, 1995, in the town of Kalocsa. Human Rights Watch/Helsinki received reports that many people had gathered to celebrate May Day in the Bishop's Garden. A group of right-wing racists, many with shaved heads, attacked a groups of Roma. More than twenty Roma were beaten, including an expectant mother who was trying to flee the scene. The police arrived at the scene two and one-half hours after being notified about the violence. Nemeth Istvan, a Roma man, was already handcuffed and in the custody of the police when, according to his account, a "skinhead" hit him in the head in front of the police. When he screamed, the policemen pressed his bloody head against the wall and told him to stop shouting because he had only injured himself by falling on some stairs.

After two years of investigation, a report filed against several police officers for severely beating Roma from the village of Orkeny was dismissed in 1995. However, six Roma were found guilty of using armed and collective force against public officials. The incident had occurred in 1993, in the village of Orkeny, when local police went to the Roma neighborhood to investigate a car theft.(No charges related to the car theft were ever filed against the Roma.) During the course of the police action, police tore out a tube from the throat of a Roma woman who needed it to facilitate breathing, a pregnant woman had a miscarriage due to be severe blows by police, and several people suffered serious injuries.

In July, in the village of Paszto, four police officers searched Laszlo Amasi's home because he was suspected of having committed a burglary. In the course of the search, the four police officers severely beat Amasi, apparently in an effort to force him to confess to the crime. Amasi died the same day from his injuries. In October 1995, the Hungarian Helsinki Committee reported that only ten cases (9 percent) of misuse of authority and ill-treatment during official procedures, out of 1,138 reported in 1994, reached the courts. What is more, reported incidents represent only a fraction of the actual number of such cases precisely because the victims know that there is almost no chance of legal redress.

A rise in the crime rate and a perceived scarcity of policemen in Hungary has spurred the creation of "citizens' guard organization" (Polarorseg). These groups of private individuals, which are organized by the law enforcement officials, are supposed to provide information on criminal activities to the local authorities. However, in some cases, groups have actively participated in law enforcement. For example, in March, in the town of Papateszer, a family was attacked by members of the local citizens' guard. In Ozd, a former industrial town that has unemploy-ment rates that exceed 80 percent for the Roma population, many Roma reported being routinely beaten by citizens' guards when they were caught foraging for wood for heating from the forest next to the town. The abusive conduct of citizens' guard organizations has been largely tolerated by local authorities.

The Right to Monitor
Human Rights Watch/Helsinki received no reports of any attempt by the government to impede the work of human rights monitors during 1995.

U.S. Policy
The State Department's *Country Reports on Human Rights Practices for 1994* was accurate and comprehensive in its portrayal of the human rights situation in Hungary.

The Work of
Human Rights Watch/Helsinki
Human Rights Watch/Helsinki's work in Hungary centered on one principal issue, human rights violations against Roma. During July and August, Human Rights Watch/Helsinki investigated many cases of violence against Roma, both by police officers and "skinheads." Human Rights Watch/Helsinki representatives traveled throughout Hungary, conducting more than 215 interviews with Roma victims, government officials, policemen, and human rights activists. A report on the findings of that mission and our recommendations were under preparation.

KAZAKSTAN

Human Rights Developments
The dissolution of parliament and removal or reduction of judicial checks and balances changed Kazakstan from a country under representative government to one ruled by presidential decree in 1995. While citizens continued to enjoy widespread free speech, some attempts to criticize these political

developments met with government repression, indicating that Kazakstan had taken a giant step backward on the road to democracy.

The erosion of legislative power began on March 6, when the Constitutional Court ruled that the popular 1994 elections that had created the parliament were unconstitutional. Within days, President Nursultan Nazarbaev, citing that ruling, dissolved parliament and governed for the rest of the year by presidential decree. His promise that new elections would take place "within two to three months" still had not materialized eight months later. On April 29 a popular referendum which some observers claimed was riddled with violations, approved the president's proposal that the electorate do away with the scheduled 1996 presidential election and allow him to retain his post uncontested until the year 2000.

On August 31, after less than a month's deliberation, reportedly 89 percent of participating voters approved a draft constitution that vastly expanded presidential prerogatives, giving Nazarbaev the authority to dissolve the parliament for something as minor as the parliament's failure to approve his nomination for prime minister, and making it all but impossible to remove the president from office. The draft also effectively dissolved the Constitutional Court, the only body that could challenge these changes.

After printing criticism of the dissolution of parliament, on March 23, the outspoken local newspaper *Karavan* was forced to close for two weeks when a fire swept through its offices in what some observers believed was political arson. On April 4, the Procurator General's office closed the newspaper *Kazakhstanskaia Pravda*, charging that it had incited ethnic hatred. On April 29, the day of the presidential referendum, B. Itterman, head of the village administration for Krasnodol'sk in Kellerovsky rayon, was assassinated "for refusing to distort the result of the referendum," according to a June 2 protest statement from the Russian Federation's Federal Assembly State Duma. On August 21, just days before the constitutional referendum, the Ministry of Internal Affairs reportedly arrested approximately half of a group on hunger strike, representing the pressure group Anti-Dictatorship Bloc and urging an election boycott, for allegedly holding an unauthorized protest. That same day, one of the strike organizers, deputy of the dissolved parliament Vladimir Chernyshev, reportedly was beaten at the entrance to his apartment, in an apparent effort to end the strike.

The Right to Monitor
There were no known impediments to human rights monitoring during 1995.

The Role of
the International Community
The European Parliament demonstrated its opposition to President Nazarbaev's dissolution of parliament in March by indicating that it would not ratify its partnership and cooperation agreement with Kazakhstan without a return to parliamentary democracy.

The U.S. response to the string of blatantly undemocratic actions was tentative and sometimes contradictory. Ambassador William Courtney hailed the March dissolution of parliament as a move "to strengthen the rule of law in Kazakhstan," according to *The Moscow Tribune* of March 14, while Defense Minister William Perry protested the move. U.S. criticism of the presidential referendum and of parts of the draft constitution was more categorical: Secretary of State Warren Christopher stated on August 31 that backsliding along the path to democracy would "affect the closeness of U.S.-Kazakstan relations."

The Work of
Human Rights Watch/Helsinki
Human Rights Watch/Helsinki focused primarily on ongoing violations of civil and political rights and the deterioration in the government's commitment to democratic reforms.

KYRGYZSTAN

Human Rights Developments

The Kyrgyzstan government's crackdown on the press during 1995 marked a sharp break from its four-year policy of encouraging the independent media. To compound last year's government-ordered closing of two newspapers, the government this year began to prosecute individual journalists. In areas other than press freedoms, Kyrgyzstan continued to foster human rights protection and monitoring and in February successfully conducted the country's first multiparty parliamentary election since becoming an independent state.

The crackdown on free speech, which began in mid-1994 with the closure of the parliamentary newspaper *Svobodnye Gory* (Free Mountains) and a newspaper insert called *Politika* (Policy), sharpened in 1995 with arrests and trials of journalists for their criticism of President Askar Akaev. On July 11, 1995, editor-in-chief of the weekly newspaper *Res Publica* Zamira Sydykova and her deputy, Tamara Slashcheva, were sentenced under article 128, part 2, of the criminal code (slander with the use of mass media) to one and a half years in prison for their articles criticizing President Akaev. Upon sentencing, they were released on their own recognizance. The court forbade both women from working as journalists, a punishment provided for under article 27 of the criminal code. According to recent reliable reports, on October 5, 1995, the prosecutor's office summoned Tamara Slashcheva and another journalist, Marina Sivashova, for interrogation in connection with an article in support of Kubanychbek Apas, former candidate to Kyrgyzstan's parliament.

Proceedings against Dr. Apas began in June 1995, also under article 128, part 2, after the newspapers *Kyrgyz Rukhu* (The Kyrgyz Spirit) and *Res Publica* published his articles sharply criticizing President Akaev. Apas's political affiliations appeared to have cut back his job prospects; a surgeon, he had not been able to find a decent job since

he defended his doctoral dissertation in late 1994.

According to the Glasnost Defense Foundation, a nongovernmental Russian organization, police beat several journalists, including Vladimir Pirogov, a correspondent for the tri-weekly newspaper *Slovo Kyrgyzstana* (The Word of Kyrgyzstan), and Zamira Sydykova during a meeting of leaders of Turkic-language countries in Bishkek on August 26-27.

The February parliamentary elections revealed some promising signs that Kyrgyzstan fostered true democracy. Twelve parties ran candidates for the parliament, collectively representing a broad array of platforms, from communist to national-patriotic. On February 27, President Akaev established an independent thirty-four-person public commission to investigate allegations of scattered voting violations.

The Right to Monitor

There were no known impediments to monitoring. On the contrary, Kyrgyzstan continued to foster human rights work.

The Role of the International Community

The international community extended humanitarian and development assistance to Kyrgyzstan this year. In December 1994, the OSCE seminar on "Free Media and Free Association" drew strong participation on these well chosen topics.

The U.S. government reportedly raised concern over the alarming backsliding in protection for free speech during meetings with Kyrgyz government officials. The State Department's *Country Reports on Human Rights Practices for 1994* gave a solid and honest analysis of current problems, such as violations of free speech and due process and corruption in the judiciary.

The Work of Human Rights Watch/Helsinki

Human Rights Watch/Helsinki focused its efforts during 1995 on monitoring free expression in the republic. The chairman of

Human Rights Watch/Helsinki's advisory board met with President Akaev and with human rights activists in Kyrgyzstan in June to discuss our concerns about, *inter alia,* restrictions on free speech.

MACEDONIA

Human Rights Developments

In 1995, Macedonia faced a number of serious obstacles associated with the transition from communism. Once a member of the Yugoslav federation, the young republic must now construct democratic institutions, revitalize its civil society and decentralize its economy—all demanding tasks in any circumstances. But Macedonia also found itself on the borders of a Balkan war. Bloody conflict in the former Yugoslavia severely affected the country by exacerbating interethnic tensions, damaging the economy and threatening stability in the region. An assassination attempt on President Kiro Gligorov in October 1995 underlined the fragility of the country's political balance. United Nations forces have been deployed in the country since 1992 to prevent a spill-over of the war.

Despite these obstacles, Macedonia has taken some significant steps toward democratization since declaring its independence four years ago. Substantive reform has opened the door to the Council of Europe and laid the foundation for a multiparty system based on the rule of law. Human rights are satisfactorily guaranteed in Macedonia's new constitution and relevant legislation. Nevertheless, while human rights are guaranteed in Macedonian law, their application has remained selective and incomplete.

The main human rights problem in 1995 was the treatment of national minorities. Macedonia has a vast number of minority groups, including Albanians, Turks, Roma, Serbs and Vlachs, all of whom reported state discrimination. While some of their complaints were politically motivated, the Macedonian government did not always take adequate steps to provide for basic minority rights, especially regarding equal access to state employment and education in minority languages. While the government addressed some of these problems in recent years, including a 1995 decision to expand the pedagogical academy in the Albanian language, the lack of improvement in many areas contributed to a deterioration in interethnic relations.

By far the largest and most vocal of the ethnic communities is the Albanians who, according to official statistics, comprised almost one quarter of the population. Despite some improvements in recent years, Albanians were still grossly under represented in the police force and state administration, even in areas where they constituted a majority of the population. For example, Albanians made up 4.12 percent of the staff of the Ministry of the Interior (which includes the police) in June 1995, only a slight improvement from 1.7 percent in 1992. In addition, some voting districts in the western part of the country, where Albanians predominate, were three times larger than districts in the east inhabited primarily by ethnic Macedonians.

One major complaint of the Albanians concerned higher education in the Albanian language. An attempt in early 1995 to open a private Albanian-language university in Tetovo was deemed illegal by the state, and the university was ordered shut down. The initiative continued nevertheless, and one Albanian man was killed during clashes with police on the first day of classes on February 17. In April, the organizers of the university were sentenced to between eight months and two and one-half years' imprisonment after a trial that violated international standards of due process. They were released on bail one month later.

But Albanians were not the only victims. All citizens of Macedonia suffered from the country's weak democratic institutions, immature political parties and economic hardships. Despite the adoption of democratic legal standards, for example, there were numerous violations of due process in Macedonian courts. Defendants were sometimes held in detention for longer than the twenty-four hours allowed by Macedonian law, did not have proper access to a lawyer or were denied the right to a fair trial. The political opposition also reported continued mistreatment by the state during 1995, including phonetapping and police harassment.

Freedom of the press also remained a concern during 1995. The state-run company Nova Makadonja maintained a virtual monopoly on printing and distribution, which severely limited the possibilities for an independent press. In May 1995, the government closed eighty-five private radio and television stations, including the most influential minority stations, allegedly for technical reasons. On December 17, the director of the private television station ART was detained and ordered to hand over a videotape of the founding of the university initiative in Tetovo. On February 17, the first day of classes in Tetovo, journalist Branko Gerovski was severely beaten by police as he left the scene of fighting between police and ethnic Albanians. The Interior Ministry subsequently disciplined the policemen responsible.

The Role of
the International Community

The United Nations and OSCE

The international community took a strong interest in Macedonia, primarily because of a fear that fighting there would spark a larger conflict in the region. To prevent this, a 1,200-member United Nations Preventive Deployment Force (UNPREDEP) and an Organization for Security and Cooperation in Europe (OSCE) monitoring mission had been deployed in Macedonia since January 1993 and September 1992, respectively, to observe and report on the internal and external threats to the country. In addition to U.N. patrols along the physical borders, both organizations attempted to assist the government with the process of democratization and occasionally to mediate among the various political forces, especially the ethnic communities. Both the government and leaders of the different ethnic communities praised the preventive role the U.N. played in helping to maintain peace.

To preserve stability, however, both the U.N. and the OSCE tended at times to downplay human rights problems within the country. Only gentle criticism was directed against a friendly Macedonian government that is seen as a stabilizing force.

U.S. Policy

The United States maintained close relations with Macedonia after its independence from Yugoslavia in 1991, although Greek pressure prevented the establishment of full diplomatic relations until October 1995. Approximately 500 American troops were based in Macedonia during 1995 as part of the United Nations preventive deployment force. They were responsible for monitoring the border in the north between Macedonia and Serbia. Officially, U.S. assistance totaled approximately $25 million a year. Military cooperation was close, with a number of joint exercises taking place during 1995 and more planned for the coming year.

The Department of State's *Country Report for Human Rights Practices in 1994* presented an accurate, though general, picture of human rights in Macedonia. Official U.S. statements on Macedonia were largely sympathetic to the government. Regarding inter-ethnic relations, the U.S. mostly called for "dialogue" and "tolerance" rather than criticize governmental actions.

The Right to Monitor

Human Rights Watch/Helsinki received no reports of Macedonian or foreign organizations that were restricted in their right to monitor human rights in the country. However, in December 1994, the ethnic Albanian organization Forum for Human Rights had 200 copies of a book titled "Evidence of Crimes Committed Against Albanians in Macedonia" confiscated on the Macedonian border as it was brought in from Albania.

The government's reason for confiscation was "not possessing a permit for importing and distributing foreign printed materials."

The Work of
Human Rights Watch/Helsinki

During 1995, Human Rights Watch/Helsinki focused primarily on raising public awareness about violations of civil and political rights in Macedonia, especially restrictions on minority rights. It also examined the work of UNPREDEP and the OSCE monitoring mission and their role in preventing the spread of war and promoting democratization in the country. A fact-finding mission to Macedonia during the summer of 1995 examined the status of minority rights, press freedom and allegations of police abuse.

ROMANIA

Human Rights Developments

Despite pressure from the international community and assurances from the Romanian government, in 1995 ethnic minorities, and especially the Roma minority, continued to face severe discrimination and mistreatment without adequate legal redress. This situation was exacerbated during the year by local officials who exploited and manipulated ethnic tensions for their own political gains. Frequent attacks on Roma were not only tolerated by law enforcement officials, but were often actually perpetrated by police officers.

On March 21, 1995, during a police raid in the Roma neighborhood of Ilfov, Emilian Niculae and his brother, whose house had been burned down in 1991 during mob violence against Roma in Bolentin Deal, were brutally assaulted by a policeman. When a police officer entered the brothers' home, they asked to see a search warrant. The policeman then beat them and took them half dressed to the Jilava police station. They were released several hours later without an explanation. No charges were filed against them. Similarly, in April, Viorel Constantin

was viciously beaten by several police officers in a bar in Tandarei, Ialomita county. He was then taken to the police station, where he was released later that night without charges or explanation.

Mob violence against Roma and impunity for the perpetrators of such crimes continued to be among the most severe human rights abuses in Romania during 1995. In the aftermath of a fight between a group of young Roma and a local Romanian family, two Roma, Maria Savu and Marinache Meclescu, were shot on January 7, 1995, in the town of Bacu. Maria Savu was taken to a nearby hospital where her leg was amputated. The following day, after villagers were called together by the tolling of church bells, a small group attacked the Roma neighborhood, burning down three Roma houses and completely destroying a fourth. The Roma whose houses were destroyed had not been involved in the incident during the previous night. Although authorities were in a position to prevent the violence and to identify the perpetrators, they did not take adequate measures to prevent the attack. As of November 1995, no one had been charged with crimes related to the violence.

During 1995, local authorities continued to provoke ethnic tensions and hostility between the Romanian majority and the ethnic Hungarian minority; among other things, the authorities attempted to remove all traces of Hungarian history and culture from several Transylvanian towns. Gheorghe Funar, the nationalist mayor of Cluj, publicly announced a series of anti-Hungarian measures in April. In 1994, Funar had sought to remove a statue of King Mathias, long a cultural symbol for the Hungarian minority. In mid-April 1995, he announced that he would place a Romanian and English-language inscription at King Mathias's birthplace, explaining that the greatest Hungarian king was Romanian. In addition, he threatened to transfer use of St. Michael's church in Cluj from the Hungarian minority to the German community.

Several laws were adopted during 1995 that severely restricted freedom of expression and also fueled ethnic tensions. For example, on September 22, the Romanian parliament approved a law that criminalized hoisting the flag, using symbols or singing the national anthem of another country in a public place. Although neutrally-worded, this law was clearly directed against the large Hungarian minority.

Furthermore, a controversial new education law that was adopted on June 29 significantly limits mother-language education. Ethnic German and Hungarian minorities criticized the law, insisting that education in the mother tongue is fundamental to preserving the identity of national minorities. The education law also made religious study compulsory for primary school children between the ages of six and ten, even if their parents do not share these religious beliefs and oppose having their children receive religious instruction.

On September 18, the Chamber of Deputies adopted Articles 205 and 206 of the penal code, which provides criminal penalties for journalists who offend public officials and will have a chilling effect on freedom of speech and the press.

Criminal sanctions against homosexual acts were eased somewhat during 1995. Amid protests by human rights and minority rights groups, on September 12 the Chamber of Deputies voted to amend the penal code to prohibit homosexual acts only if committed in public, in cases of rape, in incidents involving those under the age of consent, or if such conduct produces a public scandal. Although this language was an improvement over earlier drafts, by preserving criminal prosecution for same-sex relations that "produce a public scandal," the Chamber of Deputies adopted dangerously vague language that invites arbitrary enforcement. The law has not yet been promulgated by President Iliescu.

The Right to Monitor

Human Rights Watch/Helsinki was unaware of any instance in which the Romanian government hindered the work of human rights monitors during the year.

U.S. Policy

On May 19, the Clinton administration determined that Romania was in full compliance with the immigration criteria of the Jackson-Vanik amendment, thereby approving Most Favored Nation (MFN) trading status for Romania without the need for a waiver. Romania is now one step from being granted permanent MFN status, which is not subject to annual review. On September 26, 1995, during a meeting at the White House, Romanian President Ion Iliescu and President Clinton discussed the granting of permanent MFN status to Romania. In an improvement over 1994, the Clinton administration took this important opportunity to emphasize that permanent MFN status would be conditional on Romania's continued progress in several areas, including the treatment of the Hungarian minority. However, President Clinton failed to elicit specific human rights commitments from the Romanian government. The administration also minimized the severity of human rights abuses in Romania, especially against the Roma minority, in the U.S. Department of State *Country Reports on Human Rights Practices for 1994.*

The Work of
Human Rights Watch/Helsinki

During 1995, Human Rights Watch/Helsinki continued to focus its efforts on raising public awareness of violence against Roma and the pattern of impunity for such violence, as well as of the government's continued effort to downplay the ethnic tensions that fuel such violence. In late 1994, Human Rights Watch/Helsinki raised these concerns with the U.N. Commission on Human Rights.

RUSSIAN FEDERATION

Human Rights Developments

The Russian Federation's human rights record worsened significantly in 1995. Russian forces prosecuted a brutal war in the breakaway republic of Chechnya with total disregard for humanitarian law, causing thousands of needless civilian casualties. The Russian government also initiated a backlash against human rights in legislation and in government institutions, and made no noticeable attempt to curb police brutality, stop state-sponsored gender and racial discrimination, end abuse in the army, or improve appalling prison conditions.

Russian President Boris Yeltsin ordered 40,000 troops to Chechnya on December 11, 1994, to stop that republic's bid for independence. A December 17, 1994, government statement promised that "force [in Chechnya] will be employed with due consideration of the principle of humanity." But within one week Russian forces began bombing Grozny, Chechnya's capital, in a campaign unparalleled in the area since World War II for its scope and destructiveness, followed by months of indiscriminate and targeted fire against civilians. Russian Human Rights Commissioner Sergei Kovalyev, who remained in Grozny through much of the bombing, bore personal witness to the destruction of homes, hospitals, schools, orphanages and other civilian structures. Indiscriminate bombing and shelling killed civilians and destroyed civilian property not only in Grozny but also in other regions in Chechnya, especially in the southern mountain areas.

Russian forces attacked civilians many times throughout the war. For example, on December 17,1994, Russian troops fired on a column of refugees fleeing toward Ingushetiya, killing at least nine. The most notorious civilian massacre took place on April 7-8 in Samashki. According to a report by the independent Russian watchdog group Memorial Human Rights Center, Ministry of Internal Affairs divisions killed 103 civilians during the operation, including fifteen women and children; and the majority of men killed were summarily executed during house-to-house searches.

In the early months of the war, Russian forces arbitrarily and illegally detained and systematically beat, tortured and humiliated Chechen men suspected of being rebel fighters. Conditions in these detention centers, known as "filtration camps," were inhuman; methods of torture used to force confessions included repeated beatings with fists and rifle butts, electric shock, and attacks by dogs. According to Memorial, most of the 500 men detained were later released for lack of evidence against them.

Russian forces also repeatedly blocked or otherwise delayed the delivery of humanitarian assistance to civilians, particularly in the early stages of the war, and on at least one occasion fired on a clearly marked Médecins Sans Frontières vehicle.

Chechen forces admitted to the summary execution of captured Russian pilots throughout the war, and of at least eight Russian military detainees. Chechen forces also used civilian structures to store arms, and employed indiscriminate fire. On April 14, they reportedly summarily executed U.S. disaster relief expert Frederick Cuny, his translator, and the two doctors accompanying him. In perhaps the most heinous humanitarian law violation known to have been committed by Chechen forces, on June 14 a Chechen unit led by Shamil Basaev captured more than 1,000 civilians and held them hostage in a hospital in Budyonnovsk, in southern Russia, not far from Chechnya. They killed at least seven civilian hostages, denied them food, water and medicine, and used the civilian hospital as a shield.

OSCE-led negotiations yielded an agreement on July 30 linking Russian troop withdrawal from forward positions to disarmament of Chechen fighters, but neither side achieved significant progress. After the October 6 assassination attempt on Lieutenant General Anatoly Romanov (commander of Russian forces in Chechnya), both sides withdrew from the agreement, and low-level hostilities resumed, including aerial bombardments of villages.

Russian investigatory commissions denied the applicability of humanitarian law to the Chechen conflict altogether; however, military courts sentenced seven Russian servicemen for crimes committed against civilians, and the military prosecutor's office investigated another twenty-five crimes against civilians.

Not only did the government fail to hold commanders responsible for some of the grossest violations of human rights in Russia in the post-Soviet era, but the administration sought to dissolve by decree the Human Rights Commission, headed by Mr. Kovalyev, which documented and publicly condemned these violations, and to replace it with a group of non-specialist civil servants. As of this writing President Yeltsin had not signed the decree.

The Russian Federation's backsliding on its path to democratic reform also took the form of emasculating some government human rights mechanisms and passing legislation that encouraged abuse. On April 21, the Yeltsin administration reorganized the Department for Judicial Reform, a body that since 1992 had promoted desperately needed reform of Russia's criminal justice system. After key figures in the department were pressured to step down, its effectiveness was reduced to nil.

The April 3 passage of the Law on the Federal Security Service (or FSB, formerly the KGB),which permits the FSB to conduct searches without warrants, conduct their own investigations, arrest suspects, and run their own prisons, suspended fundamental civil rights and restored powers that were among the hallmarks of the Soviet era. The Law on Investigative Operations, signed in August, granted undercover agents the right to tap phones, open mail, establish fake organizations, infiltrate organizations, and engage in other secret activities. Their activities are effectively beyond civil control, yet evidence gathered in such operations may be used against an individual in a court of law.

This legislative *carte blanche* is especially alarming since the FSB increasingly has been involved in human rights violations. The FSB's reported refusal to question the only witness to the January 22 murder of Timofei Grigoriants, son of Sergei Grigoriants, a long-time dissident who monitors the FSB and the KGB, strongly suggests

it was involved in the murder. The Viktor Orekhov case also bears the mark of FSB intervention: Orekhov, a former KGB officer who served eight years in a labor camp for assisting dissidents in the 1970s, had participated in seminars on the KGB organized by Sergei Grigoriants. In May, Moscow police found on Orekhov an unregistered pistol, whose firing pin was reportedly broken. Police investigators grossly violated the rules of handling evidence, and when the pistol reached ballistics experts one month after the arrest, the latter ruled it fireable. A Moscow court sentenced Orekhov to three years in a maximum security labor camp, an unusually long term, in a trial prosecuted with blatant due process violations. An appeals court later reduced his sentence to one year.

Unchecked police brutality continued in 1995. A report by the Moscow-based Society for the Social Defense of Prisoners described the hundreds of police abuse claims it received every month and noted that complaints filed against the police are almost always dismissed as groundless. In July, police in Saransk reportedly suffocated a man to death in custody; two police officers were investigated, but no charges were brought against them. Human Rights Watch/ Helsinki continues to monitor this case.

Police abuse combined with the growing xenophobic mood in Russia produced a brutal, state-sponsored campaign against dark-skinned people that has been waged since at least 1993. Law enforcement agents in Moscow routinely detained, intimidated, extorted money from and beat people of color, mainly people from the Caucasus and Central Asia, who stood out in this Slavic capital.

Some policemen participated in this campaign simply to extort money or vent racist hostilities. Others acted under anti-crime measures, such as those mentioned above. Still others were enforcing city rules that require people to have a *propiska* (an obligatory residence permit, which today must be purchased at impossibly high prices). New arrivals must pay for a temporary permit and register with the city authorities, or be subject to fines and deportation. The police regularly detained people of color in mass sweeps at marketplaces and refugee hostels, more brutally and punitively in the wake of domestic unrest, such as the war in Chechnya and the Budyonnovsk hostage crisis, both of which involved dark-skinned people and violence against Russians.

Police in Budyonnovsk not only refused to protect local Chechens from retaliatory violence in the wake of the hostage crisis but actively encouraged them to leave altogether. Local Chechens were given less than twenty-four hours to gather their belongings. The Stavropol regional authorities in southern Russia forced people without propiskas to leave the area within seventy-two hours.

The war in Chechnya produced hundreds of thousands of refugees who, along with other new migrants leaving behind war, discrimination and economic hardship, were clearly unwanted in major Russian cities. Even before the outbreak of hostilities, the Moscow city government issued Ordinance No. 2154, which allowed only those individuals with Moscow propiskas to register as refugees in Moscow, an absurd proposition. The directors of newly privatized Moscow hotels forcefully evicted Armenian refugees from Azerbaijan who had been granted housing there in 1988 and 1990 by the Soviet government. The Russian government offered them no alternative housing.

Despite the 1991 court decision that rendered the propiska regime illegal, the government has made little if any effort to discontinue it in major cities. Under a July 17 order from the Council of Ministers, local authorities may refuse to register an individual for temporary or permanent residence based on a long list of conditions that are vaguely formulated and leave open ample opportunities for arbitrariness and abuse. To obey the letter of the law, anyone wishing to stay in a Russian city for more than ten days must register with authorities, in gross violation of freedom of movement.

A scathing report issued on November 16, 1994 by the United Nations Special Rapporteur on Torture has had no noticeable effect on inhumane and life-threatening conditions in Russia's overcrowded pre-trial detention facilities. By far the worst result of this negligence occurred in July at the Novokuznetsk facility, where eleven people died and dozens of others required hospital treatment for oxygen deprivation. Two people died in a labor colony (where individuals are mainly sent after conviction) in Perm, also due to oxygen deprivation.

The Moscow Center for Prison Reform and the Society for Prisoners' Social Defense both attributed the increase in overcrowding conditions to the free rein police now have to detain suspects without bringing charges and to the lack of progress in criminal justice reform, which was brought to a halt in 1995 (see above). Suspects spend on average ten months in detention during the investigatory period, and 16 percent of all pre-trial inmates languish for months or even years more awaiting trial. Convicts often remained in these facilities after conviction for lack of transportation to labor colonies or lack of space in the colonies.

The Russian army in 1995 continued to be a dangerous institution for Russian youth. The independent Soldiers' Mothers Committee reported that the rate of death due to abuse recruits remained unchanged at 3,000 for 1995. Instead of seeking an end to hazing, the Ministry of Defense won a six-month increase in service time, which affected retroactively those already serving. Young men now serve two years in the army in conditions so impoverished that, in certain areas of Siberia, recruits were given only animal feed to eat. Although the constitution provides for alternative service, the Duma has not adopted an implementing law, and the Ministry of Defense has begun prosecuting scores of men who refused to serve.

Police utterly failed to protect women from domestic and sexual violence, denying them their right to equal protection under the law. Statistics released in 1995 showed that in 1994 roughly 43 percent of female victims of violent crime suffered at the hands of their domestic partners; the prosecutor's office, however, has no official statistics on the rate of prosecution for domestic violence. A draft law on family violence which was debated in parliament in October—the first of its kind in Russia—marked a positive shift from years of relegating criminal violence to a "family matter."

Russia had a mixed record on press freedoms in 1995. The mass media brought the Chechen war in gory detail to television sets and front pages, and newspapers professing a wide variety of views continued to publish in Russia's largest cities. But provincial governments increasingly hounded the independent press, and the central government waged a campaign against the aptly named Independent Television station ("Nezavisimoe Televidenie" or "NTV"). In December 1994, authorities threatened to close NTV because of its candid reporting, and in July the prosecutor's office pressed charges against NTV journalist Elena Masyuk for withholding information on the whereabouts of a wanted criminal in connection to her interview with Chechen rebel leader Shamil Basayev. The prosecutor's office also opened an investigation of the popular satirical television program "Kukly" (Puppets) for its allegedly slanderous portrayal of government leaders. Both cases were dropped with the sacking of the acting general prosecutor. Law enforcement agencies failed to solve the execution-style March murder of celebrated television journalist Vladislav Listyev, and made little progress in the murder of Natalya Alyakina, a journalist who was shot by a Russian soldier on June 17, 1995, as she passed through a military checkpoint during the hostage siege near Budyennovsk. President Yeltsin, in a positive departure from the backlash outlined above, took a stand in defense of press freedoms in a key speech on September 1, in which he pledged personally to oppose any new draft criminal code that contained the Soviet-era article providing for the suspension of journalists' activities.

In a departure from past practice, when Russian law enforcement agencies passively cooperated with attempts by repressive Central Asian governments to harass and capture their dissidents residing in Russia, the Yeltsin government refused to extradite them: in January 1995, it dropped the investigation of two Turkmen dissidents, Murad Esenov and Khalmurad Soiunov, and in October refused to extradite a third, Shirali Nurmuradov, in all three cases concluding a lack of evidence. However, Moscow police detained Mirzo Salimov, a dissident journalist from Tajikistan, for ten days while it awaited confirmation from Tajik authorities that he was no longer on their "wanted" list (see Tajikistan section).

The Right to Monitor

Throughout January and most of February, Russian Army and Ministry of Internal Affairs (MVD) forces repeatedly blocked efforts by Memorial and Sergei Kovalyev to monitor filtration camps in North Ossetia and Chechnya. (On February 24, the MVD finally granted the group access.) On January 27, the Ministry of Defense refused to allow Sergei Kovalyev to accompany an OSCE delegation to Mozdok, North Ossetia. In another incident, an army officer reportedly threatened to kill Sergei Kovalyev if he did not leave Mozdok. MVD forces forbade humanitarian organizations, human rights monitors and journalists access to Samashki for two days after they had finished their violent search-and-seizure operation. Russian forces twice denied Human Rights Watch/Helsinki access to Mozdok and once refused it access to southern Dagestan. Russian soldiers detained two of our representatives in Grozny and confiscated audio tapes containing interviews with witnesses to human rights abuse.

Disaster relief expert Frederick Cuny was reportedly detained and summarily executed while on a mission for the Open Society Institute to assess food and medicine needs in southern Chechnya. A U.S. citizen and a member of the Human Rights Watch Arms Project Advisory Committee, he was reportedly captured by Chechen forces who may have been acting on Russian intelligence information. It is widely believed that he became a target because of his outspoken views on the abusive conduct of the war.

The Role of
the International Community

The United Nations
In January, when the war in Chechnya was at its most brutal, U.N. Secretary-General Boutros Boutros-Ghali told journalists he had "no comment" on human rights violations there. However, other U.N. committees and officials compensated throughout the year for this lapse in U.N. leadership. In February, the Commission on Human Rights issued a chairman's statement (a document weaker than a resolution) expressing "deep concern over the disproportionate use of force by the Russian Armed Forces."

Later in the year, the Human Rights Committee considered the first periodic report by Russia since the collapse of the Soviet Union. The committee's evaluation rightly chided the report's lack of information on government practice and in particular deplored violations of the right to life in Chechnya, and condemned inhuman conditions in pre-trial detention, arbitrary interference in private life by intelligence services, gender discrimination, and the propiska system.

The special rapporteur on torture's November 1994 report was presented at the 51st session of the Commission on Human Rights, held in February and March 1995. The report described in vivid detail the "infernal conditions" of Moscow pre-trial detention facilities and recommended, among other things, wider use of bail or recognizance and U.N. training for criminal justice agencies.

The European Union
The European Union distinguished itself with early activism on the Chechnya war but allowed its involvement to wane prematurely. On at least twelve occasions throughout the year, E.U. institutions deplored Russia's violations of humanitarian law, in-cluding use of indiscriminate and disproportionate force, blocking of humanitarian aid, and, in particular, atrocities committed against civilians in Samashki.

The European Commission gave teeth to its sharp public criticism of Russia's conduct in Chechnya by suspending on January 6 the ratification of the interim trade agreement that underlies the E.U.'s agreement on partnership and cooperation with Russia. The latter's article 1 clearly conditions the agreement on fulfillment of human rights principles. On January 19, the European Parliament approved this decision and called on the commission and the Council of Ministers to refrain from taking any further steps toward final ratification of the agreement until military attacks and gross violations of human rights ceased. From February through April, the Council of Ministers successfully used both trade agreements to pressure Russia to accept a semi-permanent OSCE presence in Chechnya.

In April and June, the E.U.'s Council of Ministers upheld the freeze on the interim accord, but after the Russian-Chechen negotiations began, its position softened. A European summit at Cannes in July recommended unfreezing the interim agreement before the peace agreement had been reached and in total absence of any Russian attempt to seek accountability for humanitarian law abuse. The interim agreement was signed on July 17. As military activities resumed in Chechnya in October the European Parliament again discussed the question of ratification of the partnership and cooperation agreement, but a final decision was not taken.

The OSCE
The establishment in April of the OSCE Assistance Group (AG) in Grozny, following three months of tough negotiations and field work, was a great achievement. The AG's ambitious mandate included facilitating peace talks, investigating human rights violations, and building democratic institutions in Chechnya. In accordance with its human rights mandate, it gathered information on some individual cases of human

rights abuse; forwarded cases to the Russian authorities; kept a register of missing persons; on occasion urged Russian commanders to exercise caution with respect to the civilian population; and requested, along with local NGOs, the evacuation of civilians from the Shatoi area before the commencement of military activities.

The AG also proved indispensable in forging the July 30 armistice. Severely understaffed, it was unable to deal with human rights for about half of the mission's first four months. An October 11 Permanent Council statement condemned the renewal of military activities in Grozny and the attack on the OSCE headquarters there.

The Council of Europe

The Council of Europe's Parliamentary Assembly condemned Russia's conduct in the war in Chechnya and voted on February 2 to suspend consideration of Russia's membership application. On September 26, the assembly voted to resume consideration.

U.S. Policy

The Clinton administration responded sluggishly to the slaughter in Chechnya and failed to link Russian conduct with important concessions, such as the May summit with President Yeltsin or support for IMF loans. At the same time, it promoted human rights in Russia at other official meetings through useful democracy-building programs and embassy activities.

Washington's first reaction to Chechnya was to belittle it as an "internal matter" and to make only mild statements urging restraint. Only after public criticism of its position and after its European partners deplored Russian conduct did the Clinton administration show appropriate concern. In February, Defense Secretary William Perry characterized the conflict as "wrongheaded. . .with serious human rights violations," and in April a State Department spokesman condemned the bombings in the south of Chechnya. Secretary of State Warren Christopher, at a March summit with Foreign Minister Andrei Kozyrev, suggested that the Chechnya conflict hampered Russian aspirations to join the Group of Seven nations.

President Clinton declined to use his May summit in Moscow as a forum for protesting abuse in Chechnya. Indeed, he made no significant remarks on the subject at the post-summit press conference, which had featured President Yeltsin's false proclamation that military activities had ended. President Clinton reserved his more critical remarks for a speech delivered at Moscow State University.

To its credit, the Clinton administration actively lobbied for the establishment of the AG, sent $20 million in humanitarian relief, and raised the issue of accountability in the bilateral meeting between Assistant Secretary of State for Democracy, Human Rights and Labor John Shattuck and his Russian counterpart. Neither the Clinton administration nor European governments, however, sought to link support for the $6.2 billion IMF loan to Russia with significant progress on resolving the Chechen conflict.

Much of the $342.8 million of U.S. assistance to Russia earmarked for 1995 under the Freedom Support Act funded useful programs promoting democracy, human rights and the rule of law. A cause for concern, however, was its Law Enforcement Assistance program, which organized seminars by the Federal Bureau of Investigations, the Drug Enforcement Agency, and other law enforcement agencies for their Russian counterparts on, among other things, combatting organized crime. Of the forty-eight seminars conducted in Russia and the U.S., not a single one was devoted to maintaining respect for civil rights in fighting crime, although this issue has come strongly to the fore in the past two years.

The Work of
Human Rights Watch/Helsinki

Human Rights Watch/Helsinki made Chechnya a top research priority and focused Chechnya-related advocacy efforts on the OSCE and the European Union. The first international human rights organization to report on Chechnya, we sent three missions there and published four reports in the first five months of the war. We combined publishing reports with increased, on-site public advocacy to engage intergovernmental organizations and Western governments to help end abuse in Chechnya. To this end we traveled twice to Vienna to address the OSCE Permanent Council: in February, to urge the OSCE to establish a semi-permanent mission in Grozny; and in July, to present a briefing paper pressing for criminal accountability and to urge the OSCE to appoint a special envoy to monitor and assist Russia in holding violators accountable. We also prepared a review of the AG mission for the OSCE Implementation Meeting on Human Dimension Issues in October. In July we traveled to Geneva to brief the U.N. Human Rights Committee on Chechnya.

In many written *démarches*, Human Rights Watch/Helsinki used results from fact-finding missions to urge European bodies to reconsider important concessions to Russia in connection with the conduct of the Chechnya war, a strategy that proved successful. These concessions included the European Union's interim trade agreement and Council of Europe membership. Numerous Human Rights Watch/Helsinki letters to the OSCE pressed for the speedy establishment of the AG. Also, a February letter condemned Boutros Boutros-Ghali's failure to speak out on Chechnya, and we also issued a statement at the time of the U.N. Human Rights Commission meeting urging it to take a forceful stand on Chechnya.

We repeatedly called on the Clinton administration to condemn violations in Chechnya, and on all world leaders to condemn abuse in Chechnya at the May summit. We released our last report on Chechnya at a press conference in Moscow on the eve of the summit and presented it to members of the OSCE.

Human Rights Watch/Helsinki used its Moscow office to monitor and draw public condemnation of state-sponsored discrimination in Russia: against women, ethnic minorities, and people of dissenting opinion. On March 8, International Women's Day, we released *Neither Jobs Nor Justice*, a Human Rights Watch Women's Rights Project report on gender discrimination and violence against women, at a Moscow press conference. Moscow based staff of Human Rights Watch/Helsinki participated in discussions and seminars with local women's organizations on domestic violence and developed a common advocacy strategy with them to use the draft law to raise awareness about domestic violence. We also featured the problem of domestic violence in our written intervention to the U.N. Human Rights Commission.

The Human Rights Watch/Helsinki office in Moscow closely monitored abuse of individual rights and responded to racial intolerance and threats to free speech. Our report *Crime or Simply Punishment?*, released in September at a Moscow press conference, documented police attacks on ethnic minorities in Moscow. We also submitted our findings and recommendations to the U.N. Committee reviewing Russia's compliance with the Convention on the Elimination of All Forms of Racial Discrimination in July. A letter to Prime Minister Viktor Chernomyrdin, released to the press, called on the government to preempt the threat of communal violence in the wake of the Budyennovsk tragedy. In a July 18 letter to the Minister of Justice, we urged the repeal of Articles 74 and 206-2 of the Criminal Code, which punish some types of peaceful speech, including by prison terms. We protested the charges against three journalists who wrote on racist or homosexual themes. The Ministry of Justice wrote that it was unconvinced by the free speech arguments, but the MVD showed sincere interest in at least one of the cases raised.

We urged Mikhail Krasnov, legal advisor to President Yeltsin, to intervene in the Viktor Orekhov case, spoke at a press conference organized in his defense, and attended his appeal. We also wrote Foreign Minister Kozyrev and Internal Affairs Minister Kulikov in October, urging them to expedite the release of Tajik journalist Mirzo Salimov.

THE SLOVAK REPUBLIC

Human Rights Developments

The political in-fighting between President Michal Kovac and Prime Minister Vladimir Meciar during 1995, had a decidedly negative impact on respect for human rights and the rule of law in Slovakia, particularly with regard to governmental interference with the independence of the media. Tensions between the Slovak majority and the ethnic Hungarian and Roma minorities also ran high during the year.

Friction among the political parties was highlighted on August 31, when President Michal Kovac's son was abducted from Slovakia, beaten and given electric shocks by eight unidentified men, and dropped in front of an Austrian police station. After Austrian police took him to a hospital.for treatment, they detained him on the basis of an international arrest warrant issued by a Munich court for suspicion of fraud. However, because the Slovak courts had not yet pronounced on the issue of extradition to Germany, Kovac was returned to Slovakia where his extradition case is currently pending.

During the course of the investigation into the kidnaping, Slovak police said they suspected the Slovak Information Service (SIS) had been involved. SIS chief, Ivan Lexa, a close associate of Prime Minister Meciar, refused to allow SIS members to be relieved of their oath of secrecy in order to give evidence to the police. He accused the regular police of revealing state secrets and demanded that the investigation team be replaced. As a result, three senior police officials investigating the kidnaping were dismissed from the case. The government made little effort to ascertain the truth about the SIS involvement and did not adequately investigate the serious allegations made by the police. Parliament refused to open debate on the circumstances leading up to the kidnaping.

Since the return to power of Prime Minister Meciar and his Movement for a Democratic Slovakia (KDH) after the parliamentary elections in November 1994, there has been a crackdown on free expression and the press. Shortly after the elections, parliament replaced most of the members of the State Television and Radio Council with members who were political allies. The Slovak government also used various means to prevent journalists from criticizing its policies. On March 9, thousands of demonstrators demanded the return of three widely-televised political satires, which had been taken off the air by the government.

Tensions between the Slovak majority and the Hungarian minority throughout the year reflected tensions between the Slovak and Hungarian governments. Although a basic agreement on the rights of minorities was signed by both countries in March, the Slovak government has yet to ratify the agreement, and has expressed disagreement with provisions concerning the autonomy of national minorities. Slovakia's controversial draft language law also delayed ratification of the bilateral treaty between Hungary and Slovakia. The draft language law limits the use of other languages in schools, state institutions, and both state- and privately-owned media, and was to have gone into effect on September 1, 1995. However, in September Meciar announced that the draft law would be discussed with the Council of Europe before being submitted to parliament.

The Roma minority, the second largest minority in Slovakia, experienced numerous incidents of"skinhead" violence in 1995. On September 1, 1995, a dozen Czech and Slovak "skinheads" broke into the Nevsvady home of a fifty-seven-year-old Roma man and beat him with a baseball bat and police truncheons. The Roma man suffered severe chest and elbow injuries. As of November 1995, the investigation was continuing.

In Ziar nad Hronom, the death of Mario Goral, a Roma, sparked public debate about violence against Roma. Mario Goral was set on fire on July 21 by a gang of forty youths. Goral suffered burns over 60 percent of his body. He died ten days after the attack. On August 10, in response to the incident, the Slovak government's Council for Nationalities held an extraordinary session at which it addressed the issues of racism and violence against Roma.

The Right to Monitor
Human Rights Watch/Helsinki was not aware of any interference with the work of human rights monitors by the government of the Slovak Republic during 1995.

U.S. Policy
Defense Secretary William Perry visited Slovakia in September and took that important opportunity to mention that Slovakia needed to strengthen democratic principles before it would be able to join NATO. After his meeting with government leaders, Mr. Perry said that "a test of progress toward democracy is the government tolerating diversity of opinion, fully supporting constitutional rights and providing transparency of government."

President Michal Kovac met with U.S. Vice President Al Gore on August 8, 1995. Kovac told Slovak radio that U.S. representatives were interested in the progress of democracy in Slovakia and had stressed that Slovakia is not living up to the same standards as other countries in the region. However, the U.S. did not issue a public statement concerning the meeting.

The State Department accurately commented on human rights in the Slovak Republic in its *Country Reports on Human Rights Practices for 1994.*

The Work of
Human Rights Watch/Helsinki
Human Rights Watch/Helsinki continued closely to monitor the treatment of the Roma and Hungarian ethnic minorities, as well as efforts by the Slovak government to address serious problems of discrimination on the basis of race and ethnicity. Human Rights Watch/Helsinki also closely monitored developments regarding restrictions on the press in the Slovak Republic.

TAJIKISTAN

Human Rights Developments
The political, social and economic situation in Tajikistan remained unstable in 1995, three years after the end of the Tajik civil war, which had resulted in 20,000 to 50,000 dead and produced over 800,000 refugees and displaced persons. Despite the government's ostensible goal of reconciliation, the presidential elections of November 1994, held in a climate marred by intimidation and fraud, were followed by similarly flawed parliamentary elections in February 1995. The regional animosities that exacerbated, and ultimately overshadowed, the ideological conflicts of the civil war continued to generate violence in 1995.

U.N.-sponsored peace negotiations between the Afghanistan-based Tajik opposition and the Tajik government in early 1995 and a meeting between the opposition leader Seyyed Abdollah Nuri and President Emomali Rahmanov in mid-1995 had limited success in furthering national reconciliation. The September 1994 cease-fire agreement was, however, extended to February 1996, although armed clashes continued along the Tajik-Afghan border. Failure in implementing confidence-building measures, such as prisoner exchanges, endangered the viability of further talks to be held before the end of 1995. Peace in Tajikistan was further endangered by the Tajik government's inability to exercise centralized control over large areas of the country, resulting in pro-government paramilitary and military forces' acting with near impunity even in the Kuliab area (south of Dushanbe), the residents of which dominate the government.

As in 1994, civil and political rights violations occurred throughout Tajikistan, even though there was a decline in the number of summary executions, disappearances and murders. In general, the government made no attempt to investigate such incidents or punish the perpetrators. In particular, a climate of fear and intimidation reigned over the Gharm region (northeast of Dushanbe) and in Kafarnihan (east of Dushanbe), where government forces continued to harass, detain, and abuse individuals, targeting in particular young men of Gharmi and Pamiri origin who were perceived to be opposition sympathizers. The presence of various opposition groups in the mountains of the Gharm region and a military build-up by the government there greatly increased tensions in that region.

Human Rights Watch/Helsinki received frequent reports of illegal searches of homes, as well as violations of due process rights of detainees, including the right to legal counsel, the right to a fair and public hearing by an impartial tribunal, and the right to be tried without undue delay. Many individuals detained even for short periods reported systematic beatings and torture in detention centers. In the Gharm area alone, at least six individuals died in detention or as a result of brutal beatings, torture, and shootings by the official militia forces. In addition, despite the announcement of several amnesties, the government continued to hold scores of political prisoners, and to detain without trial many who were arrested in early 1993 for having exercised their right to legitimate nonviolent dissent.

The government also maintained its suspension of opposition newspapers and continued to censor independent journalists. Editors of independent newspapers, who had already been practicing self-censorship, were regularly harassed by the government. As a result of the tight official control over the registration of new newspapers and paper distribution, no new journals emerged.

The Right to Monitor

Although more than forty associations and foundations have received official registration since 1990, including several dealing with human rights and women's issues, no indigenous nongovernmental organization confronted the government over human rights violations. Human rights were monitored by a small international community including several U.N. agencies, the International Committee of the Red Cross (ICRC), the Organization on Security and Cooperation in Europe (OSCE) mission to Tajikistan, and the International Organization for Migration (IOM). In addition, Human Rights Watch/Helsinki has had a representative stationed in Dushanbe since 1994. Despite unsatisfactory response to our written and verbal protests, government officials did not directly interfere in our activities and on numerous occasions acknowledged, albeit with reservations, the importance of our interventions. The ICRC continued to be denied universal access to prisoners. In general, however, the government cooperated with the UNHCR and IOM in the repatriation and integration of returnees.

The Role of
the International Community

The United Nations
Under the auspices of the U.N., further talks were held between the government and the opposition, with limited success. The U.N. Mission of Observers in Tajikistan (UNMOT), established by the Security Council in December 1994 for six months and later extended to December 1995, monitored the cease-fire agreement between government and opposition forces. The UNHCR played a key role in facilitating repatriation and in protecting the human rights of Tajik refugees and internally displaced persons (IDPs). But unfortunately, it also decided in September 1994 to reduce its operations in Tajikistan by late 1995, despite continued security problems facing refugee and IDP returnees, leaving protection and human rights monitoring functions to the OSCE, which lacks experience in such operations. The United Nations Development Programme (UNDP) initiated several programs to promote community development and to develop income generating projects for women.

The European Community

The OSCE mission to Tajikistan was established in December 1993 and became operational in February 1994. Despite its broad mandate including the promotion of human rights, the OSCE focused in its first year on legislative reform, evaluating a draft Tajik constitution and electoral laws, with limited success because of its inability to engage the government in a meaningful dialogue and because some of its efforts at legislative review occurred after passage of relevant laws. In July 1995, the Permanent Council of the OSCE decided to monitor and report on the human rights situation in the country, including the rights of IDP and refugee returnees. By October, however, the OSCE had failed to field the staff necessary to undertake those functions, especially with regards to monitoring the rights of those refugees and IDPs returning to the south. The OSCE also recommended that the government establish a human rights ombudsman and began reviewing a government proposal to create such a position. In general, the OSCE was reluctant to address individual cases of human rights violation, and as of this writing, it was unclear how the OSCE would be able to implement its human rights mandate without doing so.

Russian Federation Policy

The Russian government continued to take a special interest in Tajikistan. Several agreements between the Russian and Tajik governments significantly strengthened Moscow's economic ties with the republic and provided for greater military involvement. The reinforced 201st Motorized Rifle Division continued to form the bulk of the Commonwealth of Independent States (CIS) peacekeeping forces established in 1993. Despite their peacekeeping mandate, the forces are alleged by several sources to be involved in the hostilities. Russia also sought to safeguard the rights of ethnic Russians in Tajikistan.

U.S. Policy

The Tajikistan section of the State Department's *Country Reports on Human Rights Practices for 1994* described a broad spectrum of human rights abuses committed by both the government and the opposition. However, the report gave insufficient attention to the security problems facing IDP and refugee returnees in the south, an issue that would become particularly important as the UNHCR planned to turn over its monitoring and protection functions in that area to the OSCE. Representatives of the U.S. Embassy in Tajikistan frequently raised human rights concerns with the government and intervened before the government on behalf of victims of violations.

The Work of Human Rights Watch/Helsinki

Human Rights Watch/Helsinki established an office in Tajikistan in April 1994. Our goal in 1995 was to continue monitoring the post-war transition period and to urge those governments with interests in Tajikistan to condition military aid and non-humanitarian economic assistance on improvement in the government's human rights record. We also sought to engage the Tajik government, at both the national and local levels, in dialogue on human rights issues. We intervened regularly before the General Procuracy and the Ministries of Internal Affairs and Security on behalf of individuals who had suffered human rights violations, and briefed multilateral organizations, nongovernmental organizations, and journalists on the current conditions in the country. Intervention by Human Rights Watch/Helsinki in mid-1995 was instrumental in suspending the return of internally displaced persons from Badakhshan in the absence of sufficient safeguards.

In May, Human Rights Watch/Helsinki released the report *Return to Tajikistan: Continued Regional and Ethnic Tensions.* In September, we submitted to the OSCE a critique of the activities of the OSCE's mission to Tajikistan. A report on human rights violations in the Gharm region was in preparation as of this writing.

TURKEY

Human Rights Developments

Strong human rights statements by some government officials, the release of scores of political prisoners, the reform of an abusive law, and a reduction in the sheer numbers of political killings brought some improvement to the human rights situation in Turkey in 1995. Problems still remained. Free expression was still punished with arrests and imprisonment, torture was still employed as a routine instrument of police investigation, an abusive counterinsurgency campaign continued to empty Kurdish villages, and there were continued reports of disappearances. The most notable change was the October 27 amendment to the 1991 Anti-Terror Law. Under this and other laws an estimated 170 writers, intellectuals, and journalists were imprisoned for exercising their right to free expression. As of this writing eighty-two had been ordered to be released from prison, and all others convicted under that article are to have their sentences reviewed.

A multiplicity of factors influenced the drop in reported abuses. In its desire to achieve a customs union with the European Union, Prime Minister Tansu Ciller's coalition government—especially her junior partner, the Republican People's Party (CHP)—pushed for a democratization package and paid more attention to human rights concerns. Her efforts came to a standstill on September 21, however, when the CHP left its four year union with Ciller's ruling True Path Party (DYP). The same coalition was patched back together at the end of October and is expected to take the country to early elections on December 24.

There were some welcome positive statements by government officials, such as former Justice Minister Mehmet Mogultay's (CHP) April acknowledgment that extrajudicial executions do take place in Turkey and former Minister of Human Rights Algan Hacaloglu's (CHP) criticism of a deadly house raid. At the end of October Ciller suggested ending emergency rule in the ten provinces in southeastern Turkey, and in March, she ordered the Interior Ministry to guarantee due process to detainees, register prisoners in pre-trial detention to prevent disappearances, and remove "any equipment allowing ill-treatment (if there is any)." There was speculation, however, that Ciller issued the order to prevent publication of a report by the European Commission for the Prevention of Torture (CPT) based on its October 1994 investigation. Nevertheless, these orders, if properly executed, would go far to reduce torture. The changed nature of the armed conflict with the PKK was an equally important reason for the drop in reported violations. After four straight years of serious abuses (1991-94), however, it was still too early to assess the long-term impact of this year's improvements.

Serious problems still remain. The armed conflict between the PKK, the outlawed Workers Party of Kurdistan, and government forces in the mostly Kurdish southeastern Turkey, where most recent abuses have occurred, entered its eleventh year. The PKK, an armed group that has regularly violated international humanitarian law, certainly presented Turkey with a legitimate security concern, but the government's attempts to address that threat have habitually violated the basic rights of Turkish citizens. Security forces continued to depopulate villages forcibly in their counterinsurgency struggle against the PKK. Torture remained routine in most political cases, although the number of deaths in detention dropped. Reports of disappearances while in police detention or under suspicious circumstances increased. Death squad-style killings also remained a problem, albeit at a reduced level. For its part, the PKK continued to attack "village-guard villages" in which numerous civilians believed to be loyal to the Turkish government were killed or summarily executed, although also at a lower level than in 1994.

In January, Prime Minister Ciller vowed to bring Turkey in line with the European Convention for the Protection of Human Rights and Fundamental Freedoms, among other things by amending article 14 of the constitution, which broadly limits rights and freedoms that aim to violate the "indivisible unity of the state." In an April visit to the United States, she vowed to enact a "democratization package" that had stalled in 1994 in parliament and specifically mentioned changing article 8, a notorious provision of the Anti-Terror Law that punishes free speech and has sent scores of Turkish writers to jail. After weeks of debate, in July, several amendments to its restrictive, coup-era 1982 constitution were passed, the first time a civilian government—and not the military—has changed Turkey's fundamental law.

But the amendments that were passed, while increasing some freedoms, such as allowing academics and students to join political parties and permitting trade unions to collaborate with political parties (article 52), did little to address chronic human rights violations. The code of criminal procedure (CMUK), continued to allow political suspects to be held in incommunicado detention up to fifteen days in western Turkey and up to thirty days in emergency rule areas in southeastern Turkey, and is believed to encourage torture.

Freedom of expression in Turkey suffered notable setbacks in 1995, though the amendment of article 8 of the 1991 Anti-Terror Law may reverse this trend. The unamended article 8 punished writing as so-called separatist propaganda "regardless of method, aim, and intent." Although the mainstream press and television were often a lively forum for debate, some efforts by journalists, authors, and intellectuals to discuss the Kurdish issue, human rights abuses by security forces, or the armed conflict in southeastern Turkey were met with severe repression, including censorship, imprisonment and torture of journalists and writers, and the banning of newspapers.

Even Turkey's most famous writer, Yasar Kemal, was charged in January under article 8 for an article, "Campaign of Lies," that first appeared in the German weekly *Der Spiegel* and was subsequently published in the Turkish press. Other mainstream press figures also faced legal actions. In October, journalist-writer Ahmet Altan was found guilty under article 312 and given a suspended sentence for an article, "Atakurt," which posits the existence of a land called "Kurdiye," where Turks must demand their rights. By mid-1995, approximately 2,000 cases awaited trial under article 8 in State Security Courts. In August, the prosecutor in a case against ninety-nine leading intellectuals charged under article 8 for publication of *Freedom of Thought and Turkey* accepted the defendants' arguments that article 8 contradicted international conventions and appealed the constitutionality of the law to the Constitutional Court.

On October 27, the Turkish parliament passed amendments to article 8. Most importantly, the state must prove intent, a change from the old text. Sentences will also be reduced under the new amendment. Although not an amnesty, all cases were to be reviewed within a month; as of early November, at least eighty-two people convicted under article 8 were ordered to be released.

Both main pro-Kurdish dailies, *Ozgur Ulke (Free Land)*, and its successor, *Yeni Politika (New Policy)*, faced attacks and government censorship and restrictions. Journalists were detained, threatened, jailed and tortured under article 8 of the Anti-Terror Law or article 312 of the penal code. In at least one instance, on August 22, a *Yeni Politika* reporter, Sayfettin Tepe, died under suspicious circumstances in police custody. On December 3, 1994, bomb blasts struck *Ozgur Ulke* offices in Istanbul and Ankara, killing one and causing great damage. In February, authorities closed *Ozgur Ulke* under Turkey's press law. In August, *Yeni Politika* was shut down under the same statute; of the 126 issues that were published, 117 were confiscated and censored during its brief, four-month existence. Other radical, Kurdish, or left-wing publications, as well as the publishers of such material, faced similar obstacles.

Repression against Kurdish politicians also continued, although some of the imprisoned DEP parliamentarians were released.

On December 8, 1994, seven deputies from the banned Democracy Party (DEP) and one independent were found guilty on a variety of charges such as "participating in armed gangs," "knowingly giving comfort to armed gangs," and making "separatist" propaganda. Two, independent Mahmut Alinak and Sirri Sakik, were released for time served in pre-trial detention, while six others were given prison sentences of between seven and fifteen years. In October, Ahmet Turk and Sedat Yurtdas were released by the Turkish Supreme Court (Yargitay) with the ruling that they be tried again in State Security Court along with Alinak and Sakik. The court, however, ratified the fifteen year sentences of Hatip Dicle, Leyla Zana, Orhan Dogan, and Selim Sadak.

Party administrators and members of the People's Democracy Party (HADEP), the successor party to DEP, were arrested and put on trial for alleged links with the PKK and in some cases tortured. Five HADEP members were murdered in death squad-style killings during the first eight months of 1995, bringing to twelve the number of members murdered since its founding in May 1994. In June, legal proceedings were launched to close another pro-Kurdish party, the Democracy and Change Party, headed by the former head of the People's Labor Party (HEP), the party that preceded DEP, because the party "demand[ed] cultural rights for Kurds," which the prosecutor's office perceived as separatist. The chairman of the Democracy and Change Party, Ibrahim Aksoy, was arrested on his return to Turkey because of charges against him under article 8 of the Anti-Terror Law in October.

Death squad-style assassinations (so-called *actor unknown murders*) continued in 1995, albeit at a lower level then in the previous three years when a total of 1,242 individuals fell victim to such attacks. (In 1994, 423 people were killed.) As of September, there had been an estimated ninety-eight death squad murders. Targets included PKK members and sympathizers, HADEP party members and journalists, especially of radical or Kurdish papers.

During the past four years, substantial evidence has accumulated pointing toward collusion between perpetrators of death squad attacks, such as Hezbullah, a radical Islamic group, and security forces, especially in southeastern Turkey. Government efforts to bring the guilty to justice have been lax at best, with convictions in only a minority of the more than 1,000 murders. In 1994 and 1995, however, security forces arrested seventy-four Hezbullah members and charged them in at least seventy-one murders, including five of HADEP members committed in 1995. While these arrests were welcome, they have done little to refute credible allegations of police involvement in such killings or too explain the failure promptly and fully to investigate all killings. This spring, for example, a draft of a report prepared by a Turkish parliamentary commission on death squad killings and leaked to the press contained information alleging a connection between death squad killings and security forces.

The decrease in death squad killings is most likely attributable to the changed nature of the conflict, though the arrests mentioned above were also clearly a factor. After three years of almost non-stop armed conflict in southeastern Turkey, the political and actual landscape of the area where most abuses occur has changed radically. Pro-PKK villages in rural southeastern Turkey that were home to rebel sympathizers, one of the death squads' prime targets, have been forcibly depopulated. Active political life in the region, both legal and illegal, has also been curtailed, and many activists for pro-Kurdish parties like the banned DEP or guerrilla militants have either left the area, been killed, imprisoned, or gone underground.

Disappearances while in police custody or after being detained by unidentified individuals or those identifying themselves as police also continued. According to the Human Rights Foundation, in 1994 there were forty-nine such disappearances confirmed. The Human Rights Association of Turkey received 158 reports of disappearances in the first nine months of 1995. In

August, the Interior Ministry announced that a network of centers would be set up to allow family members to locate detainees, but it is too early to assess the impact of this announcement, with some reports indicating that the centers do not have access to information from Anti-Terror police units.

There were also six deaths in police custody under suspicious circumstances in the first seven months of 1995. According to the Human Rights Foundation of Turkey, thirty-four people died in police custody in 1994. Police officials often claimed that an individual committed "suicide," though autopsy reports usually indicated severe torture. Past trials against abusive police have been slow to start, lasted years, and ended in light sentences or acquittal. In at least one case in 1995, however, the Elazig Public Prosecution office in August charged eight police with torturing Sinan Demirbas to death on July 20. The trial is presently underway.

Police in Turkey continued to use excessive force in performing their duties in violation of both Turkish and international law. In mid-March, police in Istanbul fired into crowds of Alevi demonstrators, killing twenty-one. Although agitators from extreme left-wing organizations were active in the demonstration, and rocks, bottles, and molotov cocktails were thrown, the police response was not proportional to the threat faced. Alevis, members of a liberal offshoot of Shia Islam and an estimated 30 percent of Turkey's population, were protesting a March 12 armed attack by extreme right-wing groups against coffee houses frequented by Alevis and leftists that left two dead and scores wounded. The district police chief was removed from his post shortly after the shootings, and in July the trial of twenty police officers alleged to have used firearms during the demonstration "exceeding the limits of defense and obligation" began in Istanbul.

There were also several incidents in both southeastern and other areas of Turkey where police, the army, or the gendarmerie fired at vehicles at roadblocks or at individuals near military bases, alleging that they had not obeyed orders to halt. Several were killed. In one incident in early July in Tunceli province, so-called police special team (*Ozel Tim*) members fired wildly at civilians and civilian structures, causing damage and wounding at least one individual. After the incident many were reassigned, and it was announced that team members would receive human rights training. This was a welcome development, especially because special team members have routinely abused civilians with impunity since the units were organized in 1993.

Police also continued to kill suspects under suspicious circumstances in house raids. While in some instances police and suspects exchanged fire and both suffered dead and wounded, in other cases it appeared that all suspects were killed even though no armed resistance was reported. After a house raid on April 12 in Ankara left three suspected Dev-Sol (Revolutionary Left) members dead, the former Turkish Minister for Human Rights, Algan Hacaloglu, stated, "this is an extrajudicial killing."

Armed conflict in southeastern Turkey between government forces and the PKK continued, where combined Turkish army and police forces conducted major military operations against the PKK. The Turkish military also continued its policy of forced evacuations of rural settlements within Turkey to deprive the PKK of its logistical base of support: by the end of 1994, official figures put the number of totally or partially depopulated villages and hamlets in southeastern Turkey at 2,664 since the conflict started eleven years ago. While some villagers left for economic reasons and some—especially village guard settlements—left the area due to PKK pressure, most of more than 2,000 villages were forcibly evacuated by security forces. Torture, disappearances, and detentions often accompanied evacuations. While the government stated that villagers were removed for their own protection, the majority of cases indicated that forced evacuation was meant as a punishment for refusing to enter the village guard system or for aiding the PKK. There were also allegations of food embargoes, especially against villages in Tunceli province, by which security forces limited the amount of food villagers could bring back to their homes. Some village guards, a civil defense force that reached 70,000 in number, have been implicated in various killings and illegal behavior. In August, the former Minister for Human Rights stated that in 1996 some villagers would be allowed to return to their homes and would receive two heads of livestock and aid in rebuilding homes.

In spite of the PKK's December 1994 claim that it would abide by the Geneva Conventions, in 1995 the group continued to kill civilians, especially in villages that chose to form village guard units, to execute so-called "state supporters," to plant bombs in non-military targets, and to kidnap journalists and tourists whom they later released unharmed. Through August 4, PKK militants had killed at least fifty-four civilians.

Illegal radical leftist and rightist groups continued their activities. Dev-Sol executed imprisoned members and others on charges of "collaboration" with the state. The Islamic Great East Raiders Front (IBDA-C) was responsible for several bombings this year, including one in mid-January that killed two individuals including Onat Kutlar, a well-respected writer and journalist, and another in August that took the life of a Romanian tourist.

The Right to Monitor

Severe repression in 1995 impeded the human rights monitoring of both domestic and international groups in Turkey. Several members of the Turkish Human Rights Associations (HRA), a decentralized, membership-based group legally registered and operating in most of Turkey's provinces, including the Diyarbikir branch's secretary, Mahmut Sakar, were arrested during the course of the year. Many of those arrested reported being tortured and treated inhumanely in custody. Other members reported receiving death threats. The human rights group Mazlum-Der reported interference in its efforts to distribute aid to the displaced from south-

eastern Turkey.

The leadership of both the HRA and the Turkish Human Rights Foundation (THRF), which runs a documentation center and four torture treatment centers, faced prosecution primarily for their nonviolent expression. For example, in June, the former chairman of the Istanbul HRA, Eren Keskin, began serving a thirty-month sentence for an article she wrote calling for a cease-fire between the PKK and government forces; however she was released in November because of the amendment to article 8. In late 1994, the chairman of the THRF, Yavuz Onen, and research director, Fevzi Argun, were prosecuted for a book they published on torture in Turkey, and three members of the HRA, including its chairman, Akin Birdal, were prosecuted for publication of a book on Turkey's counterinsurgency campaign. Both trials ended with acquittals in January. In November, prosecutors opened another trial against Onen, HRF documentation chief Fevzi Argun, former Balikesir bureau chief Turgal Inal, and six others for insulting the laws of the republic and decisions of the parliament, under article 159/3 of the penal code, in connection with publishing and writing the book, *A Present to Emil Galip Sandalci.*

Police conducted raids on several HRA branch offices during the year, forcing several offices, including those in Diyarbikir, Mersin and Adana, to remain closed for extended periods of time.

In June, Amnesty International consultant Helmut Oberdiek was deported from Turkey while conducting research in Adana. In 1994, Amnesty International's Turkey researcher had been declared *persona non grata* by the Turkish government. Human Rights Watch was able to continue its monitoring in Turkey during 1995.

The Role of
the International Community

The European Union

The European Union and its member states took a keen interest in events in Turkey in

1995. On March 6, Turkey signed a "customs union agreement" with the E.U., which represents the closest link to the E.U. aside from full membership. However, the European Parliament must ratify the treaty, and it has insisted on an improvement in Turkey's human rights record setting three main conditions: passage of a number of constitutional amendments; abolishment of article 8; and the release of all DEP deputies imprisoned in 1994. In April 1995, the European Parliament stated that human rights abuses in Turkey were too serious to allow ratification of the agreement. In early July, the European Commission, the executive body of the E.U., issued an interim report concluding that, "the current situation in Turkey with regard to the rule of law and the respect for human rights is unsatisfactory. Despite the imperfections . . . its institutions are essentially democratic, secular, and pluralistic." The E.U. welcomed the passage of numerous amendments to Turkey's constitution in late July as a step in the right direction, but urged further reform and democratization.

The European Parliament has conditioned a positive vote ratifying the customs union agreement on improvements in Turkey's human rights record. A vote on the accord was scheduled for the end of 1995. While some members of the European Parliament were not satisfied with human rights improvements and referred to recent legal reforms as "cosmetic," both the European Commission and the European Council of Ministers were pushing hard for approval. In October, E.U. External Affairs Commissioner Hans van den Broek declared that a rejection of the customs union by the European Parliament could result in "a severe backlash in Turkey," where he said only Muslim fundamentalists are against closer ties with western Europe and that "there is now every reason for the European Parliament to approve the accord."

U.S. Policy

In 1995, the Clinton administration consistently raised human rights concerns, but also reiterated that those concerns would not outweigh Turkey's important role as an ally and a "big emerging market." Government officials, including Assistant Secretary of State John Shattuck, U.S. Ambassador to Turkey Marc Grossman, and Deputy Secretary of State Strobe Talbott publicly expressed concern about Turkey's human rights record. The State Department's *Country Reports on Human Rights Practices for 1994* was forthright in its judgment of the human rights situation in Turkey: "Despite the Ciller Government's pledge in 1993 to end torture and to establish a state based on the respect for human rights, torture and excessive use of force by security personnel persisted throughout 1994." Pursuant to a congressional request, the State Department, in consultation with the Department of Defense, issued a report on the use of U.S. weapons in Turkey's counterinsurgency and forced village evacuation campaign. The U.S. government estimated that it had supplied 80 percent of Turkey's military inventory. While the report did not acknowledge that a Turkish state policy existed to depopulate villages, its discussion of the abusive use of U.S. supplied weapons against civilians was the most compelling and critical statement on Turkey's human rights record ever made by the U.S. government.

The Clinton administration used encouragement, rather than punitive actions, to bring about an improvement in Turkey's human rights record. In February, asked if U.S. military credits would be linked with Turkish human rights actions, Assistant Secretary of State for European Affairs Richard Holbrooke bluntly stated, "I never said that. That is not something I am prepared to say." He added, "...I think it is extremely unproductive to leave the impression that human rights, while it is a major issue, is going to become something that would rupture the U.S.-Turkish relationship." In a June 1995 letter to Rep. Sonny Callahan, chair of the House Appropriations Subcommittee on Foreign Operations, Chairman of the Joint Chiefs of Staff General Shalikashvili underscored Turkey's "strategic value to the United

States" in an effort to head off congressional efforts to reduce military aid to Turkey based on human rights concerns. In an August 15, 1995, letter to Representative Lee Hamilton, (D- IN), Secretary of State Warren Christopher stated that, "Turkey's human rights record raises serious concerns, but we do not believe that it has engaged in a consistent pattern of gross violations . . . of human rights." Consequently, Christopher stated that the U.S. would not invoke Section 502B of the Foreign Assistance Act, which requires that the U.S. cut off military aid to states that grossly abuse human rights.

In fiscal year 1995, the administration proposed giving Turkey $405 million in military credits, but Congress slashed this to $364.5 million and then withheld 10 percent until the State Department presented the report on the use of U.S. weapons in Turkey mentioned above. Turkey refused to accept the 10 percent. For 1996, the administration proposed $450 million in military credits; in the foreign aid bill for fiscal year 1996, Congress slashed that to $321 million.

The Work of
Human Rights Watch/Helsinki

Our top priority during 1995 was to raise the profile of Turkey's human rights abuses and to insist that all available leverage be used to elicit human rights concessions from the Turkish government. In September, we testified before the Helsinki Commission of the U.S. Congress in hearings devoted to Turkey. In June, we sent a mission to Turkey to investigate PKK abuses and also the plight of Kurds forcibly evacuated from the southeast living in Adana, a city in western Turkey. We were forced to cancel the trip, however, after former Minister of the Interior Nahit Mentese turned what was to have been a private meeting into a press conference and made the continued work of the delegation impossible. In October, another mission was sent to Turkey to investigate torture and the process of application by Turkish citizens to the European Commission on Human Rights. Throughout the year, we followed cases of prisoners of con-

science, victims of torture, and disappearances in police custody, issuing intervention letters and press releases, which were distributed to policymakers in Europe and the United States.

TURKMENISTAN

Human Rights Developments

In 1995, illegal arrests of dissidents, elections of parliamentary candidates who ran unopposed, and the brutal dispersal and detention of the hundreds of residents who held the first protest rally in recent years confirmed Turkmenistan as one of the most repressive governments in the world. The campaign to discredit dissent took on theatrical proportions when the state charged that leading dissidents plotted to kill President Saparmurad Niyazov and labeled peaceful marchers "drug addicts."

President Niyazov, enjoying an uncontestable presidency until the year 2002, continued to rule his one-party state under the strict control of security forces and to suppress nearly all dissenting speech. In late 1994, four men reportedly associated with his political archrival, Avdy Kuliev, were charged with plotting a presidential assassination: Mukhammetkuli Aimuradov, Murat Esenov, Khoshaly Garaev and Khalmurat Soiunov. Esenov and Soiunov, who were arrested in Moscow on November 24 and 25, 1994, respectively, were cleared of charges for lack of evidence by the Russian Procuracy General on December 21, 1995. Garaev and Aimuradov, however, were extradited from Uzbekistan without due judicial review on October 28, 1994; on June 21, 1995, a Turkmenistan court sentenced them to twelve and fifteen years, respectively, in a strict-regime labor colony.

In early December 1994, Dyrdymurat Khodzhamukhammetov, co-chairman of Agzybirlik, a banned dissident political group, disappeared. It is not clear whether he was arrested or went into hiding. On August 10, 1995, the other Agzybirlik co-chairman,

Khudaiberdy Khallyev, reportedly was kidnaped, severely beaten and abandoned outside Ashgabat in a politically motivated attack.

On December 11, 1994, at the height of the political manhunt, the Turkmenistan government conducted elections for its parliament. Since all candidates were nominated by the president, the results, as reported by Agence France-Presse, were not surprising: 99.8 percent of the electorate voted, and all of the candidates won.

On July 12, 1995, a group of between several hundred and 1,000 residents held a peaceful march in the capital, Ashgabat, during which they distributed flyers calling for new popular elections and urging the police not to oppose them. According to one eyewitness, the protestors, surrounded by nearly as many police and secret service agents as there were demonstrators, proceeded for about an hour toward the presidential palace before the police began to beat them and carry them off in cars. In all, some 200 protestors reportedly were detained; roughly fifteen of them are believed to remain in custody four months later. The Turkmenistan authorities have not responded to requests for information about the charges against these individuals.

Abuses abounded in the wake of the rally. One protestor, Sukhanberdi Ishanov, approximately twenty years old, reportedly was badly beaten during interrogation, during which he incriminated at least one person as a rally organizer and apologized in a television appearance. Upon his release, Ishanov reportedly hanged himself; relatives who prepared his body for burial reported that it was covered with bruises, presumably from blows suffered during detention. Relatives who protested his death reportedly were themselves detained, interrogated and threatened.

Vladimir Kuleshov, for the last ten years the Ashgabat correspondent for the Moscow-based daily newspaper *Izvestia*, reportedly was interrogated and threatened with criminal charges by the Turkmenistan Procurator's office in the days following the march. In his coverage, he described the rally as a "protest march." (According to an *Izvestia* report of July 29, his interrogator objected, "We never had and never will have 'protest marches'.") On July 20, authorities reportedly sealed his office without a court order, and Kuleshov was forced to leave Turkmenistan. On July 18 and 25, respectively, journalists Mukhammet Myratly and Yovshan Annagurban reportedly were arrested on suspicion of involvement in the march, although authorities have failed to reveal the charges against them.

The Right to Monitor

The government finally registered the Russian community's independent advocacy group. However, it did so only on condition that the group become part of a government structure, thus depriving it of independence. Otherwise, there was no known attempt by local residents to monitor the human rights situation. On the contrary, some activists who previously had been willing to serve as sources of information asked not to be contacted in 1995 for fear of government retaliation.

The U.S. government's Helsinki Commission monitored the elections in December 1994, and the OSCE hosted a human rights legislation seminar in Ashgabat in September 1995, both without reported interference.

The Role of the International Community

The OSCE's September seminar in Ashgabat offered a rare forum for international concern about human rights in Turkmenistan and the region, which Amb. Audrey F. Glover, Director of the OSCE's Office for Democratic Institutions and Human Rights, used to advantage by raising concern over specific violations. However, the seminar suffered from a poorly chosen topic: "Central Asian human rights legislation" attracted almost exclusively mid-level officials and deflected attention from the point that in Turkmenistan abuses occur not because of inadequate legislative protections but because laws are inadequately enforced.

The U.S. remained the only country known to build human rights concerns into its bilateral agenda. However, it persisted in expressing concern only behind closed doors; thus, to the people of Turkmenistan, it seemed the U.S. tolerated widespread abuse as silently as did the rest of the international community. According to the State Department's April-June 1995 quarterly report on assistance, the U.S. kept assistance "moderate" because of "Turkmenistan's general lack of movement on political and economic reform." The State Department's failure to make its disappointment public, however—including shying from high-level diplomatic sanctions even when peaceful marchers were beaten and illegally arrested as they passed near the very gates of the U.S. Embassy in July—undermined the impact of limiting aid.

The Work of
Human Rights Watch/Helsinki

In 1995, we worked to break the silence on abuse created by censorship and nearly uniform international tolerance of human rights abuse in Turkmenistan. We held two joint press conferences in Moscow on political arrests, sent two letters of inquiry or protest to President Niyazov, raised concern in person about the welfare of specific victims at the OSCE seminar, and helped secure third-country asylum for persecuted dissidents.

UZBEKISTAN

Human Rights Developments

The government of Uzbekistan began a concerted campaign to shed the reputation of serious human rights abuser that it had gained in 1992. At this writing it remained too early to tell whether changes during 1995 marked the beginning of the end of state-sponsored human rights abuse in Uzbekistan or a mere toying with the trappings of democracy.

The government registered its first alternative parties in years and held a multiparty election and a popular referendum. It adopted institutional mechanisms for strengthening human rights and reached out diplomatically to its political opposition and to the international community far more than in previous years. These developments effected some short-term improvements, most notably the release of seven political prisoners: Pulatjon Okhunov, Otanazar Oripov, Inomjon Tursunov, Salavat Umurzakov and Nosir Zokirov (November 1994), Ibragim Buriev (April 1995) and Mukhtabar Akhmedova (June 1995).

However, the violations that earned Uzbekistan's government its stigma in the first place continued in 1995, including politically motivated arrests of political dissidents and Islamic leaders, violent abuse of opposition and human rights activists, cruel and inhuman treatment in pre-trial detention, violations of due process rights, refusal to register opposition parties and independent advocacy groups, and oppressive censorship.

The most dramatic improvements during the year were on the diplomatic front. The government welcomed the opening of an Organization of Security and Cooperation in Europe (OSCE) regional liaison office in the capital, Tashkent; began to engage in a joint project on human rights and governance with the U.N. Development Programme; in November 1995 reversed an almost three-year ban on Human Rights Watch's fieldwork by extending its representatives an invitation to return to Uzbekistan; and held high-level meetings in Washington, D.C. with Human Rights Watch and with leaders of its own political opposition, with whom there had been no dialogue in several years. These steps were welcome, but as of this writing, dialogue appeared more sustained with foreigners than with domestic critics: the scheduled follow-up meeting between the government and the opposition had not materialized six months later.

Efforts to promote human rights on the institutional level were also a promising sign but as of this writing had not yet effected real change. In February, the government created a human rights commission as part of the Supreme Council; in June set up a Commission on the Observance of the Constitutional Rights and Liberties of Citizens; and in August passed a law allowing any action or decision violating civil rights and liberties to be contested. These moves seemed to be mere window-dressing, however: the government liquidated the existing human rights commission, and the right to protection of civil liberties was already enshrined in Uzbekistan's federal and international obligations.

The government claimed—so far unconvincingly—that decentralization of political power was one of its prime advances. On December 25, 1994, it held what were hailed in the local media as the first multiparty parliamentary elections since independence, and on March 26, 1995, conducted a national referendum on the presidency. But these proved a sham. By June 3, 1995, the government had registered three parties other than the ruling Popular-Democratic Party, but did not lift its effective ban on the most vocal opposition parties, Erk (meaning Strength or Will) and Birlik (Unity) and refused to register a nascent opposition party, Adolat (Justice), indeed registering a much tamer party under that same name. Thus, while the elections were technically multiparty, differences among the party platforms were insignificant and the electorate was still denied access to the full spectrum of political options.

Moreover, the elections were held in an intimidating atmosphere. For example, Rashid Bekjon, a leader of the banned Erk Party, was arrested on December 11, 1994, reportedly in possession of flyers urging an election boycott, and was sentenced a half-year later to five years in jail on unrelated charges. Similarly, on March 31, one co-founder of the embryonic Adolat Party, Ibragim Buriev, was arrested on charges of, *inter alia*, illegal drug and arms possession, which were believed to have been falsified. He was released a month later, allegedly for health reasons, but also as a concession to

criticism of his arrest. Ultimately, 90 percent of parliamentary seats went to members of the ruling party, and in the March referendum, an implausible 99.6 percent of eligible voters approved extending President Islam Karimov's tenure to the year 2000.

Soon after the referendum, the other unregistered Adolat co-founder and a leading political opponent of President Karimov, Shukhrullo Mirsaidov, was violently assaulted for the fifth time in two years, allegedly by security agents. On April 18, he reported, he was kidnaped, drugged, stripped of his clothes, and photographed on video with a naked woman, presumably to discredit or blackmail him later, and his son was kidnapped and rendered helpless after being sprayed with gas. Saidov's unprecedented ability to hold a high-visibility press conference following the incident was a sign of the increased tolerance of critical speech the government exhibited for foreign consumption in 1995; the fact that the abuse occurred in the first place, and that no criminal investigation resulted, as of this writing, was a sign of how far the government would have to go to improve its actual human rights record.

Free, peaceful expression continued to be in jeopardy since publication of our last *World Report*. At the end of 1994, the government stripped American correspondent Steve LeVine of his journalist's accreditation and forced him to leave Uzbekistan, apparently because his writings displeased the government. Later in the year he was allowed to return to Uzbekistan but as of this writing, his accreditation had not yet been restored. On January 22, 1995, dissident Mukhtabar Akhmedova was arrested on charges of insulting a public official in connection with a letter she wrote protesting a government proposal to raze parts of the capital's old town. She was sentenced to four years in prison but amnestied on June 13.

Two cases indicated continuing abuse of criminal suspects during arrest and interrogation. On March 30, seven people associated with the unregistered Erk Party were sentenced to long prison terms stemming from allegations of involvement in a plot to overthrow the government. Reportedly, most were badly beaten during arrest and interrogation and forced to incriminate themselves and others. In July, two young women held in detention were intimidated into submitting to unwanted abortions, allegedly to elicit a confession. In a clear concession to public outcry, prison authorities released the women pending trial on October 5, and in late October reportedly ordered the head of the National Security Service (former KGB), the government agency responsible for their mistreatment, to take immediate, unplanned retirement.

The Right to Monitor

There was no reported interference in monitoring by foreign observers; on the contrary, the government actively encouraged such monitoring efforts. Domestically, the government augmented state-controlled human rights mechanisms at the same time as it continued to repress local groups and individual activists. The Ministry of Justice failed to register an independent human rights group for the third year in a row, despite repeated petitions, and effectively stripped the registered National Association "Russian Culture" of accreditation by making it submit a new application, which it then did not approve.

A small number of independent activists did monitor human rights this year, though at personal risk. To note only one case, Mikhail Ardzinov reported that security agents were probably behind the violent assault on him on March 9: two men knocked him down and drove off with his briefcase, but drove by again within minutes and threw it back to him. Trial monitoring equipment, notes he had been taking as he observed a political trial, and the iron rod he habitually carried with him to protect himself from just such attacks were missing from the briefcase.

The Role of the International Community

The European Union and the OSCE both made *démarches* during 1995 concerning the cases of forced abortion. The E.U. *démarche*, executed by the Italian embassy, was on the initiative of the Spanish mission to the OSCE, with strong support from Hungary and the U.S. On the basis of a June 12 decision, the European Commission took the first steps toward beginning negotiation of a partnership and cooperation agreement with Uzbekistan. In April, the OSCE created a liaison office in Tashkent, and that office conducted effective monitoring.

The U.S. continued to be the only country known to have kept human rights high on its bilateral agenda with Uzbekistan. The Clinton administration actively monitored human rights conditions, issued *démarches* and conducted interventions even as it welcomed the government's increased willingness to address human rights concerns. To highlight only one example, the U.S., working bilaterally and through the OSCE and the Congressional Working Group on International Women's Human Rights, vigorously protested the cases of forced abortion.

A visit in May by Deputy Assistant Secretary of State for Democracy, Human Rights and Labor Nancy Ely-Raphel, during which she reportedly raised concern about ongoing violations and met with activists, was followed by the signing of a treaty in June allowing U.S. citizens to travel freely within Uzbekistan. Through the National Democratic Institute (NDI), a government-funded organization linked to the Democratic Party, the U.S. sponsored the unprecedented meeting of official and opposition figures in January and again invited top officials to Washington for talks in June.

The administration also conveyed its distaste for Uzbekistan's practices by refusing to issue President Karimov a coveted invitation, although Vice-President Gore met with him in Washington, D.C. while President Karimov was in the U.S. in November for the fiftieth-anniversary U.N. celebrations.

The Work of Human Rights Watch/Helsinki

Human Rights Watch/Helsinki worked in

1995 to keep awareness of violations high, promote the work and safety of local human rights activists, and reverse visa denials for international monitors. In April and September, we wrote to President Karimov to protest the mistreatment of peaceful political dissidents and the abuse of detainees, and worked with the OSCE and the U.S. State Department to promote action on these cases. In May, the chairman of the Human Rights Watch/Helsinki Advisory Board traveled to Uzbekistan, in an non-affiliated capacity, and met with the Foreign Ministry and several dissidents to help reassess our monitoring efforts and pave the way for a full-fledged investigation. In June, our representatives met with the Minister of Foreign Affairs and Minister of Justice in Washington, D.C. to communicate concerns and help secure permission to re-enter Uzbekistan, which finally came in November. In September we launched a campaign urging that the two victims of unwanted abortions be released pending trial and that those responsible be prosecuted. As noted above, the women were released in October, and the head of the government agency responsible for their mistreatment reportedly was forced to retire.

FEDERAL REPUBLIC OF YUGOSLAVIA

Human Rights Developments

Human rights conditions continued to deteriorate in the Federal Republic of Yugoslavia (FRY) during 1995. Abuses against minorities, repression in Kosovo and Vojvodina, government efforts to limit entry or deny refugee status to Serbian refugees fleeing the Krajina region of Croatia and western Bosnia-Hercegovina and furthermore, press ganging large numbers of them to return and fight in the aforementioned republics were the most serious human rights abuses during the year.

After a number of military setbacks in Croatia and Bosnia-Hercegovina, which created an exodus of approximately 250,000 refugees headed for Serbia, the FRY announced in mid-August that all men of fighting age coming from Krajina would be barred from entering the country and would be redirected to the battlefields in Bosnia-Hercegovina. Reviews of their claims for refugee status were often rejected, and they were forcibly conscripted into abusive armed forces, as members of which they were likely to commit violations of international humanitarian law. Earlier in the summer, the Yugoslav police and army had arrested military-aged Serbian refugees in Serbia who were then forcibly mobilized by either the Bosnian Serb Army or, more recently, by notorious war criminal Arkan's paramilitary forces based in eastern Slavonia, Croatia. By June 22, the campaign widened to include even citizens of Serbia proper who in the past had lived or worked in Croatia or Bosnia-Hercegovina for some period of time. The scale of the governments's roundup was so large that it even prompted outrage within the parliament.

Serbian refugees and some Serbian citizens physically harassed Croats and Hungarians and forcibly evicted them from their homes in Vojvodina in reprisal for the Croatian Army's military successes in Krajina and western Slavonia in May and August, respectively.

The human rights situation in Kosovo—a region in the south of Serbia in which approximately 90 percent of the population is Albanian—continued to deteriorate. Shielded from international scrutiny, Serbian President Slobodan Milosevic's government intensified oppression of ethnic Albanians during the year. As of late 1995, eleven people ranging from ten to sixty-six years of age had been arbitrarily killed and eleven others wounded by the Serbian police and/or Yugoslav Army soldiers. There were approximately 2,400 cases of arbitrary arrests of Albanians by Serbian authorities, and thousands more summoned for "informative talks." Many of these individuals were beaten by the police; at this writing, over 200 were reportedly still in police custody under spurious charges. Serbian police continued to raid Albanian villages, conduct indiscriminate and brutal house raids without official search warrants, and arbitrarily arrest and imprison individuals. Excessive force and torture during detention were often reported. Forced expulsions from houses and apartments also continued to exacerbate tensions in the area.

A number of Albanians, particularly former government employees in the police and army, were especially targeted by the Serbian authorities during the year. During 1995, over 200 Albanians were reportedly prosecuted for, among other things, "acts of hostility against the state" and "jeopardizing the territorial integrity of the Federal Republic of Yugoslavia." In addition, some were accused "of forming a parallel Ministry of Foreign Affairs and Ministry of Interior Affairs, with the goal of jeopardizing the constitutional order and territorial integrity of Serbia and Yugoslavia." Many of the defendants were subjected to beatings and torture, were coerced into making incriminating statements, and were held for up to four days without the right to contact their lawyers or relatives.

As of late 1995, an estimated three-quarters of the overall number of formerly employed Albanians had been dismissed from their state jobs. The Kosovo Albanians continued to refuse to recognize Serbian direct rule in the province and established a "parallel society" and government, including "underground" schools, clinics and other civic institutions.

Approximately 13,000 Serbian refugees, many of whom had fled the Krajina region during the Croatian offensive or areas of northwestern Bosnia that fell to Bosnian government forces, were settled in Kosovo by the Belgrade government during the last quarter of 1995. Another 3,000 had been settled in Kosovo earlier during the year. This resettlement initiative served the government's longstanding goal of changing the demographic composition of the region. The refugees were given incentives to settle permanently in the region, including free land, jobs, credits, and in some cases Albanians' houses and apartments that were either temporarily vacant or from which Albanian tenants had been evicted.

The Right to Monitor

The Yugoslav government continued to obstruct international observers from monitoring human rights developments in Kosovo, Sandzak and Vojvodina, yet several domestic groups were able to monitor human rights in FRY throughout 1995. The Belgrade-based Humanitarian Law Fund investigated Serbian-perpetrated violations of human rights in Kosovo early in the year; the Belgrade-based Serbian Helsinki Committee and the Center for Anti-War Action launched a protest against the recently revived campaigns in Serbia to forcibly draft refugees. The Humanitarian Law Fund and the Serbian Helsinki Committee also interviewed Serbs displaced from Krajina and investigated expulsions of non-Serbs in Vojvodina. The Council for the Defense of Human Rights in Kosovo, the Kosovo Helsinki Committee, Albanian political parties, Muslim groups in Sandzak, and Croatian and Hungarian groups in Vojvodina also documented abuses committed against their respective ethnic groups, encountering sporadic interference by the government.

The Role of
the International Community

The possibility of a peace agreement for Bosnia-Hercegovina in 1995 contributed to European and U.S. leaders' reluctance to address the human rights record of the Yugoslav government and Serbia's continued material support of the Bosnian Serb army, which committed atrocities when it overran the U.N.-declared "safe area" of Srebrenica (see Bosnia section). Although Bosnian Serb leaders Radovan Karadzic and Gen. Ratko Mladic were indicted by the International Criminal Tribunal for the Former Yugoslavia (ICTY) in July, they continued to appear at Milosevic's side during meetings with U.S. and European negotiators.

Despite Milosevic's numerous past promises to the international community to seal the border with Serbian-controlled areas of Bosnia-Hercegovina and to cut all political, economic and military ties with the Bosnian Serbs, as well as U.N. certification that the border was sealed, the international press reported that the border remained porous and that Serbia continued its support for Bosnian Serb forces. According to a July 26 article in *The Independent* (London), there were frequent sightings of petrol, munitions, soldiers and vehicles with Yugoslav army registration plates crossing over from Serbia into Bosnia-Hercegovina. In January, according to U.N. representatives, more than sixty-two helicopter flights crossed the Serbian-Bosnian border, in violation of the U.N.-imposed "no-fly" zone over Bosnia. By exploiting loopholes in the border closure agreements drawn up by the international community, the FRY continued to provide important material and manpower assistance to the Bosnian Serb army.

On July 4, the *International Herald Tribune* (Paris) reported that Belgrade was, in effect, running the Bosnian and Krajina Serb war machines: in the aftermath of Croatia's offensive to retake Serbian-controlled western Slavonia, uncovered documents reportedly revealed that 300 officers were on Belgrade's payroll. Moreover, in May, a member of the Yugoslav Army's general staff—Lt. Gen. Mile Mirksic—was sent from Serbia as the replacement commander for the forces of the self-proclaimed Republic of Serbian Krajina in Croatia. In March, Milosevic sent up to 900 troops, twenty tanks, ground-to-ground rockets and other equipment from the rump Yugoslavia into the Serb-controlled area· of eastern Croatia. This was all carried out in presence of U.N. troops mandated to demilitarize the zone, who were ordered by their Russian commander not to block the movement.

At the end of May and beginning of June, after Bosnian Serbs took hostage approximately 400 U.N. soldiers, Milosevic's chief of security Jovica Stanisic was a ubiquitous figure at the Bosnian Serb-U.N. negotiations to bring about the U.N. prisoners' release. Stanisic's appearance in Pale just before each group of hostages was freed further underscored the view that Milosevic had never broken off his military and strategic support for the Bosnian Serbs despite a highly publicized feud with Karadzic.

At the outset of the year, the contact group—comprising representatives from the U.S., France, Germany, U.K. and Russia—agreed to lift sanctions imposed on rump Yugoslavia if Milosevic would recognize Bosnia-Hercegovina and Croatia and tighten its border with the Bosnian Serbs. Throughout the year, countless European—and more recently American—diplomats traveled to Belgrade, invariably attempting to convince Milosevic to recognize Bosnia-Hercegovina in exchange for a lifting of the international sanctions. Milosevic turned down such offers a number of times, insisting that sanctions be lifted first. Although the international community was not satisfied with his preconditions, Milosevic was able to score a fundamental political success for FRY: he brought an end to the country's status as an international pariah by linking his personal involvement in the Bosnian peace negotiations with the issue of lifting the international sanctions against rump Yugoslavia.

In November, the International Criminal Tribunal for the former Yugoslavia indicted three Yugoslav Army officers in connection with war crimes perpetrated during and after the fall of the city of Vukovar in Croatia in 1991.

U.S. Policy

Through most of the year, the Clinton administration's peace negotiators, led by Assistant Secretary of State Richard Holbrooke, continued to meet with President Milosevic to discuss peace in Bosnia-Hercegovina (see Bosnia section). Eagerly seeking Milosevic's cooperation in the peace process, the Clinton administration noticeably abandoned its longstanding policy, most clearly articulated by U.S. Ambassador to the United Nations Madeleine Albright, that the U.S. would not support a diminution of sanctions unless the Serbian government cooperated with the International Criminal Tribunal for the Former Yugoslavia. In fact, in late October, members of the Clinton administration suggested suspending U.N. sanctions against the FRY as an incentive for Serbia to cooperate during U.S.-led peace negotiations in Ohio. The proposal was quashed after protests from other members of the administration, notably Ambassador Albright.

The Work of
Human Rights Watch/Helsinki

Human Rights Watch/Helsinki continued to monitor Serbia's role in perpetrating human rights abuses and violations of the laws of war in conflict areas within the former Yugoslavia, and more specifically, its support for abusive rebel Bosnian and Croatian Serb forces and for individuals who have been indicted as war criminals. We also focused on the need for accountability to remain a key issue in the peace process and worked to condition the lifting of U.N.-imposed sanctions against the FRY on its cooperation with international efforts to establish accountability for war crimes and crimes against humanity in the former Yugoslavia. On January 10, Human Rights Watch/Helsinki urged the U.N. Security Council to reinstate sanctions against the FRY until it ended all direct and indirect support of forces committing human rights abuses in Bosnia-Hercegovina and Croatia and cooperated with the International Criminal Tribunal for the Former Yugoslavia. Human Rights Watch/Helsinki issued similar calls to the members of the Security Council on February 15 and June 2, protesting the international negotiators' proposal to suspend sanctions against the FRY

in return for Milosevic's recognition of Bosnia-Hercegovina and Croatia, without providing for FRY's cooperation with the tribunal. On July 31, Human Rights Watch/ Helsinki and twenty-six other humanitarian, human rights, and religious groups called for multilateral military action to stop genocide in Bosnia-Hercegovina, specifically to halt the Bosnian Serb offensive against the U.N. designated "safe areas" of Srebrenica and Zepa. The statement also called, among other things, for the stigmatization of Serbia if it could be proven to be directing, assisting and supplying abusive troops in Bosnia-Hercegovina, and the maintenance of sanctions against Belgrade until it cooperated with the investigation and extradition of indicted war criminals.

By substituting individualized guilt for the assumptions of collective ethnic guilt that now fuel the conflict, the International Criminal Tribunal for the Former Yugoslavia—the only existing fair trial venue and viable road to accountability—offered an historic opportunity to provide justice to victims of atrocities, possible deterrence against further abuse, and a basis for eventual peace in the region. In June, Human Rights Watch/Helsinki released a report critiquing domestic war crimes trials in Bosnia-Hercegovina, Croatia and the FRY, pointing to their politicization and lack of due process. The report also highlighted the paucity of trials in which members of the parties' own forces are tried for violations of human rights.

Human Rights Watch/Helsinki also focused its efforts in the FRY on monitoring and exposing abuses against non-Serbs and Serbian refugees from Krajina in the FRY. In January, we submitted written statements concerning minority rights in the FRY to the 51st Session of the U.N. Commission on Human Rights.

HUMAN
RIGHTS
WATCH

MIDDLE
EAST

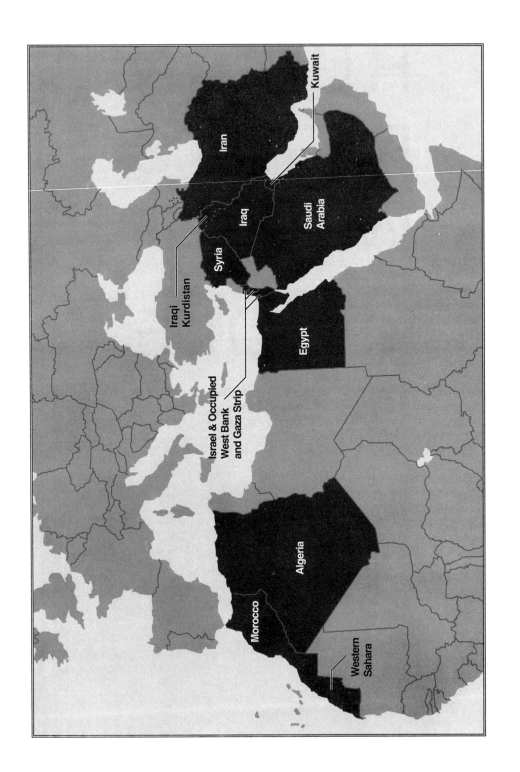

HUMAN RIGHTS WATCH/MIDDLE EAST OVERVIEW

Human Rights Developments

Human rights violations were increasingly out in the open in 1995. Many Middle East governments decided they did not have to go to great lengths to conceal abusive practices in their battle against Islamist opponents and "enemies of the peace process." With the international community largely turning a blind eye, governments facing Islamist opposition groups—violent and nonviolent— literally got away with murder. The violent groups they confronted were equally bold and bloody—deliberately killing civilians to punish or intimidate those who withheld support or were related, in any way, to the government.

The Arab-Israeli peace process, jolted by the assassination of Israel's Prime Minister Yitzhak Rabin, dominated the political picture. Elsewhere in the region the aftermath of international armed conflicts and unresolved internal conflicts took other turns, with northeast Iraq the scene of internecine warfare between Kurdish groups and a Turkish invasion; continuing violence in and around Israeli-occupied south Lebanon; Iraq's failure to release information on the almost one thousand prisoners unaccounted for since it withdrew from Kuwait; Yemen's actions to stifle criticism in the wake of its civil war; and more delays in the process to resolve the seemingly intractable dispute between Morocco and the Polisario Front over the status of the Western Sahara.

Nowhere was the conflict between an Islamist movement and a secular government more deadly than in Algeria, where tens of thousands died. Armed Islamist opposition groups in Algeria, as well as in Egypt and the Israeli-occupied territories, violated basic humanitarian norms by deliberately targeting civilians. But the response by governments to opposition groups, Islamist and secular, often failed to distinguish the violent forces from the nonviolent. In Saudi Arabia the government continued its crackdown on the largely nonviolent Islamist opposition, with hundreds of arrests. In Egypt, even nonviolent and nonpolitical organizations, including the nation's principal human rights organizations, were targeted as the government's campaign to suppress the violent Islamist movement was transformed into a blunt instrument to suppress criticism and to restrict political participation.

Elections did not in themselves mean effective political participation; opposition candidates in Egypt were thrown into prison, and in Iran, the lead-up to 1996 elections brought new restrictions on freedom of expression. Kuwait provided a human rights bright spot, with its signing of four international human rights instruments and abolition of its abusive state security courts. In Morocco, despite reforms that had brought significant improvements, law enforcement officials continued to engage in torture and due process violations. Syria's state security courts ignored defendant claims of coerced confessions, and sentenced nonviolent political dissidents to long prison terms. Despite promises that it would not adopt the abusive practices of its neighbors, the Palestinian Authority in Gaza/Jericho—at Israel's urging and with U.S. approval—set up a state security court to try militant opponents. Israel, in the areas under its direct control, continued to abuse the rights of Palestinians.

The commitment to accountability was tested across the region in 1995. Governments exhibited a disturbing confidence that if they rode out an initial storm of criticism the world would soon forget about abuses; whether it was Egypt's stubborn refusal to allow investigations of deaths in detention, or Algeria's cover-up of the Serkadji prison massacre, or Israel's hiding behind a statute of limitations in its domestic law to avoid investigating reports of the murder of prisoners of war by Israeli troops in 1956 and 1967—war crimes that should never be subject to statutes of limitations.

There was no letup in the ongoing

struggle between Middle East governments and Islamist opposition groups that called for dramatic transformations in government and society. Algeria was the scene of the bloodiest and ugliest conflict, in which thousands of civilians were deliberately killed or wounded, targeted by both sides. In Israel, radical religious parties, angrily opposed to their government's agreements with the PLO, threatened violence to stop the handover of territory to Palestinian control. The threats turned to action in November when a militant Israeli assassinated Prime Minister Rabin, after several incidents in which Israeli extremists murdered Palestinians.

Emboldened by assurances of continued political support, several governments in the Middle East intensified and broadened their attack on all who opposed the government, violent and nonviolent alike. Expanding the focus from militant activists to the political center, government crackdowns also targeted lawyers, human rights activists, journalists, intellectuals, and academics. Lawyers were beaten in Syria and forty-three were imprisoned in Egypt, some of them after torture. Political parties were banned and in Egypt candidates for parliamentary elections were imprisoned. The space for political activity or dissent was shrinking all over the region.

Nongovernmental organizations, from human rights groups to charitable societies, having emerged as a force to be reckoned with on the international scene, were increasingly restricted.

In Egypt, the Arab world's most populous country, the government of Hosni Mubarak paid little attention to domestic law, international law, or issues of accountability as its battle with the violent clandestine Islamic Group was paralleled by an expanding campaign to suppress the nonviolent opposition as well. Security forces operated with virtual impunity. Arbitrary arrests, long-term detentions, torture, hostage-taking, deaths in detention, and executions of civilians condemned to death without appeal by military courts were the main features of Egypt's human rights record. In a widely criticized move, Mubarak referred eighty-two Muslim Brothers, including former elected members of parliament and at least sixteen candidates in the upcoming election, to the Supreme Military Court for prosecution on political charges.

In Saudi Arabia the government beheaded an Islamist activist, the first Islamist opponent to be executed. He was convicted in a trial that failed miserably to meet international standards. Hundreds of other critics were arbitrarily arrested and detained without trial.

In Bahrain, demonstrations calling for restoration of constitutional rule and the release of political prisoners erupted in December 1994 and continued into the summer of 1995. While some demonstrators were implicated in acts of violence, resulting in the death and injury of members of the security forces and the destruction of property, most demonstrations were peaceful. When faced with peaceful protests, the security forces, led by former British colonial officer Ian Henderson, frequently used excessive lethal force. The government's show of force resulted in the death of at least ten protesters—including some who died under suspicious circumstances while in custody. Scores of protesters were injured when security forces used live ammunition to disperse demonstrators. Hundreds of suspected supporters of the protest movement were arrested, including Sheikh Abdel-Amir al-Jamri, a religious scholar, and members of his family. The only offense of many of those arrested appeared to be their call for restoration of the parliament and constitutional rule, suspended since 1975. By late October, while most detainees appeared to have been released, hundreds still remained in detention, including many who, after summary trials, were given lengthy prison sentences by the State Security Court. Others were summarily dismissed from their jobs.

In April, over 300 Bahraini women signed a petition calling for the restoration of democracy, respect for human rights and increased political participation for women. The government threatened the scores of signatories with the loss of their jobs if they did not withdraw their support for the effort, and subsequently some were dismissed or suspended.

Organized opposition groups continued to violate basic humanitarian law through deadly indiscriminate attacks and the targeting of civilians. In one of their bloodiest attacks yet, Algeria's Armed Islamic Group claimed responsibility for a suicide bombing near an Algiers police station. The explosion killed forty-two and injured over 200, mostly civilians. The group also murdered wives and children of police officers, teachers and other public employees. Militant Palestinian Islamist groups claimed responsibility for four suicide bombings that killed forty Israelis and wounded hundreds.

In spite of the acts of violence intended to derail the Arab-Israeli peace talks, including the assassination of Prime Minister Rabin and the attempt made on the life of Egyptian President Hosni Mubarak, ongoing efforts to negotiate and implement peace agreements between Israel and its neighbors dominated the political picture of the Middle East. Too often human rights issues and the principle of accountability were treated as irritants or obstacles to this process. While political resolutions to the region's conflicts are essential to improving human rights conditions, peace agreements and implementation plans must include at all stages human rights protections in order to have any hope of succeeding.

It would be difficult to consider the first full year of the Palestinian Authority's (PA) partial self-rule as a human rights success. While the transfer of authority reduced contact and clashes between the Israeli army and the 800,000 Palestinians living in the Gaza Strip and Jericho enclave, Israel continued to restrict Palestinians entering and leaving the occupied territories. In the West Bank areas over which Israel exercised direct control, human rights abuses such as arbitrary arrest, collective punishment and torture continued as in past years.

Meanwhile, in the Gaza Strip and Jericho, the Palestinian Authority made little progress in establishing the rule of law. The PA bypassed its existing civil court system and established a state security court to try mainly Islamist militants accused of violent activities.

As governments planned for the future peace, they were reminded—often painfully—of lingering unresolved legacies of past wars. Israel's occupation of southern Lebanon and the Golan Heights and Syria's 35,000 troops in Lebanon raised a range of human rights issues. The current and future status of Palestinian refugees required immediate attention; their precarious position was exposed when Libya expelled thousands this year, leaving entire families with nowhere to go.

The 1991 Gulf War continued to raise accountability issues. Five years after its invasion of Kuwait, Iraq had failed to account for the more than 900 "missing" Kuwaitis and other nationals rounded up during the invasion and occupation. Five years of U.N. economic sanctions imposed on Iraq and Iraq's refusal to accept the U.N.'s offer of conditional oil sale, have caused critical shortages of food and medicine and a dramatic rise in infant mortality. In northern Iraq, under the protection of an internationally enforced no-fly zone, rival Kurdish parties battled each other, killing or wounding hundreds in the process.

In Kuwait, the Bedoons—native Kuwaitis denied nationality—and Palestinian residents continue to suffer the aftershocks of the war. Collectively accused of collusion with Iraqi forces, they were subjected to a range of harassment and abuse, from heavy fines and threats to arbitrary arrest and torture, all in a concerted effort by the state to force them to leave Kuwait. For the Bedoons, this was a denial of their right to remain in, or return to, their own country.

In some cases governments adopted or continued the use of extraordinary procedures in the form of emergency law or state security courts, which by their very nature were abusive. Kuwait showed improvement in this area by abolishing its state security court, which had meted out death penalties and other harsh sentences in unfair proceedings that used coerced confessions and denied legal counsel.

In most other countries state security courts survived; in fact, thrived in their own abusive way. In Syria, for example, excruciatingly slow-paced trials of accused members of unauthorized political groups continued before the three-judge state security court. Many defendants had already spent fifteen years in prison before being charged and put on trial. Complaints of coerced confessions and torture were ignored by the judges and the accused had no access to lawyers of their choice. Verdicts could not be appealed.

In Egypt, an emergency law in effect since 1981 allowed the government to try civilians before military courts. But the expanded use of military courts to try hundreds of civilians, including leaders of civil society, caused an uproar of protest in Egyptian political and human rights circles.

Several governments encouraged the violent and intimidating activities of so-called vigilante groups supportive of government policy, especially when their actions were directed against known government critics or opponents. In Iran, the government did little to stop militant mobs from attacking, on two separate occasions, a prominent intellectual as he expressed his views on a liberal interpretation of Islamic principles. In Egypt a controversial court ruling declared a university professor an apostate because of his academic writing and ordered his separation from his Muslim wife. This decision was not only an outrageous infringement on the couple's rights; it could also embolden violent Islamist groups to attack them.

It was rare for states to openly confront or condone the use of torture. Most states claimed not to tolerate torture, despite overwhelming evidence to the contrary. A debate brewed in Israel over the government's controversial decision to allow increasingly harsh methods of interrogation, which often amounted to torture. In Iraq, where there was no such debate, a series of brutal decrees, advertised in newspapers, prescribed branding of the forehead and amputation for a range of offenses.

Prisons and detention centers, where accountability has life-and-death consequences, were often routinely used as centers for torture. Many prisoners died in detention as a consequence of torture or severe ill-treatment. Internal investigations were rarely conducted and almost never made public, doing little to show that authorities at a high level did not authorize the abusive treatment. In Egypt there was an alarming rise in the number of deaths in detention. There were at least two reported deaths in detention in the Gaza/Jericho area under the newly established Palestinian Authority.

The Algerian government not only blocked all independent investigations of a massacre in February at the Serkadji prison, it destroyed evidence, hastily buried the estimated one hundred prisoners without autopsies and prosecuted no one.

Across the region it remained difficult for human rights monitors, and at times lawyers, to gain access to prisons. There was at least one welcome exception as the International Committee of the Red Cross was finally granted access to Al-Khiam prison in south Lebanon.

Morocco's process of reform, which led to significant human rights improvements beginning in the late 1980s, stalled in 1995. Prison conditions remained abusive. The government did not account for all of the disappeared, or pay reparations to those who had been released from secret detention. Torture and due process violations continued.

Although difficult to track, use of the death penalty appeared to be increasing. In Saudi Arabia the government beheaded 192 people in the first ten months of 1995, most of whom were convicted of drug trafficking in secret trials with no appeal. That was more than in the two previous years combined.

Elections and preparations for elections were major themes in 1995. The Middle East needed no reminder of the critical human rights implications of an election process. The region's worst human rights disaster, Algeria, was precipitated in 1992 when a military-backed regime annulled parliamentary elections that the major Islamist party was poised to win. Algerians were due to return to the polls at the end of the year for the presidential election, in the face of threats against those who participate by the Armed Islamic Group. One candidate was assassinated in September.

This year human rights abuses were frequently associated with the election process. Governments often cynically manipulated elections and referenda to ensure victory, or validate their repressive rule, and the accompanying processes were riddled with violations of the right to free expression, association and assembly.

In Egypt, President Mubarak's preparation for the parliamentary election consisted of throwing opposition candidates into jail. In Lebanon, the Syrian government, with some 35,000 troops stationed in the country, apparently suggested there might not be the need for an election as long as the Lebanese government could amend the constitution to allow the existing president to serve an unprecedented third term. Despite an outcry from some quarters, the government approved the amendment and President Elias Hrawi began his third term.

In Iran's run-up to election scheduled for early 1996 the government restricted candidate eligibility and closed newspapers.

The U.N. came under sustained pressure from Morocco as it prepared for the referendum on self-determination in the Western Sahara. This threatened the fairness of the process and led to long delays. There were no delays in the September referendum in Iraq, when President Saddam Husein quickly called for a vote of confidence and received 99.9 percent of the votes cast.

The Right to Monitor

Human rights organizations, both national and international, were at the forefront of the struggle to hold governments accountable and to ensure compliance to international legal standards.

Those who had the courage to speak out in defense of human rights, criticize repressive practices, or monitor human rights conditions continued to face attacks from the government and violent opposition groups they criticized.

Two human rights activists were assassinated in Algeria, and as was the case in many of the murders there, the identities of the killers were not conclusively determined. Rampant political violence made any form of independent human rights monitoring an act of great courage.

Most countries in the region placed tight restrictions on human rights monitoring. Syria, which opened its doors to some international human rights organizations, did not allow its own citizens to monitor human rights conditions. Individuals or groups who were determined to investigate and report on human rights issues were tolerated in some countries as long as they did not cross certain lines, or were obliged to work from outside the country. Some were imprisoned for their work or killed. Although advances in telecommunication technology improved the efficiency of collecting and disseminating information from a position of exile, these groups continued to operate in the face of threats and ongoing harassment.

The large and active Egyptian human rights community came under sustained and aggressive attack in 1995 from the Mubarak government for exposing the worsening human rights conditions. Accused by the minister of the interior of "tarnishing Egypt's image," all human rights groups, domestic and international, faced restrictions, surveillance, interference, and a barrage of ridicule from the government-dominated media.

Human Rights Watch/Middle East requested access to Libya and Iraq in order to conduct fact-finding missions, but had not received a positive response.

The Role of
the International Community

The Arab-Israeli peace process dominated 1995 foreign policy objectives for most governments with interests in the Middle East, especially the U.S. and European states. But a double standard with respect to accountability politicized human rights issues, weakened the will of governments to respect the rule of law, and slowed progress. While certain states were publicly criticized for violations and subjected to unilateral or multilateral economic embargoes (Iran, Iraq, and Libya), abuses by "friendly" states were seldom acknowledged.

The double standard was clearly illustrated by U.S. actions and policies in the region: States that supported the peace process, or confronted Islamist militants were usually not criticized or held accountable for their own abuses except, to a limited extent Algeria. On the other hand, governments or groups referred to as "enemies of the peace process" and Islamist opposition groups were held to a strict standard and harshly criticized.

U.S. Assistant Secretary of State Robert H. Pelletreau could have been referring to most governments in the Middle East—especially Egypt, which receives $2.1 billion in U.S. assistance every year—when he described the situation in Algeria, "The government's reliance on repressive tactics has led to serious excesses by the security forces, alienated the Algerian people...[and] marginalized moderate elements of society..."

Many in the international community seemed to fear that the horrible violence that consumed Algeria could spread to other countries—Egypt, Tunisia and Morocco in particular. This fear muted public expressions of concern about government human rights abuses, sending a message that in the battle against Islamists brutal, arbitrary, and indiscriminate actions would be tolerated.

Governments battling opponents of the peace process were given the same latitude. This was the message delivered by U.S. Vice President Al Gore when he visited Jericho in March. He praised the Palestinian Authority for its use of state security courts, although he was well aware of their lack of due-process safeguards.

As human rights were downgraded,

economic objectives were elevated to a high priority. The U.S. government put enormous effort into winning Middle East contracts for U.S. businesses and promoting economic activity around the Arab-Israeli peace process. A U.S.-sponsored business summit held in Amman brought together more than one thousand business and government representatives. It remained to be seen whether governments and businesses in pursuit of contracts and profits will recognize their obligations to adopt socially responsible practices that defend and promote human rights.

With the human rights component to its foreign policy circumscribed by other agendas, the State Department often pointed to its annual human rights report as evidence of its continued importance. These generally accurate and comprehensive reports were valuable records of U.S. government awareness of human rights conditions, but they were no substitute for foreign policy action. The U.S. government's failure to use the findings of its own reports to hold governments accountable to a single standard of human rights behavior opened its human rights policies to accusations of bias and hypocrisy.

With the U.S. and other governments acting out of a combination of competing interests, the Middle East might have looked to the United Nations for even-handed assistance in defending human rights. But while the U.N. celebrated its fiftieth birthday this year, its performance in the Middle East was not a cause for celebration. Without the mandate or political will to resist Moroccan pressure, the U.N. risked losing control of its operation to organize a free and fair referendum in the Western Sahara.

In Iraq the U.N. was caught in a tragic dilemma; with the government of Iraq refusing to comply with Security Council resolutions, the U.N. maintained tight economic sanctions for a fifth straight year, and watched as Iraqi civilians suffered and died as a result.

The Work of
Human Rights Watch/Middle East

Through a combination of fact-finding missions, in-depth research, advocacy, and co-ordination with local organizations Human Rights Watch/Middle East promoted human rights accountability.

Human Rights Watch/Middle East's work in 1995 covered a range of issues from the government security force's practice of hostage taking in Egypt, to the institutionalized discrimination against the Bedoons of Kuwait. We examined the human rights improvements and shortcomings in Morocco since the reforms beginning in the late 1980s, and assessed the human rights record of the Palestinian Authority in its first year of in Gaza/Jericho self-rule areas.

Governments were not the only targets of our research and advocacy. The United Nation's failing operation in the Western Sahara was the object of a fact-finding mission and findings were published in an October report. A Human Rights Watch/Middle East delegation met with a Hamas spokesman in the Gaza Strip to protest the targeting of civilians by Hamas militants.

After years of making requests to the government of Syria, Human Rights Watch/ Middle East was finally allowed to conduct an official fact finding mission to Syria. The mission lasted seven weeks and included visits to several parts of the country and interviews with a wide range of Syrians. The first in a series of reports focused on the state security court, pressure on political prisoners after release, and torture.

Although priority was given to the monitoring of current conditions and rapid response interventions when the first word of an abuse was received, Human Rights Watch/Middle East also pursued issues of accountability for past abuses; for example, urging states to bring a case of genocide against the government of Iraq for its slaughter of Kurds in the late 1980s.

Human Rights Watch maintained pressure on governments all over the world, with particular attention to the U.S. and the states of the European Union, urging them to raise human rights issues in their diplomatic and trade contacts with Middle East governments.

ALGERIA

Human Rights Developments

Algeria was the scene of the bloodiest conflict raging in the Middle East and North Africa during 1995. Since the military-backed annulment of parliamentary elections that the Islamic Salvation Front (FIS) was poised to win in 1992, the government and the militant Islamist opposition have fought an increasingly ugly war that has cost the lives of thousands of civilians. It has also wiped out many of the freedoms and rights that Algerians had begun to enjoy during a period of liberalization that lasted from after the 1988 riots until the declaration of state of emergency in February 1992.

Precise data on how many persons have been killed, by whom and why they were targeted is notoriously elusive, due to strict censorship, the hazards of investigating the violence, and the fact that responsibility for most killings goes unclaimed. To complicate matters further, the sources of warnings and claims of responsibility cannot always be authenticated. Unofficial estimates place the numbers killed between 1992 and 1995 between 30,000 and 50,000. Often, killings were carried out in such a way as to maximize suffering and to terrorize others. The victims' bodies were often mutilated and dumped in public places.

Armed Islamist groups continued to kill civilians in blatant violation of the most elemental humanitarian norms, even if, as many believe, some of the killings officially attributed to them were carried out by criminal or other groups whose links to the Islamist movement were tenuous at best.

The targeting of journalists, intellectuals, teachers, and secular party activists and other visible social groups intensified in 1995. The twenty-two journalists and other media workers killed in the first ten months of the year brought the total slain since 1993 to fifty, making Algeria the most dangerous place in the world in which to practice journalism. Reporters lived a semi-clandestine life, sleeping in different places every night.

Scores of journalists fled into exile.

The targeting of civilians was pursued most avidly by the Armed Islamic Group (GIA). In March the GIA issued a warning that they would kill the women relatives of government officials and security-force members unless all women Islamist prisoners were released. Since then, bombs have gone off in residential compounds housing police families, injuring scores, and assailants have slaughtered the wives and children of policemen. The GIA also claimed responsibility for a daytime suicide bombing January 30 next to an Algiers police station, killing forty-two and injuring over 200, most of them civilian passers-by.

Most of the civilians killed in the Algerian conflict were neither professionals nor prominent figures. While some civilians were apparently killed on suspicion of being informers or for defying the material demands of armed groups, the motives in many cases remained obscure.

The GIA threatened to kill anyone who participated in the November 1995 presidential elections. One candidate was assassinated in September. Armed groups also continued their campaign of sabotage against public institutions, including schools, government offices, public-sector industries and public transport and telecommunication facilities. Armed groups set up checkpoints on the roads between cities, terrorizing, robbing, and sometimes assassinating passengers in vehicles they stopped.

In September 1994, the GIA had demanded a shutdown of the education system above the middle-school level. In July 1995, the minister of education stated that 958 schools had been totally or partially destroyed in attacks that he attributed to Islamist groups.

With growing constancy, FIS representatives in exile condemned the attacks on civilians by armed groups. (The FIS was outlawed in 1992 after its strong showing in local and parliamentary elections. Its two chief leaders were in prison in Algeria. The relations between the FIS political leadership and the armed groups remained nebu-

lous.) For example, Ja'far el-Houari, a member of FIS executive committee abroad, said in a September 14 interview in Le Figaro:

> The FIS and the GIA have nothing to do with each other. The FIS is a major political party, with a program, and figures who are known. As for the GIA, no one knows who's in charge....It's not a political party. It is not looking for electoral support. We condemn the attacks they claim, the kidnapings, and the beheadings of young women.

One exception was a statement by Anouar Haddam, head of the FIS parliamentary delegation in exile, who appeared to justify the January 30 suicide bombing by explaining that its target was the police station rather than passers-by. But Rabah Kebir, a member of the FIS executive committee in exile, unequivocally condemned the bombing. Regrettably, such condemnations had little effect on the groups that were carrying out the killings. Also, FIS representatives did not publicly repudiate the targeting by the Islamic Salvation Army, considered the FIS' armed wing, of civilians deemed to be working with the government.

Government troops also engaged in assassinations. There were reports of suspects being arrested and then turning up dead, with official news reports stating that they had been killed in a clash. There were also reports of arbitrary killings carried out by security forces that entered neighborhoods thought to be sympathetic to Islamists and executing persons who had no relation to the armed conflict.

Security forces were also responsible for disappearances. Families and friends witnessed the arrest of suspects, after which they could obtain no further information about their whereabouts.

The torture of Islamist suspects was common in interrogation centers. According to defense lawyers, judges systematically refused to order medical examinations of defendants who claimed their confessions had been extracted through torture.

In February, the government abolished the special courts created by a 1992 decree to try cases involving "terrorism" and "subversion." But the courts were abolished only after the decree's repressive provisions were incorporated into Algeria's criminal and criminal procedure codes. For example, the law now permits *garde à vue* (incommunicado) detention to last as long as twelve days in "terrorism" cases, an excessively long period that facilitates the abuse of detainees under interrogation. Lawyers reported that even this limit was commonly exceeded, with detainees being held for weeks under interrogation without having any contact with lawyers or relatives.

Another tool of repression is long-term internment without charge. The semi-official Human Rights Monitoring Body (ONDH) reported in July that 641 detainees were being held in Ain Mguel camp in the southern desert. Imprisoned FIS officials were subjected to other forms of abuse: Ali Belhadj, sentenced in 1992 for conspiring against state authority, was transferred between detention facilities without his whereabouts being disclosed, while Abdelqader Hachani spent his fourth year in detention without being brought to trial.

Despite claims by President Zeroual that abuses would not be tolerated, security forces committed excesses in a climate of impunity. Nothing illustrated this better than the aftermath of the confrontation at Serkadji prison in February that cost the lives of five guards and about one hundred prisoners. Despite evidence that vastly excessive force was used against the mutinous inmates, the authorities hastily buried the victims without autopsies, blocked all independent investigations, and prosecuted no security-force member in connection with the slaughter of prisoners. Another bloody incident at Berrouaghia prison in November 1994 was the object of an even more thorough information black-out.

The government required Algerian news organs to obtain permission to publish any "security"-related information, including all reports on clashes. Television and radio served as mouthpieces of the government, while newspapers that attempted to report independently on incidents or to report the views of Islamists were in several instances suspended or confiscated, their writers and editors hauled into court.

Authorities restricted political activity by the opposition parties that in January had signed a "National Contract" in Rome proposing negotiations with the government and a halt to the violence. Most efforts by them to hold public meetings during the year were blocked, and their activities were either ignored or ridiculed by the state-controlled broadcast media.

The abuse of women became a rallying cry for both sides of the conflict. Security sources reported that 161 women had been killed during the first seven months of 1995, in attacks they attributed to Islamists. There were allegations that Islamists had gunned down women merely for refusing to wear the headscarf, or for working in professions they considered "un-Islamic," such as that of seamstress or hairdresser. The Algerian press publicized the testimony of women who said they had been abducted, raped and enslaved by Islamist rebels, sometimes under the guise of a form of temporary marriage permitted by certain interpretations of Islam (*al-mut'a*). But it was impossible to gauge the scope of these atrocities, or to verify whether the perpetrators were in fact Islamist groups or common criminals. FIS leaders abroad repudiated the abduction and killing of women.

Women were also victimized by the security forces. Leading activists in the Islamist women's movement were taken into custody and their whereabouts not revealed. There were reports that security forces raided the homes of fugitives and, in their absence, harassed and assaulted female relatives. To cite one example, soldiers in the province of Boumerdes repeatedly visited the home of a fugitive's family, demanding to know where he was. During one visit in August, a group of soldiers confiscated all valuables from the home, and then several of them proceeded to rape the fugitive's wife.

The government fostered the growth of local civil guard and less formal "self-defense" groups in 1995. The civil guards were trained and armed by the security forces. Although created to help protect persons and property in rural areas where the military presence was light, the civil guards added a dangerous element to the armed conflict.

The Right to Monitor

The question asked by Algerians everywhere, "*Qui tue qui?*," surrounded many of the hundreds of unsolved homicides reported each month. In few countries was information about human rights as difficult to access, even though independent organizations were permitted to exist, and visas were issued to foreign groups. Obstacles to monitoring human rights included rampant political violence that made field-work dangerous and intimidated potential providers of information; strict censorship of security-related information in the press; and a thorough lack of transparency on the part of the security forces and the armed opposition.

Dangerous security conditions impeded virtually all data collection by Algeria's two independent human rights leagues, although they were able to issue statements critical of the government. The 1994 assassination of the president of one league, Youcef Fathallah, remained unsolved, and an activist with the other league, Abdel-Hafid Megdoud, was murdered in September. Also, in February, women's rights activist Nabila Djahnine, was gunned down in Tizi-Ouzou. The press reported that the GIA had claimed responsibility for her killing.

In July, the opposition parties that supported the "National Contract" were barred by the government from holding an open-door meeting in Algiers on the subject of human rights. The meeting was to have featured, *inter alia*, testimony of abuse experienced by women Islamists and female relatives of Islamists. Such testimony, if permitted, would have challenged the pro-government discourse that holds that the dangers to Algerian women come primarily from Islamists.

The work of the government-created Human Rights Monitoring Body (ONDH) simply did not reflect the gravity of security force abuses, although it made occasional allusions to them. An investigation organized by the ONDH into the incident at Serkadji prison completely ignored the central question of how one hundred prisoners were killed (see above). It was no coincidence that the ONDH-sponsored inquiry was the only one to receive any government cooperation at all.

In the absence of effective monitoring by established independent human rights organizations, ad hoc human rights networks provided a modest flow of information—usually about abuses attributed to a particular side of the conflict. A group of lawyers and families of prisoners assembled an impressive dossier on the killings at Serkadji prison. A network of activists with Islamist sympathies collected testimonies of torture, detentions and killing and published them in Islamist publications abroad and in the *White Book on Repression in Algeria 1991-1994*. Other groups collected and published sketchy data on the assassination of women and other abuses that they attributed to the Islamist rebels. But associations that tried to expose human rights abuses regardless of the alleged perpetrator were rare indeed.

The Role of the International Community

French Policy

French support for the Algerian government survived the change of French presidents and prime ministers. As the Western country most concerned by developments in Algeria, France lobbied hard to set the course of the policies of its European and North American allies toward its former colony. France reportedly resisted efforts to attach political or human rights conditions to the provision of economic assistance or the terms of debt restructuring. However, by year's end, there were signs that French policy was coming under review.

France was the leading exporter to and

the second largest importer from Algeria. It provides Algeria with US$1.2 billion annually in export credits. In late 1994, France sold Algeria nine Ecureuil helicopters, saying they were for civilian purposes. But the helicopters could be outfitted with rockets and night-vision equipment to be deployed against insurgents.

French policy was shaped partly by concern that an Islamist victory in Algeria would damage bilateral relations, radicalize the Algerian community in France, destabilize other North African countries, and spark an exodus of Algerians towards France and elsewhere. The continuing conflict has already produced some of these outcomes; visa and asylum applications from Algerians have surged in France since the violence began in 1992. (France has rejected the vast majority of both types of requests.) And in July, a wave of terrorist bombings began in metropolitan France that was widely suspected of links to the conflict in Algeria.

French public statements on human rights reflected a double standard. Senior officials frequently condemned atrocities attributed to Islamist armed groups, but refrained from criticizing security force abuses except when denouncing excesses by all parties to the conflict. The bias was made thoroughly apparent in September, when the ministry of interior banned the importation of a searing, if one-sided, report on human rights abuses by the Algerian government, committed mostly against Islamists. It said *The White Book on Repression in Algeria (1991-1994)*, published in Switzerland, might "disturb the public order" because it contained "incitement to hatred." France did not censor equally one-sided, graphic and disturbing material describing abuses committed by Islamists.

Although the "National Contract" proposal by the Algerian opposition was rejected emphatically by Algiers and received in a noncommittal manner by Paris, it obtained a more favorable response in other Western capitals (see above). It put the Algerian government on the political defensive for the first time since elections were canceled in 1992. However, Algiers was able, with much lobbying assistance from France, to negotiate three key debt relief deals during the next seven months, with private creditors (the London Club), public creditors (the Paris Club), and the International Monetary Fund.

French support for the Algerian government received minimal attention during the presidential campaign and Jacques Chirac's first months as president. The issue was forced onto center stage by the bombs that began exploding in France in July. At a July 23 press conference, President Chirac insisted, "French aid to Algeria was not aid to the Algerian state, nor a sign of any sort of approval toward it. It is aid to prevent economic chaos following upon political chaos." On August 29, Prime Minister Alain Juppé insisted that France "does not support the Algerian military," and hopes for "a democratic and stable Algeria."

Few observers accepted such professions of neutrality. There were, however, indications of French impatience with Algiers' failure to embark on a credible democratic process. Relations were strained over the handling of the hijacking of an Air France passenger jet in December 1994, claimed by the GIA. In April, before the French presidential elections, *Le Monde* reported plans to cut annual aid to Algeria by some 15 percent. And in October, the president's spokesperson said that at the approaching summit with President Zeroual, Chirac would underscore France's desire to see a "true democratic process" get under way in Algeria, including "unassailable legislative elections." On October 26, after the cancellation of their meeting provoked mutual recriminations, Chirac for the first time suggested publicly that it was "legitimate" to consider linking French aid levels to the "pace of the democratic process" in Algeria. As controversially organized presidential elections in Algeria approached, it remained to be seen whether France would become more forceful in advocating a credible democratic process.

U.S. Policy

United States policy toward Algeria was dominated by three elements: fear that the political crisis will spread beyond the national borders, the premise that its influence over developments in Algeria was quite limited, and deference toward France, the European ally that was most concerned about developments in Algeria and most supportive of the current government. Thus, while the United States position was more outspoken than France's toward human rights and the need for wider political participation in Algeria, it passed up opportunities—such as during negotiations over restructuring Algeria's international debt—to pressure the government to curtail abuses and broaden the political process.

The U.S. furnished Algeria with no military or economic grants or credits, although it provided loan guarantees for the purchase of large amounts of U.S. agricultural products. And the U.S. refused in 1995 to license the sale by U.S. companies of virtually all items requested by the Algerian government that could be used in fighting the insurgency.

On human rights, the United States on several occasions expressed strong disapproval of violations committed by the government and by Islamist armed groups. The State Department's *Country Reports on Human Rights Practices 1994* was blunt about the abuses on both sides, although quite limited in its level of documentation.

In his only major public statement about Algeria during the year, President Clinton told the incoming Algerian ambassador on March 20, "We have no illusions about the dangers of radicalism in the name of religion. We must be honest in identifying the sources of such radicalism, which include authoritarianism and repression."

Assistant Secretary of State Robert H. Pelletreau stressed this theme before the House International Relations committee on April 6. Countering the argument of Algerian officials that the armed groups thrive mainly due to help from abroad, Secretary Pelletreau told the committee, "The Government's reliance on repressive tactics has led to serious excesses by the security forces, alienated the Algerian people...marginalized moderate elements of society and empowered Islamic radicals who enthusiastically took up the fight."

The U.S. also urged the government to dialogue with the opposition forces, reacting favorably to, but not explicitly endorsing, the "National Contract" signed in Rome by the FIS and two other major political parties.

The U.S. distinguished between Islamist groups, noting that the FIS "has continued to advocate dialogue and a return to elections." In its contacts with the FIS, the U.S. pressed it to do more to disassociate itself from acts of terrorism, including those claimed by the GIA. The FIS's Anouar Haddam boasted that the FIS had resisted such pressures, and challenged the U.S. to prove that Islamist groups had in fact carried out any terrorist actions, according to *al-Sharq al-Awsat* daily of June 25.

For the government of Algeria, the main successes in the international arena during 1995 were the agreements it signed with the International Monetary Fund, private banks and state creditors to reschedule the country's US$29 billion debt. It obtained these agreements with no explicit political conditions attached to them. The U.S. went along with the rescheduling, but reportedly did not always go along with French efforts to secure for the Algerian government easier terms of repayment.

The Work of Human Rights Watch/Middle East

Human Rights Watch/Middle East worked to reinforce the efforts of Algerian human rights monitors during 1995. When our offer to participate in an investigation into the killings at Serkadji prison went unanswered, we issued a report on the incident that was based heavily on the work of the ad hoc group of prisoners' lawyers and relatives. We also organized three visits to the U.S. by Algerians active in human rights, arranging meetings for them with Congress, the executive branch, journalists, academics, Algerian-Americans, and nongovernmental organizations.

Human Rights Watch/Middle East also interviewed Algerians who had fled to Europe and North America about the risks they faced at home, and provided information to lawyers preparing asylum claims submitted by Algerians. We also gave press interviews throughout the year, particularly during the lead-up to the November 16 presidential elections.

In 1995, the Embassy of Algeria in Washington replied to the *Human Rights Watch World Report* section covering events in Algeria during 1994. The embassy stated that Algeria's police "use their weapons only in situations of legitimate defense." It denied the existence of death squads and stated that authorities "do not condone or tolerate the alleged use of torture." Human Rights Watch/Middle East replied in an open letter to the embassy in November.

EGYPT

Human Rights Developments

At the opening session of the Ninth U.N. Congress on the Prevention of Crime and Treatment of Offenders, in Cairo on April 29, President Hosni Mubarak affirmed that his government's fight against "th[e] heinous crime...of terrorism" was "within the framework of constitutional legitimacy and full respect for the principles of human rights." But these reassuring words corresponded little with the state's abusive actions.

Long-term detention without charge or trial, torture, extreme isolation of political prisoners in appalling conditions, a sharp rise in deaths in custody, and continuing executions of civilians condemned to death by military courts were features of the dismal human rights picture in 1995. The official investigation of the presumed death under torture of Islamist defense lawyer Abdel Harith Madani, in April 1994, yielded no

public information, and security forces harassed and intimidated his young widow in an attempt to force her silence about the controversial case.

The government prepared for the November 29 parliamentary elections—the first since 1990—by jailing leading opposition candidates and campaigners. The contest for the 444 seats unfolded against a backdrop of continuing emergency law and an unrelenting crackdown on the Muslim Brotherhood, the principal political opposition force in Egypt. The group, which was banned in 1954 and lacks official legal status as a party, planned to run 150 candidates as independents, in almost half of the country's electoral districts. The Brotherhood re-emerged in the 1970s under former president Anwar Sadat and, until this year's arrests, had been tolerated by authorities, its members operating openly in Egyptian public life, calling for the full adoption of Islamic law, and eschewing the use of violence. In August, President Mubarak used his emergency law powers to order the trial of forty-nine prominent Muslim Brothers before a military court, the first time in thirty years that members of the group faced military prosecutors. None of these civilian defendants were indicted for violent offenses. In October, another thirty-three Muslim Brothers, including parliamentary candidates, were referred to the military court.

In other developments, the state initiated measures to curb press freedom and control independent nongovernmental organizations (NGOs). Senior officials denied a pattern of rights violations and, instead, publicly excoriated the integrity of human rights organizations and obstructed their activities. Intellectuals and rights groups warned that a controversial court ruling in June, which declared a university professor an apostate because of his academic writings and ordered his separation from his wife, imperiled freedom of expression.

Acts of political violence punctuated the year, from the attempted assassination of President Mubarak on June 26 in Addis Ababa, Ethiopia, to bloody encounters inside Egypt in which civilians, members of the security forces, and known or suspected Islamist militants lost their lives. The clandestine Islamic Group continued its violent attacks against security forces and suspected police collaborators, and did not spare civilians when it carried out so-called revenge operations for security forces raids in which its members had been shot dead. It claimed responsibility, for example, for killing eight policemen and three civilians in four simultaneous attacks in Mallawi on January 2. In one of the attacks, the Egyptian Organization for Human Rights (EOHR) reported, armed militants stopped a pick-up truck and fired indiscriminately at the passengers. On March 22, several hours after an Islamic Group leader and two of his colleagues were killed in Minya, militants opened fire on police in a train traveling between Minya and Assyut; three civilians, two policemen, and one militant were killed in the exchange of fire.

Christians were shot dead in villages in the south by suspected Islamist extremists who went unapprehended. On July 8, pharmacist Khayri Fahmi Girges was killed in his field near Mallawi. Residents said that one month earlier Girges had received anonymous letters threatening him with death unless he reversed his decision to donate part of his land to the Coptic archdiocese of Mallawi. The influential weekly *Rose al-Yusuf* reported on September 25 that eleven Christians had been killed in Upper Egypt in September alone, all of them wealthy jewelers or landowners. The magazine criticized the news blackout about these targeted sectarian killings.

In an astounding statement, Interior Minister Hassan el-Alfi suggested that the state had the right to carry out extrajudicial executions of militants. "The security forces are very concerned about human rights," he said in an interview with *al-Wafd* on May 10. "During the past years, we have been very patient in our fight against terrorism. We could have annihilated the terrorists.... We found weapons and got full confessions from the people who are currently in prison, which

would have entitled us to kill them on the spot." Numerous extrajudicial executions have, however, been reported in recent years. In a report released on December 1, 1994, EOHR expressed "grave suspicions" that, over the previous seven months, eleven suspected Islamic Group members in Minya "were killed intentionally by gunfire shortly after their arrest, or when they were not in a position to resist." In 1995, known or suspected militants continued to be shot dead in raids by "anti-terrorism units."

Since 1992, military courts have tried and condemned to death civilians charged with acts of political violence in proceedings that have not complied with international fair trial standards. In 1995, executions were carried out swiftly after death sentences by these courts, with no appeal to a higher tribunal—in violation of international standards. Two men found guilty of the October 1994 attempted assassination of writer Naguib Mahfouz were sentenced to death on January 10 and hanged on March 29. As of August 6, forty-eight of the sixty-four civilians condemned to death by military courts since 1992 had been executed. The Egyptian Foreign Ministry informed Human Rights Watch in June 1993 that cases referred to military courts involved "terrorist groups that have committed the crimes of killing and harming public property, especially when committed on the strength of extremist beliefs." The trial that began on September 16 of forty-nine Muslim Brothers, none of whom were charged with crimes involving violence, was a significant departure from these stated guidelines.

Prison conditions, and an alarming rise in prisoner deaths, emerged as a major issue in 1995. Defense lawyers expressed extreme concern about inadequate food, lack of medical care, and physical abuse of political prisoners, particularly at new facilities such as Wadi Jedid, Aqrab, and Fayoum, where contact with outsiders was severely restricted or nonexistent. One attorney told us in July that he was permitted two minutes at Wadi Jedid earlier in the year to see Hassan Gharabawy, a lawyer detained without charge since 1989:

"They brought him to me crawling, then they told him to 'visit.' He got up, collapsed, and said: 'I do not want anything. I am dying slowly.'"

Authorities made it difficult for lawyers to collect detailed information about conditions and medical care at Wadi Jedid, first by denying entry even to those with official permits to visit and then by limiting the time with prisoners to five minutes. Visits to Aqrab and Fayoum prisons were prohibited. In August, lawyers provided us with the names of twenty-three prisoners who reportedly died at Wadi Jedid since it opened in February. One of them, thirty-five-year-old defense lawyer Mustafa Iraqi from Fayoum, was arrested in December 1992, tried and acquitted by a military court in August 1993, but never released. Authorities said that Iraqi died on June 20 of natural causes from a lung ailment, but his family and lawyer have not received a copy of the medical report. Lawyers reported that gathering information about these and other deaths was exceedingly difficult because families were intimidated by security forces and afraid to speak.

Continuing a pattern Human Rights Watch/Middle East has documented since 1992, defense lawyers who represented detained Islamist militants were subjected to intimidating surveillance, harassment and other forms of pressure by State Security Investigation (SSI), the elite internal-security arm of the interior ministry. Over forty lawyers remained imprisoned without charge or trial under emergency law detention orders, despite repeated court orders to release them, including Hassan Gharabawi (detained since November 1989), and Abdel Moneim Muhamed Muhamed and Shaaban Ali Ibrahim (detained since June 1990).

Stepped-up government pressure against the nonviolent Islamist political opposition began in late 1994. Journalist Adel Hussein, secretary general of the opposition Labor Party which works in political alliance with the Muslim Brotherhood, was summoned for questioning by state security prosecutors on December 24, 1994, on suspicion of links with extremists purportedly because Islamic Group leaflets were found "under his seat" on a flight to Cairo. He was detained until January 18, pursuant to the 1992 "anti-terrorism" amendments to the penal code. These provisions grant prosecutors the power to detain anyone for up to six months, without judicial review, for investigation of the vaguely-worded offense of promoting, by any means, the aims of groups that "seek to suspend the constitution or laws, prevent state authorities from carrying out their duties, threaten personal or public liberties, or harm national unity or social peace." After his release, Hussein termed his detention a "farce" that was designed to intimidate the political opposition.

The crackdown on the Muslim Brotherhood followed, beginning with the arrest of twenty-eight men, all of them active in public life, on January 23. They included former members of parliament Hassan el-Gamal, Dr. Eissam al-Erian (deputy secretary general of the Egyptian medical syndicate), and Dr. Ibrahim Zafarani (secretary general of the medical syndicate in Alexandria). There were additional roundups throughout the year. On July 17, former parliamentarian Dr. Muhamed el-Sayed Habib, geology professor and head of the faculty club at Assyut University, was arrested with seventeen others. On October 9, fifteen prominent figures were arrested, including lawyer Muhamed Gharib and parliamentary candidates Dr. Abdel Moneim Abul-Futuh (assistant secretary general of the Arab Doctors Union) and Mahmoud Hussein (treasurer of the engineers association), and other elected leaders of professional associations. All of the aforementioned were among the Muslim Brothers being tried before the military court (see below). On October 31, candidate Ahmad Seif Islam Hassan al-Banna, a sixty-two-year-old lawyer and bar association leader, was arrested with six others while campaigning in a Cairo neighborhood.

One aspect of the government campaign was to discredit the Brotherhood in the eyes of the Egyptian public in advance of the parliamentary elections. State ministries issued statements intended to link the Brotherhood to terrorism and violence, without providing specific information about the basis for the allegations. When 149 people were arrested at a summer youth camp near Alexandria on July 28, MENA (Middle East News Agency) said that the camp was being used by the Brotherhood, which it described as a "terrorist organization," for training "in violent physical exercises, karate, and Kung Fu....and teaching the terrorist concepts that depend on repudiating society and changing it by penetrating its vital sectors and recruiting its members to serve terrorism and extremism."

Brotherhood leaders countered with pleas for the right to participate without restrictions in Egypt's political system. "The government has arrested any Muslim Brotherhood members found distributing leaflets," official spokesman Mamoun al-Hudaybi said in an April interview in *Filastin al-Muslimah* (London). "The Muslim Brotherhood cannot organize a public meeting in a public place....How can we address the people if there are no leaflets, especially since the entire media is monopolized by the government, which exploits it to serve its candidates?"

The confrontation escalated when President Mubarak on August 31 ordered the trial before the Supreme Military Court of forty-nine well-known Muslim Brothers, including one *in absentia*. None of them were accused of crimes involving violence. But Interior Minister el-Alfi claimed that prosecutors had proof that the defendants were involved in terrorism. In an interview published in *al-Ahram* on August 26, he said: "It has been proven that the elements of the dissolved Muslim Brotherhood are involved in backing and supporting terrorism. The prosecution's interrogation of detained suspects has revealed this. Investigations disclosed many important things and substantiated evidence irrefutably." Yet, the accusations presented at the trial's opening session on September 16 were limited to nonviolent offenses such as belonging to a proscribed group, recruitment of new members, and

organizational leadership and fundraising activities. On October 30, the defense team of over sixty lawyers withdrew from the case. "There is not a single proof of criminal activity," one of the lawyers told the press the next day. "This is a political case that is not for a criminal court to decide." Earlier in the month, on October 15, President Mubarak referred another thirty Muslim Brothers to the military court. Sixteen of them were planning to run for parliament, some standing in for prospective candidates and former parliamentarians who had been arrested earlier in the year and were brought before the military court in September.

Press freedom suffered a major setback on May 27 when parliament hastily passed Law 93 of 1995, with only forty-five of 444 legislators present for the vote. The content of the new law—as well as the lack of advance notice and public debate prior to its passage—generated angry protests from journalists. The law amended the penal code, mandating fines and imprisonment for broadly defined offenses such as "publishing false or biased rumors, news and statements or disconcerting propaganda" if such material "offends social peace, arouses panic amongst people, harms public interest, or shows contempt for state institutions or officials." The law also cancelled statutes that prohibited the detention of journalists for investigation of press-related offenses, and it stiffened penalties for defamation and libel, while eliminating the burden on prosecutors to prove malicious intent. The government responded to the public furor with a compromise, deciding in June to form a special committee, appointed by the state-controlled Higher Press Council and including journalists, to review all press legislation and draft a comprehensive new law to present to parliament at the end of 1995. On October 8, the journalists' syndicate criticized the slow pace of the committee's work, warning that it would withdraw its representatives from the committee if a new law was not drafted by December 24.

There was increasing evidence of a coordinated government effort to exert greater control over independent NGOs and restrict their activities. In February, Cairo-based groups formed a coalition to call attention to moves by the state to challenge their legal status and interfere with funding from international donors. One area of concern was a legal memorandum prepared by the Ministry of Justice in January, that threatened the survival of NGOs that were registered as civil companies but were not profit-making enterprises. Some groups have used this legal option as an alternative to seeking status under the restrictive Law 32 of 1964 that governs private associations. The memorandum stated that such civil companies were in violation of the law—and subject to prosecution, imprisonment and fines for criminal offenses—because NGOs should be regulated by the Ministry of Social Affairs, pursuant to Law 32. The memorandum further stated that such groups could not legally secure funding from any foreign institution or individual. This ruling was reinforced by the Foreign Ministry, which in January called a meeting of funding organizations to stress that it was prohibited to provide grants to groups not registered under Law No. 32. There were also plans to create a government-appointed NGO coordinating council that would supervise the plans, activities and funding of the NGO community. These proposed legal and administrative mechanisms for greater control over the long term were accompanied by blatant interference throughout the year with activities scheduled by various NGOs.

The term "intellectual terrorism" was used frequently in Egypt during the year to describe the legal maneuvers of conservative Muslim activists against targeted individuals for their intellectual expression. Nothing illustrated this more dramatically than the case against Dr. Nasr Abu Zeid, a professor of Islamic Studies and Linguistics at Cairo University, who was declared an apostate by a civil appeals court in June and was ordered separated from his wife. The court's decision raised deep fears about the future of freedom of expression in Egypt because of the power of dogmatic religious forces to intimidate and silence intellectuals.

Dr. Abu Zeid, a Muslim, was first targeted in 1992, when a university committee voted to deny him promotion because one member argued that his academic writing contained "clear affronts to the Islamic faith." (This decision was reversed in May 1995, when the university council granted Dr. Abu Zeid status as a full professor.) Dr. Abu Zeid was targeted again in 1993, when an Islamist lawyer filed suit in the Giza Personal Status Court to divorce Dr. Abu Zeid from his Muslim wife, Dr. Ibtihal Unis, also a university professor, on the grounds that he was an apostate. In January 1994, the court threw out the case, ruling that the plaintiffs did not have standing. The decision was challenged before the Cairo Court of Appeals, which on June 14 cancelled the lower court's ruling and announced its controversial decision to separate Dr. Abu Zeid from his wife. The appeal court cleared the way for the decision first by ruling that the lawyers who brought the lawsuit had standing because the Islamic legal principle of *hisba*—any Muslim's right to legal action in matters considered harmful to Islam—applied in personal status matters, and then by declaring Dr. Abu Zeid an apostate.

The appellants cited Dr. Abu Zeid's academic writings, which they claimed contained heretical statements, to establish their case, and the appeals court agreed. Referring to specific passages from Dr. Abu Zeid's writings, the court found that his academic work "constitutes a direct attack against God's verses [in the Quran]." The court stated that Dr. Abu Zeid "denies the existence of devils and makes their presence a merely psychological matter in the minds of the first Islamic believers, and that the Quran merely acquiesced to their understandings and culture." Dr. Abu Zeid's writing indicated that he "refused to acquiesce to God's legislation, claiming that it is related to a specific historical period, and asking that the mind begin to exchange them with contemporary meanings that are more humane and progressive, better than the literal meanings," the court concluded.

"This dark medieval nonsense has to stop," wrote prominent sociologist Saad Eddin Ibrahim in a July editorial in the monthly *Civil Society*. EOHR termed the decision "unprecedented in the history of modern Egypt, that is, to separate a husband from his wife against their will, due to opinions expressed and adopted by one of them." In a July report, the Cairo-based Center for Human Rights Legal Aid (CHRLA) warned of the dangerous precedent set by the appeal court's acceptance of a case based on *hisba* because it "grants Muslims the right to file lawsuits in cases where, in their opinion, an exalted right of God has been violated," thus inviting "examination of the consciences of writers, intellectuals and researchers." Following the court's ruling, the clandestine Jihad Organization issued a call for the killing of Dr. Abu Zeid as an apostate, and added that anyone opposed to the death penalty for apostasy was himself an apostate.

Human Rights Watch/Middle East reported in 1994 that Muslim converts to Christianity had been questioned by the SSI about their religious beliefs and contacts with non-Christians, and that in some cases the interrogations had involved threats and violence, including torture. We continued to receive information about the harassment of Egyptian Christians by the security apparatus. On September 18, we wrote to authorities about the gross mistreatment, including sexual abuse, of a young Coptic Christian woman, who had been summoned for questioning by SSI in August and again in September. The interrogators sought information about her relationship with Muslim converts to Christianity, and the names of activists in the convert community.

The Right to Monitor

Tensions increased greatly between the state and the human rights movement in 1995. The government used the media and international fora to denigrate independent human rights monitors and reports, and the Interior Ministry escalated its direct interference with the activities of local and international human rights groups. In a February 20 written statement to the U.N. Commission on Human Rights, the government said that Human Rights Watch reports on Egypt "were based on lies and allegations circulated by terrorists and repeated by some nongovernmental organizations....[T]he aim of Human Rights Watch seems to be to publish false and biased allegations and bring some States into disrepute on a selective and unfair basis." This *note verbale* was in direct response to a written statement about cases of torture submitted by Human Rights Watch to the commission in January.

Throughout the year, Interior Minister el-Alfi criticized Egyptian and international human rights groups. "Unfortunately, these organizations obtain their information from offenders, weirdos, and people who have a vested interest," he said in an interview published in *al-Ahram* on August 26. He offered additional words of scorn following the release of EOHR's report on prisons, which was based on seventy-one visits to fifteen facilities: "The reports published by human rights organizations about prison conditions are sheer lies and fabrications, have no basis in truth and are simply aimed at tarnishing Egypt's image," *al-Ahram Weekly* reported on September 28.

The Interior Ministry monitored and restricted the activities of human rights groups throughout the year. Incidents included: instructions by SSI for the Egyptian Center for Human Rights and Consolidation of National Unity to cancel a conference on sectarian violence in Egypt (January); cancellation of a meeting at the Ibn Khaldoun Center for Development Studies for women's groups preparing for the U.N. women's conference in Beijing (May); cancellation of a previously approved training workshop sponsored by the Lawyers Committee for Human Rights and EOHR on the use of video technology (May); cancellation of a human rights training session by international experts for Egyptian lawyers, sponsored by the CHRLA (July); and the detention, blindfolding and interrogation by SSI of an EOHR lawyer who was on a fact-finding mission in Upper Egypt, during which time his notes and other documents were seized (July 13-15).

Although the internationally recognized EOHR celebrated its tenth anniversary in 1995, it was forced to continue operating without official legal status. It has appealed a lower court ruling that upheld a decision by the Ministry of Social Affairs to deny it registration as a legal NGO. In August, the High Administrative Court postponed until December 4 its decision on the EOHR appeal.

U.S. Policy

The U.S. was Egypt's largest donor and military supplier in 1995. As in past years, the country enjoyed special status as the second-largest recipient of U.S. military and economic assistance in the world, after Israel. The aid—$1.3 billion from the Foreign Military Financing Program and $815 million in Economic Support Funds—continued to flow, without conditions imposed for practical and measurable human rights improvements, despite the damning assessment of rights conditions presented in the State Department's *Country Reports on Human Rights Practices for 1994.* Following the release in February of the country report—which senior Egyptian government officials criticized as "lies" and "fabrications"—the U.S. Embassy in Cairo issued a comforting statement on February 11 that softened the sting: "The determination of the U.S. government to combat terrorism is second to none and our cooperation with the Egyptian government in this matter is extensive and of great mutual importance .... [I]t is important to emphasize that our commitment to the prosperity and security of Egypt and our close relationship with its government remain unchanged and strong." For the balance of the year, Clinton administration officials offered no public criticism of the human rights practices of the Egyptian government. President Mubarak was warmly received during his official visit to Washington, D.C., from April 1-5; regrettably, human rights were deliberately omitted from the agenda of his meeting with President Clinton.

The opening statement of Assistant Secretary of State for Near Eastern Affairs Robert H. Pelletreau to the Subcommittee on Near Eastern and South Asian Affairs of the Senate Foreign Relations Committee, on May 11, described Egypt as "our key Arab partner in efforts to achieve an Arab-Israeli peace and bolster moderate forces in the volatile Middle East." Secretary Pelletreau defended the Clinton administration's FY96 aid request by citing the mutual interest of both countries in "peace, stability, moderation, and development of the region," with no mention of human rights or Egypt's sorry performance.

U.S. Ambassador Edward Walker, in a lengthy interview published in the August 31 issue of the English-language weekly *al-Ahram,* also characterized the U.S.-Egyptian relationship as "very positive." He added apologetically: "We've had some differences in tactics from time to time, but that's very natural between countries, even with the best of friends like Egypt." The ambassador expressed concern about "the scourge of terrorism," and then offered this noncommittal comment: "You have to balance out the legal protection that people have in any society with the need of law enforcement forces to go after people."

The Work of
Human Rights Watch/Middle East

Throughout the year, we followed up on previous areas of research with advocacy initiatives—in Cairo, Geneva and Washington—designed to focus attention on SSI abuses and impunity, prison conditions, and the increasing reliance on the military justice system to prosecute civilians. We met in Egypt with human rights and other groups to discuss common concerns, including the state's intensified pressure on the NGO community.

In January, we released *Hostage-Taking and Intimidation by Security Forces* which documented illegal incommunicado detention of family members to pressure fugitive Islamist militants to surrender to authorities. The report also highlighted security forces use of arbitrary arrest, threats and other forms of intimidation to ensure their own impunity and silence family members from speaking out about cases of disappearance, deaths in detention, possible extrajudicial executions, and excessive use of lethal force. Soon after its release, SSI detained and pressured the wife of Abdel Harith Madani, who died in custody in 1994, not to speak about her husband's case to journalists and human rights organizations. In a February 10 letter to Interior Minister el-Alfi, we protested this attempt to intimidate the widow, and condemned the banning of a story about her harassment from the February 12 issue of the *Middle East Times*. In February, a Human Rights Watch/Middle East representative traveled to Cairo to gather additional information about the treatment of Madani's widow and discuss the case with lawyers, journalists and government officials. The government did not respond to our requests for meetings. In September we wrote to President Mubarak protesting the expanded use of the military justice system to prosecute civilians.

IRAN

Human Rights Developments

As international attention focused on Iran's criticism of the Arab-Israeli peace process, and other aspects of its foreign policy, inside the country Iranians were increasingly outspoken in demanding respect for basic freedoms. A few days before his death in January, the Islamic Republic's first Prime Minister, Mehdi Bazargan, who in recent years had been one of the government's most persistent internal critics, spoke of the suppression of political freedom and of "widespread, corruption into the very heart of the judiciary." He noted in an interview published in the West, "they never allowed this nation to breathe. All efforts to restore some liberty were crushed at the inception." Bazargan's words aptly described another year in Iran's long human rights crisis. The

government closed newspapers, imprisoned critics, forcibly suppressed protests, and condoned vigilante attacks against domestic opposition. Religious zealots from competing authorities interfered in people's everyday lives enforcing ever-changing rules of conduct.

The attack on freedom of expression, reported in *Human Rights Watch World Report 1995*, gathered pace. In a case that had a chilling effect on writers and creative artists, Ali Akbar Saidi-Sirjani died in detention under mysterious circumstances in November 1994. The coroner's report on the cause of death of this prominent writer was withheld.

Ayatollah Ahmad Jannati, a senior member of the Council of Guardians, denounced writers who, following the disappearance of Saidi-Sirjani, signed an open letter in October 1994, calling for an end to censorship. Speaking at Friday prayers at Tehran University, Ayatollah Jannati accused the writers of "spreading corruption," and warned them that if they continued zealous government supporters *(hezbollahi)* would act to stop them. The Council is a body of twelve clerics and experts in Islamic Law responsible for ensuring that legislation comports with Islamic principles and the Constitution of the Islamic Republic.

In December 1994, 500 journalists joined the writers' protest against censorship, objecting in particular to the summary closure of newspapers by the authorities. Nevertheless, in February 1995, the Press Supervisory Board, a government dominated body, ordered the closure of the *Jahan-e Eslam* newspaper for "acting against the security of the state, and tarnishing officials." The closure arose out of a serialized interview with former Interior Minister Ali Akbar Mohtashemi, which was highly critical of the policies of president Rafsanjani. In March, the literary journal *Takapou* was accused of violating Islamic values and closed. In August, the government closed *Payam-e Daneshju,* a weekly news magazine, also associated with the critics of the president. The magazine had gained a large circulation because of its reporting on allegations of widespread corruption within the government, and within the *Bonyad-e Mostazafin*, a foundation closely associated with the government. In October, a provincial daily, *Tous*, was closed for violating laws on defamation in its criticism of the government.

The government carried out these newspaper closures in apparent violation of press laws requiring charges against the media to be brought before a court. The government submitted the draft of a new press law to the parliament *(Majles)* in June. The new law would provide the Ministry of Islamic Guidance with powers to order the closure of publications without the need for prior court approval, thus writing into law the ministry's de-facto powers. The banned but active opposition group, the Freedom Movement of Iran, criticized the draft law because it would allow the executive to encroach on the powers of the judiciary, and would further restrict the freedom of the press.

In violation of constitutional prohibitions on government ownership of newspapers, government officials began publication of two new newspapers, *Iran* and *Akhbar*.

Restrictions on freedom of expression also extended to the cinema industry. In June, 214 filmmakers signed an open letter to the government calling for the lifting of government's restrictions on the industry. The filmmakers complained of bureaucratic interference in scripts, production, funding and distribution. The Ministry of Islamic Guidance responded to these protests by announcing at the end of June that it would ban the export of films portraying a "negative image of life in Iran." In recent years, Iranian films have won acclaim at international film festivals, but the ministry stated that these films "lack a national and Islamic identity."

In a sinister development, threatening to stifle the free exchange of ideas, hezbollahi mobs attacked intellectual Abdol Karim Soroush as he was giving a speech in Isfahan, in July, and again in Tehran in October. On both occasions, scores of youths opposed to the philosopher's ideas disrupted his scheduled university lectures, preventing him from speaking. Dr. Soroush had been criticized for his liberal interpretation of Islamic principles. The attack on Soroush followed criticism made in September by Spiritual Leader Ali Khamenei, who chided unnamed intellectuals for unjustly criticizing the clergy and "earning a living on Islam." In July, following the first attack on Soroush, 107 professors sent an open letter to President Rafsanjani urging him to uphold the constitution, and to prevent such illegal interference in people's rights.

Vigilante violence continued throughout the year, encouraged by state officials and religious spokesmen. In July, a mob attacked the memorial service for Dr. Karim Sanjabi, a leader of the National Front, and a former minister in the transitional government of Mehdi Bazargan. The authorities took no action to restrain the attackers or to pursue and prosecute them after the event.

In August, the Morgh Amin bookstore in Tehran was firebombed because it had published a book condemned by some as un-Islamic. The burning of the bookstore sparked a controversy in the press as hard-liners, like Ayatollah Jannati, praised the actions of those who burnt the store, saying that they had only done what the authorities should have done. This brought a response from supporters of president Rafsanjani, "How can a man who is a member of the legislature encourage thugs to take the law into their own hands." Others within the government responded that it was the testament of Ayatollah Khomeini that the hezbollahi should take up the task of protecting Islam whenever the authorities failed. When *Salam* newspaper entered the fray, accusing Ayatollah Jannati of "encouraging anarchy," a mob gathered outside the newspaper offices shouting "death to the enemies of Islam." In September, more than forty publishers sent an open letter to president Rafsanjani calling on the government to "deal legally with anti-cultural elements and book burners."

The president's critics were not the

only Iranians resorting to officially-sponsored vigilantism. Clerics had written an open letter to Ayatollah Khamenei in August, *Salam* newspaper reported, protesting that supporters of president Rafsanjani had formed gangs of thugs who "drove from their pulpits" Friday prayer leaders critical of government policies. Also in August, government supporters prevented Ayatollah Mohtashemi from making a speech at Tehran University.

The forthcoming elections were increasingly the focus of opposition statements. The opposition Freedom Movement called on Iranians to participate in the elections, and to change the government through the ballot box. However, in August, the authorities reconfirmed the ban on the Freedom Movement as an organization whose activities "are not in accordance with the Iranian Constitution." The authorities took no measures to secure meetings and activities organized by the Freedom Movement from attack by mobs.

The continuing economic crisis contributed to social unrest. In April residents of a shantytown in the Islamshahr suburb of Tehran demonstrated against increases in bus fares. According to Amnesty International, security forces fired on the crowd, killing up to ten people. Revolutionary Guards detained hundreds of people after the demonstration. Golam Hossein Rahbarpour, head of the Revolutionary Courts in Tehran, announced in June that fifty of the demonstrators would go on public trial before Revolutionary Courts. Nevertheless, the detainees were held incommunicado, and without charges. In response to the Islamshahr disturbances, the government was reported to have conducted military maneuvers, and formed a rapid reaction force "to crush the enemies of Islam," according to journalist Safa Ha'eri.

In July, *Salam* newspaper reported a strike by workers at the Benz Khavar auto manufacturing plant in Islamshahr. The workers' demands for increased pay were met by the deployment of troops around the factory, who broke up the demonstration after three days. The opposition Iran Nation Party reported that some of the strikers were detained, and would face trial before Revolutionary Courts. In August, workers in a privatized textile factory in Ghaemshahr, in northern Iran, staged a protest against job lay-offs. Again, Revolutionary Guards forcibly broke up the protest.

Intrusive restrictions on everyday life continued. In January, the Majles passed a law banning the possession of satellite television dishes. The law, which came into effect in March, stipulated that violators would be fined up to $2,000. The new law also gave a pretext for security forces to enter private houses to search for outlawed satellite equipment.

In September, Ayatollah Khamenei issued a *fatwa* stating that, "teaching young people to read and play music makes them depraved and leads to corruption." In accordance with the ruling, Tehran's largest public-funded cultural center canceled its music classes. However, private music schools continued to function.

In September, Ayatollah Jannati urged zealous Muslims to block traffic if they saw wedding parties that did not conform to Islamic norms. According to Reuters, the radical legislator was apparently referring to brides who appeared in public in western-style bridal gowns.

The activities of extra-governmental enforcers of Islamic orthodoxy became more prominent throughout the year, increasing the likelihood of interference in the daily life of citizens. Women continued to be hounded to comply with petty restrictions. In May, police authorities began implementation of a decree prohibiting women from riding in the front seat of taxis. More than 120 shops in northern Tehran were closed for selling female clothing "incompatible with the norms of the Islamic Republic." Detention of women for failure to observe a rigid dress code continued, but enforcement was inconsistent and unpredictable. In an interview with *Aftab-Gardoun* magazine in June, president Rafsanjani urged women to accept the "limitations" nature had imposed on them.

In May, according to *Salam* newspaper, a new court system was introduced in Tehran, in accordance with the decision to unify criminal courts within a system of General Courts *(Dadgahayeh Aam)*. The introduction of the new system brought chaos as inexperienced judges were given responsibility over both investigation and judgment, undermining legal safeguards. The government dealt severely with those who criticized the new system. Dr. Javad Tabatabai, deputy-dean of Tehran University Law School, was dismissed after criticizing the new courts. Students declared a strike to protest his removal.

In an unusual development, three women accused of the murder of Christian leaders in 1994, were brought to trial in public before Revolutionary Court. Proceedings before such courts almost invariably take place in secret. The motivation of the authorities to hold this trial in public appeared to be political, as the authorities sought to place responsibility for the killings on the violent opposition group, the People's Mojahedine Organization of Iran (PMOI). At the hearing in September, the women confessed to the murder of Protestant pastor Tateos Michaelian. The women's confessions, emphasizing their connection to the PMOI, were televised. Other unusual aspects of this trial were that the women were assigned lawyers—lawyers are normally banned from Revolutionary Courts—and the hearings were open to observers, including Western diplomats.

There were reports that political opponents of the government were sentenced to death, especially in the Kurdish areas in the northwestern provinces. For example, in September, according to the Kurdish Democratic Party of Iran, which advocates armed revolt, six of its supporters were executed in Orumieh Prison. Also in September, the Organization of Iranian People's Fedaian (Majority) announced the execution of one of its supporters in Langrud. Violent clashes between armed government opponents and the security forces continued to take place in the Kurdish areas, and in Sistan va Baluchestan province in the southeast.

Iran has long provided a haven to millions of refugees from the conflict in Afghanistan, with little assistance from the international community. In a draconian plan, the government announced that all of the estimated 1.6 million refugees must leave Iran by March 1997, inducing them to leave by refusing to renew their residency or work permits. The government's resolve to eject its Afghan population was not weakened by the continuing conflict in Afghanistan, from which the refugees had originally fled.

The government enhanced its joint security agreement with Turkey, which led in August to an exchange of dissidents, in violation of the international prohibition on *refoulement*. Iran handed over thirty-four opponents of the Turkish government and received fourteen Iranian dissidents in return. While an Interior Ministry spokesman, Ali Reza Barati, stated that cooperation with Turkey "to eradicate terrorism" would continue, these exchanges raise grave concerns about the security of Iranian refugees in Turkey who were compelled to go through processing by Turkish police in order to obtain refugee status.

The Right to Monitor

The government denied access to independent international human rights organizations, and for the forth consecutive year, the U.N. special representative on the human rights situation in Iran was not allowed to visit Iran. Domestic human rights activity was limited to government controlled groups. Human rights bodies like the Parliamentary Human Rights Committee, the Organization for Defending Victims of Violence, which was associated with the Ministry of Foreign Affairs, and the newly established Human Rights Commission within the judicial branch operate in Iran, but their activities did not substitute for independent monitoring or reporting. Nevertheless, this year saw an increasing number of groups and individuals voice public criticism of the government. In January, Grand Ayatollah Sadeq Rouhani, one of Shi'ism's pre-eminent clerical leaders, wrote an open letter to President Rafsanjani stating that life in Iran had become "unbearable for those who abide by the true principles of our Islamic faith." Grand Ayatollah Rouhani stated that he wished to leave Iran because his life was at risk from "armed criminals." In a long letter, published in London by the Arabic daily *Ash-Sharq Al-Awsat,* Grand Ayatollah Rouhani criticized specific government practices, including night raids on private houses on the pretext of searching for alcohol, and confiscation of property without due process of law.

In a second open letter in June, Grand Ayatollah Rouhani criticized arbitrary detention, beatings of prisoners and extrajudicial executions. In apparent response to Rouhani's statements, the security forces detained twenty-five of his followers in Qom in July, including his 26-year-old son, Javad. The detainees were held in an unknown location, and the authorities did not announce the charges on which they were being held. Grand Ayatollah Rouhani's movements were restricted by the authorities, as were those of other senior clerics, including Ayatollah Montazeri, the former designated successor to the Leader of the Islamic Republic. Many clerics joined in protests against these actions.

Secular critics were also active in 1995. Retired general Azizollah Amir Rahimi continued to voice dissent, even after his release from prison in March. Former minister, Dariush Foruhar openly challenged the authorities in a July telephone interview with the independent Paris-based news agency, Iranian Press Services, to permit "a peaceful transition from dictatorship to democracy," or else "face the consequences." He warned that "state hooliganism" would be confronted forcefully. Foruhar also condemned forthcoming parliamentary and presidential elections, scheduled for March and April 1996, as a facade.

Foruhar's supporters claimed that the government was preparing to kill him, pointing to an article in *Keyhan Hava'i* newspaper in which he was accused of being "in tune with Western governments," and of rejecting the Islamic Constitution. The article suggests that while in Europe, Mr. Foruhar, "may be prey to violent actions by opposition organizations."

Former deputy-Prime Minister Abbas Amir-Entezam continued to speak out from his prison cell in Evin Prison. Mr. Amir-Entezam, imprisoned since late 1979 on unproven charges of espionage for the United States, wrote to a prominent German legislator to call for worldwide condemnation of the government's violation of human rights. "Why should our people be denied the right of choosing freely its own government?" Mr. Amir-Entezam asked in his letter.

The Role of the International Community

The United Nations

The U.N. special representative on Iran was not allowed to visit Iran in 1995. Nevertheless, in March the U.N. Commission on Human Rights condemned Iran for "gross and systematic violations of human rights." The report of the special representative adopted by the Commission noted that at least 283 persons detained in 1992 in connection with unrest in Mashad remained in detention without trial. The report also detailed the persecution of religious minorities, including increased surveillance on Iranian Christians.

In August, the U.N. Subcommission on Prevention of Discrimination and Protection of Minorities adopted a resolution condemning "flagrant violations of human rights in Iran," including "excessive use of the death penalty," torture, the use of excessive force in suppressing demonstrations, the harassment and intimidation of people by street patrols, the lack of due process standards and restrictions on freedom of expression.

The European Union

In May, the European Union sought a written pledge from the Iranian government that it would take no action of any kind aimed at killing the British author, Salman Rushdie, condemned to death by a fatwa from the late Ayatollah Khomeini. The approach followed indications given by Iranian officials to Scandinavian governments that the threat to the author's life from the Iranian government could be lifted.

When put to the test, the reports proved to be without substance, and no written statement from the Iranian government was forthcoming. This led to a cooling in relations between the Scandinavian countries and the Iranian government, with Norway downgrading its diplomatic relations. However, while the E.U. expressed frustration over the failure to make progress on the Rushdie case, the European Commission announced in May its intention "to leave all lines of communication open with a country which is an important trading partner and an important regional power." Germany expressed its opposition to sanctions because they would result in Iran defaulting on debt payments. The E.U. debated lesser punitive measures, including the suspension of economic dialogue, and the cancellation of the annual meeting of foreign ministers with Foreign Minister Velayati.

U.S. Policy

On April 30 President Clinton issued an executive order imposing a total trade embargo on Iran, citing Iran's "export of terrorism," threat to the Middle East peace process, and pursuit of nuclear weapons as the reasons for his decision, which placed a new emphasis on Iran in U.S. foreign policy.

Skepticism characterized the initial international reaction to the forthright U.S. action, with the European Union declaring its intention to continue a "critical political dialogue" with the Iranian authorities, and Japan showing little enthusiasm to join any embargo. The Clinton administration's decision to act against Iran, after years of talking tough appears to have been prompted by the desire to head off anticipated congressional moves to propose even harsher measures that would have imposed a secondary embargo on companies trading with Iran, potentially causing havoc in international trade.

U.S. policy focused on preventing the transfer of nuclear technology to Iran from Russia and China. The U.S. also tried to persuade its Western allies not to take over the business it was foregoing by upholding the embargo.

The economic results of this policy were inconclusive. At the G-7 Summit in Halifax in May, the communique made no direct reference to the Iran sanctions. The U.S. made little attempt to link its sanctions policy to the internal human rights situation, and in the short term, at least, those most hostile to the West inside Iran drew credit for standing up to U.S. pressure, and could use the embargo to justify repressive internal measures. In September, Assistant Secretary of State for Near Eastern Affairs Robert Pelletreau claimed that the policy was working, pointing to pressure from other countries that denied Iran access to official credits. Pelletreau declared the U.S. intention to "raise the cost to Tehran's leaders of maintaining their destabilizing policies."

In the absence of a U.S. diplomatic presence, the State Department's *Country Reports on Human Rights Practices for 1994* relied on observation of the human rights situation from outside the country. The report contained little new information, and spoke in broad generalities.

The Work of
Human Rights Watch/Middle East

In November 1994, Human Rights Watch/ Middle East called on the Iranian government to conduct an independent autopsy into the cause of death of Ali Akbar Saidi-Sirjani, and to publish the results. It received no reply.

In January, following a statement by Prosecutor General Ayatollah Moghtadai inviting international human rights organizations to visit Iranian prisons, the organization resubmitted its request to send a delegation to Iran to assess prison conditions. It received no reply. The organization had first made this request in April 1994, following a statement from another Iranian leader inviting representatives of the international news media to visit Iran's prisons.

In June, following the United States' Executive Order on Iran, Human Rights Watch/Middle East expressed concern to Secretary of State, Warren Christopher, about obstacles that the Executive Order may pose to the exercise of freedom of expression and movement by Iranians and others, including journalists, academics, researchers, and human rights workers.

In September, Human Rights Watch/Middle East wrote to Minister of Interior, Mohamed Ali Besharati, expressing concern over the arson attack on the Morgh Amin bookstore, and Ayatollah Jannati's praise of the attack. The organization asked to be informed of the government's efforts to apprehend the perpetrators of the attack.

In a letter to the Turkish authorities, the organization expressed concern over the situation of Iranian refugees in Turkey, and urged the Turkish government to uphold its obligations under international law to safeguard refugees from being sent to countries where they faced persecution.

IRAQ AND IRAQI KURDISTAN

Human Rights Developments

Nearly 20 million Iraqis continued to suffer under the combined impact of a brutally repressive government and a fifth consecutive year of crippling economic sanctions. The government of President Saddam Hussein continued to impose arbitrary arrests, torture, lack of due process, and an expanded use of the death penalty on a population suffering from critical shortages of food and medicine, high unemployment and rampant inflation. As the year ended there was little relief in sight on both fronts. Iraqis were increasingly dependent on an abusive government that, despite high level defections, remained powerful. And in spite of credible U.N. reports of a health and nutrition crisis in Iraq, the United Nations had hardened its position to maintain sanctions, due partly to Iraq's lack of cooperation in complying with U.N. resolutions.

The Iraqi government continued to punish its citizens under a series of brutal decrees first passed in June 1994. The decrees—which impose punishments constituting torture—ordered the amputation of ears and hands, branding of foreheads and the use of the death penalty for crimes such as stealing, desertion from the military, smuggling antiquities, engaging in currency exchange, organizing prostitution and car theft. The amputations and branding were sometimes carried out in non-medical facilities and without anesthesia. Human Rights Watch/Middle East learned that physicians who refused to perform these procedures, or attempted to repair or reconstruct damage done by such punishments, were themselves punished with amputation and even execution.

New decrees broadened the application of the death penalty. Anyone receiving a third conviction for theft or surgically repairing the disfigurement brought about by branding and amputation would be executed.

In response to Human Rights Watch/Middle East's report on these decrees, Iraq's mission to the U.N. claimed that these laws were a response to the increase in crime and the deteriorating economic situation created by the U.N. sanctions. Responding to calls to repeal the decrees, the mission wrote that parties "...who are eager to cancel these decrees in the name of human rights should work to cancel the reasons that pushed [the government] in the direction of legislating them, and lifting the economic blockade over Iraq will certainly produce new conditions that will lead to canceling the punishments."

In the face of worsening conditions hundreds of thousands of Iraqis fled their country and many others tried to leave. In response to this major exodus of the mainly middle class, the government took several steps. To stem the flow of government employees to other countries the government enacted laws restricting their right to exit Iraq. And to keep state employees from taking better paying jobs in the private sector, the government prevented them, by law, from resigning from their positions. Iraq also placed onerous exit taxes on professionals, especially doctors and dentists, to prevent them from easily leaving the country.

Even Iraqis who managed to flee to Jordan were still vulnerable to Iraqi intelligence agents who operated relatively freely and effectively there. For several months in 1995, Iraqi agents occupied an apartment across the street from the United Nations High Commissioner for Refugees (UNHCR) offices in Amman in order to monitor and photograph Iraqis seeking asylum.

Human Rights Watch/Middle East spoke with a number of Iraqis in Jordan who received threats, either from staff at the Iraqi Embassy in Amman or from officials coming from Baghdad directly. Pressured to cease any type of activity considered critical of the government, these individuals were threatened with direct action, such as bodily harm or abduction; or indirect action like harassment of relatives who still resided in Iraq. Prior to August, when Iraq was told to drastically reduce the number of its embassy staff, the government of Jordan appeared to turn a blind eye to these activities.

At the end of 1994, the Iraqi government detained Air Force Brigadier General Turk Ismail Dulaimi along with several other Air Force officers for allegedly plotting a coup. Dulaimi was released in April; then rearrested two weeks later and summarily executed. When his body was returned to his family in the town of Ramadi, it reportedly bore marks of torture. This triggered angry demonstrations by members of Dulaimi's family and relatives. The Iraqi government immediately put down the disturbances and afterwards, according to reports from Ramadi, mounted a campaign of arbitrary detentions, torture and summary executions against persons presumed to have links to the coup plot and protests.

In July 1995 the government announced two general amnesties, in part to cope with severe prison overcrowding. The first amnesty related to criminal offenders. The second was offered to political prisoners and government opponents living abroad or in hiding in Iraq. The release of political prisoners and others unjustly imprisoned is usually a welcome development. However, because political opponents were required to register with the Iraqi government in order to qualify for the amnesty, there was legitimate skepticism about the government's real intentions. This would not be the first time that Iraq used an amnesty as a ruse to round up opponents. After the 1991 uprising in the south, Iraq issued an amnesty for which people had to apply. About 3,000 individuals who came forward and registered in Najaf were placed on trucks and have not been heard of since. Some political prisoners were released in 1995 under the amnesty, but most remained in prison.

In spite of the amnesty the government continued to harass, threaten and arrest people on political grounds. Freedom of expression was tightly restricted. Writers who criticized or questioned government policies were detained. For example, Aziz Said Jasim, a political theorist and writer, and Dhargham Hashim, a journalist who published an article favorably portraying Marsh Arabs, remained in prison.

Five years after its invasion of Kuwait, Iraq has yet to provide significant information regarding the condition and location of more than 900 Kuwaitis and others rounded up during the invasion and occupation of Kuwait. Iraq maintains that as of January 1992 all Kuwaitis held in Iraq had been released. But the Kuwaiti government claims that more than 600 Kuwaitis were still being held by Iraq; an independent organization places the figure at more than 900 individuals, including non-Kuwaitis and Kuwaiti Bedoons who were not included in the government's count.

On July 10, the Iraqi government submitted to the U.N. Security Council a memorandum promising to cooperate with an investigation of the disappeared Kuwaitis. It said that it had prepared a response to 230 files submitted by Kuwait through the International Committee of the Red Cross (ICRC). The government said it would act on the remaining files in cooperation with the ICRC, "provided that there is complete compliance with the requirement of secrecy and avoidance of politics in resolving the matter and that the information provided is credible." This would suggest that, despite earlier denials, Iraq has information on the disappeared.

In August, Lt. General Hussein Kamel Hassan Majeed, minister of minerals and industries and head of Iraq's weapons program, defected to Jordan. Joining him was his brother Saddam Hassan, head of the presidential guard; their wives (Saddam Hussein's eldest daughters); and an entourage of thirty people. While the international community was not sure what to make of this unprecedented development, the Iraqi government acted decisively; it immediately rounded up scores of individuals related to or associated with Hussein Kamel, including soldiers and officers of the elite Republican Guards as well as Mohammad Dhiyab al-Ahmad, minister of housing and reconstruction and Amir Rashid al-Saadi, minister of industry.

Hussein Kamel publicly claimed that he defected in order to serve the interests of Iraq and its people. But, intimately involved in the Iraqi leadership for several years, Kamal and his brother had played direct roles in the government's severe human rights violations. Hussein Kamel directed the destruction of the Shia holy places after the uprisings in 1991, and he was directly responsible for developing Iraq's biological weapons program. Saddam Kamel oversaw the infamous Radwaniyya prison where thousands have been detained without trial and tortured; and many were executed. It was reported that Saddam Kamel personally executed several prisoners.

The government continued to repress Iraq's minority populations. Focusing on the northern city of Kirkuk, the authorities maintained a policy of "Arabization" designed to displace the resident Kurds and establish Arabs as the city's majority; the Kurdish leadership has argued that Kirkuk be placed in the Autonomous Region under Kurdish control. Since 1991, the government has expelled Kurdish families from the city and seized their homes and property.

Other minorities such as the Turkomen, Assyrians and Chaldeans were coerced to list their ethnicity as Arab in a government effort to erase their distinct identities and increase the number of Arabs in the census. Turkomen neighborhoods were confiscated and inhabitants forced to relocate.

In a similar manner, the government subjugated the Shi'a Muslim population, despite the fact that they constitute a majority. Shi'a were prevented from buying homes in Baghdad and some were expelled. In addition, the government moved large numbers of Shi'a to areas in the north, such as Kirkuk, in order to dilute the resident Kurdish majority, "Arabize" the area, and weaken the Shi'a power in southern Iraq.

Although Iraq historically has not targeted Christians, in 1995 Human Rights Watch/Middle East received reports including first hand testimony and documents about abuses against Iraqi Jehovah Witnesses. A group of five Jehovah Witnesses were detained and held without trial by the Intelligence Agency and the General Security force. During their more than two months of detention, they were reportedly beaten and whipped, subjected to severe overcrowding and denied adequate food. Released from prison, their ordeal has not ended; they still suffer periodic harassment, threats of imprisonment, and extortion.

The Right to Monitor

The freedom to monitor or disseminate information about government violations of human rights does not exist in Iraq. Harsh laws punished those who were found to insult or demean government or Ba'th Party institutions, subjecting them to arrest, detention, imprisonment and even the death penalty. As far as we know, no independent human rights organization openly operated within government-controlled Iraq in 1995.

Iraqi exiles monitor human rights developments primarily from Tehran, Damascus, and London. The Iraqi National Congress, a London-based coalition of opposition parties; the Organization for Human Rights in Iraq, a private London-based group; the Documental Center on Human Rights in Iraq, affiliated with the Supreme Assembly of the Islamic Revolution in Iraq; and Gulf War Victims, a private relief organization located in Tehran, were principal sources of information about human rights conditions.

The U.N. special rapporteur for human rights in Iraq, Max Van der Stoel, has since 1992 been refused permission by Iraq to conduct investigations. Iraq said in a letter from its U.N. mission that during his last visit in early 1992, Van der Stoel "...behaved in a way which was far from neutrality and objectivity that his mission demands..." The letter provided nothing to support these allegations.

The Role of
the International Community

The United Nations

In February, Special Rapporteur Van der Stoel issued an interim report on the situation of human rights in Iraq. He was extremely critical of the use of amputations and brandings by the Iraqi government. He strongly rejected Iraq's argument that such measures were necessary to prevent crime. He decried the treatment of the Shi'a population, condemning the ongoing destruction of the marsh region, military assaults on Shi'a villages, and ongoing "interference in the conduct of religious affairs."

In April, the Security Council passed Resolution 986, under which Iraq would be permitted to sell $2 billion worth of oil every 180 days in order to buy food and medicine for its people. The conditions for this sale included the requirement that most of the oil flow through Turkey and that 30 percent of the proceeds go toward war reparations, U.N. humanitarian assistance programs, U.N. ad-

ministrative costs, and a separate relief operation in the Kurdish governorates in the northern "safe haven." Iraq rejected the resolution, saying that the conditions infringed on its sovereignty and national unity.

In September the World Food Programme (WFP) issued a report on its August mission to Iraq. "Alarming food shortages are causing irreparable damage to an entire generation of Iraqi children," according to a WFP statement.

The crisis could no longer be ignored or merely blamed on Baghdad. International organizations and some states recognized that if U.N. imposed sanctions were even partly responsible for the deteriorating health and nutritional conditions, then international action—either in the form of stepped up relief or adjustments to the sanctions—was necessary to alleviate the suffering. But hopes of seeing sanctions lifted anytime soon were dashed in August when the defection of Husein Kamel shook loose new information about Iraq's weapons program which had been withheld by Iraq. Compliance seemed to be a long way off and the mood in the Security Council turned sharply against efforts to ease sanctions.

United States Policy

While the U.S. held firm to its policy of isolating Iraq and maintaining economic sanctions for the fifth consecutive year, 1995 saw an increasing number of states—mainly in the Middle East, but also in Europe—express serious concern about the impact of economic sanctions on the welfare of Iraqi civilians. The momentum to consider an easing of sanctions received a boost early in the year when it appeared that Iraq was moving closer to compliance with conditions, outlined in U.N. Security Council Resolutions, for lifting sanctions. France and Russia, keenly interested in reestablishing trade relations with Iraq, led this initiative. It was met with determined opposition from the U.S. which insisted on strict compliance with all U.N. resolutions before lifting sanctions, especially the requirement to provide all relevant information on Iraq's past and current chemical and biological weapons capabilities.

Serious humanitarian reasons for easing the crippling effects of sanctions were matched by principled arguments that Iraq had been offered, but refused to accept, arrangements through which oil sales would resume, strictly regulated by the U.N., allowing Iraq to meet the basic needs of its people. It was argued that lifting sanctions without strict control would remove pressure needed to hold Iraq accountable for its aggression against Kuwait and to ensure the elimination of its weapons of mass destruction. Trade and economic considerations increasingly emerged as factors in the sanctions debate, although these were not often openly discussed. As some states eagerly anticipated the end of sanctions to establish lucrative trade deals with Iraq, others appeared to be more interested in maintaining sanctions to preserve the status quo, in particular, protecting Saudi Arabia's paramount position in the oil market.

The Work of
Human Rights Watch/Middle East

In June, Human Rights Watch published a report detailing the government's enactment and implementation of harsh punishments including amputation, branding, and the death penalty. Also, in June, after learning of a planned trip to Iraq by the U.N. High Commissioner for Human Rights, we sent a letter reminding the commissioner that his visit should not be seen as an alternative to Van der Stoel's blocked human rights investigations and urging him to press the government to allow the visit of the special representative.

In August, Human Rights Watch/ Middle East conducted an investigative mission to meet with a wide segment of the Iraqi exile community in Amman, Jordan.

On the basis of evidence gathered from more than eighteen tons of seized government documents and two years of field research on Iraq's campaign of genocide against the Kurds, Human Rights Watch continued to pursue the goal of bringing a case for violations under the Genocide Convention against the Government of Iraq at the International Court of Justice.

IRAQI KURDISTAN

Human Rights Developments

Human rights conditions in the Kurdish controlled region of Iraqi Kurdistan continued to deteriorate during 1995. Thousands of civilians fell victim to the internal fighting that plagued northern Iraq throughout the year.

In December 1994, armed skirmishes between the two principal parties, the Patriotic Union of Kurdistan (PUK) and Kurdistan Democratic Party (KDP), broke a tenuous cease-fire. Fighting continued into 1995, concentrated around Erbil, seat of the Kurdistan Regional Authority. Eventually Erbil fell entirely under the control of the PUK.

Another cease-fire brought the heaviest fighting to an end in March. In June, both the KDP and the PUK showed some progress in reconciliation, but in July, the cease-fire was broken and armed hostilities resumed.

In March, the Turkish military launched a major operation sending 35,000 troops into northern Iraq in search of rebels of the Turkish Kurdish Workers Party (PKK). This unprecedented deep incursion triggered human rights concerns and a call on Turkey to abide by the standards set out in the Geneva Conventions. Rejecting the applicability of the conventions, Turkey stated it only targeted PKK rebels; however, Kurdish civilians from both Turkey and Iraq were casualties in the fighting. After completing a full withdrawal in May, the Turkish military invaded again in July and withdrew soon afterwards.

Compounding difficulties caused by fighting between the Kurdish parties and the invasion of northern Iraq by Turkey, the Iraqi military launched attacks along the southern area of the "safe zone" in March. In addition, there were persistent reports of Iraqi government agents acting in northern Iraq, using thallium sulfide poison against political opponents. In January, members of the Iraqi National Congress in northern Iraq reportedly became ill from thallium poisoning and one died before receiving sufficient treatment. In August, it was reported that seven persons affiliated with the Supreme Council for the Islamic Revolution in Iraq were poisoned in the village of Maidana; one died.

On February 11, Dr. Sa'di Barzanji, a professor of law at the University of Salahaddin, was physically assaulted and kidnaped by four armed PUK members. He was held in incommunicado detention for two days before Jalal Talabani, the secretary general of the PUK, secured his release. However, he was kept under house arrest in Suleimaniya and was not permitted to return to Erbil.

The Right to Monitor

Although the Kurdish regional authorities have expressed openness to human rights monitoring by international organizations, the volatile atmosphere makes it dangerous and difficult to conduct investigative missions. International relief agencies continue to close their operations in the region due to the severity of the clashes between the parties.

The Kurdistan Human Rights Organization sought to document abuses throughout the region. Its staff have suffered direct threats and intimidations by all the parties to the conflict for their reporting of violations and their cooperation with international human rights organizations. Several Kurdish activists were forced to flee the region in 1995 and seek political asylum because of specific threats against them.

The Role of
the International Community

European Union Policy

The European Parliament issued a resolution on the situation in northern Iraq, calling for a cessation of the fighting that brought "grave violations of human rights by both the KDP and the PUK and also by the Islamic Movement" including a bomb explosion in a crowded market in Zakho which killed over seventy people. In another resolution, the parliament "condemned" Turkey's military intervention in northern Iraq and the resulting violation of international law and human rights."

United States Policy

In January, David Litt, a U.S. State Department official visited northern Iraq. In his meeting with the Kurdish leadership, he urged the PUK and the KDP to accept the Iraqi National Congress as the mediator in their conflict and establish a cease-fire.

The U.S. has continued to maintain the no-fly zone in northern Iraq, but stepped aside when Turkey invaded northern Iraq to attack Turkish Kurdish insurgents.

The Work of
Human Rights Watch/Middle East

On January 9, Human Rights Watch/Middle East sent a letter to Mr. Talabani, leader of the PUK, Mas'oud Barzani, president of the Kurdistan Democratic Party and Abduallah Rasoul, prime minister of the Kurdistan Regional Government expressing concern over the fighting in northern Iraq.

On February 21, Human Rights Watch/Middle East sent letters to Talabani, Barzani and Rasoul, regarding the abduction of Dr. Barzanji. It discussed our concerns regarding violations of the laws of war during recent fighting, including the treatment of civilians.

On March 2, Human Rights Watch/Middle East issued a press release and two letters regarding Dr. Barzanji. In a letter to Talabani, we protested Barzanji's continued detention under house arrest. In a letter to Rasoul, we informed him that as the de facto authority it was obligated to protect the rights of civilians, and that the continued detention violated the PUK's obligations under international humanitarian law. To date Human

Rights Watch/Middle East has not received a response to either letter.

On April 20, we sent a letter to Erdal Inonu, the Turkish foreign minister, protesting Turkey's denial of the applicability of the laws of war in northern Iraq. The letter outlined Turkey's obligations under the Geneva Convention.

ISRAELI-OCCUPIED WEST BANK AND GAZA STRIP

Human Rights Developments

Implementation of the interim agreement between Israel and the Palestine Liberation Organization (PLO) dominated both political and human rights developments. The assassination of Israeli Prime Minister Yitzhak Rabin on November 4 cast doubt on the future pace and course of the peace process.

In 1995, the 800,000 Palestinians of the Gaza Strip and the West Bank enclave of Jericho spent their first full year under Palestinian rule. In the rest of the West Bank, the transfer of formal authority to the Palestinians over local security matters got under way after the "Oslo II" agreement was signed in September. Elections for an eighty-two member legislative council were planned for early 1996, the first elections for public office to be held in the West Bank and Gaza Strip in two decades.

For Palestinians living in the areas affected, the incremental transfer of authority reduced direct contact with the Israeli Defense Forces (IDF). Community life and work were no longer disrupted by prolonged round-the-clock curfews, which had been so often imposed by the IDF during the Palestinian uprising. Clashes with soldiers, and the attendant casualties, decreased. Israeli security forces killed thirty-four Palestin-ians during the first ten months of 1995, compared to 108 in all of 1994.

Slightly under 5,000 Palestinians remained in Israeli prisons after the initial prisoner releases stemming from the "Oslo II" accord; but due to continuing arrests throughout the year, this figure was only slightly below the number in prison at the same time one year earlier.

Israel continued to maintain stringent control, if at a distance, over aspects of the lives of Palestinians no longer under its direct rule. The most onerous controls were on freedom of movement; Israel continued to restrict Palestinians entering and leaving the occupied territories, as well as traveling within the territories, through a system of permits and checkpoints.

Israeli security forces, in those areas where they continued to exercise direct control, committed the same kinds of abuses as in past years: they arbitrarily arrested hundreds of civilians, tortured suspects during interrogation; and employed excessive and often fatal force in confronting demonstrators.

The first part of this section covers the practices of the Israeli occupation authorities. A separate subsection examines the conduct of the Palestinian Authority (PA). Both sections focus on political and civil rights. Some prominent issues in the Israeli-Palestinian conflict, such as the future boundaries of a Palestinian entity and how the right to self-determination is to be exercised, lie outside the mandate of Human Rights Watch.

Some commentators argue that the interim accords have ended the state of military occupation. In our view, Israel, in its actions that affect Palestinian civilians anywhere in the West Bank and Gaza Strip, continues to be bound by the obligations of a military occupier, especially the humanitarian law requirements of the Fourth Geneva Convention. Militant opposition groups, such as the Islamic Resistance Movement (Hamas) and the Islamic Jihad, must also abide by customary humanitarian norms, especially the unconditional prohibition on acts of violence against civilians.

The increase in attacks on Israelis by Palestinian groups opposed to the Israeli-PLO accord, particularly of deadly suicide bombings, led to an intense Israeli crackdown on suspected Hamas and Islamic Jihad members. Hundreds of suspects were arrested and interrogated, often abusively.

In October 1994, the government of Israel announced that it would allow the General Security Service (GSS) to employ harsher interrogation methods. The new powers remained classified, as did the GSS's standing interrogation guidelines. But according to the testimony of Palestinians who underwent interrogation, the methods used in 1995 involved a more intensive use of those already practiced: primarily a combination of sleep deprivation, hooding, prolonged standing or sitting in unnatural positions, threats, beatings and violent whiplashing of the head. Some combination of these methods were used on most of the hundreds of Palestinians who were taken in for interrogation during the year, including those who were later released without charge. Applied in combination, these methods often amounted to torture.

In April, Abd al-Samed Harizat, a suspected Hamas activist, became the first Palestinian to die under Israeli interrogation since 1993. A Justice Ministry inquiry determined that Harizat had died from fatal brain damage caused by his interrogators violently shaking his head back and forth. Nevertheless, the state attorney declined to prosecute the interrogators, explaining that death from the shaking technique was so rare that the interrogators could not have anticipated that their actions would lead to fatal results.

According to reports in the Israeli media, the government renewed throughout the year its authorization for interrogators to employ the harsher methods, including whiplashing, but only in "exceptional" cases and only with permission from superiors.

In August, the GSS held a rare press conference to claim that the use of the harsher methods had enabled the agency to crack a Hamas ring responsible for a string of suicide bombings. Attorney General Michael Ben Yair entered the public controversy in October, telling the press that shaking should be restricted to rare cases because of its severe nature. "I am not ready to see every black-bearded Palestinian youngster who is detained for interrogation end up with brain damage," he said.

The army's pursuit of "dangerous" fugitives was also the subject of unprecedentedly blunt words, although the fatal shooting of fugitives declined in 1995. In April, the army's commander of the West Bank forces told an Israeli newspaper that the goal of such operations was to kill certain wanted men. Human rights organizations have long charged that special army units had summarily killed scores of fugitives since 1989 without making an effort to capture them alive, challenging official assertions that force was used only as a last resort.

In February, authorities lengthened the maximum period of administrative detention (internment without charge) from six months to one year, renewable. Among the nearly 200 Palestinians in administrative detention as of October, the longest-held had been detained without charge for over three years.

Israeli-imposed restrictions on movement constrained the lives of virtually all Palestinians in the West Bank and Gaza Strip. The stated grounds for these restrictions were security concerns, which were exacerbated by the rise in deadly bombings inside Israel that had been carried out by residents of the West Bank and Gaza Strip. At the same time, these restrictions were imposed indiscriminately on all Palestinians, without regard to individual guilt or to the extreme hardship that particular individuals faced as a result. Appeals procedures for Palestinians denied a permit were neither efficient nor transparent. Given its inflexible and indiscriminate nature, the closure policy constituted a form of collective punishment that harmed Palestinians living in both the self-rule areas and those under direct Israeli rule.

During most of the year, only the small number of Palestinians who held valid Israeli-issued permits were allowed to enter Israel or Israeli-annexed East Jerusalem. They were also effectively the only ones permitted to travel between the West Bank and the Gaza Strip, since that trip required crossing through Israeli territory.

There were extended periods during the year when no Palestinians, even those holding permits, were permitted to leave the West Bank or Gaza Strip. According to Palestinian human rights organizations, between May 1994, when the first agreement on the transfer of authority was signed (the "Cairo Agreement"), and August 30, 1995, the Israeli authorities imposed seventeen total closures on the West Bank and Gaza Strip for a total of seventy-four days.

The closure policy severely disrupted Palestinian life and caused economic hardship. The number of Palestinian workers employed inside Israel continued to dwindle because their permits had been canceled or non-Palestinian workers had been hired to replace them. Many Gaza students could not pursue their university studies on the West Bank. Other Palestinians could not reach Jerusalem to meet business contacts, submit visa requests at foreign consulates, or obtain specialized medical care.

Tensions over Israeli settlements continued to simmer, fueled by the approaching transfer of authority to the Palestinians over parts of the West Bank. Tensions were highest in Hebron, where the IDF continued to respond to settler-Palestinian strife by subjecting Palestinians—but not settlers—to curfews, road closures, and delays at checkpoints. Settlers continued to vandalize Palestinian property, throw stones at Palestinian homes and otherwise harass Palestinians, with little risk of the harsh treatment that authorities administered to Palestinians suspected of similar acts against Jews.

During the first ten months of 1995, Palestinians killed eleven Israeli civilians and one tourist inside pre-1967 Israel. Hamas claimed responsibility for some of these attacks, openly targeting Israeli civilians and thereby violating one of the most elemental customary norms of humanitarian law.

The number of Palestinians killed by their brethren as suspected collaborators with Israel continued to decline. Two Palestinians were killed as suspected collaborators in the first eight months of the year, according to the Associated Press. In addition, in October, two human rights organizations, al-Haq and the Mandela Institute, expressed concern about three Palestinian detainees inside Israeli prisons who appeared to have died from physical torture inflicted during questioning by other detainees.

The Palestinian Authority (PA)

Human rights in the areas under Palestinian rule remained in a precarious state. Although Palestinians savored freedoms they had not known during the years of the direct Israeli occupation, the PA made little progress in establishing a rule of law. Violations of human rights included physical abuse of detainees, newspaper closures, and closed-door trials of opposition suspects that violated basic due-process norms. There were also acts of violence and intimidation against Palestinians by the over-staffed security agencies, and by members of the Fatah faction of the PLO, who while not formally integrated into the security agencies, were allowed freedom of operation as such by Yasir Arafat, who chairs both the PA and the PLO.

Under pressure from Israel and the United States to prevent and punish attacks on Israeli targets from the areas he administered, Chairman Arafat arrested suspected members of opposition groups, primarily from Hamas and Islamic Jihad, throughout the year and imprisoned them without formal charges for weeks or months at a time. Other suspects were put on trial in the newly-created state security courts. In these courts, which stood outside the existing Palestinian civil and military court system, trials usually took place at night and were closed. The proceedings, which often lasted only minutes, were presided over by security force officers with no previous judicial experience. Defendants, who were mostly accused of planning or taking part in violent activities on behalf of the Islamist opposition, were given insufficient notice of the charges and were not represented by lawyers of their own choosing. Most of the trials ended in convictions and prison terms.

During the first ten months of the year, two Palestinians died under suspicious circumstances during or after interrogation by the Palestinian security services; two others were killed shortly after their release from detention. In at least one of these two cases, there was suspicion of security force complicity in the death. In one death-in-detention case, involving a U.S. citizen of Palestinian origin, the U.S. government pressed for a serious inquiry and the PA announced that five security-force members had been detained. But investigations into the deaths lacked transparency, raising doubts about the commitment of the PA to exposing the facts and punishing abuse in its ranks.

The PA grew more aggressive in pressuring Palestinian media to temper criticism of the Israeli-PLO accord and the authority's record. Journalists were briefly arrested, and newspapers were suspended on at least five occasions for articles deemed damaging to the authority. In May, the Gaza state security court sentenced the editor of Hamas-affiliated *al-Watan* newspaper to two years in jail on charges of incitement against the authority. He was still in prison when a ban on *al-Watan* was lifted in October.

The various security agencies came under scrutiny not only for their conduct within the self-rule areas of Gaza and Jericho but also beyond their borders. The Israeli human rights organization B'Tselem issued a report in August 1995 accusing the Palestinian Preventive Security Service (PSS) of conducting policing activities throughout the West Bank, even though the Cairo Agreement gave them responsibility for internal security only in the self-rule areas. The PSS was accused of arresting residents without warrants, holding them in detention for long periods without bringing charges against them, and torturing them during interrogation. B'Tselem pointed out that the PSS was,

with Israeli acquiescence, filling a vacuum in that Israeli occupation forces had largely neglected law enforcement in criminal matters. The PSS denounced the B'Tselem report as "baseless," and denied that the abuses it documented were the work of PSS agents.

U.S. Policy

Just as human rights in the occupied territories was never a focus of U.S. policy toward Israel, in 1995 it became apparent that it was not a focus of U.S. policy toward the PA, either. With the exception of suicide bombings that killed Israelis, the administration kept largely silent in the face of serious violations, as if it feared that interventions on human rights issues might undermine the peace process it backed so strongly.

Human rights violations are not merely "symptoms" of a conflict to be addressed by focusing exclusively on long-term political goals. While a just political solution to the Israeli-Palestinian conflict can of course improve the state of human rights, abuses must also be confronted in the present. They cause enormous suffering, constitute violations of the legal obligations of the abusive parties, and contribute to the kind of political turmoil that undermines peace prospects.

The U.S. has provided Israel each year with more than three billion dollars in economic and military assistance, making it the largest beneficiary of U.S. bilateral assistance. The U.S. also became the largest bilateral donor to the PA when, in 1993, it pledged $500 million in development projects and loan guarantees over five years, including $24 million in 1995 for "democracy-building" programs. In our view, this aid gives the U.S. influence it should use to promote greater respect for human rights by the Israeli and Palestinian authorities.

The U.S. downgrading of human rights was best illustrated by its response to two salient issues in 1995: Israel's adoption of explicitly more abusive interrogation methods and the PA's creation of the state security courts.

The rise in suicide bombings prompted

the government of Israel to ease restraints on interrogation methods. This represented another step backward by a state that had ratified the Convention against Torture in 1991 but had continued to use torture systematically. The State Department's *Country Reports on Human Rights Practices for 1994* called "credible" the reports that Israeli interrogators were responsible for "widespread abuse, and in some cases torture." Except in the *Country Reports*, the U.S. refrained from clarifying publicly where it stood on this core rights issue, despite preliminary evidence that the eased guidelines had led to an increase in torture, the death of a Palestinian under interrogation in April, and the debate in Israel around the new guidelines.

Toward the PA, the U.S. effectively endorsed Israel's position of repeatedly urging Chairman Arafat to do more to prevent and punish attacks by armed opposition groups on Israelis, while showing little interest in the human rights consequences of how this goal was achieved. The highest U.S. official to visit the area during the first ten months of 1995, Vice President Al Gore, conveyed this message clearly. On March 24 in Jericho, Gore hailed Chairman Arafat's promise to set up state security courts as "an important step forward in helping to build confidence in the peace process and in the effort by authorities on all sides to control violence and stop terrorism and defeat the enemies of the peace process." On April 4 the vice president sidestepped reports of the courts' lack of due-process safeguards, telling a Washington audience, "I know there has been some controversy over the Palestinian security courts, but I personally believe that the accusations are misplaced and that they are doing the right thing in progressing with prosecutions."

One week later the State Department spokesperson alluded weakly to the problem, responding to a journalist's question, "The establishment of the rule of law, including respect for human rights, is a very important element in the development of Palestinian self-rule....We know that Chair-

man Arafat and the Palestinian authorities are grappling with these issues."

There was no doubt that attacks on Israelis posed a grave threat to the peace process. It was also true that in attempting to stop the attacks, the new and financially strapped PA lacked some of the means and institutions that can help to safeguard human rights. But by endorsing a security policy that resulted in arbitrary mass arrests and summary, closed-door trials, the U.S. appeared to attach little priority at this formative stage to the need to build human rights protections in the self-rule areas.

To its credit, the U.S. Embassy and Jerusalem consulate staff took an active interest in human rights conditions, meeting regularly with local rights groups and producing a well-researched chapter in the *Country Reports on Human Rights Practices for 1994*. And although John Shattuck, the assistant secretary of state for democracy, human rights and labor, did not visit Israel or the occupied territories in 1995, his staff met in October in Washington with Col. Jibril Rujoub, Chief of the Palestinian Preventive Security Service in Jericho. According to Bureau staff, much of the meeting was devoted to human rights concerns.

The Right to Monitor

Israeli, Palestinian and international human rights organizations were permitted to exist and operate in the occupied territories. During 1995, they collected and disseminated information with little interference from the Israeli authorities. The main impediment to fact-finding was the tight Israeli control over the movement of Palestinians, including human rights workers and journalists (see above). One al-Haq worker, Sha'wan Jabarin, completed an eight-month term in administrative detention in February 1995.

Human rights organizations continued to work in the Palestinian self-rule areas. However, several incidents occurred to suggest that official tolerance for human rights fact-finding and criticism was limited.

Following the release of a critical statement on the decree to establish the Palestinian state security courts in February 1995, Raji Sourani, then-director of the Gaza Center for Rights and Law (GCRL), was detained overnight for questioning. A seminar organized by the GCRL to examine the state security courts was barred by the PA on the pretext that a requisite permit had not been obtained. No observers were permitted to attend trials of the state security courts in the self-rule areas.

Bassem Eid, a field-worker at the Israeli human rights organization B'Tselem, was attacked by name by Colonel Rujoub. Following the August 1995 release of B'Tselem's critical report on human rights violations by the PSS, Col. Rujoub, denounced the report and publicly accused Eid, a Palestinian resident of Jerusalem, of being an agent of the Israeli police. Many rights groups protested this remark as a malicious and unsubstantiated allegation that could endanger Eid's personal safety. The PA gave assurances that human rights groups were free to work in the self-rule areas, but did not formally retract the accusation.

The ombudsman-like Palestinian Independent Commission for Human Rights enjoyed greater access and influence with the PA than did other Palestinian rights groups. Since Dr. Hanan Ashrawi stepped down as head of the commission, it may become clear whether the authorities' responsiveness to its interventions was due to their respect for the institution itself or to the immense personal prestige of Dr. Ashrawi.

The Work of
Human Rights Watch/Middle East

Seeking to keep attention directed toward human rights during a transitional year, Human Rights Watch/Middle East published a report in February assessing human rights conditions in the self-rule areas. The report addressed both Palestinian and Israeli authorities, reminding the latter that their humanitarian obligations toward residents of the self-rule areas did not end abruptly with the transfer of partial powers to the Palestinians. The report emphasized restrictions on freedom of movement. It also documented abuses by the Palestinians, including beatings in detention, arbitrary arrests, and censorship, and stressed the need to strengthen the rule of law.

Prior to releasing the report, representatives of Human Rights Watch/Middle East met with Palestinian human rights organizations, Palestinian officials in the Gaza Strip and Israeli officials in Jerusalem to discuss our findings. We also met with a Hamas spokesman in Gaza to protest the targeting of Israeli civilians by Hamas militants. A follow-up mission to confer with Israeli and Palestinian human rights workers was conducted in August.

A global report on communal violence contained a chapter on Israeli judicial leniency toward acts of violence committed by Jewish settlers in the West Bank.

In written interventions and published articles, Human Rights Watch/Middle East took its concerns to the authorities and before international public opinion. For example, in response to revelations that Israelis soldiers had executed Egyptian prisoners of war in 1956 and 1967, we urged the Israeli government to investigate thoroughly and not to rule out criminal prosecutions. A letter to Chairman Arafat urged a retraction of Col. Rujoub's dangerous accusation that human rights field-worker Bassem Eid was an Israeli police agent.

KUWAIT

Human Rights Developments

While 1995 was marked by significant improvements in the human rights picture in Kuwait, there remained serious systematic abuses. There was no change in the government's policy to pressure the Bedoons, Kuwait's longtime native residents, to leave the country. Although a limited franchise was granted to male naturalized citizens, early promises to give women the right to vote were not fulfilled, despite Kuwait's signing of the Convention on the Elimination of All Forms of Discrimination Against

Women, which mandates gender equality. Although practical steps were taken to improve conditions for Asian maids, they remained without legal protection from abusive employers.

During 1995, the Kuwaiti government took several steps to improve human rights conditions in the country. It abolished the State Security Court, which in the past handed down death penalties and other harsh punishments in proceedings falling far short of international standards for fair trials, including the use of coerced confessions and denial of the right to legal counsel. Also during 1995, Kuwait signed the International Covenant on Civil and Political Rights, the International Covenant on Social, Economic and Cultural Rights and the Convention against Torture and Other Cruel, Inhuman or Degrading Treatment or Punishment. However, the signing of these instruments was not accompanied by any steps to permit local human rights groups, dissolved since 1993, to resume their activities legally.

Kuwait for the first time extended a limited franchise to "second-class" male citizens—Kuwaitis who were either naturalized or otherwise deemed ineligible for first class citizenship because they failed to prove that they or their ancestors settled in Kuwait before 1920. The parliament granted naturalized male citizens the right to vote after twenty years of their naturalization. In another significant step, male children of naturalized citizens born after their father's acquisition of Kuwaiti citizenship were also granted the right to vote. Women, whether of the first or second class, remained disenfranchised, as did male children born before their fathers were naturalized.

Iraqi threats against Kuwait were cited in 1995 by Kuwaiti officials as justifications for continued human rights abuses and delays in dealing with past violations. Those tensions and Iraq's refusal to provide information on hundreds of Kuwaitis who remain unaccounted for since their detention during the Iraqi occupation contributed to a hostile atmosphere for groups suspected as a whole of holding Iraqi sympathies, including the Bedoon and Palestinian communities. This led to renewed pressure on these populations to leave the country; they were denied freedom of movement, employment and education for their children.

There was no perceptible change in 1995 in the government's refusal to account for the hundreds of extrajudicial executions, disappearances and torture cases which took place during the post-liberation martial-law period (February through June 1991).

In July, the parliament dissolved the State Security Court, established in 1970 and mandated to try a variety of offenses broadly defined in the State Security Act of 1970. After the end of the war in February 1991 and until it was disbanded, the court tried scores of Iraqis, Palestinians, Bedoons and others charged with collaboration with the Iraqi occupying forces. Throughout its history, trials before this court were characterized by serious shortcomings, including the use of confessions obtained through torture, the denial of legal counsel of the defendants' own choosing and a limited right of appeal. Relying primarily on evidence provided by the notorious State Security Investigations Apparatus, the court handed down scores of death penalties and other harsh punishments, disregarding defendants' claims of torture and ill-treatment.

During 1995, hundreds of foreign residents and Kuwaiti Bedoons were administratively detained without charge or trial in the Talha Deportation Prison and then given a choice between leaving the country voluntarily or remaining in the overcrowded makeshift detention facility indefinitely. Some had been held since the end of the war, including many who were stateless or refugees. The promise made by the prime minister in June 1993 to improve conditions and relocate Talha inmates, after some of its residents went on a hunger strike, went largely unfulfilled, despite urging from the National Assembly's human rights committee. Although already crowded in 1994, with an average population of 650, the number of detainees doubled during 1995 at the Talha facility, a former school converted into a detention center in 1991.

The Kuwaiti government continued to employ a range of actions to induce Iraqi and Palestinian residents and Bedoons to leave the country. Measures of intimidation included arbitrary arrest and detention, torture and ill-treatment of prisoners, unlawful searches, heavy fines, threats, public humiliation and the denial of employment. Having succeeded in reducing the nearly 400,000-strong Palestinian community to about 33,000, the Kuwaiti government has sought to achieve similar results with the Bedoon community. During the year, it escalated pressure on the Bedoons to secure citizenship elsewhere if they wanted to remain in Kuwait lawfully. Most Bedoons were long-term residents of Kuwait who were born in Kuwait and have lived there all their lives, but were not officially deemed to qualify for Kuwaiti citizenship. From a total population of over 300,000, only half remain in Kuwait. The rest, most of whom left during the Gulf conflict, were stranded in exile, mostly in Iraq, because Kuwait refuses to permit their reentry.

Accused as a group of aiding the Iraqi occupying forces, Bedoons were targeted for retribution, although many had in fact been killed by the Iraqi occupiers for acts of resistance. Since liberation, Bedoons have been prevented from sending their children to government schools and threatened with expulsion from the only country they have ever known. All those employed by the government were dismissed from their jobs. The military and the police, which before the invasion were largely composed of Bedoons, rehired only a small fraction of their prewar employees—depriving the community of its chief source of income. In 1995, Bedoons found outside the remaining Bedoon slums were detained and pressured to leave the country in exchange for the government dropping the charges of illegal residence. The government remained opposed to reopening the citizenship application process to give Bedoons an opportunity to make their claims.

Many of the Palestinians still in Kuwait were stateless refugees who came originally from the Gaza Strip, but were not allowed by Israel to return. Despite the agreements signed between Israel and the Palestinians granting them autonomous rule over Gaza and parts of the West Bank, Israel retained control over the borders, preventing most stateless Palestinians from returning. During 1995 in Kuwait, many Gazans were harassed, threatened with imprisonment, denied employment and education, or subjected to fines for every day they stayed in Kuwait.

Another vulnerable group of foreign residents subjected to mistreatment was made up of nearly 200,000 Asian maids, mainly from the Philippines, Sri Lanka, India and Bangladesh. They were expressly excluded from the protection of labor legislation, and in practice also left at the mercy of their private employers with regard to violent abuse. Hundreds of abused Asian expatriates sought refuge in their respective embassies, charging their employers with rape, physical assault, unlawful confinement or withholding wages. Abuses by employers recorded in 1995 included cases of murder, rape and other sexual abuse, beatings, confinement and passport confiscation. While in 1995 the Kuwaiti government brought charges against some employers accused in the murder or wrongful death of their maids, most lesser abuses went unpunished. In a positive step, in September, Ahmed al-Kulaib, minister of social affairs and labor, conducted surprise inspections and threatened abusive employers and employment agencies with fines and other penalties. However, without a legal mandate to extend labor law to the maids, it was not clear how the ministry could penalize employers where criminal law could not be invoked.

The Dasma Police Station, used to hold maids pending their deportation or the resolution of their claims, became extremely overcrowded during the first half of 1995, with a population of 300 maids. Kuwaiti law requires maids who complain about their employers to either stay with their employers until the conflict is resolved or be detained. Most of those complaining, who were not in their countries' embassy shelters, were detained until their cases were resolved: this sometimes took months, leading many maids to drop their complaints and accept repatriation. Responding to criticism of the crowded conditions at Dasma detention and deportation facility, and dismal conditions at embassy shelters, the Kuwaiti government agreed to repatriate the maids without the required consent of their employers and the return of their original residency permits which were regularly withheld by the employers. Between June and August, several hundred maids were repatriated. To facilitate their departure, most had to forfeit their claims to back wages and drop criminal charges against their employers.

In 1995, the Kuwaiti government reiterated its ban on political parties and took steps to enforce a 1985 moratorium on the formation of new private associations, including human rights groups. The government enforced its 1993 decision to close down over fifty unlicensed private organizations, including six human rights groups. The authorities prevented the unauthorized groups from holding public functions or advertising their activities.

The Right to Monitor

The right to monitor was dealt a severe blow with the closure in August 1993 of all human rights groups in Kuwait, including the Kuwaiti Association to Defend War Victims (KADWV) and the Kuwaiti Association for Human Rights (Kuwait's branch of the Cairo-based Arab Organization for Human Rights). Established immediately after the Gulf War, KADWV had been the most vocal local human rights group. The Kuwaiti government, which never formally recognized the organization's legal existence, ordered KADWV and the other human rights and humanitarian groups to close down on the grounds that they had not been licensed.

Although the order was directed at all unlicensed organizations, government officials cited only human rights and humanitarian organizations and singled out KADWV

for criticism. Groups that attempted to defy the ban in 1995 were threatened with the use of force if they held public meetings or conducted public activities. Newspapers were barred from publishing advertisements for the dissolved organizations, and licensed groups were ordered not to host activities by them. In 1995, the government evicted KADWV, the League of Families of POWs and the Missing, the Popular Committee for Solidarity with POWs and the Missing and Amnesty International's Kuwait group from the public building they had occupied since 1991. Nevertheless, KADWV continued to work privately, as have some of the other banned groups, albeit in a much reduced capacity.

Included in the government's ban were four other human rights and humanitarian groups: the Mutual Assistance Fund for the Families of the Martyrs and POWs, the Pro-Democracy Committee, Supporters of Single-Citizenship Committee, and the Women Married to Non-Kuwaitis Support Association.

In 1995, while the Parliamentary Committee for the Defense of Human Rights continued its activities under its limited mandate, there was little cooperation from the executive branch to facilitate its investigations. In June, the Committee's chair, Deputy Muhammed al-Marshad, resigned from the committee, reportedly in protest of the government's failure to cooperate.

While severely restricting the activities of local independent groups, the Kuwaiti government in 1995 began efforts to establish a semi-governmental human rights group and permitted outside human rights groups to visit Kuwait.

U.S. and European Policies

Since the end of the 1991 Gulf War, the U.S. has been the main force protecting Kuwait from renewed Iraqi attack and Kuwait's chief arms supplier. Under a 1991 military agreement, the U.S. maintained a substantial naval presence nearby and held frequent U.S.-Kuwaiti maneuvers. These exercises amount to a semi-permanent presence in light of their frequency, their duration and the large number of troops involved. The U.S. has pre-positioned a large amount of war materiel in Kuwait and integrated Kuwaiti facilities with those of the U.S. In one such exercise in March, code-named "Intrinsic Action 95-2," about 1,350 U.S. armored troops took part in a "rapid-reaction" joint effort with Kuwaiti forces. The exercise lasted for six weeks and used the U.S. weapons pre-positioned in Kuwait, according to Navy Lt. Cmdr. Scott Campbell, a Defense Department spokesman. In addition to pre-positioned materiel, the U.S. maintains two A-10 Thunderbolt ("tank-killer") squadrons in Kuwait since they were deployed there the previous October, in the wake of Iraq's threatening movement of armored divisions near the Kuwaiti border.

During March, Defense Secretary William Perry visited Kuwait to discuss joint defense cooperation in the face of reported Iraqi buildup. Defense officials said that these exercises were part of ongoing preparations by the United States and Kuwait to meet quickly any sudden military threat from Iraq or Iran.

In addition to military ties, commercial interests appeared to dominate the bilateral relationship, with U.S. companies accounting for nearly half of foreign investment in Kuwait, according to U.S. officials. Despite the extensive military, political and economic contacts between the two countries, no public criticism of human rights abuses in the country was voiced, with the exception of the cataloguing of human rights abuses in the State Department's *Country Reports on Human Rights Practices*.

France, Russia and the United Kingdom also signed military agreements with Kuwait undertaking to defend its independence and territorial integrity. In 1995, the three countries competed with the U.S. in providing the Kuwaiti military with advanced hardware and in securing a sizable share of Kuwait's government and private sector contracts, but failed to voice public concern over human rights abuses in Kuwait. France and the U.K., both of which were visited in May by the Emir of Kuwait, Shaikh Jaber al-Ahmed al-Sabah, were among Kuwait's top five trade partners and after the U.S. were the next two top suppliers of military equipment. In 1994, France exported 4.5 billion francs ($461 million) in non-military goods to Kuwait. Its imports from Kuwait amounted to 959 million francs ($93 million) and its military sales included advanced missile-carrying warships for the Kuwaiti navy. During the same year, Britain exported £312 million ($490 million) in non-military goods to Kuwait. Its imports from Kuwait amounted to £239 million ($375 million) and its recent military sales included 250 British armored cars. In addition, the Kuwaiti government was reportedly the largest single shareholder of the British Petroleum Company.

The Work of
Human Rights Watch/Middle East

In 1995, Human Rights Watch/Middle East combined research with advocacy to improve the observance of human rights in Kuwait, publishing a report on the country while engaging in substantive discussions with Kuwaiti officials and following up previous published reports. While there was significant progress during the year on a number of issues, others remained to be resolved.

In July, Human Rights Watch published *The Bedoons of Kuwait: "Citizens Without Citizenship,"* a 105-page detailed study of the conditions under which Bedoons have been forced to live after they were effectively denationalized by the Kuwaiti government.

Also in July, the Kuwaiti government abolished the State Security Court, a tribunal that had been repeatedly criticized by Human Rights Watch/Middle East for failing to meet international standards for fair trials. We worked closely with Kuwaiti jurists who had campaigned for its abolition.

During 1995, Human Rights Watch/Middle East appealed, unsuccessfully, with Kuwaiti officials to rescind orders preventing local human rights and humanitarian groups from continuing their activities.

Human Rights Watch/Middle East continued its efforts, begun immediately after the liberation of Kuwait, to urge Kuwaiti and U.S. officials to take steps to improve conditions for Asian maids in Kuwait. In 1994, the Overseas Private Insurance Corporation had decided to withhold its approval of insurance for investment in Kuwait until the State Department conducted a high level dialogue with Kuwaiti officials on workers' rights and made future commitments contingent on positive steps taken by the Kuwaiti government. In August, Human Rights Watch/ Middle East contributed a section on the mistreatment of Asian maids in Kuwait to the *Human Rights Watch Global Report on Women's Human Rights*. Without addressing the underlying issue of the legal vacuum in labor law, the Kuwaiti government took several steps to improve conditions for the maids, including the repatriation of several hundred maids stranded in embassy shelters and deportation detention facilities. In addition, Kuwaiti prosecutors demonstrated more vigor in 1995 in investigating serious abuses.

In the United States, there was a landmark ruling on the treatment of maids. On June 1, in a case on which we worked closely with the U.S. Justice Department, the U.S. Court of Appeals (first circuit) in *United States v. Alzanki* upheld a district court's conviction of Talal al-Zanki, a Kuwaiti citizen living in Boston, of holding a Sri Lankan maid he had hired in Kuwait in involuntary servitude in violation of the 13th amendment of the U.S. constitution and statutes. Al-Zanki was sentenced to one year and one day in prison, plus restitution. This was the first case of its kind to be decided on 13th amendment grounds since the 1988 *United States v. Kozminski* case. The al-Zanki case was widely discussed in Kuwait, with many calling for improvement of the treatment of maids to prevent a similar outcome.

In July, Human Rights Watch/Middle East wrote to the Iraqi government urging it to provide full accounting for nearly one thousand Kuwaitis and others who disappeared and were believed detained by Iraqi authorities during the occupation of Kuwait.

MOROCCO AND THE WESTERN SAHARA

Human Rights Developments

Despite significant improvements in its human rights record, Morocco's transition to a democratic state complying with international human rights standards was far from complete. In the late 1980s and early 1990s, the government took steps that significantly enhanced the rights of Moroccans and created a more open climate with respect to human rights. However, the momentum for progress appeared to have stalled in 1995, as government officials emphasized past progress rather than addressing continuing violations.

Procedural safeguards introduced in 1991 contributed to reduce the degree and number of abuses during incommunicado detention, but torture, ill-treatment and due process violations still occurred with disturbing frequency. There were at least two deaths in detention in 1995. Mohammed Ahmadi died in the police station of Nador, reportedly due to ill-treatment, and Hamza Dagdoug died the day after his arrest on January 18, 1995. According to the police, Dagdoug had committed suicide in the central police station of Tangiers, using a tie that had "inadvertently" been left in the toilets. Investigations that had been opened in at least half a dozen of the twenty-five deaths in detention since 1989 did not yield any results.

In addition, the forty-eight hour maximum normally permitted for incommunicado detention was illegally prolonged in many cases. The police at times falsified their records to indicate incorrect arrest dates, in order to give the impression that they were complying with this provision. The *"procès verbal,"* or official statement taken by the police during incommunicado detention, was often coerced or fabricated, but often constituted the basis for a conviction. As in the past, most abuses, particularly ill-treatment and torture, tended to occur during incommunicado detention, when lawyers were absent. However, procedural violations also took place during the subsequent "preliminary interrogation," where lawyers were present, but were often not permitted to ask questions or include their observations or objections as part of the official record.

Human rights abuses occurred in a number of high-profile arrests and trials. For example, Khadija Benameur, a young labor union activist who was beaten and arrested during a peaceful factory strike in March 1995, was subsequently kept in pre-trial detention in excess of the permitted forty-eight hour period, denied the right to call witnesses at trial and refused a legally required medical examination, despite signs that she had been tortured. In another case, defendants charged with carrying out a series of armed attacks during 1993 and 1994 on behalf of militant Islamists were convicted in flawed proceedings on January 28, 1995. They were held in incommunicado detention for an illegally prolonged period, the investigating judge refused to order a medical examination to investigate signs of torture, and interrogations and confessions were made in Arabic, although several of the defendants had been raised in France and reportedly did not speak fluent Arabic.

Torture and ill-treatment continued in 1995, albeit with less frequency than before. Such abuses occurred not only in political or security cases, but also in ordinary criminal cases, and were most acute in rural areas. Inadequate investigations and the failure to prosecute law enforcement officials responsible for abuses during detention created little incentive for change. Moreover, law enforcement officials who had been accustomed to committing torture and ill-treatment with impunity for decades, received little, if any, training and education regarding international human rights standards or Moroccan law. Finally, Morocco did not take the required steps to make the Convention against Torture and other Cruel, Inhuman or Degrading Treatment or Punishment, which it had ratified in June 1993, enter into the country's official laws. Nor did Morocco take the legislative and administrative steps required to meet its affirmative obligation to place domestic laws in compliance with the convention.

Prison conditions in Morocco remained poor, due to severe overcrowding, ill-treatment of prisoners and a lack of medical attention. When a rebellion broke out in Khenifra prison on January 29, 1995 to protest conditions, prison officials responded with firearms, wounding prisoners and causing a number to be hospitalized. Following the rebellion, the Moroccan Organization for Human Rights demanded, and was authorized, to conduct an unprecedented visit to the prison site. The group released a report concluding that the policy followed in the prison was one of punishment and repression, and that ill-treatment, malnutrition and inadequate medical treatment were rampant. Moreover, although the government reported that prison deaths in 1994 and 1995 were all attributable to natural causes, many were actually due to poor detention conditions, including four deaths in the span of a single week in the civil prison of Oukacha in March 1995. Several prisoners went on lengthy hunger strikes to protest their conditions.

On April 18, 1995, government spokesperson Driss Alawi announced that the government had decided to take steps to improve the prison situation. Human Rights Minister Mohammed Ziane accompanied journalists on visits to several civil prisons in April, May and October 1995. While the public acknowledgment of the gravity of prison conditions was an important step forward, the government failed to follow these statements with concrete actions. For example, by November the government had still not presented to parliament proposed modifications to the outdated prison code. The government had received draft amendments from the Consultative Council on Human Rights in March 1994.

The government did not address the

issue of at least fifty prisoners who had been arrested on political charges but were arbitrarily excluded from a general amnesty in July 1994. Abdessalam Yacine, the leader of the outlawed Islamic group al 'Adl wa al-Ihsan, was held under house arrest for the fifth year. Yacine had been arrested pursuant to an extrajudicial, administrative order and no criminal charges were brought against him. The government also failed to resolve the issue of forced disappearances in Morocco. With the exception of a small stipend provided by the armed forces to twenty-eight former military officers who survived the notorious "Tazmamart" secret detention center, none of the over three hundred other victims of forced disappearances released in June 1991, or the families of victims who did not survive, received reparations for the suffering endured in up to two decades of secret detention. Hundreds of Moroccan and Western Saharan families continued to search for missing relatives, many of whom had "disappeared" into Moroccan custody over two decades ago. Moreover, the government made no efforts to provide details on these cases or investigate human rights abuses in the secret detention centers; as a result, those guilty of committing torture and "disappearance" were not held accountable for their crimes.

Many former prisoners and those who had been "disappeared" continued to be denied passports and national identity papers following their release, preventing them from exercising their right to freedom of movement. Abraham Serfaty, one of the most well-known of Morocco's former political prisoners, who was stripped of his Moroccan nationality following his release from prison in 1991, remained in exile in France. The supreme court did not act upon an appeal that had been submitted by Serfaty's attorney in November 1991. The authorities repeatedly harassed Ahmed Marzak, who was released from Tazmamart in 1991 after more than eighteen years of secret detention, and confiscated his passport when he attempted to travel to France for medical attention in July 1995. Marzak was reportedly kidnaped by

the police and taken to the outskirts of Rabat, where he was subjected to ill-treatment for thirty-six hours and interrogated, particularly about his relations with foreign nationals.

The Moroccan judiciary did not function independently and was susceptible to bribes and influence from high government officials. Judges also refused to order medical examinations, although the right to such examinations was provided in the Code of Penal Procedure, or to investigate allegations of torture, even when detainees showed visible signs substantiating their claims. Members of the judiciary were able to engage in illegal acts with impunity, as the judiciary was not generally subject to controls, supervision or penalties. The fact that judges were under qualified and the judiciary was insufficiently funded further undermined the judicial system. As it had done with respect to prison conditions, the government acknowledged these shortcomings. On April 18, 1995, government spokesperson Driss Alawi announced plans to carry out a structural reorganization of the Ministry of Justice in order to enhance the independence and credibility of the judiciary. On April 24, 1995, the king gave a speech addressing the serious problems facing the Moroccan judicial system and noted, in particular, the problem of low salaries and corruption. However, the government ultimately took no public steps to improve the judicial system.

Laws that discriminated against women remained on the books, including commercial and criminal laws and provisions of the *Moudawana* or Family Code regarding matrimonial tutelage, marital repudiation and physical and legal guardianship over children of divorced women. Cultural, economic and family pressures often prevented women from knowing their legal rights or seeking redress, even when their rights were protected by law. In the workplace, women complained about unequal salaries and their lack of representation in managerial positions, whether in the private or public sector. Domestic violence remained prevalent but went unaddressed by the government, which failed to adopt specific measures to protect women or ensure that violators were prosecuted to the full extent of the law. Police and judges failed to treat domestic violence as a serious problem, and showed a reluctance to assist women who had been physically assaulted in exercising their legal rights.

The press continued to test the new, open climate in Morocco and political discourse took place openly. However, the government still controlled the public media, including the Maghreb Arabe Presse news agency, which only reflected official positions. In addition, restrictive press laws remained on the books, such as overly-broad defamation laws, and Article 77 of the Press Code, which permitted the minister of the interior to order the seizure or suspension of a publication without a judicial decision. On January 6, 1995, for example, an issue of the weekly *Maroc Hebdo*, which had excerpted a speech given by a Moroccan prince at an American university, was seized pursuant to this law. In addition, three subjects remained "taboo" in Morocco: criticizing the king or Islam, or challenging Morocco's claim to sovereignty over the Western Sahara—an issue of utmost sensitivity in Morocco (see the Western Sahara section). For example, Abdelkadir Chidoudi was sentenced to three years on June 30, 1995, and Ma'ghi Hicham, was sentenced to six months on July 28, 1995, both for having allegedly insulted the king.

Despite constitutional guarantees of the right to free assembly and association, the government frequently interfered with the activities of a range of legally-existing organizations, including labor unions and Berber organizations. Throughout the year, the authorities also banned public performances of the enormously popular singer and humorist Ahmed Snoussi ("Bziz"), who often parodied governmental figures and policies.

In addition to a number of pro-government political parties, several opposition parties continued to operate and were represented in parliament, including Istiqlal and the Socialist Union of Popular Forces (USFP).

However, Le Parti Maghrébin, a new political party, was denied authorization in March/April 1995. In addition, a de facto ban on Islamist political parties continued. Islamist groups kept most of their activities underground, but a publicized Islamist conference on Chechnya was banned in February.

The Right to Monitor

Several independent or opposition-affiliated human rights organizations, including the Moroccan Organization for Human Rights (OMDH) and the Moroccan Association for Human Rights (AMDH), operated freely in Morocco and expressed open criticism of governmental policies and actions. These organizations did not experience interference with their activities but stated that efforts at dialogue with the government had been ineffective. The Consultative Council on Human Rights (CCDH), which was created by the king in May 1990 to provide counsel on matters related to human rights, did not make independent decisions, rarely met and was slow to act.

After nearly four years of denying permission to Human Rights Watch/Middle East to conduct a fact-finding mission to Morocco, Moroccan authorities agreed to this request in April 1994, and a Human Rights Watch/Middle East mission took place the following spring. We were able to meet freely with government officials, members of the political opposition, human rights groups and other citizens. Amnesty International began the process of organizing groups of local members throughout Morocco. However, in accordance with Amnesty International policy, these groups would not work on Moroccan cases.

The Role of
the International Community

The apparent lack of political will on the part of the Moroccan government to pursue further meaningful improvements in its human rights practices coincided with a reduction or elimination of pressure from Western countries with respect to continuing human rights violations. As neighboring Algeria fell deeper into instability and violence, the West grew more protective of Morocco, despite its continuing record of human rights abuses, citing the importance of the Moroccan regime as a buffer against the spread of Islamic militancy. For the United States, Morocco's cooperative role in the Palestinian-Israeli peace process served as an additional justification for refraining from criticism. The State Department's *Country Report on Human Rights Practices for 1994* on Morocco was quite critical and documented human rights violations extensively but, with one exception, the U.S. government did not use this information to exert public pressure on King Hassan. The U.S. Ambassador to Morocco did intervene following the arrest and harsh sentences handed down to eight peaceful demonstrators in the Western Sahara, which may have been a factor in the king's subsequent decision to commute the defendants long prison sentences to one year. United States military sales to Morocco for 1995 were estimated at US$36.2 million and commercial military sales were estimated at US$5.9 million. In addition, the United States provided military education and training (IMET) to Morocco and was expected to transfer over $58 million in used military equipment, at little or no charge. The United States also continued to provide over $50 million in annual economic assistance, and agreed to create a US$250 million investment fund guaranteed by the Overseas Private Investment Corporation (OPIC).

France was Morocco's largest trade partner during 1995, engaging in both commercial and military sales, and the two governments enjoyed very good relations. The French government was silent regarding recent human rights violations in Morocco. Commercial interests also dominated the relationship between Morocco and the European Union (E.U.). In April, for example, the E.U. made two loans for infrastructure investments, totaling ECU 135 million. The E.U. did call for stepping up the dialogue on human rights with countries with which it had economic cooperation agreements, such as Morocco, and placed human rights, which

are always part of E.U. policy, on the agenda for the November Barcelona conference, aimed at creating a Euro-Mediterranean partnership. In July, Moroccan Prime Minister Abdellatif Filali criticized the E.U.'s preparatory document for the conference, saying that it overemphasized political relations, while only superficially discussing economic cooperation, partnership and social problems.

The Work of Human Rights Watch/Middle East

Human Rights Watch/Middle East sought to draw the attention of the international community to the serious abuses that continued during 1995, despite improvements in Morocco's human rights record. Human Rights Watch/Middle East followed several trials in Morocco and monitored due process violations that took place before and during trial. Human Rights Watch/Middle East worked closely with other independent and nongovernmental organizations to assess progress on cases of disappearances. Human Rights Watch/Middle East conducted a fact-finding mission to Morocco in the summer of 1995 and released a report and detailed recommendations based on its findings.

THE WESTERN SAHARA

Human Rights Developments

Little progress was made towards holding a scheduled referendum in the Western Sahara, intended to resolve the twenty year conflict between Morocco and the Popular Front for the Liberation of Saguia el Hamra and Rio de Oro (the Polisario Front, the Western Saharan liberation movement.) The referendum, which is to be conducted by the United Nations Mission for the Referendum in the Western Sahara (MINURSO), will ask

Sahrawis (Western Saharans) to choose between independence or integration into Morocco. In addition to extremely slow progress in the process to identify those eligible to vote, which had started almost three years behind schedule in August 1994, the fairness of the referendum was threatened. While both parties routinely created obstacles, Morocco, which was the stronger of the two parties both militarily and diplomatically and physically controlled most of the Western Sahara, regularly engaged in actions that compromised the fairness of the process. At the same time, the U.N. mission failed to fulfill its obligation to ensure the fairness of the upcoming referendum.

Citing slow progress in the voter identification process, the U.N. secretary-general repeatedly recommended the postponement of a transitional period, during which the U.N. was to have had powers including the responsibility for monitoring law and order in the territory, as well as the right to ensure that laws or measures that could obstruct a free and fair referendum were suspended. This delayed indefinitely the U.N. mission's assumption of powers essential to its effective supervision of the voter identification process.

Moroccan security forces routinely prevented Sahrawis seeking to submit voter applications from entering U.N. headquarters and the identification center in the Western Saharan capital of Laayoune. Applicants going through the identification process in the Moroccan-controlled Western Sahara were not permitted to come to the identification center on their own; rather, they were gathered in a central location and brought to the identification center in Moroccan vans. The U.N. did not formally investigate reports that Morocco had intimidated applicants who had come forward to be identified in the Moroccan-controlled Western Sahara, such as allegations that registration receipts had sometimes been illegally confiscated by Moroccan authorities.

Western Saharan (Sahrawi) tribal leaders involved in the identification process reported that Morocco had pressured Sahrawi tribal leaders living in the Moroccan-controlled Western Sahara on how they should rule in individual cases. This reportedly occurred through intimidation, either in advance or by Moroccan observers present in the identification room, who often signaled to tribal leaders. In addition, members of the MINURSO identification commission reported that they had come under pressure from certain senior U.N. staff members to make decisions on voter eligibility that favored Morocco and were contrary to the accepted procedures. In order to be eligible to vote in the referendum, applicants had to prove that they met one of five criteria agreed to by the parties, including membership in a Sahrawi tribe, or proving that their father was a Sahrawi born in the territory. A large number of the applicants submitted by Morocco had no documents proving links to the Western Sahara, were not familiar with the tribal structure of the region and had clearly memorized answers to the factual and biographical questions posed by the Commission. Many of these applicants were among the 40,000 people Morocco had transferred to the Western Sahara in 1991, in violation of the terms of the Settlement Plan, stating that they were Sahrawis who wanted to vote in the referendum. For the fourth year, this population lived under twenty-four hour guard in tent cities in the Western Sahara, and received food and other benefits from the Moroccan government. Access to the tent cities was tightly restricted by Moroccan police and secret service agents. Despite indications that individuals with questionable ties to the Western Sahara were being presented for identification, there was little opportunity to scrutinize the U.N.'s procedures or guidelines for making the final decisions on eligibility. Although the general criteria for eligibility were known, the U.N.'s final decisions were made behind closed doors, and no decisions were announced on the over 50,000 applicants who had already been identified by the U.N.

On January 25, 1995, Ambassador Frank Ruddy, former deputy chairman of the MINURSO identification commission, testified before the United States Congress, alleging MINURSO mismanagement and obstructionist actions by Morocco. In response to Ruddy's allegations, the U.N. under-secretary-general for internal oversight services conducted an investigation and issued a report on April 5, 1995 (the "internal oversight services report"), confirming some of Ruddy's allegations, but failing to find evidence of mismanagement.

In a September 8, 1995, report to the Security Council, the secretary-general stated that progress in the identification process had been "disappointing," but recommended the extension of MINURSO's mandate to January 31, 1996. The Security Council did so, but noted the secretary-general's intention to present the Security Council with alternative options before the expiration of the mandate, including a possible withdrawal of MINURSO if conditions necessary for the start of the transitional period were not in place.

Morocco continued to engage in human rights abuses in the Moroccan-controlled Western Sahara. On May 11, 1995, eight young men were arrested in Laayoune following a peaceful, pro-independence demonstration, and sentenced to fifteen to twenty years imprisonment by a military court in Morocco. Citing this incident and other "violations of the peace process," Polisario temporarily suspended its participation in the identification process on June 23, 1995. On July 9, 1995, the king commuted the eight Sahrawis' sentences to one year.

Hundreds of Sahrawis who had been victims of forced disappearances but were released in June 1991 still had not received any compensation from the Moroccan government by the end of 1995. Moreover, hundreds of cases of Sahrawis who reportedly disappeared up to two decades ago remained unresolved and the government made no effort to investigate or hold accountable those responsible for disappearances.

In 1995, up to 165,000 Sahrawis lived in desert camps in southwestern Algeria. They had taken refuge in these camps twenty years earlier, when armed conflict had broken out between Morocco and the Polisario Front. The refugees received humanitarian assistance from international relief organizations, U.N. agencies and the European Community. Polisario administered these camps and appeared to provide assistance to Sahrawi refugees on a timely and equitable basis.

Although living conditions in the desert were difficult and the location of the Polisario camps was remote and desolate, there was no evidence of food shortages, epidemics or other major health problems. Although most refugees expressed openly their unhappiness with the difficulties of living in the camps, there was no evidence that the Polisario was keeping refugees there forcibly. Rather, most of the difficulties and restrictions faced by the refugees were a result of their remote situation and the harsh climate in the desert, the economic and political difficulties of the region and the realities of being a stateless refugee population. Some refugees have returned to the Moroccan-controlled Western Sahara, and some Sahrawis have left the Moroccan-controlled Western Sahara since the original exodus, to join Polisario and live in the camps.

On May 8, 1989, prior to the signing of the U.N. Settlement Plan, Polisario released 200 elderly, ill and disabled Moroccan combatants captured and held during the war— in some cases for more than two decades. For the sixth straight year, Morocco denied these released prisoners, who were camped near the border, the right to return to Morocco; eight of them had died by 1995. Over 2,300 other Moroccan prisoners of war and up to 300 Polisario prisoners of war were still being held in Morocco and in Algeria. The ICRC has visited both sets of prisoners regularly since May 1993, with some interruptions. Human Rights Watch/Middle East visited two Polisario prisoner camps, where it found detention conditions to be extremely harsh, particularly due to the desolate desert location, intense heat, and the constant threat of sudden sandstorms. Some prisoners complained about their physical treatment at the hands of prison guards, while others emphasized that this had improved in the past five or six years. All the prisoners complained about insufficient food and medication, as well as about compulsory, unpaid labor, which was required for long hours, in a harsh climate.

The Right to Monitor

Opportunities for independent outsiders to observe and analyze the U.N. identification process in the Moroccan-controlled Western Sahara were strictly limited. Although no authorization was officially required for entering the Moroccan-controlled Western Sahara, local officials in fact required authorization from Rabat. Journalists and representatives of nongovernmental organizations were permitted to spend no more than thirty minutes in the MINURSO identification center in Laayoune, a period that was too brief to permit meaningful observation of a complex process. MINURSO staff members, including military observers, were subjected to constant surveillance. Until U.N. officials intervened, Moroccan security forces prevented Human Rights Watch/Middle East from entering the U.N. headquarters, stating that entry had to be cleared with local Moroccan authorities first. Moroccan authorities also detained the Human Rights Watch/Middle East representative at the entry to one of the "tent cities" in Laayoune and then held her at a police station. Moroccan authorities' harassment of Human Rights Watch/Middle East, as well as their strict surveillance of its activities, impeded the organization's ability to conduct a thorough investigation of human rights abuses in the Moroccan-controlled Western Sahara. The obstruction of the work of independent observers sent the signal that the U.N. mission was acquiescing to Moroccan interference in the referendum process and that the process was not being carried out in a transparent manner.

In Polisario refugee camps in Algeria, Human Rights Watch/Middle East was encouraged by members of Polisario to move about freely in the camps and speak to whom-ever it chose, but the remoteness of the camps, the unfriendly desert terrain and the absence of private transportation ultimately made Human Rights Watch/Middle East dependent upon Polisario for moving about. Although Polisario had agreed to provide access to all of the locations where Moroccan prisoners of war were being held in Algeria, Human Rights Watch/Middle East was only permitted to visit two such locations.

The Role of the International Community

U.N. Policy

The U.N.'s investigation into the allegations raised by Frank Ruddy provided an opportunity to expose shortcomings in the MINURSO operation and make constructive recommendations aimed at ensuring the credibility and fairness of the referendum process. Instead, the internal oversight services report had a defensive tone, and failed to provide a strong critique of the process or useful recommendations. Despite longstanding allegations of misconduct and unfairness associated with the MINURSO operation, the Security Council did not raise these concerns in any of its resolutions, or initiate any investigation until June 1995, when it sent a fact-finding delegation to the region to "assess progress and identify problems." The delegation issued a report that focused primarily on the slow pace of identification, and only alluded to issues related to the fairness of the referendum.

The U.S. and Argentine missions to the U.N. took the lead in pressing the Moroccan government to permit the 184 remaining prisoners of war released by Polisario to return to Morocco, in accordance with the internationally-guaranteed right to enter one's own country. However, by November, the Moroccan government had not responded to this initiative.

U.S. Policy

United States policy with regard to the Western Sahara was guided by the fact that this region was not a foreign policy priority, and that one party to the conflict—Morocco—is a close ally. The United States did not probe into the fairness and transparency of the referendum. However, citing mismanagement and the lack of progress in operations such as MINURSO, Republican Party legislators took the lead in calling for cuts in U.S. funding for U.N. peacekeeping operations. Due, in part, to pressure from Congress, the U.S. mission to the United Nations raised objections to continued funding for MINURSO, creating uncertainty prior to the September 22 Security Council vote as to whether the MINURSO mandate would be extended. However, like the Security Council, the U.S. mission focused on the lack of progress in voter identification and the issue of financial resources, but failed to call on the Moroccan government to stop undermining the fairness of the referendum process.

The Work of
Human Rights Watch/Middle East

Human Rights Watch/Middle East conducted a fact-finding mission to southwestern Algeria and the Moroccan-controlled Western Sahara in August 1995, and released a report on its findings. Although Human Rights Watch takes no position on the issue of self-determination, we sought to draw attention to the fact that the free and fair nature of the referendum process had been significantly compromised, and that the identification process was not being carried out in a transparent manner. Prior to the Security Council's September vote on extension of MINURSO's mandate, Human Rights Watch/Middle East wrote a letter to all members of the Security Council, urging them to reexamine and modify the mandate of MINURSO in order to ensure a free, transparent and fair referendum. The letter also called on the Security Council to send a strong signal to the Moroccan government that it must stop obstructing and compromising the fairness of the referendum process. We also provided interviews to the press, and information to other nongovernmental organizations interested in visiting the refugee camps in southwestern Algeria or in observing the U.N. operation in Algeria and in the Moroccan-controlled Western Sahara.

SAUDI ARABIA

Human Rights Developments

In 1995 Saudi Arabia experienced further deterioration in human rights observance. There was a four-fold increase in the number of executions, mostly of foreign suspected drug traffickers. One Islamist opposition activist was also beheaded, the first activist to be put to death since the rise of Islamist opposition during the Gulf War. Arbitrary arrest, detention without trial and ill-treatment of prisoners remained the norm during the year, especially for those accused of political offenses. Several hundred Islamist opponents were arbitrarily detained without trial. The ban on free speech, assembly and association was strictly enforced; violators were jailed, deported, banned from travel or dismissed from their government positions. Restrictions on the employment and movement of women were strictly observed, and harassment of non-Muslims and Muslims who do not follow the kingdom's strict religious code continued unabated.

The government's crackdown on peaceful dissent by Islamist groups, begun in 1993, continued during the year. Most detainees were held without trial. Those who were put on trial were tried before secret tribunals without the benefit of legal counsel. On August 11, 1995, the government of Saudi Arabia beheaded Abdalla al-Hudhaif, a supporter of the Committee for the Defense of Legitimate Rights (CDLR), a banned Saudi opposition group established in May 1993 by Islamist jurists and professors. He was convicted in a secret trial in which nine other Islamists were given lengthy prison sentences. The execution marked the first time an Islamist activist was executed in Saudi Arabia since the rise of Islamist opposition during the Gulf War. Al-Hudhaif, a thirty-three-year-old businessman and father of six, was accused of throwing acid on an intelligence officer, possession of firearms, and "fomenting dissension" by supporting the London-based CDLR and distributing its leaflets. This attack was the only incident of violence that the government attributed to the Islamist opposition since the beginning of its public activity, which has been otherwise restricted to peaceful means, including public rallies, speeches and the distribution of leaflets and audio cassettes.

The Saudi government, in announcing the verdicts of the secret tribunal, accused its opponents of rebellion and heresy—capital offenses in Saudi Arabia. The judicial proceedings were marred throughout by violations of due process of law, including the use of coerced confessions, denial of legal counsel and blatant interference by government officials. For example, at first, the tribunal sentenced al-Hudhaif to twenty years in prison, but the Ministry of Interior protested the lightness of sentence and demanded a retrial. The judiciary complied, and in the second review, al-Hudhaif was sentenced to death.

The defendant was informed of the first sentence in May 1995, but the decision to put him to death—which was reportedly made in early July and ratified by King Fahd on July 10—was kept secret until August 12, a day after the execution. The beheading was carried out in secret, an exception to the rule of public executions. The authorities reportedly rejected al-Hudhaif's family's requests to hand over his body to conduct religious burial services. Instead, he was buried by the government, fueling speculation that he had been tortured before he was killed. The government justified this unprecedentedly harsh sentence by citing the need to combat dissension and maintain the security and stability of the state. It cited other offenses that the condemned man had allegedly committed, including the possession of weapons and his support for CDLR and the distribution of its publications, which were usually highly critical of Saudi leaders.

In a reference to the CDLR, the government's statement and the court judgment referred repeatedly to the defendant's "support for the so-called Committee for the Defense of Rights, a group that has declared disobedience to the rulers and recanted the pledge of loyalty to the ruler of the nation" and his "distribution of its publications and sheltering those who did." It also referred to his "disrespect and disobedience to the ruler of the community and to the nation's religious scholars, who have condemned this group as an illegitimate entity, warned of its dangers and called for fighting it."

Nine other Islamists, including two university professors and a lecturer, were given lengthy prison sentences by the same tribunal, which cited their support for CDLR among the grounds for the conviction. Two of the convicted were accused of conspiracy to attack the intelligence officer although they had already been in detention for weeks when the attack took place. Other than the defendants' apparent support for CDLR, the government presented no evidence that the attack was authorized by CDLR, which was not known to advocate the use of violence.

The campaign against the nonviolent Islamist opposition continued during 1995. Several hundred religious opponents of the government were arrested. In almost all cases, the arrests and accompanying searches were conducted without warrants and suspects were held without charge or trial. None of the detainees were allowed visits by legal counsel.

Most of the detainees were suspected supporters of the two jailed opposition leaders, Shaikh Salman al-Audah and Shaikh Safar al-Hawali, both university professors and religious leaders who had been banned from speaking in public, dismissed from their academic posts in September 1993, and were detained since September 1994. Those detained also included founders and supporters of CDLR.

Although no formal charges were filed against most of the detainees, government statements cited their public speaking in defiance of previous bans and "fomenting dissension and civil strife." Salman al-

Audah's book *Kissinger's Promise* was cited in an official statement as evidence of subversion, as were audiocassettes and handbills distributed clandestinely, in defiance of government prohibitions. An August 12, 1995, official statement branded the Islamist opponents as heretics, referring to the CDLR as a group that has "strayed beyond the pale of Islam by sowing the seeds of dissension when they declared their disobedience to the ruler of the nation to whom they had pledged loyalty and expressed their utter disregard for the Ulema, whom they accused of failing to perform their duty." The government had already secured an opinion from the Council of Senior Scholars denouncing the CDLR as a heresy. If convicted as heretics, many of the detained Islamist opponents could face severe punishments, including the death penalty.

There was a marked increase during 1995 of reports of torture and ill-treatment of detainees during interrogation by the secret police and the religious police. To compel prisoners to provide information they were frequently beaten with bamboo sticks and plastic-covered truncheons. Ill-treatment included prolonged incommunicado detention, sleep deprivation for long periods, threats of violence and execution, and insults. Visits by family members or lawyers were often denied for long periods.

There was a four-fold increase in the number of executions during 1995 over the previous year. During the first nine months, 182 people were executed, compared to fifty-three in all of 1994. Most were beheaded in public. Most were foreigners who were suspected of smuggling drugs, including mild sedatives, sleeping pills and stimulants, into the country. The summary proceedings which resulted in these harsh sentences fell far short of international standards for fair trials. Most of the defendants were not represented by lawyers at the trials or assisted in preparing their defense. In 1995, there was also a marked increase in the application of judicially-ordered corporal punishment, including flogging for a variety of crimes and amputations for theft.

Under the Imprisonment and Detention Law No. 31 of 1978 and its 1982 bylaws, issued by the minister of interior, detainees may be held indefinitely without trial or judicial review. Although families were often able to find out informally if one of their members had been detained, rarely was there formal notification. This practice applied equally to foreigners, many of whom had no family in Saudi Arabia to notice that they were missing. Saudi authorities did not notify foreign missions of the arrest of their nationals and declined to sign international or bilateral consular agreements mandating such notification or allowing immediate access by foreign consulates.

It was equally rare for a detainee to be informed of the charges against him or her. Saudi law permits interrogation of detainees without the benefit of counsel, and the use of force to elicit confessions was commonplace in the Saudi security system. The law explicitly sanctions flogging, indefinite solitary confinement, and deprivation of family visits, as methods for disciplining prisoners.

Foreigners, their number estimated officially at about five million (27 percent of the population), faced special hardships, including a ban on travel within the country or abroad without written permission from their employers. Hundreds of foreigners accused of violating the stringent visa regulations by overstaying their residency permits or changing their employers were being held in crowded, substandard deportation facilities throughout the kingdom. Most were subsequently expelled without judicial review. Since regulations required that aliens secure clearance from their former employers before being permitted to leave the country, many were kept in deportation facilities awaiting these clearances.

Human rights abuses were facilitated by the absence of an independent judiciary and the lack of scrutiny by an elected representative body or a free press. The royal family's concentration of power and the absence of a free press or parliament left government officials and members of the royal family immune to criticism and free to abuse their positions. In 1994, there were several reports of unpunished abuses by members of the royal family, including murder and beatings of Saudi citizens and foreign residents.

Not surprisingly, the newly appointed Consultative Council failed to address human rights concerns. Almost all of the sixty-one members of the new council were government loyalists, the majority of them long-time government employees. According to the Consultative Council's own bylaws, the Council's members retain their positions in the executive branch while serving their terms in the Consultative Council. By virtue of its mandate, composition and bylaws, the Council did not appear likely to provide a forum for significant political discussion or act as a check on human rights abuses. Although all of the Council's meetings—after the inaugural session—were held in secret, Human Rights Watch/Middle East learned that the Council did not make any independent decisions regarding civil rights or other controversial issues. Few officials were instructed by King Fahd to brief the council in private sessions, and no members were known to have seriously questioned government policy in these sessions.

As a result of the government's crackdown, opposition activity went nearly completely underground or into exile. Mosque sermons, books, leaflets and audiocassettes, which in the past openly criticized corruption and favoritism and called for more political participation, were muted during 1995, as the government enforced its strict ban on public speaking, assembly, and association. In addition to arresting hundreds of Islamists, the government dismissed many from their teaching jobs and banned many others from travel. It also introduced measures to tighten its control over the flow of information in and out of the country. In several statements issued by the Ministry of Interior, the government warned citizens and residents against publicly criticizing the state's "internal, foreign, financial, media or other policies," or "communicating with anyone outside the country, or any activist inside the country, by telephone or fax." The ban included religious sermons, university lectures and the distribution or ownership of "hostile" writings or audiocassettes.

The Saudi government owns and operates all radio and television stations in the kingdom, and it keeps the privately owned local press on a very short leash, preventing criticism of government policies. Foreign publications, including daily newspapers and weekly magazines, were barred from the country in 1994 for publishing such views. The government exercises considerable influence over major regional and international news organizations. Royal family members and their close associates owned key news organizations, including United Press International; al-Hayat, a major daily in the Middle East; and MBC, a London-based satellite television network. The Ministry of Information signed an agreement with Radio Monte Carlo's Middle East Division, a major source of news in the kingdom, to highlight positive elements of government policy. MBC in turn acquired the Arab Network of America (ANA), previously a private radio and television cable network with services in most U.S. metropolitan areas. After it changed owners, ANA canceled programs that aired views critical of Saudi policies. During 1995, there were reports that the British Broadcasting Corporation Arabic Television, a joint venture between the BBC and a company owned by a member of the Saudi royal family, canceled programs unfavorable to the Saudi government.

Although the Saudi government banned the importation and the use of satellite dishes in 1994, it has not moved to confiscate those already in use in the kingdom. In March 1994, a royal decree banned television satellite dishes, imposing a fine equivalent to US$26,667 for possessing and $133,333 for importing the equipment. In June, in an apparent response to satellite-transmitted criticism of the government, the Ministry of Interior gave those who already owned dishes a month to re-export or otherwise dispose of them before imposing the fines.

The Right to Monitor

Since monitoring human rights violations was considered by the government as political activity, Saudi Arabian law and practice strictly prohibited such an undertaking. Saudi associations of any kind wishing to report on human rights violations in the kingdom had to work either clandestinely inside the country, at the risk of arrests, or operate outside the kingdom. In 1995, the ability to monitor human rights abuses in Saudi Arabia was handicapped by the continued shutdown of opposition groups reporting abuses and the arrests of opposition activists attempting to monitor violations.

However, new opposition groups established in 1994 outside the kingdom provided a steady stream of news and commentary on violations of the rights of dissidents and government opponents. The mainstream Islamist opposition group, CDLR, resumed its activities from London, publishing regular reports on arrests of Islamist activists. Another Islamist group, the Advice and Reformation Committee, was established in London, led by Usama bin Ladin, a Saudi businessman who was accused of supporting radical groups in the region and stripped of his Saudi citizenship in 1994.

The Reform Movement, the main Shi'a opposition group, refrained from conducting any public activities in 1995 outside Saudi Arabia, in exchange for government promises to improve conditions for the Shi'a minority. Before they were suspended, the movement's activities had included the publication of a magazine in Arabic and another in English, and the distribution of human rights information by groups affiliated with the movement. During the year, the Holy Shrines Center, run by a smaller Shi'a opposition group, continued to issue occasional reports on violations of the rights of the Shi'a minority.

No human rights organizations were permitted to visit Saudi Arabia in 1995. Saudi government offices consistently failed to respond to Human Rights Watch/Middle East's inquiries and requests for information. However, in October, Prince Bandar ibn Sultan, the Saudi Ambassador to the United States, reversed a long standing policy and extended a conditional invitation to Human Rights Watch/Middle East to visit Saudi Arabia.

U.S. and European Policies

By virtue of an important strategic relationship with Saudi Arabia spanning over fifty years, the United States was uniquely well-placed to help curb human rights abuses in Saudi Arabia. Although the Clinton election campaign had cited Saudi Arabia as a target for human rights attention, the Clinton administration largely failed to criticize publicly Saudi violations, and occasionally praised the kingdom's rulers. Subordinating human rights principles to strategic and commercial interests, the increased level of military and commercial activity during the year was not accompanied by public candor in assessing the human rights record of Saudi Arabia. During the year, high level meetings regularly took place between the two governments, but U.S. officials refrained from publicly expressing any concern over human rights violations.

The defense of Saudi Arabia was a key goal of U.S. foreign policy that the Clinton administration emphasized from the beginning of its term and repeated several times during 1995. This commitment was demonstrated during the year through the assignment of a large number of U.S. military advisers with the Saudi military, delivery of sophisticated U.S.-made weapons to Saudi Arabia, holding of military exercises by U.S. forces in the Gulf, regular high level visits by military officials of both countries, and the overall upgrading of the permanent U.S. military presence in the Gulf—renamed the Fifth Fleet. Secretary of Defense William Perry visited Saudi Arabia in March and Prince Sultan ibn Abdel Aziz, minister of defense and second deputy prime minister, visited the United States in late October and met with senior administration officials, including President Clinton and Vice President Gore.

In March, after his visit to Riyadh,

Defense Secretary William Perry said that he had received guarantees from Saudi Arabia for U.S. military access to its ports and airfields after he had shared with Saudi officials spy photo evidence of Iraq's new military infrastructure. "We agreed that continued United States access to Saudi bases and ports is the key to quick, forceful response to aggression," Secretary Perry said, adding that Iraq had been using what limited revenues it had to rebuild the military infrastructure destroyed during the 1991 Gulf War. Secretary Perry said that the two nations, which enjoyed "good relations for over fifty years," shared the belief that the six states of the Gulf Cooperation Council (Bahrain, Kuwait, Oman, Qatar, Saudi Arabia and the United Arab Emirates) should improve their military readiness in the face of potential threats from Iraq and Iran. "Saudi Arabia is an island of stability in a sea of trouble," Secretary Perry said, adding that Washington and Riyadh were committed to working together to maintain stability for the region. The Secretary said that he had received expressions of support for basing supplies for a U.S. armored division in the Gulf region. Supplies for three brigades would support an entire U.S. armored division—about 15,000 soldiers. Equipment for one brigade had already been stored in Kuwait, while another agreement was being negotiated to store a second brigade in Qatar. Secretary Perry said that no formal agreement was reached on storing the equipment in Saudi Arabia, but that he was confident the issue would be worked out in time.

The bilateral military arrangements included the sale of sophisticated weapons, with Saudi Arabia accounting for over one fourth of total U.S. military sales. In September, Saudi Arabia received the first group of seventy-two F-15S fighter bombers contracted for immediately after the Gulf War.

In addition to military hardware, Saudi Arabia was a major source of large commercial contracts with U.S. companies. After intensive lobbying by senior administration officials, including President Clinton, Saudi Arabia awarded the Boeing Company and the McDonnell-Douglas Corporation with a $6 billion dollar contract and gave American Telephone and Telegraph a $4 billion dollar contract to expand the kingdom's telephone network. U.S. firms in general increased their investments in Saudi Arabia, making the U.S. by far the largest single foreign investor in the kingdom.

In September, Raymond Mabus, U.S. ambassador to Saudi Arabia, participated in a tour of major U.S. cities aimed at encouraging U.S. businesses to invest in the region, especially in the countries that were considered to be promoting the peace process. In his speeches Mabus praised the Saudi government's support for the peace process and reassured U.S. businesses that although Saudi Arabia lives among some "bad neighbors," referring to Iran and Iraq, the internal situation in the country was "very stable," emphasizing that Saudi Arabia plays a major role in supporting the U.S. in an area of vital interest to the U.S.

Occasional references to the need for promoting human rights in the Middle East in general were never followed by statements of concern about serious human rights violations in Saudi Arabia or the lack of political participation in the kingdom, where no elections of any kind were held and no public independent expression was permitted. With the exception of the annual recitation of human rights abuses in the kingdom in the U.S. Department of State's *Country Reports on Human Rights Practices for 1994*, U.S. officials refrained from commenting on human rights, even when Saudi Arabia beheaded Abdalla al-Hudhaif in August—the first opposition activist to be executed—and when the rate of execution in the country for nonviolent drug offenses quadrupled during the year.

The policies of major European powers toward human rights in Saudi Arabia paralleled those of the U.S. in subordinating human rights to military and commercial ties. Both the United Kingdom and France assiduously cultivated the Saudi government for additional military and commercial contracts. In October, Charles Million, France's minister of defense, visited Saudi Arabia to promote French-Saudi military cooperation, including France's proposal to sell large numbers of France's advanced battle tanks. Million's visit was to be followed later in the year by visits by ministers of interior and foreign affairs, in preparation for a visit by French President Jacques Chirac scheduled for early 1996. France has been a major source of weaponry for the Saudi Arabian navy, which since 1980 has purchased French-made warships, missiles, and naval attack helicopters. In November 1994, France and Saudi Arabia signed a US$3.8 billion contract for military equipment and training. Despite the many occasions in which Saudi and French officials met during 1995, French officials refrained from publicly voicing concerns over human rights abuses.

In an apparent effort to safeguard its close military and economic ties with Saudi Arabia, the British government was also silent on human rights abuses. In addition, during 1995, the British government took measures to prevent Saudi citizens from expressing their opposition to their government from London. The British authorities expelled Ahmed al-Zahrani, a former Saudi diplomat who defected and sought asylum in the U.K. after his book on Saudi policy was criticized by the Saudi ministry of interior. The British government also attempted to deport Dr. Muhammed al-Mas'ari, another Saudi dissident and spokesman of the CDLR, but was thwarted by British courts.

The Work of
Human Rights Watch/Middle East

In 1995, despite the Saudi government's failure to approve Human Rights Watch/Middle East's request for an official mission to the kingdom, we continued our monitoring of human rights conditions and advocacy on behalf of victims of abuse in Saudi Arabia.

In July and August, a Human Rights Watch/Middle East representative investigated the repressive measures taken by the Saudi government against its political opponents since 1993. A report on the results of the investigation was pending.

In August, Human Rights Watch/Middle East issued a statement protesting the execution of the first Saudi Islamist opponent since the rise of Islamist opposition during the Gulf War. It also condemned the secret trial that resulted in harsh sentences for nine other Islamists.

In October, the Saudi ambassador to the United States reversed a longstanding policy and extended a conditional invitation for Human Rights Watch/Middle East to visit Saudi Arabia.

SYRIA

Human Rights Developments

Syria remained a tightly controlled society, with little space for its seventeen million citizens to exercise the full range of civil and political rights. A state of emergency, in force since 1963, still provides a convenient legal mantle for suspending basic constitutional freedoms. Open political activity was a privilege enjoyed only by the ruling Ba'th Party and the six smaller parties allied with it in the National Progressive Front. Unauthorized opposition groups—their ranks decimated by arrests throughout the 1980s—continued to operate clandestinely, their capacity to organize, disseminate information, and otherwise make their views known severely limited.

The country's legal system lacks procedures by which a group can obtain status as a party, and criminalizes peaceful political dissent. Since 1992, criminal statutes have been used to prosecute before a court of exception—the state security court—hundreds of known or suspected members of unauthorized political groups for vaguely formulated offenses such as "opposing any of the goals of the Revolution" and membership in organizations "created to change the economic or social structure of the state or the fundamental fabric of society."

Extremely slow-paced, unfair trials of those accused of membership in unauthorized political groups continued in Damascus before the three judge state security court, whose verdicts cannot be appealed to a higher tribunal. Many of the defendants had been imprisoned without charge since the 1980s. In trial sessions observed by Human Rights Watch/Middle East in April, judges ignored defendants' complaints about coerced confessions and torture under interrogation; there was limited or no access to competent lawyers prior to and during trials; and key stages of some proceedings—such as presentation of evidence by the prosecutor—took place outside the public courtroom, with the defendants not present. Fifteen-year sentences handed down by the court could keep some political and human rights activists imprisoned until the year 2002.

For the fifteenth year, authorities maintained their relentless punishment of a leading opposition figure, sixty-five-year-old lawyer Riad al-Turk, the head of the Communist Party-Political Bureau. He was arrested in October 1980 and remained detained without charge in an isolation cell in the basement of the Military Interrogation Branch in Damascus. In May, Human Rights Watch/Middle East received information that al-Turk's health had seriously deteriorated and his life was in danger. In a letter to President Hafez al-Asad, we urged his release on humanitarian grounds, and took the position that detention without charge for nearly fifteen years represented a blatant contradiction of Syria's stated commitment to the rule of law.

Releases in 1994 and 1995 reduced the already small group of Syria's longest serving known political prisoners to three. In January 1995, authorities freed Fawzi Rida, Abdel Hamid Muqdad, and former minister Muhamed 'Id Ashshawi, all of them detained without charge since 1970. The remaining three continued to be held despite the completion of their prison sentences over ten years ago. Jalal al-Din Mirhij and Mustafa Tawfiq Fallah, both of whom were reported in poor health in Mezze military prison, were arrested in 1970 and sentenced by the security court in 1971 to fifteen-year prison terms.

Khalil Brayez, a former Syrian army officer and author of two books critical of Syrian military operations during the 1967 war with Israel, was abducted from Lebanon in 1970 and sentenced to fifteen years imprisonment in 1972. He too was held in Mezze prison. The continued detention of these men appears to be wholly arbitrary and they should be released. Interior Minister Muhammed Harba did not allow Human Rights Watch/Middle East to visit al-Turk, Fallah and Brayez when we requested access in April.

An estimated 500 to 600 political prisoners were freed in March and April, the largest number since the dramatic releases of several thousand long-term detainees in late 1991. While this was a welcome action, a prisoner's punishment did not end with his release. Former prisoners continued to be harassed and intimidated by the security apparatus. They have been summoned for questioning, threatened, asked to serve as informers, and warned to keep silent, explaining the reluctance of many to provide information to human rights investigators. Some prisoners were pressured to "give up politics" prior to release and to sign written loyalty oaths as a condition for release. Those convicted of offenses by the security court have been penalized with an accessory ten-year deprivation of civil rights following the completion of their prison sentences. They were barred by law from work in the state sector, even if they formerly held government jobs. They cannot vote, run for office, or serve in councils of syndicates or sects.

Some of the prisoners released in 1995 had been held incommunicado at Tadmor military prison since the early 1980s, in abysmally harsh conditions in the desert 200 kilometers northeast of Damascus. Many prisoners did not survive the depradations at Tadmor. The body of one of them, Ahmad Khoula, was delivered to his family in Aleppo on October 28, 1994. Khoula, a teacher of Arabic, was thirty-one years old when he was arrested by security forces in Aleppo on June 5, 1980. It was not known if Khoula was alive or dead until 1991, when released prisoners brought news that he was in

Tadmor. They said that he walked with a limp because one of his legs, fractured when he was tortured under interrogation in 1980, had never been properly treated. Authorities did not explain the circumstances of Khoula's death and provided no information about why he had been detained for over fourteen years.

We received reports during the year about incommunicado detention, but in some cases families were too afraid to release names and other details. In January, a man in his twenties from a village near Jableh was arrested upon arrival at Damascus airport. Waiting family members were given his luggage, and he was held incommunicado for over two months, then released without charge. He was reportedly arrested because he had written his family from Cyprus, where he had been employed, describing the contents of newspaper articles about Syria published there. A Jordanian citizen who entered Syria in 1993, to obtain information about the whereabouts of his older brother who was arrested in Damascus in 1985 and held incommunicado, was himself taken into custody by security forces at the border. For the next month, family members made inquiries at various security agencies in Damascus, only to be told repeatedly that there were no records of his detention. In a meeting with the family in March 1995, we confirmed that the man was still "disappeared" as of that date.

In early 1995, there were incidents of violence against lawyers in Latakia. On February 14, two prominent lawyers, Dr. Burhan Zreg and Muhamed Radoun, were beaten in Sheikh Dhaher police station in the city center when visiting on behalf of a client who had been repeatedly harassed after he refused to pay one of the officers a large bribe. When the lawyers arrived, they were punched, kicked, and severely beaten by a dozen policemen, including officers, then dragged into the detention area and locked up for two hours. They were freed when members of the lawyers syndicate council arrived at the police station and facilitated their release. Following the attack, some 150 lawyers sent letters of protest to the national lawyers syndicate in Damascus. They were concerned and fearful because this was not an isolated case. In January, fifty-five-year-old lawyer Adam Aloush from Latakia had been beaten in the state security office, where he was visiting on behalf of a client. Colleagues said that his injuries kept him out of work for a month but that he remained silent. "He did not dare to complain. They threatened him," one lawyer told us. A March 1 order, signed by Interior Minister Harba and sent to the lawyers syndicate and all police stations, reminded the police to be "well mannered when dealing with people," but emphasized that lawyers were not permitted to interfere in police affairs.

The government did not ease its unrelenting grip on civil society, and the country remained bereft of independent institutions. Syrian daily newspapers and electronic media were state controlled, books were subjected to pre-publication censorship, and academic freedom was limited. Operatives from security agencies scrutinized the activities of private associations registered with the Ministry of Social Affairs and Labor. They attended meetings and sometimes demanded information about the political affiliations of members.

There were arbitrary restrictions on freedom of movement of suspected dissidents and former political prisoners. According to lawyers, there was one blacklist for those prohibited from obtaining passports, and another for persons barred from travel abroad without permission of one or more security services. There was no semblance of due process when the right to travel was curtailed: the Interior Ministry did not provide reasons for the rejection of passport applications and exit permits.

Syria's Kurdish minority continued to suffer acute discrimination under the law. The consequences of a special census conducted in 1962 in northeastern Hassakeh governorate, which has the largest concentration of Kurds in Syria, remained a major issue. The village-by-village census arbitrarily stripped over 100,000 Kurds of their

Syrian citizenship, reclassifying them as "foreigners," in violation of international law. Kurds with this status, who have been issued special red identity cards, were unable to obtain passports, were barred from employment in the state sector, and could not own property or businesses. This mass denationalization has affected an increasing number of Kurds over the years because the legal status of parents was passed on to their Syrian-born children, who have been deprived by the state of their right to a nationality.

As of March 1995, there were 334,870 officially registered Palestinian refugees in Syria, with some 28 percent residing in ten refugee camps administered by the United Nations Relief and Works Agency. Information-gathering about human rights conditions in this community was exceedingly difficult. There were no independent Palestinian nongovernmental organizations in Syria, and the Damascus-based, anti-Arafat Palestinian political factions does not criticize the practices of their host President Asad. The refugee camps were reportedly under the surveillance of plainclothes forces from Military Intelligence, Political Security, and a joint body composed of representatives of both branches.

The Right to Monitor

The Syrian government does not recognize the right of its citizens to carry out independent monitoring and reporting of human rights abuses. When an emerging human rights movement became too vocal in late 1991, the state moved quickly and harshly to crush it. Suspected members and supporters of the Committees for the Defense of Democratic Freedoms and Human Rights in Syria (CDF) were arrested by security forces. In March 1992, fourteen were sentenced to prison terms ranging from three to ten years, following a trial before the state security court that did not meet international fair trial standards. Other than monthly visits with immediate family members, these activists have had no contact with the outside world. Two of them, forty-four-year-old lawyer

Aktham Naissa (sentenced to nine years imprisonment) and thirty-three-year-old writer Nizar Nayouf (sentenced to ten years), were said to be suffering from medical problems that have not being adequately treated. The government did not allow visiting Human Rights Watch/Middle East representatives to meet with the men.

Although Syrian rights activists languished in prison, the government allowed international human rights organizations to carry out research. Human Rights Watch/Middle East was notified in January that a long-standing request to conduct a fact-finding mission had been granted. During the mission, which began in March, no restrictions were placed on the freedom of movement of our investigators and there was no overt surveillance of their activities.

Authorities were, however, unresponsive on issues such as access to prisons and political prisoners which were still deemed sensitive. In October 1994, a Human Rights Watch/Middle East representative had discussions in Damascus with senior government officials, including the interior minister, about visiting places of detention and meeting with prisoners, including Syrian rights activists. The request was not turned down at that time. On March 29, while the mission was in progress, Justice Minister Hussein Hasoun informed us that we would be allowed to visit any civilian prison in the country that was under the supervision of his ministry. All facilities where political prisoners were being held, however, were closed to us as they were under military or security apparatus control: they included Tadmor, Sednaya, and Mezze prisons, the Damascus detention center of the Military Interrogation Branch of Military Intelligence, and the section of Adra prison controlled by Political Security. We responded on April 1, with a letter to Interior Minister Harba requesting a meeting to discuss access to these facilities and political prisoners. The letter was not answered.

The Role of
the International Community

Diplomatic efforts to secure the long-sought Israeli-Syrian peace deal once again eclipsed any sustained focus on the Asad government's human rights performance. Overwhelming public silence marked the approach of both the U.S. and European Union toward specific aspects of Syria's human rights record. There appeared to be an unspoken agreement to keep specific human rights concerns off-limits while peace-process negotiations continued. We were aware of no vigorous bilateral or multilateral efforts in 1995 to press Syrian authorities for measurable human rights improvements. The government's decision to welcome visits by international organizations and allow them access to security court trials and senior officials, while a positive step, was no substitute for substantive reforms to ensure civil and political rights.

The European Union

On June 15, the European Parliament passed a strongly worded resolution, citing "continued violations of human rights" in Syria. The resolution deplored the fact that the European Commission had not yet submitted to the parliament a report on human rights in Syria and the results of the November 1994 meeting between the Syrian foreign minister and European Union (E.U.) foreign ministers. In July, Human Rights Watch/Middle East urged the European Council of Ministers and the European Commission to present the progress report on human rights in Syria to the European Parliament, in accordance with the commitment made by the commission during the December 1993 debate on the Fourth Protocol on financial and technical cooperation with Syria. The approval of this protocol released a five-year E.U. aid package of over $178 million to the Asad government.

The United States

The improved bilateral relationship between the U.S. and Syrian governments—and continuing high-level diplomatic contacts between the two states—presented an important opportunity for a more assertive and vocal U.S. role in addressing ongoing rights violations. Yet, aside from the strong language in the State Department's *Country Reports on Human Rights Practices for 1994*, there were no public statements from Clinton administration officials during the year about human rights in Syria, except in the most general, inscrutable terms. "We have a number of serious differences with Syria on a variety of issues. We continue—frequently and at the highest levels—to make our position on issues such as human rights ... clear to the Syrian government," was the written answer of Assistant Secretary of State Robert H. Pelletreau to a question for the record submitted by Representative Lee Hamilton of the House of Representatives International Relations Committee on August 2.

U.S. diplomats, however, did have a positive reaction to our July recommendation to all embassies in Damascus that representatives attend security court trials. As of this writing, Human Rights Watch/Middle East understands that the U.S. embassy in Damascus was actively considering how to implement this recommendation in coordination with other interested governments.

The United Nations

Human Rights Watch/Middle East understood that gross violations of human rights in Syria were under examination through the confidential Resolution 1503 procedure of the U.N. Economic and Social Council.

The Work of
Human Rights Watch/Middle East

Our work during the year combined extensive field research in Syria with continuing contact with Syrian government officials and advocacy efforts urging greater activism on behalf of human rights by the U.S. and European Union. In November 1994, we circulated a briefing paper in advance of the November 28 meeting in Brussels between European Union foreign ministers and Syrian Foreign Minister Farouq al-Shar'a. It expressed concern about the absence of human rights as an official agenda item for the meeting. We had learned that human rights would only be raised in a "discreet manner" following the meeting, during bilateral talks between the Syrian foreign minister and the European Union Presidenct, then German Foreign Minister Klaus Kinkel, and European Commission President Jacques Delors. We sent the briefing document to Kinkel and Delors, and urged that the issues it raised be seriously discussed during the bilateral talks.

Human Rights Watch/Middle East conducted a fact-finding mission in Syria from March 23 to May 8. In July, we published *Syria: The Price of Dissent*, a fifty-four-page report on security court trials, torture, and the continuing pressures on political prisoners after release. The report, based on information collected during the mission and observation of security court proceedings, included the Syrian government's response to a detailed written summary of the major findings which we provided prior to publication.

Our representatives returned to Syria from July 19-25, following the publication of the report. Despite repeated contacts prior to and during this visit with the Syrian Foreign Ministry in Damascus and the Syrian embassy in Washington, D.C., there was no response to our request to meet with government officials to discuss the report.

On July 12, we wrote to the Syrian Ministry of Foreign Affairs and expressed our desire to return to Syria later in 1995 to undertake additional research. As of this writing, we were waiting for an affirmative response from the government.

HUMAN
RIGHTS
WATCH

UNITED STATES

Human Rights Developments

The climate for human rights in the United States worsened in 1995, marked by mounting evidence of the persistence and pervasiveness of racism in the criminal justice system, expanded use of the death penalty, increased reliance on incarceration and harsher conditions of confinement, and attacks on due process and freedom of expression by the new Republican majority in Congress.

The sharp differences in the way African-Americans and whites reacted to the acquittal of African-American celebrity O.J. Simpson of murder charges highlighted the systematic abuse of minority citizens by police and ongoing racism in the criminal justice system. The experience of discrimination at the hands of law enforcement officials and courts led many minorities to deeply distrust institutions of justice. In addition, minority rights were weakened over the year by three Supreme Court decisions that reduced protections in voting, education, and employment, and by a concerted Republican-led attack on "affirmative action" programs designed to increase the representation of minorities in workplaces and higher education.

Concerns over police misconduct throughout the country grew during the year. Police officers in a number of cities were accused of serious human rights violations, including murder, brutality, and rape, with many victims asserting that these abuses were racially motivated. Despite the seriousness of the allegations, far too often police leadership as well as state and federal prosecutors failed in their duties to vigorously pursue and prosecute cases of police misconduct.

The debate over racial disparities in prison terms for drug offenses erupted into public view in October when inmates rioted in four federal prisons after Congress rejected the recommendations of the United States Sentencing Commission to modify the differential treatment between crack and powder cocaine in mandatory federal drug sentences. Among the commission's other disturbing findings: although whites and African-Americans used both forms of cocaine, whites were arrested and prosecuted mainly for federal powder cocaine crimes while African-Americans made up 90 percent of those convicted for crack cocaine offenses.

The federal crimes of possession and distribution of crack cocaine carried much harsher penalties than similar offenses involving powder cocaine. This two-tiered sentencing scheme, though facially neutral, had a significant discriminatory impact on the African-American community. The disparate impact of drug laws on African-Americans was heightened by the pattern of narcotics law enforcement, which was largely concentrated in minority neighborhoods in U.S. cities. As a result African-Americans were arrested, prosecuted, convicted, and imprisoned for drug crimes far out of proportion to their numbers among the general population or the population of drug users, and were the principal recipients of the harsher sentences that applied to crack use and sale.

The April 19 bombing of the federal building in Oklahoma City at first caused a xenophobic reaction, as many commentators assumed that Islamic militants were responsible. Although home-grown adherents of radical right-wing movements were ultimately charged in the case, the Clinton administration and members of Congress nevertheless exploited public fear and anxiety over the bombing to press for passage of a repressive "anti-terrorism" bill that would establish new courts, using secret evidence, to deport non-citizens suspected of "terrorist" activity, and limit inmates condemned to death to one appeal in federal courts. The administration, having succeeded in 1994 in expanding to sixty the number of federal crimes for which the death penalty may be imposed, moved quickly to seek it in the Oklahoma case. Elsewhere in the United States the pace of executions quickened, with New York's new governor signing a bill that ended the state's longstanding moratorium on executions. The national total of forty-two executions by the end of September broke the modern annual record of thirty-eight set in 1993.

The increasing use of the death penalty was particularly troubling in light of extensive evidence that showed it to be administered in a racially discriminatory manner at both state and federal levels. For example, all ten of the defendants approved by the attorney general for capital prosecution under the Federal Anti-Drug Abuse Act were African-Americans, and, at the state level, racial minorities accounted for almost 50 percent of all those executed during the first ten months of 1995.

Another highly disturbing aspect of death sentencing in the United States was the continuing execution of juvenile offenders—convicted of crimes committed before the age of eighteen—in blatant violation of international legal instruments, including the International Covenant on Civil and Political Rights (ICCPR), the American Convention of Human Rights, and the U.N. Convention on the Rights of the Child. The United States faced strong international condemnation for this practice.

The trend to curb the due process rights of inmates continued during 1995. Prisoners in the United States traditionally had three successive procedures to challenge their convictions or sentences: appellate review, state habeas corpus review, and federal habeas corpus review. In recent years, the courts as well as state and national legislatures have increasingly restricted the availability of federal habeas corpus review for both state and federal inmates. Congressional initiatives in 1995, including the anti-terrorism legislation and a revised crime bill, would, if passed and signed into law, restrict the federal appeals process for all condemned federal and state inmates and make it harder for federal judges to reverse convictions or sentences handed down by state courts.

The most significant human rights abuses in U.S. prisons during 1995 stemmed from the exploding prison population and concomitant extreme overcrowding of prison facilities. In August 1995, the U.S. Justice Department announced that the nation's prison population had soared above the one-million mark for the first time, more than doubling since 1985. The increases reflected tougher sentencing for a range of crimes as well as a greater proportion of drug arrests leading to longer prison terms. Overcrowding meant that most facilities built with single occupancy cells had two prisoners per cell and prison dormitories were often triple-bunked. Overcrowding also led to a deterioration in physical and sanitary conditions, the spread of airborne diseases, and reduced levels of basic necessities such as staff supervision and delivery of health services.

In another disturbing and regressive development, the state of Alabama reintroduced prison chain-gangs after a hiatus of some thirty years. Groups of prisoners shackled and chained together at the ankles cleared ditches, cut grass, picked up litter, and mended fences for twelve hours a day, five days a week, with hourly water breaks and a brief lunch, under the supervision of armed guards. Such treatment violates the Convention Against Torture and Other Cruel, Inhuman, or Degrading Treatment or Punishment and the ICCPR's prohibition against degrading treatment of prisoners.

The federal and state prison systems in recent years have made increasing use of super-maximum security facilities, informally known as "supermaxes" or "maxi-maxis." Supermaxes subject prisoners to extreme social and sensory deprivation, including near-total isolation from other prisoners, surroundings designed to reduce visual stimulation, minimal or no time outdoors, frequent denial of reading material, and complete lack of recreational facilities. At one such prison facility, the Maximum Control Complex in Westville, Indiana—which has identical cell blocks centered on control booths from which all the cells are visible—a number of inmates interviewed by a Human Rights Watch team in June 1995 complained of feeling like experimental guinea pigs in a laboratory. Prisoners were never in the presence of other people, including fellow inmates, except during rare visits or when being moved by guards.

In January 1995, conditions at the Security Housing Unit (SHU) of another notoriously harsh prison, California's Pelican Bay facility, were held, in a landmark federal court ruling, to "cross the constitutional line." The strongly worded opinion detailed eleven shockingly violent assaults on inmates by guards and described the SHU as a "windowless labyrinth of cells and halls sealed off from the outside world," where prisoners routinely endured conditions of total social isolation and sensory deprivation that "may press the outer bounds of what most humans can psychologically tolerate." Despite findings like these, legislation to curb the power of the courts to order remedies in cases involving inhumane and unconstitutional conditions in adult prisons and juvenile detention facilities was nearing congressional approval.

Over the year Congress also took steps that would impair freedom of expression in the country, including a proposed constitutional amendment—the first revision of the First Amendment right to free speech in U.S. history—to permit prosecution of protesters who burn or desecrate the nation's flag and a pending bill to restrict "indecent" expression on the Internet.

Gender discrimination remained a pervasive problem in the United States during 1995. U.S. constitutional and statutory law consistently failed to provide adequate legal protection for women who, particularly in the sectors of employment, health care, and prison facilities and programs, faced discrimination on account of their sex. Under the United States Constitution, as interpreted by the Supreme Court, discrimination based on gender merited a lower level of judicial scrutiny than discrimination based on race or national origin. Women were also inadequately protected by U.S. statutory law, since many U.S. anti-discrimination statutes failed to proscribe gender-based classifications. Although gender discrimination law applied equally to men and women, in practice women were far more likely to receive inferior treatment on account of their sex. Less stringent than the standard applicable to discrimination by race or nationality, the U.S. legal standard for sex discrimination violated article 3 of the International Covenant on Civil and Political Rights, which mandates equal access to civil rights protections for men and women.

Immigrants to the United States were targets of campaigns to limit their rights in 1995. Although immigration policy has historically fallen within the domain of the federal government, state legislatures increasingly asserted control over certain aspects of immigration with a view to circumvent federally mandated due process rights for non-citizens. For example, despite a Supreme Court ruling that public assistance could not be withdrawn without a prior hearing, California's Proposition 187 statute, approved in a November 1994 referendum, instructed state facilities to cut off medical aid, welfare funds, and schooling for supposed illegal migrants without explicitly providing for a hearing. Major provisions of Proposition 187 were judicially enjoined in December 1994, pending a determination of their constitutionality. The statute, as applied, would potentially violate the antidiscrimination principle of article 26 of the ICCPR.

Meanwhile, as immigration issues moved to the forefront of the national debate, undocumented immigrants, refugees, legal residents and U.S. citizens continued to be subjected to abuse by Border Patrol agents and inspectors of the U.S. Immigration and Naturalization Service (INS), including severe beatings and arbitrary detentions. Victims of abuse faced many barriers to filing or pursuing complaints due to structural flaws in the INS's investigatory and disciplinary processes. As a result of its defective complaint and agent review procedures the agency consistently failed to enforce its stated policies and hold abusive agents accountable. Nevertheless, the Clinton administration and Congress poured new resources into the INS to vastly increase the number of agents, without requiring sufficient improvements in the agency's abysmal human rights record.

In a positive development in 1995, the INS convened a Citizens' Advisory Panel (CAP) in April, June, and October. Although the CAP directly heard the concerns of human rights advocates and focused on improving the INS's flawed complaint intake system, the INS countered the momentum for accountability by pushing to gain sole control of the complaint and agent review process and advocating the elimination of the oversight function performed by the Office of the Inspector General for the Department of Justice. The panel was expected to submit formal recommendations to the attorney general in early 1996.

On May 2, 1995, the United States announced its intention to grant humanitarian parole to most of the approximately 21,000 Cuban asylum seekers interned since August 1994 at the U.S. naval base in Guantánamo Bay, Cuba. At the same time, the U.S. announced a new policy, adopted after negotiating a migration agreement with the Cuban government, to repatriate automatically all Cubans intercepted at sea. Those claiming to fear persecution would be instructed to apply for refugee status through the U.S. Interests Section's already overwhelmed in-country processing program in Havana. The new policy initially did not permit adequate screening to protect Cubans qualifying as refugees from involuntary repatriation as required by the international law principle of non-*refoulement*. The administration subsequently expanded the shipboard screening procedures instituted under the policy to consider the internationally recognized definition of a refugee. Concerns remained, however, about the difficulties in assuring a fair hearing posed by shipboard, rather than land-based, screening and the mistaken reliance on in-country refugee processing as a substitute for strict adherence to the the principle of non-refoulement.

In January, following the return to office of President Jean-Bertrand Aristide, the U.S. initiated forcible repatriations of over 3,700 Haitians from detention camps at Guantánamo, despite ongoing security concerns in Haiti. The cursory interview U.S. officials accorded the Haitians immediately prior to their repatriation was publicly decried by the United Nations High Commissioner for Refugees as insufficient protection from refoulement. In addition to the Guantánamo repatriations, the U.S. returned roughly 200 Haitians intercepted on the high seas between October 1994 and October 1995 without any refugee screening, denying them even the shipboard procedures in place for Cubans interdicted in similar circumstances.

The Right to Monitor

While civil liberties and human rights groups operated freely in the United States, two moves by Congress threatened the ability of some advocacy groups to function. One was the abolition of federal funding for legal centers in many states that provided representation for indigent death-sentenced inmates. There was considerable evidence that Congress acted not from fiscal considerations, but due to the centers' role in prolonging condemned inmates' appeals and overturning some death sentences. In addition, at this writing Congress was considering legislation which would discontinue federal grants for organizations that engaged in "political advocacy" even with their own private funds. Lobbying with federal money was already prohibited, but the proposed legislation would contravene the rights to impart information and ideas of all kinds and to take part in the conduct of public affairs conferred by articles 19 and 25 of the ICCPR.

The Role of
the International Community

Restrictions placed by the United States on its ratification of the International Covenant on Civil and Political Rights (ICCPR)—first, limiting the domestic applicability of the covenant, and second, overriding the prohibition on the execution of persons for crimes committed when they were younger than eighteen—drew considerable objection from other nations, including Germany,

France, Italy, Belgium, Norway, the Netherlands, Portugal, Spain and Sweden.

The scheduling of Mumia Abu-Jamal's execution by the state of Pennsylvania for August 17, 1995, sparked an international campaign for clemency in his case. Abu-Jamal, a former radio journalist and African-American political activist, had remained on death row since 1982 when he was convicted—amid widespread accusations of racial bias in the courtroom, inadequate representation, and prosecutorial misconduct—of the 1981 killing of a Philadelphia police officer. Abu-Jamal continued to proclaim his innocence. The governments of Germany and Belgium appealed to U.S. authorities on his behalf, President Chirac authorized the French ambassador to Washington to take "any step that might help to save the life of Mr. Mumia Abu-Jamal," and Italian parliamentary deputies passed a Lower House motion urging their government to press the United States to lift Abu-Jamal's death sentence. Although the governor of Pennsylvania rejected all intercessions, a court of common pleas judge granted a stay of execution to enable Abu-Jamal to complete his appeals process.

The Work of
Human Rights Watch

In 1995, Human Rights Watch expanded its investigation and advocacy on the U.S. with two principal areas of emphasis: U.S. compliance with international human rights treaties and human rights in the criminal justice system, including race discrimination in policing, sentencing and incarceration, impunity for brutality by law enforcement officials, inhumane conditions of confinement, and use of the death penalty.

In March, on the eve of the United Nations Human Rights Committee's first hearing on U.S. compliance with the ICCPR, Human Rights Watch and the American Civil Liberties Union (ACLU) submitted to the committee a detailed memorandum evaluating the United States record and criticizing the U.S. government's first periodic report to the committee. Human Rights Watch and the ACLU noted that by qualifying its ratification of the ICCPR through a series of reservations, declarations, and understandings, and by designating the treaty non-self-executing, the United States had effectively denied its citizens the rights conferred by it. Although the U.S. justified this virtual nullification of ICCPR rights for Americans on grounds of the sufficiency of domestic legislation, many convention provisions actually provided broader protection than was available under U.S. law, as interpreted by the Supreme Court.

The U.N. Human Rights Committee had taken the same view as Human Rights Watch on the U.S. conditions on ratification, in a November 1994 General Comment highly critical of states parties' attaching reservations to the ICCPR. In its March presentation to the committee, the U.S. castigated this position as going "much too far" and insisted that "reservations are an essential part of a state's consent to be bound" that could not "simply be erased."

Human Rights Watch and the ACLU found significant shortcomings in U.S. compliance with ICCPR standards in many substantive areas, including racial and gender discrimination, prison conditions, administration of the death penalty, treatment of Haitian and Cuban detainees, children's rights, freedom of expression, the rights of minority language speakers, limitations on aliens' rights to due process, and prisoners' rights.

Human Rights Watch similarly pressed the U.S. government regarding compliance with the International Convention on the Elimination of All Forms of Racial Discrimination (CERD). In October, in a joint letter and report to Secretary of State Warren Christopher, Human Rights Watch and two colleague organizations—the International Human Rights Law Group and the NAACP Legal Defense Fund—identified four issues of race discrimination in the criminal justice system and urged the United States to address them in its forthcoming submission to the CERD Committee. The three organizations' *Summary of Concerns About Race*

Discrimination in the U.S. Criminal Justice System lauded U.S. ratification of the CERD in 1994 as a first step toward applying international human rights law to the problem of racial discrimination in the country, but opposed the Clinton administration's declaration—similar to the one entered for the ICCPR—that the convention was not self-executing.

The three groups urged that the United States' first annual report as well as subsequent submissions to the CERD Committee include extensive statistical data concerning the experience of racial minorities within the justice system, and identified four areas where data would be particularly helpful in evaluating the disparate racial impact of specific policies: super-maximum security prisons, administration of the death penalty, police misconduct, and drug prosecutions. With respect to the disproportionate assignment of racial minorities to supermaximum security prisons, race disparities in the administration of the death penalty, and police abuse of minority citizens, Human Rights Watch and the two other organizations asked the executive branch to provide the CERD Committee with data on the numbers and racial backgrounds of nonviolent inmates assigned to supermax prison units, statistics revealing the racial breakdown of capital prosecutions and convictions, and similar statistics drawn from a sampling of local police departments regarding police stops, arrests, and physical confrontations between police and civilians. In addition, the joint report pointed out that there have been numerous domestic legal challenges to the racially disparate impact of the powder cocaine/crack distinction in federal sentencing statutes and guidelines, but almost all have foundered on the lack of sufficient evidence of intentional discrimination. CERD condemns laws and practices with a racially discriminatory *effect*, regardless of intent, and requires the elimination of laws with an unjustifiable adverse impact on particular racial or ethnic groups, so Human Rights Watch and its colleague groups urged that the United States' report to the CERD Committee address the issue of the disparate racial impact of U.S. drug laws and describe any intended remedial steps.

During 1995, Human Rights Watch undertook investigations and advocacy efforts on several facets of the administration of capital punishment. In a March 1995 report, *United States: A World Leader in Executing Juveniles*, the Human Rights Watch Children's Rights Project urged the U.S. government to abolish the death penalty for both juvenile and adult offenders and recommended that, as a first step toward abolition, the United States enact legislation to end executions of persons who, at the time they committed their crimes, were below the age of eighteen, and that federal and state prosecutors refrain from seeking the death penalty in such cases. The Children's Rights Project report pointed out that the harsh treatment accorded juvenile offenders in the criminal justice system contrasted sharply with U.S. civil laws, which were based on the premise that minors generally do not have the same level of intellectual and psychological maturity as adults and hence require special protections.

During the year Human Rights Watch sent letters to Pennsylvania Gov. Thomas Ridge and Superintendent James Price of the Waynesburg State Correctional Institute to express grave concern about the then-impending execution of Mumia Abu-Jamal and to protest the curbs imposed on his free expression rights by prison authorities. In the letter to Governor Ridge, Human Rights Watch expressed its opposition to the death penalty in all circumstances and urged him to withdraw the execution warrant against Abu-Jamal. Although the organization did not take a position on the underlying criminal charges against Abu-Jamal, it noted serious concerns about the fairness of his trial, particularly the heavy reliance during the sentencing phase on information regarding his political beliefs and associations.

In September, Human Rights Watch joined with Physicians for Human Rights and several members of the medical, legal, academic, and public service communities in a letter calling on the American Psychiatric Association (APA) to formulate and articulate its own definitive stance on the ethics of psychiatrists assessing the competence of prisoners for purposes of approving their execution. The action was in response to the APA's support for an argument that physician involvement in the administration of the death penalty is not necessarily unethical, propounded in a report by the American Medical Association's Council on Ethical and Judicial Affairs (CEJA), which endorsed such psychiatric assessment. The letter reiterated the position we took in the 1994 Human Rights Watch/Physicians for Human Rights/American College of Physicians report, *Breach of Trust*, that physician participation in capital punishment conflicts acutely with the caring and curing missions that are central to the medical profession.

Human Rights Watch persisted in its work to end human rights abuses by INS Border Patrol agents and inspectors on the premise that until abusive officials were held accountable for their actions, rights violations along the country's southern borders would continue. In our third report on the issue since 1992, *Crossing the Line: Human Rights Abuses Along the U.S. Border with Mexico*, Human Rights Watch revealed that INS Border Patrol agents deployed along the western segment of the U.S.-Mexico border continued to abuse their authority and committed serious human rights violations including murder, rape, unjustified shootings, severe beatings, and arbitrary detentions, with impunity. The April 1995 report also documented physical abuse and harassment perpetrated by INS inspectors at U.S. border posts in Arizona and California, which, though less endemic than border patrol violence, occurred in a similar climate of impunity.

In response to our 1993 report on border violations, the INS had assured Human Rights Watch that it would address the issue of agent misconduct, which had developed into one of the worst police abuse problems in the country. The latest report exposed failure by the INS to address the problem adequately; the few reforms undertaken were of a cosmetic nature and remained largely ineffective. Although during the year the INS periodically convened a Citizens' Advisory Panel (CAP) required by law, it continued to reject the option of independent civilian review that Human Rights Watch consistently advocated in all three reports.

Human Rights Watch staff testified at the first two, and submitted documentation for all three, CAP meetings. The organization's initial concerns about the CAP's limited mandate were mitigated when nongovernmental members of the panel addressed serious shortcomings in the INS's complaint and review procedures and the inadequacy, as a result of increased hiring, of training programs for INS supervisors, a fact reportedly admitted by the INS at CAP's October meeting.

In view of the enduring problem of police abuse throughout the U.S., Human Rights Watch initiated a nationwide field research project on police violence and the barriers to accountability. The organization also stepped up advocacy efforts for more extensive and effective local civilian review of police practices. In October, Human Rights Watch testified before the City Council of the District of Columbia opposing the council's earlier decision to suspend the Civilian Complaint Review Board and transfer its operating budget to the internal review apparatus of the Metropolitan Police Department itself. Human Rights Watch stressed that, were the police allowed to investigate allegations of police misconduct without any external oversight, the customs of solidarity within the ranks of the force would serve to weaken any pressure for accountability. The organization also made several concrete recommendations to streamline and invigorate the civilian panel's operations and to heighten its impact.

An October 1995 Human Rights Watch Children's Rights Project report, *United States: Children in Confinement in Louisiana*, documented the abusive conditions in which children were confined in Louisiana's four post-adjudication correctional facilities, in violation of international legal standards and, in important respects, national laws as well. The report disclosed that children at all four facilities were periodically restrained by handcuffs, regularly physically abused by guards, and kept in isolation for long periods of time. Moreover, being housed in dormitories of forty to fifty children with no privacy, even when using toilet facilities, stripped the child detainees of a basic sense of dignity. In addition, virtually every child interviewed by Human Rights Watch complained of hunger. We made several recommendations to end the physical and psychological abuse of children and to promote the goal of rehabilitating them in an environment that fosters respect and dignity, including the establishment of a functioning complaint mechanism to enable the children to seek redress for abuse and the provision of adequate programming to educate, train, and counsel them.

Between 1993 and late 1995, the Human Rights Watch Women's Rights and Prison Projects investigated a grave and potentially explosive national problem of custodial sexual misconduct in United States prisons. Human Rights Watch found that in state women's prisons in California, Georgia, Illinois, Michigan, New York, and the District of Columbia, ill-trained male officers guarded female prisoners with little appropriate guidance or oversight regarding sexual misconduct. The result was a highly sexually charged custodial environment in which the officers further stepped over the line with respect to the prisoners and engaged in rape, sexual assault, other forms of sexual contact, and inappropriate visual surveillance of the women while they were dressing, showering, or using the toilet. A detailed report on these findings was in preparation at this writing. Given the steadily rising female prison population—the number of women in prison grew by 75 percent between 1987 and 1992—the national and state governments must acknowledge the magnitude of the problem of custodial sexual abuse and devote the necessary financial and human resources to secure its speedy eradication.

THE ARMS PROJECT

The Human Rights Watch Arms Project was established in 1992 to monitor and seek to prevent the transfer of weapons and the provision of military assistance and training to governments or armed groups that commit gross violations of internationally recognized human rights or the laws of war. A corollary of this is to promote freedom of expression and freedom of information about arms and arms transfers worldwide. In addition, the Arms Project seeks to eliminate weapons which as a class are, or should be, prohibited by the laws of war, without consideration of the human rights record of the country or group possessing them. These are weapons that are by their very nature indiscriminate or cruel and inhumane.

The Human Rights Watch Arms Project is unique because it straddles the human rights movement (from which we derive our basic philosophy, motivating energy, fact-finding methodology, and expertise in international law) and the arms control community (from which we draw our expertise in the arms trade and the development of weapons systems). Through our research and advocacy, we put the spotlight on violations of human rights and the laws of war, and place the legal and moral responsibility for these violations at the doorstep of governments that have supplied weapons or other forms of military support to the violators.

We attempt to document the link between weapons used in specific abuses to the supply of these weapons through a combination of documentary research (including, in the U.S., analysis of documents obtained under the Freedom of Information Act) and field investigation. By combining our ability to uncover new information with the capabilities of Human Rights Watch to advocate change, we have become increasingly effective in stigmatizing governments or forces that are guilty of, or complicit in, weapons-related abuse. Our methodology encompasses research into the full range of weapons, including weapons of mass destruction. Field research to date has focused on the trade in light weapons and small arms, bringing to these weapons a small reflection of the attention given to the tracking of non-conventional and major conventional weapons through the International Atomic Energy Agency and the United Nations conventional arms register. Except for artillery (for example, in the cases of Bosnia and Angola), it is light weapons and small arms that are used most frequently in human rights abuses and violations of the laws of war.

In 1995, the Human Rights Watch Arms Project developed its program to elaborate existing projects (landmines), expand into new areas (chemical and biological weapons, and blinding lasers), and vigorously pursue more effective campaign strategies. During the past year it was the Arms Project's capacity to reveal new information on the transfer and use of arms that led to a series of concrete successes. After our reports, a sale of U.S. cluster bombs to Turkey was stopped and the attention of the U.N. Security Council was drawn to the re-arming, by France, Zaire and others, of the perpetrators of the Rwandan genocide. The United States agreed to new prohibitions in international law on blinding lasers after the Arms Project publicized the secret development of tactical laser weapons in the U.S.; and not long afterward, the U.S. halted the production of the Laser Countermeasure System (LCMS), a portable laser weapon singled out by the Arms Project for its capability to blind persons within a range of 3,000 feet. The Arms Project also contributed to decisions by the U.N. General Assembly to adopt a resolution endorsing the goal of the eventual elimination of antipersonnel landmines, and by the U.S. Senate to pass an amendment mandating a one-year moratorium on use of antipersonnel landmines by U.S. forces.

The Work of the Arms Project

Targeting Weapons Systems

Under international humanitarian law, the use of weapons that are inherently indiscriminate (or prone to indiscriminate use) or cause unnecessary suffering is banned. The Arms Project has gone further in seeking a total ban on the production, stockpiling and trade of such weapons.

In 1995, the Arms Project initiated new programs on chemical and biological weapons and on blinding laser weapons. Meanwhile, as a member of the steering committee of the International Campaign to Ban Landmines we continued research and advocacy efforts aimed at obtaining a total ban on antipersonnel landmines and attended the Review Conference on the 1980 Convention on Prohibitions or Restrictions on the Use of Certain Conventional Weapons Which May Be Deemed to Be Excessively Injurious or to Have Indiscriminate Effects, or the Convention on Conventional Weapons (CCW), in Vienna in September-October 1995.

Landmines

The Arms Project has singled out antipersonnel landmines as inherently indiscriminate weapons deserving of a total ban on production, stockpiling, trade and use. Landmines stay in the ground long after a conflict has ended, causing untold suffering to civilians for decades. Current estimates are that some one hundred million antipersonnel landmines lie buried in the soil in Cambodia, Angola, Afghanistan, Iraq, Bosnia, Nicaragua and some sixty other countries.

During 1995, the landmines crisis worsened. During the last year, approximately 100,000 landmines were removed in mine clearance operations while approximately 2.5 million new mines were laid down by warring factions. At the same time, there have been some stunning developments toward a ban on antipersonnel landmines. In the past year, the number of nongovernmental organizations (NGOs) endorsing a ban has grown from under sixty to more than 350. There are now organized national campaigns in approximately thirty nations, with recent launches in Afghanistan and South Africa. After President Clinton embraced the goal of the eventual elimination of antipersonnel landmines by the U.S. in a speech at the U.N. in September 1994, the U.N. General Assembly adopted a resolution endorsing a similar goal in December 1994. In March 1995, Belgium became the first nation to enact legislation to ban production, export and use of mines. Seventeen other nations have declared support for an immediate and comprehensive ban, while thirty nations have announced a moratorium on the export of mines. In July 1995, both the European Parliament and the Organization of African Unity passed resolutions calling for a comprehensive ban on antipersonnel mines. At the end of October, the U.S. House-Senate conference committee on the Foreign Operations bill accepted the Leahy amendment mandating a one-year moratorium on the use of antipersonnel landmines by U.S. forces. The bill had yet to be voted on by both the House and Senate, and signed by President Clinton, before the law will take effect.

As a member of the steering committee of the International Campaign to Ban Landmines, the Arms Project has played an important role in these developments. Our advocacy efforts continue to be centered on four main areas: international legal and diplomatic initiatives; public education and organizing activities to build the International Campaign to Ban Landmines; coalition building to increase participation in the campaign by organizations from the developing world; and public education and organizing to create a more broad-based U.S. campaign.

At the Review Conference on the 1980 Convention on Conventional Weapons in Vienna in September-October 1995, we urged governments to adopt a total ban, and failing that, to strengthen Protocol II on landmines by adopting new verification and compliance provisions, expanding the scope of the protocol to cover non-international conflicts,

mandating regular and frequent review of the CCW, and other measures. Regrettably, the conference unexpectedly ended in deadlock, with nations unable to agree even on modest changes. The conference is expected to reconvene in January and April 1996. During the coming year, the Arms Project intends to continue to work at both the international and national levels to enhance prospects for a comprehensive ban on antipersonnel landmines.

Blinding Laser Weapons

In 1995, the Arms Project took on the issue of tactical laser weapons following appeals from the International Committee of the Red Cross in Geneva, which had been alone in undertaking medical and legal analysis on these weapons systems. We felt that the Arms Project might contribute something important by presenting evidence of active laser weapon programs in the United States and elsewhere, and thought that the September 1995 Review Conference on the 1980 Convention on Conventional Weapons might offer an opportunity to seek a ban on such weapons. In our view, tactical laser weapons should be banned because their primary effect in certain circumstances is to blind anyone at whom they are directed; the injury is irreversible and therefore, in comparison with other injuries that may occur on the battlefield and in light of alternative weapons systems available to the modern military, inflicts suffering that is cruel and unnecessary. Until 1995, the U.S. government had barely acknowledged the presence of these weapons in its arsenal, and was loath to discuss any form of restrictions on their use.

In the spring of 1995, the Arms Project discovered from documents obtained under the Freedom of Information Act that the United States has been developing at least ten separate tactical laser weapon systems. In a May 1995 report publicizing these systems, *U.S. Blinding Laser Weapons*, we drew a great deal of media attention to this previously unknown and undiscussed issue, with coverage in *The New York Times, The Financial Times, Jane's Defense Weekly, De-*

fense News, and other U.S. and foreign newspapers and specialized publications. The Arms Project had several meetings with U.S. government officials to express our concern about these weapons, as well as with officials of Britain, France, Germany, Sweden, Belgium, Ireland, NATO, the European Commission, the European Council, and members of the European Parliament. We also worked hard to bring together individuals and organizations in the United States and Europe on the issue of blinding laser weapons, urging them to raise it with their governments and within their communities.

In June 1995, the European Parliament passed a resolution calling for a ban on laser weapons that can cause blindness. More significantly, following our disclosures, the U.S. government announced a formal policy on blinding lasers on September 1, reversing both its opposition to any regulation of laser weapons and its previous position that intentional blinding is a legal and acceptable method of warfare. However, the new policy statement contained a loophole designed to permit continued use of laser weapons categorized as "anti-optical" or "anti-sensor" systems. In fact, the day before the surprise release of the policy statement, the U.S. Army awarded a seventeen million dollar contract for initial production of a laser weapon known as the Laser Countermeasure System (LCMS), an "anti-optical" weapon mounted on an M-16 rifle which the Army acknowledges fires a laser beam powerful enough to burn out human retinas from 3,000 feet away.

Just prior to the September-October 1995 Review Conference of the CCW, the Arms Project released its second report on lasers, *Blinding Laser Weapons: The Need to Ban a Cruel and Inhumane Weapon*. This report made new revelations about U.S. and other laser weapon programs, gave a comprehensive analysis of the military, humanitarian, and legal considerations surrounding blinding lasers, and evaluated possible protocol language. Sustained advocacy efforts by Human Rights Watch, the ICRC, and others, were instrumental in gaining acceptance of a new protocol on blinding laser weapons at the Review Conference. One year ago, very few observers would have believed that passage of a protocol was possible. While weaker than Human Rights Watch would like, the new protocol establishes the crucial principle that deliberate blinding is barbaric and an unacceptable way to wage war. Unfortunately, the new protocol contains the same loophole as the new U.S. policy statement, and allows an entire category of laser weapons to escape regulation.

However, in another sudden reversal, the U.S. announced on October 12 that it was canceling the LCMS program. It is ironic that the decision to terminate LCMS was made at the very time that the U.S. delegation in Vienna was insisting that the protocol include a loophole through which the LCMS could be used. Human Rights Watch believes that the LCMS cancellation reflects both a recognition at the highest levels of the Pentagon of the lack of military utility of this weapon system and concern about pursuing this weapon in light of the new policy against blinding.

Chemical and Biological Weapons

In the spring of 1995, the Arms Project launched a major new endeavor by establishing its chemical and biological weapons program. The objective of the program is to strengthen efforts to prevent the proliferation of weapons of mass destruction by introducing a human rights component into the debate. We envision doing so in a number of ways: providing a human rights analysis of the proliferation question; helping to better enforce an existing norm by further stigmatizing chemical and biological weapons as indiscriminate, cruel and abhorrent to the human conscience; and lending our investigative skills to attempts to uncover evidence of illegal chemical/biological weapons production, stockpiling, trade or use.

During the first half year of the program, efforts centered on two main areas of work: the building of a network of experts, and a preliminary investigation into cases of alleged CW or BW use. Moreover, the Arms Project has made contact with a number of nongovernmental organizations, both in the human rights and arms control communities in the United States and Europe, to exchange information, and has met with government officials, attended unclassified government meetings on CBW, submitted Freedom of Information Act requests to several branches of the U.S. military for information on chemical and biological issues, and collected reports and testimony on CBW issues and proliferation concerns.

The emerging network has enabled us to begin to develop a capability to respond to allegations of CBW production, stockpiling, trade and use. Depending on the outcome of future investigations, the Arms Project will seek to highlight the use of CBW in modern conflicts, despite the existing prohibitions, and lend its weight to efforts by those who seek ratification of the Chemical Weapons Convention and the addition of a verification regime to the Biological Weapons Convention. Additionally, the Arms Project intends to monitor the international trade in CW and BW components, much as we monitor the trade in conventional weapons. Finally, we intend to serve as an address and source of protection for whistle-blowers, or will blow the whistle ourselves, in cases where we obtain evidence of illegal manufacturing or transfer of chemical and biological weapons.

Field Investigations

As with all of Human Rights Watch's work, the Arms Project begins with field investigation. In carrying out its research, the Arms Project routinely works in cooperation with the regional divisions of Human Rights Watch which provide local expertise and maintain extensive archives on countries and their human rights records. Through on-site investigations in war-torn regions, abusive countries and arms-producing countries, the Arms Project attempts to document abuses committed with particular weapons and to link those abuses to the weapons suppliers: both the companies that manufacture them

and the governments that fund or authorize their sale.

In seeking to curb the proliferation of light weapons to human rights abusers, our work contributes to regional arms control, peace and stability. Because arms-supplying governments are often sensitive to embarrassing publicity and do not want to be stigmatized by the international community, shining a spotlight on policies that permit such arms transfers encourages governments to cut off the arms flow to abusive forces and halt one of the worst forms of proliferation. In addition, our presence in the field allows us to identify the role of arms flows in fostering serious tensions and potentially explosive situations at an early stage, and thus positions us best for work on early warning and conflict prevention.

Rwanda

In 1995, the Arms Project undertook a thorough investigation into the supply of arms to the former Rwandan government, military and militias—the perpetrators of the Rwandan genocide—who have been regrouping their forces in refugee camps in eastern Zaire. This was a follow-up to research conducted in 1993 on the impact of the arms trade on the human rights situation in Rwanda. The Arms Project's first report, issued in January 1994, documented the flow of French, Egyptian and South African arms to the Habyarimana government and alerted the international community to the possibility of a disaster of major proportions.

In 1994-1995, after the genocide in Rwanda, an Arms Project consultant spent four months in Rwanda and Zaire, interviewing scores of United Nations and NGO representatives, Rwandan and Zairian government officials, members of the exiled Rwandan forces responsible for the genocide, and persons involved in the arms trade. In a report released in May 1995, *Rearming with Impunity: International Support for the Perpetrators of the Rwandan Genocide*, we implicated France, Zaire, South Africa, China and the Seychelles for either directly providing arms to the Rwandan Hutu forces, or for facilitating shipments of arms from other sources. Subsequent to the report, Human Rights Watch wrote to U.N. Secretary-General Boutros Boutros-Ghali apprising the Security Council of our findings, and we met with officials at various missions to the U.N., including the French mission. We also met with the chairman of the U.N. sanctions committee on Rwanda, Ambassador Nugroho Wisnumurti, who is the representative of Indonesia to the U.N.

The report had tremendous resonance, receiving wide coverage in the international media. The United Nations Security Council incorporated three of our key recommendations in Resolution 997 of June 9, 1995: a call for consultations with the governments of neighboring countries on the possibility of the deployment of U.N. military observers at airports in eastern Zaire; an affirmation that the arms embargo under Resolution 918 (1994) applies to forces in states neighboring Rwanda if such weapons are intended for use within Rwanda; and a call for effective measures to prevent military activities by Rwandan nationals in neighboring states aimed at destabilizing Rwanda, and to prevent them from receiving arms.

In Europe, the report was widely circulated among members of the European Parliament, and several members raised questions related to the report in its Development Committee, Sub-committee on Human Rights, Foreign Affairs Committee and others. In South Africa, the government denied the allegations made in our report, but at the same time launched an official inquiry. In August, it instituted new procedures for arms exports. The parastatal arms export agency, Armscor, which was not mentioned in our report, also issued a denial, but suggested that arms manufactured in South Africa could have found their way clandestinely to Rwanda and Burundi. Armscor also opened files documenting arms sales to Rwanda totaling one hundred million South African rand in the five years preceding August 1993—well before the U.N. arms embargo on Rwanda, but all the same this should be seen as a step

toward greater transparency in arms transactions. The French Ministry of Foreign Affairs issued a flat denial at the end of May, but to our knowledge the French government did not carry out a serious inquiry into any of the allegations we made in our report. A separate statement by officials at the Ministry of Cooperation suggested that French arms shipments had in fact taken place.

In Zaire, President Mobutu Sese Seko reacted to the Human Rights Watch report on May 30 by pledging that "Zaire will never be the base for the reconquest of another land." Zaire's prime minister, Kengo wa Dondo, declined to either confirm or deny allegations of arms supplies reaching the Rwandan Hutu exile forces in Zaire, but said that those making the accusations had not provided his government any evidence of the allegations. Kengo wa Dondo then called on the U.N. to send a fact-finding mission to Zaire to investigate charges that Hutu extremists were conducting military training exercises in eastern Zaire. Zaire rejected a request by the Security Council to permit the deployment of U.N. military observers under Resolution 997. In June, Human Rights Watch met with the U.N. Special Rapporteur on Zaire, Ambassador Roberto Garretón, to brief him on the militarization of the refugee camps and arms transfers in eastern Zaire.

In a letter to the Security Council in August during the debate on lifting the arms embargo on Rwanda, Human Rights Watch expressed concern that the measure would result in a greater flow of arms to the Great Lakes region and further destabilize the situation. The embargo was suspended for one year on August 16 under Resolution 1011. On September 7, the Security Council voted to approve the establishment of an international commission to investigate allegations of arms flows to former Rwandan government forces in the Great Lakes region. The six-member commission traveled to the region in early November. The creation of the commission was a positive development but fell short of our principal demand to have U.N. military observers deployed at key airports in Zaire.

Turkey

In late 1994, the Arms Project conducted research on an intended sale of 493 CBU-87 cluster bombs by a U.S. company, Alliant Techsystems, to Turkey. The CBU-87 is the latest and most deadly cluster bomb in the U.S. arsenal; it can saturate an area the size of a football field with 202 small, individual bomblets. The Arms Project is opposed to the transfer of cluster bombs and other weapons to Turkey because of Turkey's horrendous human rights record, well documented over the years by Human Rights Watch/Helsinki, and because of the indiscriminate nature of cluster bombs, especially when used in counterinsurgency efforts. During our research we discovered that, whereas the private contract had been signed, approval for an export license was still pending with the U.S. government.

In December 1994, the Arms Project published a report about the sale, *U.S. Cluster Bombs for Turkey?*, offering much detail on the nature of cluster bombs. In a letter to Secretary of State Warren Christopher accompanying the report, we urged the United States to deny the company's request for an export license in light of Turkey's record and, in particular, our concern that Turkey would use these weapons indiscriminately in its conflict with the Kurdish Workers Party (PKK). The report received wide coverage in the press and specialized defense magazines. Partly as a result of our disclosure of the pending sale, the deal was canceled. In addition to attempting to block this particular sale, the Arms Project also urged the U.S. to monitor carefully the use of the lethal equipment that it provides Turkey, and to introduce end-use monitoring as a consistent and highly visible element of any U.S. military assistance to Turkey in the future.

In the spring of 1995, the Arms Project began an in-depth investigation of arms transfers to the government of Turkey in light of the increasingly violent and abusive conflict between the Turkish army and the PKK. Both sides have committed gross abuses of human rights and the laws of war, targeting civilians as if they were combatants. More-over, the Turkish military has undertaken a scorched earth campaign in the Kurdish countryside, destroying hundreds of villages and forcibly relocating the rural population, while engaging in extrajudicial executions and torture. Turkey continues to enjoy great support from NATO for political and military reasons, and this has cushioned the government from international rebuke for its treatment of its Kurdish population.

In June 1995, the U.S. Department of State issued a ground-breaking report ("Report on Allegations of Human Rights Abuses by the Turkish Military And on the Situation in Cyprus") admitting that Turkey engages in gross abuses such as torture, extrajudicial executions and forced village evacuations. The report also conceded that "U.S.-origin equipment, which accounts for most major items of the Turkish military inventory, has been used in operations against the PKK during which human rights abuses have occurred." The report, which was not based on original investigative research, failed to provide concrete proof of the use of U.S. weapons in specific violations, however, and understated the role of U.S. weapons in the village eradication campaign.

The Arms Project sent a consultant to Turkey in June 1995 to obtain detailed information about the forced evacuation of Kurdish villages, focusing on the use by Turkish security forces of U.S. and other weaponry. In a report released in November 1995, the Arms Project presented the results of this investigation. Drawing on twenty-nine case studies of events that occurred between 1992 and 1995, the report linked specific weapons systems to individual incidents of Turkish violations. Supplemented by interviews with former Turkish soldiers, U.S. officials and defense experts, the report concluded that U.S. weapons, as well as those supplied by other NATO members, are regularly used by Turkey to commit severe human rights abuses and violations of the laws of war in the southeast.

Angola

In November 1994, the Arms Project published *Angola: Arms Trade and Violations of the Laws of War since the 1992 Elections.* This report was the result of an on-going investigation by a researcher with Human Rights Watch/Africa on behalf of the Arms Project. The report (which included a summary in Portuguese) concluded that Angola's "forgotten war," in which an estimated 100,000 civilians have lost their lives, was fueled by a steady supply of weapons to both sides. Indeed, before the recent peace accords, the government of Angola was the largest arms purchaser in sub-Saharan Africa, mortgaging its future oil production to finance an estimated U.S.$3.5 billion worth of weapons imports in 1993 and 1994. The rebel movement National Union for the Independence of Angola (UNITA) also was involved in large purchases of weapons from both private dealers and foreign governments. The report named the following countries as having supplied weapons or other forms of military assistance to the two parties to this conflict: Russia, Brazil, North Korea, Spain, Portugal, Bulgaria, the Czech Republic, Ukraine, Uzbekistan, South Africa, Zaire, Namibia and the United States.

The report, the release of which was timed to coincide with the signing of a peace treaty by the Angolan government and UNITA, succeeded in crystallizing international attention on the need for human rights monitors as part of the U.N. mission to Angola—one of the report's main recommendations. In its deliberations on November 20, 1994, the Security Council relied on facts and figures provided in our report before deciding to send peacekeepers to Angola and calling on both the government and UNITA to cease acquisition of arms—another of our key recommendations. Moreover, British soldiers being prepared for their participation in that mission were put through an intensive human rights monitoring course based, *inter alia*, on the findings of our report, which became required pre-deployment reading. In 1995, the researcher returned to Angola for a follow-up investigation into continuing arms flows to Angola.

Georgia/Abkhazia

In March 1995, the Arms Project, in collaboration with Human Rights Watch/Helsinki, released *Georgia/Abkhazia: Violations of the Laws of War and Russia's Role in the Conflict* following an investigation into the fratricidal war between Georgia and its breakaway, unrecognized Abkhaz republic in 1992-1994. We concluded that both sides in the conflict had shown a reckless disregard for the protection of the civilian population and were responsible for gross violations of international humanitarian law. Moreover, in a pattern eerily reminiscent of the war in the former Yugoslavia, the combination of indiscriminate attacks and targeted terrorization of the civilian population marked deliberate efforts by both sides to force the population of the other party's ethnic group out of areas of strategic importance. We also concluded that the Russian Federation played a significant role in the conflict, and was in various ways responsible for escalating human rights abuse.

The report (which included a summary in Russian) was released at a press conference in Moscow in March 1995. Prior to that, the Arms Project and Human Rights Watch/Helsinki had presented the organization's findings to the principal actors in the conflict in the Georgian capital Tbilisi, in Sukhumi, the capital of the Abkhaz region, and in Moscow while carrying out a field investigation into further abuses during the post-war period. In conversations with government officials, we pressed the following issues: investigation and prosecution of war crimes by both sides; accountability of irregular forces; the return of internally displaced persons; the extension of the mandates of U.N. forces and Russian forces operating under the aegis of the Commonwealth of Independent States; a halt to continuing violence in the Gali region along the frontline between the opposing forces; and the need for vastly expanded efforts to demine the conflict zone to allow for the repatriation of some 200,000 remaining displaced persons. We also met with the U.N. special envoy to Georgia and with members of the

Organization for Security and Cooperation in Europe's Permanent Council, and wrote to the U.N. secretary-general and to senior officials of the U.N. High Commissioner for Refugees. Human Rights Watch continues to inject human rights considerations into the on-going peace process.

Cambodia

In March 1995, the Arms Project, in collaboration with Human Rights Watch/Asia, released *Cambodia at War*, a study based on two missions to Cambodia in 1994 and 1995. The report documents severe abuses by both government forces and the Khmer Rouge, and highlights the role of Thailand, Indonesia and other governments in supplying weapons, military aid and other support to either party to the conflict. We called for an end to the provision of arms and military equipment to the warring parties, as well as for the abolition of the use, acquisition and stockpiling of antipersonnel landmines. We also called on international donors to insist that the Cambodian government hold its officials—civilian and military—accountable for gross violations of human rights. The Cambodian government has now announced its support for a complete ban on landmines and has reportedly ordered military units to cease laying mines. Despite the new policy, Human Rights Watch continues to receive reports that government soldiers are using mines. There will therefore be a need for ongoing monitoring of compliance with the official orders.

Israel/Lebanon

The Arms Project continued to monitor the conflict between Israel and Lebanese guerrilla forces in southern Lebanon. In August 1995, a researcher with Human Rights Watch/ Middle East traveled to southern Lebanon to obtain information about civilian casualties from recent indiscriminate attacks launched from territory occupied by Israeli military forces or its proxy South Lebanon Army. The investigation, which included research into the use by Israeli forces of antipersonnel weapons, was a follow-up to research undertaken in 1993-1994 into the fighting in southern Lebanon in which both Israeli forces and Lebanese militias committed violations of the laws of war by targeting population centers.

The United Nations and International Standards

Competition in the global arms sales market has continued to intensify in the post-Cold War period. Data released in mid-1995 by the U.S. Congressional Research Service indicate that in 1994 developing nations (where the negative impact of arms trade tends to be the greatest) purchased more than twenty-five billion dollars in weapons, roughly the same as the previous year. In 1994, France ranked first in new arms transfer agreements with the developing world ($11.4 billion, or 45 percent), while the United States ranked first in arms deliveries to the developing world ($6.7 billion, or 47 percent). These data underscore the need for further controls on conventional weapons.

During three weeks in September and October, state parties to the 1980 Convention on Conventional Weapons met in Vienna for the CCW's first review since the treaty came into force. The focus of the review conference was on new restrictions on use of landmines, but nations were unable to reach agreement on even modest changes in the Landmines Protocol and will have to resume negotiations in January and April 1996. An important new protocol restricting use and transfer of blinding laser weapons was adopted (see above).

The U.N. Register of Conventional Arms was in its third year of operation in 1995. Despite inaccurate submissions by some nations, and noncompliance by others, the register continues to be a major source of information on global arms trade and an important mechanism toward greater transparency and accountability, as well as greater trust between nations. The register covers only seven types of major conventional weapons systems, however, and contains no information on light weapons or small arms.

In 1995, the U.N. maintained arms

embargoes on Iraq (imposed as part of a full trade embargo imposed in 1990), states of the former Yugoslavia (1991), Somalia (1992), Libya (1992), Liberia (1992), and Angola (1993). The arms embargo imposed on Rwanda in 1994 was modified in June 1995 to apply to "the sale or supply of arms and *matériel* to persons in the States neighboring Rwanda, if that sale or supply is for the purpose of the use of such arms or *matériel* within Rwanda." In August 1995, the U.N. Security Council suspended the arms embargo on the supply of arms to the government of Rwanda for the period of one year, until September 1, 1996 (see above).

In 1995, the Chemical Weapons Convention, which was opened for signature in January 1993, garnered more ratifications, although the two critical countries in this regard, the United States and the Russian Federation, have yet to decide on ratification. As of September 1995, thirty-eight states had ratified the convention, out of sixty-five ratifications that are required for the convention to enter into force.

In July 1995, state parties to the 1972 Biological Weapons Convention met in Geneva as part of the second session of the Ad Hoc Group of BWC State Parties to discuss definitions of terms and objective criteria, confidence-building and transparency measures, measures to promote compliance/verification, and measures related to Article X on technological cooperation. A third session was scheduled for the end of November 1995. The Ad Hoc Group is mandated to develop a proposal for a legally binding verification protocol in preparation for the fourth review conference of the BWC, which is now expected to take place toward the end of 1996.

United States Policy

In February 1995, the Clinton administration announced its Conventional Arms Transfer Policy, proclaiming that "[a] critical element of U.S. policy is to promote control, restraint and transparency of arms transfers," but emphasizing the potential economic benefits of arms sales. The new policy was notable in that it instituted no new controls on arms sales. In effect, the new policy was designed to make it easier for U.S. arms industries to market their wares abroad by lending administration support to this effort. As has been the case in previous administrations, human rights considerations have taken a back seat in arms trade decisions to economic, military, or other political factors. Since the 1970s, there have been only a few occasions when the executive branch has restricted arms sales on human rights grounds, or when Congress insisted that it do so. Many sales occur unnoticed by the public, and in some cases, by the Congress (see Turkey section above).

In March, the U.S. Congress ratified the Convention on Conventional Weapons, including the CCW's Protocol I on undetectable fragments and Protocol II on landmines. The Clinton administration has not sent Protocol III on incendiary weapons to Congress. After the international community agreed to the adoption of a new protocol (Protocol IV) on laser weapons in October, the U.S. government will be expected to ratify that protocol as well. The U.S. also had yet to ratify the Chemical Weapons Convention. Ratification has been held up in Congress by the office of Senator Jesse Helms, the chairman of the Senate Foreign Relations Committee.

In May 1995, the House Committee on International Relations narrowly defeated (18-17, with eight members not voting) a proposed Code of Conduct on U.S. arms transfers, sponsored by Rep. Cynthia McKinney. A similar proposal, sponsored by Senator Mark Hatfield (bill S.326), had not yet been introduced in the Senate as of early November 1995. The Hatfield/McKinney proposal is part of an international campaign by nongovernmental organizations (NGOs) to rein in the arms trade. In May 1995, a coalition of European NGOs launched an appeal for the European Union to adopt a stricter code of conduct on the sale of arms and establish an effective E.U. arms export control regime. In September, Nobel Peace Prize laureate Oscar Arias Sánchez announced that a group of Nobel Peace Prize winners was planning to introduce a new proposal, aimed at establishing a code of conduct to govern the international arms trade, at the U.N.

THE CHILDREN'S RIGHTS PROJECT

Human Rights Watch established the Children's Rights Project in April 1994 to work with the organization's regional divisions and other thematic projects to uncover abuses that uniquely affect children and for which unique campaigning initiatives are required. The project deals with abuses carried out or tolerated by governments and also those perpetrated by armed opposition groups, such as the use of children as soldiers.

The project grew out of recognition that children are frequently victims of abuse that springs directly from their being children. For the most part, international children's aid groups that sponsor welfare and development projects have not dealt with these abuses because they cannot afford to antagonize host governments. Human rights groups, for their part, have focused largely on the rights of adults. As the human rights movement has addressed the plight of political dissidents, it has tended to neglect those, like children, whose persecution is generally unrelated to their political views. Human Rights Watch created the Children's Rights Project to fill this important gap by devising effective research and advocacy strategies to decrease and work toward the eventual elimination of the abuses of the civil and political rights of children. Moreover, the project serves as a link between international and national children's groups and the human rights community.

Children are particularly vulnerable to exploitation. In many countries children, some as young as eight, are forced to become soldiers, to kill or be killed, to be victims of atrocities or, sometimes, to take part in them. In other countries, children serve as bonded laborers, their childhood mortgaged as they work to pay off loans made to their families. In many countries children are forced into prostitution, snatched by strangers, or sold by their families and even trafficked from one country to another while governments ignore their plight.

The Human Rights Watch Children's Rights Project works to hold governments accountable for failing to respect and protect children's basic human rights.

The Work of the Children's Rights Project

During 1995 the Children's Rights Project, working with the organization's regional divisions, researched and campaigned to bring to light conditions in correctional institutions for children in Louisiana, the use of children as soldiers and slaves in Sudan, the use of the death penalty against juveniles in the United States, and the global scope of the phenomenon of child soldiers. The findings of research into these issues, including fact-finding missions to Louisiana and the Sudan, were published with recommendations for urgent change and for the mobilization of those who can bring this about. At the end of the year we sent a fact-finding mission to India to look into bonded child labor.

Child Soldiers

Many thousands of children around the world are used as soldiers. Often these children are armed with fully-automatic assault rifles; many take part in atrocities as well as confronting and killing opposing fighters. Children themselves are killed or gravely injured, suffer psychological trauma, and are deprived of schooling and a normal childhood. Many are unable, at the conflict's end, to reintegrate into their communities.

Some children are forcibly recruited; some "volunteer" in order to survive. Many are treated brutally by the forces with which they serve, through casual beatings or torture. Some are forced to kill or torture others.

The United Nations Convention on the Rights of the Child and Protocols I and II to the Geneva Conventions of 1949 forbid the recruitment of children under fifteen as soldiers. Human Rights Watch believes that no one under the age of eighteen should serve in armed conflict.

The work that began in 1994 with the launch (with Human Rights Watch/Africa) of reports and campaigning on child soldiers in Liberia and Sudan continued in 1995 with further fact-finding and advocacy.

In January 1995 we presented to the United Nations Human Rights Commission a statement on the use of children as soldiers, and recommended that the commission press all member states and warring factions to take steps to halt the practice. These steps were to disarm and demobilize immediately all child soldiers and to refrain from further such exploitation of children; to take part in the U.N. Working Group drafting an optional protocol to the U.N. Convention on the Rights of the Child that would raise the minimum age for participation in armed conflict from fifteen to eighteen; and to raise in their own countries the minimum age of participation in armed conflict to eighteen.

In September we released, with Human Rights Watch/Africa, *Children in Sudan: Slaves, Street Children and Child Soldiers.* The report describes the recruitment of young boys by government and opposition forces alike. The rebel SPLA was continuing its practice of inducting boys as young as eleven, using them as child soldiers or keeping them in a form of reserve, with thousands of boys in SPLA camps separated from their families and denied an education and a normal life. The government, in turn, was found to recruit children from buses and recreation sites; some recruitment was conducted from camps established to hold boys rounded up in random sweeps through city streets and marketplaces.

We plan to release a short report designed in part for the use of the U.N. working group now developing a protocol on the minimum age at which one can take part in armed conflict. The report will pull together the work that Human Rights Watch has done on child soldiers since 1989, including country-by-country information on the practice in Angola, Burma, El Salvador, Ethiopia, Liberia, Mozambique, Peru, and Sudan.

The project aimed to raise international awareness of child soldiers, the abuses they themselves suffer and the dangers that they present to others. As part of this effort we assisted *Newsweek* staff with a cover story on child soldiers and briefed other print and electronic media on the issues. We worked with local and international children's and human rights groups and with the U.N. experts preparing a report to be presented to the General Assembly in 1996 on the impact of armed conflict on children. Work with governments and inter-governmental organizations to stop the use of child soldiers is outlined below.

Bonded Child Labor

Hundreds of thousands of children work as bonded child laborers in countries around the world; the full extent of the problem has yet to be shown. Bonded labor, normally debt bondage or peonage, is outlawed by the 1956 U.N. Supplementary Convention on the Abolition of Slavery, the Slave Trade, and Institutions and Practices Similar to Slavery. Bonded labor of children typically arises when parents receive an advance payment or a reduction in debt in exchange for their child's labor. But the workplace is often structured so that "expenses" and/or "interest" are deducted from a child's earnings in such amounts that it is almost impossible for a child to repay the debt. Moreover, some children work to pay off debts inherited by their families from past generations. Many are subjected to severe physical abuse, as in a case cited in the July 1995 Human Rights Watch/Asia report, *Contemporary Forms of Slavery in Pakistan*:

Two years ago at the age of seven, Anwar started weaving carpets in a village in Pakistan's province of Sindh. He was given some food, little free time, and no medical assistance. He was told repeatedly that he could not stop working until he earned enough money to pay an alleged family debt. He was never told who in his family had borrowed money nor how much he had borrowed. Any time he made an error with his work, he was fined and the debt increased. Once when his work was considered to be too slow, he was beaten with a stick. Once after a particularly painful beating, he tried to run away, only to be apprehended by the local police who forcibly returned him to the carpet looms.

On another level, we met with children's and human rights groups, as well as representatives from the United Nations Children's Fund (UNICEF), the International Labor Organization (ILO), the World Bank, and other organizations, to try to develop a holistic strategy to prevent children from losing their childhood, education, and opportunities by being entrapped in bonded labor. We worked with others to develop a campaign to educate consumers about products made with bonded child labor, and to persuade companies not to use or sell these products.

The Children's Rights Project worked to provide to children's organizations and international advocacy groups objective on-the-spot reporting to support efforts to effect change.

Slavery

In *Children of Sudan: Slaves, Street Children and Child Soldiers*, Human Rights Watch interviews describe the use of children as slaves in Sudan. Children tell in their own words of having been stolen from their families by government forces during raids on their villages in the war zones. These children were taken as booty by soldiers and militia members who returned to western and northern Sudan. There the children were

frequently beaten and performed unpaid labor inside the soldiers' houses or herding their animals. Some told of running away only to be caught and returned to the families abusing them. Some captors branded the children they exploited.

We found that army officers, soldiers, militia members and others who held children in slavery operated with impunity from government prosecution. The Sudan government failed to live up to its obligations to prevent and punish such abuses, as set forth in the Convention on the Rights of the Child, the 1926 Slavery Convention as amended, the 1956 Supplementary Convention on the Abolition of Slavery, the 1930 International Labor Organization (ILO) Forced Labor Convention (No. 29) concerning Forced or Compulsory Labor, the 1957 ILO Convention (No. 105) concerning the Abolition of Forced Labor, the African Charter on the Rights and Welfare of the Child, and the International Covenant on Civil and Political Rights (ICCPR).

Our strategy is to inform relevant national and international organizations and to raise public awareness of the children's plight. We have recommended action to examine and end slavery in Sudan to UNICEF, the ILO, the Committee on the Rights of the Child, the Working Group on Contemporary Forms of Slavery, and the U.N. Special Rapporteur on Sudan, and have taken part in many forums and press interviews concerning slavery in Sudan.

Children in Conflict with the Law

International standards provide both broad and specific protections for children in the justice system. These include the Convention on the Rights of the Child (art. 40), the ICCPR (art. 10,14), the Standard Minimum Rules for the Administration of Juvenile Justice, the U.N. Rules for the Protection of Juveniles Deprived of their Liberty, the U.N. Guidelines for the Prevention of Juvenile Delinquency, the Standard Minimum Rules for the Treatment of Prisoners, and the African Charter on the Rights and Welfare of Children (art. 16, 17).

These treaties and standards require governments to hold detained or imprisoned children separate from adults, and to incarcerate children only as a last resort and in humane conditions. They forbid torture and other cruel, inhuman, and degrading treatment of children by police and security forces. They recognize that children need special consideration because of their physical and mental immaturity.

The Children's Rights Project's work for children caught up in the justice system focused in 1995 on the conditions in children's penal institutions in the state of Louisiana, and on juveniles facing the death penalty in the United States. Campaigning for change in Jamaica continued, following up our 1994 report on children in police lockups there. Many of the children we met during the 1994 mission were confirmed to have been released shortly after the report's publication, while the government ordered significant reforms.

Louisiana

In March and May, the Children's Rights Project sent fact-finding missions to Louisiana to look into the conditions in which children are confined in state correctional institutions (prisons for children). In October we released a report, *United States: Children in Confinement in Louisiana*. Our researchers visited all four state "training schools" and interviewed more than sixty children as well as state officials, judges, lawyers, social workers and others concerned with juvenile justice. We found that physical brutality is pervasive and that there is no functioning complaint system by which children can bring abuses to the attention of authorities.

Moreover, children are confined unnecessarily in restraints such as handcuffs and shackles, and are kept in isolation for as long as five days, contrary to international standards. In addition, many children told us they were hungry. The overall environment of the institutions failed to meet the primary goal required by international standards for any form of juvenile incarceration: to create an environment that will ensure children's successful reintegration into society.

The Children's Rights Project recommended the adoption by both the state of Louisiana and the federal government of mandatory standards that at a minimum comply with international standards. Our detailed recommendations included the monitoring and training of guards to make effective the prohibition of physical abuse, and the establishment of an effective complaint procedure that will ensure that children can seek redress and that staff are appropriately disciplined for abuses.

The report was widely covered by the media in Louisiana. The head of the corrections department attended the press conference at which the report was released, acknowledged the existence of physical abuse by guards and announced plans for change.

This report is the first of what we hope, resources permitting, will be a series on conditions in juvenile detention facilities for children in the U.S. Our strategy is two-fold. First, we plan to issue reports that document the ways in which children's rights are violated, raising public awareness. No other organization in the United States is carrying out such a program.

Second, we plan to work with children's advocates, local, national, and international, to address the human rights issues surrounding the detention of juveniles, and to work for change. We will continue to work with children's advocates in Louisiana who are eager to work toward reform, with national organizations, and with international groups like Defense for Children International and the International Save the Children Alliance, both in Geneva. We have submitted a report to the U.N. Committee on the Rights of the Child, detailing our findings on children in custody.

We will press both the government of Louisiana and the federal government to enact mandatory standards for children's correctional institutions. Under the Juvenile Justice and Delinquency Prevention Act the federal government is required to issue such standards and to monitor their implementation, but it has failed to do so.

Death Penalty

Human Rights Watch opposes the death penalty in all circumstances because of its inherent cruelty. We strongly oppose the imposition of the death penalty on juvenile offenders, those whose crimes were committed before they were eighteen.

In March the Children's Rights Project released a short report, *United States: A World Leader in Executing Juveniles*. The report revealed that nine juvenile offenders have been executed in the U.S. since the death penalty was reinstated by the U.S. Supreme Court in 1976; four of these were executed during the last six months of 1993, indicating that such executions are on the rise.

Only eight other countries have carried out such executions in the past fifteen years: Bangladesh, Barbados, Iran, Iraq, Nigeria, Pakistan, Saudi Arabia, and Yemen. The United States continues to execute juveniles in clear contravention of international agreements and standards prohibiting this, including the ICCPR (art. 4(5)), the American Convention on Human Rights (art. 4(5)), the Convention on the Rights of the Child (art. 37(a)), the Standard Minimum Rules for the Administration of Juvenile Justice (art. 2,17), and the African Charter on the Rights and Welfare of Children (art. 5(3)). The death penalty, by its nature irreversible and inherently cruel, is inappropriate for individuals who were not physically and emotionally mature at the time they committed their crimes.

Our report was timed for release just before the first meeting of the U.N. Human Rights Committee at which the U.S. was to report on its compliance with the provisions of the ICCPR. Members of the committee used our report extensively to question government officials and, later, to condemn the U.S. strongly for executing juveniles.

Work with the United Nations

The U.N. Committee on the Rights of the Child, the treaty body charged with monitoring compliance with the Convention on the Rights of the Child, is a forceful and effective group that welcomes input from nongovernmental organizations (NGOs). The committee receives reports from signatories to the convention, questions officials closely on the state's compliance, and makes cogent recommendations for change. In addition, the committee persuaded the U.N. General Assembly to create a special study on the impact of armed conflict on children. It also persuaded the U.N. Human Rights Commission to establish the working group on the minimum age for armed conflict.

The Children's Rights Project has submitted to the committee reports on the treatment of juveniles in the justice systems in Jamaica, Northern Ireland, and the state of Louisiana (the committee agreed to receive the latter although the U.S. is not yet a party to the convention). The committee has in some cases urged the offending government to take the steps recommended in Human Rights Watch submissions. A representative of the Children's Rights Project appeared before the committee to testify on Jamaica and Northern Ireland. In November the committee held a theme day on juvenile justice; we appeared before the committee and submitted written recommendations based on our work on conditions for detained or incarcerated children.

The Children's Rights Project recommended that the Human Rights Commission create a special rapporteur on child soldiers. We also recommended that the new Special Rapporteur on the Sale of Children, Child Prostitution and Child Pornography continue to include the issue of child soldiers in her portfolio. We have recommended to the special rapporteurs, experts, and special representatives appointed to address specific country situations that, where relevant, they address the issue of child soldiers in internal armed conflict.

We have recommended to the U.N. Subcommission on the Prevention of Discrimination and Protection of Minorities and its Working Group on Contemporary Forms of Slavery that it study the issue of child soldiers, recommend the appointment of a special rapporteur on child soldiers, and recommend to governments and armed opposition groups that they end the practice of using children under eighteen as soldiers.

We have recommended to the U.N. High Commissioner for Refugees that it study the issue of recruitment of children from refugee camps, and that it take steps to protect children in its camps from recruitment.

U.S. Policy

One hundred seventy-seven of the 185 member states of the United Nations have ratified or acceded to the Convention on the Rights of the Child. In February 1995 the Clinton administration signed the convention; it has not, however, forwarded the convention to the Senate for ratification. Jesse Helms, the chair of the Foreign Relations Committee, has described the convention as a "pernicious document" and has vowed not to hold hearings on its ratification.

Human Rights Watch supports the ratification of the convention and will urge members of the Senate to do so.

The U.S. has been a major stumbling block in the meetings of the U.N. working group to draft the optional protocol to the Convention on the Rights of the Child that would raise the permissible age for taking part in armed conflict. The U.S. permits seventeen-year-olds to enlist in the armed forces with parental permission, and is opposed to raising the minimum age to eighteen. The U.S. has also argued for requiring twenty-five signatures for the Optional Protocol to take effect, while other countries are opting for ten signatures. The working group will meet again in January 1996; the Children's Rights Project will attempt to persuade the administration to change its positions.

U.S. officials appeared before the U.N. Committee on Human Rights for the first time in March to report on U.S. compliance with the ICCPR. Questioned by the committee about the use of the death penalty against juveniles, the U.S. challenged our report and denied—incorrectly—that nine juvenile offenders had been executed in the U.S. since the resumption of the death penalty in 1976. In addition, the State Department's legal adviser told the committee that the American people support the execution of persons who committed crimes as minors.

In a more positive vein, the U.S. Department of Labor held hearings in 1994 and 1995 on the use of child labor, including bonded child labor, in the manufacture of products that are imported into the United States, and has issued reports on the hearings. At the first hearing, Human Rights Watch testified on bonded child labor in the carpet industry in Pakistan.

THE FREE EXPRESSION PROJECT

In 1995, the Free Expression Project focused on promoting freedom of expression principles and standards in "cyberspace," and, joined by the Association of American Publishers, investigated freedom of expression in Albania and Cuba. (More detailed accounts of those investigations are found in the Helsinki and Americas sections of this report.) The Project also managed the work of the Committee for International Academic Freedom and administered the Hellman/Hammett grants to writers who have been victimized by political persecution.

Free Expression in "Cyberspace"

Prior to the G-7 Ministerial Conference on the Information Society held in Brussels on February 25 and 26, 1995, the Free Expression Project prepared a letter, co-signed by other U.S. and international civil liberties groups, to Vice President Al Gore, who represented the United States at the summit. The letter to Vice President Gore, who had initially called for the conference to formulate a unified policy for building a "global information infrastructure" (GII), urged him to press the G-7 ministers to adhere to international free expression principles in any multilateral agreement regarding the development, content, control, and deployment of the proposed GII. The letter noted the extraordinary opportunity presented by new communications technologies to "motivate citizens to become more involved in decision-making at local and global levels as they organize, debate and share information unrestricted by geographic distances or national borders." It called upon the United States to work against any censorship and to promote diverse ideas and viewpoints on the GII. In particular, the letter called for a prohibition on prior censorship of online communications and for limiting restrictions of online speech to expression that directly and immediately incites acts of violence. The letter also called for nondiscriminatory access to online technology and enforceable legal protections against unauthorized scrutiny and use by private or public entities of personal information on the GII.

Following receipt of the letter, Mr. Gore's prepared remarks were amended to include support for free expression standards.

Hellman/Hammett Grants

The Free Expression Project administers a program of annual grants to writers from around the world who have been victims of political persecution and are in financial need. First established in 1989, the grant program is funded by the estates of Lillian Hellman and Dashiell Hammett, American writers who were victimized for their political beliefs and associations during the U.S. anti-communist "purges" of the early 1950s. With this experience in mind, Ms. Hellman left a legacy to provide support for writers who have been persecuted for expressing political views.

In addition to offering financial assistance, the Hellman/Hammett grants publicize individual cases, helping focus attention on repression and censorship around the world. In some cases, however, writers must request anonymity because of the dangerous circumstances in which they and their families are living.

The 1995 recipients, a diverse group of forty-eight poets, novelists and journalists from twenty-three countries, received grants totaling about $175,000. There were four recipients from Vietnam, four from Iran, eight from countries that were formerly part of the Soviet Union, and thirteen recipients from the Peoples Republic of China. The recipients include: Kenneth Best, founder of Liberia's first independent newspaper, who was imprisoned three times and deported to two countries before coming to the United States, where he is working to return to Liberia; Fatos Lubonja, an Albanian writer imprisoned for seventeen years after the government declared his writings "decadent"; Father Ricardo Rezende, a Brazilian parish priest and author whose work with landless rural workers has put his name on a "death list"; Mumia Abu-Jamal, a U.S. journalist on death row in Pennsylvania, who was convicted of killing a police officer in a trial that raises questions about fairness, especially during the sentencing phase which relied heavily on information about Jamal's political associations and beliefs; Bonor Tigor Naipospos, an Indonesian journalist sentenced to eight and one- half years in prison on charges that included expressing Marxist views in his writing; and Koigi wa Wamwere, poet, novelist and journalist,who was arrested and charged with treason for articles deemed "seditious" by the state. The three recipients from Turkey—Fikret Baskaya, Ismet G. Imset, and Aysenur Zarakolu—all wrote or spoke out about the country's Kurdish minority.

Human Rights Watch awarded the annual Hellman/Hammett grants after nominations were reviewed by a five-person selection committee composed of writers and editors who are members of the Free Expression Project advisory committee. In the course of the year, the selection committee approved an additional ten grants to writers who needed emergency funds to help them leave countries where they were in immediate danger or to provide urgently needed medical or legal assistance.

The Free Expression Project also wrote protest letters on behalf of writers in Burma, Pakistan and Sierra Leone who had received Hellman/Hammett grants in prior years and were being persecuted again in 1995.

Committee for International Academic Freedom

The Committee for International Academic Freedom was formed in 1991 by Human Rights Watch and a group of U.S. university presidents and scholars in recognition of the critical role that education plays in the development of civil society and the frequent targeting of educators and students by the world's more repressive regimes. When professors, teachers and students are harassed or imprisoned for exercising their rights of free expression and inquiry, when their work is censored, or when universities are closed for political reasons, the Committee sends protest letters and cables to appropriate government officials and publicizes the abuses in the academic community.

In 1995, the Committee wrote about situations in Cuba, the Dominican Republic, Burma, Israel, Bahrain and Tunisia. Two letters were sent to Cuban President Castro, one protesting the firing of six professors who had written about the relationship between the country's economic plight and emigration, and the second protesting the denial of exit visas to four other professors who were scheduled to present papers at the annual meeting of the Latin American Studies Association. The Committee urged Israeli President Rabin to establish a process for issuing travel permits to students who live in Gaza while attending schools in the West Bank and followed up seven months later after a new term had started and guidelines for student travel permits still had not been defined. Other Committee letters dealt with the "disappearance" of a lecturer at the Autonomous University of Santa Domingo; the harassment of Dr. Moncef Marzouki of the Medical School in Sousse, Tunisia; the suspension of Associate Professor of Sociol-

ogy Munira Ahmed Fakhro after she signed the "Bahraini Women's Petition"; and the arrest of a Burmese student whose private letters were characterized as "incriminating documents."

The Committee is composed of twenty-three university presidents and scholars and co-chaired by Jonathan Fanton of the New School for Social Research, Hanna Holborn Gray of the University of Chicago, Vartan Gregorian of Brown University and Charles Young of the University of California at Los Angeles.

THE WOMEN'S RIGHTS PROJECT

The Women's Rights Project of Human Rights Watch was established in 1990 to work in conjunction with Human Rights Watch's regional divisions to monitor violence against women and discrimination on the basis of sex that is either committed or tolerated by governments. The project grew out of Human Rights Watch's recognition of the rampant levels of gender-based violence and discrimination around the world and of the past failure of human rights organizations, and the international community, to hold governments accountable for abuses of women's basic human rights. The project monitors the performance of specific countries in securing and protecting women's human rights, highlights individual cases of international significance, and serves as a link between women's rights and human rights communities at both national and international levels.

Much of our advocacy work in 1995 focused on networking with women's human rights organizations to ensure that women's human rights were given priority attention at the Fourth World Conference on Women. We also released the *Human Rights Watch Global Report on Women's Human*

Rights, a compilation of five years of work with women's rights and human rights groups investigating abuses of women's rights around the world. Covering abuses such as rape in war, abuses against women in custody, domestic violence, and relating to women's reproductive and sexual lives, the report sets forth a conceptual framework for integrating women's human rights into international human rights practice. It also applies this approach to specific violations of women's rights in a score of countries around the world, and crafts national and international remedies for pervasive women's rights abuse. The report was released in September at the Fourth World Conference on Women in Beijing.

Women's Human Rights Developments

This section does not evaluate progress in women's human rights throughout the world, but describes developments in countries most closely monitored by the Women's Rights Project in 1995: Russia, the United States, Kenya, South Africa, Mexico, Haiti, Nigeria, Thailand, Turkey, and Botswana. During 1995 we conducted three missions, in Morocco, Japan, and Singapore and continued investigations in Nigeria and the U.S.

Russia

On International Women's Day, March 8, 1995, Human Rights Watch released *Neither Jobs Nor Justice: State Discrimination Against Women in Russia* in English and Russian at a Moscow press conference. The report documented how economic and political changes in Russia have adversely affected women's enjoyment of their fundamental human rights. Russian women face widespread employment discrimination that is practiced, condoned, and tolerated by the government. Government employers have fired women workers in disproportionate numbers and have also refused to employ women because of their sex. Far from attacking sex discrimination, the Russian government has actively participated in discriminatory action and failed to enforce laws prohibiting such practices.

The Russian government, and particularly its law enforcement agencies, also have denied women their right to equal protection of the law by failing to investigate and prosecute violence against women. In particular, law enforcement agencies and police have been largely indifferent to domestic violence and sexual assault. Local law enforcement officials scoff at reports of violence by domestic partners and refuse to intervene in what they identify as "family matters." In some instances, police themselves have mistreated and harassed women who report such crimes as a way to intimidate them and stop them from filing complaints.

The assumption that political and economic change would improve the protection of human rights generally in Russia has generally proven to be true in some aspects, such as people's ability to exercise their freedom of association or speech. But women's human rights, far from being better protected in a rapidly changing Russia, are frequently being abridged and denied.

Since the release of *Neither Jobs Nor Justice,* Russian officials have failed to end their participation in the widespread employment discrimination that has contributed to the impoverishment of female-headed households. They have, however, turned their attention in unprecedented ways to violence against women, by recognizing publicly the significant dimensions of the problem and taking initial steps to respond to it. In June 1995, the Russian government released the first-ever official figures on domestic violence, revealing that 14,500 women died at the hands of their husbands in 1993 and that another 56,400 women were disabled or seriously injured consequent to domestic violence. Some members of Russia's lower house of parliament repeatedly revised draft legislation on domestic violence (first introduced in 1994), but until October, they refused to make public the draft law and to seek the input of women's organizations. Parliamentary officials have since indicated their interest in cooperating with NGOs.

United States

In an eighteen-month investigation, from 1993 to 1995, Human Rights Watch documented the sexual abuse of women in state prisons in California, Georgia, Illinois, Michigan, New York, and the District of Columbia. We found that women incarcerated in state prisons in these areas face a serious and potentially pervasive problem of sexual misconduct by prison officials. Male officers have engaged in rape, sexual assault, inappropriate sexual contact, verbal degradation, and unwarranted visual surveillance of female prisoners. Our findings, while profoundly troubling, scratched only the surface of the problem of sexual misconduct in the state correctional systems that we investigated. The need to address this problem is particularly urgent given that the female prison population in the United States is increasing at almost double the rate of the male population.

In virtually every prison that we visited, state prison authorities were allowing male officers to hold contact positions over female prisoners with no clear definition of sexual misconduct, no clear rules and procedures with respect to it, and no meaningful training in how to avoid it. Prison officials also were failing to equip female prisoners to deal with the potential abuse in the cross-gender guarding situation. They rarely, if ever, informed female prisoners of the risk of sexual misconduct in custody. Nor did they advise them of the mechanisms available— to the extent that any existed—to report and remedy such practices.

Two prison systems that we investigated, in Georgia and the District of Columbia, had taken initial steps to address this problem. But most states were failing to address adequately custodial sexual misconduct and had yet to train officers to avoid such misconduct or to put in place administrative measures and, where appropriate, to apply criminal sanctions to prohibit and punish this abuse. Moreover, the federal government was failing to meet its international obligations to ensure that custodial sexual violence was not only prohibited but also remedied by states. In fact, the United States government had allowed custodial sexual misconduct at the state level to fall into a kind of legal and political vacuum where in large measure neither international, nor federal, nor state law was seen to apply.

Kenya

Our 1993 report, *Seeking Refuge, Finding Terror*, documented the Kenyan government's indifference to cases of sexual abuse, notably rape, against Somali refugee women in refugee camps in Kenya's Northeastern Province. A follow-up mission in September 1994 found that the monthly incidence of rape had decreased from double-digit numbers to a handful. The mission also showed that the Kenyan government and the United Nations High Commissioner for Refugees (UNHCR) adopted many of our recommendations for improving women's safety in the camps.

Nonetheless, as of late 1995, although the number of night-time attacks had decreased, women continued to be vulnerable when they left the camp to fetch firewood or to herd goats. Since young girls were often sent out to perform these tasks, they constituted a large proportion of 1995 rape victims. Kenyan police officers continued to be unable or unwilling to investigate and prosecute rape claims effectively. Lack of housing continued to impede the assignment of any women police officers to the camps.

South Africa

In January 1995 the Women's Rights and Africa divisions of Human Rights Watch sent a mission to South Africa to investigate the problems of violence against women and to evaluate the state's efforts to stem such abuse. The mission to South Africa came almost one year after the country's first multiracial general election in April 1994 that brought sweeping political changes and ended the repressive apartheid policies of the past. The recently elected government of national unity, led by the African National Congress (ANC), was legally committed under the interim constitution (brought into effect on the first day of the elections) to the achievement of full equality for women. At the highest policy-making levels the government had specifically expressed a commitment to addressing the problem of violence against women.

However, despite the new government's pledge to prioritize the problem of violence against women, the Women's Rights Project found in its report titled *Violence against Women in South Africa* that an enormous gap existed between policy and practice. The legacy of state violence that underpinned the apartheid state had resulted in extremely high levels of violence throughout society, including against women. South African women's organizations underscored the pervasive nature of this abuse: approximately one in every three South African women has been raped, and perhaps as many as one in six South African women is being abused by her partner.

South African women victims of violence frequently experienced indifference or hostile treatment from police officers when they attempted to report rape or domestic abuse. Ignorance of the laws protecting women was common in many police stations and among court clerks. Within the courts, the testimony of rape survivors was often discounted or rapists given lenient sentences. The apartheid policies of the past continued to affect victims of domestic violence and rape. Lingering state racism and sexism prejudiced black women in particular in their interactions with police and judicial authorities. In the rural areas, where black women have the least education and work under the worst conditions, access to redress against perpetrators of violence was even more restricted than for white, "colored," or Indian women. In the townships, inaction by the police led to a dangerous reliance on young "comrades" to mete out vigilante "justice" against alleged perpetrators of violence, including violence against women, further undermining the rule of law.

The South African government had given less attention to violence against women than it had, for example, to the more

overt political violence during the transition period and under the new government. Despite a number of encouraging initiatives, as of this writing, there was no coordinated national strategy to address the problems in the criminal justice, law enforcement, health, and welfare systems in a systematic fashion. Moreover, the current government had not firmly committed itself to providing funds for training of police and judicial officers and improved services to women victims of violence.

Mexico

In March 1995, the Women's Rights Project conducted a mission to Mexico to investigate allegations of widespread state-tolerated discrimination against women assembly workers in the export-oriented assembly plant sector along the Mexico/U.S. border. Despite clear Mexican and international law prohibiting such conduct, we found that personnel and administrators at these *maquiladora* factories—most of them owned by foreign companies—routinely discriminated against both prospective and actual female employees. Employers regularly required female job applicants to verify their pregnancy status by submitting to pregnancy tests and to detailed and intrusive questioning with regard to their sexual activity, contraception use, and menses schedule. Women found to be pregnant were denied work. Moreover, in some cases, maquiladora personnel and management mistreated and sometimes forced women workers to resign when they became pregnant.

Over 250,000 women work in Mexico's maquiladora plants. Most have only a primary school education and minimal formal work experience. As such they view the *maquila* work as perhaps the only viable income available to them. Work in other likely sectors, such as domestic service or in stores, often involves worse conditions than those prevalent in the maquiladoras. Consequently, the women are particularly vulnerable to (and reluctant to denounce) the discrimination and difficult working conditions they face in these factories.

We found that rather than address the abuse of women workers, the Mexican government had failed not only to enforce international and domestic prohibitions against sex discrimination but also to ensure women effective protection from such discrimination when it occurred in the workplace. Although workplace discrimination was legally prohibited, the Mexican government provided no means by which women who were denied jobs because they were pregnant could contest this abuse. Mexico's existing conciliation and arbitration boards heard cases only where a labor relationship had been established. Furthermore, the head of one conciliation and arbitration board in Tijuana told Human Rights Watch that " . . . the owner is right to try to avoid the cost [of hiring a pregnant worker]."

Haiti

From Haitian President Jean-Bertrand Aristide's October 1994 return to Haiti to November 1995, the time of this writing, not one rape committed during the coup period had been investigated and tried. Nonetheless, Aristide took several steps to address human rights violations committed in his absence and to examine in particular the status of women in the country. He created a Ministry on the Status and Rights of Women, headed by Dr. Lise Marie Dejean, which was responsible for, among other things, the coordination and implementation of policies aimed at promoting the rights of women; the facilitation of women's access to education, health, economic opportunity, and professional training; and the coordination of policies aimed at preventing violence against women. In addition, he created a National Commission for Truth and Justice, the charter of which committed the commission to investigate politically motivated, gender-based crimes against women. The commission's mandate was limited, however; while it could, given sufficient evidence, name names of actual perpetrators of violations of human rights, it had no judicial authority to prosecute cases.

Thailand

During 1995, the Women's Rights Project continued to monitor the trafficking of Burmese women and girls into forced prostitution in Thailand. We worked with local Thai groups to investigate the government's efforts to reduce such trafficking. The Thai cabinet did send a draft anti-prostitution bill to parliament for approval, but as of late 1995, no further action had been taken.

There were many problems with the proposed bill. For example, although the fines on procurers and brothel owners had increased dramatically, the potential prison sentences were shorter. Further, while the bill imposed penalties on convicted prostitutes, clients who hired prostitutes over eighteen years old were not subject to any such penalties. Since most prostitutes are women and most clients are men, this factor constituted discrimination on the basis of sex.

More important, Thai police still largely failed to enforce existing laws against trafficking. Police conducted occasional brothel raids, but did little to punish traffickers and continued to detain and summarily deport trafficking victims as illegal immigrants. Even though the Thai government had taken steps to improve conditions in the Immigration Detention Center, conditions in the local jails—where trafficking victims often were detained pending deportation—remained abysmal. Local organizations reported that once the women and girls were detained in these facilities, they were extremely hard to contact and, therefore, stood at greater risk of custodial abuse. The nongovernmental organizations themselves found that Thai government cooperation with their efforts was difficult to obtain and that some activists had been harassed by the government for their anti-trafficking work.

Nigeria

In late 1994, the Women's Rights Project and Human Rights Watch/Africa sent research teams to Nigeria to investigate discrimination against widows in the south and forced child marriage in the north. In some areas of the south, we found that widows were forced to endure humiliating rituals when their husbands died and that they were denied inherited property under discriminatory customary law.

In five northern states that we visited, we found that girls are customarily forced by their families into marriage, frequently before puberty, despite the girls' express objections or attempts to run away. Many child brides are compelled to engage in sexual relations as soon as they are married and, as a consequence, they become pregnant and give birth before they are physically mature. This can not only increase their risk of death in childbirth, but also cause serious medical complications due to early pregnancy, including obstetric or vesico-vaginal fistula (an abnormal communication between the bladder and the vagina that causes fluids to pass uncontrolled from one to the other). Girls suffering from these complications smell from the constant leakage of urine, and many are abandoned by their husbands and families. The Nigerian government has taken few steps to eradicate these abuses, failing to pass laws setting a minimum age of marriage or protecting individuals' right to consent to marriage.

Turkey

Less than one year after the June 1994 release of our report on the Turkish government's use of forced gynecological exams to control women's virginity, the Ministry of Education proposed regulations authorizing virginity exams for schoolgirls under eighteen when required by school authorities. Opposition from women and students in Turkey prompted some government officials to oppose the measure, which ultimately was dropped. A regulation remained, however, that empowered Turkish school authorities to monitor the morality of students in their charge, a vague provision interpreted by some school officials to allow them to instigate virginity exams.

In early 1995, Turkey's women's minister, Onay Alpago, proposed to parliament new laws to eradicate statutory sex discrimination. The draft laws proposed to eliminate legal provisions establishing the husband as the head of the family household, allow women to retain their family names after marriage, provide equal property rights in cases of divorce, treat men and women equally in cases of adultery, and put in place new protections for victims of domestic violence. The proposed legislation was being reviewed by a parliamentary commission at this writing, although early passage seemed unlikely.

Finally, the torture and inhuman treatment of women in custody continued in Turkey. On August 14, 1995, the Human Rights Foundation of Turkey reported that twenty-four-year-old Leman Celikaslan had been raped repeatedly while in police custody in Ankara. Celikaslan was detained by police July 21, 1995 in a raid on the house where she was staying as a guest and was held in Ankara Central Closed Prison. Following her detention by Anti-Terror Police, she was taken to a wood, stripped, and sexually abused. She alleges that later three Anti-Terror police raped her in her cell. To our knowledge, the Turkish government had made no effort to prevent the ongoing torture and ill treatment of women in detention. In no instance of which we are aware were police investigated or punished for their participation in forced virginity exams or in sexual assault of women in custody.

Botswana

In September 1994, the Women's Rights Project and Human Rights Watch/Africa released *Second Class Citizens: Discrimination against Women Under Botswana's Citizenship Act.* The report condemned the Botswana government for discriminating against women in its Citizenship Act, which denied citizenship to children of Botswana women married to foreign men, and failing to comply with a high court decision that found this discrimination unconstitutional.

Just a year later, in August 1995, after a concerted campaign by local and international women's rights activists, the National Assembly of Botswana amended the Citizenship Act to eliminate its discriminatory provisions. The amendment granted citizenship to children, born in or outside of Botswana, whose mother or father is a citizen of Botswana. However, it did not apply to persons born prior to the adoption of the amendment, although it permitted expedited naturalization of minor children who were not Botswana citizens but had a parent who was a Botswana citizen. The amendment also revised the act to grant foreign wives and husbands of Botswana citizens the same naturalization requirements.

The Role of
the International Community

The United Nations

The year was marked by the U.N. Fourth World Conference on Women, held in Beijing in September. The themes of the Women's Conference—equality, development, and peace—had been addressed at previous U.N. world conferences on women, although with little or no reference to human rights. By contrast, at the 1995 world conference, the protection and promotion of women's human rights emerged as a central concern of both government and nongovernmental participants.

The growing importance of human rights as a key element in global policy-making with respect to women reflected the mounting influence of an increasingly organized and effective international women's human rights movement. Women activists from around the world went to the Beijing conference—as both governmental and nongovernmental delegates—to affirm the importance of women's human rights and to demand that governments integrate women's rights in the U.N.'s system-wide activity, refrain from abusing the human rights of women, and ensure not only that such abuse be prohibited, but also that when it occurs, it be denounced and remedied.

However, the potential of nongovernmental delegates in particular freely and safely to participate in the Beijing conference was compromised to some degree by the host Chinese government, a number of

other government delegations, and the inaction of the United Nations. The Chinese government, while attempting to use the official U.N. conference to boost its international image and deflect attention from its worsening human rights record, undermined the nongovernmental forum. Serious problems complicated the accreditation process for nongovernmental organizations (NGOs). NGOs that were critical of China's policies, abortion rights groups, and others were initially denied accreditation. Following strong protests which resulted in the reversal of some accreditation decisions, the Chinese government denied and delayed entry visas to numerous accredited participants, lowering the number of NGO representatives that attended the conference. The NGO site was moved by the Chinese government to Huairou, some sixty kilometers away from the official U.N. conference site in Beijing. The move severely hampered the NGOs' ability to meet government delegations, to coordinate their own work between the NGO and official conferences, and to influence the content of the Platform for Action. The Chinese government largely reneged on promises to provide adequate transportation between Huairou and the official conference site in Beijing, simultaneous translation, and even adequate space for workshops.

At the NGO Forum in Huairou and at off-site locations, Chinese security agents followed participants, harassed them, confiscated their materials, disrupted their workshops, and intimidated them. In hotels off the forum site, some participants were forbidden to have meetings or press interviews in their rooms, were watched by hotel security, and in some cases, found that their belongings had been searched. A number of international journalists also encountered difficulties obtaining visas and receiving clearance to bring in electronic equipment. Once in Beijing, they were relegated to certain hotels and subjected to Chinese security surveillance.

In addition, prior to and during the conference, the Chinese government heightened repression within the country and detained some Chinese political activists, largely to prevent them from meeting conference participants. Chinese security officials also acted to maintain "public order" by executing sixteen common criminals in Beijing to create a "secure environment" for the U.N. gathering.

Both the United Nations Conference Secretariat and Secretary-General Boutros Boutros-Ghali's representatives failed adequately to address these problems. Prior to the conference, the U.N. failed to act to ensure NGO participation until pushed to do so by NGOs and some governments. At first, the U.N. Conference Secretariat denied numerous NGOs accreditation for the Women's Conference without granting them the opportunity to appeal the decision. This was of particular concern because the secretariat's decisions appeared to exclude organizations based on their political agendas and not on their failure to conform to the technical criteria for accreditation. Human Rights Watch expressed concern that the U.N. not succumb to pressure from abusive governments to restrict NGO participation in the conference. Ultimately, governments at the March Commission on the Status of Women meeting allowed NGOs denied accreditation to appeal the Secretariat's initial decision, and ECOSOC voted to accept many of these groups. Nonetheless, in the weeks immediately prior to the conference, the U.N. failed to prevent China from excluding many NGO delegates via the visa denials and delays described above.

After the Chinese government suddenly relocated the NGO Forum to Huairou, the U.N. was late stepping in to mediate with the Chinese government. Again, only after NGOs demanded that the U.N. support their call for an NGO Forum site that would provide both the necessary facilities and permit access to the official conference did the secretary-general's envoy, Ismat Kittani, go to China to meet with officials. Prior to the NGO outcry, the U.N. made excuses for China's failure to offer a site with adequate facilities for the gathering of 35,000 activists.

Then in Huairou at the NGO Forum itself, when NGO participants were faced with varying levels of China-sponsored or China-tolerated intimidation and interference that prevented them from participating fully and openly in the NGO Forum, the U.N. refused to intervene to ensure the inviolability of the NGO process. Instead, the U.N. offered the disingenuous excuse that the NGO Forum was not a U.N. conference and therefore the U.N. had no responsibility for what happened there. This stance contradicted its constructive, public intervention when China changed the NGO Forum site from Beijing to Huairou in March. Where the U.N. had an opportunity both to go beyond rhetoric in its support for NGOs and to demand respect for the conference participants' fundamental human rights of freedom of association and expression, it utterly failed.

Despite these obstacles, nongovernmental participants worked closely with government delegates to produce a Platform for Action that identified the economic, social and political problems facing women and recommended government action for improving women's status over the next decade. During debates over the platform, a number of governments strongly resisted the growing international consensus that in order to advance women's status, governments must protect and promote their human rights. Several official delegations—most notably the Holy See, Iran, Sudan, Guatemala, and Malta—made concerted efforts to modify or abridge women's human rights in light of religion, culture, or national law. These delegations promoted the concept that women have a "special" role in society and the family as an excuse to deny women their equality, civil liberties, and the right to be free from violence.

Ultimately, the Platform for Action did reaffirm the universality and indivisibility of human rights, asserted that these rights extend to women's reproductive and sexual lives, and reiterated that culture, religion, and national law cannot be used to justify the denial of women's fundamental rights. The platform, however, made no clear commitment to the provision of adequate funding for the implementation of these protections. Moreover, it neither guaranteed equal inheritance rights for girls nor extended international protection to internally displaced women.

Although the conference gathered NGOs and governments together to craft rights-based ways of improving women's status, it also highlighted the intense resistance of many governments to women's equality and the full realization of their human rights, particularly within family structures and as concerns women's sexual and reproductive lives. The conference starkly demonstrated the ongoing need to identify and end abuses against women worldwide. While the governments ultimately made commitments in principle to advance this goal, what remained to be seen was whether they would do so in practice.

U.S. Policy

In 1995 the Clinton administration was a vocal proponent of women's human rights, particularly at the Fourth World Conference on Women in Beijing, China. At the conference, First Lady Hillary Rodham Clinton denounced specific violations of women's human rights and called upon governments to recognize and act on their responsibility for such abuses. However, in its own foreign policy, the administration made only small steps toward integrating concern for women's human rights into its relations with abusive governments. Moreover, the U.S. did not back up its commitment to promote women's rights around the world when it came to domestic policy; it continued to deny American women access to international human rights protections by failing to ratify important human rights treaties and limiting its accountability under those treaties that it did ratify.

This lack of progress in U.S. policy was not due to lack of information: the State Department's *Country Reports on Human Rights Practices for 1994* demonstrated improved reporting on violations of women's human rights. Although some problems remained, the 1994 report was more comprehensive both with regard to the types of abuses discussed and the countries in which gender-related abuses were documented.

In the months prior to the Women's Conference, the Clinton administration played a key role in promoting full NGO participation in the conference and its preparatory processes. Human Rights Watch pressed the Clinton administration to demonstrate a similar level of support for the goal of advancing human rights at the conference itself and with respect to the host country. Once the First Lady announced her plans to attend the conference, we urged her to move beyond the role of observer, to be a strong public leader on women's human rights, and to speak out publicly against human rights abuses in China in order to minimize any public relations pay-off enjoyed by the Chinese government consequent to her visit. The U.S. sent a strong delegation to the conference—including U.S. Ambassador to the United Nations Madeleine Albright, Secretary of Health and Human Services Donna Shalala, Administrator of the Environmental Protection Agency Carol Browner and Undersecretary of State for Global Affairs Timothy Wirth—and chose U.S. Ambassador to the U.N. Human Rights Commission Geraldine Ferraro to negotiate for strong protection of women's human rights.

In Beijing, the U.S. pledged to establish a White House inter-agency council on women to implement the Platform for Action; to launch a $1.6 billion initiative to fight crimes of violence against women in the U.S.; to combat threats to American women's health and security; to maintain its commitment to reproductive health rights; to improve working conditions for women in the U.S.; to promote access to financial credit for American women; to use Agency for International Development (AID) programs to increase women's political participation and the enforcement of women's legal rights worldwide; and, finally, to speak out publicly in defense of human rights.

Important as many of these initiatives may prove to be, they fell short of providing the concrete steps needed to ensure that U.S. policies, at home and abroad, promoted respect for women's human rights. The U.S. made no pledge to integrate women's rights concerns into its aid and trade relationships with abusive governments, offered no financial support for improving the international mechanisms that are supposed to protect women's rights, and underestimated the need for guaranteeing international human rights protection to women in the U.S. itself. Although the commitments did place high priority on ratification of CEDAW, the Clinton administration made a similar pledge at the U.N. Human Rights Conference in Vienna in 1993, yet in 1995 the U.S. remained the sole industrialized nation that had failed to ratify the treaty. This problem was made that much more acute—and the administration's active support for ratification made that much more necessary—by the fact that the treaty was being vigorously opposed by extreme conservatives in the U.S. Congress.

Several of the U.S. commitments, at least as presented in Beijing, were too preliminary to connote any substantial progress on promoting women's human rights within the United States. For example, to our knowledge the campaign to improve conditions for women in the workplace initially consisted only of Labor Department efforts to solicit pledges from employers to change their policies and practices. Moreover, while other commitments such as the $1.6 billion in federal resources were more developed, they could be blocked by Congress, which was divided on whether to fund or cut support for the important Violence Against Women Act (VAWA).

As important as domestic initiatives to combat violence against women was the protection provided by international standards. Such protection was denied to American women as a result not only of the U.S. failure to ratify CEDAW, but also because of its compromised ratification of the International Covenant on Civil and Political Rights (ICCPR), which effectively denied U.S. citizens the ability to assert the rights protected by the covenant in U.S. courts (see United States section).

The only other concrete measure offered by the U.S. in Beijing to promote women's human rights at the international level was a women's legal rights initiative by AID. The goal of this initiative—attacking obstacles to the full realization of women's rights through education and support for local NGOs—was essential, but funding was not guaranteed. Moreover, for this program to be effective, it must be backed up by the thorough integration of concern for women's legal rights into AID's own programs. As the case of Russia indicated (see below), AID itself still failed fully to promote women's equal rights as an integral component of its economic and political development programs.

The administration was less than diligent in monitoring and reporting on women's human rights violations in the United States. For example, in its first appearance before the United Nations Human Rights Committee, pursuant to it obligations under the ICCPR, the administration stated that the problem of sexual abuse of women in prison was "addressed through staff training and through criminal statutes prohibiting such activity." The U.S. failed altogether to inform the committee of ongoing sexual abuse of women in a number of state prisons across the country, abuse that the Justice Department was itself investigating in several states.

In January 1995, the Clinton administration reported to the Senate Appropriations Committee on efforts by the Thai government to control sex trafficking. The administration's report concluded that, although there was no systematic involvement of the Thai government in the trafficking of Burmese women and girls, criminal trafficking networks flourished thanks to police corruption, the direct participation of individual police officers in trafficking networks, and Thailand's failure to enforce its laws. According to the State Department report, Thai government efforts to combat trafficking had been limited to creating a special police unit and introducing legislation to increase penalties for traffickers. In February 1995, Rep. Louise Slaughter, with fifty-five co-sponsors, introduced a resolution urging the State Department to consider the Thai government's efforts to hold police and immigration officials accountable for abuses against Burmese women and girls when distributing military aid to the Thai government.

The U.S. directed millions of dollars to Russia in 1995 for economic aid, military conversion, and programs designed to develop democratic institutions. With some important exceptions, U.S. support for Russian public and private sector initiatives failed to raise women's human rights concerns. AID had worked to ensure women's participation in training for professionals and had implemented guidelines to overcome obstacles that might keep women from benefiting from U.S. technical assistance. Yet many other AID programs that contributed to the introduction of market-based reforms and the restructuring of certain sectors of the economy—including energy and defense—failed to ensure that women did not suffer discrimination as reforms were implemented. Nor had they required U.S. and Russian partners to prohibit sex discrimination in their workplaces. AID had also directed insufficient attention to the longstanding problem of gender bias in the legal system in its programs to promote human rights, judicial independence, and reform of criminal laws.

In Haiti, respect for human rights improved markedly after the U.S.-led international intervention restored President Aristide to office. Nonetheless, more effort was needed to assure accountability for past abuses and to deter future abuse. The U.S. strongly condemned rampant abuse, including the rape of women as a tool of political repression under the Cédras regime. Yet, despite two promises—in May and September 1995—to provide assistance to the National Commission for Truth and Justice, a body established by President Aristide to investigate and prosecute human rights violations, the U.S. had not delivered this support as of this writing. At the same time, the U.S.-sponsored training of interim police cadets had incorporated women's rights, to the extent that recruits were shown how to gather forensic evidence to support a rape allegation.

In 1994 concerns over the executive branch's inconsistent record on protecting and promoting women's human rights led Congress to call for the appointment of a State Department senior advisor who would work to ensure the full integration of women's human rights into U.S. foreign policy. In November 1994, a senior coordinator for international women's issues was appointed to the office of the under secretary for global affairs, Tim Wirth. Unfortunately, a State Department decision to expand this post's mandate beyond women's human rights to a broad range of "women's" issues undercut its effectiveness. The result was that, as demonstrated by the above examples of Thailand, Russia, and Haiti, the U.S.'s willingness to raise women's human rights concerns did not translate into consistent action to protect and promote rights as an integral component of U.S. foreign policy. The senior coordinator's role could include coordinating the work of the Human Rights Bureau with other State Department bureaus as well as federal agencies outside the State Department to ensure that information on women's human rights is factored into political decision-making. For this to be effective, however, the coordinator would require greater institutional support within the State Department and a clearer focus on human rights.

Members of the U.S. Congress, who played a key role in the struggle to advance women's rights in both foreign and domestic policy, harshly criticized the Chinese government for its interference with NGO participation in the Women's Conference in Beijing. Congress directed U.S. delegates publicly to support NGOs subjected to harassment or restrictions on their activities and to protest actions by the Chinese government aimed at punishing Chinese citizens who sought to express their views or meet with delegates during the conference. At a

March press conference, the Congressional Caucus for Women's Issues called for a fair and open accreditation process for nongovernmental organizations seeking to participate in the conference, thus turning the spotlight on the importance of NGO participation at a moment when it was under siege by repressive governments.

In 1995, the bipartisan Congressional Working Group on International Women's Human Rights denounced violations of women's human rights in four countries: Botswana, Mexico, Uzbekistan and Bahrain. The working group, formed in April 1994, sends urgent letters in support of women who are at imminent risk of abuse or who require international support in their search for justice for past abuse.

In May 1995 the Immigration and Naturalization Service (INS) adopted guidelines to assist asylum officers in adjudicating the claims of female asylum seekers—one year after numerous organizations, including Human Rights Watch, proposed such guidelines in order to remedy procedural and substantive obstacles to asylum claims of women victims of gender-related persecution. The guidelines represent a critical step toward making the asylum process less hostile to female applicants fleeing human rights violations and recognizing, as a matter of law, that women are targeted for gender-related abuses that may amount to persecution. The value of the guidelines, however, could only be fully realized if the INS followed up at the highest levels with clear and consistent support for incorporating them into consideration of asylum claims.

Unfortunately, a lack of just such leadership in implementing the guidelines came to light in August when the INS challenged an immigration judge's decision to grant asylum to a woman who feared persecution on gender-related grounds; the INS appealed a decision that relied on its own guidelines. Following significant public outcry, the INS withdrew its appeal. Several months earlier, and prior to the adoption of the guidelines, another immigration judge denied asylum to a woman who claimed gender-related persecution resulting from her opposition to female genital mutilation (FGM), her own forced circumcision as a teen, and her fears for her daughters. In denying the claim, the judge opined that the claimant could choose to acquiesce to the practice of FGM, that not all cultures view FGM as harmful and that her dispute was with tribal custom, and thus that her anticipated harm was both highly subjective and not a matter for state intervention. In order to minimize such inconsistent application of the law and to ensure that female asylum seekers could receive a fair hearing, the INS message to those responsible for resolving women's asylum claims would need to be much clearer in directing them to implement the agency's guidelines.

The Work of the Women's Rights Project

Much of our advocacy work in 1995 focused on ensuring that women's human rights be given priority attention at the Fourth World Conference on Women. As in previous years, our efforts also focused on securing accountability for specific violations of women's human rights raised in our monitoring and reports. In addition, we continued our efforts to strengthen U.S., regional and international mechanisms for monitoring and remedying violations of women's human rights.

The Women's Rights Project worked in conjunction with Human Rights Watch/Asia and our U.N. representative to ensure the ability of women from around the world to participate in the Women's Conference and to push governments gathered at the conference to commit to end violations of women's human rights and to hold abusers accountable. Concerned that many nongovernmental organizations (NGOs) were being deliberately excluded from the conference and its preparatory processes, Human Rights Watch coordinated a January 1995 sign-on letter from twenty-five women's and human rights organizations to Secretary of State Warren Christopher urging the State Department to ensure the broadest possible NGO access to the Women's Conference. In a March letter to U.N. Secretary-General Boutros Boutros-Ghali, we protested the U.N.'s role in allowing repressive governments to dictate which NGOs could participate in the conference. In May we called again on the secretary-general to guarantee full and meaningful NGO participation in the conference by ensuring that the Chinese government provided appropriate facilities for the NGO Forum. We also joined other women's and human rights organizations in a letter to Boutros-Ghali calling on the U.N. to ensure that China provideNGO participants with an appropriate site for the NGO Forum and with access to the official proceedings. At a March press conference called by the Congressional Caucus on Women's Issues, the Women's Rights Project urged the U.S. and other governments to ensure an open accreditation process for NGOs seeking to participate in the U.N. conference.

In June we worked with a number of human rights advocates to call on U.N. High Commissioner for Human Rights José Ayala Lasso to make public statements supporting a platform for action at the Beijing conference that would stress the universality and indivisibility of women's fundamental human rights, challenge efforts to undermine women's right to equality and commit governments to implementing specific measures to improve the protection of women's rights.

The Women's Rights Project stressed two priority goals at the women's conference: governments must recognize their obligation to respect women's rights in order to advance women's status in all spheres—political, social and economic—and they must make concrete commitments to promote and protect those rights in practice. Prior to the March meeting of the Commission on the Status of Women, the Women's Rights Project prepared a critique of the draft Platform for Action and distributed this to members of the U.S. and other government delegations. We also wrote to the U.S. State Department's senior coordinator for international women's issues and the director of its Global Conference Secretariat, urging the U.S. delegation to take a leading role in promoting women's human rights at the conference. We met with First Lady Hillary Clinton's staff to discuss priority women's human rights concerns and participated in two meetings with Assistant Secretary of State John Shattuck to discuss the U.S. position on key human rights provisions in the Beijing draft Platform for Action.

Human Rights Watch also pressed European governments to promote meaningful NGO participation in the Women's Conference and to recognize the key role of eliminating women's human rights abuse in efforts to advance women's status. In May 1995, Human Rights Watch's Brussels office helped to secure European Parliament's adoption of a resolution that called on the Chinese government to guarantee freedom of speech to NGOs and press attending the conference; to refrain from excluding women because of their political views, national origin or sexual orientation; and to provide an NGO Forum site that would allow easy communication between the NGO and government meetings.

Following the conference, the Women's Rights Project briefed members and staff of the Congressional Caucus on Women's Issues about the implications of the conference for women's human rights and the need for strong U.S. leadership in implementing government commitments made in Beijing. We also met with Amb. Geraldine Ferraro to press for follow-up to the commitments made in Beijing and wrote to Mrs. Clinton urging that women's human rights be more fully integrated into U.S. bilateral aid and trade relations.

Our first *Global Report on Women's Human Rights*, released in September in Beijing, reflected five years of research and advocacy on issues such as rape and violence against women during armed conflict, domestic violence, trafficking of women and girls into forced prostitution and marriage, and abuses against women workers in some twenty countries. It also offered concrete recommendations to governments, the United Nations and the regional human rights bodies for steps to halt gender-based violations and secure the full protection of women's human rights.

In order to press for the elimination of sex discrimination in Russia and to support efforts by local groups to invoke international human rights law to this end, we worked closely with our colleagues in Russia to publicize the findings of our report, *Neither Jobs Nor Justice*, then use the report in workshops and at conferences to share information and develop human rights advocacy skills. In August 1995, Human Rights Watch's Moscow representative participated in a preparatory conference to the Women's Conference in Beijing where Russian women prepared for the substantive debates over women's human rights and learned about the potential obstacles to NGO participation in the conference. In the U.S., project staff presented the findings of our report to AID and urged officials to promote respect for women's rights through their programs.

In Haiti, we continued to seek accountability for the use of rape as a tool of political repression under the military rule of Raoul Cédras, by pressing President Aristide to ensure that rape and other assaults on women were among those crimes investigated and prosecuted by his administration. In January 1995, we met with Robert Gelbard, assistant secretary of state for international narcotics and law enforcement, to discuss the role of women in Haiti's interim police force, the incorporation of women's human rights into police training and the screening out of former police alleged to have committed rape.

In February 1995 the Women's Rights Project continued its monitoring of the use of rape by Peru's security forces with a letter to President Alberto Fujimori, calling on him to act on his promise to punish soldiers and police officers who commit rape. Evidence gathered by the project and local activists indicated that rape against women in detention continued unabated, uninvestigated and unprosecuted. The letter documented six cases of women detained by the security forces and raped, sometimes repeatedly, during their incarceration. To our knowledge, none of the women's claims had been investigated by the Peruvian authorities.

The Women's Rights Project also contributed to Human Rights Watch efforts to oppose passage of the Stop Turning Out Prisoners Act (STOP), legislation that would severely limit the ability of prisoners in the U.S. to seek redress for serious violations of human and civil rights. The project was particularly concerned that this legislation, approved by Congress in late 1995, would cut off some of the minimal remedies available to women victims of rape and sexual assault committed by prison guards and staff.

In March 1995 Human Rights Watch protested the death sentence passed on Flor Contemplacion, a Filipina domestic worker in Singapore, and urged President Ong Teng Cheong to commute her sentence. Contemplacion was sentenced to death in January 1993 for the murder of another Filipino domestic worker and her employer's four-year-old son. Human Rights Watch received information indicating that there were serious doubts about the fairness of her trial. Despite international outcry calling for a new trial to ensure Contemplacion's right to due process, the Singapore government executed her in March.

The Women's Rights Project continued its efforts to press member states of the United Nations to integrate women's human rights into the U.N.'s system-wide human rights activities. In February, we submitted a written statement to the U.N. Human Rights Commission supporting the work of the special rapporteur on violence against women and calling attention to specific instances of government-sponsored or -tolerated violence against women. The project has supplied the special rapporteur with extensive documentation of human rights abuses against women to assist her in preparing her first report on the extent, causes, and consequences of violence against women.

The project also continued its efforts to publicize the need for protection programs that can prevent rape and other abuse in refugee camps. We called on the UNHCR to put into place mechanisms to institute programs similar to those undertaken in Kenya in other refugee camps around the world. In 1995 project staff had met several times with the UNHCR, including individuals assessing the Women Victims of Violence program in the Kenyan refugee camps. We also raised the problem of women refugees' physical safety with U.N. High Commissioner Sadako Ogata in July at a U.S. Congressional briefing. In the U.S., we participated in a forum sponsored by the U.S.-based Women's Commission on Refugee Women and Children to strengthen the UNHCR Guidelines on the Protection of Refugee Women. In August, we presented our findings at a UNIFEM-sponsored conference in Ethiopia on the protection of refugee and internally displaced women in Africa.

In 1995 the Women's Rights Project increased its participation in training activities with colleagues from around the world. We began working with women's rights activists in 1994 to develop strategies for applying human rights documentation and advocacy methods to gender-specific human rights violations. Women's Rights Project staff participated in training workshops with the Center for Women's Global Leadership in New Jersey with women activists from around the world and with members of WiLDAF (Women in Law and Development in Africa) from fifteen African countries in Uganda. In 1995 we participated in Albania's first international forum on women's human rights, outlining and assessing methods for deterring domestic violence with human rights advocacy, and we presented women's rights case studies to a conference in Trinidad on how to document women's human rights abuses. Project staff also led several workshops at the NGO Forum in Huairou, China on using human rights advocacy to ensure government accountability for abuses against women. Finally, we began a joint effort with the Institute for Women, Law and Development to produce a training manual for women's human rights activists.

SPECIAL INITIATIVES

The complexity that human rights work has acquired, and the diversity of opportunities for advocacy and action, have increasingly demanded that Human Rights Watch undertake initiatives involving a specialized focus or expertise. At times, those initiatives consist of a single opportunity to make our voice heard on a crucial issue, but often they take the form of sustained campaigns. Some of these activities undertaken in 1995 included the following.

Prisons

The Human Rights Watch Prison Project has conducted specialized prison research and campaigns for prisoners' rights since 1987, to focus international attention on prison conditions worldwide. Drawing on the expertise of the regional divisions of Human Rights Watch, our prison project has investigated conditions for sentenced prisoners, pre-trial detainees, immigration detainees, and those held in police lockups. The work is distinctive in the international human rights field in that it examines conditions for all prisoners, not only those held for political reasons.

In addition to pressing for improvement in prison conditions in particular countries, the prison project seeks to place the problem of prison conditions on the international human rights agenda. We believe that a government's claim to respect human rights should be assessed not only by the political freedoms it allows but also by how it treats its prisoners, including those not held for political reasons. Our experience has repeatedly shown that a number of democratic countries that are rarely if ever a focus of human rights scrutiny are in fact guilty of serious human rights violations within their prisons.

The prison project has a self-imposed set of rules for prison visits: investigators undertake visits only when they, not the authorities, can choose the institutions to be visited; when the investigators can be confident that they will be allowed to talk privately with inmates of their choice; and when the investigators can gain access to the entire facility to be examined. These rules are adopted to avoid being shown model prisons or the most presentable parts of institutions. When access on such terms is not possible, reporting is based on interviews with former prisoners, prisoners on furlough, relatives of inmates, lawyers, prison experts and prison staff, and on documentary evidence. The prison project relies upon the U.N. Standard Minimum Rules for the Treatment of Prisoners as the chief guideline by which to assess prison conditions in each country. Prison investigations are usually conducted by teams composed of a member of the project's staff or advisory committee and a member of a Human Rights Watch regional division's staff with expertise on the country in question. Occasionally, the prison project invites an outside expert to participate in an investigation.

The project publishes its findings in reports that are released to the public and the press, both in the United States and in the country in question, and sent to the government of that country.

In previous years, the project conducted studies and published reports on prison conditions in Brazil, Czechoslovakia, Egypt, India, Indonesia, Israel and the Occupied Territories, Jamaica, Mexico, Poland, Romania, South Africa, the former Soviet Union, Spain, Turkey, the United Kingdom, the United States (including Puerto Rico, with a separate short report published), Venezuela, and Zaire.

The Enforcement of Standards

The U.N. Standard Minimum Rules for the Treatment of Prisoners is the most widely known and accepted document regulating prison conditions. Unfortunately, these standards, although known to prison administrators virtually all over the world, are seldom fully enforced. Based on extensive research over the years, we concluded in our 1993 *Human Rights Watch Global Report on Pris-*

ons that the great majority of the millions of persons who are imprisoned worldwide at any given moment, and of the tens of millions who spend at least part of the year behind bars, are confined in conditions of filth and corruption, without adequate food or medical care, with little or nothing to do, and in circumstances in which violence—from other inmates, their keepers, or both—is a constant threat. Despite international declarations, treaties and standards forbidding such conditions, this state of affairs is tolerated even in countries that are more or less respectful of human rights, because prisons, by their nature, are out of sight, and because prisoners, by definition, are outcasts. To strengthen the enforcement of standards, Human Rights Watch has continued to advocate creating a U.N. human rights mechanism to inspect prisons and to strengthen the mechanism for enforcement of standards and the prevention of abuses.

Human Rights Watch staff participated in the 1995 session of the Working Group on the Optional Protocol to the Convention against Torture, convened by the U.N. Commission on Human Rights to devise a universal system of visits to places of detention. Despite our reservations regarding the confidentiality of the proposed system, we endorsed the effort and strove to ensure its maximum effectiveness.

Beginning in 1993, the Human Rights Watch specialist in prisons regularly participated in an international effort by representatives of about a dozen nongovernmental and intergovernmental organizations to strengthen standards regarding prison conditions; the goal is to make these standards more effective in safeguarding the human rights of detainees. A representative of the prison project was among the drafters of an international handbook on the human rights of people imprisoned or detained. The document was presented during the Ninth U.N. Congress on the Prevention of Crime and the Treatment of Offenders, held in Cairo in April 1995.

Fact-Finding: Japan and the U.S.

In March, the prison project and Human Rights Watch/Asia released a report titled *Prison Conditions in Japan*. Based on interviews conducted in Tokyo, Kobe, Osaka, Niigata and Asahikawa, the report condemned the widespread use of solitary confinement, the restrictions on contacts between prisoners and the outside world, the obsessiveness about rules, and the draconian punishments that have characterized the Japanese correctional system. It catalogued numerous cases in which the prison authorities had imposed harsh penalties for the most trivial rule violations, such as one prisoner who was punished with ten days in solitary confinement for looking at a guard. Concluding that from the moment of arrest through to the end of imprisonment "a prisoner in Japan is deprived of the most basic rights," the report urged Japan to undertake a serious reform of its prison system. A project representative returned to Tokyo in March to release the report simultaneously in Japanese and English. She participated in a press conference and presented two public lectures on prison conditions in Japan.

For several years the prison project has monitored the treatment of prisoners and other detainees in the United States. The project continued collecting information on U.S. prison conditions in 1995, with a particular focus on the proliferation of super-maximum security institutions (or "maxi-maxis"), a problem to which Human Rights Watch first called attention in its 1991 report on prison conditions in the United States.

In June, the project conducted a mission to a maxi-maxi facility in the state of Indiana, the Maximum Control Complex (MCC). Having received distressing reports of abuses at the MCC since it opened in 1991, the project had repeatedly asked to be allowed to inspect the facility, but the state's commissioner of corrections had persistently refused to grant permission for such a visit. When a new superintendent took charge of the facility in 1995, however, this permission was granted. On inspecting the institution and speaking privately with a number of prisoners, the Human Rights Watch delegation found that many of the worst abuses of the MCC's first years (when it was a "horror show," in the words of a prisoner who in 1992 was left in four-point mechanical restraints spread-eagled to his bed for days at a time) had been remedied or ameliorated. Nonetheless, the basic structural problems of prolonged social isolation and severe sensory deprivation still persisted. Held in solitary confinement in small, sterile, continuously lit cells, and deprived of almost all human contact over a period of years, MCC prisoners were treated in a manner that was injurious to their human dignity and that boded poorly for their eventual reintegration into society.

Our prisons expert and staff of the Human Rights Watch Women's Rights Project also concluded in 1995 an extensive study of sexual abuse of women in U.S. prisons. Having interviewed witnesses, including prisoners, former prisoners, prisoner rights advocates, lawyers and government officials in five states, investigators determined that women incarcerated in U.S. state prisons face a serious and potentially pervasive problem of sexual misconduct by prison officials. In particular, the abuses found included rape, sexual assault, inappropriate sexual contact, verbal degradation, and the unwarranted visual surveillance of undressed women prisoners. Equally troubling, most states had not adopted even preliminary measures to address these problems.

Business and Human Rights

As we noted in last year's *World Report*, some proponents of international trade and investment have argued that human rights should receive lower priority than fast-track, investment-driven development. While several Asian governments were the earliest to articulate this viewpoint a few years ago— arguing for an "Asian concept of human rights"—Western governments also direct their foreign policies with a strong bias toward "commercial diplomacy." In this line of reasoning, economic growth by itself would improve human rights; boosting trade would advance human rights by creating a middle class that ultimately would demand a greater political voice. This argument, however, ignores the fact that, for every liberalizing Taiwan there is a Singapore, Indonesia, China or Peru where economic growth has simply bolstered an authoritarian regime. Indeed, even if economic development could be correlated in the long term with improved respect for human rights—an unproven proposition—that would offer little solace to those imprisoned and tortured in the meantime.

A government's promotion of corporate investment abroad regardless of human rights conditions in the prospective host country sends a signal to businesses that human rights are neither a proper concern of theirs nor an issue of importance to their governments. And abusive leaders receive the same signals, which does the opposite of encourage reform. But once a corporation invests in a country, that country's human rights problems inevitably affect corporate practices and the exercise of workers' rights, including rights of free association and expression.

Recognizing that the increased importance of globalized trade in creating an ever-closer link between the corporate practices and human rights conditions in a growing number of countries, Human Rights Watch began in 1994 to examine this connection and develop ways of addressing it. In 1995 our work linking business and human rights expanded to country situations as diverse as Guatemala, Egypt, the West Bank/Gaza Strip, Nigeria, and China.

Two overarching principles have guided the work on business and human rights. We stress the absolute principle that corporations must avoid complicity in governmental human rights abuse. And we urge corporations to use their often considerable influence to increase respect for human rights in the course of their business operations.

In Nigeria, Human Rights Watch/Africa researched the role of the Royal Dutch Shell Petroleum Corporation in serious abuses against the Ogoni people in the country's southeastern Rivers State. On the basis of our findings, Human Rights Watch set forth a number of policy recommendations for foreign oil companies operating in Nigeria. This generated international press attention to Shell's role and responsibility. Our recommendations included a call to oil companies to criticize publicly the use of excessive force by the Nigerian security forces. To follow up our research, Human Rights Watch representatives met with officials of multinational oil companies, and those discussions continued at this writing. Human Rights Watch co-sponsored an ad that appeared in *The New York Times* protesting the death sentence issued for Ken Saro-Wiwa, the principal leader of the Ogonis, whom the authoritarian government of Nigeria had accused, without due process, of murder (see Nigeria section). Human Rights Watch/Africa pressed Royal Dutch Shell and other oil companies operating in Nigeria to protest Ken Saro-Wiwa's death sentence. After the Abacha government rushed to execute Saro-Wiwa despite a concerted international outcry on his behalf, we called for oil companies to publicly condemn the execution.

With respect to China, while continuing discussion with corporations over particular issues, Human Rights Watch/Asia called on investment banks that planned to finance the mammoth Three Gorges dam to avoid any involvement with the project until the Chinese government provided verifiable guarantees to protect the rights of the more than one million people scheduled to be forcibly relocated to make way for the dam. Human Rights Watch raised these concerns with institutional investors, including public pension funds, and insisted that investment banks be accountable for their decisions on this project. Responding to coverage of our concerns in investment journals in the U.S. and elsewhere, the president of the Three Gorges Dam Corporation acknowledged that criticisms on human rights and environmental grounds made it more difficult to generate foreign funding for the dam.

Human Rights Watch/Middle East

raised the issue of corporate social responsibility for human rights at the Middle East/North Africa Economic Summit in Amman in October. We distributed to both conference participants and the press a detailed statement of concerns highlighting the link between respect for basic human rights and a climate conducive to investment, including an account of worker-related human rights abuse in Egypt and the issues of freedom of movement and discrimination resulting from Israeli policies in the West Bank, Gaza Strip, and Israel.

Regarding Guatemala, Human Rights Watch/Americas wrote a letter to the president of Western Atlas, a Houston-based oil exploration company conducting a seismic study in the Ixcán area, expressing our concerns about the company's employment of a known human rights violator and fugitive from justice. We believed the employment of this man contributed to a cycle of impunity for rights abuse. As far as we could ascertain, the company terminated his employment.

Drugs and Human Rights

As drug trafficking has spread around the world, with ever more countries affected by the production, shipment and consumption of psychoactive drugs, national and international counternarcotics programs have also proliferated. Unfortunately, these programs by and large have escaped close human rights scrutiny.

In early 1995, Human Rights Watch began a multi-year project to document and challenge human rights violations caused or exacerbated by efforts to curtail drug trafficking. The project focused initially on international counternarcotics programs supported or encouraged by the United States. Although Human Rights Watch has taken no position on the merits of counternarcotics objectives, we have insisted that those objectives—like all national and international political goals—be pursued within the framework of internationally recognized human rights. By raising our findings and concerns with the media, policy analysts, public offi-

cials and the general public, Human Rights Watch pressed for the incorporation of human rights considerations into the drug policy debate.

Human Rights Watch's first report on counternarcotics policies and programs, titled *Bolivia: Human Rights Violations and the War on Drugs*, was published in July 1995. Based on a mission to Bolivia in March and April 1995, the report examined Bolivian counternarcotics laws, institutions, and strategies and the central role of U.S. pressure and funding. Although the United States government insisted that U.S. counternarcotics assistance could advance human rights objectives, in Bolivia that assistance was supporting programs deeply flawed by human rights violations. For example, under Law 1008, the country's anti-drug statute, Bolivians charged with drug offenses were imprisoned without the possibility of pretrial release and, even if acquitted, were forced to remain imprisoned until their trial courts' decisions were reviewed by the Supreme Court, a process that routinely took years. In Chapare, the rural area in which most of Bolivia's coca is grown and cocaine base is produced, the antinarcotics police had run roughshod over the population, conducting arbitrary searches and seizures, manhandling and beating residents, stealing their goods and money. Some Bolivians detained on drug trafficking charges had alleged complicity in abusive interrogations by agents of the U.S. Drug Enforcement Administration (DEA). DEA personnel acknowledged to Human Rights Watch that they do not intervene to stop abuse by Bolivian agents. We found that impunity for abuses by the antinarcotics police was the norm. Even complaints of serious human rights violations, including torture, and of abuses by DEA agents, were rarely investigated.

The report received widespread publicity in Bolivia and contributed to the growing public debate over the course of that country's counternarcotics efforts. Reforms to Law 1008 that would remedy some of its more serious adverse effects on human rights were being discussed by the Bolivian government and parliament as of this writing.

Human Rights Watch, through the drugs and human rights initiative, also researched the racial impact of drug-law enforcement in the United States and urged the U.S. government to address that impact in its first submission to the United Nations Committee on the Elimination of Racial Discrimination, pursuant to U.S. ratification of the Convention on the Elimination of all Forms of Racial Discrimination (see United States section). Ongoing research in the United States focused on the linkages between counternarcotics operations, corruption, and police brutality.

Lesbian and Gay Rights

In 1994, Human Rights Watch adopted a policy opposing state-sponsored and state-tolerated violence, detention and prosecution on the basis of sexual orientation, and in 1995 expanded its work on discrimination to cover discriminatory treatment of lesbians and gays. In 1995, three Human Rights Watch regional divisions spoke out against persecution of lesbian and gay individuals and organizations.

Human Rights Watch/Americas protested armed raids on the offices of FUNDASIDA, the only nongovernmental AIDS organization in El Salvador, and subsequent death threats and attacks against members of the gay men's group Entre Amigos (Among Friends), whose membership records were taken in the raid. Human Rights Watch/Africa criticized President Robert Mugabe's order banning the organization Gays and Lesbians of Zimbabwe from the Zimbabwe International Book Fair, and condemned offensive anti-homosexual remarks that the president made at the fair's opening ceremonies. Human Rights Watch/Helsinki called on the Russian Federation to repeal two criminal laws used to harass a journalist and outspoken gay rights activist, Yaroslav Mogutin, denounced by Russian authorities as a "corrupter of public morals" and threatened with blacklisting. The division also condemned police detention and beating of members of an Albanian gay rights organization, Gay Club Albania, and called for the repeal of all Albanian criminal penalties for homosexual acts.

Standard-Setting and Mechanisms of International Law

Human Rights Watch contributes to the progressive development of human rights standards in international law. The organization has contributed to the drafting and negotiation of multilateral treaties, has sought precedent-setting judgments by courts and treaty bodies, and has promoted acceptance and ratification of such standards by all states in the international community. There is already an important body of substantive norms, both in the international law of human rights and in international humanitarian law (the laws of war); unfortunately, enforcement of those standards lags far behind. For that reason, our work in standard-setting has increasingly focused on the development of adequate and effective mechanisms to redress violations of human rights.

The International Criminal Court

The United Nations has developed a comprehensive list of "international crimes," behavior by individuals that affects all nations and peoples and therefore injures the interests of the international community as a whole. Among those crimes are the most egregious violations of human rights: genocide, crimes against humanity, and war crimes. At the same time, those are crimes for which there is a pervasive impunity because, almost by definition, domestic courts have been unwilling or unable to investigate, prosecute and punish them. The idea of an international criminal court to act when domestic remedies fail has been discussed for much of this century, without significant progress. Since 1992, however, it has gained new currency due to the need to confront ghastly episodes of massive deprivation of life occurring in the past decade. The creation of international criminal tribunals for the former Yugoslavia and for Rwanda in 1994 and 1995 renewed expectations that the international community was not helpless to bring the perpetrators of egregious crimes to justice. On the other hand, the political limitations of creating *ad hoc* courts under the peace and security powers of the United Nations, have persuaded many nations that it is time to move forward in the creation of a permanent international criminal court.

A concrete proposal was placed on the agenda of the United Nations General Assembly in late 1994. By consensus, the General Assembly decided to convene an Ad Hoc Committee (to which all members states could send delegates) to meet twice during 1995 and engage in discussion of the draft statute drawn by the International Law Commission. Each meeting lasted about two weeks and was attended by delegations of fifty to sixty countries. The mandate of the ad hoc committee did not allow it to engage in negotiations or propose amendments to the draft statute. As a result, there were important discussions but little progress toward consensus. Significantly, the delegates were reluctant to recommend a firm timetable for completing a draft treaty and convening a diplomatic conference at which it could be signed. An active majority of participating states seemed intent on maintaining the momentum so far achieved and moving steadily toward the creation of the court, but a minority of states demanded further discussion, and—as is often the case at the United Nations—the consensus that was actually achieved represented the lowest common denominator. The delegations that sought to slow down the process included states traditionally hostile to the development of human rights standards on the basis of sovereignty or on argued cultural relativism. On this issue, they were joined by the United Kingdom, the United States and Japan, governments that otherwise professed to contribute to the progress of international law. Distrust of an international criminal court by the United States contrasted sharply with the staunch support it provided to the two existing ad hoc tribunals. Perhaps it was easier to support judicial bodies before which American officials were not likely to be brought.

In support of the prompt creation of an international criminal court, Human Rights Watch joined a loose coalition of nongovernmental organizations (NGOs) interested in the subject, monitored the daily sessions of the ad hoc committee, prepared and distributed commentaries to the draft statute that were well received by the delegates, and met informally with many delegations to express our points of view. We also sent letters to bar associations and legal scholars, urging them to express their views to the representatives of their governments on the need for action on this matter. As the issue came back to the General Assembly in late October 1995, we distributed a commentary on the report produced by the ad hoc committee and insisted on the need for progress in drafting a final treaty.

On the substance of the draft, we have advocated restricting the subject matter jurisdiction of the court to genocide, crimes against humanity and war crimes (in the latter case both in international and internal conflict), and leaving out narcotics offenses, terrorism and aggression. We have also urged that the court be granted inherent jurisdiction not only on genocide but also on war crimes and crimes against humanity, and that—although its competence would be subsidiary to that of national courts—the court itself should be empowered to decide whether domestic remedies have been attempted in good faith as a bar to its own jurisdiction. We have strenuously objected to a stance adopted by the United States that would allow the Security Council to decide which cases might be heard by the court; in our view, that would deprive the court of its indispensable independence from political organs. During 1995 Human Rights Watch worked with other NGOs developing plans to help build citizens' support throughout the world for this initiative in the coming years.

Declaration on Forced and Involuntary Disappearances

In 1982, the U.N. Human Rights Commission set up a Working Group on Forced and Involuntary Disappearances, in an effort to address that cruel and dramatic practice. Over the years, the working group devised innovative ways of responding to the problem. It has published periodic reports listing the complaints it receives each year, sought and obtained permission to conduct on-site visits, and created a simple but effective mechanism to act on urgent requests. On the other hand, it never had a specific mandate to analyze petitions or review evidence; as a result, the working group does not establish governmental responsibility on any given case, but exposes governments that practice or tolerate disappearances only through statistical information that shows how many cases have been "resolved" in a given period.

In 1992, the U.N. General Assembly approved a Declaration on Forced and Involuntary Disappearances, at the behest of the Commission on Human Rights. Though non-binding, this instrument advanced the standards on this particularly cruel practice, and delineated the obligations of the state to address its consequences. In early 1995, the Commission on Human Rights asked its Working Group on Disappearances to propose means of supervising compliance by states with the standards set forth in the declaration. In turn, the working group asked NGOs for their input.

In August 1995, we submitted a detailed proposal to the working group, urging it to consider setting up a complaint mechanism by which affected families could seek its intervention. The working group would then seek the cooperation of the relevant national authorities to conduct an investigation, and eventually issue a resolution on the record, determining whether the facts as ascertained by the working group constituted a violation of the declaration, and formulating recommendations.

International Criminal Tribunals

Impunity for the most egregious violations of human rights continues to be the norm, despite the international community's pronouncements condemning "ethnic cleans-

ing" killings in the former Yugoslavia, genocide in Rwanda and massive violations of the laws and customs of war in Chechnya, to name only the most visible examples. Though international law has long ago developed principles designed to ensure accountability for crimes against humanity, such as universal jurisdiction, so far there has been a manifest lack of political will to enforce them. Almost by definition, domestic courts are unavailable, unwilling or incapable of dealing effectively and fairly with these crimes. Under those circumstances, the international community must provide the means for redress to the victims while strictly respecting standards of fair trial. The Security Council has created ad hoc international criminal tribunals for the former Yugoslavia and Rwanda, and all nations are duty-bound to cooperate with them and with the Office of the Prosecutor. While insisting on each country's obligation to investigate, prosecute and punish these crimes, we have also urged the international community to make accountability a reality through effective enforcement of international law.

Throughout 1995, Human Rights Watch supported the work of the two international criminal tribunals set up by the United Nations for Rwanda and the former Yugoslavia. We met regularly with the general prosecutor, Justice Richard Goldstone, and his staff and provided them with documentation from our on-site investigations so that the prosecutors can develop it into evidence to be used at trial or in support of indictment requests. We also paid close attention to the budgetary and funding problems that the tribunals faced at the United Nations, and urged the missions of key nations to insist on full funding for their activities. At the meeting of the U.N. Commission on Human Rights in Geneva, we publicly called on all governments to support the tribunals and to cooperate with their work. Our researchers on the ground met often with investigators and other staff of the tribunals, and we hosted meetings in our New York office with Chief Justice Antonio Cassese and other judges. On several occasions, we urged the Security

Council not to lift sanctions on Serbia and Montenegro until such time as the government has effectively lived up to its obligation to cooperate with the tribunal and the general prosecutor and has allowed their staff to conduct proper investigations in its territory. We also reacted publicly to statements by foreign governments that reflected hostility toward the tribunals.

Legal Advocacy

Increasingly, our efforts to promote corrective action to address human rights abuses led us to take part in judicial proceedings or in submissions before bodies set up in international law to hear individual complaints. Human Rights Watch strongly believes that courts and international protection mechanisms provide not only a useful forum to publicize instances of human rights violation but also the opportunity to advance principles of protection of rights so that they become part of international law.

The International Court of Justice and the Kurds

In 1995 Human Rights Watch pursued its efforts to bring a genocide case to the International Court of Justice against the government of Iraq for its 1988 "Anfal" campaign in which 50,000 to 100,000 people were killed, hundreds of thousands of villagers were forcibly displaced, and 2,000 villages were destroyed in an effort to eliminate the Kurdish population in northern Iraq. During the year, Human Rights Watch met and discussed the case with representatives of a number of prospective plaintiff states in the effort to build a coalition to litigate the case before the court.

To facilitate governments' consideration of the available evidence, and to demonstrate the strength of that evidence, Human Rights Watch prepared an evidentiary memorandum linking the documents and testimonies we had gathered with the essential elements of genocide to underline both the requisite acts and intent by Baghdad to eliminate an ethnic group. The evidentiary memorandum was drafted to enable prospective plaintiff states to gauge the strength of the legal merits according to article 2 of the Genocide Convention.

Litigation in United States Federal Courts

United States law allows federal courts to hear cases in tort brought against foreign nationals for "crimes against the law of nations" committed in foreign lands. This unique feature of the country's legal system has become an important tool in stigmatizing perpetrators of crimes against humanity by making sure that United States soil does not become a safe haven for them when they leave office in their countries. Since 1980, several cases have been brought against torturers and abusers of other fundamental rights, and successive court victories have turned this litigation strategy into an important advocacy tool. In the late 1980s, Human Rights Watch joined other organizations and law firms in bringing three such complaints against the former "lord of life and death" of Buenos Aires, Gen. Carlos Guillermo Suárez Mason, who had fled Argentina shortly after the return to democracy and was living in golden exile in San Francisco. We won default judgments for our clients, and eventually Suárez Mason was extradited to Argentina.

In 1995 we found new opportunities to apply the strategy. We took advantage of opportunities to represent plaintiffs in cases brought under the Alien Tort Claims Act and the Alien Victim Protection Act, which confer jurisdiction on federal courts to hear suits in damages against perpetrators of crimes "in violation of the law of nations" committed in foreign lands, as long as the defendant is present in the territory of the United States. With the assistance of the New York law firms of Debevoise & Plimpton and Carter, Ledyard & Milburn, we undertook to represent several Rwandan nationals who had lost family members in the genocide of April and May 1994, in a case called *Mushikiwabo v. Barayagwiza*, in the Southern District of New York. The defendant, Jean Bosco Barayagwiza, was leader of one of the extremist political factions that prepared and then unleashed the massacres. Mr. Barayagwiza was served in 1994, when he visited the United Nations before the fall of the genocidal regime. Since then, he has resided in France and in Zaire. In 1995, the court entered a default judgment against him. Our side filed a detailed request for compensatory and punitive damages, and for oral hearings on the matter.

Requests under the Freedom of Information Act

Under the Freedom of Information Act it is possible to force disclosure of information and documentation that exists in United States government archives. We pursue administrative requests for release of material that we consider vital to human rights research or the protection of persons whose rights have been violated. While attempting to monitor the conditions for Haitian and Cuban refugees held in the Guantánamo Bay naval base, we heard allegations of acts of violence by American troops against Haitian minors. We also sought to obtain information on the practices followed with respect to segregation of refugees in the camp. We then filed two FOIA requests: one requesting a copy of the Administrative and Segregation Policies and Procedures to be followed by Joint Task Force 160 (the unit charged with running the camps), and another one to obtain a copy of a report of an investigation conducted by the task force on allegations of abuse against Haitian minors.

In July, U.S. Ambassador to the U.N. Madeleine Albright showed satellite and aerial photographs at a closed session of the Security Council. The pictures reportedly show Bosnian civilians from the Srebrenica camp being rounded up in a soccer field before being killed. In August, we joined several organizations filing an FOIA request demanding disclosure of this evidence.

Briefs Amicus Curiae

By filing briefs as *amicus curiae*, or "friend of the court," Human Rights Watch provided courts with an international human rights analysis of the legal questions at issue in selected cases. Our international human rights perspective is relevant not only in cases brought, for example, under the Alien Tort Statute, in which courts directly examine international human rights standards, but also in cases where domestic law and practice arguably contravene international norms. In such cases, Human Rights Watch calls the court's attention to international legal obligations that limit domestic authority: obligations that may function both as a constraint on and as a guide to the interpretation of domestic legal norms.

CABA v. Christopher: In this case against U.S. Secretary of State Warren Christopher and others, Human Rights Watch filed an amicus brief in support of 35,000 Cuban detainees held indefinitely at the Guantánamo Bay naval base after their 1994 attempts to immigrate to the U.S. by sea. Emphasizing the United States' international treaty obligations, particularly its obligation not to repatriate any Cuban who would face political persecution, we supported the Cubans' claims that they had been wrongly denied access to refugee processing and to legal counsel for such processing. In a disappointing ruling, however, the Eleventh Circuit held that these treaty obligations were non-enforceable in court and that the detainees had no right to refugee screening. A few months later, the administration reversed its policy and decided to admit the Guantánamo Cubans to the United States.

Doe v. Karadzic: In 1993, two citizens of Bosnia-Herzegovina filed a class action lawsuit against Radovan Karadzic, the leader of the Bosnian Serbs, on behalf of the thousands of victims of the "ethnic cleansing" carried out under his leadership. The suit was based on the Alien Tort Claims Act and other statutes conferring jurisdiction over torts committed in violation of international law. Without notice to the parties and without the benefit of briefing on the relevant points of law, the district court in New York dismissed the action. Demonstrating a basic lack of familiarity with international legal standards, it ruled categorically that "acts committed by non-state actors do not violate the law of nations." Characterizing the entity headed by Karadzic as a "warring military faction," as opposed to a recognized state, the court found that Karadzic's actions did not violate international law. On the plaintiffs' appeal of this ruling, Human Rights Watch filed an amicus brief arguing that the defendant need not represent a *recognized* state to be subject to international law constraints on state actors, and that many international human rights standards do bind non-state actors, so that the court's blanket dismissal of the case was mistaken. In October 1995, the Second Circuit reversed the lower court's ruling, and the case was remanded to the district court for further action.

Office of the Special Prosecutor of the Transitional Government of Ethiopia v. Mengistu: The government of Ethiopia from 1974 to 1991—known as the Derge—became notorious for its brutal and systematic human rights violations, including widespread use of torture and extrajudicial executions against political opponents, journalists, union leaders and scholars. The Derge also employed starvation as a weapon of war. President Mengistu Haile Mariam and some high Derge officials fled to Zimbabwe, while others were detained in Ethiopia. The new Ethiopian government requested that Zimbabwe extradite those officials that fled and, in an effort to bring justice to the victims of Derge's abuses, began in 1994 to prosecute members of the Derge for crimes against humanity. In March 1995, Human Rights Watch filed an amicus brief with the Ethiopian Supreme Court in support of the prosecution's effort, arguing in particular that Ethiopian penal provisions that codified the international law prohibition on crimes against humanity were applicable in the current prosecutions.

Freedom To Travel Campaign v. Newcomb: In 1994, the U.S. government's ban on citizens' travel to Cuba was challenged in federal district court as unconstitutional. Although the court dismissed the challenge, its ruling was appealed to the Ninth Circuit Court of Appeals. Human Rights Watch joined the American Civil Liberties Union and other groups in filing an amicus brief in support of the petitioners, the Freedom To Travel Campaign, arguing that the travel restrictions violate article 19 of the International Covenant on Civil and Political Rights. Article 19 protects freedom of expression, defined as including "freedom to seek, receive and impart information and ideas of all kinds, regardless of frontiers." As article 19 suggests, one of the key methods by which information is shared is through travel and the free exchange of ideas. The right of U.S. citizens to travel to Cuba is critical to their ability to participate fully in public debate on foreign policy matters, to share their views with Cubans, and to return to the United States capable of informing their fellow citizens of conditions in Cuba.

The ESMA case: Although family members of thousands of people detained and disappeared during Argentina's "dirty war" (1976-1983) have filed *habeas corpus* petitions in hopes of determining the whereabouts or fate of their loved ones, such legal efforts have almost always proven unavailing. Even when democracy was reestablished in Argentina, the specific fate and whereabouts of each disappeared person were still concealed and have remained so up to the present day. In March 1995, Navy Capt. Adolfo Scilingo publicly confessed to having thrown "disappeared" people out of airplanes into the sea—a confession that forced the reopening of criminal cases that had been closed by virtue of impunity laws and pardons issued in the late 1980s. In one such case, the district court ordered officials of the Navy and other entities to obtain or reconstruct lists of the disappeared persons held at the ESMA, a notorious concentration camp run by the navy. Human Rights Watch filed an amicus brief in support of the petition made by human rights leader Emilio

Mignone, whose daughter disappeared at the ESMA camp, to the Federal Court of Appeals (Criminal Panel) for Buenos Aires. The brief argued that, in accordance with an emerging "right to the truth" in international human rights law, the government of Argentina had a responsibility to investigate the disappearances and inform the victims' family members, as well as society in general, of the results of that investigation. It further argued that discharge of that obligation was not barred by statutes designed to immunize certain individuals from prosecution. It was the first amicus brief ever accepted by an Argentine court and, so far as we know, by any court in Latin America. Unfortunately, the appellate court later reversed its order when the Menem administration responded that it could not find documentary archives. A similar ruling in a companion case was appealed to the Supreme Court.

Makawanyane & Mchunv v. State: The newly created Constitutional Court of South Africa heard, as its first case, a challenge to the death penalty, which the new constitution had not directly abolished. The NAACP Legal Defense and Educational Fund and Human Rights Watch filed an amicus brief; because non-South African institutions did not have standing to appear as amicus, our brief was submitted to the court as part of several memoranda brought to its attention by a colleague organization in South Africa, the Legal Resources Centre. Borrowing from the experience in death penalty litigation in the United States, our brief postulated that in a society beset by racial inequalities, there is no way to apply the death penalty without racial discrimination. In sum, we argued that the death penalty invariably subordinates "the values which underlie an open and democratic society based on freedom and equality," in the words of the new South African Constitution. In June 1995, the Constitutional Court declared the South African death penalty statute unconstitutional. It did so by the unanimous, individually reasoned vote of each one of its justices. The decision will surely become a landmark in the worldwide struggle to abolish capital punishment.

CONGRESSIONAL CASEWORK

Human Rights Watch continued to work closely with three groups of members of the United States Congress that regularly take up cases of victims of human rights abuse and related issues. These are the Congressional Friends of Human Rights monitors, the Congressional Committee to Support Writers and Journalists, and the Congressional Working Group on International Women's Human Rights. The three casework groups are made up of members of the Senate and the House of Representatives, from both major political parties, who are interested in protecting threatened individuals and promoting respect for human rights throughout the world. Human Rights Watch assisted in the formation of these groups to enable concerned members to respond rapidly to human rights emergencies. The congressional casework groups send letters of concern to governments which abuse, or fail to protect from abuse, human rights monitors, writers, journalists or women who suffer gender specific violations of their human rights. In addition, the groups address legislation which contributes to human rights violations, such as laws that grant impunity for human rights abusers or suppress free speech. Human Rights Watch identifies and investigates appropriate cases, and works with each group's steering committee which determines which cases they will pursue. Once approved, letters are signed by the steering committee (4-5 members) and released on letterhead containing the names of all committee members.

The committees serve four important functions. First, and most importantly, the groups' letters pressure governments to stop the persecution of specific human rights monitors, writers, journalists, and women who are victims of gender specific abuses or take action to stop others who are doing so. By raising concerns about the safety of threatened individuals with heads of state and other high ranking officials, the committees provide protection by making it known that the case is being followed by members of the U.S. Congress. Second, by drawing the connection between legislation passed or pending in a given country and human rights violations there, the groups send a clear message that members of Congress are aware of these measures and strongly disapprove. Third, the letters keep members of Congress informed about the nature of human rights violations occurring in countries around the world, information which may later affect United States legislative decisions. Finally, the letters are an important advocacy tool in the countries where abuses occur. Human Rights Watch, and our local partners, seek to publicize congressional letters in the country where the abuses occur. Press accounts of U.S. congressional interest in human rights violations can bolster local efforts to promote rights and protect persecuted individuals. Also, by providing copies to the U.S. ambassador in each country, the groups' letters are often followed up by personal diplomatic inquiries.

The Congressional Friends of Human Rights Monitors

The Congressional Friends of Human Rights Monitors, formed in 1983, was composed of twenty-seven Senators and 112 Members of the House of Representatives in the 1st Session of the 104th Congress. The Steering Committee members were Sen. Daniel Patrick Moynihan, Sen. James Jeffords, Rep. Tony Hall, and Rep. Constance A. Morella. In 1995, the group focused its attention on assassinations, attacks, and threats against human rights monitors, and on legislation which shielded the perpetrators of such abuses.

In three letters sent between December 1994 and November 1995, the Congressional Friends continued to express their concern over forced disappearances, mur-

ders, and death threats against human rights monitors in Guatemala. In August, the Congressional Friends wrote to President de León Carpio providing detailed information regarding a series of murders, death threats, and kidnappings directed against human rights monitors associated with the Presbyterian church in the Department of Chimaltenango. The group reported that the June 23 killing of Manuel Saquíc Vásquez, a Presbyterian minister, and the August 1 killing of Pascual Serech, a member of the Human Rights and Verification Committee of Comalapa, Chimaltenango, were believed to be part of a year-long campaign of intimidation and murder carried out by Victor Román Cutzal, the military commissioner of Panabajal, Chimaltenango, and his associates in the civil self-defense patrols. The Congressional Friends urged the Government of Guatemala to investigate the killing of Manuel Vásquez, and to prosecute those found responsible. In addition, the group urged the government to rearrest and prosecute Victor Román Cutzal, who had previously been charged with the killing of Serech, as a suspect in both that murder and the killing of Vásquez. The Congressional Friends requested appropriate measures to protect members of the Panabajal Human Rights Committee, the Defensoría Maya of the Kakchiquel Presbytery, and CIEDEG, who had been threatened with death by military commissioners, including Victor Román, civil patrollers, and a death squad called Jaguar Justiciero. The group concluded "that only concrete steps to end the impunity enjoyed by human rights violators will enable Guatemala to guarantee the safety and physical integrity of human rights monitors and all Guatemalan citizens."

On August 10, the Congressional Friends wrote to President Alberto Fujirmori of Peru to express their concern over the passage of the Amnesty Law (Law 26479, 1995), and over death threats received by Tito Guido Gallegos Gallegos, a human rights lawyer. Gallegos Gallegos, who works with a church-based human rights organization in the town of Juli in the Department of Puno, received a death threat which read in part, "we have never bothered you but we have learned that you are promoting the non-application of the Amnesty Law." Focusing on the connection between the Amnesty Law, which exempts from criminal liability military and police forces that committed human rights violations over a fifteen year period, expunging their convictions and sentences or preventing their prosecution, the Congressional Friends wrote, "in our judgment, the threat against Mr. Gallegos Gallegos is a result of the climate of impunity created by passage of the Amnesty Law." The group went on to urge President Fujimori to investigate the threats against him, and to prosecute those found responsible. In addition, the Congressional Friends urged President Fujimori to pledge his government's commitment to prosecuting those found responsible for human rights violations, and to work toward the repeal of the Amnesty Law.

The government of Peru responded on August 22, in the form of a letter from Francisco Tudela van-Breugel-Douglas, the minister of foreign affairs, who wrote the Congressional Friends at "the special request of the president." In his letter, Minister van Breugel-Douglas wrote that "the main purpose of the law is to consolidate the peace..., [and] guarantee the necessary climate of political stability, within a process of democratic bolstering," and that the law was "aimed at reaffirming the process of national reconciliation." Moreover, the minister asserted that "the government of Peru is very closely identified with the cause of human rights."

The Embassy of Peru in Washington also requested a meeting with Congressional Friends of Human Rights Monitors staff to discuss the concerns highlighted in the August 10 letter, and the government's response. In the meeting, on August 29, Human Rights Watch and Congressional Friends staff reiterated their concern for the safety of Gallegos Gallegos. In addition, they provided new information regarding the alleged involvement of military personnel in the threats against him.

On November 1, the Congressional Friends sent a follow-up letter to Foreign Minister van-Breugel-Douglas reiterating some of the concerns outlined at the August 29 meeting, and respectfully disagreeing with the minister's assertions, expressing their belief that "the long term interests of democracy and stability are best served by sending a strong message to human rights violators that society will not provide impunity for their crimes under any circumstances."

In December 1994, the Congressional Friends wrote to Bulgarian President Zhelyu Zhelev to express their concern over threats made against Dimitrina Petrova, and other members of The Human Rights project of Bulgaria, an organization which monitors violence against the Roma Gypsy Minority. The threats against Petrova and her colleagues began in April 1994 after a neo-Nazi skinhead interrupted a press conference in which The Human Rights Project released a statement condemning violence against the Roma. In the days and months following the April 15 press conference, a swastika was painted on the mailbox of the organization's office, and threatening phone calls were received. Petrova filed complaints with the police in Sofia, but was told that they would be "unable to protect" members of her organization. In addition, a member of the Council of Ministers, Mr. Matanov, was quoted in the *Continent*, a daily newspaper, stating, "Bulgaria does not need foreign enemies as long as it has domestic human rights monitors." The Congressional Friends denounced "the atmosphere of impunity" created by such statements from high officials and by police indifference.

Dimitrina Petrova reported a number of changes following the release of the Congressional Friends letter. First, the threats against The Human Rights Project stopped. Second, threats against human rights monitors became an issue in the media (most of the major daily newspapers reported on the letter at the time of its release). Third, Mihail Ivanov, an advisor to the president, called a meeting with Petrova to discuss the situation. Fourth, the U.S. embassy offered to assist Petrova. Fifth, the Ministry of Internal Affairs started a check into the threats.

In addition to the letters on Guatemala, Peru and Bulgaria the Congressional Friends sent letters to Colombia, China, Turkey, Pakistan, Tunisia and Brazil between December 1994 and November 1988.

The Congressional Committee to Support Writers and Journalists

The Congressional Committee to Support Writers and Journalist was formed in 1988 and was composed of seventeen Senators and seventy-four Members of the House of Representatives in the 1st session of the 104th Congress. The Steering Committee was composed of Sen. Bob Graham, Rep. Jim Leach, and Rep. John Lewis. The committee focused their attention on attacks against journalists and on foreign legislation aimed at censoring free expression.

In May, the committee wrote to Indonesian Ambassador Arifin M. Siregar, to express concern over the Indonesian government's crackdown on members of the Alliance of Independent Journalists (AIJ). The AIJ was established in August 1994 in response to the 1994 banning of the independent publications *Detik, Tempo,* and *Editor.* In 1994, the committee wrote to the Indonesian government to protest the revocation of publishing licenses for the three publications. According to the committee's May letter, on March 16, four members of the AIJ, including the group's Secretary General Ahmad Taufik, were arrested and charged with publishing without a license, forming an unauthorized association, and other "crimes." The committee expressed their belief that the arrests "were a part of a broader crackdown by Indonesian Intelligence officials against critics of top officials of [the] government, particularly Minister of Research and Technology Habbie, Minister of Information Harmoko, and President Soeharto..." The committee went on to call for a cease to the apparent crackdown on publications critical of government policies or officials. The committee also asked the government to "immediately release Ahmad

Taufik, and other members of the Alliance of Independent Journalists if they have been detained simply for exercising their internationally recognized right to freedom of expression."

On June 22, Ambassador Siregar responded to the committee's May 15 letter. He wrote, "As we see it, the main issue at hand is not a case of restricting the freedom of the press. Rather, it relates to a violation of Indonesia's law." He went on to confirm that the four members of the AIJ were being prosecuted because they formed an association, and published and distributed their materials without obtaining the required licenses. However, in a revealing aside, the ambassador added that the "charges against members of this group also include allegations that the nature of the publications is such that they could be considered to be misinformative and designed to foment public unrest."

In July, the committee wrote to Egyptian President Husni Mubarak to express concern over a bill, approved by the Egyptian Parliament on May 27, that imposes stiff penalties on any journalist who publishes information that the authorities deem "false" or "aggravating." The committee stated that "such legislation may violate the right to freedom of expression, protected under article 19 of the International Covenant on Civil and Political Rights (ICCPR), to which Egypt is a state party." The legislation imposes prison terms of up to five years and a maximum of 10,000 Egyptian pounds (U.S.$2,000) for violating the statute. The committee's letter quoted a statement from the Egyptian Parliament which said, "the punishment is against the publication of rumors, false or opposing information and aggravating publications that effect the status quo, or cause undue panic, or harm any public office, or the country's economy." The committee wrote, "if accurate, such a statement indicates that the Egyptian Parliament intended the bill as a serious restraint to freedom of expression. The ICCPR and the Universal Declaration of Human Rights establish a right to 'impart' information. Any undue restriction on that right is a violation of Egypt's commitments under international law." The committee urged President Mubarak not to sign the legislation into law, and to publicly express opposition to any legislation which violates the internationally recognized right to freedom of expression.

President Mubarak responded to the committee's letter on August 21. In a short letter, he reaffirmed Egypt's commitment to human rights and stated that Egypt "strictly observe[s] and protect[s] the rights of journalists because we believe they are serving a very good cause and performing a crucial role in society." His letter did not address the draft legislation newly passed by Parliament, nor did it reveal his intentions with respect to signing the bill into law.

In addition to the letters to Indonesian Ambassador Siregar and Egyptian President Mubarak the Congressional Committee to Support Writers and Journalists wrote letters concerning violations of the right to freedom of expression in Colombia, Guatemala, Venezuela, Tunisia and Burma.

The Congressional Working Group on International Women's Human Rights

The Congressional Working Group on International Women's Human Rights, which was formed in April 1994, is a bipartisan group composed of twenty-four Senators and thirty-six members of the House of Representatives. It was created to promote accountability for violations of women's rights worldwide. The four members of the working group's steering committee are Sen. Patty Murray, Sen. Olympia J. Snowe, Rep. Jan Meyers and Rep. Joe Moakley.

In the past year, the working group denounced violations of women's human rights in four countries: Botswana, Mexico, Uzbekistan and Bahrain.

The Working Group expressed its concern over discrimination against women in Botswana's Citizenship Act, which until recently allowed Botswana men married to foreign women, but not Botswana women married to foreign men, to pass Botswana citizenship to their children. The working group wrote a letter to the president of Botswana calling for attention in particular to the case of Unity Dow, a citizen of Botswana whose husband is a U.S. national. On this basis, her children were denied Botswana passports by the attorney general. The Botswana Court of Appeal ruled that the discriminatory provision in the Citizenship Act was both unconstitutional and violative of international human rights norms. The working group's letter urged the government of Botswana to implement the Court of Appeal's decision by amending the discriminatory section of the Citizenship Act. In addition, they urged the government to issue Botswana passports to the children of Unity Dow and of other Botswana women who are married to foreign men. Encouraged by pressure from local and international groups, in August 1995 the National Assembly of Botswana amended the Citizenship Act to eliminate such discriminatory provisions.

The working group wrote to the president of Mexico to press for a prompt and impartial investigation and prosecution in a case involving the alleged rape of three Tzeltal women by members of the Mexican National Army. A mother and her three daughters were detained at a military checkpoint in Chiapas. The four women, who were returning to their home from selling fruits and vegetables near the town, were detained and interrogated by soldiers from the Mexican National Army as suspected sympathizers of the Zapatista National Liberation Army. According to adffidavit testimony given by the three sisters, they were locked in a room and beaten and raped by several dozen soldiers who accused them of being Zapatistas. The case was being investigated in a military court. The letter urged the president of Mexico to turn the investigation and prosecution of the case over to civilian authorities, in accordance with the Mexican Constitution and international law. Article 13 of the Mexican Constitution states, "When a crime of lack of military discipline involves a civilian, the corresponding civilian authority shall hear the case." The working group also called for the protection of the well-being and safety of the four women who were told by the soldiers not to report the attack.

In September 1995, the working group conveyed its deep concern over the condition and treatment of two women held in custody by the Uzbekistan government. While in detention, the women, who were pregnant at the time of their arrest, were threatened with forced abortions in order to coerce them into changing their plea from innocent to guilty. It was reported that both women were forced by prison officials to undergo abortions. Individuals familiar with the case believe that this was ordered because Uzbekistan law requires that pregnant women be released pending trial. The working group called on the government of Uzbekistan to condemn this cruel and inhuman treatment of the female prisoners. The letter also urged the government to release the two women into the custody of their relatives or other individuals acceptable, to the defendant and the court; to initiate an investigation into their treatment by law enforcement agents; and to punish their abuse to the fullest extent of the law. As a result of the international outcry over the gross mistreatment of the female prisoners, authorities at the National Security Service (former KGB) prison in the Central Asian state of Uzbekistan released the two women.

In October, the working group wrote to the government of Bahrain to raise concern regarding the suspension of Dr. Munira Ahmed Fakhro from her teaching position at the University of Bahrain. Dr. Munira Fakhro is a well-regarded academic and author of numerous works on issues related to the cause of women and democratic change in Bahrain. Her suspension from her university position resulted from her refusal to withdraw support for a petition calling for a greater degree of democracy and women's participation in the political process in Bahrain. The petition was signed by over 300 Bahraini women. Approximately ninety women were instructed by the Bahraini government to sign statements apologizing for signing the petition and to refrain from further political activity. The working group appealed to the president of Bahrain to order the immediate restoration of Dr. Munia Fahkro to her teaching position. The letter urged the government to restore the jobs of two other women who were dismissed as a result of refusing to withdraw their support for the petition and to permit them to exercise their internationally recognized right to express their views freely. To date the government has taken no measures to restore the women to their positions.

HUMAN RIGHTS WATCH INTERNATIONAL FILM FESTIVAL

The Human Rights Watch International Film Festival was created to advance public education on human rights issues and concerns using the unique medium of film. Each year, the Human Rights Watch International Film Festival exhibits the finest human rights films and videos in commercial and archival theaters and on public and cable television throughout the United States. Highlights of the festival are also presented in various cities abroad, reflecting the increasingly global appeal that the project has generated.

In selecting films for the festival, Human Rights Watch concentrates equally on artistic merit and human rights content. The festival encourages filmmakers around the world to address human rights subject matter in their work and presents films and videos from both new and established international human rights filmmakers. Each year, the festival's programming committee screens more than 700 films and videos to create a program that represents a wide number of countries and issues. Once a film is nominated for a place in the program, staff of the relevant division of Human Rights Watch also view it to confirm its accuracy in the portrayal of human rights concerns.

The Human Rights Watch International Film Festival was established in 1988, in part to mark the tenth anniversary of the founding of what has become Human Rights Watch. After a hiatus of three years, it was resumed in 1991 and has since been presented annually. The 1995 festival season marked the beginning of new collaborative ventures between the festival and the Film Society of Lincoln Center which now presents the series annually in New York and the Museum of Tolerance which will host the series each year in Los Angeles. Thirty films and videos (of which twenty-three were premieres) from more than twenty countries were presented over a two-week period. A majority of the screenings were followed by discussions with the filmmakers and Human Rights Watch staff on the human rights issues represented in each work. The festival included feature length fiction and documentary films as well as works-in-progress and experimental and animated films.

In 1992, Human Rights Watch created Film Watch, in association with the Film Festival and a group of American filmmakers to monitor and protect the human rights of filmmakers around the world. Over the years, Film Watch has written letters of protest to governments that have attempted to abuse the rights of filmmaker or to censor their films. Most recently, Film Watch publicized the Chinese government's blatant attempt at censorship when it "asked" the 33rd New York Film Festival not to include in its program the film, *The Gate of Heavenly Peace,* a documentary that examines the events and the complex political process leading up to the massacre in Tiananmen Square. The New York Film Festival did not submit to the Chinese government's request and the documentary was shown at the Festival.

Each year the festival opens its New York run with an opening night fundraising celebration. In conjunction with the opening night festivities, the festival annually awards a prize in the name of cinematographer and director Nestor Almendros, who was a cherished friend of the festival. The award, which includes a cash prize of $5,000, goes to a deserving new filmmaker in recognition of his or her contributions to human rights. The 1995 recipient was Chilean director Carmen Castillo whose outstanding work, *La Flaca Alejandra (In a Time of Betrayal),* re-examines the effects of Pinochet's dictatorship, during and after his reign. This very powerful, personal film also became the centerpiece of the festival's Women's Day Program—a day and night exclusively devoted to films and videos that address women's rights around the world.

In 1995, in honor of Irene Diamond, a longtime board member and supporter of Human Rights Watch, whose lifetime dedication to human rights and filmmaking has been invaluable to our work, the festival launched a new award, "The Irene Diamond Lifetime Achievement Award," which will be presented annually to a director whose life's work illuminates an outstanding commitment to human rights and film. The 1995 award went to the renowned international director, Costa Gavras.

Highlights of the 1995 festival included a retrospective of the work of acclaimed Cuban director Tomas Gutierrez Alea, whose latest film, *Frese y Chocolate (Strawberry and Chocolate),* was nominated for an Academy Award and, who is noted for his satirical critiques of government bureaucracy from "inside the Revolution." The High School Project, now in its third year, offers daytime screenings for students followed by interactive discussions between students, teachers, filmmakers and Human Rights Watch staff; it was expanded this year to include public and private schools in the Los Angeles area as well as in New York. Joining forces with the Human Rights Watch Children's Rights Project, a selection of the festival's program was also presented to young people at Spofford Detention Center and Riker's Island (both in New York).

In September, the festival exhibited works by and about women as part of the

Non-Governmental Organization's Forum (NGO Forum) at the Fourth International Conference on Women in Beijing, China. The films reached across borders and spoke about the universality of human rights. The festival plans to send highlights from the past six festivals, in a package entitled, "Archive Alive," to ten of the NGO groups that attended the conference. Also in September, segments from the festival program appeared in Bogota, Boston, Guatemala City and Florence (Italy). Showcases of the festival will appear in Seattle, North Carolina, London, Hong Kong and Port-au-Prince later in 1995 and in early 1996.

MISSIONS

Human Rights Watch/ Africa

January-February/ Rwanda: Investigated the 1994 genocide and current human rights abuses.

January-February/ Belgium and France: Conducted an advocacy trip to Brussels and Paris to press for greater attention by European governments to human rights abuses in Africa.

February/ Rwanda: Set up a field office to document the 1994 genocide and to monitor current human rights violations.

February-March/ Mozambique and Zimbabwe: Joint mission with the Arms Project to research landmines legacy in southern Africa.

March /South Africa: Investigated violence in the KwaZulu-Natal and its effects on the new democracy.

March/ Angola: Joint mission with the Arms Project to investigate continued arms flows and human rights abuses since the November 1994 Lusaka Protocol.

March/ Nigeria: Conducted a mission to southeast Nigeria to investigate the military crackdown in Ogoniland.

March/ Sudan: Conducted research in southern Sudan and Kenya concerning human rights abuses by the government of Sudan.

April/ Rwanda: Investigated the 1994 genocide and current human rights abuses.

April /South Africa: Conducted a joint mission with the Women's Rights Project to investigate domestic violence.

May-June/ Sudan: Investigated human rights conditions in northern Sudan, and documented abuses against children, especially street children, child soldiers, and the use of slavery.

June/ Rwanda: Investigated the 1994 genocide and current human rights abuses.

June/ South Africa and Mozambique: Conducted a joint mission with the Arms Project to further research into the landmines legacy and jointly organized a conference on landmines with the University Eduardo Mondlane.

July/ Ethiopia: Investigated the progress of the trials of the former Mengistu regime.

August/ Rwanda: Investigated the 1994 genocide and current human rights abuses.

October/ Austria: Conducted a joint mission with the Arms Project to attend the Review Conference on Conventional Weapons (CCW) as an observer.

October/ Rwanda: Investigated the 1994 genocide and current human rights abuses.

Human Rights Watch/ Americas

December-January/ Brazil: Investigated police and military violence in the *favelas* (slums) of Rio de Janeiro.

February/ Cuba: (in cooperation with the Free Expression Project) Investigated violations of the right to freedom of expression and freedom of association.

February/ Mexico: Conducted preliminary research on labor rights violations, particularly violations of the right to organize labor unions.

March/ Guatemala: Investigated the work of the U.N. human rights mission and cooperation between the government and guerrillas.

March/ Haiti: Investigated the selection, training, and performance of interim and permanent Haitian police.

March/ Brazil: Opened the Human Rights Watch/Americas office in Rio de Janeiro. Held a press conference in Sao Paulo to release Human Rights Watch/Americas' agenda for the administration of newly elected Brazilian President Fernando Henrique Cardoso. Traveled to Boa Vista to monitor the status of the government investigation into the July 1993 massacre of sixteen Yanomani Indians. Investigated police raids and the extrajudicial execution of a detainee by off-duty police officers in Rio Grande do Sul.

March and April/ Bolivia: (in cooperation with the Drug Project) Investigated human rights abuses committed in the context of the "war on drugs."

March-April/ Haiti: Advocacy on interim and permanent police and the change from a multinational force to a U.N. peacekeeping mission. Released *Haiti: Security Compromised: Recycled Haitian Soldiers on the Police Front Line* in Port-au-Prince.

March-April/ Mexico: Investigated human rights violations in Chiapas. Interviewed government and military officials.

April/ Colombia (in cooperation with the Arms Project): Investigated crimes committed by members of paramilitary groups in Colombia and connections between those groups and the Colombian armed forces.

April/ Guatemala: Met with government officials regarding human rights conditions.

April/ Brazil: Together with other human rights groups and nongovernmental organizations, Human Rights Watch/Americas' Brazil director met with Brazilian President Fernando Henrique Cardoso in the U.S.

April-May/ Cuba: (with the Foundation France Libertés, the Federation Internationale des Droits de l'Homme [FIDH], and Médecins du Monde) Interviewed prisoners and met with President Fidel Castro and other government officials.

April-May/ Haiti: Investigated violence and procedural irregularities relating to the impending June parliamentary and local elections.

June/ Haiti: Advocacy on electoral concerns and research on accountability issues, particularly the Haitian truth commission. Released *Haiti: Human Rights Concerns Prior to the June 1995 Elections* in Port-au-Prince.

June/ Brazil: Conducted fact-finding on rural violence and development in Brasília.

July/ Peru: Met with government officials and the press, following up on the July publication, *Peru: The Two Faces of Justice.*

July/ Brazil: Participated in a conference in Porto Alegre on women's rights, presenting a paper on the use of international human rights instruments to advance women's human rights.

July-August/ Bolivia: (in cooperation with the Drug Project) Met with Bolivian and U.S. officials and held press conferences to release spanish version of the report, *Bolivia: Human Rights Violations and the War on Drugs.*

July-August/ Chile: Conducted an advocacy mission regarding the amnesty law and the Contreras case.

August/ Argentina: Conducted an advocacy mission regarding issues of truth and justice in Argentina; met with press and human rights organizations.

August/ Brazil: Conducted an advocacy mission in Rio de Janeiro, Brasília, and São Paulo; met with senior government officials and human rights organizations. Testified in Brasília before the federal congress on Brazil's international obligation to investigate, prosecute, and punish cases of forced disappearance committed by state agents.

August/ Guatemala: Investigated civil patrol violence against repatriating refugees in the Ixcán region.

August-September/ Mexico: Investigated the June massacre of peasants in Guerrero; updated information on alleged Zapatistas detained in February, and began research into labor-related human rights violations.

September/ Costa Rica: Presented preliminary objections before the Inter-American Court of Human Rights in *Castillo Paez v. Peru* and *Maria Elena Loayza v. Peru.*

September/ Brazil: Appeared before

the Inter-American Commission on Human Rights in Washington in cases against the Brazilian government.

September-October/ Brazil: Investigated police violence in Rio de Janeiro's favelas.

November/ Colombia: Conducted an advocacy mission and met with press and government officials.

Human Rights Watch/Asia

January-February/ Burma: Investigated abuses linked to the offensive against the Karen ethnic rebels following the fall of their headquarters; also investigated attacks on the 10,000 new refugees who arrived in Thailand.

May/ Burma: Conducted an advocacy mission from the London office to Brussels and Amsterdam following the release of our report in March.

May/ Cambodia: Attended a regional conference on human rights and development in the Mekong River basin in May; met with regional and local human rights advocates to discuss the plans and priorities of NGOs in Cambodia specifically, and in Southeast Asia more generally.

May/ India: Met with government officials, local human rights groups and members of the official National Human Rights Commision.

May/ Sri Lanka: Attended a regional NGO conference on human rights and development designed to set priorities for advocacy for groups throughout Asia in the upcoming year; met with local colleagues to discuss human rights concerns in Sri Lanka.

June/ Burma: Traveled to Paris, to meet with Foreign Ministry officials regarding the French position, as chair of the European Union, toward Burma; also met with French human rights groups.

June/ South Korea: Investigated labor rights violations in the Republic of Korea.

July-September/ Thailand: Began an investigation into abuses against migrant workers from Burma and elsewhere.

August-September/ Burma: Visited Burmese refugee camps in Thailand, includ-

ing the "safe area" for political dissidents; traveled to Japan to continue discussions with the ministry of foreign affairs on Japanese policy toward Burma.

August/ China: (in cooperation with the Women's Rights Project) Sent two delegates to Beijing for the U.N. Fourth World Conference on Women.

September/ Hong Kong: Investigated the intensification of religious repression in China.

September/ Japan: Continued dialogue with government officials, Diet members and others on Japan's human rights policies.

November/ Hong Kong: Conducted a mission to investigate the human rights situation in the lead-up to the July 1997 transition to Chinese sovereignty.

November/ Japan: Participated in NGO conferences on human rights and worker rights in relationship to the APEC summit in Osaka.

November/ Sri Lanka: Attended two conferences. The first was a consultation of Asian NGO representatives to discuss international and domestic advocacy strategies for the upcoming year, the second was an international meeting of NGOs concerned about deteriorating conditions in Sri Lanka.

Human Rights Watch/ Helsinki

January/ Georgia: Conducted additional advocacy work against torture and advocacy work for the protection of due process.

January/ Chechnya: Investigated abuses by both sides in the war.

February/ Chechnya: Continued investigations of abuses by both Russians and Chechens in the war.

February-March/ Moscow, Brussels and Vienna: Conducted advocacy on Chechnya with the European Union and the Organization for Security and Cooperation in Europe (OSCE). Addressed all the ambassadors to the OSCE in Vienna (the first time that an NGO was allowed to do so).

March/ Vienna and Austria: Met with the OSCE as a group and several member states on a bilateral level to do more advocacy work on Georgia.

April/ Khasavyurt, Dagestan: Interviewed refugees to gain information about continued and intensifying humanitarian law violations, mostly by Russian forces, in the war in Chechnya.

April-May/ Albania: (in cooperation with the Free Expression Project) Investigated freedom of the press issues.

May/ Croatia: Investigated violations of the rules of war and other human rights abuses following the Croatian Army offensive in western Slavonia.

May-June/ Moscow: Gathered information on police brutality and state-sponsored violence against dark-skinned people in Moscow and violations of freedom of movement, as well as violations of the rights of refugees and internally displaced persons in the Russian Federation.

June-July/ England: Investigated xenophobic violence and police brutality against foreigners.

June/ Prague, Czech Republic: Attended a meeting on Roma in Eastern Europe.

June/ Armenia: Gathered information on the Armenian government's crackdown on the opposition since December 1994.

June/ Turkey: Investigated PKK abuses and the conditions of forced Kurdish migrants in Adana, a western Turkish city. The mission was called off due to a manipulative press conference called by the Interior Ministry that misstated the goals of Human Rights Watch/Helsinki as an organization.

July-August/ Macedonia (Albania and Kosovo): Investigated the situation of civil and political rights in the country including the rights of ethnic minorities and the state of inter-ethnic relations; freedom of the press and expression; police violence and prison conditions; and the role of the international community in the country.

July-September/ France: Investigated xenophobic violence; treatment of asylum seekers; treatment of immigrants in detention centers; police brutality and harassment at the border; and racial discrimination.

July/ Geneva and Vienna: Conducted an advocacy trip to discuss Chechnya with the U.N. Human Rights Committee and the OSCE.

July-August/Tuzla, Bosnia-Hercegovina: Interviewed the displaced from Srebrenica and Zepa.

August-September/ Serbia: Investigated the displacement of Serbs from the Krajina area in Croatia; the expulsions of Croats and Hungarians from the Serbian province of Vojvodina; and the drafting of Krajina refugees into military and paramilitary forces.

September-November/ United Kingdom, Germany, France, Belgium and Turkey: Investigated cases of Turkish citizens who have applied to the European Commission on Human Rights and have been harassed by police, tortured, or in at least one case killed; also investigated torture and Turkey's progress on ending torture in light of the European Committee to Prevent Torture's harsh December 1992 report condemning torture in Turkey as a systematic problem.

November/ Croatia: Investigated further violations of the rules of war and human rights in the Krajina region of Croatia.

November-December/ Tajikistan and Afghanistan: Investigated conditions in Tajik refugee camps and conditions for returnees from those camps.

November/ Uzbekistan: Conducted first follow-up field investigation since the organization was banned in early 1993, and met for the first time with government officials.

November/ Chechnya: Investigated the human rights situation in Chechnya one year after the beginning of the conflict there.

November/ Oslo, Norway: Presented a paper at a conference on "Conflict in the Caucasus" regarding NGOs and conflict.

Human Rights Watch/ Middle East

February/Israel, the West Bank and the Gaza Strip: Briefed officials on new report on human rights in the Palestinian self-rule areas and released the report.

February/Egypt: Investigated government intimidation of civilians mentioned in recent reports on Egypt.

March/Egypt: Held meetings with

Egyptian human rights organizations and other NGOs; collected information about the harassment of defense lawyers.

March/Jordan: Collected information about Jordanians held in Syrian prisons.

March-May/Syria: Observed state security court trials; investigated prison conditions; the treatment of released political prisoners; and the treatment of the Kurdish minority.

April/Egypt: Conducted a mission to mark the anniversary of the death in detention of an Egyptian lawyer, and participated in a press conference criticizing further arrests of lawyers.

May-June/Morocco: Investigated human rights abuses including due process violations, torture, the status of political prisoners and the "disappeared."

June-July/ France: Conducted interviews on Algeria and initiated research for a Helsinki division report on the treatment of immigrants in France.

July/Saudi Arabia: Conducted investigation on the repression of Islamist dissidents and limits on peaceful expression.

July/Egypt: Collected information about the increasing harassment of Egyptian NGOs, including human rights group.

July/Syria: Met with diplomats in Damascus to discuss the report on Syria released the same month.

August/Jordan: Conducted research on human rights conditions in Iraq.

August/Algeria-Western Sahara: Interviewed Sahrawi refugees and Moroccan prisoners of war in Algeria, and investigated the U.N. operation organizing the referendum to be conducted in the Western Sahara.

August/ Bahrain: Investigated government harassment of pro-democracy activists.

August-September/ Lebanon: Investigated civilian casualties in south Lebanon from indiscriminate attacks by Israeli forces and the South Lebanon Army; collected information about the treatment of the Palestinian refugee population; and met with Lebanese human rights groups and lawyers.

The Arms Project

January-March/ Rwanda/Zaire: Investigated arms flows to the perpetrators of the Rwandan genocide in Zaire; uncovered evidence of weapons shipments by France, Zaire and others in violation of a United Nations arms embargo.

March/ Georgia/Abkhazia: (in cooperation with Human Rights Watch/Helsinki): Released report on laws of war violations and conducted follow-up research on recent developments, including non-repatriation of internally displaced persons, the problem of landmines, and continuing hostilities along the frontline.

April and August-October/ Colombia: Conducted investigation into the nature and scope of the relationship between the Colombian military and paramilitary groups, which are particularly abusive of human rights, and United States assistance to the Colombian military.

June-July/ Turkey: Investigated use of NATO-supplied weapons in Turkey's war in the southeast, in particular the use of such weapons in gross violations of international humanitarian law and human rights. Found evidence of critical role of U.S. equipment, such as fighter planes, helicopters and automatic rifles, in the village depopulation campaign and attendant abuses, such as extrajudicial executions and torture.

The Children's Rights Project

March and May/ United States: Investigated conditions in Louisiana correctional institutions for children.

October/ United States: Held press conferences to release report on Louisiana correctional institutions for children; met with state officials and nongovernmental organizations on follow-up to the report.

October/ Italy: Took part in international conference on child labor in Pisa.

November-December/ India: (in cooperation with Human Rights Watch/Asia) Began investigation into the use of bonded child labor.

November-December/ India: (in cooperation with Human Rights Watch/Asia)

Began investigation into the treatment of street children by police.

November/ Geneva: Took part in theme day on juvenile justice of U.N. Committee on the Rights of the Child.

The Prison Project

June/ United States: Interviewed prisoners at the Maximum Security Complex, a "maxi-maxi" facility in Westville, Indiana.

November/ Geneva: Participated in U.N. Working Group on the Draft Optional Protocol to the Convention Against Torture.

The Women's Rights Project

March/ Mexico: Investigated gender discrimination in the export oriented factories along the U.S./Mexico border.

April /South Africa: Conducted a joint mission with Human Rights Watch/Africa to investigate domestic violence.

May/ Japan: Investigated government sponsored or tolerated abuse against Thai women trafficked into Japan for the purpose of prostitution.

May and June/ Singapore and Hong Kong: Examined abuse of migrant domestic women workers in Hong Kong, Singapore and Taiwan.

August/ China: (in cooperation with the Human Rights Watch/Asia) Sent delegates to Beijing for the U.N. Fourth World Conference on Women.

October/ Morocco: Investigated sex discrimination under the Moroccan Family Code.

1995 Publications

To order any of the following titles, please call our Publications Department at (212) 986-1980 and ask for our publications catalog.

Human Rights Watch

Playing the "Communal Card": Communal Violence and Human Rights, 4/95, 176 pp.

Slaughter Among Neighbors: The Po-litical Origins of Communal Violence, 10/95, 202 pp.

Human Rights Watch/Africa
Kenya

Old Habits Die Hard: Rights Abuses Follow Renewed Foreign Aid Commitments, 7/95, 15 pp.

Nigeria

The Ogoni Crisis: A Case-Study of Military Repression in Southeastern Nigeria, 7/95, 44 pp.

Rwanda

The Crisis Continues, 4/95, 15 pp.

Somalia

Somalia Faces the Future: Human Rights in a Fragmented Society, 4/95, 72 pp.

South Africa

Threats to a New Democracy: Continuing Violence in KwaZulu-Natal, 5/95, 38 pp.

Violence against Women in South Africa: The State Response to Domestic Violence and Rape, 11/95, 144 pp.

Sudan

Child Soldiers in Sudan: Slaves, Street Children and Child Soldiers, 9/95, 128 pp.

Human Rights Watch/Americas
Bolivia

Human Rights Violations and the War on Drugs, 7/95, 42 pp.

Cuba

Improvements without Reform, 10/95, 34 pp.

Guatemala

Disappeared in Guatemala: The Case of Efraín Bámaca Velásquez, 3/95, 15 pp.

Haiti

Security Compromised: Recycled Haitian Soldiers on the Police Front Line, 3/95, 27 pp.

Human Rights Conditions Prior to the

June 1995 Elections, 6/95, 20 pp.

Human Rights after President Aristide's Return, 10/95, 33 pp.

Mexico

Army Officer Held "Responsible" for Chiapas Massacre: Accused Found Dead at Defense Ministry, 6/95, 13 pp.

Peru

The Two Faces of Justice, 7/95, 52 pp.

United States

Crossing the Line: Human Rights Abuses Along the U.S. Border with Mexico Persist Amid Climate of Impunity, 4/95, 37 pp.

Human Rights Watch/Asia

Burma

Abuses Linked to the Fall of Manerplaw, 3/95, 30 pp.

Entrenchment or Reform?: Human Rights Developments and the Need for Continued Pressure, 7/95, 39 pp.

Cambodia

Cambodia at War, 3/95, 168 pp.

The War Against Free Speech: Letter from Human Rights Watch and the New Cambodian Press Law, 9/95, 15 pp.

China

Enforced Exile of Dissidents: Government "Re-entry Blacklist" Revealed, 1/95, 22 pp.

The Three Gorges Dam in China: Forced Resettlement, Suppression of Dissent and Labor Rights Concerns, 2/95, 48 pp.

Keeping the Lid on Demands for Change, 6/95, 13 pp.

"Leaking State Secrets": The Case of Gao Yu, 7/95, 32 pp.

General

Human Rights in the APEC Region: 1995, 11/95, 46 pp.

India/Nepal

Rape for Profit: Trafficking of Nepali Girls and Women to India's Brothels, 7/95, 96 pp.

Indonesia

Deterioriating Human Rights in East Timor, 2/95, 13 pp.

Soeharto Retaliates against Critics: Official Reactions to Demonstrations in Germany, 5/95, 7 pp.

Press Closures in Indonesia One Year Later, 7/95, 6 pp.

Japan

Prison Conditions in Japan, 3/95, 112 pp.

Pakistan

Contemporary Forms of Slavery in Pakistan, 7/95, 96 pp.

South Korea

Labor Rights Violations under Democratic Rule, 11/95, 31 pp.

Sri Lanka

Stop Killings of Civilians, 7/95, 10 pp.

Vietnam

The Suppression of the Unified Buddhist Church, 3/95, 16 pp.

Human Rights in a Season of Transition: Law and Dissent in the Socialist Republic of Vietnam, 8/95, 19 pp.

Human Rights Watch/Helsinki

Albania

The Greek Minority, 2/95, 20 pp.

Bosnia-Hercegovina

The Fall of Srebrenica and the Failure of U.N. Peacekeeping, 10/95, 58 pp.

Croatia

The Croatian Army Offensive in Western Slavonia and its Aftermath, 7/95, 17 pp.

Civil and Political Rights in Croatia, 10/95, 176 pp.

Georgia

Trial in Georgia Draws to a Close, 1/95, 14 pp.

Georgia/Abkhazia: Violations of the Laws of War and Russia's Role in the Conflict, 3/95, 56 pp.

Germany

"Germany for Germans": Xenophobia and Racist Violence in Germany, 4/95, 120 pp.

Russia

Russia's War in Chechnya: Victims Speak Out, 1/95, 8 pp.

War in Chechnya: New Report from the Field, 1/95, 14 pp.

Three Months of War in Chechnya, 2/95, 26 pp.

Partisan War in Chechnya on the Eve of the WWII Commemoration, 5/95, 19 pp.

Crime or Simply Punishment?: Racist Attacks by Moscow Law Enforcement, 9/95, 32 pp.

Tajikistan

Return to Tajikistan: Continued Regional and Ethnic Tensions, 5/95, 30 pp.

Former Yugoslavia

War Crimes Trials in the Former Yugoslavia, 6/95, 45 pp.

Human Rights Watch/Middle East

Algeria

Six Months Later, Cover-Up Continues in Prison Clash that Left 100 Inmates Dead: Report by Defense Lawyers Charges Inmates Were Deliberately Massacred, 8/95, 18 pp.

Egypt

Hostage-Taking and Intimidation by Security Forces, 1/95, 41 pp.

Iraq

Iraq's Crime of Genocide: The Anfal Campaign against the Kurds, 5/95, 406 pp.

Iraq's Brutal Decrees: Amputation, Branding and the Death Penalty, 6/95, 16 pp.

Israel & Israeli-Occupied Territories

The Gaza Strip and Jericho: Human Rights under Palestinian Partial Self-Rule, 2/95, 50 pp.

Kuwait

The Bedoons of Kuwait: "Citizens without Citizenship," 8/95, 120 pp.

Morocco

Human Rights in Morocco, 10/95, 42 pp.

Syria

The Price of Dissent, 7/95, 54 pp.

Western Sahara

Keeping it Secret: The United Nations Operation in the Western Sahara, 10/95, 42 pp.

Human Rights Watch Arms Project

Cambodia

Cambodia at War, 3/95, 168 pp.

General

Blinding Laser Weapons: The Need to Ban a Cruel and Inhumane Weapon, 9/95, 49 pp.

Georgia

Georgia/Abkhazia: Violations of the Laws of War and Russia's Role in the Conflict, 3/95, 56 pp.

Rwanda

Rearming with Impunity: International Support for the Perpetrators of the Rwandan Genocide, 5/95, 19 pp.

Turkey

Weapons Transfers and Violations of the Laws of War in Turkey, 11/95, 184 pp.

United States

U.S. Blinding Laser Weapons, 5/95, 16 pp.

Human Rights Watch Children's Rights Project

Sudan

Child Soldiers in Sudan: Slaves, Street Children and Child Soldiers, 9/95, 128 pp.

United States

A World Leader in Executing Juveniles, 3/95, 22 pp.

Children in Confinement in Louisiana, 10/95, 152 pp.

Human Rights Watch
Free Expression Project

Banned, Censored, Harassed and Jailed Writers Receive Grants: 48 Writers from 23 Countries Recognized by Lillian Hellman/ Dashiell Hammett Funds, 6/95, 8 pp.

Human Rights Watch Prison Project
Japan

Prison Conditions in Japan, 3/95, 112 pp.

Human Rights Watch
Women's Rights Project
General

The Human Rights Watch Global Report on Women's Human Rights, 8/95, 480 pp.

Russia

Neither Jobs Nor Justice: State Discrimination Against Women in Russia, 3/95, 30 pp.

South Africa

Violence against Women in South Africa: The State Response to Domestic Violence and Rape, 11/95, 144 pp.

STAFF AND COMMITTEES

Human Rights Watch

Staff

Executive: Kenneth Roth, Executive Director; Gara LaMarche, Associate Director; Jennifer Hyman, Executive Assistant.

Advocacy: Holly J. Burkhalter, Advocacy Director; Lotte Leicht, Brussels Office Director; Joanna Weschler, United Nations Representative; Allyson Collins, Research Associate; Tuhin Roy and Marti Weithman, Associates.

Communications: Susan Osnos, Communications Director; Robert Kimzey, Publications Director; Suzanne Guthrie, Publications Manager; Fitzroy Hepkins, Mail Manager; Karen Sorensen, Online Research Associate; Lenny Thomas, Production Manager; Sobeira Genao, Publications Associate; Liz Reynoso, Communications Associate; Kathleen Desvallons, Part-Time Assistant.

Development: Derrick Wong, Development Director; Desiree A. Colly, Regional Development Director; Rachel Weintraub, Special Events Director; Bob Zuber, Foundations Relations Director; James Holland, Coordinator of Individual Giving; Marianne Law, Special Events Coordinator; Wendy Worthington, Associate.

Finance and Administration: Derrick Wong, Director; Barbara Guglielmo, Director of Finance; Maria Pignataro Nielsen, Administrative Manager; Walid Ayoub, Systems Administrator; Anderson Allen, Office Manager, Washington; Urmi Shah, Office Manager, London; Isabelle Tin-Aung, Office Manager, Brussels; Emanuel Smallwood, Bookkeeper; Iris Yang, Junior Accountant; Mia Roman, Receptionist/Office Assistant, New York; Michaela Harrison, Receptionist/Office Assistant, Washington; Christina Pena, Part-Time Assistant.

General Counsel: Juan E. Méndez, General Counsel; Marti Weithman, Associate.

Program: Cynthia Brown, Program Director; Michael McClintock, Deputy Program Director; Jeri Laber, Senior Advisor; Jemera Rone, Counsel; Allyson Collins, Research Associate; Richard Dicker, Associate Counsel; Jamie Fellner, Associate Counsel; Joanne Mariner, Associate Counsel; Nandi Rodrigo, Associate.

International Film Festival: Bruni Burres, Director; Heather Harding, Associate Director.

1995 Fellowship Recipients: Michael Bochenek, Leonard H. Sandler Fellow; Samya Burney, W. Bradford Wiley Fellow; Mercedes Hernandez-Cancio, Women's Law and Public Policy Fellowship; Ada Cheng, Henry R. Luce Fellow; Robin Levi, Sophie Silberberg Fellow; Milbert Shin, Orville Schell Fellow; Joyce Wan, Henry R. Luce Fellow.

Human Rights Watch/Helsinki

Staff
Holly Cartner, Executive Director; Erika Dailey, Rachel Denber, Guissou Jahangiri-Jeannot, Ivana Nizich, Christopher Panico, Research Associates; Ivan Lupis, Research Assistant; Anne Kuper, Alexander Petrov, Shira Robinson, Lenee Simon, Associates.

Advisory Committee
Jonathan Fanton, Chair; Alice H. Henkin, Vice Chair; M. Bernard Aidinoff; Roland Algrant; Robert L. Bernstein; Charles Biblowit; Martin Blumenthal; Roberta Cohen; Lori Damrosch; Istvan Deak; Adrian W. DeWind; Fr. Robert Drinan; Stanley Engelstein; Ellen Futter; Willard Gaylin. M.D.; Michael Gellert; John Glusman; Paul Goble; Robert K. Goldman; Jack Greenberg; Rita E. Hauser; Robert James; Rhoda Karpatkin; Stephen L. Kass; Bentley Kassal; Marina Pinto Kaufman; Joanne Landy; Margaret A. Lang; Leon Levy; Wendy Luers; Theodor Meron; Deborah Milenkovitch; Toni Morrison; John B. Oakes; Herbert Okun; Jane Olson; Yuri Orlov; Srdja Popovic; Bruce Rabb; Peter Reddaway; Stuart Robinowitz; John G. Ryden; Herman Schwartz; Stanley K. Sheinbaum; Jerome J. Shestack; George Soros; Susan Weber Soros; Michael Sovern; Fritz Stern; Svetlana Stone; Rose Styron; Liv Ullman; Gregory Wallance; Rosalind C. Whitehead; William D. Zabel; Warren Zimmermann.

Human Rights Watch/Middle East

Staff
Christopher E. George, Executive Director; Eric Goldstein, Research Director; Aziz Abu-Hamad, Virginia N. Sherry, Associate Directors; Fatemah Ziai, Research Associate; Sarvenaz Bahar, Elahé S. Hicks, Brian Owsley, Bashar Tarabieh, Pamela Pensock, Consultants; Shira Robinson, Awali Samara, Associates.

Advisory Committee
Gary G. Sick, Chair; Lisa Anderson, Bruce Rabb, Vice Chairs; Shaul Bakhash; M. Cherif Bassiouni; Hyman Bookbinder; Paul Chevigny; Helena Cobban; Patricia Derian; Stanley Engelstein; Edith Everett; Mansour Farhang; Robert K. Goldman; Rita E. Hauser; Rev. J. Bryan Hehir; Edy Kaufman; Marina Pinto Kaufman; Samir Khalaf; Judith Kipper; Pnina Lahav; Ann M. Lesch; Richard Maass; Stephen P. Marks; Philip Mattar; David K. Shipler; Sanford Solender; Shibley Telhami; Sir Brian Urquhart; Andrew Whitley; Napoleon B. Williams, Jr..

Human Rights Watch Arms Project

Staff
Joost R. Hiltermann, Director; Steve D. Goose, Program Director; Ann Peters, Research Associate; Kathleen Bleakley, Ernst Jan Hogendoorn, Research Assistants; William M. Arkin, Kathi L. Austin, James Ron, Monica Schurtman, Frank Smyth, Consultants; Selamawit Demeke, Associate.

Advisory Committee
Ken Anderson; Nicole Ball; Frank Blackaby; Frederick C. Cuny; Ahmed H. Esa; Bill Green; Di Hua; Frederick J. Knecht; Edward J. Laurance; Vincent McGee; Janne E. Nolan; Andrew J. Pierre; David Rieff; Kumar Rupesinghe; John Ryle; Mohamed M. Sahnoun; Gary G. Sick; Thomas Winship.

Human Rights Watch Children's Rights Project

Staff
Lois Whitman, Director; Arvind Ganesan, Mina Samuels, Lee Tucker, Consultants.

Advisory Committee
Roland Algrant; Michelle India Baird; James Bell; Albina du Boisrouvray; Rachel Brett; Nicole Burrowes; Bernadine Dohrn; Fr. Robert Drinan; Sanford J. Fox; Lisa Hedley; Anita Howe-Waxman; Kela Leon; Alan Levine; Hadassah Brooks Morgan; Prexy Nesbitt; Elena Nightingale; Martha J. Olson; Marta Santos Pais; Janet A. Phoenix; Susan Rappaport; Jane Green Schaller; Robert G. Schwartz; Mark I. Soler; Lisa Sullivan; William L. Taylor; Geraldine Van Bueren; Peter Volmink; James D. Weill.

Human Rights Watch
Free Expression Project
Staff

Gara LaMarche, Director; Marcia Allina, Program Associate.

Advisory Committee

Roland Algrant, Chair; Peter Osnos, Vice Chair; Alice Arlen; Robert L. Bernstein; Tom A. Bernstein; Ellen Bettman; Hortense Calisher; Geoffrey Cowan; Dorothy Cullman; Patricia Derian; Adrian W. DeWind; Irene Diamond; E. L. Doctorow; Norman Dorsen; Frances FitzGerald; Jack Greenberg; Vartan Gregorian; S. Miller Harris; Alice H. Henkin; Pam Hill; Joseph Hofheimer; Lawrence Hughes; Ellen Hume; Mark Kaplan; Stephen L. Kass; William Koshland; Judith F. Krug; Anthony Lewis; William Loverd; Wendy Luers; John Macrae, III; Kati Marton; Michael Massing; Nancy Meiselas; Arthur Miller; Rt. Rev. Paul Moore Jr.; Toni Morrison; Bruce Rabb; Geoffrey Cobb Ryan; John G. Ryden; Steven R. Shapiro; Jerome Shestack; Nadine Strossen; Rose Styron; John Updike; Luisa Valenzuela; Nicholas A. Veliotes; Kurt Vonnegut, Jr.; Deborah Wiley; Roger Wilkins; Wendy Wolf.

Human Rights Watch Prison Project
Staff

Joanne Mariner, Associate Counsel.

Advisory Committee

Herman Schwartz, Chair; Nan Aron; Vivian Berger; Haywood Burns; Alejandro Garro; William Hellerstein; Edward Koren; Sheldon Krantz; The Hon. Morris Lasker; Benjamin Malcolm; Diane Orentlicher; Norman Rosenberg; David Rothman; Clarence Sundram.

Human Rights Watch
Women's Rights Project
Staff

Dorothy Q. Thomas, Director; Regan E. Ralph, Staff Attorney; LaShawn R. Jefferson, Research Associate; Binaifer Nowrojee, Consultant; Kerry McArthur, Evelyn Miah, Associates.

Advisory Committee

Kathleen Peratis, Chair; Nahid Toubia, Vice Chair; Mahnaz Afkhami; Abdullahi An-Na'im; Helen Bernstein; Alice Brown; Charlotte Bunch; Rhonda Copelon; Lisa Crooms; Patricia Derian; Gina Despres; Joan Dunlop; Mallika Dutt; Martha Fineman; Claire Flom; Adrienne Germain; Leslie Glass; Lisa Hedley; Zhu Hong; Stephen Isaacs; Helene Kaplan; Marina Pinto Kaufman; Wangari Maathai; Joyce Mends-Cole; Marysa Navarro-Aranguren; Donna Nevel; Susan Peterson; Celina Romany; Margaret Schuler; Jeane Sindab; Domna Stanton.

Human Rights Watch California
Staff

Desiree A. Colly, Regional Development Director; Kristina Hudson, Outreach Coordinator; Wendy Worthington, Associate.

Advisory Committee

Stanley K. Sheinbaum, Honorary Chair; Mike Farrell, Jane Olson, Co-Chairs; Clara A. "Zazi" Pope, Vice Chair; Joan Willens Beerman; Rabbi Leonard Beerman; Justin Connolly; Alan Gleitsman; Danny Glover; Paul Hoffman; Barry Kemp; Maggie Kemp; Lynda Palevsky; Tracy Rice; Vicki Riskin; Cheri Rosche; Pippa Scott; Sid Sheinberg; Andrea Van de Kamp; Francis M. Wheat; Dianne Wittenberg; Stanley Wolpert.

Help expose human rights abuses in over 70 countries worldwide.

Support *Human Rights Watch!*

□ **YES!** I want to do what I can to support the important work that Human Rights Watch is doing around the world.

I am enclosing my tax-deductible gift made payable to **Human Rights Watch** in the amount of:

□ US $200 □ US $100 □ US $50 Other: _____

Please charge my VISA or MC account.

Account #: _____ Exp. Date _____

Signature: _____

Your US $50 donation will guarantee that you will receive the next 10 issues of Human Rights Watch's Update.

WR96

Name _____

Address _____

City/State/Zip/Country _____

Phone _____

Please mail this coupon, your gift and all correspondence to:

Attn: Marcia Holland, HUMAN RIGHTS WATCH 485 Fifth Avenue, New York, NY 10017 USA

□ **Please send me a copy of your Publications Catalog.**